WORKSHOPS IN COMPUTING
Series edited by C. J. van Rijsbergen

Also in this series

ALPUK91, Proceedings of the 3rd UK Annual Conference on Logic Programming, Edinburgh, 10–12 April 1991
Geraint A.Wiggins, Chris Mellish and Tim Duncan (Eds.)

Specifications of Database Systems
International Workshop on Specifications of Database Systems, Glasgow, 3–5 July 1991
David J. Harper and Moira C. Norrie (Eds.)

7th UK Computer and Telecommunications Performance Engineering Workshop
Edinburgh, 22–23 July 1991
J. Hillston, P.J.B. King and R.J. Pooley (Eds.)

Logic Program Synthesis and Transformation
Proceedings of LOPSTR 91, International Workshop on Logic Program Synthesis and Transformation, University of Manchester, 4–5 July 1991
T.P. Clement and K.-K. Lau (Eds.)

Declarative Programming, Sasbachwalden 1991
PHOENIX Seminar and Workshop on Declarative Programming, Sasbachwalden, Black Forest, Germany, 18–22 November 1991
John Darlington and Roland Dietrich (Eds.)

Building Interactive Systems: Architectures and Tools
Philip Gray and Roger Took (Eds.)

Functional Programming, Glasgow 1991
Proceedings of the 1991 Glasgow Workshop on Functional Programming, Portree, Isle of Skye, 12–14 August 1991
Rogardt Heldal, Carsten Kehler Holst and Philip Wadler (Eds.)

Object Orientation in Z
Susan Stepney, Rosalind Barden and David Cooper (Eds.)

Code Generation – Concepts, Tools, Techniques
Proceedings of the International Workshop on Code Generation, Dagstuhl, Germany, 20–24 May 1991
Robert Giegerich and Susan L. Graham (Eds.)

Z User Workshop, York 1991, Proceedings of the Sixth Annual Z User Meeting, York, 16–17 December 1991
J.E. Nicholls (Ed.)

Formal Aspects of Measurement
Proceedings of the BCS-FACS Workshop on Formal Aspects of Measurement, South Bank University, London, 5 May 1991
Tim Denvir, Ros Herman and R.W. Whitty (Eds.)

AI and Cognitive Science '91
University College, Cork, 19–20 September 1991
Humphrey Sorensen (Ed.)

5th Refinement Workshop, Proceedings of the 5th Refinement Workshop, organised by BCS-FACS, London, 8–10 January 1992
Cliff B. Jones, Roger C. Shaw and Tim Denvir (Eds.)

Algebraic Methodology and Software Technology (AMAST'91)
Proceedings of the Second International Conference on Algebraic Methodology and Software Technology, Iowa City, USA, 22–25 May 1991
M. Nivat, C. Rattray, T. Rus and G. Scollo (Eds.)

continued on back page...

Krysia Broda (Ed.)

ALPUK92

Proceedings of the 4th UK Conference on Logic Programming, London, 30 March – 1 April 1992

Published in collaboration with the British Computer Society

Springer-Verlag
London Berlin Heidelberg New York
Paris Tokyo Hong Kong
Barcelona Budapest

Krysia Broda, BSc, MSc, PhD
Department of Computing
Imperial College of Science, Technology and Medicine
180 Queen's Gate
London, SW7 2BZ, UK

ISBN-13: 978-3-540-19783-6 e-ISBN-13: 978-1-4471-3421-3
DOI: 10.1007/978-1-4471-3421-3

British Library Cataloguing in Publication Data
ALPUK92: Proceedings of the 4th UK Conference on Logic Programming, London, 30 March–1 April 1992. – (Workshops in Computing Series)
I. Broda, Krysia II. Series
005.133

Library of Congress Cataloging-in-Publication Data
A catalog record for this book is available from the Library of Congress

Typesetting: Camera ready by contributors

34/3830-543210 Printed on acid-free paper

Preface

Under the auspices of the UK branch of the Association of Logic Programming, the 4th ALPUK Conference was held in London between March 30th and April 1st 1992. The conference was evenly divided between invited papers, submitted papers and tutorials. The submitted papers were refereed prior to acceptance and the invited papers have been refereed since their presentation.

The submitted papers selected for the conference were from a diversity of areas (both geographical and technical). Several papers were from the broad area of program analysis. Shyamasundar et al describe the use of term rewriting as a means of analysing the termination of logic programs. Jacquet ascribes a metric semantics for contextual logic programs, which allow for inheritance between modules. Bsaïes looks at deriving properties required for the synthesis of programs from Horn clause specifications, whilst Lu and Greenfield give an algorithm for efficiently generating abstract models of programs.

Several papers addressed language and implementation issues. Antoniou and Sperschneider discuss the modularisation of logic programs and detail an approach that combines both specification and implementation. Chen and Staples give an intuitively appealing discussion of 'soft-typing' logic programs. The important (and controversial) implementation issue of error-handling is considered by Shih et al. Succi et al give a WAM-based compiler for SEL, a language based on sets and equations.

Although logic programming is popularly identified with Prolog, there is an ever growing interest in concurrent logic languages. A particularly clear exposition of constraint and process algebra semantics of these languages is given in the invited paper of de Boer and Palamidessi. They give a compositional semantics which is based on linear sequences and discuss its properties. The submitted paper by Pimentel and Troya discusses a parallel language which is all but consumed by object-oriented features. Concurrent logic languages should not be confused with the concurrent execution of Prolog; Clocksin discusses a distributed implementation technique for the latter and describes the experience of implementing the method. His paper gives performance results for a varying number of processors and different classes of programs.

Hodges, in his invited paper, examines the significance of Horn clauses for computer science. He discusses the properties of Horn clauses and puts forward some personal views for the reasons behind the contemporary success of Horn clause logic. He also suggests some generalisations, which will surely provide a good basis for future discussion.

Another theme of the invited papers was logic programming in contexts other than classical first order. Gabbay and Ohlbach present an approach for transition from a Hilbert calculus for a logic to its model theoretic semantics which preserves soundness and completeness. Their method uses predicate calculus as a metatheory for both, and the various steps of their method are clearly described. They illustrate the application of their algorithm with many examples.

In their paper, Pym and Wallen lay the foundations for a taxonomy of proof systems; in particular they argue that computational solution of problems can be divided into two phases, proof search and answer extraction. Differing techniques for the two phases permit the computational solution of problems to be extended. They illustrate with a simple propositional language and compare SLD proof search with a more general procedure.

Jiang and Richards introduce an interval temporal logic IQ-C, which includes terms that refer to times and has other special features, and give an interim account of its semantics. They outline a technique for Skolemisation, which has an interesting history, and discuss a resolution-like proof procedure for IQ-C.

A comprehensive tutorial introduction to the language Gödel is given by Bowers and Hill whose paper includes many examples which were demonstrated at the conference, while a tutorial introduction to parallel logic programming (STRAND) is given by Florentin and Gittins.

The conference contributed to the ever-widening frontier of logic programming and the proceedings should be of interest to all workers in the field. As the frontier widens, so does the scope for interaction between different camps within logic programming, and between logic programming and other related disciplines. In the end, it is from the fruits of such interaction that many novel ideas are born.

The conference organisers wish to thank the sponsors: ALP-UK, Imperial College, Polytechnic of North London, AII, BIM, LPA, ISL and ESL.

August 1992 Krysia Broda

Conference Chair

Graem Ringwood

Programme Chair

Krysia Broda

Local Organiser

David Gilbert

Referees

Marcello d'Agostino
Trevor Bench-Capon
Krysia Broda
Derek Brough
Ines de Castro Dutra
Mike Clark
Tim Clement
Tony Dodd
Marc Eisenstadt
Dov Gabbay
David Gilbert
Steve Gregory
Wilfrid Hodges
Chris Hogger
John Lloyd
Chris Mellish
Jeremy Pitt
Graem Ringwood
Jon Rowson
Fariba Sadri
Vitor Santos Costa
Murray Shanahan
Harold Simmons
Raed Sindaha
Stan Wainer
Lincoln Wallen
David Warren
Rong Yang

Contents

Applications in Logic

Tutorials

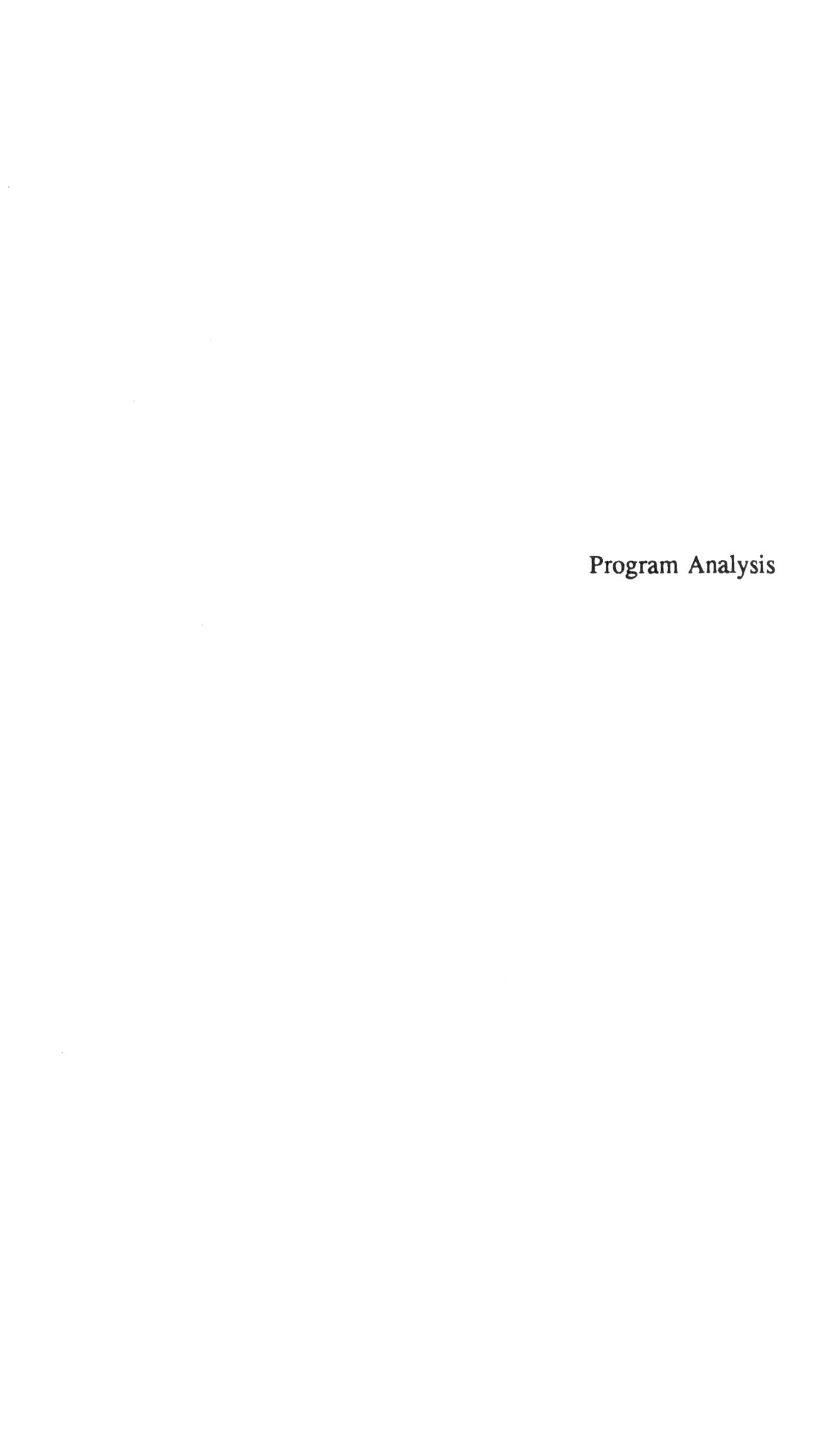

Program Analysis

Rewriting Concepts in the Study of Termination of Logic Programs

R. K. Shyamasundar
Computer Science Group
Tata Institute of Fundamental Research
Colaba, BOMBAY 400 005, INDIA

M. R. K. Krishna Rao
Computer Science Group
Tata Institute of Fundamental Research
Colaba, BOMBAY 400 005, INDIA

Deepak Kapur*
Department of Computer Science
State University of New York at Albany, NY 12222†

Abstract

A characterization of terminating logic programs is proposed. The approach is to relate the termination property of logic programs with that of term rewriting systems and use various termination techniques of rewriting in characterizing and proving termination of logic programs. The characterization is given using a new concept, *unification closure*. The concept of unification closure is closely related to the concepts of *forward closure* and *overlap closure* used in term rewriting literature to characterize the termination of *linear* term rewriting systems. Equivalence of our characterization with that based on level mappings is proved. Computability of the unification closure for a class of logic programs satisfying the *bounded term-size property* is established. The mechanizability and practicality of the approach is discussed.

1 Introduction

Checking termination of logic programs is an important problem, much like the termination of imperative programs. Since writing logic programs can be viewed as more like writing specifications of computations, there can be a debate about whether it is meaningful to talk about verifying logic programs. It will be, however, difficult to justify arguments against ensuring termination of logic programs. In fact any one who has written logic programs has to confront,

*Partially supported by NSF Grant nos. CCR-8906678 and INT-9014074.

†e-mail addresses: {shyam, krishna}@tifrvax.bitnet, kapur@cs.albany.edu

sooner or later, the possibility of a program unleashing an infinite computation either because of a bug in one's program or due to the idiosyncracies of an interpreter being used for a logic programming language.

There have been several attempts in characterizing termination of logic programs [20,4,18,3]. It is not quite clear how most of these methods can be mechanized. The goal of this research is to associate a term rewriting system with a logic program and study the termination properties of logic programs by analyzing properties related to termination of term rewriting systems (TRS). The termination property of rewrite systems is well-studied compared to that of logic programs and a good number of implementations are available for checking termination of rewrite systems. It is hoped that by developing suitable transformations of logic programs to rewrite systems, it will be possible to effectively use techniques for showing termination of term rewrite systems in studying termination of logic programs. And, we already have considerable success in applying this approach, especially to well-moded sequential logic programs and guarded Horn clause programs.

In our earlier paper, Krishna Rao et al [12], we developed a transformational methodology for proving termination of *well-moded* logic programs under a class of selection rules. This methodology has some advantages over those proposed by Ullman and van Gelder [19] and Pluemer [17] (a brief review of the transformation and the comparison with [19] and [17] is provided in the next section). The practicality and usefulness of our approach has been illustrated in [14] by proving the termination of the Prolog implementation of a compiler for **ProCoS** level 0 language PL_0 developed at Oxford university [9,10].

In this paper, we extend our approach for studying termination of logic programs without the restriction of well-modedness. Further, we study *termination in the strong sense*, i.e., termination of a program for a given query *irrespective of the selection/search rule* employed by the underlying interpreter. In a later section, the approach is extended to include the selection rule used by the interpreter.

We characterize termination of logic programs through the concept of *unification closure*, which is closely related to concepts of *forward closure* [6] and *overlap closure* [8] used in studying termination of rewrite system. In particular, we show that a given logic program terminates on a given goal if and only if the associated unification closure is finite and does not contain any pair of the form $\langle a_1, a_2 \rangle$ such that a_1 and a_2 are variants of each other. We prove the equivalence of our characterization with that of Bezem [4] and thereby show that the class of programs which satisfy the above condition on unification closure is large *enough to compute every total recursive function.*

Unification closure is proved to be finite for function- free programs and programs satisfying the *bounded term-size property* of Van Gelder [7]. It is proved that an *nvi* logic program (i.e., a program without local variables) terminates for all ground queries if the associated rewrite system terminates. However, local variables play a crucial role in the paradigm of logic programming (as place holders for intermediate values in sideways-information-passing) and it is not possible to give an effective procedure for transforming programs containing local variables into *nvi*-programs [17]. To deal with programs containing local variables, we introduce the notion of ***boundedness*** and prove that a logic program (with local variables) terminates for all ground (in fact, bounded) queries if the associated rewrite system is terminating and bounded. Intuitively, boundedness of a term eliminates the possibility of infinite ascending chains over the set of instances of that term.

Our characterization is ***syntactical*** and ***mechanizable*** as compared to the characterizations given in Bezem [4] and Apt and Pedreschi [3]. Owing to the strong relationship between termination of logic programs and that of rewrite systems established in this paper, it is possible to use many termination techniques (and implementations such as RRL and REVE) proposed in the term rewriting literature for proving termination of logic programs.

The rest of the paper is organized as follows: Section 2 gives preliminary definitions and relevant results on termination of rewriting systems. In section 3, we briefly review the results of [12] and give an outline of the termination proof for the **ProCoS** complier. In section 4, we define the notion of ***unification closure*** and characterize ***universal termination*** of logic programs. In section 5, we analyze various properties of unification closure, such as computability and the relationship with level mappings. Conditions are identified for reducing the termination problem of logic programs to that of rewrite systems. In section 6, selection rule is included in the termination analysis. Section 7 concludes paper with a discussion on relationship with other related works, practicality of the approach and the ongoing work. We follow the notation of Lloyd [16] and Dershowitz [6] throughout the paper.

2 A Brief Review of Term Rewriting Systems

In this section, we give some basic definitions of term rewriting systems and discuss some results on termination of rewriting systems. For more details, reader is referred to [8] and [6].

Definition 1: Let $\mathcal{F}$ be a set of function symbols and $\mathcal{X}$ be a set of variables. A term rewriting system R over the set of terms $\mathcal{T}(\mathcal{F},\mathcal{X})$ is a finite set of *rewrite rules* of the form $l \rightarrow r$, where l and r are terms in $\mathcal{T}(\mathcal{F},\mathcal{X})$ such that $Var(r) \subseteq Var(l)$ and l is not a variable.

A rule $l \rightarrow r$ applies to term t in $\mathcal{T}$ if a subterm s of t matches with l through some substitution σ, i.e. $s = l\sigma$, and the rule is applied by replacing the subterm s in t by $r\sigma$. If the resulting term is u, we say t is rewritten to u in one step and denote the step by $t \Rightarrow u$.

Definition 2: A term rewriting system R is ***terminating*** if and only if it does not admit any infinite chain of the form $t_0 \Rightarrow t_1 \Rightarrow \cdots \Rightarrow t_i \Rightarrow t_{i+1} \Rightarrow \cdots$.
If R admits such an infinite chain, then it is ***nonterminating***.

The termination of term rewriting systems in general is undecidable (for instance, it is proved in [5] that one can simulate a Turing machine using a single rewrite rule). However, a wide variety of heuristics and techniques have been proposed for proving termination of classes of term rewriting systems (for a survey of such techniques, see [6]). The key idea is to show that terms decrease under a well-founded ordering after each rewriting step. Many well-founded orderings discussed in [6] exploit the syntactic structure of terms. Simplification orderings [6] such as *recursive path ordering, lexicographic path ordering* are good examples of such orderings and are implemented in theorem provers based on the rewriting paradigm such as RRL [11], REVE [15] etc.

3 Termination of Well-moded Logic Programs

A general technique for proving termination of any program is to prove that values of some arguments in a recursive call decrease under some well-founded ordering. The presence of local variables used for sideways-information-passing in logic programs poses a few problems for such an approach. See [12] or [17] for a thorough discussion on the problem of local variables.

To cope with the problem of local variables, Ullman and van Gelder [19] proposed a methodology for proving termination of a logic program for a query with a given moding information, using inter-argument inequalities of the predicates. Pluemer [17] generalized the form of inequalities and extended Ullman et al's method to generate a set of predicate-inequalities whose satisfaction ensures the termination of a given well-moded program for all well-moded queries.[1]

Pluemer's method assumes that the given logic program is *normalized* (no variable occurs more than once in a literal) and *free of mutual recursion.* Thus, preprocessing is needed to eliminate mutual recursion and make programs *normalized.* Further, Pluemer's method needs a program to satisfy a property called the 'existence of an admissible solution graph for each clause.' This property is generally violated by clauses in which a variable occurs in input positions of more than one literal in the body. For example, the last clause of the following multiplication program (taken from [17]) with moding information *add* (in, in, out) and *mult* (in, in, out) violates this property (the variable Y occurs in the input positions of *add* and *mult*) *and Pluemer's method cannot prove its termination.*

$add(0, Y, Y) \leftarrow$
$add(s(X), Y, s(Z)) \leftarrow add(X, Y, Z)$
$mult(0, Y, 0) \leftarrow$
$mult(s(X), Y, Z) \leftarrow mult(X, Y, Z1),\ add(Z1, Y, Z)$

In our earlier paper [12], we proposed a transformational methodology for proving termination of well-moded programs, which overcomes the drawbacks of [19] and [17] (*it does not need any preprocessing and assumes no property*). It basically transforms a given logic program into a *TRS* eliminating local variables through Skolemization. This process of Skolemization heavily exploits moding information and well-modedness of the programs. We informally describe the transformation, illustrate it through an example and show that there

[1] We consider Pluemer's work as an extension and refinement of Ullman and Van Gelder's work, and most of our remarks about Pluemer's method also hold for Ullman and Van Gelder's method (in slightly different form).

are *definite advantages* in relating termination of logic programs with that of rewrite systems.

Well-moded programs: A *mode* m of an n-ary predicate p is a function from $\{1, \cdots, n\}$ to the set $\{in,\ out\}$. And $\{i \mid m(i) = in\}$ is the set of input positions of p (similarly output positions are defined). For a clause $c\ :\ A \leftarrow B_1, \cdots, B_k$ and a variable X in c, B_i is *consumer* (*producer*) of X if X occurs in an input (output) position of B_i and A is *consumer* (*producer*) of X if X occurs in an output (input) position of A. The producer-consumer relation of c is $\{\ (B_i,\ B_j)\ \mid\ B_i$ and B_j $(i \neq j)$ are producer and consumer of a variable X in $c\ \}$. A clause c is *well-moded* if (a) its producer-consumer relation is *acyclic* and (b) every variable in c has a producer. A program P is *well-moded* if every clause in it is well-moded. A well-moded query is a well-moded clause without head.

A selection rule (or computation rule) gives the next literal to be resolved among the literals (subgoals) in the current goal. This notion of selection rule can be extended for a clause, as a rule which gives an evaluation order among the literals in the body of the clause. It can be captured by a partial order (if $l_i < l_j$ in the partial order, it means that l_i should be selected before selecting l_j). *A selection rule is implied by the moding information of a well-moded program if and only if its partial order for each clause in the program is an extension of the producer-consumer relation of that clause.*

Transformation Procedure

Step 1: Corresponding to each output position of a predicate in the given program, we introduce a function symbol. For example, consider a 5-ary predicate p of mode $\{in, out, in, in, out\}$. We introduce two function symbols p'_1 and p'_2 of arity 3 (the number of input positions in p) corresponding to the first and second output positions respectively.

Step 2: Corresponding to each clause in the program, we derive a set of rewrite rules using the producer-consumer relation.[2]

A formal description of the transformation procedure is given in [12]. It may be noted that the transformation given in [1] (for different purposes) is a special case of ours in the following sense: [1] can transform well-moded logic programs into rewrite system only if (a) predicates have *exactly one output position* and (b) producers of a variable precede its consumer in the textual order.

The main theorem of [12] is given below without proof. This theorem establishes a sufficient condition for the termination of well-moded logic programs.

Theorem 1: *A well-moded logic program terminates for all well-moded queries under any selection rule implied by the moding information, if the derived rewrite system is terminating.*

Illustration of the transformation: Intuitively, the transformation produces a set of rewrite rules from the above *multiplication* program as follows.

[2]Producer-consumer relation can be represented by *literal dependency graph* [17] of the clause. This graph is much simpler compared to the *AND/OR-solution graph* used in Pluemer's method and Variable/Argument graphs used in [19].

1. Since the output of predicate *add* for inputs 0 and Y is Y, we get **add 1(0, Y) → Y**.
   Similarly, from the third clause, we get **mult 1(0, Y) → 0**.
2. From the second clause, we can see that the output of *add* for inputs $s(X)$ and Y is $s(Z)$, where Z is the output of *add* for inputs X and Y. So we get **add 1(s(X), Y) → s(add 1(X, Y))**.
3. From the last clause, we can see that the output of *mult* for inputs $s(X)$ and Y is Z, where Z is the output of *add* for the inputs $Z1$ and Y, where $Z1$ is the output of *mult* for inputs X and Y. So we get **mult 1(s(X), Y) → add 1(Z1, Y)**, where **Z1 = mult 1(X, Y)**. So the resulting rule is
   mult 1(s(X), Y) → add 1(mult 1(X, Y), Y).

It is very easy to prove the termination of this rewrite system using the recursive path ordering with precedence $\mathbf{s} < \mathbf{add}'_1 < \mathbf{mult}'_1$. (see [12] for the complete proof).

Compared to the methods of [19] and [17], this method has certain advantages: (a) no preprocessing is needed (b) it can handle programs in which a variable occurs in input positions of many atoms in the body of a clause.

Using this approach, we are able to prove termination of *append, split, fair-split, quick-sort, merge-sort* etc. Further, we [14] are able to prove termination of a Prolog implementation of a compiler for **ProCoS** level 0 language PL_0 [9,10]. The code for this compiler extensively uses local variables and cut operator, and no termination proof (a crucial part in the correctness proof) has existed until now. We proved *termination* of the compiler by proving termination of the derived rewrite system using the *lexicographic path ordering* [6]. (Actually, we proved a stronger result than needed. The cuts (!) are essentially used to restrict the search. We proved that the compiler terminates even without cuts, which implies the termination in the presence of cuts).

However, the above Skolemization procedure needs moding information and does not work for non-well-moded programs. Since Prolog programs are often written without giving moding information (most of the Prolog interpreters do not use moding), there is a need to relax the requirement of *well-modedness* in the termination analysis. The following sections study termination without the requirement of *well-modedness*.

4 Universal Termination of Logic Programs

In this section, we define the notion of *universal termination* of logic programs and obtain a characterization of it using the notion of *unification closure*.

Definition 3: A logic program P is called *universally terminating with respect to a goal* Q if all the SLD-derivations from P starting with Q are finite *irrespective* of the selection rule used to select the literals from the goals. Further, P is called *universally terminating* if P is universally terminating with respect to every goal Q.

Note: This notion of *universal termination* is referred to as *strong termination* in [20].

The universal termination of logic programs, is captured by the following lemma:

Lemma 1: *There is an infinite derivation for the query* $\leftarrow q_1, q_2, \cdots, q_n$ *if and only if there is an infinite derivation for at least one of the queries* $\leftarrow q_i, 1 \leq i \leq n$.

Proof: Follows from definitions of SLD derivation and universal termination.

In the following, we define the notion of ***unification closure***.

Definition 4: Let P be a given logic program. For each clause $A \leftarrow B_1, \cdots, B_n$ in P, construct a set of rewrite rules $\{\ A \rightarrow B_i \mid 1 \leq i \leq n\}$. For each unit clause $p_i(\cdots) \leftarrow$, construct $\{\ p_i(\cdots) \rightarrow True\ \}$. The union of these sets of rewrite rules constructed for each clause of the program is denoted by RR_P and is called the ***associated term rewriting system*** of P.

Definition 5: Let P be a given program and $Q = \leftarrow q_1, q_2, \cdots, q_m$ be a given query. Let SIG_Q be the *set of initial subgoals*, $\{q_i | 1 \leq i \leq m\}$. The ***unification closure*** of program P with respect to query Q, is denoted by UC_{P_Q}, and is inductively defined as follows:

1. For each $q_i \in SIG_Q$ and for each rule $l \rightarrow r$ in RR_P, if q_i unifies with l through a most general unifier σ, then $\langle q_i\sigma, r\sigma\rangle \in UC_{P_Q}$, and
2. If $\langle p_1, p_2\rangle \in UC_{P_Q}$ and $l \rightarrow r \in RR_P$ such that l unifies with p_2 through a mgu σ then
(i) $\langle p_1\sigma, r\sigma\rangle \in UC_{P_Q}$ as well as
(ii) $\langle l\sigma, r\sigma\rangle \in UC_{P_Q}$.

Unification closure construction is illustrated through the following examples.

Example 1: Let P be the program

$p(f(X)) \leftarrow p(X)$

For a query $Q = \leftarrow p(f\ n(a)),\ n \in N$, the unification closure UC_{P_Q} is given by

$$\begin{array}{l} \{\quad \langle p(f\ n(a)),\ p(f\ n-1(a))\rangle, \\ \quad\ \ \langle p(f\ n(a)),\ p(f\ n-2(a))\rangle, \\ \quad\ \ \langle p(f\ n(a)),\ p(f\ n-3(a))\rangle, \\ \quad\ \ \vdots \\ \quad\ \ \langle p(f\ n(a)),\ p(a)\rangle\ \} \quad \cup \quad \{\langle p(f\ k(a),\ p(f\ k-j(a))\rangle \mid 1 \leq j < k < n\ \}. \ \square \end{array}$$

Informally speaking, $\langle s,\ t\rangle \in UC_{P_Q}$ captures the information that s is reachable in some SLD derivation from Q, and t can be reached from s. Later, we will prove that the unification closure is transitive. The need for the subclause (ii) of clause (2) in the definition of the unification closure becomes clear from the following example.

Example 2: Consider the program P containing the following clauses:

$p(X) \leftarrow q(Z)$
$q(Y) \leftarrow q(Y)$
and the query $\leftarrow p(X)$.

The unification closure of the rewriting system associated with this program includes a pair $\langle q(Y),\ q(Y)\rangle$ indicating that the program P goes into an infinite loop through the derived subgoal $q(Y)$.

If the pair $\langle l\sigma,\ r\sigma\rangle$ had not been included in UC_{P_Q} as per the subclause (ii) of clause (2), UC_{P_Q} would have been finite and would not contain any *variant-pair*[3] (in fact every pair would have $p(\cdots)$ as the first component), thereby leading to a (wrong) conclusion of termination by Theorem 3 given in the sequel. The purpose of subclause (ii) is to check whether any of the subgoals reachable from the query itself can have an infinite SLD-derivation. □

We do not distinguish between pairs that differ just in variables (i.e., they are variants of one another). This is explained in the following example.

Example 3: Let P be the following program and the query Q be $\leftarrow p(a)$
$p(X) \leftarrow p(Y)$

We take UC_{P_Q} as the finite set $\{\ \langle p(a),\ p(Y)\rangle,\ \langle p(Y),\ p(Y1)\rangle\}$ but not the infinite set $\{\ \langle p(a), p(Y)\rangle,\ \langle p(Y), p(Y_1)\rangle,\ \langle p(Y_1), p(Y_2)\rangle, ..., \langle p(a), p(Y_1)\rangle,\ \langle p(a), p(Y_2)\rangle, ...\}$ because $\langle p(a), p(Y_i)\rangle$, $i > 1$ are variants of $\langle p(a),\ p(Y)\rangle$ and $\langle p(Y_i),\ p(Y_j)\rangle$, $i \neq j$ are variants of $\langle p(Y),\ p(Y_1)\rangle$. □

The following results are established in Shyamasundar et al [18]. To meet the space limitations, we skip the proofs of many theorems.

Lemma 2: if $\langle s, t\rangle \in UC_{P_Q}$ and $\langle t, u\rangle \in UC_{P_Q}$ then $\langle s, u\rangle \in UC_{P_Q}$.

An atom C is a descendent of atom A if C occurs in an SLD-derivation starting with query $\leftarrow A$.

Lemma 3: Let A and C be atoms in the Herbrand universe of a program P. If C is a descendent of A, then there is a pair $\langle A\sigma,\ C\rangle$ in UC_{P_Q} for some substitution σ,[4] where $Q = \leftarrow A$.

Proof: By induction on the number of resolution steps needed to get C from $A\sigma$ in the SLD-derivation. □

The following theorem relates SLD-derivations to the unification closure. The theorem essentially says that, corresponding to every atom in an SLD-derivation starting with a query Q, there is a pair in UC_{P_Q}, and corresponding to every pair in UC_{P_Q} there is an atom in an SLD-derivation starting with Q.

Theorem 2: Given a logic program P and a query $Q = \leftarrow q_1, \cdots, q_m$,

1. if an atom $a \notin \{q_1, \cdots, q_m\}$ appears in a node of an SLD derivation of P starting with Q, then there is a q_j, $1 \leq j \leq m$ such that $\langle q_j\sigma, a\rangle$ is in UC_{P_Q} for some substitution σ , and

[3] We write *variant-pair* to mean a pair of the form $\langle a_1,\ a_2\rangle$ such that a_1 and a_2 are variants of each other.

[4] In fact, σ is the composition of the mgu's in the SLD-derivation from A to C.

2. for every pair $\langle s, t\rangle$ in UC_{P_Q}, there is a node containing the subgoal t in some SLD-derivation of P starting with Q.

Proof: First part follows from Lemma 3. Second part is proved by induction on the number of applications of the UC_{P_Q} definition needed for generating the element $\langle s, t\rangle$. □

The following theorem gives a necessary and sufficient condition for the universal termination of logic programs.

Theorem 3: *A logic program P is universally terminating with respect to a query Q if and only if UC_{P_Q} is finite and does not contain any pair of the form $\langle a_1, a_2\rangle$ such that a_1 and a_2 are variants of each other.*

Proof: Let the query Q be $\leftarrow q_1, q_2, \cdots, q_n$.

(if): Let us assume that UC_{P_Q} is finite and does not contain any pair of the form $\langle a_1, a_2\rangle$ such that a_1 and a_2 are variants of each other and P is not terminating with respect to the query Q. Since there are only a finite number of clauses in a program, in any infinite derivation, at least one clause (say C) will be applied infinite times. Now there are three possibilities; either (a) C is resolved with some atom repeatedly, or (b) C is resolved every time with a different variant of the same atom, or (c) C is resolved every time with a different atom (and all these atoms are not variants of each other).

In case (a) the repeated atom is a descendent of itself and by Lemma 3, there should be a reflexive pair in UC_{P_Q} and a reflexive pair is by definition a variant-pair, so it contradicts the assumption. Similarly in case (b) there should be a variant-pair in UC_{P_Q}, contradicting the assumption. In case (c), by Theorem 2, UC_{P_Q} should be infinite – again a contradiction.

(only if): Assume that the program P is terminating with respect to the query Q. By the definition of universal termination, all the SLD-derivations starting with Q are of finite length. So the set of reachable subgoals are finite and hence by Theorem 2, UC_{P_Q} is finite.

If there is a variant-pair, say $\langle l, l'\rangle$ in UC_{P_Q} then the clause whose head unifies with l (and hence *with l' also*) can be applied repeatedly. This gives an infinite SLD-derivation contradicting the assumption of termination. Hence there is no variant-pair in UC_{P_Q}. □

5 Unification Closure, RR$_P$, and Level Mappings

From Theorem 3, it is evident that the termination of logic programs with respect to a query Q is decidable whenever UC_{P_Q} is finite and is semidecidable in general. It is interesting to look for sufficient conditions for the finiteness of UC_{P_Q}. The following theorem establishes the finiteness of unification closure for the class of programs satisfying the *bounded term-size property* [7].

Definition 6: (Van Gelder [7]): A logic program has the *bounded term-size* *property* if there is a function $f(n)$ such that whenever the top level goal has no argument of size greater than n, then no subgoal in any top-down (e.g. SLD) derivation has an argument of size greater than $f(n)$, whether the derivation is successful or not. (The size of a term is the count of its functors, constants and variables.)

Theorem 4: *If a logic program P has the bounded term-size property then the unification closure UC_{P_Q} of P is finite for any query Q.*

Proof: Since number of constant, function and predicate symbols in a program is finite, the number of terms of size less than $f(n)$ is finite (modulo variables renaming) for any finite n. And the number of distinct atoms (modulo variable renaming) that can occur in any SLD-derivation of P is finite and hence by Theorem 2, the unification closure UC_{P_Q} is finite. □

As a corollary, it can be easily seen that unification closure is finite and computable for function-free programs. Hence universal termination[5] is decidable for these classes of programs.

5.1 Level Mappings and Unification Closure

We relate our characterization with that of Bezem [4] after introducing the needed concepts.

Definition 7: A *level mapping* for a logic program P is a function $|\ | : B_P \rightarrow \mathcal{N}$, where B_P is the Herbrand base of P. For $A \in B_P$, we denote by $|A|$, the *level* of A.

Definition 8: Let P be a logic program and $|\ |$ a level mapping for P. We call *P recurrent with respect to* $|\ |$ if for every ground instance $B \leftarrow A_1, \cdots, A_n$, of a clause in P, $|B| > |A_i|$, $1 \leq i \leq n$. P is called *recurrent* if P is recurrent with respect to some level mapping.

Definition 9: An atom A is called ***bounded*** with respect to a level mapping $|\ |$ if $|\ |$ is bounded on the set $[A]$ of ground instances of A. If A is bounded, $|[A]|$ denotes the maximum that $|\ |$ takes on $[A]$. A goal G is bounded if every atom in it is bounded.

Bezem [4] proved that every SLD-derivation of a recurrent program starting with a bounded goal terminates and every total recursive function can be computed by recurrent programs. We show the equivalence of our condition for termination to the level mapping condition of recurrent programs. Such an equivalence proves that the class of programs which satisfy our condition is large enough to compute every total recursive function.

Theorem 5: *If P is recurrent, then for every bounded query Q, UC_{P_Q} is finite and does not contain any pair of the form $\langle a_1,\ a_2 \rangle$ such that a_1 and a_2 are variants of each other.*

Proof: It follows from the fact that every SLD-derivation starting with a

[5]Remember that we are yet to include the computation (selection) rule into our analysis of termination.

bounded goal is finite for recurrent programs. □

Theorem 6: *A logic program P is recurrent if for every ground query Q, UC_{P_Q} is finite and does not have a pair of the for m $\langle a_1, a_2 \rangle$ such that a_1 and a_2 are variants of each other.*

Proof: Let us assume that for every ground query Q, UC_{P_Q} is finite and does not have any pair of the form $\langle a_1, a_2 \rangle$ such that a_1 and a_2 are variants of each other. Then we can define a level mapping $|\;| : B_P \rightarrow \mathcal{N}$ as follows. For every atom $A \in B_P$

$$|A| = |UC_{P_Q}|, \quad \text{where} \quad Q \quad \text{is} \leftarrow A$$

It is easy to see that this level mapping is well defined and P is recurrent w.r.t. it. □

The following theorem follows from the above two theorems and it shows the equivalence of our condition based on unification closure with that of Bezem based on level mappings.

Theorem 7: *A logic program P is recurrent* if and only if *for every bounded query Q, UC_{P_Q} is finite and does not contain any pair of the form $\langle a_1, a_2 \rangle$ such that a_1 and a_2 are variants of each other.*

Proof: The only-if part follows from Theorem 5.

If- part: Since every ground query is a bounded query, unification closure is finite and does not contain variant-pairs for every ground query (hypothesis of this theorem). Therefore, P is recurrent by Theorem 6. □

5.2 Terminating RR_P

It is easy to see that, *if a program P is recurrent, its RR_P terminates* (we can use the level mapping of P as the termination ordering for RR_P). However, the converse is not true as illustrated by the following example. In this subsection, we identify a class (*nvi*) of programs for which the converse holds, and obtain a condition (*boundedness*) that ensures the termination of a non-*nvi* logic program for a class of queries, whenever the associated RR_P terminates.

Example 4: The following program P does not terminate for the query $\leftarrow p(2,4)$ (third clause can be repeatedly applied after the goal $\leftarrow q_2(Z,4)$ is derived), whereas the RR_P terminates.

The logic program P	Corresponding RR_P
$p(0,4) \leftarrow$	$p(0,4) \rightarrow True$
$p(X,Y) \leftarrow q_1(X,Z), q_2(Z,Y)$	$p(X,Y) \rightarrow q_1(X,Z)$
	$p(X,Y) \rightarrow q_2(Z,Y)$
$q_2(s(X),Y) \leftarrow q_2(X,Y)$	$q_2(s(X),Y) \rightarrow q_2(X,Y)$
$q_2(1,2) \leftarrow$	$q_2(1,2) \rightarrow True$
$q_1(X,Y) \leftarrow$	$q_1(X,Y) \rightarrow True$

Definition 10: A clause C is *non-variable introducing* (*nvi*, for short) if every variable that appears in the body of C also appears in the head of C. Further,

a program P is said to be *nvi* if every clause in P is *nvi*.

It is important to observe that for a *nvi* program, all the goals in an SLD-derivation starting with a ground query are ground. The following theorem exploits this fact.

Theorem 8: A *nvi* program P terminates on ground queries if RR_P terminates.

Proof: Each step in an SLD-derivation starting with a ground query for a nvi program is just a *rewriting* of the selected atom by the body of the clause (properly instantiated) whose head unifies with selected atom. So, from any infinite SLD-derivation starting with a ground query, one can easily construct an infinite rewriting sequence (contradicting the termination of RR_P) and hence the theorem is proved by contradiction. □

From the above theorem, it is clear that for proving termination of *nvi*-programs, it is sufficient to prove the termination of RR_P. But for programs containing local variables (variables which appear only in the body of a clause), termination of RR_P is not sufficient for the termination of P. In the following, we establish a condition (based on the notion of *boundedness*), which along with termination of RR_P ensures termination of P for a class of queries. Boundedness of a term t essentially eliminates the possibility of an infinite ascending chain in the set of instances of t.

Definition 11: A term t (or an atom A) is *bounded with respect to a well-founded ordering* $\prec$ if and only if for every ground instance g of t, there is a maximal element m (w.r.t. $\prec$) in the set of ground instances of t (denoted by $[t]$) such that $g \preceq m$.

It is easy to show that every ground term is *bounded* w.r.t $\prec$, and that if t is bounded w.r.t $\prec$, then $t\sigma$ is bounded w.r.t $\prec$ for every substitution σ.

Definition 12: A rewrite rule $l \rightarrow r$ is *bounded* with respect to a well-founded ordering $\prec$ if for every substitution σ, *$r\sigma$ is bounded w.r.t $\prec$* if *$l\sigma$ is bounded w.r.t $\prec$*.
A rewrite system is *bounded* w.r.t $\prec$ if every rule in it is bounded w.r.t $\prec$.
A query $\leftarrow q_1(\cdots), \ldots, q_n(\cdots)$ is *bounded with respect to* $\prec$ if each $q_i(\cdots)$, $1 \leq i \leq n$, is bounded w.r.t. $\prec$.

The following two results are proved in [18].

Lemma 4: *If P is a logic program with bounded RR_P, all intermediate goals in an SLD-tree starting with a bounded query are bounded.*

The following theorem gives a sufficient condition for termination of a program for a class of queries. It essentially says that, if we can prove the termination of RR_P using a well-founded ordering (say $\prec$) and RR_P is bounded w.r.t $\prec$, then P terminates for all bounded (w.r.t $\prec$) queries and hence for all ground queries.

Theorem 9: *Let P be a logic program and $\prec$ be a stable[6] well-founded ordering. Then P terminates for all bounded (w.r.t. $\prec$) queries if*

[6] A well-founded ordering is *stable* if $s \prec t$ implies $s\sigma \prec t\sigma$ for every substitution σ.

1. RR_P is bounded w.r.t. $\prec$ and
2. $r \prec l$ for every rule $l \rightarrow r \in RR_P$ (i.e., RR_P is terminating).

Proof (by contradiction): omited for space limitations. It uses the above lemma and the fact that there cannot be an infinite ascending chain over the set of instances of a *bounded* term. □

Example 5: Let P be the following program computing Ackermann's function (taken from [4]) .

$p(0, Y, s(Y), W) \leftarrow$
$p(s(X), 0, Z, W) \leftarrow p(X, s(0), Z, W)$
$p(s(X), s(Y), Z, s(W)) \leftarrow p(s(X), Y, Z', W), p(X, Z', Z, s(W))$

$$RR_P = \{ \quad \begin{array}{l} p(0, Y, s(Y), W) \rightarrow True \\ p(s(X), 0, Z, W) \rightarrow p(X, s(0), Z, W) \\ p(s(X), s(Y), Z, s(W)) \rightarrow p(s(X), Y, Z', W) \\ p(s(X), s(Y), Z, s(W)) \rightarrow p(X, Z', Z, s(W)) \quad \} \end{array}$$

We can prove the termination of RR_P using the well-founded ordering $\prec$ defined as:
$p(X, u_2, u_3, Y) \prec p(s(X), v_2, v_3, s(Y))$,
$p(s(X), u_2, u_3, Y) \prec p(s(X), v_2, v_3, s(Y))$, and
$p(X, u_2, u_3, s(Y)) \prec p(s(X), v_2, v_3, s(Y))$,
It can be shown that the RR_P is bounded under $\prec$. So this program terminates for all bounded queries (i.e., $\leftarrow p(u_1, u_2, u_3, u_4)$, where u_1 and u_4 are ground terms). □

Termination of the RR_P of example 4 can be proved using the well-founded ordering $\prec$ defined as follows: $q_1(\cdots) \prec p(\cdots)$, $q_1(\cdots) \prec p(\cdots)$, $q_2(X, Y) \prec q_2(s(X), Y)$. But the RR_P is not bounded as the second rule is not bounded ($p(2, 4)$ is bounded but $q_2(Z, 4)$ is not bounded because its set of ground instances has no maximal element). Hence, the program does not terminate for $\leftarrow p(2, 4)$. □

The results in this section have established a strong relation between the termination of logic programs and that of the associated term rewrite systems. Termination techniques of rewrite system discussed in [6] can be used in proving termination of logic programs.

6 Incorporating a Selection Rule

So far we have studied the termination of a logic program ignoring the selection rule and the search strategy. In the following, we take the selection rule into account in the termination analysis. We show that we can use a similar approach for establishing termination of a logic program under a given selection (or computation) rule. The basic idea is to derive the associated rewriting system for a given logic program with respect to a given selection rule. For simplicity, here we consider *Prolog's left-to-right* selection rule.

To incorporate Prolog's left-to-right selection rule, we should control the rewriting so that an atom will be rewritten only when all its predecessors have succeeded (i.e. they are reduced to *True*). This control can be achieved by associating with each atom some control information. For this purpose, we add an additional integer argument to every predicate symbol. The control information for the selection of atoms (or subgoals) in a goal is given as follows. The first (leftmost) atom gets 1 as its last (newly added) argument, the second atom gets 2 as its last argument and in general, the $i\ th$ atom in the goal gets i as its last argument. We allow an atom to be rewritten only when the last argument is 1. This ensures that the leftmost atom can only be rewritten. When the leftmost atom succeeds (i.e., reduced to *True* in the rewrite system), the last arguments of the remaining atoms will be updated by decrementing them by 1. This is formalized in the following definitions.

Definition 13: The associated rewrite system RR_{PS_Q} of a logic program P and a query $Q = \leftarrow q_1(\cdots), \cdots, q_n(\cdots)$ with respect to Prolog's selection rule is constructed as follows.

1. Add a new clause $query \leftarrow q_1(\cdots), \cdots, q_n(\cdots)$ to the program and denote the resulting program by P'.
2. For every k-ary predicate symbol p in P', introduce a new function symbol p' of arity $k+1$.
3. For each unit clause of the form $p(\cdots)$ in P', put $p'(\cdots, 1) \rightarrow True$ in RR_{PS_Q}.
4. For each clause of the form $p(\cdots) \leftarrow p_1(\cdots), p_2(\cdots), \cdots, p_n(\cdots)$, in P', include the following set of rewrite rules in RR_{PS_Q}

$$\begin{aligned} \{ \quad & p'(\cdots,1) \rightarrow f_{p_1}(p'_1(\cdots,1),\cdots,p'_n(\cdots,n)) \\ & f_{p_1}(True, p'_2(\cdots,2),\cdots,p'_n(\cdots,n)) \rightarrow \\ & \qquad\qquad f_{p_2}(p'_2(\cdots,1),\cdots,p'_n(\cdots,n-1)) \\ & \qquad \vdots \\ & f_{p_{n-1}}(True, p'_n(\cdots,2)) \rightarrow p'_n(\cdots,1) \quad \}, \end{aligned}$$

where $f_{p_1}, \cdots, f_{p_{n-1}}$ are new function symbols of arity $n, n-1, \cdots, 2$, respectively.

Definition 14: The ***unification closure*** of program P for query $Q = \leftarrow q_1(\cdots), \cdots, q_n(\cdots)$ with respect to a selection rule S, denoted as UC_{PS_Q}, is defined inductively as follows:

1. $\langle Q, f_q(q_1(\cdots,1), \cdots, q_m(\cdots, m))\rangle \in UC_{PS_Q}$
2. If $\langle t_1, t_2\rangle \in UC_{PS_Q}$ and $l \rightarrow r \in RR_{PS_Q}$ and t_2 has a subterm s within some context u such that s unifies with l via a most general unifier σ then (i) $\langle t_1\sigma, u\sigma[r\sigma]\rangle \in UC_{PS_Q}$ as well as (ii) $\langle l\sigma, r\sigma\rangle \in UC_{PS_Q}$

The following theorem [18] establishes a necessary and sufficient condition for termination of logic programs under a given selection rule.

Theorem 10: *A logic program P terminates for the query Q under a given selection rule S if and only if UC_{PS_Q} is finite and does not contain any pair of the form $\langle t_1,\ t_2\rangle$ such that t_1 is variant of a subterm of t_2.*

Example 6: Let P be the following program computing transitive closure.

$s(a,b) \leftarrow$
$s(b,c) \leftarrow$
$tc(X,Y) \leftarrow s(X,Y)$
$tc(X,Y) \leftarrow s(X,Z), tc(Z,Y)$
and the query Q be $\leftarrow tc(a,c)$

The RR_{PS_Q} and UC_{PS_Q} under Prolog's left-to-right selection rule are given below.

$$RR_{PS_Q} = \{\ \begin{array}{l} s'(a,b,1) \rightarrow True \\ s'(b,c,1) \rightarrow True \\ tc'(X,Y,1) \rightarrow s'(X,Y,1) \\ tc'(X,Y,1) \rightarrow f_1(s'(X,Z,1), tc'(Z,Y,2)) \\ f_1(True, tc'(Z,Y,2)) \rightarrow tc'(Z,Y,1) \\ query'(1) \rightarrow tc'(a,c,1) \quad \} \end{array}$$

$UC_{PS_Q} = T \ \cup \ \{ \langle Q,\ t\rangle \ \mid \ \langle tc'(a,c,1),\ t\rangle \in T \}$, where T is given by

$$T = \{\ \begin{array}{l} \langle\ Q,\ tc'(a,c,1)\ \rangle \\ \langle\ tc'(a,c,1),\ s'(a,c,1)\ \rangle \\ \langle\ tc'(a,c,1),\ f_1(s'(a,Z,1),tc'(Z,c,2))\ \rangle \\ \langle\ tc'(a,c,1),\ f_1(True,tc'(b,c,2))\ \rangle \\ \langle\ s'(a,b,1),\ True) \\ \langle\ tc'(a,c,1),\ tc'(b,c,1)\ \rangle \\ \langle\ f_1(True,tc'(b,c,2)),\ tc'(b,c,1)\ \rangle \\ \langle\ tc'(a,c,1),\ s'(b,c,1)\ \rangle \\ \langle\ f_1(True,tc'(b,c,2)),\ s'(b,c,1)\ \rangle \\ \langle\ tc'(b,c,1),\ s'(b,c,1)\ \rangle \\ \langle\ tc'(a,c,1),\ True\ \rangle \\ \langle\ tc'(b,c,1),\ True\ \rangle \\ \langle\ f_1(True,tc'(b,c,2)),\ True\ \rangle \\ \langle\ s'(b,c,1),\ True\ \rangle \\ \langle\ tc'(a,c,1),\ f_1(s'(b,Z,1),tc'(Z,c,2))\ \rangle \\ \langle\ f_1(True,tc'(b,c,2)),\ f_1(s'(a,Z,1),tc'(Z,c,2))\ \rangle \\ \langle\ tc'(b,c,1),\ f_1(s'(b,Z,1),tc'(Z,c,2))\ \rangle \\ \langle\ tc'(a,c,1),\ f_1(True,tc'(c,c,2))\ \rangle \\ \langle\ f_1(True,tc'(b,c,2)),\ f_1(True,tc'(c,c,2))\ \rangle \\ \langle\ tc'(a,c,1),\ tc'(c,c,2)\ \rangle \\ \langle\ f_1(True,tc'(b,c,2)),\ tc'(c,c,2))\ \rangle \quad \} \end{array}$$

This program P terminates for the query Q since UC_{PS_Q} is finite and does not contain any variant-pair. □

Example 7: It is easy to see that the above program does not terminate for the query $\leftarrow tc(a,c)$, if we add a unit clause $s(a,a) \leftarrow$ to it. Let P' be the resulting program. The $UC_{P'S_Q}$ contains the following set (containing a reflexive pair) in addition to UC_{PS_Q} of the example 6, reflecting the nontermination.

$$\{ \quad \langle Q,\ f_1(True, tc'(a,c,2)) \rangle \\ \langle tc'(a,c,1),\ f_1(True, tc'(a,c,2)) \rangle \\ \langle s'(a,a,1),\ True \rangle \\ \langle Q,\ tc'(a,c,1) \rangle \\ \langle tc'(a,c,1),\ tc'(a,c,1) \rangle \\ \langle f_1(True, tc'(a,c,2)),\ tc'(a,c,1) \rangle \} \qquad \square$$

7 Conclusion

This paper makes *two specific contributions*; firstly, it studies termination of non-well-moded programs and secondly it gives a theoretical foundation for an overall approach of studying termination of logic programs (sequential and parallel) by transforming them into suitable term rewrite systems.

The works of Bezem [4] and Apt and Pedreschi [3] also address the problem of termination of logic programs and Prolog programs. Bezem uses the notion of level mappings to characterize universal termination whereas Apt and Pedreschi use level mappings and models to characterize the termination of logic programs under Prolog's selection rule. Though the simplicity of these two characterizations is appealing, they suffer from a common draw back in that they are not mechanizable.

On the other hand, our characterizations are *purely syntactical and mechanizable*. The results on termination of *nvi*-programs and the results related to the boundedness show the *mechanizability* of our approach. The fact that we are able to prove termination for a bunch of benchmark programs and **ProCoS** compiler demonstrates the *practicality* of the approach.

As an extension of this work, we are studying termination of parallel logic programs such as guarded Horn clauses (GHC-programs) using rewriting concepts [13]. The results are very encouraging and we are able to treat a collection of benchmark programs such as *append, split, fair-split, permutation, quick-sort, merge-sort*.

Acknowledgements: The presentation of the paper has greatly benefited from the live discussions with Prof. K.R. Apt and Prof. J.W. Klop during the second author's stay at CWI, Amsterdam. In fact, our interest in the termination of parallel logic programs was stimulated by Prof. K.R. Apt. We thank both of them for their constructive suggestions. The second author also thanks CWI for partially supporting the visi t.

References

[1] F. Alexandre, K. Bsaies and A. Quere (1991) *On using mode input-output for transforming logic programs*, Workshop on Logic Program Synthesis

and Transformations LOPSTR'91 (proceedings to appear in the LNCS Series of Springer- Verlag).

[2] K. R. Apt, R. N. Bol, and J. W. Klop (1989), *On safe termination of PROLOG programs*, Proc. Sixth International Conference on Logic Programming, pp. 353-368.

[3] K. R. Apt and D. Pedreschi (1990), *Studies in pure PROLOG: Termination*, Proc. Symp. on Computational Logic, Basic Research series 1, Springer-Verlag, pp. 150-176.

[4] M. Bezem (1989), *Characterizing termination of logic programs*, Report CS-R89199, CWI, Amsterdam. Also in Proc. of *North American Logic Programming Conf. 1989.*

[5] M. Dauchet (1989), *Simulation of Turing Machines by a left-linear rewrite rule.*, in Proc. of Rewrite Techniques and Applications conference, RTA'89, Lecture Notes in Computer Science Vol. 355, pp. 109-120.

[6] N. Dershowitz (1987), *Termination of rewriting*, Journal of Symbolic Computation, Vol. 3, pp. 69-116.

[7] A. Van Gelder (1988) *Negation as failure using tight derivations for general logic programs*, in Foundations of Deductive Databases and Logic Programming, Edited by J.Minker, Morgan Kaufmann Publishers, pp. 149-176.

[8] J. V. Guttag, D. Kapur and D. Musser (1983), *On proving uniform termination and restricted termination of rewriting systems*, SIAM J. Computing Vol. 12, pp. 189-214.

[9] He Jifeng and C. A. R. Hoare (1989), *Operational Semantics for ProCoS level 0 language*, **ProCoS** Project Document, OU HJF 1/3, Oxford University.

[10] He Jifeng, P. Pandya and J. Bowen (1990), Compiling specification for ProCoS Programming language Level 0, **ProCoS** Workshop, Malente, April 1990 (Also as Project Document, OU HJF 4/2).

[11] D. Kapur and H. Zhang (1989), *An Overview of Rewrite Rule Laboratory (RRL)* , Proc. of Rewrite Techniques and Applications conference, RTA'89, Springer-Verlag LNCS vol. 355, pp 559-563.

[12] M. R. K. Krishna Rao, D. Kapur and R. K. Shyamasundar (1991), *A transformational methodology for proving termination of logic programs*, Proc. 5th conf. on Computer Science Logic, CSL '91, to appear as LNCS volume.

[13] M. R. K. Krishna Rao, D. Kapur and R. K. Shyamasundar (1992), *Proving termination of guarded Horn clause programs*, submitted for publication.

[14] M. R. K. Krishna Rao, R. K. Shyamasundar and P. Pandya (1992), *Termination proof for ProCoS level 0 language* PL_0 *compiler*, TR, Tata institute of Fundamental Research, Bombay, India (in preparation).

[15] P. Lescanne (1986), *REVE: a rewrite rule laboratory*, Proc. of Conf. on Automated Deduction, CADE'86, Springer LNCS Vol. 230, pp. 695-696.

[16] J. W. Lloyd (1987), *Foundations of Logic Programming*, Springer-Verlag.

[17] L. Pluemer (1990), *Termination proofs for logic programs*, Ph. D. thesis, University of Dortmund, Also appears as Springer Verlag LNCS vol. 446.

[18] R. K. Shyamasundar, M. R. K. Krishna Rao and D. Kapur (1990), *Termination of Logic Programs*, TR, Tata institute of Fundamental Research, Bombay, India, August 1990 (Revised version appears as TR/TIFR May 1991).

[19] J. D. Ullman and A. Van Gelder (1988), *Efficient tests for top-down termination of logical rules*, JACM, 35(2), pp. 345-373.

[20] T. Vasak and J. Potter (1986), *Characterization of terminating logic programs*, IEEE Symposium on Logic Programming, pp. 140-147.

Appendix: A Sample clause from **ProCoS** level 0 language PL_0 compiler.

```
ce(E1/E2, S, F, M, Psi, [Loc | Omega]) :-
                ce(E1, S, L1, M1, [Loc | Omega]),
                mtrans(stl(Loc), L1, L2, M2),
                ce(E2, L1, L2, M3, Omega),
                mtrans(ldl(Loc), L3, L4, M4),
                mtrans(rev, L4, L5, M5),
                mtrans(div, L5, L6, M6),
                mtrans(stoperr, L6, F, M7),
                flatten([M1, M2, M3, M4, M5, M6, M7], M), !.
```

Metric Characterizations of Contextual Logic Programs

Jean-Marie Jacquet
Department of Computer Science
University of Namur, Namur, Belgium

Abstract

The aim of this paper is twofold: to characterize contextual logic programs by means of metric semantics and to argue the usefulness of metric characterizations for formally reasoning about program properties.

A new denotational semantics of contextual logic programs is proposed. It is defined compositionally, without any help of any declarative paradigm and of any transition system. Following the lines of [7], it uses metric spaces rather than cpo's and processes as semantic domains. It is shown to be well-suited to tackle extra-logical features and abstract enough for program analysis.

A methodology of program analysis is derived from the denotational metric charaterization of programs. It is suggested that most program properties can be proved by using the equalities defining the denotational semantics and by using inductive reasoning. Properties of the computed answer substitutions can also be established by reasoning about the substitutions reported by the semantics. Those claims are argued through the study of the universal termination property of several classical procedures.

1 Introduction

One of the most appealing features of logic programming is probably the ideal possibility of writing programs in a purely declarative style, that is by only considering the logic of the knowledge embodied in the programs and by paying no attention to their execution. As a result, the semantics of logic programs should be made in a purely logical way by using so-called Herbrand models or least fixed points of so-called immediate consequence operators on those models (see e.g. [18], [4], [12]).

However, as shown in [8], this ideal is not completely realizable in practice. Among the reasons are the introduction of extra-logical features such as Prolog cut and the semi-decidable nature of Horn clauses. Hence, in practice, one has to take care of the control of the execution and, when building semantics applicable to the analysis of logic programs, of the order in which computed answer substitutions and infinite derivations occur. As proved in [8], this does not however exclude the use of logic to build logic programs.

Another weakness of pure logic programs concerns the lack of structure of these programs and, associated with it, the lack of structure in the derivations. This has been recently solved in [13] through so-called contextual logic programming. This paper tries to achieve a better understanding of these structured programs in giving a semantic characterization of them and in applying it to the analysis of program properties, especially, of the termination property. To that end, a denotational semantics is first developed. It is of a compositional nature and, in contrast with the declarative semantics, can be adapted to tackle extra-logical features like the cut. We believe that it is also well-suited for the analysis of contextual logic programs and, as a justification, apply it to the termination study of several logic programs.

For simplicity of the exposition, sequential contextual logic programs using a Prolog-like search strategy are only examined here. However, we strongly believe that our method can be extended to cope with concurrent programs and properties related to concurrent executions such as those of deadlock- and starvation-freedom. Furthermore, as shown later, it can also be applied in the context of Prolog programs, to be seen as particular cases of contextual logic programs.

The original features of our work are best suggested by comparing it with related work.

To our best knowledge, semantics for contextual logic programs have only been presented in [13] and in [11]. Semantics just handling sets of computed answer substitutions have only been presented in the former work. As suggested before, more expressive semantics are needed for program analysis and we will present one after. The latter paper presents and compare several semantics for a parallel version of contextual logic programming. Beside semantics describing only computed answer substitutions, an operational and a denotational semantics tackling infinite derivations and multiple occurrences of computations are described there. They differ from two respects with the semantics presented here. On the one hand, in [11], no restriction is imposed on the way in which clauses are selected for reduction: they are used simply as alternatives. In contrast, in the sequential version we consider here, the Prolog top-to-bottom order is imposed. This results in the introduction of a new operator and in a modification of the semantics, allowing us, for instance, to treat the cut. On the other hand, the streams are assigned different meanings. In [11], the substitutions composing a stream correspond to the mgu's progressively computed during a reduction whereas here they represent (final) computed answer substitutions, the order in which they are listed in the stream representing the order in which they are produced.

The termination of logic programs has already been studied in [1, 2, 3, 5, 6, 10, 14, 15, 16, 17, 19]. A first difference with our work is that all these papers have only tackled logic programs, even mostly Prolog programs, and, therefore, not contextual logic programs. However, contextual logic programming introduces the overriding of predicate definitions, which requires fresh solutions, presented hereafter.

Discarding the contextual logic extension, the work closest to ours is probably [5]. It also proposes a denotational semantics issued from an imperative tradition and, based on it, a study of program termination. However, cpo's are used there whereas we shall use complete metric spaces and contractions.

In [19], Vasak and Potter distinguish between the existential termination of logic programs and the universal termination of logic programs. As a snapshot, the first form of termination requires that a given goal either finitely fails or that at least one answer substitution is eventually computed whereas the latter requires that, for a given goal, all the possible derivations are finite. Furthermore, they give a recursive characterization of the set of atomic goals for which a logic program universally terminates for that goal and for all its instances, under selected computation rules. As pointed out in [5], the clause selection strategies are not taken into account and there is thus no hope to extend Vasak and Potter's method to programs involving extra-logical features like Prolog cut - whereas we can do here.

Another attempt to reason about the universal termination of logic programs is described in [10] but the method proposed there is not really general.

Aiming at an automatic verification, Ullman and van Gelder ([17]) first generates a sufficient set of inequalities between the sizes of the arguments of relation symbols and then verifies whether these inequalities indeed hold. This technique is improved in [15] where the form of the inequalities and the measure of the size of the arguments are generalized. As suggested, we shall follow a quite different approach requiring no generation of testing inequalities.

Following [1] and [6], Apt and Pedreschi ([2, 3]) propose a model characterization of the termination of logic programs. It has recently been extended in [14] in order to cope with Prolog built-in primitives. In contrast with this approach, we will follow a more imperative tradition which has the merit over [2, 3, 14] of being easily extensible to tackle any kind of extra-logical features.

In this volume, [16] proposes an alternative approach based on term rewriting.

Finally, Deville also analyzes the termination of Prolog programs in his book [8]. For that purpose, he uses mode and multiplicity information. Our proposal does not require that information but is able to derive less information about the programs.

The remainder of this paper is organized as follows. Section 2 recalls the basis of contextual logic programming and specifies the sequential version under study. Section 3 introduces the metric tools used in the paper. Section 4 progressively defines the denotational semantics, firstly for a language without extra-logical features, then including Prolog cut and finally involving extra-logical features. Section 5 presents our methodology for the analysis of programs. Finally, section 6 states our conclusions and suggests work for future research.

2 Contextual Logic Programming

Contextual logic programming ([13]) is an extension of logic programming providing both local and context-dependent predicate definitions. On the one hand, the clauses of a program are distributed over several modules or units, as they are called in [13], and in that sense a predicate definition is local to the unit where the corresponding clauses occur. On the other hand, the definition of a predicate may depend on predicates not defined in the same unit, and in that case, the definitions available in a so-called context are assumed by default.

To further describe the contextual extension, let us explain a bit our notations and introduce the basic notions of contextual logic programming. The interested reader is referred to [13] (on which this section is based) for further details.

2.1 Syntax

As usual in logic programming, the contextual logic language under consideration in this paper comprises denumerably infinite sets of *variables*, *functions* and *predicates*, subsequently referred to as *Svar*, *Sfunct* and *Spred*, respectively. It also includes a set *Sunit* of so-called *unit names*, characterized by the property that every element u has attached a finite subset of Spred, called the *sort* of u and denoted by *sort*(u). The sets *Svar*, *Sfunct*, *Spred* and *Sunit* are assumed to be pairwise disjoint but, for two unit names u_1, u_2, the sorts $sort(u_1)$ and $sort(u_2)$ need not be disjoint.

The notions of term, atom, substitution, ... are defined as usual. The corresponding sets are respectively referred to as *Sterm, Satom, Ssubst*, ... We do not recall these notions here but rather specify some notions related to contextual logic programming as well as some useful notations.

An *extension formula* is a formula of the form $u \gg \overline{G}$ where u is a unit name and $\overline{G}$ is a finite conjunction of atomic or extension formulae. A *general atom* (*g-atom*) is an atomic or an extension formula. It is typically denoted by the letters A, B, C, ... The set of g-atoms is subsequently denoted by *Sgatom*. A *general goal* (*g-goal*) is a finite conjunction of g-atoms. It is typically denoted by the symbols $\overline{A}$, $\overline{B}$, $\overline{C}$, ..., $\overline{G}$, ... The empty g-goal is denoted by the Δ symbol. The set of g-goals is referred to as *Sggoal*. Clauses take here the form $H \leftarrow \overline{B}$ and allow extension formulae to occur in their bodies. Given an atom $A=p(t_1,\ldots,t_m)$, we denote by *name*(A) the predicate name of A, namely p. A set of clauses is said to *define* a predicate p if it contains a clause whose head name is p. A *unit* is a formula of the form $u : U$, where $u \in Sunit$ and U is a finite set of clauses such that the set of predicates defined in U is $sort(u)$. We call u the *name* or *head* of the unit and U its *body*. A *system of units* is a set $\mathcal{U}$ of units such that no two distinct units in $\mathcal{U}$ have the same name. For a unit in $\mathcal{U}$ with name u, we denote its body by $|u|_{\mathcal{U}}$, or simply $|u|$ if $\mathcal{U}$ is understood. In the sequel we will often abuse language and refer to u as a unit in $\mathcal{U}$ when in fact we mean the unit u: $|u|$. Systems of units will subsequently play the role of programs so that we will refer to them under the name of program. Following these lines, the set of systems of units (or the set of programs) is subsequently referred to as *Sprog*.

A *context* is a stack of units. It is referred to by its name, consisting of an arbitrary sequence of unit names. The set of context names, *Scontext*, is thus the free monoid $\mathrm{Sunit}^{<\omega}$. Context names are represented by juxtaposition, as in uv. The empty sequence λ is employed as the name of the *empty* context. The context resulting from *extending* the context c with unit u (i.e. by putting u on top of the stack) is denoted by uc.

2.2 Derivation relation semantics

This terminology given, the contextual extension to logic programming can now be defined. This is achieved by means of the following derivation relation $c \vdash_{\mathcal{U}} \overline{G}\ [\theta]$, defined for a system of units $\mathcal{U}$, a context name c, a g-goal $\overline{G}$ and a substitution θ. Its intended meaning is that there is a (successful) *derivation of* $\overline{G}$ *in* c *from* $\mathcal{U}$ *with computed answer substitution* θ. More formally, the derivation relation $c \vdash_{\mathcal{U}} \overline{G}\ [\theta]$ is defined by means of rules of the form

$$\frac{Assumptions}{Conclusion} \quad \textit{if} \quad Conditions,$$

asserting the *Conclusion* whenever the *Assumptions* and *Conditions* hold. (Note that *Assumptions* or *Conditions* may be absent from some rules.) Precisely, it is defined, by case analysis on the form of $\overline{G}$ as the smallest relation of *Sprog* × *Scontext* × *Sggoal* × *Ssubst* satisfying the following rules (N-T) to (E-T). The symbol ϵ is used to denote the empty (identity) substitution and $c \vdash_{\mathcal{U}} \overline{G}\ [\theta]$ is written simply as $c \vdash \overline{G}\ [\theta]$, for readability.

Null formula

(N-T) $$\frac{}{c \vdash \Delta\ [\epsilon]}$$

Conjunction

(C-T) $$\frac{c \vdash A\ [\theta],\ c \vdash (A_1,\ldots,A_m)\theta\ [\sigma]}{c \vdash A,A_1,\ldots,A_m\ [\theta\sigma]}$$

Atomic formula—local reduction

(R-T) $$\frac{uc \vdash \overline{B}\theta\ [\sigma]}{uc \vdash A\ [\theta\sigma]} \quad \textit{if} \quad \begin{cases} H \leftarrow \overline{B} \in |u|^{1} \\ A \text{ and } H \text{ unify with mgu } \theta \end{cases}$$

Atomic formula—contextual definition

(X-T) $$\frac{c \vdash A\ [\theta]}{uc \vdash A\ [\theta]} \quad \textit{if} \quad name(A) \notin sort(u)$$

Extension formula

(E-T) $$\frac{uc \vdash \overline{G}\ [\theta]}{c \vdash u \gg \overline{G}\ [\theta]}$$

The first two rules are essentially the same as for Horn clause logic. On the one hand, rule (N-T) states that the empty conjunction Δ can be derived in any context, with the empty substitution as computed answer substitution. On the other hand, rule (C-T) states that a conjunction is derivable if its conjuncts are, each in turn.

The last three rules (R-T), (X-T) and (E-T) explain the contextual extension. Rule (R-T) states that, in order to derive an atom in a context whose top unit defines the corresponding predicate, one has to reduce the atom in the unit and to derive the induced instance of the body of the clause used for the reduction. Rule (X-T) states that in case the treated atom has no definition in the top unit, then the atom has to be reduced in the context with the top unit removed. Finally, rule (E-T) states that an extension formula is derivable in a context if the "inner" conjunction is derivable in the context extended with the unit mentioned in the extension formula.

Particularly notice that, as a consequence of the above rules, the usual logic programming derivation of a goal $\overline{G}$ for a program P is obtained by the contextual reduction of $u \gg \overline{G}$ for the unit u consisting of the clauses of P. In that sense, contextual logic programming subsumes logic programming and the general methods we will develop for contextual logic programming can be applied in the restricted case of logic programming, as well.

---

[1] As usual, a suitable renaming of the clauses is assumed.

2.3 Sequential version under study

Although the units are ordered sequentially in the contexts and therefore for the reductions, the above rules impose no order of selection of clauses from the same unit. We will do however in the sequential version considered in this paper and will adopt a Prolog top-to-botom strategy of selection of clauses. Furthermore, we will consider in section 4 – and consequently assume to be included in the language – the Prolog cut and the usual extra-logical features.

3 Metric spaces

Throughout this paper, metric spaces will be used as important semantic tools. The reason for their introduction arises from the following fact: it is quite natural to identify two histories the more, the greater their common prefix is. This observation naturally leads to a distance between them, as formalized in example 2, and therefore to metric spaces. The reader is assumed to be familiar with metric spaces as well as with their related notions of convergent sequences, closed and compact subsets, completeness, ... and is referred to [9], when need be. For the sake of completeness, we just specify hereafter some practical language misuses, describe examples of metric spaces employed subsequently and recall the notion of contraction and its very useful property (due to S. Banach) of having one and only one fixed point in complete metric spaces.

Convention 1 *We only use subsequently metric spaces whose metric is bounded by 1 i.e metric spaces (M,d) such that for all $x, y \in M$, $d(x,y) \leq 1$. In view of this, we refer to them more simply as metric spaces. Furthermore, their metric d is often omitted when it is clearly understood.* ∎

Example 1 *For any set S, the mapping $d_{disc} : S \times S \rightarrow [0,1]$ defined by*

$$d(x,y) = \begin{cases} 0 & \textit{if } x = y \\ 1 & \textit{otherwise} \end{cases}$$

for any $x, y \in S$, defines a distance on S, called the discrete distance. Furthermore, the space (S, d_{disc}) is a complete metric space. In case no distance has been explicitly defined, any set is assumed subsequently to be endowed with the discrete distance. ∎

Example 2 *Let A be an alphabet and let $A^{\leq\omega}$ denote the set of all finite and infinite words over A. Furthermore, let, for any $x \in A^{\leq\omega}$, $x[n]$ represent the prefix of x of length n. Define the mapping $d_{stream} : A^{\leq\omega} \times A^{\leq\omega} \rightarrow [0,1]$ as follows: for any $x, y \in A^{\leq\omega}$: $d_{stream}(x,y) = 2^{-sup\{n : x[n]=y[n]\}}$, with the convention that $2^{-\infty} = 0$. Then, $(A^{\leq\omega}, d_{stream})$ is a complete metric space.* ∎

Example 3 *Let X be some set and (M,d), (M_1,d_1), (M_2,d_2) be complete metric spaces. Define the mapping d_{funct} on the set $X \rightarrow M$ of all functions from X to M and the mapping d_{cart} on the cartesian product $M_1 \times M_2$ as follows: for any $f_1, f_2 \in X \rightarrow M$, $(x_1,x_2), (y_1,y_2) \in M_1 \times M_2$,*

$$\begin{aligned} d_{funct}(f_1,f_2) &= \sup_{x \in X} d(f_1(x), f_2(x)) \\ d_{cart}((x_1,x_2),(y_1,y_2)) &= max\{d_1(x_1,y_1), d_2(x_2,y_2)\}. \end{aligned}$$

The spaces $(X \rightarrow M, d_{funct})$ and $(M_1 \times M_2, d_{cart})$ are complete metric spaces. In case no distance has been explicitly defined, the distances d_{funct} and d_{cart} are implicitly taken for the sets $X \rightarrow M$ and $M_1 \times M_2$, respectively. ∎

Definition 2 *Let (M_1, d_1) and (M_2, d_2) be two metric spaces. A function $f : M_1 \rightarrow M_2$ is called a* contraction *iff there is a real number $c \in [0,1)$ such that, for all $x, y \in M$, $d_2(f(x), f(y)) \leq c.d_1(x, y)$.* ∎

Proposition 3 (Banach's theorem) *Let (M,d) be a complete metric space. Any contraction $f : M \rightarrow M$ has a unique fixed point.* ∎

4 Denotational Semantics

The semantics we will use for the semantic analysis of contextual logic programs is of a denotational type. Its main features are that it is defined compositionally and without any help of any transition system or reference to any declarative paradigm. Besides the challenge they constitute in the design of the semantics, we believe that these properties are both natural and necessary requirements for the analysis of programs. Indeed, compositionality is a key issue in software engineering. As already explained, declarative semantics are also not well-suited for coping with extra-logical features as well as flow of control. Finally, reasoning about computations is best abstracted from the detailed transition steps defined by transition systems.

As already suggested, another desire – met by our semantics – is that extra-logical features can be treated easily. For the ease of exposition, the semantics is first presented in the pure contextual logic framework involving no extra-logical feature. It is then extended to tackle Prolog cut, and thereby negation implemented according to the negation-as-failure rule. It is finally augmented in order to cope with built-in primitives.

4.1 Pure sequential contextual logic programming

The denotational semantics should ideally report the answer substitutions in the order in which they are computed as well as indicate infinite derivations when they occur. The first property is modelled by delivering, as semantics for goals, sequences partly composed of substitutions. They intend to represent the computed answer substitutions and the order in which they occur is intended to reflect the order in which they are computed. The divergence requirement is fulfilled by inserting internal actions in the sequences. They represent the unifications and context modifications performed during the reductions. They are subsequently represented by the τ letter. Infinite derivations thus corresponds to the infinite sequence of τ's.

Summing up, the semantic domain to be used is composed of sequences of the form

$$\tau. \cdots .\tau.\theta_1. \cdots .\tau. \cdots .\tau.\theta_m. \cdots$$

either finite and ending by a substitution or infinite and possibly ending by an infinite number of τ's. Among them, four types are worth pointing out. Firstly, the empty sequence, subsequently denoted by λ, is associated with a computation with no internal step and no computed substitution; it corresponds to an immediately failing computation. Secondly, finite sequences are associated with goals whose resolutions finitely terminate; the substitutions reported therein correspond to the answer substitutions actually computed. Finally, infinite computations may be of two kinds: those ending with the infinite sequence of τ's and those consisting of the infinite repetition of (finite) sequences of the form $\tau. \cdots .\tau.\theta$. The former corrrespond to diverging computations. The latter are associated with goals whose resolutions produce an infinite number of computed answer substitutions.

The following definition formalizes the semantic domain just introduced.

Definition 4 *Define the set of computation histories Shist as the set of words* $Scas^{\leq\omega} \cup (Scas^{<\omega} \times \{\tau^\omega\})$ *where the set of computed answer sequences Scas is defined as the set of words* $\{\tau\}^{<\omega} \times Ssubst$. *We will subsequently consider the cartesian products of this definition as suffixing mechanisms and use the stream distance introduced in example 2. By doing so, the set Shist is turned into a complete metric space.* ∎

Giving a compositional semantics requires the identification of semantic operators which provide counterparts at the semantic level for the syntactic operators. Two syntactic operators are employed in the sequential contextual logic language under consideration: the sequential union of clauses in the programs and the sequential composition of general atoms in goals. We now describe their semantic counterparts.

The semantic counterpart of the union of clauses, subsequently denoted by $\oplus$, consists of concatenating the sequences reported by the semantic analysis of the clauses. To be more specific, consider the program composed of the following unit $\mathtt{u}_p$:

```
u_p:  p(a).
      p(b).
```

The contributions of the clauses for `p(X)` given the context $\mathtt{u}_p$ are $\tau.\{\mathtt{X/a}\}$ and $\tau.\{\mathtt{X/b}\}$, respectively, where the τ's are used to denote the unifications. In total, the (global) semantics to report for `p(X)` is $\tau.\{\mathtt{X/a}\}.\tau.\{\mathtt{X/b}\}$ i.e. the concatenation of the two sequences.

Although the concatenation of sequences may be defined directly, we will use a recursive definition in the aim of getting the reader acquainted with our techniques. A direct recursive definition leads to the following equation, for any $h_1, h_2 \in Shist$,

$$h_1 \oplus h_2 = \begin{cases} c.(h_r \oplus h_2) & \text{if } h_1 = c.h_r \text{ , with } c \in \{\tau\} \cup Ssubst \\ h_2 & \text{otherwise,} \end{cases}$$

or, equivalently, using prefix notations,

$$\oplus\,(h_1, h_2) = \begin{cases} c.(\oplus\,(h_r, h_2)) & \text{if } h_1 = c.h_r \text{ , with } c \in \{\tau\} \cup Ssubst \\ h_2 & \text{otherwise.} \end{cases}$$

As required, these equations state

i) that concatenating a non empty sequence $h_1 = c.h_r$ ($c \in \{\tau\} \cup Ssubst$) with h_2 gives the sequence whose first element is c and whose tail is obtained by recursively concatenating h_r with h_2 *(first case of the equations)*;

ii) and that concatenating the empty sequence with h_2 gives h_2 *(second case of the equations)*.

However, such a direct definition is ill-defined because of the possibly infinite nature of the streams. This difficulty is circumvented by using a higher-order function, of the same recursive nature, but that turns out to be a well-defined contraction. The actual concatenation function $\oplus$ is then defined as the (unique) fixed point of this contraction.

Definition 5 *Define* Ψ_{cl} : $[Shist \times Shist \rightarrow Shist] \rightarrow [Shist \times Shist \rightarrow Shist]$ *as the following function: for any* $F : Shist \times Shist \rightarrow Shist$, *any* $h_1, h_2 \in Shist$,

$$\Psi_{cl}\,(F)(h_1, h_2) = \begin{cases} c.F(h_r, h_2) & \textit{if } h_1 = c.h_r\ ,\ \textit{with } c \in \{\tau\} \cup Ssubst \\ h_2 & \textit{otherwise.} \end{cases}$$ ■

Proposition 6 *The function* Ψ_{cl} *is a contraction.* ■

Definition 7 *Define the function* $\oplus$: $Shist \times Shist \rightarrow Shist$ *as the unique fixed point of* Ψ_{cl} . ■

The semantic counterpart of the sequential composition of atoms in goals is slightly more complicated. Basically, given two goals $\overline{G}_1$ and $\overline{G}_2$, the semantics of $\overline{G}_1$, $\overline{G}_2$ is obtained by taking all the computed answer substitutions for $\overline{G}_1$ in the semantics delivered for $\overline{G}_1$ and by replacing them with the semantic sequences for the induced instances of $\overline{G}_2$. Note that this replacement is actually a concatenation that suitably handles internal steps, possibly combined in infinite sequences. As an illustration, let us consider the goal

$$(\mathtt{u}_p \gg \mathtt{p(X)})\ ,\ (\mathtt{u}_q \gg \mathtt{q(X)})$$

and the program composed of the following units $\mathtt{u}_p$ and $\mathtt{u}_q$:

```
u_p :  p(f(X)).          u_q :  q(f(a)).
       p(g(X)).                 q(Y) ← q(Y).
```

The semantics for $\mathtt{u}_p \gg \mathtt{p(X)}$ reports the two substitutions $\alpha = \{\mathtt{X/f(V)}\}$ and $\beta = \{\mathtt{X/g(W)}\}$. They are actually preceded by two internal actions representing the context extensions and the clause unifications so that the actual semantics will be $\tau.\tau.\alpha.\tau.\beta$. The semantics for $\mathtt{q(X)}\alpha$ produces the substitution $\gamma = \{\mathtt{V/a}\}$, preceded by two internal actions for the context and the clause unification and then diverges. It is thus $\tau.\tau.\gamma.\tau.\tau.\cdots$. The semantics for $\mathtt{q(X)}\beta$ diverges. As easily checked, the semantics for the above goal is $\tau.\tau.\tau.\tau.\gamma.\tau.\ \cdots\ .\tau.\tau$ i.e. it is indeed the result of respectively replacing α and β by the sequences $\tau.\tau.\gamma.\tau.\ \cdots\ .\tau.\ \cdots$ and $\tau.\ \cdots\ .\tau.\ \cdots$ in the sequence $\tau.\tau.\alpha.\tau.\beta$.

As the semantics are built compositionally, the semantics of $\overline{G}_2$ is defined independently of the answer substitutions computed for $\overline{G}_1$. We are thus led to combine in the way just explained not sequences but sequences with functions that map some given substitutions to sequences.

A direct recursive definition leads to the following equation, for any $h \in$ *Shist* and any $f : Ssubst \rightarrow Shist$,

$$h \otimes f = \begin{cases} \lambda & \text{if } h = \lambda \\ \tau.(h_r \otimes f) & \text{if } h = \tau.h_r \\ f(\theta) \oplus (h_r \otimes f) & \text{if } h = \theta.h_r \end{cases}$$

or, equivalently, using prefix notations,

$$\otimes (h, f) = \begin{cases} \lambda & \text{if } h = \lambda \\ \tau.(\otimes (h_r, f)) & \text{if } h = \tau.h_r \\ f(\theta) \oplus (\otimes (h_r, f)) & \text{if } h = \theta.h_r \end{cases} .$$

These equations support the following intuitive reading.

i) In the first case, the goal $\overline{G}_1$ is associated with the empty sequence λ, and hence directly fails. The goal $\overline{G}_1$, $\overline{G}_2$ thus directly fails whatever $\overline{G}_2$ is, and the semantics to be reported for it is therefore λ.

ii) In the second case, the goal $\overline{G}_1$ is associated with a sequence of the form $\tau.h_r$ and thus performs an internal action first. The semantics to be reported for $\overline{G}_1$, $\overline{G}_2$ is therefore composed of this first internal action followed by the result of a recursive treatment of h_r with respect to the semantics of G_2.

iii) In the last case, the recursive reasoning has reached, in the semantics of $\overline{G}_1$, a subsequence of the form $\theta.h_r$, with θ a substitution. In this situation, according to the above example, the corresponding part of the semantics for $\overline{G}_1$, $\overline{G}_2$ is obtained by

- by replacing θ by the semantics of $\overline{G}_2$ i.e. $f(\theta)$, this replacement actually consisting of a concatenation,
- and by treating recursively the remainder h_r with respect to the semantics of $\overline{G}_2$.

However such a direct definition is again ill-defined because of the possibly infinite nature of the streams. A correct definition is provided, here too, by a suitable higher-order contraction, of the same recursive nature.

Definition 8 *Define* Ψ_{seq} : $[Shist \times (Ssubst \rightarrow Shist) \rightarrow Shist] \rightarrow [Shist \times (Ssubst \rightarrow Shist) \rightarrow Shist]$ *as the following function: for any* $F : Shist \times (Ssubst \rightarrow Shist) \rightarrow Shist$, *any* $h \in Shist$, *any* $f : Ssubst \rightarrow Shist$, *any* $\theta \in Ssubst$,

$$\Psi_{seq} (F)(h, f) = \begin{cases} \lambda & \textit{if } h = \lambda \\ \tau.F(h_r, f) & \textit{if } h = \tau.h_r \\ f(\theta) \oplus F(h_r, f) & \textit{if } h = \theta.h_r \end{cases}$$

■

Proposition 9 *The function* Ψ_{seq} *is a contraction.* ■

Definition 10 *Define the function* $\otimes$: $Shist \times (Ssubst \rightarrow Shist) \rightarrow Shist$ *as the unique fixed point of* Ψ_{seq} . ■

We are now in a position to define the denotational semantics. As suggested above, it is best viewed as a function, mapping, for a given program, a given goal in a given environment to an history. Previous developments suggest that the environment to consider is composed of a substitution, summing up the values computed so far for the variables, and of a context, according to which the goal should be reduced. The denotational semantics is thus of type

$$Sprog \rightarrow Sggoal \rightarrow Scontext \rightarrow Ssubst \rightarrow Shist$$

In view of the operators $\oplus$ and $\otimes$, the definition of the denotational semantics amounts to stating the semantics of the basic cases, that is of generalized atoms and of the empty goal. The semantics of the latter is quite clear: the current substitution is simply reported. The semantics of atoms reflect rules (R-T) and (X-T):

i) in case there are clauses unifiable with the atom under consideration in the top unit of the considered context, the semantics consists of the concatenation of the sequences of the induced instances of the clause bodies, previously preceded by τ to indicate the unification step;
ii) in case the current context is not empty and there are no clauses defining the atom in the top unit, the semantics consists of the semantics of the atom in the context with the top unit removed, this sequence being preceded by τ to indicate the context update;
iii) otherwise, the semantics reports failure i.e. the empty sequence λ.

Finally, the semantics of an extension formula $u \gg \overline{G}$ reflects rule (E-T): it is the semantics of $\overline{G}$ in the context extended with u, preceded by τ to indicate the context update.

Again, the infinite nature of streams make a direct recursive definition ill-defined and the problem is circumvented by using a higher-order contraction. The above intuition is then more clearly reflected by substituting $\Psi_{den}(F)$ and F by Den in the following equations.

Definition 11 *Define* Ψ_{den} : $[Sprog \rightarrow Sggoal \rightarrow Scontext \rightarrow Ssubst \rightarrow Shist] \rightarrow [Sprog \rightarrow Sggoal \rightarrow Scontext \rightarrow Ssubst \rightarrow Shist]$ *as the following function: for any* $F : Sprog \rightarrow Sggoal \rightarrow Scontext \rightarrow Ssubst \rightarrow Shist$, *any* $P \in Sprog$, *any* $A \in Satom$, *any* $A_1, \ldots, A_m \in Sgatom$ $(m > 1)$, *any* $\overline{G} \in Sggoal$, *any* $c \in Scontext$, *any* $\sigma \in Ssubst$,

i) $\Psi_{den}(F)(P)(A)(c)(\sigma) =$
$$\begin{cases} \tau.F(P)(B_1)(c)(\sigma\theta_1) \oplus \cdots \oplus \tau.F(P)(B_m)(c)(\sigma\theta_m) & \textit{if } Cond_1, \\ \tau.F(P)(A)(c')(\sigma) & \textit{if } Cond_2, \\ \lambda & \textit{otherwise} \end{cases}$$

ii) $\Psi_{den}(F)(P)(u \gg \overline{G})(c)(\sigma) = \tau.F(P)(\overline{G})(u.c)(\sigma)$

iii) $\Psi_{den}(F)(P)(A_1, A_2, \cdots, A_m)(c)(\sigma) =$
$$\Psi_{den}(F)(P)(A_1)(c)(\sigma) \otimes F(P)(A_2)(c) \otimes \cdots \otimes F(P)(A_m)(c)$$

iv) $\Psi_{den}(F)(P)(\Delta)(c)(\sigma) = \sigma$

where the $Cond_i$*'s stand for the following conditions* [2]

- $Cond_1$: $c = u.c'$, *A is defined in u and* $(H_1 \leftarrow \overline{G}_1)$, ..., $(H_m \leftarrow \overline{G}_m)$ *are the clauses of P unifiable with* $A\sigma$, *say with mgu's* $\theta_1, \ldots, \theta_m$, *respectively;*

[2] As usual, suitable renamings of the clauses are assumed.

- *$Cond_2$:* $c = u.c'$ *and A is not defined in u.*

∎

Proposition 12 *The function* Ψ_{den} *is a contraction.* ∎

Definition 13 *Define the denotational semantics Den : Sprog → Sggoal → Scontext → Ssubst → Shist as the unique fixed point of* Ψ_{den} *. For the clarity of the exposition, given* $P \in Sprog$, $\overline{G} \in Sggoal$, $c \in Scontext$, $\theta \in Ssubst$, *the denotational semantics* $Den(P)(\overline{G})(c)(\theta)$ *will often be rewritten as* $[\![\overline{G}]\!](P)(c)(\theta)$ *and the program P will moreover be often omitted when it is implictly understood.* ∎

4.2 Adding the cut

We now extend the denotational semantics in order to cope with Prolog cut. From a syntactic point of view, it is introduced as a new operator " ! " combining atoms in goals and binding them tighter than the sequential composition operator " , ". Intricate use of brackets will be avoided by assuming a left-associativity rule.

From the semantic point of view, the cut operator has the effect of discarding some solutions. Precisely, it behaves as a predicate that always succeeds but with the side-effect of removing all the choice points created since it appears in the derivations. Restated in other terms, the success of the cut operator modifies the behavior of goals and the use of clauses as follows. On the one hand, for $\overline{G} = \overline{G}_1 \,!\, \overline{G}_2$, the first solution reported by the evaluation of $\overline{G}_1$ will be considered for the evaluation of $\overline{G}$; the others will be discarded. On the other hand, if p is defined by means of the clauses $c_1, \ldots, c_m$ and if the body of c_k contains a cut, then the reduction of this cut leads to the discarding of $c_{k+1}, \ldots, c_m$ as alternative clauses for reducing p.

This behaviour can be easily modelled in the denotational semantics. As far as goals are concerned, the cut has the flavour of a sequential composition operator: the only difference with the operator " , " is that it only considers the first substitution computed by the first goal component instead of all of them. As far as clauses are concerned, it has the effect of discarding the contribution of some of them. This is subsequently modelled by introducing a termination symbol related to the cut: " | ". When adding (i.e. concatenating) the contribution of clauses, its effect is to discard any history that would follow it. Of course, several cuts can be inserted in a program and it is certainly dangerous to mix several " | " symbols related to several cuts. Fortunately, thanks to the compositional way in which the semantics is constructed, it is possible to eliminate these symbols in such a way that no clashes will actually appear. As an interesting side effect, the final denotational semantics will be free from such terminators.

Semantic histories to be considered now are thus finite sequences of the form

$$\tau. \cdots .\tau.\theta_1. \cdots .\tau. \cdots .\tau.\theta_m$$

possibly suffixed by " | ", or infinite sequences either repeating infinitely sequences of the form $\tau\ n.\theta$ for some finite n or τ's from some moment on. This is formalized in the following definition, extending the semantic domain of definition 4.

Definition 14 *Define the set of extended histories Sehist as the set of words* $Scas^{\leq\omega} \cup (Scas^{<\omega} \times \{\tau^{\omega}, \mid\})$ *and endow it with the same distance as Shist. It is also a complete metric space.* ■

The previous operators " $\oplus$ " and " $\otimes$ " need to be extended to this new domain. This is achieved as follows according to the intuition just sketched and to the recursive reasoning of section 4.1

Definition 15 *Define* Ψ_{ecl} : [*Sehist*×*Sehist* → *Sehist*] → [*Sehist*×*Sehist* → *Sehist*] *as the following function: for any* F : *Sehist* × *Sehist* → *Sehist, any* $h_1, h_2 \in$ *Sehist,*

$$\Psi_{ecl}\,(F)(h_1,h_2) = \begin{cases} c.F(h_r,h_2) & \text{if } h = c.h_r \text{ , with } c \in \{\tau\} \cup Ssubst \\ \mid & \text{if } h_1 = \mid \\ h_2 & \text{otherwise.} \end{cases}$$ ■

Proposition 16 *The function* Ψ_{ecl} *is a contraction.* ■

Definition 17 *Define the function* $\overline{\oplus}$: *Sehist* × *Sehist* → *Sehist as the fixed point of* Ψ_{ecl} . ■

Definition 18 *Define* Ψ_{eseq} : [*Sehist* × (*Ssubst* → *Sehist*) → *Sehist*] → [*Sehist* × (*Ssubst* → *Sehist*) → *Sehist*] *as the following function: for any* F : *Sehist* × (*Ssubst* → *Sehist*) → *Sehist, any* $h \in$ *Sehist, any* f : *Ssubst* → *Sehist, any* $\theta \in$ *Ssubst,*

$$\Psi_{eseq}\,(F)(h,f) = \begin{cases} \lambda & \text{if } h = \lambda \\ \mid & \text{if } h = \mid \\ \tau.F(h_r,f) & \text{if } h = \tau.h_r \\ f(\theta)\,\overline{\oplus}\,F(h_r,f) & \text{if } h = \theta.h_r \end{cases}$$ ■

Proposition 19 *The function* Ψ_{seq} *is a contraction.* ■

Definition 20 *Define the function* $\otimes_e$: *Sehist* × (*Ssubst* → *Sehist*) → *Sehist as the unique fixed point of* Ψ_{eseq} . ■

Desired properties are that the functions $\overline{\oplus}$ and $\otimes_e$ are proper extensions of the functions $\oplus$ and $\otimes$ to *Sehist*. This is indeed the case, as claimed by the following proposition.

Proposition 21 *For any* $h, h_1, h_2 \in$ *Shist,* f : *Ssubst* → *Shist, one has* $h_1 \,\overline{\oplus}\, h_2 = h_1 \oplus h_2$ *and* $h \otimes_e f = h \otimes f$. ■

To keep the definition of the denotational semantics compositional, a counterpart has to be defined for the cut operator. The similarity of the cut with respect to the sequential composition operator makes a direct definition possible. This is achieved in the following definition where the operator " $\ominus$ " is defined as the semantic counterpart for the operator " ! " by means of the operator " $\overline{\oplus}$ ".

Definition 22 *Define* $\ominus$: *Sehist* × (*Ssubst* → *Sehist*) → *Sehist as the following function: for any* $h \in$ *Sehist, any* f : *Ssubst* → *Sehist,*

$$h \ominus f = \begin{cases} h & \text{if } h = \tau\,\omega \text{ or } h = \lambda \\ f(\theta)\,\overline{\oplus}\,\mid & \text{if } h = \tau\; n.\theta.h_r \end{cases}$$ ■

A final operator is needed to remove the cut marks " | ". It is defined as the following operator *uncut*. On the way, its combination with the operator " $\overline{\oplus}$ " is defined as the operator " $\oplus_e$ ".

Definition 23

1) Define uncut : Sehist → Shist as the following function: for any $h \in Sehist$,

$$uncut(h) = \begin{cases} h_r & \text{if } h = h_r.\mid \text{ with } h_r \in Scas^{<\omega} \\ h & \text{otherwise.} \end{cases}$$

2) Define $\oplus_e$: Sehist×Sehist → Shist as the following function: for any $h_1, h_2 \in Sehist$, $h_1 \oplus_e h_2 = uncut(h_1 \overline{\oplus} h_2)$. ∎

We are now in a position to define the extended version of the denotational semantics. In view of the operators " $\oplus_e$ ", " $\otimes$ " and " $\ominus$ ", this consists of straightforwardly extending definitions 11 and 13.

Definition 24 *Define Ψ_{eden} : [Sprog → Sggoal → Scontext → Ssubst → Sehist] → [Sprog → Sggoal → Scontext → Ssubst → Sehist] as the following function: for any F : Sprog → Sggoal → Scontext → Ssubst → Sehist, any $P \in Sprog$, any $A \in Satom$, any $\overline{G}, \overline{G_1}, \overline{G_2} \in Sggoal$, any $c \in Scontext$, any $\sigma \in Ssubst$,*

i) $\Psi_{eden}(F)(P)(A)(c)(\sigma) =$

$$\begin{cases} \tau.F(P)(B_1)(c)(\sigma\theta_1) \oplus_e \cdots \oplus_e \tau.F(P)(B_m)(c)(\sigma\theta_m) & \text{if } Cond_1, \\ \tau.F(P)(A)(c')(\sigma) & \text{if } Cond_2, \\ \lambda & \text{otherwise} \end{cases}$$

ii) $\Psi_{eden}(F)(P)(u \gg \overline{G})(c)(\sigma) = \tau.F(P)(\overline{G})(u.c)(\sigma)$

iii) $\Psi_{eden}(F)(P)(\overline{G_1}, \overline{G_2})(c)(\sigma) = \Psi_{eden}(F)(P)(\overline{G_1})(c)(\sigma) \otimes_e F(P)(\overline{G_2})(c)$

iv) $\Psi_{eden}(F)(P)(\overline{G_1} \,!\, \overline{G_2})(c)(\sigma) = \Psi_{eden}(F)(P)(\overline{G_1})(c)(\sigma) \ominus F(P)(\overline{G_2})(c)$

v) $\Psi_{eden}(F)(P)(\Delta)(c)(\sigma) = \sigma$

where the $Cond_i$'s stand for the following conditions [3]

- *$Cond_1$: $c = u.c'$, A is defined in u and $(H_1 \leftarrow \overline{G_1})$, ..., $(H_m \leftarrow \overline{G_m})$ are the clauses of P unifiable with $A\sigma$, say with mgu's θ_1, ..., θ_m, respectively;*
- *$Cond_2$: $c = u.c'$ and A is not defined in u.*

∎

Proposition 25 *The function Ψ_{eden} is a contraction.* ∎

Definition 26 *Define the denotational semantics Den_e : Sprog → Sggoal → Scontext → Ssubst → Sehist as the unique fixed point of Ψ_{eden}. For the clarity of the exposition, given $P \in Sprog$, $\overline{G} \in Sggoal$, $c \in Scontext$, $\theta \in Ssubst$, the denotational semantics $Den_e(P)(\overline{G})(c)(\theta)$ will often be rewritten as $[\![\overline{G}]\!]_e(P)(c)(\theta)$ and the program P and the subscript "e" will moreover be often omitted when they are implictly understood.* ∎

Another desired property is that the denotational semantics does not report the auxiliary symbol " | ". This is indeed the case, as stated by the following property.

[3] As usual, suitable renamings of the clauses are assumed.

Proposition 27 *For any $P \in Sprog$, $\overline{G} \in Sggoal$, $c \in Scontext$, $\sigma \in Ssubst$, one has $Den_e(P)(\overline{G})(c)(\sigma) \in Shist$.* ■

4.3 Adding built-in primitives

The denotational semantics can finally be extended to tackle built-in primitives. Handling them consists simply of adding new basic cases to those of definition 24. For instance, for handling the **var** built-in primitive, it is sufficient to add the following equation:

$$\Psi_{eden}\,(F)(P)(\mathtt{var(X)})(c)(\sigma) = \begin{cases} \sigma & \text{if } \mathtt{X}\sigma \text{ is a variable} \\ \lambda & \text{otherwise.} \end{cases}$$

5 Reasoning about programs

This section aims at arguing that the denotational semantics developed in the previous section can be used as the basis for formal reasoning about program properties. In our opinion, most program properties can indeed be proved by using the equalities of definitions 11 and 24 and by using inductive reasonings. Properties of the computed answer substitutions can also be established by reasoning about the substitutions reported in the semantic histories. Due to lack of space, we will support our claim here through the study of the universal termination property of some elementary and classical procedures. However, more complex procedures can be treated by using similar reasonings.

Our first example illustrates inductive reasoning on the denotational semantics. It tackles the classical `partition` procedure, defined as follows:

```
up  partition(X,[],[],[]).
    partition(X,[Y|L],[Y|S],G)  ←  Y≤X , partition(X,L,S,G).
    partition(X,[Y|L],S,[Y|G])  ←  Y>X , partition(X,L,S,G).
```

The expected claim is stated in the following proposition.

Proposition 28 *For any real number* `x`*, any ground list* `l` *of real numbers, any variables* `S`, `G`*, any context c with u_p as top element, the evaluation of the call* `partition(x,l,S,G)` *terminates successfully by binding* `S` *and* `G` *to lists of reals of length less than or equal to* `l`.[4]

Proof The proof amounts to establishing that, under the conditions of the proposition and for any substitution θ leaving `S` and `G` free, $[\![$`partition(x,l,S,G)`$]\!](c)(\theta)$ contains at least one substitution and that all its substitutions bind `S` and `G` to lists of reals of length less than or equal to that of `l`. This is achieved by induction on the length of `l`, say $\mathcal{L}$.

Basic case: $\mathcal{L} = 0$. In this case, `l` is the empty list `[]`, `partition(x,l,S,G)` unifies only with the first clause and $[\![$`partition(x,l,S,G)`$]\!](c)(\theta) = \tau.\gamma$ with $\gamma = \theta\circ\{\mathtt{S/[\,]},\mathtt{G/[\,]}\}$. The thesis is then established.

[4]The length of a list is assumed to be defined as usual.

Induction case: $\mathcal{L} > 0$. In this case, `l` is non-empty. It is thus of the form `[y|l']`, for some real `y` and some list of reals `l'` of length strictly less than $\mathcal{L}$. It follows that the call `partition(x,l,S,G)` unifies with the last two clauses and that

$$
\begin{aligned}
&[\![\texttt{partition(x,l,S,G)}]\!](c)(\theta) = \\
&\quad \tau.[\![\texttt{y} \le \texttt{x}, \texttt{partition(x,l',S',G)}]\!](c)(\theta\circ\{\texttt{S/[y|S']}\}) \\
&\quad \overline{\oplus}\ \tau.[\![\texttt{y} > \texttt{x}, \texttt{partition(x,l',S,G')}]\!](c)(\theta\circ\{\texttt{G/[y|G']}\})
\end{aligned}
$$

for some lists S' and G'. According to the compositional nature of definition 11, the denotational semantics of the right-hand side of the equality are obtained from that of the inequalities `y` $\le$ `x`, `y` $>$ `x`, and from that of the recursive calls `partition(x,l',S',G)` and `partition(x,l',S,G')`. As an application of section 4.3, the denotational semantics of the inequalities is defined as

$$
[\![I]\!](c)(\sigma) = \begin{cases} \sigma & \text{if } I \text{ is verified} \\ \lambda & \text{otherwise} \end{cases}
$$

where I stands for the inequalities. Moreover, according to the inductive reasoning, the semantics of the recursive calls contain at least one substitution and all their substitutions bind the two last variable-argument to lists of reals of length strictly less than $\mathcal{L}$. The thesis then results from the definition of the operator $\overline{\oplus}$. ■

Two remarks are here worth noting. On the one hand, it is easy to extend the previous proof to further qualify the lists `S` and `G`, for instance, as being composed of elements less than or equal to `x` and strictly greater than `x`, respectively. On the other hand, the previous example does not use that much the contextual extensions. However, it is also easy to extend the previous reasoning in order to cope with more evolved programs such as:

```
ua :    append([],L2,L2).
        append([X|L1],L2,[X|L]) ← append(L1,L2,L).


uqs :   qsort([],[]).
        qsort([X|L],Ls)  ←  up ≫ partition(X,L,S,G),
                            qsort(S,Ss), qsort(G,Gs),
                            ua ≫ append(Ss,[X|Gs],Ls).
```

Let us now turn to a more complicated example involving fixed-point reasoning. Consider the procedure **even** computing the series of even numbers.

```
ue :    even(0).
        even(s(s(X))) ← even(X).
```

Let us prove the following result.

Proposition 29 *For any context c with* u_e *as top unit, any variable* X*, the evaluation of* even(X) *in the context c delivers an infinite number of computed answer substitutions successively binding* X *to* $s^{2k}(0)$*, for* $k = 0, 1, 2, \cdots$.

Proof The proof amounts to establishing that, under the conditions of the proposition and for any substitution θ leaving X free, the denotational semantics $[\![\texttt{even(X)}]\!](c)(\theta)$ yields an infinite sequence of substitutions successively binding X to $s^{2k}(0)$, for $k = 0, 1, 2, \cdots$. Indeed, in view of definition 11, the denotational semantics verifies the following equality

$$[\![\texttt{even(X)}]\!](c)(\theta) = \tau.(\theta \circ \{\texttt{X/0}\}) \oplus \tau.[\![\texttt{even(X')}]\!](c)(\theta \circ \{\texttt{X/s(s(X'))}\}) \quad (1)$$

A solution of this equation is given by

$$\tau.\theta_1.\tau.\tau.\theta_2.\tau.\tau.\tau.\theta_3.\cdots.\tau^n.\theta_n.\cdots$$

where

$$\begin{aligned}
\theta_1 &= \theta \circ \{\texttt{X/0}\} \\
\theta_2 &= \theta \circ \{\texttt{X/s(s(X}_1\texttt{))}\} \circ \{\texttt{X}_1\texttt{/0}\} \\
\theta_3 &= \theta \circ \{\texttt{X/s(s(X}_1\texttt{))}\} \circ \{\texttt{X}_1\texttt{/s(s(X}_2\texttt{))}\} \circ \{\texttt{X}_2\texttt{/0}\} \\
&\ldots \\
\theta_n &= \theta \circ \{\texttt{X/s(s(X}_1\texttt{))}\} \circ \{\texttt{X}_1\texttt{/s(s(X}_2\texttt{))}\} \circ \cdots \circ \{\texttt{X}_n\texttt{/0}\} \\
&\ldots
\end{aligned}$$

It is the only solution thanks to the uniqueness of the fixed-points of contractions and to proposition 12. It also obviously verifies the thesis. ■

It is here worth noting that, in contrast with methods based on cpo's, the fortunate property of contractions of having a unique fixed-point liberates the previous proof of a fixpoint induction reasoning as well as of the proof that the proposed solution for the equation 1 is indeed the least one.

As our last example, let us modify the **even** procedure to get an infinite derivation. To that end, let us simply permutate the positions of the s(s(X)) and X arguments in the last clause:

```
even(X) ← even(s(s(X)).
```

Proposition 29 should now be reformulated as follows.

Proposition 30 *For any context c with* u_e *as top unit, any variable* X*, the evaluation of* even(X) *in the context c produces an answer substitution binding* X *to* 0 *and then enters an infinite loop.*

Proof The proof is conducted as for proposition 29 but equation 1 should now be replaced by the equation

$$[\![\texttt{even(X)}]\!](c)(\theta) = \tau.(\theta \circ \{\texttt{X/0}\}) \oplus \tau.[\![\texttt{even(s(s(X)))}]\!](c)(\theta)$$

and be completed by the equation

$$[\![\texttt{even(s(s(X)))}]\!](c)(\theta) = \tau.[\![\texttt{even(s(s(s(((X))))))}]\!](c)(\theta)$$

These equations accept, as unique solution, the infinite sequence

$$\tau.(\theta\circ\{\mathtt{X}/\mathtt{0}\}).\tau.\ \cdots\ .\tau.\ \cdots$$

This establishes the thesis. ∎

6 Conclusion

The paper has characterized contextual logic programs by means of metric semantics. Precisely, a denotational semantics of a sequential version of contextual logic programs has been presented first and, based on it, a methodology for semantic studies of the properties of those programs has been developed next.

The denotational semantics, issued from the metric branch of the imperative approach to semantic design, is of a compositional nature and rests on no declarative framework and on no transition system. Rather, it is based on processes similar to those introduced in [7]. In contrast with declarative semantics, it is well-suited to tackling extra-logical features as well as infinite derivations. Although it necessarily reflects some operational behaviours, it is also more abstract than step operational semantics directly derived from transition systems.

We believe that this semantics is well-suited for the analysis of contextual logic programs and that it can be used as the basis of formal reasonings about program properties. As a justification, we have suggested a methodology for the analysis of programs and have applied it in the study of the universal termination property of some classical procedures. Although sequential programs subject to a Prolog-like search strategy have only been examined here, we strongly believe that our methodology can be extended to concurrent programs and to properties related to concurrent executions such as those of deadlock- and starvation-freedom. Our future work will be concerned with such issues. Other subjects for future work include extensions of the method to languages incorporating object-oriented features such as inheritance.

Acknowledgments

The research reported herein has been partially supported by Esprit BRA 3020 (Integration). The author like to thank the members of the C.W.I. concurrency group, headed by J.W. de Bakker, for their weekly intensive discussions. He also wishes to thank B. Le Charlier for his interest in his work.

References

[1] K.R. Apt and M.Bezem. Acyclic Programs. In D.H.D. Warren and P.Szeredi, editors, *Proc. 7 th Int. Conf. on Logic Programming*, pages 617–633, Jerusalem, Israel, 1990. The MIT Press.

[2] K.R. Apt and D./ Pedreschi. Studies in pure Prolog: termination. In J.W. Lloyd, editor, *Symposium on Computational Logic*, pages 150–176. Springer-Verlag, 1990.

[3] K.R. Apt and D.Pedreschi. Proving Termination of General Prolog Programs. In T.Ito and A.Meyer, editors, *Proceedings of the International Conference on Theoretical Aspects of Computer Software*, volume 526 of *Lecture Notes in Computer Science*, pages 265–289. Springer-Verlag, 1991.

[4] K.R. Apt and M.H. van Emden. Contributions to the theory of logic programming. *Journal of ACM*, 29(3):841–862, 1982.

[5] M.Baudinet. Proving Termination Properties of Prolog Programs: a Semantic Approach. In *Proc. 3 rd Symp. on Logic In Computer Science*, pages 336–347, Edinburgh, Great-Britain, 1988. IEEE Computer Society Press.

[6] M.Bezem. Characterizing Termination of Logic Programs with Level Mappings. In E.L. Lusk and R.Overbeek, editors, *Proc. of the North American Conference on Logic Programming*, pages 69–80, Cleveland, USA, 1989. The MIT Press.

[7] J.W. deBakker and J.I. Zucker. Processes and the Denotational Semantics of Concurrency. *Information and Control*, 54:70–120, 1982.

[8] Y.Deville. *Logic Programming: Systematic Program Development*. International Series in Logic Programming. Addison-Wesley, 1990.

[9] R.Engelking. *General Topology*. Heldermann Verlag, 1989.

[10] C.J. Hogger. *Introduction to Logic Programming*. Academic Press, 1984.

[11] J.-M. Jacquet and L.Monteiro. Comparative Semantics for a Parallel Contextual Logic Programming Language. In S.Debray and M.Hermenegildo, editors, *Proc. of the North American Conference on Logic Programming*, pages 195–214, Austin, USA, 1990. The MIT Press.

[12] J.W. Lloyd. *Foundations of Logic Programming*. Springer-Verlag, second edition, 1987.

[13] L.Monteiro and A.Porto. Contextual Logic Programming. In G.Levi and M.Martelli, editors, *Proc. 6 th Int. Conf. on Logic Programming*, pages 284–302, Lisboa, 1989. The MIT Press.

[14] C.Palamidessi, E.Marchiori, and K.R. Apt. *Semantics and Proof Theory of First-Order Built-in's of Prolog*. Technical report, Centre for Mathematics and Computer Science (CWI), Amsterdam, The Netherlands, 1992. To appear.

[15] L.Plümer. *Termination Proofs for Logic Programs*, volume 446 of *Lecture Notes in Artificial Intelligence*. Springer-Verlag, 1990.

[16] R.K. Shyamasundar, M.R.K. Rao, and D.Kapur. Rewriting Concepts in the Study of Termination of Logic Programs. *This volume*.

[17] J.D. Ullman and A.van Gelder. Efficient tests for top-down termination of logical rules. *Journal of ACM*, 35(2):345–373, 1988.

[18] M.H. van Emden and R.A. Kowalski. The semantics of predicate logic as a programming language. *Journal of ACM*, 23(4):733–742, 1976.

[19] T.Vasak and J.Potter. Characterization of Terminating Logic Programs. In *Proc. 3rd Symp. on Logic Programming*, pages 140–147, Salt Lake City, USA, 1986. IEEE Computer Society Press.

Static Analysis for the Synthesis of Eureka Properties for Transforming Logic programs

Khaled Bsaïes
Centre de Recherche en Informatique de Nancy (CNRS) and INRIA-Lorraine
BP 239, 54506 Vandœuvre lès Nancy Cedex, FRANCE
e-mail : bsaies@loria.crin.fr

Abstract

Much research has been devoted to logic program transformation using Unfold/Fold transformations. However there has been relatively little work on the use and the synthesis of so-called *Eureka properties*. Experience has shown that in many cases Unfold/Fold transformations are not sufficient to produce efficient logic programs and we have to consider the application of suitable properties. This paper deals with the way to discover these properties. First we introduce notions of a well-behaved clause and definite program. We prove that under certain conditions the application of the Unfold/Fold transformations preserves the notion of well-behavedness. We introduce a strategy based on static program analysis for the synthesis of *Eureka properties* for a class of logic programs called *candidate programs*. Finally we illustrate this strategy by a complete example.

Key Words: logic programs, transformation, correctness, mode input-output, strategy, definite program, folding, unfolding, property.

1 Introduction

Our initial specification is made in terms of Horn clauses and our objective is to obtain, by successive applications of Unfold/Fold transformations, a correct and more efficient program. Correctness (if they solve the right problem) and performance (how fast they run, and how much space they use) are the two factors by which programs may be judged. Transformation techniques based on Unfold/Fold transformation are fruitful for producing correct and more efficient programs [11], [5], [23]. Obtaining a recursive definition is in general a cause of improved efficiency. Recursion is an essential mechanism in logic programming, as it is mentioned in one form or another by Hogger [13] [12], Clark & Darlington [6], Clark & Sickel [7], Lau & Prestwich[16] and Pettorossi & Proietti [20].

Experience has shown that in many cases Unfold/Fold transformations are not sufficient to produce efficient logic programs. We have to consider the application of suitable properties. However, the synthesis of properties for a given program requires substantial creativity and appears to be a difficult task for an automatic system. In this paper we mainly propose a strategy to find such properties by *using static program analysis* (mode and type). This method requires in the beginning a fixed recursive pattern form of the desired target recursive definition version. Such a pattern is called a *target_schema*. Here our approach is similar to that taken by Feather for pattern_directed Fold/Unfold transformation used for developing programs in recursion equations [10] and Lau & Prestwich for the synthesis of recursive logic procedures from first-order logic specifications [16]. Balzer suggests that the user-direct application of a transformation may serve as the goal whenever the transformation is inapplicable to the current state of the program [4]. In which case the user is given the option of entering a subgoaling mode with the objective of applying other transformations to make possible the suspend transformation step. This idea is called *jittering* or *conditioning*. The strategy finally proposes a set of *candidate properties*. If one of them is valid, we obtain a recursive definition of the initial program. The correctness of the target program w.r.t. the initial one is guaranteed. This method is a powerful technique which is successful for numerous cases.

This paper is organized as follows: In section 2 we give some preliminary definitions and notations; Section 3 deals with the static program properties; section 4 is devoted to the definition of *properties*. In section 5 we describe our strategy to find properties.

2 Preliminaries

2.1 Notations and Definitions

In the following, we assume that the reader is familiar with the basic terminology of first order logic such as *term, atom, formula, substitution, matching, most general unifier* (mgu) and so on. A *constant* is a 0-ary function symbol. A *term* is a variable or a constant or of the form $f(t_1, ..., t_n)$ where f is an n-ary function symbol and $t_1, ..., t_n$ are terms. An *atom* is of the form $p(t_1, ..., t_n)$, where p is an n-ary predicate symbol and $t_1, ..., t_n$ are terms. An *expression* is either a term, atom, conjunction of atoms. We assume knowledge of the semantics of Prolog, minimum Herbrand model...[17], [3]. We adopt the following notations:

• x, y, z for variables.
• $\bar{t}$ denotes $(t_1, ..., t_n)$
• p, q, r *and identifiers (plus,...)* for predicate symbols.
• A, B for atoms and Γ, Δ, Λ, Φ for ordered conjunctions of atoms. For example, let Γ be $B_1, \ldots, B_n$ where "," stands for the logical connector "and". A definite clause (or Horn clause) has the following form: $A \leftarrow \Gamma$. A is called the clauses *head* and Γ the clause *body*. A definite program is a sequence of definite clauses. A definition of the predicate symbol p is the set of clauses whose heads are atoms with predicate symbol p.
• $card(E)$ gives the number of elements in the set E, $card(\emptyset) = 0$.
• $\mathcal{M}(P)$ for the least Herbrand model for the program P.
• $\mathcal{P}(P)$ (resp. $\mathcal{F}(P)$) denotes the set of predicate (resp. function) symbols used in the program P.
• c, cc, d, rr, e, w for clauses.
• $\mathcal{V}(E)$ is the set of the variables occurring in the expression E.
• An atom A is *linear* for x if x has at most one occurrence in A. An *expression*

(an atom or a term) is said to be linear if it is linear for all its variables.

• If V is a countable set of variables and F a finite set of function symbols, $T_F(V)$ is the set of the terms built with the symbols of F and the symbols of V.

• $A \leftarrow$, is called a unit clause.

• Let $c: A \leftarrow \Delta$ be a definite clause, $internal(c) = \mathcal{V}(\Delta) \setminus \mathcal{V}(A)$.

• $\mathcal{S}(t)$ denotes the set of subterms of the term t. $\mathcal{S}$ is defined by:
$\mathcal{S}(x) = \{x\}$, $\mathcal{S}(f(t_1, ..., t_n)) = \mathcal{S}(t_1) \cup ... \cup \mathcal{S}(t_n) \cup \{f(t_1, ..., t_n)\}$.
$\mathcal{S}(c) = (\mathcal{S}(A_0) \cup ... \cup \mathcal{S}(A_n)) \setminus \{A_0, .., A_n\}$ where c is a definite clause of the form $A_0 \leftarrow A_1, ..., A_n$.

• A *substitution* σ is a morphism of $T_F(V)$, such that $x\sigma = x$ except for a finite set of variables. The application of σ to the term t is denoted by $t\sigma$. We denote a substitution σ by a set $\{(x_1/t_1), ..., (x_n/t_n)\}$, where each x_i is a variable and each t_i is a term such that x_i does not occur in t_i. The *domain* and the *image* of the substitution σ are respectively the sets $Dom(\sigma) = \{x_1, ..., x_n\}$ and $Im(\sigma) = \{t_1, ..., t_n\}$.

• A substitution σ is called a *variable_pure* substitution if $\forall\ t \in Im(\sigma)$, t is a variable.

• Let E and F be expressions, i.e. atom or term. We say E and F are *variants* if there exist substitutions θ and σ such that $E = F\theta$ and $F = E\sigma$. Let E be an expression; a renaming substitution for E is a *variable_pure substitution* $\{(x_1/y_1), ..., (x_n/y_n)\}$ such that $\{x_1, ...x_n\} \subseteq \mathcal{V}(E)$, the y_i are distinct and $(\mathcal{V}(E) \setminus \{x_1, ...x_n\}) \cap \{y_1, ..., y_n\} = \emptyset$

2.2 Transformations

Unfold/fold transformations were introduced by Burstall & Darlington [5] in the context of the functional languages and generalised and applied by Clark & Sickel [7] for logic programs as just special cases of logical deduction. The unfold/fold transformation method is formulated for logic programs in such a way that the transformation always preserves the equivalence of programs as defined by the least model semantics by Tamaki & Sato [23]. The main difference between our transformations and those defined by Tamaki & Sato is that the order of atoms in the body of a clause is significant for our transformations. Our basic transformations are:

Definition 2.1 (Unfolding)
Unfolding consists of applying SLD-resolution to a clause w.r.t. an atom of its body. Let (c_1)*:* $A \leftarrow \Gamma,\ B,\ \Delta$ *and* $(c_2) : C \leftarrow \Phi$ *be two clauses such that there exists* σ*, an mgu of* B *and* C*; the result of unfolding the atom* B *with the clause* (c_2) *is the following clause* (c_3)*:* $(A \leftarrow \Gamma, \Phi\ , \Delta)\sigma$.

Definition 2.2 (Folding)
Folding consists of replacing an instance of the body of a clause by the corresponding head instance of this clause: Let (c_1)*:* $A \leftarrow \Gamma,\ \Delta,\ \Phi$ *and* $(c_2) : B \leftarrow \Lambda$ *be two clauses and* σ *a substitution such that* $\Lambda\sigma = \Delta$*, the folding of* (c_2) *in* (c_1) *is the clause* (c_3)*:* $A \leftarrow \Gamma,\ B\sigma,\ \Phi$.

Definition 2.3 (Introduction of a new definition)
This consists of the introduction of a new predicate in terms of already existing

ones. Indeed we introduce a new clause of the form: $p(t_1, ..., t_k) \leftarrow A_1, ..., A_n$ *where p is a new predicate symbol and* $A_1, ..., A_n$, $t_1, ..., t_k$ *uses symbols already existing.*

3 Static program properties

3.1 Mode input-output

In this section we introduce the mode input-output which is a static program property. It can be derived or verified by static analysis. In general, logic programs are undirected, i.e. there is no concept of *input* and *output* arguments to a predicate. An argument may be used either as an *input* or as an *output* argument. It is often the case, however, that in a particular logic program, a predicate is called in one direction only, i.e. it is called with a particular set of ground arguments (the *input* arguments), while another set of arguments may or may not be ground when the program is called, but will definitely be ground after the program has succeed (the *output* arguments). In our context, mode analysis allows us to distinguish the arguments of the predicates; some arguments will be *output* while others will be *input*. It is well known that the evaluation of a query of a given *Prolog* program depends on the position of atoms in the body of clauses. By analyzing the *mode* of a program we can describe the *flow of data* among the body atoms of its clauses. Much research has been devoted to the *modes*; some are involved in the area of optimisation of compilers [8], [9], [18] others in the area of program transformations [21], [2]. In the following section, we give some definitions.

Definition 3.1 (Mode of predicate)
Let p be a predicate symbol of arity n, a mode m for p is a n_tuple $(m_1, \ldots, m_n)$ *over the set* $\{in, out\}$. *An* $i \in \{1,...,n\}$ *such that* $m_i = in$ *(resp.* $m_i = out$*) is called an input (resp. output) position for p. A predicate p with a mode m is called moded.*

Remark 3.1
Let $A = p(t_1, ..., t_n)$ be an atom and $m = (m_1, ..., m_n)$ a given mode of p.

$$\mathcal{V}_{in}(A) = \bigcup_{1 \le i \le n \text{ and } m_i = in} \mathcal{V}(t_i), \quad \mathcal{V}_{out}(A) = \bigcup_{1 \le i \le n \text{ and } m_i = out} \mathcal{V}(t_i)$$

$$\mathcal{T}_{in}(A) = \bigcup_{1 \le i \le n \text{ and } m_i = in} \{t_i\}, \quad \mathcal{T}_{out}(A) = \bigcup_{1 \le i \le n \text{ and } m_i = out} \{t_i\}$$

In $p(t_1, ..., t_n)$ an occurrence x in t_i is an out-occurrence (resp. in-occurrence) if $m_i = out$ (resp. $m_i = in$).

Definition 3.2 (Mode of clause and program)
A clause (resp. program) is called moded if all its predicates (resp. clauses) are moded.

Definition 3.3 (Well-behaved clause)
Let $c: \ A_0 \leftarrow A_1, ..., A_n$ *be a moded clause w.r.t. a given mode m, c is called well-behaved w.r.t. the mode m if the following conditions hold:*

1) if c is a non unit clause,
$\forall\ x\ \in\ \mathcal{V}_{in}(A_0),\ x \in (\mathcal{V}_{in}(A_1,...,A_n) \setminus \mathcal{V}_{out}(A_1,...,A_n)),$
else (c is a unit clause) $\mathcal{V}_{out}(A_0) = \mathcal{V}_{in}(A_0)$.

2) $\forall\ x\ \in (\mathcal{V}(c)\ \setminus\ \mathcal{V}_{in}(A_0))$ *x has one and only one out-occurrence in the body of c.*

3) $\forall i \in [1,n], \forall x \in (\mathcal{V}_{in}(A_i) \setminus \mathcal{V}_{in}(A_0)), (\exists j \in [1,i-1], x \in \mathcal{V}_{out}(A_j))$.

4) $\forall\ x\ \in (\mathcal{V}(c)\ \setminus\ \mathcal{V}(A_0)),\ \ x\ \in \mathcal{V}_{in}(c)$

5) $\forall\ i\ \in\ [1..n]\ \mathcal{V}_{in}(A_i) \neq \emptyset$

Remarks 3.1
a) The well-behaved programs cover a broad range of logic programs typically encountered in practice.

1. The condition (1) of the definition (3.3) expresses that each *in* variable of the head of a non unit clause must be used at least once in *in* position and does not appear in *out* position in the body of the clause. For the unit clause we must have the same variables in *in* position and in *out* position in A_0.
2. The condition (2) of the definition (3.3) expresses that each occurrence *out* of a variable in the body of a clause is computed exactly once in the body of the clause.
3. The condition (3) of the definition (3.3) expresses that each internal variable must be computed before it is used.
4. The condition (4) expresses that an internal variable occurs at least once at *in* occurrence (by condition 2 we are sure that it is used at *out* occurrence) in the body of c.
5. The last condition expresses the fact that we can not have a predicate with mode $(out, ..., out)$.

b) The well-behaved clause definition is more subtle than the well-moded clause definition introduced in [2]. We recall this definition:

Definition 3.4 (well-moded clause)
Let $c:\ A\ \leftarrow\ A_1,...,A_n$ *a moded clause, c is called well-moded if the following conditions hold:*
1) $\forall\ x\ \in\ \mathcal{V}_{in}(A)$, *all occurrences of x in the body of c are in-occurrences.*
2) $\forall\ x\ \in (\mathcal{V}(c)\ \setminus\ \mathcal{V}_{in}(A))$ *x has one only out-occurrence in the body of c.*
3) $\forall\ i\ \in\ [1,n],\ \forall\ x\ \in\ \mathcal{V}_{in}(A_i)\ \setminus\ \mathcal{V}_{in}(A)\ \ (\exists j\ \in\ [1,i-1],\ \ x\ \in\ \mathcal{V}_{out}(A_j))$.

Example 3.1
The clause: $times(x,s(y),v)\ \leftarrow\ times(x,y,z),\ plus(z,x,v)$ is well-behaved w.r.t. the mode m defined by $m_{times} = m_{plus} = (in, in, out)$.
The clause $p(x,y)\ \leftarrow\ r(z), p(x,z), q(z,t)$ is not well-behaved w.r.t. the mode m defined by $m_p = m_q = (in, out)$ and $m_r = (in)$.

Definition 3.5 (Well-behaved program)
A given program is called well-behaved w.r.t. a given mode m iff all its clauses are well-behaved w.r.t. the mode m.

Definition 3.6 (p_substitution)
A p_substitution *is a substitution σ such that*
(1) σ is idempotent i.e.: $\mathcal{V}(Im(\sigma)) \cap \mathcal{V}(Dom(\sigma)) = \emptyset$
(2) $\forall\ x, y \in Dom(\sigma)\quad x \neq y \Rightarrow \mathcal{V}(x\sigma) \cap \mathcal{V}(y\sigma) = \emptyset$
(3) $\forall\ x\ \in\ Dom(\sigma)$ $x\sigma$ is linear.

Proposition 3.1
Let c be a well-behaved clause w.r.t. a given mode m and a p_substitution σ, then the clause $c\sigma$ is well-behaved w.r.t. the mode m.

Proof:
Let x be in $\mathcal{V}(c\sigma)$.
- If $x\ \in\ \mathcal{V}(c)$, x is invariant by σ (condition 1 of the definition of p_substitution), therefore the set of the occurrences of x in c is identical to the set of occurrences of x in $c\sigma$. Then $c\sigma$ is well-behaved.
- If $x\ \notin\ \mathcal{V}(c)$. $\exists\ z\ \in\ \mathcal{V}(c)$ such that $x\ \in\ \mathcal{V}(z\sigma)$.
The number of occurrences of z in c is identical to the number of occurrences of x in $c\sigma$ (condition 2 and 3 of p_substitution) and the mode of those occurrences is preserved by the application of σ; $c\sigma$ is then well-behaved.
□

3.2 Types

The logic programs we consider are typed; much research has been devoted in this direction [19]. The concrete types are sets of closed terms which are solutions of fixpoints equations. For example the *natural number* type is defined by the equation: $N = \{0\} \cup s(N)$, where 0 and s are the constructors of the *natural number* type.
Let π be the function which gives the domain and codomain of a predicate or function symbol, π is defined as follow:
• $\pi(f) = (\underline{T}_1, ..., \underline{T}_{n+1})$, $\underline{T}_i$ are types and intuitively f is the function symbol, $f: \underline{T}_1, ..., \underline{T}_n\ \rightarrow\ \underline{T}_{n+1}$, where $\underline{T}_1, ..., \underline{T}_n$ is the domain of f and $\underline{T}_{n+1}$ is the codomain of f.
• $\pi(p) = (\underline{T}_1, ..., \underline{T}_n, \mathcal{B})$, $\underline{T}_i$ are types and $\mathcal{B}$ is the boolean type, intuitively p is the predicate symbol, $p: \underline{T}_1, ..., \underline{T}_n\ \rightarrow\ \mathcal{B}$, where $\underline{T}_1, ..., \underline{T}_n$ is the domain of p and $\mathcal{B}$ is the codomain of p.

Definition 3.7 (Typed term, atom, clause)
Let t (resp. A (resp. c)) be a term (resp. an atom (resp. a definite clause)). We suppose that for all $x\ \in \mathcal{V}(t)$ (resp. $\mathcal{V}(A)$ (resp. $\mathcal{V}(c)$)) x is declared i.e. type(x) is the type associate with x. For all expressions of the form $h(t_1, ..., t_n)$, we have $type(h(t_1, ..., t_n)) = last(\pi(h))$ where $last(\underline{T}_1, ..., \underline{T}_{n+1}) = \underline{T}_{n+1}$.
t (resp. A (resp.c)) is said to be typed iff
for all expression $h(t_1, ..., t_n)$ in $\mathcal{S}(t)$ (resp. $\mathcal{S}(A)$ (resp. $\mathcal{S}(c)$)),
$\forall i \in [1..n]$ $type(t_i) = \pi(h)|i$ (i^{th} projection).

Definition 3.8 (Typed program)
Let P be a definite program. P is said to be typed iff:

- *the predicate and function symbols used in P are declared.*
- *all its clauses are typed.*

We suppose that the programmer gives the domain and codomain of the predicate and function symbols used in the program.

Remarks 3.2
1) We can infer the type of variable symbols occurring in the clauses of the program from the declaration of predicate and function symbols.
2) The basic transformations preserve the notion of typed program (proposition 3.5 and 3.6 and 3.7).

Definition 3.9 (Typed_substitution)
Let σ be a substitution and type be the application which associates with $x \in \mathcal{V}(Dom(\sigma) \cup Im(\sigma))$ the type of x. σ is typed iff $\forall x$, $x\sigma$ is typed and $type(x) = type(x\sigma)$.

3.3 The transformations preserve the well-behaved notion

Proposition 3.2 (Folding)
Let $c_1 : A \leftarrow \Gamma, \Delta, \Lambda$ and $c_2 : B \leftarrow \Delta'$ two non unit clauses such that:

1. *c_1 and c_2 are well-behaved w.r.t. a given mode m*
2. *there exists a p_substitution σ such that $\Delta'\sigma = \Delta$*
3. *σ substitutes distinct variables for the internal variables of c_2, and these variables do not occur in A, Γ, Λ.*
4. *$B\sigma$ is out-linear, i.e. $B\sigma$ is linear for all $x \in \mathcal{V}_{out}(B\sigma)$*
5. *$((\mathcal{V}_{out}(B\sigma) \setminus \mathcal{V}_{out}(A)) \cap \mathcal{V}_{in}(\Delta)) \subset \mathcal{V}_{in}(\Lambda)$*

then $c_3 : A \leftarrow \Gamma, (B\sigma), \Lambda$, is well-behaved w.r.t. the mode m.

Proof:
The proof is made by case analysis on the positions of the atoms in the body of c_3; let us verify the conditions of the definition of well-behaved for the clause c_3:

1. Let $x \in \mathcal{V}_{in}(A)$ we have to prove:
   a) if $x \in \mathcal{V}_{in}(A)$ then $x \in \mathcal{V}_{in}(\Gamma, B\sigma, \Lambda)$ and
   b) if $x \in \mathcal{V}_{in}(A)$ then $x \notin \mathcal{V}_{out}(\Gamma, B\sigma, \Lambda)$

   let us prove a); as c_1 is well-behaved we have:

   - if $x \in \mathcal{V}_{in}(\Gamma, \Lambda)$ it is OK..
   - else $x \in \mathcal{V}_{in}(\Delta)$ then $x \in \mathcal{V}_{in}(\Delta'\sigma)$, we distinguish two cases:
     1) $x \in \mathcal{V}_{in}(B\sigma)$, it is OK.
     2) $x \notin \mathcal{V}_{in}(B\sigma)$ then $x \in \mathcal{V}_{out}(\Delta)$, in contradiction with the fact that c_1 well-behaved ($x \in \mathcal{V}_{out}(\Delta)$ and $x \in \mathcal{V}_{in}(\Delta)$).

   let us prove b)

If $x \in \mathcal{V}(B\sigma)$. let us suppose that $x \in \mathcal{V}_{out}(B\sigma)$. By hypothesis $c_2\sigma$ is well-behaved then x has one occurrence out in $(\Delta'\sigma)$, which contradicts the fact that c_1 is well-behaved.

2. Let $x \in \mathcal{V}(c_3) \setminus \mathcal{V}_{in}(A)$ and let us prove: x has exactly one out-occurrence in $\Gamma, B\sigma, \Lambda$. We remark that as $c_2\sigma$ is well-behaved we have

$$\text{if } x \notin \mathcal{V}(c_1) \text{ then } x \notin \mathcal{V}(c_3)$$

in fact if $x \notin \mathcal{V}(c_1)$ then $x \notin \mathcal{V}(A, \Gamma, \Delta, \Lambda)$; as $c_2\sigma$ is a non unit clause and $c_2\sigma$ is well-behaved we have $x \notin \mathcal{V}(\Delta)$, then $x \notin \mathcal{V}(B\sigma)$.

$x \in \mathcal{V}(c_1)$ x has once only out-occurrence in Γ, Δ, Λ (c_1 is well-behaved);

- if this out-occurrence is in Γ, Λ: $x \notin \mathcal{V}_{out}(\Delta)$ and according to $c_2\sigma$ is well-behaved; $x \notin \mathcal{V}_{out}(B\sigma)$, then x has once only out-occurrence in $\Gamma, (B\sigma), \Lambda$.
- if this out-occurrence is in Δ: $x \in \mathcal{V}_{out}(\Delta)$ and according to $c_2\sigma$ is well-behaved; $x \notin \mathcal{V}_{in}(B\sigma)$; if $x \in \mathcal{V}_{out}(B\sigma)$ as $B\sigma$ is out-linear the result holds else $x \notin \mathcal{V}(B\sigma)$; according to the hypothesis (3) of the proposition $x \notin \mathcal{V}(A, \Gamma, \Lambda)$ therefore x does not occur in c_3, then we have a contradiction.

3. Let $c_3 : A \leftarrow \underbrace{A_1, \ldots, A_{k-1},}_{\Gamma} \underbrace{A_k}_{B\sigma}, \underbrace{A_{k+1}, \ldots, A_n}_{\Lambda}.$

Let $x \in \mathcal{V}_{in}(A_i) \setminus \mathcal{V}(A)$ and let us prove:

$$(1) \quad \exists j \ 1 \leq j < i \qquad x \in \mathcal{V}_{out}(A_j)$$

- If $i \leq k-1$ the existence of j for (1) is assured since c_1 is well-behaved.
- If $i = k$ $x \in \mathcal{V}_{in}(B\sigma)$ therefore $x \in \mathcal{V}(\Delta)$, and as $c_2\sigma$ is well-behaved, all the occurrences of x in Δ are *in*, and as c_1 is well-behaved, for each *in−occurrence* of x in an atom H of Δ there exists one *out − occurrence* of x in an atom previous H in the body of c_1. This atom is necessarily an atom of Γ (since all the occurrences of x in Δ are in).
- If $i > k$ $x \in \mathcal{V}_{in}(\Lambda)$.
  As c_1 is well-behaved we have: $x \in \mathcal{V}_{out}(\Gamma, \Lambda)$ *or* $x \in \mathcal{V}_{out}(\Delta)$. If $x \in \mathcal{V}_{out}(\Gamma, \Lambda)$ the result holds, else, let us suppose that $x \in \mathcal{V}_{out}(\Delta)$. We have $x \notin \mathcal{V}_{in}(B\sigma)$. If $x \in \mathcal{V}_{out}(B\sigma)$, the result holds ($B\sigma = A_k$ *and* $k < i$) else $x \notin \mathcal{V}(B\sigma)$, by the hypothesis $x \notin \mathcal{V}(A, \Gamma, \Lambda)$, in contradiction with $x \in \mathcal{V}_{in}(\Lambda)$.

4. We consider that c_3 is written in the same form as in the previous point.

Let $x \in \mathcal{V}(A_i) \setminus \mathcal{V}(A))$ and let us prove:

$$(2) \quad \exists j \ i < j \leq n \qquad x \in \mathcal{V}_{in}(A_j)$$

- If $k < i \leq n$, the existence of j for (2) is assured since c_1 is well-behaved.

- If $i = k$, let $x \in (\mathcal{V}_{out}(B\sigma) \setminus \mathcal{V}(A))$; as $c_2\sigma$ is well-behaved then $x \in \mathcal{V}_{out}(\Delta)$ and as c_1 is well-behaved $x \in \mathcal{V}_{in}(\Delta,\ \Lambda)$. If $x \in \mathcal{V}_{in}(\Lambda)$ the result holds it is OK, else $x \notin \mathcal{V}_{in}(\Lambda)$, so we have $x \in \mathcal{V}_{in}(\Delta)$ since c_1 is well-behaved, which contradicts the hypothesis $((\mathcal{V}_{out}(B\sigma) \setminus \mathcal{V}_{out}(A)) \cap \mathcal{V}_{in}(\Delta)) \subset \mathcal{V}_{in}(\Lambda)$.
- If $i < k$, $x \in \mathcal{V}_{out}(\Gamma)$ and $x \notin \mathcal{V}(A)$; as c_1 is well-behaved $x \in \mathcal{V}_{in}(\Gamma, \Delta, \Lambda)$.

  if $x \in \mathcal{V}_{in}(\Gamma, \Lambda)$, it is OK. else $x \in \mathcal{V}_{in}(\Delta)$ then $x \in \mathcal{V}_{in}(\Delta'\sigma)$
  we distinguish two cases:
  - $x \in \mathcal{V}_{in}(B\sigma)$, it is OK.
  - $x \notin \mathcal{V}_{in}(B\sigma)$ then $x \in \mathcal{V}_{out}(\Delta'\sigma) \Rightarrow x \in \mathcal{V}_{out}(\Delta)$, in contradiction with $x \in \mathcal{V}_{in}(\Delta)$ and c_1 well-behaved.

5. The condition 5 of the definition of well-behaved clause is obvious for c_3 since c_1 and $c_2\sigma$ are well-behaved.

□

Remark 3.2
If the condition 5 of the previous proposition does not hold then the clause c_3 resulting from the *Folding* of c_2 in c_1 is not well-behaved. For example suppose that we have the two well-behaved clauses: $c_1 : p_1(y,x) \leftarrow r(y,t),\ q(t,x)$ and $c_2 : p_2(y,x,t) \leftarrow r(y,t),\ q(t,x)$ respectively w.r.t.. The mode m defined by: $m_{p_1} = m_r = m_q = (in, out)$ and $m_{p_2} = (in, out, out)$. The clause $c_3 : p_1(y,x) \leftarrow p_2(y,x,t)$ is not well-behaved w.r.t. the mode m.

Proposition 3.3 (Unfolding)
Let $c_1 : A \leftarrow \Gamma,\ B,\ \Lambda$ and $c_2 : B' \leftarrow \Delta$, be two well-behaved clauses w.r.t. a given mode m and c_1 is a non unit clause and there exists $\theta = mgu(B, B')$ such that θ is a p_substitution and $\mathcal{V}(c_1) \cap \mathcal{V}(c_2) = \emptyset$ then $c_3 : (A \leftarrow \Gamma,\ \Delta,\ \Lambda)\theta$ is well-behaved w.r.t. the mode m.

Proof:
The proof is made by case analysis on the positions of the atoms in the body of c_3. □

Proposition 3.4 (Introduction of new definition)
The transformation introduction of a new definition preserves the notion of well-behaving if the introduced clause is well-behaved w.r.t. the mode of the current program.

3.4 The transformations preserve the typed notion

Proposition 3.5 (Folding)
Let P be a typed program and $c_1 : A \leftarrow \Gamma,\ \Delta,\ \Lambda$ and $c_2 : B \leftarrow \Delta'$ two clauses of P such that:
- *there exists a substitution σ such that $\Delta'\sigma = \Delta$*
- *$\mathcal{V}(c_1) \cap \mathcal{V}(c_2) = \emptyset$*

then $c_3 : A \leftarrow \Gamma,\ (B\sigma),\ \Lambda$, is typed.

Proposition 3.6 (Unfolding)
Let P be a typed program and $c_1 : A \leftarrow \Gamma, B, \Lambda$ and $c_2 : B' \leftarrow \Delta$, be two clauses of P, if there exists $\theta = mgu(B, B')$ and $\mathcal{V}(c_1) \cap \mathcal{V}(c_2) = \emptyset$ then $c_3 : (A \leftarrow \Gamma, \Delta, \Lambda)\theta$ is typed.

Proposition 3.7 (Introduction of new definition)
The transformation introduction of a new definition preserves the notion of typedness if the introduced clause is typed.

4 Properties

Definition 4.1 (Property)
Let P be a program; a property of P is a first order formula of the form:
(1) $\forall x_1, ..., \forall x_n(\exists y_1, ..., \exists y_m \, \Delta \Leftarrow \exists z_1, ..., \exists z_k \, \Lambda)$ *where:*
$\{x_1, ..., x_n\} = \mathcal{V}(\Delta) \cap \mathcal{V}(\Lambda)$, $\{y_1, ..., y_m\} = \mathcal{V}(\Delta) \setminus \mathcal{V}(\Lambda)$ *and*
$\{z_1, ..., z_k\} = \mathcal{V}(\Lambda) \setminus \mathcal{V}(\Delta)$
which is valid in the least Herbrand model of P. We denote this property by $(\Delta \Leftarrow \Lambda)$.

Definition 4.2 (Validity of a property)
The logic formula (1) is valid in $\mathcal{M}(P)$, if the following condition holds: for all ground substitution σ of the variables $x_1, ..., x_n$ if there exists a ground substitution θ of the variables $z_1, ..., z_k$ such that $(\Lambda\sigma)\theta$ is valid in $\mathcal{M}(P)$ then there exists a ground substitution δ of the variables $y_1, ..., y_m$ such that $(\Delta\sigma)\delta$ is valid in $\mathcal{M}(P)$

Example 4.1
The associativity of the predicate *plus* can be expressed by the properties:
$plus(x, y, u),\ plus(u, t, z) \Leftarrow plus(y, t, v),\ plus(x, v, z)$ and
$plus(y, t, v),\ plus(x, v, z) \Leftarrow plus(x, y, u),\ plus(u, t, z)$

The symmetry relation of the predicate *rev* (reverse list) can be expressed by the property: $rev(x, y) \Leftarrow rev(y, x)$

Definition 4.3 (The transformation Applying_a_Property)
Let $(c) : A \leftarrow \Gamma, \Delta', \Phi$ be a clause of (P) and $(\Delta \Leftarrow \Lambda)$ a property of P and σ exist such that $\Delta\sigma = \Delta'$, satisfying:
$\forall x \in \mathcal{V}(\Lambda) \setminus \mathcal{V}(\Delta)$, σ substitutes x with distinct variables of Δ' and these variables do not occur in A or in Γ or in Φ, then the result of the application of the property $(\Delta \Leftarrow \Lambda)$ on (c) is the clause $(c') : A \leftarrow \Gamma, \Lambda\sigma, \Phi$.

Proposition 4.1
The application of the transformation applying_a_property preserves the semantics of the program (P) in the sense of the least Herbrand model of (P).

Proof:
The proof is made by using the Tamaki & Sato [23] proof tools. □

Example 4.2
If the condition of application of the transformation *applying_a_property* does not hold, we can in certain case increase the set of solutions of the transformed program w.r.t. the initial program. Let us consider the following program P_1:

$$\begin{array}{lcl} p(x,y) & \leftarrow & q(x,y,y),\ r(y) \\ q(c,a,b) & \leftarrow & \\ q(a,b,b) & \leftarrow & \\ h(c) & \leftarrow & \\ h(a) & \leftarrow & \\ r(b) & \leftarrow & \end{array}$$

$\mathcal{M}(P_1) = \{p(a,b), q(a,b,b), q(c,a,b), h(c), h(a), r(b)\}$

let $P : \ q(x,y,z) \ \Leftarrow \ h(x)$ a property of P_1. Let P_2 be the resulting program of the application of the property P to the program P_1. P_2 is then:

$$\begin{array}{lcl} p(x,y) & \leftarrow & h(x),\ r(y) \\ q(c,a,b) & \leftarrow & \\ q(a,b,b) & \leftarrow & \\ h(c) & \leftarrow & \\ h(a) & \leftarrow & \\ r(b) & \leftarrow & \end{array}$$

We have $\mathcal{M}(P_2) = \{p(c,b), p(a,b), q(a,b,b), q(c,a,b), h(c), h(a), r(b)\}$

5 Synthesis of Eureka properties

5.1 Formalisation

Given a logic program P and a clause c which defines p, ($p(\bar{t})$ is the head atom of c), our strategy will attempt to find a recursive definition of p. This strategy requires the user to specify the following beforehand: the head of the required recursive definition is an instance of $p(\bar{t})$. By specifying the head of the desired recursive definition, we restrict the search space. This step is called specifying the *target_schema*. Indeed, the system requires the user to specify the form of the instance of $p(\bar{t})$ which will be the head of the recursive definition to be derived from $p(\bar{t})$.

Formally, we start with a definition of p of the following form $c : p(\bar{t}) \ \leftarrow \ \Gamma$. Then given an instance $p(\bar{t})\theta$ of $p(\bar{t})$, the *target_schema* is $p(\bar{t})\theta$ where the body Δ of the clause $p\theta \ \leftarrow \ \Delta$, which will contain among its atoms the recursive call, can be thought of as a result of some unfolding transformations of atoms in the body of c followed by a folding transformation. We have to determine Δ. Let us introduce some definitions:

Definition 5.1 (Projection of a program w.r.t. a set of predicates) *Let P be a definite program and $F \subset \mathcal{P}(P)$. The program P_F projection of P w.r.t. F is obtained from P in this way:*

- *the definition of p, such that $p \notin F$ is removed from P*
- *atoms $p(\bar{t})$, such that $p \notin F$ are removed from clauses where they appear.*
- *each predicate symbol p in P is renamed p_F in P_F.*

Remark 5.1
If c is a clause of P such that the head predicate symbol is in F then the corresponding clause in P_F is c_F.

Example 5.1
The projection of the (Div) program (see section 5.4) w.r.t. $F = \{div, less, times\}$ is:

$$
\begin{array}{lll}
1 & div_F(a,b,q,r) & \leftarrow \; less_F(r,b),\; times_F(b,q,t) \\
4 & times_F(0,x,0) & \leftarrow \\
5 & times_F(s(x),y,z) & \leftarrow \; times_F(x,y,t) \\
6 & less_F(0,s(x)) & \leftarrow \\
7 & less_F(s(x),s(y)) & \leftarrow \; less_F(x,y)
\end{array}
$$

Definition 5.2 (Linear recursive clause)
Let c be a definite clause of the form: $c : p_0(\overline{t_0}) \leftarrow p_1(\overline{t_1}), ..., p_k(\overline{t_k})$;
c is called:
- *recursive iff there exist i in [1..k] such that* $p_i = p_0$
- *linear recursive iff there exists exactly one* $i \in [1..k]$ *such that* $p_i = p_0$.

Definition 5.3 (Linear recursive predicate)
A definition of a predicate is linear recursive if it contains a unique non unit clause which is linear recursive.

Example 5.2
The definition of the predicate ***plus*** defined in the program *Div* (i.e the clauses (2) and (3) in section 5.4) is linear recursive.

Let us characterise the candidate programs to be processed by our strategy.

Definition 5.4 (Candidate program)
Let P be a definite program and $c : p_0(\overline{t_0}) \leftarrow p_1(\overline{t_1}), ..., p_n(\overline{t_n})$, *be the definition of* p_0 *in P. P is a candidate program w.r.t. c if:*
- *P is well-behaved w.r.t. a given mode m*
- *P is typed.*
- *for all i in [1..n] the definition of the predicates* p_i *are linear recursive.*
- *c is not recursive.*

Remark 5.2
In the previous definition, we mark each recursive call in the $p_1, ..., p_n$ definitions "recursive atom" and we mark the atoms $p_1(\overline{t_1}), ..., p_n(\overline{t_n})$ in c "recursive atom".

Definition 5.5 (Unfolding of marked atoms)
c_1, c_2 *and* c_3 *are clauses used in the definition 2.1 of the unfolding transformation (see section 2)*
- *if* $p(\overline{t}) \neq B$ *is marked "recursive atom" in* c_1, *then in* c_3, $p(\overline{t})\theta$ *is marked "recursive atom"*
- *if* $p(\overline{t})$ *is marked "recursive atom" in* Φ, *then in* c_3, $p(\overline{t})\theta$ *is marked "recursive atom".*

Definition 5.6 (Generalisation of a set of atoms)
Let $E = \{p_1(\overline{t}_1), ..., p_n(\overline{t}_n))\}$ *be a set of atoms, the generalisation of E denoted by* $GEN(E)$ *produces the set* $\{p_1(\overline{x}_1), ..., p_n(\overline{x}_n)$, *such that for* $1 \leq l, i \leq n$, $1 \leq j \leq arity(p_i)$ *and* $1 \leq m \leq arity(p_l)$, $\overline{x}_i|j \neq \overline{x}_l|m$[1] *and* $arity(h)$ *gives the arity of h.*

[1] $\overline{x}|j$ is the jth projection w.r.t. $\overline{x}$

Example 5.3
Let $E = \{plus(s(x), y, z),\ less(s(x), s(y))\}$,
$GEN(E) = \{plus(s_1, s_2, s_3),\ less(s_4, s_5)\}$.

Definition 5.7 (Set of non-foldable predicates)
Let P be a candidate program w.r.t. $c:\ p_0(\overline{t_0}) \leftarrow p_1(\overline{t_1}), ..., p_n(\overline{t_n})$ and $d:\ p_0(\overline{t'_0}) \leftarrow \Delta_0,\ p_1(\overline{t'_1}),\ \Delta_1, ...,\ \Delta_{n-1},\ p_n(\overline{t'_n}),\ \Delta_n$. d is the clause obtained by applying the unfolding transformation to atoms of the body of c. Let $E = \{p_1, ..., p_n\}$ then $NFP(c,d)$ is the set of F, $F \subset E$, such that:

1) in $P_{\mathcal{P}(P)\setminus F}$, $c_{\mathcal{P}(P)\setminus F}$ is foldable in $d_{\mathcal{P}(P)\setminus F}$ and $\mathcal{V}(head(d_{\mathcal{P}(P)\setminus F})) \cap \mathcal{V}(body(d_{\mathcal{P}(P)\setminus F})) \neq \emptyset$
2) $\forall L$, such that $L \subset F$, we have in $P_{\mathcal{P}(P)\setminus L}$, $c_{\mathcal{P}(P)\setminus L}$ is not foldable in $d_{\mathcal{P}(P)\setminus L}$.

$NFP(c,d)$ is called the set of non foldable predicates w.r.t. the clauses c, d.

If $NFP(c,d) = \emptyset$, then the *folding* of c in d is possible in P.

Example 5.4
In the (Div) example of the section 5.4
$c:\ div(a,b,q,r) \leftarrow less(r,b),\ times(q,b,t),\ plus(t,r,a)$ and
$d:\ div(a,b,s(x),r) \leftarrow less(r,b),\ times(x,b,u),\ plus(b,u,v1),\ plus(v1,r,a)$
$NFP(c,d) = \{\{times\},\ \{plus\}\}$

5.2 How to find properties?

Let us present the schema of the proposed strategy described in an algorithmic form. Let P be a *candidate program* w.r.t. $c:\ p_0(\overline{t_0}) \leftarrow p_1(\overline{t_1}), ..., p_n(\overline{t_n})$ which is the *definition* to derive. The goal of the strategy is to find a linear recursive definition of p_0.

Our strategy is based on the following steps:

1. ***target_schema step***

- The user proposes a *target_schema* which is the head of the desired recursive definition and it has the following form: $p_0(\overline{t_0})\theta$. In the next steps, we try to find the body Δ of the recursive clause, whose head is the proposed *target_schema*: $(p_0(\overline{t_0})\theta \leftarrow \Delta)$.
- By applying the unfolding transformation to some of the atoms occurring in the body of c, we seek a clause d with head $p_0(\overline{t_0})\theta'$ where $p_0(\overline{t_0})\theta'$ and $p_0(\overline{t_0})\theta$ are variants; if this operation does not succeed then choose another *target_schema* (goto step 1). Otherwise, from the body of d we try to find Δ, (Δ is in fact in the following form Γ, $p_0(\overline{t_0})\sigma$, Σ, where σ is a substitution, $p_0(\overline{t_0})\sigma$ is the recursive call and Γ, Σ are conjunctions of atoms).
- Let $AN := NFP(c,d)$

<u>*If*</u> $AN \neq \emptyset$
<u>*then*</u>

2. *enriching the target_schema step*

- Let $Q \in AN$. Let $F = (\mathcal{P}(P) \setminus Q)$. The *Folding* of c_F in d_F produces the clause e in P_F. Let $AN := (AN \setminus Q)$
- The variables having only one occurrence in $(\mathcal{V}(e) \setminus \mathcal{V}(p_0(\overline{t_0})\sigma))$ are substituted by different fresh variables $s_1, ..., s_l$. Let ee be the resulting clause and l be the number of these fresh variables.
- Let $\mathcal{A} := \{p(\overline{t})$ *in the body of* d, $p(\overline{t})$ is not marked "recursive atom" and $p \in Q\}$; add to the body of the clause ee the atoms of $GEN(\mathcal{A})$; let $s_{l+1}, ..., s_k$ be the fresh variables introduced by $GEN(\mathcal{A})$.

3. *static analysis step*

We will use static analysis for instantiating arbitrary variables $s_1, ..., s_k$, such that the resulting clause will be typed and well-behaved w.r.t. a given mode. Let $index := 0$ ($index$ is the number of the "repeat" loop execution), for each loop we use a new mode for the predicate symbols used in program P.

<u>***Repeat***</u>

Let m be a mode of the predicate symbol p_0. Infer the mode of all predicates used in P and rearrange atoms in the body of ee, such that ee will be well-behaved w.r.t. the mode m.
Arbitrary variables s_i, $i \in [1..k]$ must be substituted by a *typed_substitution* σ.
$index := index + 1$.
We distinguish the following cases;
Let ee be in the following form $ee: A_0 \leftarrow A_1, ..., A_n$
1) **for** $i \in [1..n]$, **if** $s_j \in \mathcal{V}_{in}(A_i)$ **then**
if $(card(\mathcal{V}_{in}(A_0) \setminus \mathcal{V}_{in}(A_1, ..., A_n)) = 1)$ **then**
$Y_{index,j} := \{u \in \mathcal{S}(\mathcal{T}_{in}(A_0)) \setminus \mathcal{S}(\mathcal{T}_{in}(A_1, .., A_n))$ and $type(s_j) = type(u)\}$
else
$Y_{index,j} := \{u \in \mathcal{S}(\mathcal{T}_{in}(A_0)) \cup \mathcal{S}(\mathcal{T}_{out}(A_1, .., A_{i-1}))$ and $type(s_j) = type(u)\}$
2) **for** $i \in [n..1]$,
if $s_j \in \mathcal{V}_{out}(A_i)$ **then**
if $\mathcal{V}_{in}(A_{i+1}, ..., A_n) \subset \mathcal{V}_{in}(A_0)$ **then**
$Y_{index,j} := \{u \in \mathcal{S}(\mathcal{T}_{out}(A_0)) \setminus \mathcal{S}(\mathcal{T}_{out}(A_1, ..., A_{i-1}, A_{i+1}, ..., A_n))$ and $type(s_j) = type(u)\}$
else if $\mathcal{V}_{out}(A_0) \subset \mathcal{V}_{out}(A_1, .., A_{i-1}, A_{i+1}, .., A_n)$
then
$Y_{index,j} := \{u \in \mathcal{S}(\mathcal{T}_{in}(A_{i+1}, ..., A_n)) \setminus$
$(\mathcal{S}(\mathcal{T}_{in}(A_0)) \cup (\mathcal{S}(\mathcal{T}_{out}(A_1, ..., A_{i-1})) \cap \mathcal{S}(\mathcal{T}_{in}(A_{i+1}, ..., A_n)))$

and $type(s_j) = type(u)\}$
else
$Y_{index,j} := \{u \in \mathcal{S}(\mathcal{T}_{out}(A_0)) \setminus (\mathcal{S}(\mathcal{T}_{out}(A_0)) \cap \mathcal{S}(\mathcal{T}_{out}(A_1, .., A_{i-1}, A_{i+1}, ..., A_n))) \cup (\mathcal{S}(\mathcal{T}_{in}(A_{i+1}, ..., A_n)) \setminus (\mathcal{S}(\mathcal{T}_{in}(A_0)) \cup (\mathcal{S}(\mathcal{T}_{out}(A_1, ..., A_{i-1})) \cap \mathcal{S}(\mathcal{T}_{in}(A_{i+1}, ..., A_n)))))$
and $type(s_j) = type(u)\}$
if $index > 1$ **then** for $i := 1..k$,
$Y_{index,i} := (Y_{(index-1),i} \cap Y_{index,i})$

Until $((\forall i \in [1..k], card(Y_{index,i}) = 1)$ or $(\exists i,\ Y_{index,i} = \emptyset)$ or (*we have used all the possible modes of the program P*))

If $(\exists i,\ Y_{index,i} = \emptyset)$ then if $AN \neq \emptyset$ go to step 2 else the *target_schema* is not interesting, so go to step 1, otherwise there exist $num\_sub = \prod_{1 \le i \le k} card(Y_{index,i})$ possibilities to substitute the k unknown variables.
Let $\psi := \{\sigma_i$, typed_substitution $i \in [1..num\_sub]$, $\sigma_l \neq \sigma_j$ for $l \neq j$ and σ_i is in the following form
$\{s_1/u_1, ..., s_k/u_k\}\ u_j \in Y_{index,j},\ j \in [1..k]\}$
Let $e_i := ee\sigma_i,\ i \in [1..num\_sub],\ \sigma_i \in \psi$.

4. simplification step
For i:=1 to *num_sub*
do

Choose the mode m of the initial program. Rename internal variables of d such that $internal(e_i) \cap internal(d) = \emptyset$, rearrange the atoms of each e_i such that e_i are well-behaved w.r.t. the mode m and add the atoms of the body of d in the right part of the bodies of e_i, let w_i be the resulting clause having the following form $B_0 \leftarrow B_1, ..., B_h$. Apply as far as possible the simplification rules. We can remove B_m $m \in [1..h]$ if one of the following conditions holds:

1) $\exists\ j,\ 0 < j < m,\ B_m = B_j$ or
2) $\mathcal{V}_{out}(B_m) \cap \mathcal{V}_{out}(B_0) = \emptyset$ and $\mathcal{V}_{out}(B_m) \cap \mathcal{V}_{in}(B_{m+1}, ..., B_h) = \emptyset$ or
3) $\mathcal{V}_{out}(B_m) \subset \mathcal{V}_{out}(B_1, ..., B_{m-1})$ or
4) $\mathcal{V}_{in}(B_m) \not\subset (\mathcal{V}_{in}(B_0) \cup \mathcal{V}_{out}(B_1, ..., B_{m-1}))$.

end_do
5. generation step

Let c_i $i \in [1..num\_sub]$ be the resulting clauses of the simplification of w_i. c_i are in the following form: $p_0(\bar{t}_0)\theta \leftarrow \Delta_i$ and d is of the following form $d: p_0(\bar{t}_0)\theta \leftarrow \Gamma$. We generate the set of candidate properties in the following way: $\Gamma \Leftarrow \Delta_j,\ j \in [1..num\_sub]$. If there exists $i \in [1..num\_sub]$ such that $\Delta_i = p_0(\overline{t_0})\theta$ then remove this property from the set of candidate properties. If one of the candidate properties is valid, the *target_schema* is validated and the recursive definition is obtained, else if $AN \neq \emptyset$ then go to step 2 else the *target_schema* is not interesting and go to step 1.

<u>*else*</u> ($NFP(c,d) = \emptyset$) by applying the folding transformation we obtain a recursive definition.

Remark 5.3
We use two heuristics in our strategy. In the first one, the arbitrary variables are substituted by subterms of terms occurring in the clause *ee* or by fresh variables representing internal variables. In the second one, if there exists i such that $Y_{index,i} = \emptyset$ or if all the properties generated in the fifth step are not valid then the *target_schema* is not the suitable one and we came back to the firt step of the strategy.

5.3 Correctness of the proposed Strategy

Proposition 5.1
The proposed strategy is correct.

Proof:
If a valid property exists among those generated by the strategy and if the condition for applying the transformation *applying_a_property* holds, then the obtained program P' is correct w.r.t. the initial program P, and we have $\mathcal{M}(P') \subset \mathcal{M}(P)$. □

Remark 5.4
The termination of the proposed strategy is not guaranteed because we can have an infinite number of non interesting *target_schemas*.

Example 5.5

$$
\begin{array}{lll}
1 & p(x,y) & \leftarrow p_1(x,y,z),\ p_2(z) \\
2 & p_1(s(x),y,s(z)) & \leftarrow p_1(x,y,z) \\
3 & p_2(s(z)) & \leftarrow p_2(z)
\end{array}
$$

If the user proposes the following *target_schema* $p(x, s^n(y))$ with $n > 0$, by applying the unfolding transformation to some atoms of the body of the clause (1) we can not have a clause whose head matches with $p(x, s^n(y))$. Such schemas are called *loop_schemas*.

5.4 A complete example: the *Div* program

Let us consider the (*Div*) program.

$$
\begin{array}{lll}
1 & div(a,b,q,r) & \leftarrow less(r,b),\ times(q,b,t),\ plus(t,r,a) \\
2 & plus(0,x,x) & \leftarrow \\
3 & plus(s(x),y,s(z)) & \leftarrow plus(x,y,z) \\
4 & times(0,x,0) & \leftarrow \\
5 & times(s(x),y,z) & \leftarrow times(x,y,t),\ plus(y,t,z) \\
6 & less(0,s(x)) & \leftarrow \\
7 & less(s(x),s(y)) & \leftarrow less(x,y)
\end{array}
$$

This problem is not foldable i.e. we can not find a sequence of unfolding which makes it possible the application of the folding transformation. Intuitively, in this example if we destroy the relationship between terms in different atoms by introducing new variables we can not fold. By unfolding the atom $times(q,b,t)$, we introduce a new variable and we destroy the relationship between the first argument in the *plus* predicate and the third one of the *times* predicate. On the other hand, the unfolding of $less(r,b)$ or $plus(t,r,a)$ produces change in the terms occurring in the atom with *times* predicate, and the folding operation is not possible.

The *Div* program is *well – behaved* w.r.t. the mode m defined by: $m_{div} := (out, in, in, out)$, $m_{less} := (out, in)$, $m_{times} := m_{plus} := (in, in, out)$. *Div* is also a typed program. Let us describe step by step the strategy. c is the clause: $div(a,b,q,r) \leftarrow less(r,b),\ times(q,b,t),\ plus(t,r,a)$, the recursive predicates of *div* are *less*, *plus* and *times*. We mark the atoms in the body of c "recursive atoms" and the recursive call of clauses 3, 5 and 7, "recursive atoms".

1. ***target_schema step***:
   - The user proposes the *target_schema* $div(a,b,s(x),r)$
   - By unfolding the atom $times(b,q,t)$ in c we have the clause $d:\ div(a,b,s(x),r) \leftarrow less(r,b),\ times(x,b,u),\ plus(b,u,v1),\ plus(v1,r,a)$
2. ***enriching the target_schema step***:
   - $NFP(c,d) := \{\{times\},\{plus\}\}$, $Q := \{plus\}$, $F = \{div, less, times\}$. In Div_F we fold c_F in d_F; let w_F be the resulting clause $div_F(a,b,s(x),r) \leftarrow div_F(v_1,b,x,r)$
   - v_1 *is in* $(\mathcal{V}(w_F) \setminus \mathcal{V}(div(a,b,s(x),r))$ and it is used with one and only one occurrence in the body of w_F, so it is substituted by the variable s_1.
   - $plus(b,u,v_1)$ is not marked "recursive atom" and $plus \in Q$, so $GEN(plus(a,b,v_1) = plus(s_2,s_3,s_4)$; we add the atom $plus(s_2,s_3,s_4)$ to the body of w_F, and we get the clause: $ee:\ div(a,b,s(x),r) \leftarrow plus(s_2,s_3,s_4),\ div(s_1,b,x,r)$
3. ***static analysis step***:
   - If we consider the following mode for the predicate *div*: $m_{div} := (out, in, in, out)$, we infer the mode of *less*, *plus*, *times* : $m_{less} := (out, in)$, $m_{plus}(in, in, out)$, $m_{times} := (in, in, out)$. We arrange w.r.t. this mode m the atoms in the body of the clauses defining the program *Div* such that *Div* conserves the well-behaved notion w.r.t. the mode m:

1	$div(a,b,q,r)$	$\leftarrow$	$less(r,b),\ times(q,b,t),\ plus(t,r,a)$
2	$plus(0,x,x)$	$\leftarrow$	
3	$plus(s(x),y,s(z))$	$\leftarrow$	$plus(x,y,z)$
4	$times(0,x,0)$	$\leftarrow$	
5	$times(s(x),y,z)$	$\leftarrow$	$times(x,y,t),\ plus(y,t,z)$
6	$less(0,s(x))$	$\leftarrow$	
7	$less(s(x),s(y))$	$\leftarrow$	$less(x,y)$

ee is then: $ee: div(a,b,s(x),r) \leftarrow div(s_1,b,x,r),\ plus(s_2,s_3,s_4)$

1) $s_4 \in \mathcal{V}_{out}(plus(s_2,s_3,s_4))$ then $s_4 \in \{a\}$

2) $s_2 \in \mathcal{V}_{in}(plus(s_2,s_3,s_4))$ then $s_2 \in \{b,x,s(x),s_1,r\}$

3) $s_3 \in \mathcal{V}_{in}(plus(s_2,s_3,s_4))$ then $s_3 \in \{b,x,s(x),s_1,r\}$

4) $s_1 \in \mathcal{V}_{out}(div(s_1,b,x,r))$ then $s_1 \in \{s_2,s_3\}$

this first step gives $Y_{1,1} := \{s_2,s_3\}$, $Y_{1,2} := \{b,x,s(x),s_1,r\}$, $Y_{1,3} := \{b,x,s(x),s_1,r\}$ and $Y_{1,4} := \{a\}$.

- if we consider another mode $m_{div} := (in, in, out, out)$ then the synthesis of the corresponding mode of the predicate symbols used in the program gives: $m_{less} := (out, in)$, $m_{times} := (out, in, in)$; for the predicate *plus* it is used in the clause 1 by the mode (out, in, in) and in the clause 5 by the mode (in, out, in). We rename[2] the predicate symbol *plus* used in the clause 5 with the predicate symbol *minus* and we rearrange the atoms in the body of clauses defining the program *Div* such that *Div* is well-behaved w.r.t. the mode *m*:

1	$div(a,b,q,r)$	$\leftarrow$	$less(r,b),\ plus(t,r,a),\ times(q,b,t)$
2	$plus(0,x,x)$	$\leftarrow$	
3	$plus(s(x),y,s(z))$	$\leftarrow$	$plus(x,y,z)$
4	$times(0,x,0)$	$\leftarrow$	
5	$times(s(x),y,z)$	$\leftarrow$	$minus(y,t,z),\ times(x,y,t)$
6	$less(0,s(x))$	$\leftarrow$	
7	$less(s(x),s(y))$	$\leftarrow$	$less(x,y)$
8	$minus(0,x,x)$	$\leftarrow$	
9	$minus(s(x),y,s(z))$	$\leftarrow$	$minus(x,y,z)$

ee is then: $ee: div(a,b,s(x),r) \leftarrow minus(s_2,s_3,s_4),\ div(s_1,b,x,r)$

1) $s_2,\ s_4 \in \mathcal{V}_{in}(div(a,b,s(x),r))$ then $s_2,\ s_4 \in \{a,b\}$

2) $s_1 \in \mathcal{V}_{in}(div(s_1,b,x,r))$ then $s_1 \in \{a,b,s_3\}$

3) $s_3 \in \mathcal{V}_{out}(minus(s_2,s_3,s_4))$ then $s_3 \in \{s_1\}$

this step gives $Y_{2,1} = \{s_3,a,b\}$, $Y_{2,2} = \{a,b\}$, $Y_{2,3} = \{s_1\}$, $Y_{2,4} = \{a,b\}$.

With this second step

$Y_{2,1} = \{s_2,s_3\} \cap \{s_3,a,b\} = \{s_3\}$,

$Y_{2,2} = \{a,b\} \cap \{b,x,s(x),s_1,r\} = \{b\}$,

$Y_{2,3} = \{s_1\} \cap \{b,x,s(x),s_1,r\} = \{s_1\}$,

$Y_{2,4} = \{a\} \cap \{a,b\} = \{a\}$.

The resulting clause is $e_1: div(a,b,s(x),r) \leftarrow plus(b,s_1,a),\ div(s_1,b,x,r)$

$\psi := \{\sigma = \{s_1/s_1,\ s_2/b,\ s_3/s_1,\ s_4/a\}\}$

4. ***simplification step***:

   If we add the atoms of the body of *d* in the right part of the body of e_1, we get:

$$cc: div(a,b,s(x),r) \leftarrow plus(b,s_1,a),\ div(s_1,b,x,r),\ times(x,b,u),\ plus(b,u,v1),\ plus(v1,r,a),\ less(r,b)$$

[2]as it is defined in section 3, a predicate has one and only one mode in a program. If we use a predicate symbol with more than one mode in a program (to be sure that the program remains well-behaved) then we have to rename this predicate.

We can verify that we can remove the atoms:
$times(x,b,u)$, $plus(b,u,v1)$, $plus(v1,r,a)$, $less(r,b)$ from the body of cc

cc is then: $cc: div(a,b,s(x),r) \leftarrow plus(b,s_1,a),\ div(s_1,b,x,r)$

5. *generation step*

   We generate the property:

   $times(x,b,u),\ plus(b,u,v1),\ plus(v1,r,a),\ less(r,b) \Leftarrow plus(b,s_1,a),\ div(s_1,b,x,r)$.
   This property is valid in the least Herbrand model of the program *Div* [3]. Then we have validated the proposed *target_schema*. We finally obtain the program:

4	$plus(0,x,x)$	$\leftarrow$	
5	$plus(s(x),y,s(z))$	$\leftarrow$	$plus(x,y,z)$
8	$less(0,s(x))$	$\leftarrow$	
9	$less(s(x),s(y))$	$\leftarrow$	$less(x,y)$
12	$div(a,b,0,a)$	$\leftarrow$	$less(a,b)$
15	$div(a,b,s(x),r)$	$\leftarrow$	$plus(b,u,a),\ div(u,b,x,r)$

6 Conclusion

This work has been done in the context of the **Spes** project [1]. The interesting features of this work are the way it allows a user to use a *target_schema* as *meta_goal* to specify the head of the required recursive definition and the static analysis step which permits us to instantiate unknown variables. It provides an interesting method to make explicit suitable *Eureka properties*. Compared with previous transformational approaches, the contribution of this paper could be summarized as follows:
1) the definition of a new strategy guided by *mode and type analysis*,
2) the ability to generate interesting properties by using a syntactic approach.

The strategy we propose produces correct programs w.r.t. the initial specifications. The method has been extended in order to synthesize *tail_recursive* defined programs by applying *Eureka properties*.

We can easily mechanise this strategy by combining the automatic generation of *target_schemas* and the automatic generation of modes for the predicate occurring in the program in order to conserve the well-behaved notion of the program.

The key idea proposed in this article, consisting of the proposition of a *target_schema*, can be extended to a general use in logic program transformation by proposing a *guided schema methodology for transforming logic programs*. This method has the advantage of directing the transformation process, so problems like the number of *unfolding* steps can be avoided by this approach. Current work is under development in this direction.

Further work will also lead to the development of strategies and the use of plans to guide inductive proofs for the generated properties. Much research has been devoted to the problem of proving automatically inductive theorems [15], [22], [14]. We believe that combining the two formal systems (the first for transforming logic programs, and the second for proving inductive properties) will offer a more powerful environment for automatic programming.

---

[3]This property can be simplified to the associativity property of the predicate *plus*
`plus(x,y,t) & plus(t,z,w) <= plus(y,z,u) & plus(x,u,w)`

Acknowledgements

I would like to thank *Alain Quéré* and *Francis Alexandre* for their helpful remarks, and the referees for their helpful comments which have improved this paper considerably.

References

[1] F. Alexandre, K. Bsaïes, J.P. Finance, and A. Quéré. SPES: A System for Logic Program Transformation. In *Proc. of the International Conference on Logic Programming and Automated Reasoning (LPAR'92)*, Lecture Notes in Artificial Intelligence. Springer-Verlag, July 1992. St. Petersburg.

[2] F. Alexandre, K. Bsaïes, and A. Quéré. On Using Mode Input-output for Transforming Logic Programs. In K-K. Lau and T. Clement, editors, *Proceedings of the LoPSTr 91 Workshop on Logic Program Synthesis and Transformation, University of Manchester.*, pages 129–147. Workshops in Computing Series, Springer-Verlag, 1991. Manchester, UK.

[3] K.R. Apt and M.H Van Emden. Contribution to the Theory of Logic Programming. *Journal of the Association for Computing Machinery*, 29(3):841–862, 1982.

[4] R. Balzer. Transformational Implementation: An Example. *"IEEE", Transaction on Software Engineering*, SE-7(1):3–14, 1981.

[5] R.M Burstall and J.A Darlington. Transformation System for Developing Recursive Programs. *Journal of the Association for Computing Machinery*, 24(1):44–67, 1977.

[6] K.L. Clark and J. Darlington. Algorithm Classification through Synthesis. In *The Computer Journal 23(1)*, pages 61–65, 1980.

[7] K.L. Clark and S. Sickel. Predicate Logic: A Calculus for the Derivation of Programs. In *Proc. IJCAI-77*, pages 419–420, 1977.

[8] S.K. Debray and D.S. Warren. Detection and Optimization of Functional Computations in Prolog. In E. Shapiro, editor, *Proceedings of the Third International Conference on Logic Programming, London*, volume 225 of *LNCS*, pages 490–504. Springer-Verlag, 1986.

[9] S.K. Debray and D.S. Warren. Automatic Mode Inference for Logic Programs. *Journal of Logic Programming*, 5:207–229, 1988.

[10] M.S. Feather. A System for Assisting Program Transformation. *ACM TOPLAS*, 4(1):1–20, 1982.

[11] M.S. Feather. A Survey and Classification of some Program Transformation Techniques. In *Proc. TC2 IFIP Working Conference on Program Specification and Transformation, Bad-Tölz, F.R.G*, 1986.

[12] C.J. Hogger. Derivation of Logic Programs. *Journal of the Association for Computing Machinery*, 28(2), April 1981.

[13] C.J. Hogger. *Introduction to Logic Programming*. Academic Press, 1984.

[14] J. Hsiang and M. Srivas. Automatic Inductive Theorem Prooving Using Prolog. *Theoretical Computer Science*, 54:3–28, 1987. North-Holland.

[15] E. Kounalis and M. Rusinowitch. Mechanizing Inductive Reasoning. In *Proc. 8 th Conf. of American Association in Artificial Intelligence (AAAI).*, pages 240–245, Boston, 1990. AAAI Press and the MIT Press.

[16] K.K. Lau and S.D. Prestwich. Top-down Synthesis of Recursive Logic Procedures from First-order Logic Specifications. In *International Conference on Logic Programming*, pages 667–684, israel, 1990. MIT Press.

[17] J.W. Lloyd. *Foundations of Logic Programming*. Springer-Verlag, 1988.

[18] C. S. Mellish. Some Global Optimizations for a Prolog Compiler. *Journal of Logic Programming*, 1:43–66, 1985.

[19] A. Mycroft and R.A. O'Keefe. A Polymorphic Type System for Prolog. *Artificial Intelligence*, 1984(23):295–307, 1984.

[20] A. Pettorossi and M. Proietti. Decidability Results and Characterization of Strategies for the Development of Logic Programs. In G. Levi and M. Martelli, editors, *6th International Conference on Logic Programming*, Lisbon (Portugal), 1989. MIT Press.

[21] U. S. Reddy. Transformation of Logic Programs into Functional Programs. In *International Symposium on Logic Programming, Atlantic City*, pages 187-196, 1984.

[22] A. Sakurai and H. Motoda. Proving Definite Clauses without Explicit Use of Inductions. In K. Furukawa, H. Tanaka, and T Fujisaki, editors, *Proceedings of the 7th Conference, Logic Programming '88*, Tokyo, Japan, April 1988. LNAI 383, Springer-Verlag.

[23] H. Tamaki and T. Sato. Unfold/Fold Transformation of Logic Programs. In *Proceedings of the 2nd International Logic Programming Conference, Uppsala*, 1984.

An Algorithm for Finite Approximations of Definite Programs and its Implementation in Prolog

Lunjin Lu*
School of Computer Science, The University of Birmingham
Birmingham, The United Kingdom

Peter Greenfield
School of Computer Science, The University of Birmingham
Birmingham, The United Kingdom

Abstract

In this paper, we first review a bottom-up abstract interpretation framework for finite approximations of definite programs that are characterised by abstraction functions. For each such abstraction function α, a finite approximation of the least fixpoint semantics is given as the least fixpoint of a function $\Phi_{P,\alpha}$ over an abstract domain in a similar way that the least fixpoint semantics is given as the least fixpoint of a function T_P over the concrete domain. Then the derivation of an algorithm for the computation of $lfp(\Phi_{P,\alpha})$ is detailed and its implementation in Prolog is presented. The final algorithm is efficient in both storage usage and time usage. The efficiency in its storage usage is obtained by formulating another function $\Psi_{P,\alpha}$ and establishing that $lfp(\Psi_{P,\alpha}) = lfp(\Phi_{P,\alpha})$. The time efficiency is obtained by using heuristic knowledge derived from program text and information accumulated during the computation of $lfp(\Phi_{P,\alpha})$. The time efficiency is exemplified through depth abstractions and stump abstractions.

1 Introduction

Let us assume that we are dealing with a definite program P, and that its Herbrand universe, Herbrand base and least fixpoint semantics are U_P, B_P and M_P respectively. Let $C_1, \ldots, C_N$ be the clauses of P. Let $C_i = A_{i,0} \leftarrow A_{i,1} \wedge \cdots \wedge A_{i,m_i}$. Let the set of ground instances of an atom A be denoted as $[A]$, i.e. $[A] = \{A\sigma | \exists\sigma.A\sigma \in B_P\}$.

The fixpoint semantics of definite programs given by van Emden and Kowalski [11] may be rewritten as follows.

Definition 1.1 (van Emden and Kowalski) The fixpoint semantics of a definite program P is the least fixpoint of function $T_P : \wp(B_P) \mapsto \wp(B_P)$ defined as follows.

$$T_P(I) = \{A_{i,0}\sigma \;| \exists\sigma.\exists C_i \in P.(A_{i,1}\sigma \wedge \ldots \wedge A_{i,m_i}\sigma \in I \wedge A_{i,0}\sigma \in B_P)\} \quad (1)$$

*Supported by the Sino-British Friendship Scholarship Scheme.

The size of $M_P = lfp(T_P)$ is usually infinite for a non-trivial program. This makes the computation infeasible. So, finite approximations of $lfp(T_P)$ must be used to derive program properties for program analyses.

Sato *et al.* [10] define a class of finite approximations of definite programs by means of depth abstractions. Xu *et al.* [12] present another class of finite approximations of definite programs by means of stump abstractions. Each of these abstractions is characterised by an abstraction function from a concrete domain to an abstract domain. Each element in the abstract domain represents a set of elements in the concrete domain.

Lu and Greenfield [5] generalise Sato's depth abstractions and Xu's stump abstractions and present a bottom-up abstract interpretation framework for finite approximations. In this paper, we derive an algorithm for the computation of such finite approximations and present its implementation as a Prolog meta-program. Section 2 reviews the bottom-up abstract interpretation framework. Section 3 presents the derivation of an algorithm for the computation of such finite approximations. Section 4 outlines an implementation of the algorithm as a Prolog meta-program. Section 5 exemplifies the algorithm developed through depth abstractions and stump abstractions. Section 6 concludes the paper.

2 A class of finite approximations

This section presents an abstract fixpoint semantics of a definite program for an abstraction function α.

Let $Terms$ be the set of terms, α be a function from $Terms$ to $\mathcal{T}erms$, the set of abstract terms. The concrete domain we consider is a sub-lattice of $(\wp(Terms), \subseteq)$ and the abstract domain a sub-lattice of $(\wp(\mathcal{T}erms), \subseteq)$. Throughout this paper, abstract objects are denoted by bold face lowercase letters or calligraphic uppercase letters.

The abstraction function α induces an equivalence relation $\equiv_\alpha$ on $Terms$, $t_1 \equiv_\alpha t_2$ iff $\alpha(t_1) = \alpha(t_2)$. When $t_1 \equiv_\alpha t_2$, t_1 (or t_2) is called α-equivalent to t_2 (or t_1). It is possible that two or more instances of a term t belong to the same equivalent class, i.e., there exist some θ_1 and θ_2 such that $t\theta_1 \equiv_\alpha t\theta_2$. The fact that $t\theta_1 \equiv_\alpha t\theta_2$ is denoted as $\theta_1 \simeq_{\alpha,t} \theta_2$.

We generalise the definition of function α from $Terms \mapsto \mathcal{T}erms$ to $\wp(Terms) \mapsto \wp(\mathcal{T}erms)$ with definition $\alpha(S) = \{\alpha(s) | s \in S\}$. We define a concretion function $\gamma : \mathcal{T}erms \mapsto \wp(Terms)$ as $\gamma(\mathbf{t}) = \{t | t \in Terms, \mathbf{t} = \alpha(t)\}$, and generalise γ from $\mathcal{T}erms \mapsto \wp(Terms)$ to $\wp(\mathcal{T}erms) \mapsto \wp(Terms)$ with definition $\gamma(\mathcal{S}) = \cup_{\mathbf{s} \in \mathcal{S}} \gamma(\mathbf{s})$.

$\alpha(M_P)$ is an ideal approximation of M_P with respect to α. That is, any other correct approximation of M_P is a superset of $\alpha(M_P)$ and hence less precise than $\alpha(M_P)$. However, it is impossible to obtain $\alpha(M_P)$ without actually calculating M_P. So, M_P must be approximated in another way. Lu and Greenfield [5] define an approximation of M_P for each abstraction function α as follows and establish its correctness.

Definition 2.1 The finite approximation of P characterised by the abstraction function α is the least fixpoint of function $\Phi_{P,\alpha} : \wp(\alpha(B_P)) \mapsto \wp(\alpha(B_P))$ defined as the following.

$$\Phi_{P,\alpha}(\mathcal{I}) = \left\{ \alpha(A_{i,0}\sigma) \middle| \begin{array}{l} \exists\sigma.\exists C_i \in P. \\ (A_{i,0}\sigma \in B_P \wedge \ldots \wedge A_{i,m_i}\sigma \in B_P \wedge \\ \alpha(A_{i,1}\sigma) \in \mathcal{I} \wedge \ldots \wedge \alpha(A_{i,m_i}\sigma) \in \mathcal{I}) \end{array} \right\} \tag{2}$$

$\Phi_{P,\alpha}$ is a monotone and $(\wp(\alpha(B_P)), \subseteq)$ is a complete lattice with set union $\cup$ as least upper bound operator. So, $\Phi_{P,\alpha}$ has the least fixpoint $lfp(\Phi_{P,\alpha}) = \cup_{i=0}^{i=\infty} \Phi^i_{P,\alpha}(\emptyset)$.

3 An Algorithm for Computing $lfp(\Phi_{P,\alpha})$

In this section we present in detail the derivation of an efficient algorithm for the computation $lfp(\Phi_{P,\alpha})$. In sub-section 3.1, an inefficient but intuitive algorithm is presented and several possible improvements in its storage usage and time usage are suggested. In sub-section 3.2, the improvement in storage usage is justified and an improved algorithm is formulated. In sub-section 3.3, the improvements in time usage are made by using heuristics derived from the program text resulting in a more efficient algorithm.

In order to compute $lfp(\Phi_{P,\alpha})$, the definition of $\Phi_{P,\alpha}$ is reformulated as follows.

$$\Phi_{P,\alpha}(\mathcal{I}) = \left\{ \mathcal{A} \middle| \begin{array}{l} \exists\sigma.\exists C_i \in P. \\ \alpha(A_{i,1}\sigma) \in \mathcal{I} \wedge \cdots \wedge \alpha(A_{i,m_i}\sigma) \in \mathcal{I} \wedge \mathcal{A} \in \alpha([A_{i,0}\sigma]) \end{array} \right\} \tag{3}$$

The equivalence between equation 3 and equation 2 may be established in a straightforward manner by mathematical induction.

3.1 An intuitive algorithm

We now present an inefficient but intuitive algorithm for the computation of $lfp(\Phi_{P,\alpha})$ from which the final efficient algorithm evolves.

Definition 3.1 $(\phi_{C_i,\alpha} : \alpha(B_P) \mapsto \alpha(B_P))$

$$\phi_{C_i,\alpha}(\mathcal{I}) = \left\{ \mathcal{A} \middle| \begin{array}{l} \exists\sigma.\alpha(A_{i,1}\sigma) \in \mathcal{I} \wedge \cdots \wedge \alpha(A_{i,m_i}\sigma) \in \mathcal{I} \wedge \\ \mathcal{A} \in \alpha([A_{i,0}\sigma]) \end{array} \right\} \tag{4}$$

The reading of $\phi_{C_i,\alpha}(\mathcal{I})$ is the set of α-abstractions of the ground atoms that may be derived in one step from $\gamma(\mathcal{I})$ and C_i. The following results from equation 3 and equation 4.

$$\Phi_{P,\alpha} = \phi_{C_1,\alpha} \cup \ldots \cup \phi_{C_N,\alpha} \tag{5}$$

Equation 5 can be utilised for the computation of $lfp(\Phi_{P,\alpha})$ resulting in the algorithm 3.1. $lfp(\Phi_{P,\alpha})$ is obtained by computing $\Phi^1_{P,\alpha}(\emptyset), \Phi^2_{P,\alpha}(\emptyset), \ldots$ until $\Phi^n_{P,\alpha}(\emptyset) = \Phi^{n+1}_{P,\alpha}(\emptyset)$ for some n.

Algorithm 3.1 An algorithm for computing $lfp(\Phi_{P,\alpha})$.

$\mathcal{J} \leftarrow \emptyset$
repeat
  $\mathcal{I} \leftarrow \mathcal{J}$
  $\mathcal{J} \leftarrow \Phi_{P,\alpha}(\mathcal{I}) = \phi_{C_1,\alpha}(\mathcal{I}) \cup \ldots \cup \phi_{C_N,\alpha}(\mathcal{I})$
until $\mathcal{J} = \mathcal{I}$
return $\mathcal{J}$

Before we discuss algorithm 3.1, let us consider the relation between the partial results in the algorithm.

Lemma 3.1 For any $n \geq 0$, $\Phi^n_{P,\alpha}(\emptyset) \subseteq \Phi^{n+1}_{P,\alpha}(\emptyset)$.

Proof The proof can be done in a straightforward manner by induction on n. □

Algorithm 3.1 is inefficient in its storage usage since it is necessary to store two partial results $\mathcal{I}$ and $\mathcal{J}$ when computing $\Phi^n_{P,\alpha}(\emptyset)$. We shall later show that only one partial result is needed.

Algorithm 3.1 is also inefficient in its time usage for the following reasons.

- It is possible that $\phi_{C_i,\alpha}(\Phi^n_{P,\alpha}(\emptyset))$ generates some elements that are already in $\Phi^n_{P,\alpha}(\emptyset)$. The time devoted to generating these elements is wasted since $\Phi^n_{P,\alpha}(\emptyset) \subseteq \Phi^{n+1}_{P,\alpha}(\emptyset)$ by lemma 3.1 and these elements need not to be generated.
- It is possible that $\phi_{C_i,\alpha}(\Phi^n_{P,\alpha}(\emptyset))$ does not generate any elements that are not in $\Phi^n_{P,\alpha}(\emptyset)$. The time devoted to the application of such $\phi_{C_i,\alpha}$ is wasted.

The above discussion suggests that improvements can be made to algorithm 3.1. This paper addresses the following.

1. Because each $\phi_{C_i,\alpha}$ is monotonic, the elements in each $\phi_{C_i,\alpha}(\Phi^n_{P,\alpha}(\emptyset))$ can be added to the previous partial result. Thus only one partial result needs to be stored. We show that the algorithm thus obtained is correct.
2. It is not necessary to apply every $\phi_{C_i,\alpha}$ in every application of $\Phi_{P,\alpha}$; only the $\phi_{C_i,\alpha}$ corresponding to those clauses whose bodies contain subgoals which might unify with some recently generated elements should be applied.
3. Regeneration of the elements in the previous partial result should be avoided whenever possible.

3.2 Improvement in storage usage

We now present an improved algorithm that incorporates improvement 1 outlined in sub-section 3.1. To justify this improvement, we formulate a new function $\Psi_{P,\alpha} : \alpha(B_P) \mapsto \alpha(B_P)$ and prove that $lfp(\Psi_{P,\alpha}) = lfp(\Phi_{P,\alpha})$.

Definition 3.2 ($\psi_{C_i,\alpha} : \alpha(B_P) \mapsto \alpha(B_P)$)

$$\psi_{C_i,\alpha}(\mathcal{I}) = \mathcal{I} \cup \phi_{C_i,\alpha}(\mathcal{I}) \tag{6}$$

Each $\psi_{C_i,\alpha}$ is monotonic.

Observation 3.1 The following hold.

$$\forall \mathcal{I}.\psi_{C_i,\alpha}(\mathcal{I}) \supseteq \mathcal{I} \tag{7}$$

$$\forall n \geq 0.(\psi_{C_i,\alpha}(\Phi^n_{P,\alpha}(\emptyset)) \subseteq \Phi_{P,\alpha}(\Phi^n_{P,\alpha}(\emptyset))) \tag{8}$$

Definition 3.3 **($\Psi_{P,\alpha} : \alpha(B_P) \mapsto \alpha(B_P)$)** Let $\circ$ denote function composition.

$$\Psi_{P,\alpha} = \psi_{C_N,\alpha} \circ \psi_{C_{N-1},\alpha} \circ \cdots \circ \psi_{C_1,\alpha} \tag{9}$$

$\Psi_{P,\alpha}$ is monotonic since each $\psi_{C_i,\alpha}$ is monotonic. Before we use $\Psi_{P,\alpha}$ to compute $lfp(\Phi_{P,\alpha})$, we need to establish that $lfp(\Phi_{P,\alpha}) = lfp(\Psi_{P,\alpha})$

Lemma 3.2 For any $n \geq 0$, $\Phi^n_{P,\alpha}(\emptyset) \subseteq \Psi^n_{P,\alpha}(\emptyset)$.

Proof The proof is by induction on n. First, the result holds for $n = 0$ since $\Phi^0_{P,\alpha}(\emptyset) = \Psi^0_{P,\alpha}(\emptyset) = \emptyset$.

Now suppose that the result holds for $n-1$. Let $\mathcal{A} \in \Phi^n_{P,\alpha}(\emptyset)$. Then there exist some σ and some clause C_i such that $\mathcal{A} \in \alpha([A_{i,0}\sigma])$ and $\alpha(A_{i,j}\sigma) \in \Phi^{n-1}_{P,\alpha}(\emptyset)$ for $1 \leq j \leq m_i$. By the induction hypothesis, $\alpha(A_{i,j}\sigma) \in \Psi^{n-1}_{P,\alpha}(\emptyset)$ for $1 \leq j \leq m_i$. By equation 6, $\mathcal{A} \in \Psi^n_{C_i,\alpha}(\emptyset)$. This, together with the monotonicity of $\Psi_{P,\alpha}$ and equation 9, implies $\mathcal{A} \in \Psi^n_{P,\alpha}(\emptyset)$. This completes the proof of the lemma. □

Lemma 3.3 For any $n \geq 0$, letting N be the number of clauses, there is some $0 \leq m \leq n \times N$ such that $\Psi^n_{P,\alpha}(\emptyset) \subseteq \Phi^m_{P,\alpha}(\emptyset)$.

Proof The proof is by induction on n. The result holds for $n = 0$ since $\Psi^0_{P,\alpha}(\emptyset) = \emptyset$ with $m = 0$.

Suppose that $\Psi^{n-1}_{P,\alpha}(\emptyset) \subseteq \Phi^{m_1}_{P,\alpha}(\emptyset)$ and $m_1 \leq N \times (n-1)$. If suffices to show that, for any $\mathcal{A} \in \Psi^n_{P,\alpha}(\emptyset)$, $\mathcal{A} \in \Phi^m_{P,\alpha}(\emptyset)$ for some $0 \leq m \leq n \times N$. If $\mathcal{A} \in \Psi^{n-1}_{P,\alpha}(\emptyset)$, then by the induction hypothesis, $\mathcal{A} \in \Phi^{m_1}_{P,\alpha}(\emptyset)$. If $\mathcal{A} \notin \Psi^{n-1}_{P,\alpha}(\emptyset)$, then there is some clause C_i such that $\mathcal{A} \in \psi_{C_i,\alpha} \circ \cdots \circ \psi_{C_1,\alpha}(\Psi^{n-1}_{P,\alpha}(\emptyset))$. By the induction hypothesis and the monotonicity of $\psi_{C_j,\alpha}$ for $0 < j \leq i$, we have $\mathcal{A} \in \psi_{C_i,\alpha} \circ \cdots \circ \psi_{C_1,\alpha}(\Phi^{m_1}_{P,\alpha}(\emptyset))$. So, by equation 8, $\mathcal{A} \in \Phi^{m_1+i}_{P,\alpha}(\emptyset)$. Letting $m = m_1 + i$, we have $\mathcal{A} \in \Psi^n_{P,\alpha}(\emptyset) \Rightarrow \mathcal{A} \in \Phi^m_{P,\alpha}(\emptyset)$ and $0 \leq m \leq n \times N$ since $0 \leq i \leq n$ and $0 \leq m_1 \leq (n-1) \times N$. □

Theorem 3.1 $lfp(\Psi_{P,\alpha}) = lfp(\Phi_{P,\alpha})$.

Proof By lemma 3.2 we have $lfp(\Phi_{P,\alpha}) \subseteq lfp(\Psi_{P,\alpha})$. By lemma 3.3 we have $lfp(\Psi_{P,\alpha}) \subseteq lfp(\Phi_{P,\alpha})$. So, $lfp(\Psi_{P,\alpha}) = lfp(\Phi_{P,\alpha})$. □

Using theorem 3.1, we can compute $lfp(\Psi_{P,\alpha})$ when $lfp(\Phi_{P,\alpha})$ is needed. Doing this results in algorithm 3.2 as an alternative for the computation of $lfp(\Phi_{P,\alpha})$.

Algorithm 3.2 An algorithm for the computation of $lfp(\Psi_{P,\alpha})$

$\mathcal{J} \leftarrow \emptyset$, $i \leftarrow 1$
repeat
  $\mathcal{J} \leftarrow \psi_{C_i,\alpha}(\mathcal{J})$
  $i \leftarrow i+1$, **if** $i > N$ **then** $i \leftarrow 1$
until the last application of each $\psi_{C_i,\alpha}$ does not add any new elements.
return $\mathcal{J}$

Algorithm 3.2 needs only one partial result to be retained. $\psi_{C_i,\alpha}(\mathcal{J})$ adds to $\mathcal{J}$ those elements which can be derived from C_i and $\mathcal{J}$ in one step. The variable i is used to ensure that each $\psi_{C_i,\alpha}$ gets its turn to be applied. The correctness of algorithm 3.2 results from the fact that when no $\psi_{C_i,\alpha}$ generates any new elements, the least fixpoint is reached.

3.3 Improvements in time usage

In fact, the order in which $\psi_{C_i,\alpha}$ is applied has nothing to do with the correctness as long as each $\psi_{C_i,\alpha}$ gets its turn to be applied to the final result. It is possible that some applications of $\psi_{C_i,\alpha}$ in algorithm 3.2 do not contribute to $lfp(\Psi_{P,\alpha})$ and time devoted to such application is wasted. So, it is desirable to avoid such applications whenever possible. Whilst it is impossible to predict whether an application will contribute to $lfp(\Psi_{P,\alpha})$ without actually applying it, it is possible to predict whether an application is *likely* to contribute to $lfp(\Psi_{P,\alpha})$. These observations are utilised to effect improvements 2 and 3 outlined in sub-section 3.1 which result in algorithm 3.3.

Before we present algorithm 3.3, we give the following definition to simplify the presentation.

Definition 3.4 Let the *name/arity* of $A_{i,j}$ in $C_i = A_{i,0} \leftarrow A_{i,1} \wedge \cdots \wedge A_{i,m_i}$ be $p_{i,j}/n_{i,j}$. We define $C_r \prec C_s$ if $p_{r,0}/n_{r,0} = p_{s,k}/n_{s,k}$ for some $1 \leq k \leq m_s$. C_r is said to activate C_s.

The reading of $C_r \prec C_s$ is that the elements generated by $\psi_{C_r,\alpha}$ might be used by $\psi_{C_s,\alpha}$ to generate elements that are not already in the partial result. We now present the improved algorithm.

Algorithm 3.3 An improved algorithm for the computation of $lfp(\Psi_{P,\alpha})$ by intelligent selection of the order in which $\psi_{C_i,\alpha}$ is applied.

$\mathcal{J} \leftarrow \emptyset$, $F \leftarrow \{C_1, \ldots, C_N\}$
repeat
  $C \leftarrow SELECT(F)$
  $F \leftarrow F - \{C\}$
  $\mathcal{J} \leftarrow \psi_{C,\alpha}(\mathcal{J})$
  if $\psi_{C,\alpha}$ generates some new elements
  then $F \leftarrow F \cup \{C_j | C \prec C_j\}$
until $F = \emptyset$
return $\mathcal{J}$

There are two major differences between algorithm 3.2 and algorithm 3.3. First, the former applies $\psi_{C_i,\alpha}$ in a fixed order whilst the latter decides the order by means of a selection function. Second, the former applies all the functions $\psi_{C_1,\alpha}, \ldots, \psi_{C_N,\alpha}$ repeatedly whilst the latter applies only those which are *likely* to generate some new elements.

Algorithm 3.3 keeps an agenda F that contains all the clauses whose corresponding functions might generate some new elements. A selection function $SELECT$ selects a clause C from the agenda and this clause is then removed from the agenda. The algorithm applies $\psi_{C,\alpha}$ to the partial result. If and only if the application of $\psi_{C,\alpha}$ contributes some new elements to $lfp(\Psi_{P,\alpha})$, then each clause C_j satisfying $C \prec C_j$ is added into the agenda F because it is necessary to check if the application of $\psi_{C_j,\alpha}$ to the latest partial result generates any new element.

Whilst algorithm 3.3 avoids applying any $\psi_{C,\alpha}$ that does not generate new elements, the speed of the algorithm depends on the intelligence of $SELECT$, the function that selects clauses. It is desirable to select a clause C that generates more new elements than any other clause in F because of the monotonicity of $\psi_{C_i,\alpha}$.

We now formulate a selection function $SELECT$ that uses two heuristics to select clauses. For each clause C in F, letting m ($m \neq 0$) be the number of goals in the body of C, we add the following information.

- $n' = n/m$, where n is the number of clauses that have activated C since the last time that C was added into F. Intuitively, the more subgoals in a clause that are likely to be resatisfied, the more new elements is the clause likely to generate.

- $t' = t/m$, where t is the total number of new elements generated by the clauses that have activated C since the last time that C was added into F. It is also intuitively justifiable that the more likely each subgoal in a clause is to be resatisfied, the more new elements is the clause likely to generate.

- m, where m has been added so as to make the updating of the agenda easier.

The agenda thus augmented is denoted as $\mathcal{F}$ and each of its elements is a quadruple (n', t', m, C). The reason we use $n' = n/m$ and $t' = t/m$ instead of n and t is that intuitively, a clause with more conditions requires more resources to draw a new conclusion.

For a clause representing a fact ($m = 0$), n' and t' are given initial values to ensure that such a clause is considered before any clause representing an implication. This is accomplished by initialising $\mathcal{F}$ with $\mathcal{F}_0$ that has one entry $(n'_0, 0, m, C)$ for each clause C, where $n'_0 = 2$ when $m = 0$ or $n'_0 = 1/m$ when $m \neq 0$.

Definition 3.5 we define the operator $\uplus$ as follows.

$$\mathcal{F}_1 \uplus \mathcal{F}_2 = \left\{ (n', t', m, C) \;\middle|\; \begin{array}{l} ((C \notin F_1 \cap F_2) \wedge ((n', t', m, C) \in \mathcal{F}_1 \cup \mathcal{F}_2)) \vee \\ (C \in F_1 \cap F_2) \wedge (\exists (n'_1, t'_1, m, C) \in \mathcal{F}_1. \\ \exists (n'_2, t'_2, m, C) \in \mathcal{F}_2.(n' = n'_1 + n'_2, t' = t'_1 + t'_2)) \end{array} \right\}$$

Algorithm 3.4 This is a reformulation of algorithm 3.3 with heuristically based selection of the order in which $\psi_{C_i,\alpha}$ is applied.

$\mathcal{J} \leftarrow \emptyset$, $\mathcal{F} \leftarrow \mathcal{F}_0$
repeat
  Select clause C from $\mathcal{F}$ with the largest (n', t')
  $\mathcal{F} \leftarrow \mathcal{F} - \{(n', t', m, C)\}$
  $\mathcal{J} \leftarrow \psi_{C,\alpha}(\mathcal{J})$
  if $\psi_{C,\alpha}$ generates t_C new elements
  then $\mathcal{F} \leftarrow \mathcal{F} \uplus \{(1/m_j, t_C/m_j, m_j, C_j) | C \prec C_j\}$
until $\mathcal{F} = \emptyset$
return $\mathcal{J}$

The selection can be accomplished by maintaining $\mathcal{F}$ as a sorted list. There are several small overheads introduced in algorithm 3.4 for deriving and storing the relation $\prec$, to remember how many new elements have been generated by each application of each $\psi_{C_i,\alpha}$ and to accomplish the operator $\uplus$. The overheads are much smaller than the cost of the applications of those $\psi_{C_i,\alpha}$ that do not generate any new elements.

So far, we have developed algorithm 3.4 for computing $lfp(\Phi_{P,\alpha})$. The algorithm is suitable for any abstraction function as long as $\alpha(B_P)$ is finite and an ancillary algorithm for the computation of $\psi_{C,\alpha}$ is provided.

4 The implementation

We first discuss the representations of the data structures used in the algorithm. There are four data structures: the program P, the approximation of the program $lfp(\Phi_{P,\alpha})$, the relation $\prec$ to be derived from the program text and the agenda $\mathcal{F}$. $\mathcal{F}$ is represented as a sorted list of quadruples, each clause C_i is represented by $(-n_i/m_i, -t_i/m_i, m_i, i)$. Negative numbers have been used to represent heuristics to take advantage of the built-in predicate *sort*.

Each clause C_i of P is represented as ':-'$(A_{i,0}, (A_{i,1}, \ldots, A_{i,m_i}))$. A static syntactic analysis procedure *syn_pg* translates the clause into (i, m_i, ':-'$(A_{i,0}, (A_{i,1}, \ldots, A_{i,m_i}))$). *syn_pg* also calculates abstraction dependent information and the relation $\prec$, representing $C_i \prec C_j$ as $act(i, j)$. Procedure *copy* renames the variables in a clause, procedure *member* enumerates the elements in a list and procedure *delete* deletes an element from a list.

The implementation of algorithm 3.4 is presented as program 4.1 in Edinburgh Prolog [4]. The function of each procedure is described by the comments just preceding it. An abstraction dependent predicate *psi* is to be provided to use the program. The reading of *psi*(+Info, $+C$, $+\mathcal{I}$, $-\mathcal{J}$, -NN) is that applying $\psi_{C,\alpha}$ to $\mathcal{I}$ results in $\mathcal{J}$ with NN being the number of new elements generated.

Program 4.1 Prolog code that implements algorithm 3.4.

```
/* lfp(+P, -LFP) computes the finite approximation LFP of P.  */
lfp(P, LFP) :-
        syn_pg(P, Info, PgN),       /* analyses and transforms P*/
        init_agenda(PgN, F0),
```

```
        sort(F0, F),
        compute(PgN, Info, F, [], LFP).

/* compute(+Program, +Info, +Agenda, +ParResB, -ParResA)       */
/* repeatedly calls procedure psi with the clause specified by*/
/* the first job of the Agenda and modifies the Agenda and     */
/* maintains it as a  sorted list.                              */
compute(_Pg, _Info, [], ParRes, ParRes).    /* agenda is empty*/
compute(Pg, Info, [(_N,_T,_M,I)|Ag], ParResB, ParResA) :-
        member((I,_,CLAUSE), Pg),          /*   find the clause */
        copy(CLAUSE, CLAUSECOPY),          /* rename the clause */
        psi(Info, CLAUSECOPY, ParResB, ParResI, NN),
        (  NN =\= 0
           ->   jobs_activated(Pg, Info, I, NN, Jobs),
                update_agenda(Ag, Jobs, NewAg),
                sort(NewAg, AgN),
                compute(Pg, Info, AgN, ParResI, ParResA)
            ;   compute(Pg, Info, Ag, ParResI, ParResA)
        ).

/* jobs_activated(+Pg, +Info, +I, +NN, -Jobs) generates the    */
/* Jobs for the clauses activated by clause I.                  */
jobs_activated(Pg, info(Heu, _Oth), I, NN, Jobs) :-
        setof(Job, find_one_job(Pg,Heu,I,NN,Job),Jobs1)
        -> Jobs = Jobs1
        ;  Jobs = [].
find_one_job(Pg, Heu, I, NN, (NJ,TJ,MJ,J)) :-
        member(act(I,J), Heu),
        member((J,MJ,_Clause), Pg),
        NJ is -1/MJ,                    /* MJ can't be 0  otherwise*/
        TJ is -NN/MJ.                   /* J cannot be activated   */

/* update_agenda(+F1,+F2,-F3) applies the operator  in          */
/* definition 3.5 to F1 and F2 to result in F3.                 */
update_agenda(F1,[],F1).
update_agenda(F1,[(N,T,M,I)|F2],[(N,T,M,I)|F3]):-
        \+ member((_,_,_,I),F1),
        update_agenda(F1,F2,F3).
update_agenda(F1,[(N,T,M,I)|F2],[(N1,T1,M,I)|F3]) :-
        member((N0,T0,M,I), F1),
        N1 is N + N0,
        T1 is T + T0,
        delete((N0,T0,M,I),F1,F10),
        update_agenda(F10,F2,F3).

/* init_agenda(+Program,-F0) sets up the initial agenda.        */
init_agenda([],[]).
init_agenda([(I,MI,_C)|Pg],[(NI,0,MI,I)|F0]) :-
        (  MI=\=0
           ->   NI is -1/MI
```

```
        ;     NI is -2        /* give priority to unit clauses*/
      ),
      init_agenda(Pg,F0).
```

5 Two examples

In this section, we show how to use program 4.1 for the computations of finite approximations through an example program and depth abstractions and stump abstractions.

Definition 5.1 (depth k abstraction) Let t be a term. The depth k abstraction of t, denoted by $d_k(t)$, is obtained by replacing each depth k sub-term of t with a newly created variable. Each such variable is denoted by an '_'. A term thus obtained is called a depth k abstract term.

Any depth k abstract term in $d_k(B_P)$, $d_k(U_P)$ or $d_k(M_P)$ does not have any variable at any level less than k. Such a term is called a canonical depth k abstract term.

Definition 5.2 (n-stump abstraction) Let t be a term and t' be a sub-term of t with f being its primary functor. t' has repetition depth (RD) 0 if the primary functor of any super-term of t' is different from f. t' has RD n if (a) t' has a super-term t'' with f as its primary functor and the RD of t'' is $n-1$ *and (b)* no super-term of t' with f as its primary functor has RD more than $n-1$.

The n-stump of a term results from replacing each argument of each of its sub-terms with RD n with a newly created variable. The function that maps a term to its n-stump is called an n-stump abstraction mapping, denoted as s_n.

We have implemented one abstraction-dependent predicate *psi* for any depth abstraction and another for any stump abstraction. Consider the following small program.

```
1    q(g(X,Y),g(Y,X)).
2    r(f(g(a,a))).
3    r(f(X)) :- r(X).
4    r(g(X,X)) :- r(X).
5    p(X):- q(X,Y),r(Y).
```

Figure 1 shows the difference between the performance of the heuristic algorithm 3.4 and that of the non-heuristic algorithm 3.2 for $lfp(\Phi_{P,d_3})$. It lists the clause number and the new elements generated for each application of $\psi_{C_i,\alpha}$ in the two algorithms. There are some empty lines for the heuristic algorithm because it avoids some non-productive applications. The heuristic algorithm invokes *three* non-productive calls to *psi* while the non-heuristic algorithm invokes *eight* such calls.

Figure 2 shows the difference between the performance of the heuristic algorithm 3.4 and that of the non-heuristic algorithm 3.2 for $lfp(\Phi_{P,s_1})$. The format of this figure is the same as figure 1. The heuristic algorithm invokes *two* non-productive calls to *psi* while the non-heuristic algorithm invokes *nine* such calls.

In both figure 1 and figure 2, q(g(X,Y),g(Y,X)) has been chosen to represent the set of abstract atoms that are abstractions of the ground instances of $q(g(X,Y),g(Y,X))$. For the depth abstraction d_3, q(g(X,Y), g(Y,X)) represents the following nine abstract atoms.

$$\left\{\begin{array}{c} q(g(a,a),g(a,a)),\ q(g(a,f(\_)),g(f(\_),a)),\ q(g(a,g(\_,\_)),g(g(\_,\_),a)), \\ q(g(f(\_),a),g(a,f(\_))),\ q(g(f(\_),f(\_)),g(f(\_),f(\_))), \\ q(g(f(\_),g(\_,\_)),g(g(\_,\_),f(\_))),\ q(g(g(\_,\_),a),g(a,g(\_,\_))), \\ q(g(g(\_,\_),f(\_)),g(f(\_),g(\_,\_))),\ q(g(g(\_,\_),g(\_,\_)),g(g(\_,\_),g(\_,\_))) \end{array}\right\}$$

For the stump abstraction s_1, (g(X,Y), g(Y,X)) represents the following 25 abstract atoms.

$$\left\{\begin{array}{c} q(g(a,f(a)),g(f(a),a)),\ q(g(f(f(\_)),f(g(\_,\_))),g(f(g(\_,\_)),f(f(\_)))), \\ q(g(a,a),g(a,a)),\ q(g(f(g(\_,\_)),f(g(\_,\_))),g(f(g(\_,\_)),f(g(\_,\_)))), \\ q(g(a,f(f(\_))),g(f(f(\_)),a)),\ q(g(f(g(\_,\_)),f(a)),g(f(a),f(g(\_,\_)))), \\ q(g(a,f(g(\_,\_))),g(f(g(\_,\_)),a)),\ q(g(f(f(\_)),f(a)),g(f(a),f(f(\_)))), \\ q(g(f(a),a),g(a,f(a))),\ q(g(g(\_,\_),f(g(\_,\_))),g(f(g(\_,\_)),g(\_,\_))), \\ q(g(f(a),f(a)),g(f(a),f(a))),\ q(g(g(\_,\_),g(\_,\_)),g(g(\_,\_),g(\_,\_))), \\ q(g(f(a),f(f(\_))),g(f(f(\_)),f(a))),\ q(g(f(a),g(\_,\_)),g(g(\_,\_),f(a))), \\ q(g(f(f(\_)),a),g(a,f(f(\_)))),\ q(g(f(a),f(g(\_,\_))),g(f(g(\_,\_)),f(a))), \\ q(g(a,g(\_,\_)),g(g(\_,\_),a)),\ q(g(f(f(\_)),f(f(\_))),g(f(f(\_)),f(f(\_)))), \\ q(g(f(g(\_,\_)),a),g(a,f(g(\_,\_)))),\ q(g(f(f(\_)),g(\_,\_)),g(g(\_,\_),f(f(\_)))), \\ q(g(f(g(\_,\_)),f(f(\_))),g(f(f(\_)),f(g(\_,\_)))), \\ q(g(f(g(\_,\_)),g(\_,\_)),g(g(\_,\_),f(g(\_,\_)))),\ q(g(g(\_,\_),a),g(a,g(\_,\_))), \\ q(g(g(\_,\_),f(a)),g(f(a),g(\_,\_))),\ q(g(g(\_,\_),f(f(\_))),g(f(f(\_)),g(\_,\_))), \end{array}\right\}$$

The heuristics used in algorithm 3.4 avoid some of the non-productive calls to *psi*. The number of such calls avoided depends on the program analysed and and the abstraction function. The time difference between the heuristic algorithm and the non-heuristic algorithm will be considerable for a larger program or a bigger $\alpha(B_P)$ because *psi* searches through the whole partial result m_i times whenever it is applied with clause C_i.

There exist some non-productive calls to *psi* in the heuristic algorithm because the heuristics used in the algorithm are conservative. More sophisticated heuristics could be used to further reduce non-productive calls to *psi*. For example, for the example program, the applications of ψ_{C_5} could be delayed until no new elements can be generated by $\psi_{C_1}, \ldots, \psi_{C_4}$. However, the task of gathering the information needed to use such heuristics would be much more complicated. So, it is uncertain if the use of such heuristics results in better performance. Furthermore, not all non-productive calls to *psi* can be avoided. There is always at least one non-productive call to *psi* before the least fixpoint is reached.

6 Conclusions

We have presented an abstract interpretation framework for a class of finite approximations of definite programs. Each finite approximation is characterised by an abstraction function and the finite approximation is given as the least fixpoint of a function over the abstract domain induced by the abstraction function. The development of a heuristic algorithm for the computation of

heuristic		non-heuristic	
clause	elements	clause	elements
1	q(g(X,Y),g(Y,X))	1	q(g(X,Y),g(Y,X))
2	r(f(g(_,_)))	2	r(f(g(_,_)))
3	r(f(f(_)))	3	r(f(f(_)))
4	r(g(f(_),f(_)))	4	r(g(f(_),f(_)))
5	p(g(f(_),f(_)))	5	p(g(f(_),f(_)))
3		1	
4	r(g(g(_,_),g(_,_)))	2	
3		3	
4		4	r(g(g(_,_),g(_,_)))
5	p(g(g(_,_),g(_,_)))	5	p(g(g(_,_),g(_,_)))
		1	
		2	
		3	
		4	
		5	

Figure 1: *The comparison of the performance of the heuristic algorithm 3.4 with that of the non-heuristic algorithm 3.2 for* $lfp(\Phi_{P,d_3})$

such finite approximations has been given in detail and the implementation of the algorithm in Prolog has been outlined.

The work presented is concerned with the computation of finite approximations by means of a bottom-up abstract interpretation framework. The problem of finite approximations has also been studied in other ways. For example, the problem of type inference is in essence a problem of finite approximations. There have been many type inference methods proposed for logic programs [7, 12, 1]. However, there has been no general framework in which to put them. Heintze and Jaffar [3] put some type inference methods in their Cartesian closure framework, whilst others [6, 2] put some type inference methods in various abstract interpretation frameworks. Our abstract interpretation framework has been generalised from depth abstractions and stump abstractions and both abstractions have been used in type inference systems [10, 12]. It is our speculation that the framework can also be used to explain some other type inference methods.

Peyton-Jones and Clack's [9] approach to the efficient calculation of fixpoints comprises an efficient representation and detection of fixpoints. Our approach to the problem is to use heuristics derived from the program to avoid non-productive computations. The two approaches can be combined to result in a more efficient solution.

O'Keefe [8] presents an algorithm for a more general class of fixpoint problems. When applied to find the least fixpoint of $\Phi_{P,\alpha}$, O'Keefe's algorithm corresponds to a variation of our algorithm 3.3 with a selection function that always selects the most recently activated clause from the agenda. This is accomplished by maintaining the agenda as a stack. The clause is selected by

heuristic		non-heuristic	
clause	*elements*	*clause*	*elements*
1	q(g(X,Y),g(Y,X))	1	q(g(X,Y),g(Y,X))
2	r(f(g(a,a)))	2	r(f(g(a,a)))
3	r(f(f(_)))	3	r(f(f(_)))
4	r(g(f(g(_,_)),f(g(_,_)))) r(g(f(f(_)),f(f(_))))	4	r(g(f(g(_,_)),f(g(_,_)))) r(g(f(f(_)),f(f(_))))
5	p(g(f(g(_,_)),f(g(_,_)))) p(g(f(f(_)),f(f(_))))	5	p(g(f(g(_,_)),f(g(_,_)))) p(g(f(f(_)),f(f(_))))
3	r(f(g(f(_),f(_))))	1	
4	r(g(g(_,_),g(_,_)))	2	
3	r(f(g(g(_,_),g(_,_))))	3	r(f(g(f(_),f(_))))
4		4	r(g(g(_,_),g(_,_)))
5	p(g(g(_,_),g(_,_)))	5	p(g(g(_,_),g(_,_)))
3		1	
		2	
		3	r(f(g(g(_,_),g(_,_))))
		4	
		5	
		1	
		2	
		3	

Figure 2: *The comparison of the performance of the heuristic algorithm 3.4 with that of the non-heuristic algorithm 3.2 for* $lfp(\Phi_{P,s_1})$

popping it off the top of the stack. The newly activated clauses are pushed onto the stack. For each clause C in the agenda, our algorithm 3.4 evaluates the probability that the clause may produce new elements and selects that clause with the largest probability.

Acknowledgements

The authors are grateful to the anonymous referees for their many constructive criticisms and suggestions.

References

[1] Azzoune H. Type inference in Prolog. In Lusk E, Overbeek R (ed) *Proceedings of the Ninth International Conference on Automated Deduction.* Springer-Verlag, 1988, pp 258-277 (Lecture Notes in Computer Science no. 310)

[2] Bruynooghe M, Janssens G, Callebaut A, Demoen B. Abstract interpretation: towards the global optimisation of Prolog programs. In *Proceedings of the 1987 Symposium on Logic Programming.* The IEEE Society Press, 1987, pp 192-204

[3] Heintze N, Jaffar J. A finite presentation theorem for approximating logic programs. In *Conference Record of the Seventeenth Annual ACM Symposium on Principles of Programming Languages.* The ACM Press, 1990, pp 197-209

[4] Hutching AMJ, Bowen DL, Byrd L, et al. Edinburgh Prolog (The New Implementation) User's Manual. AI Applications Institute, University of Edinburgh, 1987

[5] Lu L, Greenfield P. Abstract fixpoint semantics and abstract procedural semantics of definite logic programs. In *Proceedings of IEEE Computer Society 1992 International Conference on Computer Languages.* The IEEE Computer Society Press, 1992, pp 147-154

[6] Marriott K, Søndergaard H. Bottom-up abstract interpretation of logic programs. In Kowalski RA, Bowen KA (ed) *Proceedings of the Fifth International Conference and Symposium on Logic Programming.* The MIT Press, 1988, pp 733-748

[7] Mishra P. Towards a theory of types in Prolog. In *Proceedings of the IEEE international Symposium on Logic Programming.* The IEEE Computer Society Press, 1984, pp 289-298

[8] O'Keefe RA. Finite fixed-point problems. In Lassez JL (ed) *Proceedings of the Fourth International Conference on Logic Programming*, Volume 2. The MIT Press, 1987, pp 729-743

[9] Peyton-Jones S, Clack C. Finding fixpoints in abstract interpretation. In Abramsky S, Hankin C (ed) *Abstract interpretation of declarative languages.* Ellis Horwood Limited, 1987, pp 246-265

[10] Sato T, Tamaki H. Enumeration of success patterns in logic programs. *Theoretical Computer Science*, 34:227-240, 1984

[11] Van Emden MH, Kowalski RA. The semantics of predicate logic as a programming language. *Artificial Intelligence*, 23:733-742, 1976

[12] Xu J, Warren DS. A type inference system for Prolog. In Kowalski RA, Bowen KA (ed) *Proceedings of the Fifth International Conference and Symposium on Logic Programming*, The MIT Press, 1988, pp 604-619

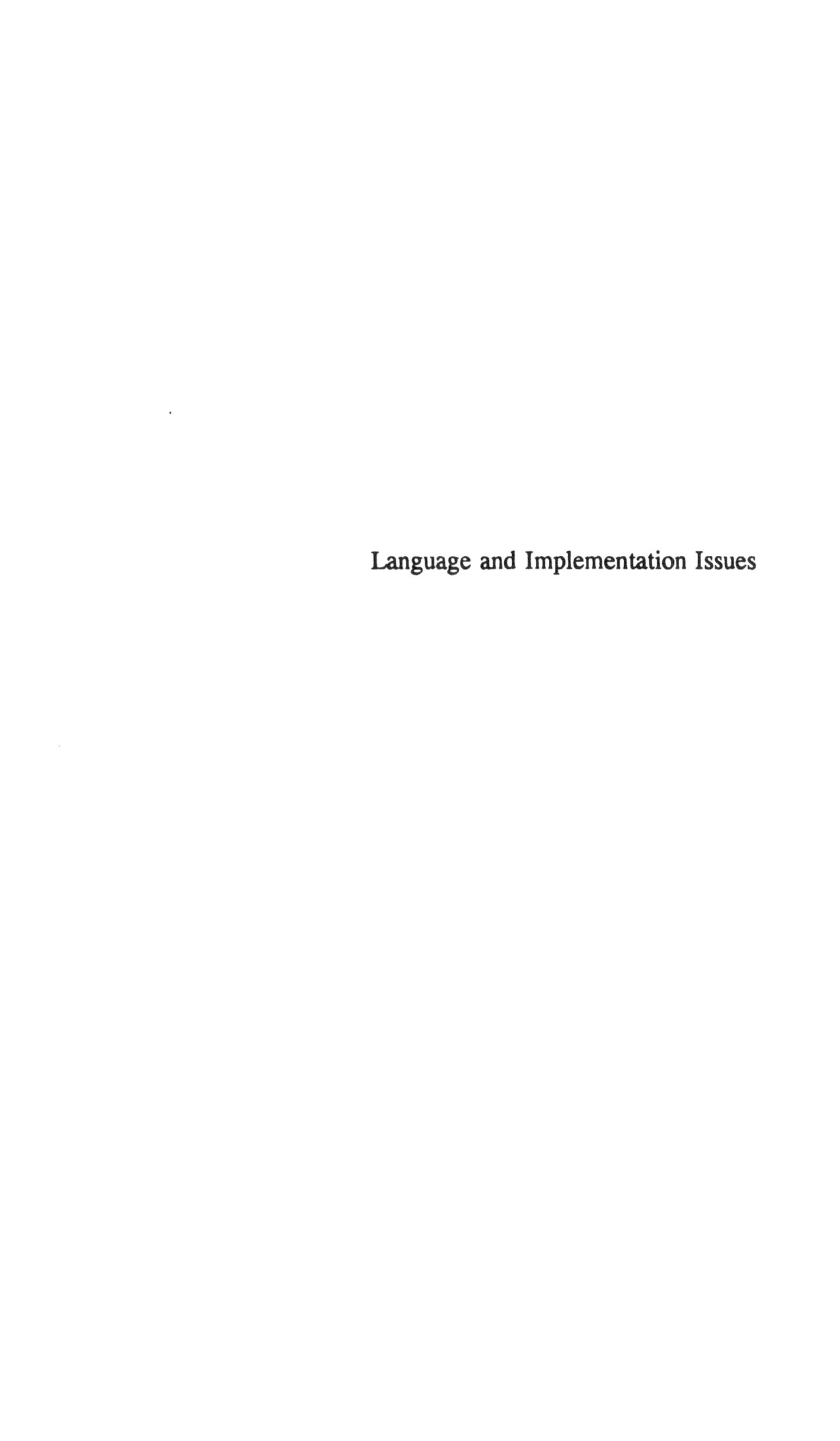

Language and Implementation Issues

Soft Sorting in Logic Programming

Jian Chen
Software Verification Research Centre
Department of Computer Science, The University of Queensland
Brisbane, Australia 4072

John Staples
Software Verification Research Centre
Department of Computer Science, The University of Queensland
Brisbane, Australia 4072

Abstract

Integrating sorts (types) into logic programming languages increases their expressiveness and evaluation efficiency. The sort structures usually considered are strict, in the sense that whenever an expression has a subexpression which is not properly sorted, the expression is classified as ill-sorted, and in effect is regarded as meaningless. Typically a logic programming language with strict sorting is incomplete, in the sense that some intuitively meaningful programs and queries are ill-sorted and hence are not part of the language.

This paper outlines the development of a concept of non-strict sorting for first-order languages, which we call soft sorting because it is in the same direction as Cartwright and Fagan's soft typing [1]. We develop on that basis a declarative semantics for sorted logic programs and queries with negation. The declarative semantics modifies Clark's completion semantics. Static sort checking is insufficient in this framework. We demonstrate that ordinary unsorted query evaluation is not always adequate for our sorted logic programs and queries. Two other procedural semantics, unsorted evaluation with sort predicates and sorted evaluation with sort constraints, are described briefly. This paper is restricted to polymorphic many-sorting. It is intended to discuss soft order-sorting separately.

1 Introduction

Integrating sorts (types) into logic programming languages increases the expressiveness and evaluation efficiency of logic programs.

The declarative semantics of traditional sorted logic programs is based on strictly sorted first-order languages, whose syntax is restricted by well-sortedness rules. Only well-sorted expressions are included in such a language, and all subexpressions of a well-sorted expression must be well-sorted. This restricts the expressiveness of the language. As the following example illustrates, some meaningful expressions are ill-sorted and hence are not part of the language.

Example 1.1 Consider the following definition of a predicate `r` in a logic program (here and below, explicit syntax from formal systems is shown in typewriter font):

```
r(X) <- p(X)
r(X) <- q(X)
```

According to the Clark semantics, the logical meaning of this definition is:

`(forall x)(r(x) <-> p(x) or q(x))`.

Suppose now that the arguments of `r`, `p`, `q` are required to be of sorts `u`, `c`, `d`, respectively, where `u` is a sort variable, and `c` and `d` are different ground sorts such that no value has both sorts. In strict sorting, the above completion is ill-sorted, and hence the program is ill-sorted. However it has a clear intuitive meaning.

One could argue that a new sort `e`, the union of sort `c` and `d`, could be introduced and both `p` and `q` associated with `e`. Then the above completion becomes well-sorted with the variable sorting `e` for `x`. But expressive power is lost in doing so, if we intended to associate sort `c` to `p` and `d` to `q`. □

This paper develops semantics for sorted logic programs, based on a non-strict concept of many-sorted languages [2]. We call it soft sorting because it has similarities with the soft typing of Cartwright and Fagan [1]. Soft sorting overcomes limitations of strict sorting such as that illustrated above.

Throughout the paper we consider only sort languages with a finite number of sort constructors.

In a softly sorted language, although each language symbol is associated with sorts, there is no *a priori* sort restriction in the definition of the language's expressions. Those expressions whose arguments do not satisfy the specified sort restrictions have interpretations. In particular, we interpret such a term which does not satisfy the language's sort restrictions as having an abnormal value *bad*, and an atomic predicate which does not satisfy the language's sort restrictions is interpreted as having a truth value *false*.

When a formal notation for the abnormal value *bad* is desired, it is denoted `bad`, and sort whose domain contains only *bad*, denoted `wrong`, is introduced.

In our approach a term or atom (atomic formula) is either well-sorted (its outermost sort restrictions are satisfied) or ill-sorted (the outermost sort restrictions can never be satisfied) or well-sortable (the outermost sort restrictions can be satisfied under certain conditions). Formulas can be either well-sorted, F-sorted, T-sorted, or well-sortable. In both cases the sortedness categories provide a simple abstract interpretation of the syntax. In the case of terms, the two abstract values "well-sorted" and "ill-sorted" are convenient. In the case of formulas however it turns out to be more useful to recognise the three values "well-sorted", "F-sorted" and "T-sorted". Intuitively, F-sortedness means that the formula is known statically to have the truth value *false* in all interpretations. Similarly T-sorted means that the formula is *true* in all interpretations. For atoms, ill-sorted implies F-sorted.

It is statically decidable whether a term is well-sorted, ill-sorted, or well-sortable, and whether a formula is well-sorted, T-sorted, F-sorted, or well-sortable. Moreover, in the case of a well-sortable term (formula), there exists a nonempty complete finite representation of sort substitutions under which the term (formula) is well-sorted [2].

Example 1.2 Following Example 1.1, and using subscripts to indicate the associated sorts of symbols,

1. $\mathtt{p_c(X_c)}$ is well-sorted;

2. $\mathtt{p_c(X_d)}$ is F-sorted, while **not** $\mathtt{p_c(X_d)}$ is T-sorted;

3. $\mathtt{p_c(X_u)}$ is well-sortable. It becomes well-sorted under the sort substitution $\{\mathtt{u/c}\}$ but F-sorted under $\{\mathtt{u/d}\}$;

4. $\mathtt{r_u(X_u)}$ `<->` $\mathtt{p_c(X_u)}$ `or` $\mathtt{q_d(X_u)}$ is well-sortable. It becomes well-sorted under $\{\mathtt{u/c}\}$, and under $\{\mathtt{u/d}\}$. □

Several sorted logic programming languages have been developed over the last ten years. Mycroft and O'Keefe first gave a polymorphic type system for Prolog in [10]. Their initial intention was to treat types merely as "syntactic sugar" and their language is not strictly a sorted one. Lakshman and Reddy reconstructed Mycroft and O'Keefe's language based on (strict) many-sorting [7]. In both works, well-sortedness can be statically checked. The ordinary unsorted unification and resolution algorithms are correct for evaluation of well-sorted programs and queries. Dietrich and Hagl [4] introduced subtypes (order-sorting) into Mycroft and O'Keefe's type system, and also treated types as syntactic sugar with no effect on the semantics of programs and queries. Consequently they needed additional (mode) restrictions on well-sortedness. Hanus [5] discussed many-sorted logic programming languages based on sorted Horn clauses. He gave a procedural semantics but not a declarative semantics. Recently, Hill and Topor introduced a declarative semantics for parametric order-sorted logic programs with negation [6]. They discussed three procedural semantics. Hill and Topor's sorting is strict.

Our declarative semantics of softly sorted logic programs and queries is a modification of Clark's completion semantics. It extends Lakshman and Reddy's work [7] and Hill and Topor's, in the case of parametric many-sorting [6]. In general, static sort checking is insufficient for soft sorting. We demonstrate that ordinary unsorted query evaluation is not always adequate for our sorted logic programs and queries. Two other procedural semantics, unsorted evaluation with sort predicates and sorted evaluation with sort constraints, will be introduced.

In order to introduce in the simplest way the application of soft sorting to logic programs, this paper is restricted to polymorphic many-sorting. It is intended to discuss soft order-sorting separately.

In section 2 we outline the syntax and semantics of softly many-sorted first-order languages. A syntax and declarative semantics for logic programs and queries with soft sorting are introduced in section 3, and their procedural semantics is described briefly. We conclude and give further research directions in section 4.

2 Softly Many-Sorted First-Order Languages

A detailed discussion of softly many-sorted first-order languages and their properties will be found in [2]. Here we give a summary.

2.1 Sort Languages

A sort language is an ordinary first-order language, intended to describe a sort structure. Thus its intended interpretations are in terms of subsets of a universe of discourse U. In our work we assume a distinguished object *bad* occurs in U, which is suitable as a value for terms which may be regarded as ill-sorted. If no suitable object *bad* exists initially in U, U should be augmented.

A *sort alphabet*, denoted $\mathcal{SA}$, is an nonempty finite set of *sort constructors*. Each sort constructor has an associated non-negative integer called its *arity*. Sort constructors of arity 0 are called *base sorts*. In soft sorting the base sort **wrong** is optional.

We assume that there is a denumerable set $\mathcal{SV}$ of *sort variables*.

We use **c**, **d**, ..., as meta variables which range over base sorts, and **k**, **l**, ..., as meta variables which range over other sort constructors. Individual sort variables are denoted **u**, **v**, ..., and meta variables which range over sort variables are denoted **u**, **v**, ... We use **s**, **s**′, ..., for meta variables which range over sorts, as defined below.

The *sort language* $\mathcal{SL}$ based on a given sort alphabet $\mathcal{SA}$ is the set of *sorts*, recursively defined as follows.

1. Each base sort $\mathbf{c} \in \mathcal{SA}$ is a sort.

2. Each sort variable $\mathbf{u} \in \mathcal{SV}$ is a sort.

3. If $\mathbf{k} \in \mathcal{SA}$ has arity $n \geq 1$, and if $\mathbf{s}_1, \ldots, \mathbf{s}_n$ are sorts in $\mathcal{SL}$, then $\mathbf{k}(\mathbf{s}_1, \ldots, \mathbf{s}_n)$ is a sort in $\mathcal{SL}$.

A sort in which no sort variable occurs is called a *ground sort*.

A *sort substitution* is a finite set $\{\mathbf{u}_1/\mathbf{s}_1, \ldots, \mathbf{u}_n/\mathbf{s}_n\}$ of *bindings* $\mathbf{u}_i/\mathbf{s}_i$, for distinct variables $\mathbf{u}_i$, where $\mathbf{s}_i$ is a sort distinct from $\mathbf{u}_i$, $i = 1, \ldots, n$. A *ground sort substitution* is a sort substitution, all of whose values $\mathbf{s}_i$ are ground sorts. Sort substitutions are denoted Θ, Φ, Ψ, ... *Sort variants*, the *solvability* of a set of sorts, *sort unifiers*, *sort solutions*, and the *solvability* of a set of sort substitutions are also defined as usual as for a first-order language [9].

A sort language $\mathcal{SL}$ has the following properties, whose justifications are given in [2].

Proposition 2.1 *It is decidable whether a set of sorts is solvable. If solvable, there exists a unique most general solution, and it is computable.*

Proposition 2.2 *It is decidable whether a set of sort substitutions is solvable. If solvable, there exists a unique most general solution, and it is computable.*

An interpretation *si* of a sort language $\mathcal{SL}$, based on a universe of discourse U, is a function which maps all ground sorts to disjoint, nonempty subsets of U, such that $si(\mathbf{wrong}) = \{bad\}$, where *bad* is the abnormal value in U. Writing $\mathcal{S}$ for the range of *si*, we call the members of $\mathcal{S}$ *sort domains*, or briefly *domains*.

From si, a function from constructors with arity n to $\mathcal{S}^n \to \mathcal{S}$ can be defined for each $n \geq 0$. We loosely call it si also: for a constructor $\mathbf{k}$ with arity n, and a set of domains $D_1, \ldots, D_n$ in $\mathcal{S}$, $si(\mathbf{k})(D_1, \ldots, D_n) = si(\mathbf{k}(D_1, \ldots, D_n))$.

A *sort variable valuation* sv, is a function $\mathcal{SV} \to \mathcal{S}$. We write $\mathcal{SVV}$ for the set of sort variable valuations.

Given a sort interpretation si, an *extended sort interpretation* si^* is the function

$$\mathcal{SL} \to (\mathcal{SVV} \to \mathcal{S})$$

recursively defined as follows.

1. For each base sort $\mathbf{c}$, $si^*(\mathbf{c})(sv) = si(\mathbf{c})$.
2. For each sort variable $\mathbf{u}$, $si^*(\mathbf{u})(sv) = sv(\mathbf{u})$.
3. For each sort $\mathbf{k}(\mathbf{s}_1, \ldots, \mathbf{s}_n)$,

$$si^*(\mathbf{k}(\mathbf{s}_1, \ldots, \mathbf{s}_n))(sv) = si(\mathbf{k})(si^*(\mathbf{s}_1)(sv), \ldots, si^*(\mathbf{s}_n)(sv)).$$

The following is proved in [2].

Proposition 2.3 *A set of sorts S is solvable if and only if for each sort interpretation si there exists a sort variable valuation sv, under which each sort in S is assigned the same domain.*

2.2 Syntax of Softly Many-Sorted Languages

Let $\mathcal{A}^0$ be an unsorted alphabet, let $\mathcal{V}^0$ be a set of unsorted variables, and let $\mathcal{SL}$ be a sort language.

A sort declaration $\mathcal{R}$ for $\mathcal{A}^0$ is defined as follows.

1. $\mathcal{R}$ assigns to each constant symbol a tuple $< \mathbf{s} >$, where $\mathbf{s}$ is a ground sort.
2. $\mathcal{R}$ assigns to each $\mathbf{f}$ with arity n, $n \geq 1$, a tuple $< \mathbf{s}_1, \ldots, \mathbf{s}_n, \mathbf{s} >$, where $\mathbf{s}_1, \ldots, \mathbf{s}_n, \mathbf{s}$ are sorts and where each variable $\mathbf{u}$ that occurs in $\mathbf{s}_i$ also occurs in $\mathbf{s}$, $i \in \{1, \ldots, n\}$.
3. $\mathcal{R}$ assigns to each $\mathbf{p}$ with arity $n \geq 1$, a tuple $< \mathbf{s}_1, \ldots, \mathbf{s}_n >$, where $\mathbf{s}_1, \ldots, \mathbf{s}_n$ are sorts.

All instances of the declared sorts of a symbol are called *associated sorts* of the symbol. We call an unsorted symbol with one of its associated sorts a *sorted symbol.*

Given an unsorted alphabet $\mathcal{A}^0$, a sort language $\mathcal{SL}$ and a sort declaration $\mathcal{R}$, a *sorted alphabet* $\mathcal{A}$ is the set of all sorted symbols derived from $\mathcal{A}^0$ and $\mathcal{SL}$ with respect to $\mathcal{R}$. It is optional to have a sorted constant **bad**, called the *abnormal constant*, declared with sort **wrong**.

It is convenient to write s for the sort tuple $< \mathbf{s} >$ associated with a sorted constant symbol. Similarly the sort tuple $< \mathbf{s}_1, \ldots, \mathbf{s}_n, \mathbf{s} >$ of a function symbol may be written $\mathbf{s}_1, \ldots, \mathbf{s}_n \to \mathbf{s}$, and $< \mathbf{s}_1, \ldots, \mathbf{s}_n >$ of a predicate symbol may be written $\mathbf{s}_1, \ldots, \mathbf{s}_n$. We often write an associated sort of a sorted symbol as a subscript of the symbol. For example a constant **bad** with associated sort **wrong** may be written $\mathbf{bad}_{\mathbf{wrong}}$.

Variables of $\mathcal{V}^0$ will be assigned sorts. A variable has a unique most general sort assigned to it which we call its declared sort. Likewise, instances of the declared sort of a variable will be called associated sorts of the variable. A *sorted variable* is a variable symbol of $\mathcal{V}^0$ together with an associated sort. The set of all sorted variables is denoted $\mathcal{V}$. When we refer to *distinct* sorted variables we mean that the variable symbols are different.

Terms, *atoms*, *literals*, and *formulas* are defined as usual for an unsorted first-order language [9]. We may call them *sorted* to emphasise that they are based on sorted symbols and variables. The *logical connectives* are written `not`, `or`, `&`, `->`, and `<->`. We use `<-` sometimes for convenience. The *logical quantifiers* are written `forall` and `exists`.

We write $\mathbf{a}$, $\mathbf{b}$, ... for meta variables which range over sorted constants, $\mathbf{t}, \mathbf{t}_1, \mathbf{t}_2, \ldots$ for variables which range over terms, $\mathbf{A}$, $\mathbf{B}$, ... for variables which range over atoms, and $\mathbf{F}$, $\mathbf{F}_1, \ldots$ for variables which range over formulas.

Given a sort substitution Θ, its application to a term or a formula is defined as follows.

1. For a sorted constant, $\mathbf{a_s}\Theta$ is $\mathbf{a_s}$. Note that since $\mathbf{a}$ is a constant, $\mathbf{s}$ is a ground sort and so $\mathbf{s}\Theta = \mathbf{s}$.
2. For a sorted variable, $\mathbf{x_s}\Theta$ is $\mathbf{x}_{\mathbf{s}\Theta}$.
3. For a term, $\mathbf{f}_{\mathbf{s}_1,\ldots,\mathbf{s}_n\to\mathbf{s}}(\mathbf{t}_1,\ldots,\mathbf{t}_n)\Theta$ is $\mathbf{f}_{\mathbf{s}_1\Theta,\ldots,\mathbf{s}_n\Theta\to\mathbf{s}\Theta}(\mathbf{t}_1\Theta,\ldots,\mathbf{t}_n\Theta)$.
4. For an atom, $\mathbf{p}_{\mathbf{s}_1,\ldots,\mathbf{s}_n}(\mathbf{t}_1,\ldots,\mathbf{t}_n)\Theta$ is $\mathbf{p}_{\mathbf{s}_1\Theta,\ldots,\mathbf{s}_n\Theta}(\mathbf{t}_1\Theta,\ldots,\mathbf{t}_n\Theta)$.
5. For other formulas,
   (a) (`not` $\mathbf{A}$)Θ is (`not` $\mathbf{A}\Theta$),
   (b) ($\mathbf{F}_1$ `&` $\mathbf{F}_2$)Θ is ($\mathbf{F}_1\Theta$ `&` $\mathbf{F}_2\Theta$),
   (c) ($\mathbf{F}_1$ `or` $\mathbf{F}_2$)Θ is ($\mathbf{F}_1\Theta$ `or` $\mathbf{F}_2\Theta$),
   (d) ((`forall` $\mathbf{x_s}$) $\mathbf{F}$)Θ is ((`forall` $\mathbf{x}_{\mathbf{s}\Theta}$) $\mathbf{F}\Theta$),
   (e) ((`exists` $\mathbf{x_s}$) $\mathbf{F}$)Θ is ((`exists` $\mathbf{x}_{\mathbf{s}\Theta}$) $\mathbf{F}\Theta$).

2.3 Interpretations of Softly Many-Sorted Languages

Let $\mathcal{L}$ be a sorted language with underlying sort language $\mathcal{SL}$. Given a universe of discourse U and a sort interpretation si of $\mathcal{SL}$ based on U, we make the following definitions.

An interpretation I of $\mathcal{L}$ is a function from the alphabet of $\mathcal{L}$ whose values are functions with domain $\mathcal{SVV}$, defined as follows.

1. For each sorted constant $\mathbf{a_s}$, $I(\mathbf{a_s})(sv)$ is in $si^*(\mathbf{s})(sv)$.
2. For each sorted function symbol $\mathbf{f}_{\mathbf{s}_1,\ldots,\mathbf{s}_n\to\mathbf{s}}$, $I(\mathbf{f}_{\mathbf{s}_1,\ldots,\mathbf{s}_n\to\mathbf{s}})(sv)$ is a mapping $U^n \to U$ such that for every n-tuple $< t_1,\ldots,t_n >$ of values in $si^*(\mathbf{s}_1)(sv) \times \cdots \times si^*(\mathbf{s}_n)(sv)$,

   $$I(\mathbf{f}_{\mathbf{s}_1,\ldots,\mathbf{s}_n\to\mathbf{s}})(sv)(t_1,\ldots,t_n) \in si^*(\mathbf{s})(sv).$$

   Also, at other $< t_1,\ldots,t_n >$, $I(\mathbf{f}_{\mathbf{s}_1,\ldots,\mathbf{s}_n\to\mathbf{s}})(sv)(t_1,\ldots,t_n) = bad$.

3. For each sorted predicate symbol $\mathbf{p}_{\mathbf{s}_1,\ldots,\mathbf{s}_n}$, $I(\mathbf{p}_{\mathbf{s}_1,\ldots,\mathbf{s}_n})(sv)$ is a mapping $U^n \rightarrow \{true, false\}$ such that for every n-tuple $< t_1, \ldots, t_n >$ of values in $si^*(\mathbf{s}_1)(sv) \times \cdots \times si^*(\mathbf{s}_n)(sv)$ and in the domain of $I(\mathbf{p}_{\mathbf{s}_1,\ldots,\mathbf{s}_n})(sv)$,

$$I(\mathbf{p}_{\mathbf{s}_1,\ldots,\mathbf{s}_n})(sv)(t_1, \ldots, t_n) = true.$$

At other $< t_1, \ldots, t_n >$,

$$I(\mathbf{p}_{\mathbf{s}_1,\ldots,\mathbf{s}_n})(sv)(t_1, \ldots, t_n) = false.$$

A *(sorted) variable valuation* v is a function $\mathcal{V} \rightarrow (\mathcal{SVV} \rightarrow U)$ such that for every sorted variable $\mathbf{x}_\mathbf{s}$, $v(\mathbf{x}_\mathbf{s})(sv)$ is a value in $si^*(\mathbf{s})(sv)$. We write $\mathcal{VV}$ for the set of variable valuations.

An extended interpretation I^*, based on I, is a function whose domain is terms and formulas. Its values on terms are functions $\mathcal{SVV} \rightarrow (\mathcal{VV} \rightarrow U)$ and its values on formulas are functions $\mathcal{SVV} \rightarrow (\mathcal{VV} \rightarrow \{true, false\})$. More specifically, I^* is defined as follows.

1. For each sorted constant $\mathbf{a}_\mathbf{s}$, $I^*(\mathbf{a}_\mathbf{s})(sv)(v)$ is $I(\mathbf{a}_\mathbf{s})(sv)$.
2. For each sorted variable $\mathbf{x}_\mathbf{s}$, $I^*(\mathbf{x}_\mathbf{s})(sv)(v)$ is $v(\mathbf{x}_\mathbf{s})(sv)$.
3. For each sorted term, $I^*(\mathbf{f}_{\mathbf{s}_1,\ldots,\mathbf{s}_n \rightarrow \mathbf{s}}(\mathbf{t}_1, \ldots, \mathbf{t}_n))(sv)(v)$ is

$$I(\mathbf{f}_{\mathbf{s}_1,\ldots,\mathbf{s}_n \rightarrow \mathbf{s}})(sv)(I^*(\mathbf{t}_1)(sv)(v), \ldots, I^*(\mathbf{t}_n)(sv)(v)).$$

4. For each sorted atom $\mathbf{p}_{\mathbf{s}_1,\ldots,\mathbf{s}_n}(\mathbf{t}_1, \ldots, \mathbf{t}_n)$, if

$$< I^*(\mathbf{t}_1)(sv)(v), \ldots, I^*(\mathbf{t}_n)(sv)(v) >$$

is in $I(\mathbf{p}_{\mathbf{s}_1,\ldots,\mathbf{s}_n})(sv)$, then $I^*(\mathbf{p}_{\mathbf{s}_1,\ldots,\mathbf{s}_n}(\mathbf{t}_1, \ldots, \mathbf{t}_n))(sv)(v) = true$, otherwise *false*.

5. The interpretations for (**not F**), ($\mathbf{F}_1$ **&** $\mathbf{F}_2$), ($\mathbf{F}_1$ **or** $\mathbf{F}_2$), ($\mathbf{F}_1$ **->** $\mathbf{F}_2$), ($\mathbf{F}_1$ **<->** $\mathbf{F}_2$), ((**forall** $\mathbf{x}_\mathbf{s}$) **F**), and ((**exists** $\mathbf{x}_\mathbf{s}$) **F**) are defined as usual for classical first-order logic.

2.4 Well-Sortedness

Well-sortedness and ill-sortedness of terms and atoms are defined as follows.

1. A sorted constant $\mathbf{a}_\mathbf{s}$ or variable $\mathbf{x}_\mathbf{s}$ is well-sorted and is of sort $\mathbf{s}$.

2. If $\mathbf{t}_i$ is of sort $\mathbf{s}_i$, $i \in \{1, \ldots, n\}$, then $\mathbf{f}_{\mathbf{s}_1,\ldots,\mathbf{s}_n \rightarrow \mathbf{s}}(\mathbf{t}_1, \ldots, \mathbf{t}_n)$, is well-sorted and is of sort $\mathbf{s}$. If there does not exist any sort substitution Θ such that $\mathbf{t}_i\Theta$, is of sort $\mathbf{s}_i\Theta$, $i \in \{1, \ldots, n\}$, then $\mathbf{f}_{\mathbf{s}_1,\ldots,\mathbf{s}_n \rightarrow \mathbf{s}}(\mathbf{t}_1, \ldots, \mathbf{t}_n)$, is ill-sorted. If **wrong** is in $\mathcal{SL}$, an ill-sorted term is of sort **wrong**.

3. If $\mathbf{t}_i$ is of sort $\mathbf{s}_i$, $i \in \{1, \ldots, n\}$, then $\mathbf{p}_{\mathbf{s}_1,\ldots,\mathbf{s}_n}(\mathbf{t}_1, \ldots, \mathbf{t}_n)$ is well-sorted. If there does not exist any sort substitution Θ such that $\mathbf{t}_i\Theta$ is of sort $\mathbf{s}_i\Theta$, $i \in \{1, \ldots, n\}$, then $\mathbf{p}_{\mathbf{s}_1,\ldots,\mathbf{s}_n}(\mathbf{t}_1, \ldots, \mathbf{t}_n)$ is ill-sorted.

For formulas, well-sortedness, F-sortedness, and T-sortedness are defined as follows.

1. Formula `true` is T-sorted and formula `false` is F-sorted.

2. If **F** is an atom **A** and **A** is well-sorted (ill-sorted), then **F** is well-sorted (F-sorted).

3. If **F** is (`not` **F**′), then: if **F**′ is well-sorted, then **F** is well-sorted; if **F**′ is F-sorted, then **F** is T-sorted; and if **F**′ is T-sorted, then **F** is F-sorted.

4. If **F** is ($\mathbf{F}_1$ `or` $\mathbf{F}_2$), then: if one of $\mathbf{F}_1$ and $\mathbf{F}_2$ is well-sorted and the other F-sorted, or if both of them are well-sorted, then **F** is well-sorted; if either of $\mathbf{F}_1$ or $\mathbf{F}_2$ is T-sorted, then **F** is T-sorted; if $\mathbf{F}_1$ and $\mathbf{F}_2$ are both F-sorted, then **F** is F-sorted.

5. If **F** is ($\mathbf{F}_1$ `&` $\mathbf{F}_2$), then: if $\mathbf{F}_1$ and $\mathbf{F}_2$ are both well-sorted, or if one of them is well-sorted and the other T-sorted, then **F** is well-sorted; if either $\mathbf{F}_1$ or $\mathbf{F}_2$ is F-sorted, then **F** is F-sorted; if $\mathbf{F}_1$ and $\mathbf{F}_2$ are both T-sorted, then **F** is T-sorted.

6. If **F** is ($\mathbf{F}_1$ `->` $\mathbf{F}_2$), then **F** is well-sorted, F-sorted, or T-sorted according as the formula ((`not` $\mathbf{F}_1$) `or` $\mathbf{F}_2$) is well-sorted, F-sorted, or T-sorted.

7. If **F** is ((`forall` $\mathbf{x_s}$) **F**′) or **F** is ((`exists` $\mathbf{x_s}$) **F**′), then **F** is well-sorted, F-sorted, or T-sorted according as **F**′ is well-sorted, F-sorted, or T-sorted.

A term or atom which is neither well-sorted nor ill-sorted is called *well-sortable*. A formula which is not well-sorted, F-sorted, or T-sorted is also called well-sortable. This choice of name is justified in Proposition 2.7.

In this paper *expressions* refers generally to both terms and formulas. A sort substitution Θ agrees with an expression E if its domain is the set of sort variables occurring in E. If a well-sortable expression is well-sorted (ill-sorted with respect to a sorted term or atom; F-sorted, T-sorted with respect to a sorted formula) under a sort substitution Θ, then we call Θ a *well-sorter* (*ill-sorter* with respect to a sorted term or atom; *F-sorter, T-sorter* with respect to sorted formula) of the expression. A *finite complete representation of well-sorters (ill-sorters with respect to a sorted term or atom; F-sorters, T-sorters with respect to a sorted formula)* of a sorted expression E is a set $\Sigma = \{C_1, \ldots, C_n\}$ of sort constraints, such that each C_i is of the form

$$\mathbf{u}_1 = \mathbf{s}_1, \ldots, \mathbf{u}_m = \mathbf{s}_m, \mathbf{u}_{m+1} \neq \mathbf{s}_{m+1}, \ldots, \mathbf{u}_k \neq \mathbf{s}_k$$

and which satisfies the following condition: for all ground sort substitutions Θ agreeing with E, Θ is a well-sorter (ill-sorter with respect to a sorted term or atom; F-sorter, T-sorter with respect to a sorted formula) of E if and only if Θ satisfies some $C_i \in \Sigma$, $i \in \{1, \ldots, n\}$.

A *complete finite explicit representation of well-sorters (ill-sorters with respect to a sorted term or atom; F-sorters, T-sorters with respect to a sorted formula)* Σ' of a sorted expression is a finite set $\{\Theta_1, \ldots, \Theta_p\}$ of sort substitutions with the following property:

Θ is a ground well-sorter (ill-sorter, F-sorter, T-sorter) if and only if there exist

$$\{\mathbf{u}_1/\mathbf{s}_1, \ldots, \mathbf{u}_m/\mathbf{s}_m\} \in \Sigma'$$

and Ψ such that

$$\Theta = \{\mathbf{u}_1/\mathbf{s}_1\Psi, \ldots, \mathbf{u}_m/\mathbf{s}_m\Psi\}.$$

Some useful results, proved in [2], are as follows.

Proposition 2.4 *It is decidable whether a sorted term or atom is well-sorted, ill-sorted, or well-sortable. In the case of sorted formulas, it is decidable whether a sorted formula is well-sorted, F-sorted, T-sorted, or well-sortable.*

Proposition 2.5 *A sort substitution instance of a well-sorted (ill-sorted) term or atom is also well-sorted (ill-sorted). A sort substitution instance of a well-sorted (F-sorted, T-sorted) formula is also well-sorted (F-sorted, T-sorted).*

Proposition 2.6 *An ill-sorted atom is assigned the truth value false in every sorted interpretation. A F-sorted (T-sorted) formula is assigned the truth value false (true) in every sorted interpretation.*

Proposition 2.7 *(Complete Finite Representations of Soft Sorters)*

1. *For a well-sortable term or atom, a nonempty complete finite representation of well-sorters and a complete finite representation of ill-sorters can be computed.*

2. *For a well-sortable formula, a nonempty complete finite representation of well-sorters, and either a complete finite representation of F-sorters or a complete finite representation of T-sorters can be computed.*

3. *There exists an algorithm which will produce a finite explicit representation for a sort constraint if one exists. Otherwise it will halt with failure.*

3 Softly Many-Sorted Logic Programming

We first give a syntax for softly sorted logic programs and queries. The formal syntax is again presented in typewriter font. A declarative semantics is then given based on softly sorted languages. We also discuss sort checking and procedural semantics.

3.1 Syntax

We assume that there is a underlying sort language $\mathcal{SL}$, and a sorted language $\mathcal{L}$. As in [9], we use `<-` rather than `->`. Unless stated otherwise, all variables occurring in an expression are considered to have distinct sort variables as associated sorts.

A *sorted clause* is defined as

$$\mathbf{H} \;\texttt{<-}\; \mathbf{L}_1 \;\&\; \cdots \;\&\; \mathbf{L}_n \tag{1}$$

where $n \geq 0$, $\mathbf{H}$ is a sorted atom, and each $\mathbf{L}_i$, $i \in \{1, \ldots, n\}$, is a sorted literal. We call $\mathbf{H}$ the *head* and $\mathbf{L}_1 \,\&\cdots\&\, \mathbf{L}_n$ the *body* of the sorted clause. For the special case $n = 0$, the sorted clause

$$\mathbf{H} \;\texttt{<-} \tag{2}$$

is regarded as abbreviating $\mathbf{H}$ <- **true**, which is logically equivalent to $\mathbf{H}$; we call it a *sorted fact*.

A *sorted query* is defined as

$$\texttt{<-}\; \mathbf{L}_1 \;\&\; \cdots \;\&\; \mathbf{L}_n \tag{3}$$

which is regarded as abbreviating **false** <- $\mathbf{L}_1 \;\&\; \cdots \;\&\; \mathbf{L}_n$, where $n \leq 1$ and $\mathbf{L}_i$, $i \in \{1, \ldots, n\}$, is a sorted literal. Resolution-style provers as used in logic programming find refutable instances of queries, or in other words, provable instances of $\mathbf{L}_1 \;\&\; \cdots \;\&\; \mathbf{L}_n$.

A *softly many-sorted logic program with negation* is a finite set of sorted clauses. In a sorted program, the set of all sorted clauses with a given head predicate symbol is called *the definition* for that predicate.

3.2 A Declarative Semantics

We define a declarative semantics for sorted logic programs with negation, following Clark's completion semantics [3] for unsorted logic programs.

Suppose that

$$\mathbf{p}(\mathbf{t}_1, \ldots, \mathbf{t}_n) \;\texttt{<-}\; \mathbf{L}_1 \;\&\; \cdots \;\&\; \mathbf{L}_m \tag{4}$$

is a sorted clause, where $\mathbf{p}$ is a sorted predicate symbol with associated sorts $(\mathbf{s}_1, \ldots, \mathbf{s}_n)$. Let = be the equality relation with declared sorts $(\mathbf{u}, \mathbf{u})$, where $\mathbf{u}$ is a sort variable, and let $\mathbf{x}_1, \ldots, \mathbf{x}_n$ be variable symbols distinct from other variable symbols occurring in the sorted clause. Then the above clause is equivalent to the sorted clause

$$\mathbf{p}(\mathbf{x}_1, \ldots, \mathbf{x}_n) \;\texttt{<-}\; (\mathbf{x}_1 = \mathbf{t}_1) \;\&\; \cdots \;\&\; (\mathbf{x}_n = \mathbf{t}_n) \;\&\; \mathbf{L}_1 \;\&\; \cdots \;\&\; \mathbf{L}_m. \tag{5}$$

Let $\mathbf{y}_1, \ldots, \mathbf{y}_l$ be all the variables occurring in (4). The *general form* of the sorted clause is

$$\begin{aligned} \mathbf{p}(\mathbf{x}_1, \ldots, \mathbf{x}_n) \;\texttt{<-}\; &(\texttt{exists } \mathbf{y}_1 \;\cdots\; \texttt{exists } \mathbf{y}_l) \\ &((\mathbf{x}_1 = \mathbf{t}_1) \;\&\; \cdots \;\&\; (\mathbf{x}_n = \mathbf{t}_n) \;\&\; \mathbf{L}_1 \;\&\; \cdots \;\&\; \mathbf{L}_m). \end{aligned} \tag{6}$$

For the definition of a sorted predicate $\mathbf{p}$ with k sorted clauses, $k \geq 1$, let

$$\begin{aligned} &\mathbf{p}(\mathbf{x}_1, \ldots, \mathbf{x}_n) \;\texttt{<-}\; \mathbf{E}_1 \\ &\qquad\qquad \cdots \\ &\mathbf{p}(\mathbf{x}_1, \ldots, \mathbf{x}_n) \;\texttt{<-}\; \mathbf{E}_k \end{aligned} \tag{7}$$

be the general forms of these clauses, as in (6).

Recall that for an unsorted logic program, the completed definition of an unsorted predicate $\mathbf{p}^0$ in the Clark semantics, is

$$(\mathtt{forall}\ \mathbf{x}_1^0 \cdots \mathtt{forall}\ \mathbf{x}_n^0)(\mathbf{p}^0(\mathbf{x}_1^0,\ldots,\mathbf{x}_n^0) \mathtt{<->} \mathbf{E}_1^0\ \mathtt{or} \cdots \mathtt{or}\ \mathbf{E}_k^0) \quad (8)$$

where $\mathbf{p}^0$, $\mathbf{x}_i^0$, $\mathbf{E}_j^0$, for all $i \in \{1,\ldots,n\}$ and $j \in \{1,\ldots,k\}$, are respectively unsorted predicate symbols, variables and conjunctions of unsorted literals.

This notion of completion is inappropriate for a softly sorted language, for example because the left side of <-> in (8) may be F-sorted and the right side not F-sorted. This may introduce inconsistency, as illustrated by the following example.

Example 3.1 Consider the following logic program:

```
p(X) <- q(X)

q(red) <-

q(7) <-
```

According to (8), the logical meaning of p(X) is the completion:

$$(\mathtt{forall}\ \mathtt{x})(\mathtt{p}(\mathtt{x}) \mathtt{<->} (\mathtt{exists}\ \mathtt{y})((\mathtt{x} = \mathtt{y})\ \&\ \mathtt{q}(\mathtt{y}))).$$

Suppose that there are two sorts, colour with a domain {red, yellow, blue} and digit with {0, ..., 9}, and suppose the two 1-place predicates p and q have declared sorts colour and u, respectively. Here u is a sort variable ranging over all sorts.

If X is of sort digit, then p(X) is F-sorted and interpreted to false in soft sorting. But q(X) is well-sorted under sort substitution {u/digit} and is true when X is replaced by 7. □

The intuition of the completion semantics is to use the meaning of the right side of <-> in defining the meaning of the left side which is a predicate. Taking the viewpoint that the sort declaration of the predicate symbol defined by a completion is a constraint on the truth of the right side of <->, we impose that constraint in defining p. Given a predicate $\mathbf{p}(\mathbf{x}_1,\ldots,\mathbf{x}_n)$ where p is a sorted predicate symbol with declared sorts $(\mathbf{s}_1,\ldots,\mathbf{s}_n)$, and $\mathbf{x}_1,\ldots,\mathbf{x}_n$ are sorted variables with associated sorts $\mathbf{u}_1,\ldots,\mathbf{u}_n$ respectively, the sort restriction on the truth of p is

$$\mathtt{sort}_{\mathbf{s}_1}(\mathbf{x}_1)\ \&\ \cdots\ \&\ \mathtt{sort}_{\mathbf{s}_n}(\mathbf{x}_n),$$

where $\mathtt{sort}_{\mathbf{s}_i}(\mathbf{x}_i) = \mathtt{exists}\ \mathbf{z}_i\ (\mathbf{z}_i = \mathbf{x}_i)$ and $\mathbf{z}_i$ and $\mathbf{x}_i$ are sorted variables with associated sorts $\mathbf{s}_i$ and $\mathbf{u}_i$ respectively, $i = 1,\ldots,n$.

Hence we modify the completion semantics for softly sorted programs as follows.

The *completion* of the above predicate p in a softly sorted language is defined as the formula

$$(\mathtt{forall}\ \mathbf{x}_1 \cdots \mathtt{forall}\ \mathbf{x}_n)(\mathbf{p}(\mathbf{x}_1,\ldots,\mathbf{x}_n) \mathtt{<->} \\ \mathtt{sort}_{\mathbf{s}_1}(\mathbf{x}_1)\ \&\ \cdots\ \&\ \mathtt{sort}_{\mathbf{s}_n}(\mathbf{x}_n)\ \&\ (\mathbf{E}_1\ \mathtt{or} \cdots \mathtt{or}\ \mathbf{E}_k)). \quad (9)$$

3.3 Static and Dynamic Sort Checking

Although soft sorting requires dynamic sort checking in general, the concepts of T-sorted and F-sorted provide a basis for some static sort checking in some cases, as we now discuss.

In the definition (9) of the completion of a predicate of a sorted program, suppose that $\mathbf{y}_1, \ldots, \mathbf{y}_q$ are the sorted variables occurring in ($\mathbf{E}_1$ `or` $\cdots$ `or` $\mathbf{E}_k$). Recall that these sorted variables are associated with distinct sort variables. Both the left side of `<->` and ($\mathtt{sort}_{\mathbf{s}_1}(\mathbf{x}_1)$ `&` $\cdots$ `&` $\mathtt{sort}_{\mathbf{s}_n}(\mathbf{x}_n)$) are well-sortable. In general, however, ($\mathbf{E}_1$ `or` $\cdots$ `or` $\mathbf{E}_k$) might be not well-sorted, and it is possible that for some Θ, ($\mathbf{E}_1$ `or` $\cdots$ `or` $\mathbf{E}_k$)Θ is F-sorted or T-sorted. In the F-sorted case, the right side of `<->` is also F-sorted. In the T-sorted case, the right side is equivalent to ($\mathtt{sort}_{\mathbf{s}_1}(\mathbf{x}_1)$ `&` $\cdots$ `&` $\mathtt{sort}_{\mathbf{s}_n}(\mathbf{x}_n)$).

Furthermore, even when ($\mathbf{E}_1$ `or` $\cdots$ `or` $\mathbf{E}_k$)Θ is well-sorted, the sorted formula ($\mathtt{sort}_{\mathbf{s}_1}(\mathbf{x}_1)$ `&` $\cdots$ `&` $\mathtt{sort}_{\mathbf{s}_n}(\mathbf{x}_n)$)$\Theta$ may be F-sorted. If this is the case, then again the right side of `<->` is F-sorted.

As F-sorted (T-sorted) formulas are always assigned *false* (*true*) in soft many-sorting, we do not need to evaluate F-sorted or T-sorted formulas at run-time. This can be used both to perform some static sort checking, and to improve efficiency generally. As we mentioned in Section 2.4, it is decidable whether a sorted formula is well-sorted, F-sorted, T-sorted, or well-sortable. If the right side is well-sorted then conjuncts within $\mathbf{E}_i$'s which are T-sorted or F-sorted are equivalent to *true* or *false* respectively and the program and its completion can be simplified accordingly, at compile-time.

If ($\mathbf{E}_1$ `or` $\cdots$ `or` $\mathbf{E}_k$) is F-sorted, then it is equivalent to *false* and the completion is equivalent to

$$(\mathtt{forall}\ \mathbf{x}_1\ \cdots\ \mathtt{forall}\ \mathbf{x}_n)(\mathbf{p}(\mathbf{x}_1, \ldots, \mathbf{x}_n)\ \texttt{<->}\ \mathtt{false}\ ).$$

If ($\mathbf{E}_1$ `or` $\cdots$ `or` $\mathbf{E}_k$) is T-sorted, then the right side of (9) is equivalent to ($\mathtt{sort}_{\mathbf{s}_1}(\mathbf{x}_1)$ `&` $\cdots$ `&` $\mathtt{sort}_{\mathbf{s}_n}(\mathbf{x}_n)$) and the completion is equivalent to

$$(\mathtt{forall}\ \mathbf{x}_1\ \cdots\ \mathtt{forall}\ \mathbf{x}_n)(\mathbf{p}(\mathbf{x}_1, \ldots, \mathbf{x}_n)\ \texttt{<->}$$
$$\mathtt{sort}_{\mathbf{s}_1}(\mathbf{x}_1)\ \texttt{\&}\ \cdots\ \texttt{\&}\ \mathtt{sort}_{\mathbf{s}_n}(\mathbf{x}_n)).$$

Note that ($\mathbf{E}_1$ `or` $\cdots$ `or` $\mathbf{E}_k$) is T-sorted only if there exists $i \in \{1, \ldots, k\}$, such that $\mathbf{E}_i$ is a conjunction of negative literals which are all T-sorted.

In fact, the subformulas $\mathbf{p}(\mathbf{x}_1, \ldots, \mathbf{x}_n)$ and ($\mathtt{sort}_{\mathbf{s}_1}(\mathbf{x}_1)$ `&` $\cdots$ `&` $\mathtt{sort}_{\mathbf{s}_n}(\mathbf{x}_n)$) have the same sortedness under every sort substitution. Thus $\mathbf{p}(\mathbf{x}_1, \ldots, \mathbf{x}_n)\Theta$ is F-sorted if and only if ($\mathtt{sort}_{\mathbf{s}_1}(\mathbf{x}_1)$ `&` $\cdots$ `&` $\mathtt{sort}_{\mathbf{s}_n}(\mathbf{x}_n)$)$\Theta$ is F-sorted. Hence ($\mathbf{E}_1$ `or` $\cdots$ `or` $\mathbf{E}_k$) is T-sorted then the completion (9) is T-sorted under Θ. This property justifies some static simplifications of sorted programs, as follows.

Since a complete finite representation of all well-sorters of $\mathbf{p}(\mathbf{x}_1, \ldots, \mathbf{x}_n)$ is $\{\ \mathbf{u}_1 = \mathbf{s}_1, \ldots, \mathbf{u}_n = \mathbf{s}_n\ \}$, a complete finite explicit representation exists and is $\{\Psi = \{\mathbf{u}_1/\mathbf{s}_1, \ldots, \mathbf{u}_n/\mathbf{s}_n\}\}$. From Proposition 2.7, we know that the sortedness of a formula is statically decidable, and after static sort checking, we need to evaluate only well-sortable and well-sorted queries. This means that in evaluation we need only the part of (9) where $\mathbf{x}_1, \ldots, \mathbf{x}_n$ are associated with $\mathbf{s}_1, \ldots, \mathbf{s}_n$ respectively:

$$(\mathtt{forall}\ \mathbf{x}_1\ \cdots\ \mathtt{forall}\ \mathbf{x}_n)(\mathbf{p}(\mathbf{x}_1, \ldots, \mathbf{x}_n)\ \texttt{<->}\ \mathbf{S}\ \texttt{\&}\ \mathbf{E}), \tag{10}$$

where $S = \texttt{sort}_{s_1}(x_1)$ & $\cdots$ & $\texttt{sort}_{s_n}(x_n)$ and where $E = (E_1 \texttt{ or } \cdots \texttt{or } E_k)$.

If the right side of (10) is well-sortable, a nonempty finite complete representation of well-sorters can be computed, as mentioned in Proposition 2.7 (2). There may also exist a complete finite explicit representation of well-sorters. We can check if one does exist by Proposition 2.7 (3), and if so compute one such explicit representation, say $\{\Theta_1, \ldots, \Theta_r\}$. Then (10) is equivalent to the conjunction of the following r sorted formulas:

$$\begin{array}{l}((\texttt{forall } x_1 \cdots \texttt{forall } x_n)(p(x_1, \ldots, x_n) \texttt{<->} S \,\&\, E))\Theta_1 \\ \qquad\qquad\qquad\qquad \cdots \\ ((\texttt{forall } x_1 \cdots \texttt{forall } x_n)(p(x_1, \ldots, x_n) \texttt{<->} S \,\&\, E))\Theta_r\end{array} \tag{11}$$

where $E = (E_1 \texttt{ or } \cdots \texttt{ or } E_k)$.

As in the well-sorted case these formulas can be simplified statically by recognising T-sorted and F-sorted subformulas.

From such equivalence transformations of (10), compile-time transformations of predicate definitions can be derived. That is beyond the scope of this paper, but here is a simple example.

Example 3.2 We extend Example 3.1 in Section 3.2 by introducing a third 1-place predicate `r` with declared sort `v`, where `v` is a sort variable. Consider the following program.

```
r(X) <- q(X) & (not p(X))

p(X) <- q(X)

q(red) <-

q(7) <-
```

Note that the associated sorts of `r`, `p`, `q`, and `X` are `v`, `colour`, `u`, and `u1` respectively. The first clause is well-sortable and the following is a complete finite representation of its well-sorters:

$$\{\{\texttt{v} = \texttt{u1}, \texttt{u1} = \texttt{u}, \texttt{u1} = \texttt{colour}\}, \{\texttt{v} = \texttt{u1}, \texttt{u1} = \texttt{u}, \texttt{u1} \neq \texttt{colour}\}\}.$$

In this example, there is also a complete finite explicit representation for the above representation, as follows:

$$\begin{array}{l}\{\ \Theta_1 = \{\texttt{v/colour}, \texttt{u/colour}, \texttt{u1/colour}\}, \\ \ \ \Theta_2 = \{\texttt{v/digit}, \texttt{u/digit}, \texttt{u1/digit}\}\ \}.\end{array}$$

A compile-time transformation of the clause is thus possible. The clause can be translated to two clauses as follows.

C1: $\texttt{r(X)}\Theta_1$ `<- (q(X) & (not p(X)))`Θ_1

C2: $\texttt{r(X)}\Theta_2$ `<- (q(X) & (not p(X)))`Θ_2

The negative literal in **C2** is T-sorted. Thus **C1** and **C2** can be further transformed to the following two clauses.

C1: $\texttt{r(X)}\Theta_1$ `<- (q(X) & (not p(X)))`Θ_1

C2': r(X)Θ_2 <- q(X)Θ_2

When there is a complete finite explicit representation of well-sorters, we can derive most general variable sortings from the representation. These variable sortings for the first clause are {X/colour} and {X/digit}. However, when an explicit representation does not exist, we use the 2-place predicate **sort** in Section 3.4.2 and Section 3.4.3. Variable sortings can be seen as special cases of such sorting constraints.

We shall illustrate shortly in Example 3.3 that dynamic sort checking is needed in general. In Section 3.4.2 and Section 3.4.3 we show how to combine dynamic sort checking with evaluation procedures for sorted logic programs. □

3.4 Procedural Semantics

We describe three query evaluation procedures for sorted logic programs based on a softly sorted language. These are ordinary unsorted evaluation, unsorted evaluation with sort predicates, and sorted evaluation with sort constraints.

3.4.1 Ordinary Unsorted Evaluation

If no negative literal occurs in the body of any clause, if the base sort **wrong** does not occur in the associated sort of any sorted symbol in a program, and if all clauses whose head predicate symbols are associated with their declared sorts are well-sorted, then we have essentially Mycroft and O'Keefe's well-typed logic programs. These conditions can be checked at compile time. It is proved in [6, 10] that the ordinary unsorted query evaluation procedure is correct ("*A well-typed program does not go wrong.*"). But if the stated restrictions on our more general framework are not satisfied, then such a procedural semantics is not correct, as illustrated by the following example.

Example 3.3 Following Example 3.1 in Section 3.2, the sorted program

```
p(X) <- q(X)

q(red) <-

q(7) <-
```

is well-sorted under the (most general) variable sorting {X/colour}. A sorted query <- p(X) is also well-sorted under the same variable sorting.

Using an unsorted evaluation, the computed answers of the query <- p(X) are {X/red} and {X/7}. However the only correct answer of the query according to the declarative semantics is {X/red}. □

3.4.2 Unsorted Evaluation with Sort Predicates

It is possible to translate a sorted logic program into an unsorted logic program, then correspondingly translate queries when they are made. We use a new 2-place predicate symbol **sort**, and include the syntax for sorts in the vocabulary of the unsorted program.

A clause

$$\mathbf{p}(\mathbf{t}_1,\ldots,\mathbf{t}_q) \texttt{ <- } \mathbf{L}_1 \;\&\; \cdots \;\&\; \mathbf{L}_n,$$

where $\mathbf{s}_1,\ldots,\mathbf{s}_q$ are the declared sorts for **p**, is translated into the unsorted clause

$$\mathbf{p}(\mathbf{t}_1,\ldots,\mathbf{t}_q) \texttt{ <- } \mathbf{L}_1 \;\&\; \cdots \;\&\; \mathbf{L}_n \;\&\; \mathtt{sort}(\mathbf{t}_1,\mathbf{s}_1) \;\&\; \cdots \;\&\; \mathtt{sort}(\mathbf{t}_q,\mathbf{s}_q).$$

If a finite complete explicit representation of well-sorters for the clause is available, we can do the following transformation.

Suppose that $\mathbf{x}_1,\ldots,\mathbf{x}_m$ are all the variable symbols occurring in

$$\mathbf{p}(\mathbf{t}_1,\ldots,\mathbf{t}_q) \texttt{ <- } \mathbf{L}_1 \;\&\; \cdots \;\&\; \mathbf{L}_n,$$

and suppose that this clause is well-sorted under the finite set of variable sortings

$$\{\mathbf{x}_1/\mathbf{s}_{11},\ldots,\mathbf{x}_m/\mathbf{s}_{1m}\}$$

$$\cdots$$

$$\{\mathbf{x}_1/\mathbf{s}_{l1},\ldots,\mathbf{x}_m/\mathbf{s}_{lm}\}.$$

Then the clause may be translated into the finite set of unsorted clauses

$$\mathbf{p}(\mathbf{t}_1,\ldots,\mathbf{t}_q) \texttt{ <- } \mathbf{L}_1 \;\&\; \cdots \;\&\; \mathbf{L}_n \;\&\; \mathtt{sort}(\mathbf{x}_1,\mathbf{s}_{11}) \;\&\; \cdots \;\&\; \mathtt{sort}(\mathbf{x}_m,\mathbf{s}_{1m})$$

$$\cdots$$

$$\mathbf{p}(\mathbf{t}_1,\ldots,\mathbf{t}_q) \texttt{ <- } \mathbf{L}_1 \;\&\; \cdots \;\&\; \mathbf{L}_n \;\&\; \mathtt{sort}(\mathbf{x}_1,\mathbf{s}_{l1}) \;\&\; \cdots \;\&\; \mathtt{sort}(\mathbf{x}_m,\mathbf{s}_{lm}).$$

A sorted logic program *P* translated in this way also includes clauses for the sort predicate, as follows.

1. For each constant **a** with the declared (ground) sort **s**:

   $$\mathtt{sort}(\mathbf{a},\mathbf{s}) \texttt{ <-}.$$

   Note that there should exist at least one constant for each base sort **s**.

2. For each sorted function symbol **f** with declared sort $\mathbf{s}_1,\ldots,\mathbf{s}_n \rightarrow \mathbf{s}$:

   $$\mathtt{sort}(\mathbf{f}(\mathbf{x}_1,\ldots,\mathbf{x}_n),\mathbf{s}) \texttt{ <- } \mathtt{sort}(\mathbf{x}_1,\mathbf{s}_1) \;\&\; \cdots \;\&\; \mathtt{sort}(\mathbf{x}_n,\mathbf{s}_n),$$

   and if **wrong** is included in the sort syntax, then also:

   $$\mathtt{sort}(\mathbf{f}(\mathbf{x}_1,\ldots,\mathbf{x}_n),\mathtt{wrong}) \texttt{ <- not } \mathtt{sort}(\mathbf{x}_1,\mathbf{s}_1),$$

   $$\ldots,$$

   $$\mathtt{sort}(\mathbf{f}(\mathbf{x}_1,\ldots,\mathbf{x}_n),\mathtt{wrong}) \texttt{ <- not } \mathtt{sort}(\mathbf{x}_n,\mathbf{s}_n).$$

Such a translation of *P* is called the *associated unsorted form* of *P*. If **wrong** is not part of the sort syntax then the above definition of the **sort** predicate is the same as in the restriction to parametric many-sorting of Hill and Topor's analysis [6]. However, because soft sorting does not include restrictions (occurring in [6]) on sortings of head atoms, the sortedness properties of the two approaches are different, as the following example shows.

Example 3.4 Suppose that predicate symbol p has declared sort **colour** and predicate symbol q has declared sort u. The clause

```
q(X) <- p(X),
```

where q is associated with **colour**, is well-sorted under variable sorting **colour** for X in soft sorting. Thus the clause is translated to

```
q(X) <- p(X) & sort(X, colour).
```

In Hill and Topor's approach, any well-sorting s for X must be a sort variant of the declared sort u of q. There does not exist such a well-sorting for q(X) <- p(X). Thus the clause is ill-sorted. □

Example 3.5 The associated unsorted form P_0 of the program P in Example 3.3 consists of clauses

```
p(X) <- q(X) & sort(X, colour)
q(red) <-
q(7) <-
sort(red, colour) <-
sort(yellow, colour) <-
sort(blue, colour) <-
sort(1, digit) <-
...
sort(9, digit) <-.
```

The associated unsorted form G_0 of <- p(X) is <- p(X) & sort(X, colour). By using unsorted evaluation on $P_0 \cup \{G_0\}$, we get the answer {X/red}. □

In this evaluation procedure, dynamic sort checking is implemented at source code level. Ordinary unsorted evaluation can then be applied to the associated unsorted forms of programs and queries. The correctness of the procedural semantics, relative to the declarative semantics, is discussed in [2].

3.4.3 Sorted Evaluation with Sort Constraints

An alternative to the method of Section 3.4.2 is to evaluate a sorted program directly, by combining the evaluation of unsorted programs with a sort constraint solver, which can run in parallel with the unsorted query evaluation.

A clause

$$\mathtt{p}(\mathtt{t}_1,\ldots,\mathtt{t}_q) \texttt{ <- } \mathtt{L}_1 \;\&\; \cdots \;\&\; \mathtt{L}_n,$$

where $\mathtt{s}_1,\ldots,\mathtt{s}_q$ are the declared sorts for p, has the sort constraint

$$\mathtt{sort}(\mathtt{t}_1,\mathtt{s}_1) \;\&\; \cdots \;\&\; \mathtt{sort}(\mathtt{t}_q,\mathtt{s}_q).$$

When a finite complete explicit representation of well-sorters for the clause is available, we can do the following transformation.

Suppose $\mathbf{x}_1, \ldots, \mathbf{x}_m$ are all the variables occurring in a sorted clause or query, which is well-sorted under the finite complete set of variable sortings

$$\{\mathbf{x}_1/\mathbf{s}_{11}, \ldots, \mathbf{x}_m/\mathbf{s}_{1m}\}$$
$$\ldots$$
$$\{\mathbf{x}_1/\mathbf{s}_{l1}, \ldots, \mathbf{x}_m/\mathbf{s}_{lm}\}.$$

Then the current sort constraint for the clause or query can be summarised as

$$(\texttt{sort}(\mathbf{x}_1, \mathbf{s}_{11}) \ \& \cdots \& \ \texttt{sort}(\mathbf{x}_m, \mathbf{s}_{1m}))$$
$$\texttt{or} \cdots \texttt{or}$$
$$(\texttt{sort}(\mathbf{x}_1, \mathbf{s}_{l1}) \ \& \cdots \& \ \texttt{sort}(\mathbf{x}_m, \mathbf{s}_{lm})).$$

The sort constraint of a clause or query is **true** if the clause or query is well-sorted under all variable sortings, for example, p(red) <- in Example 3.1. For a sorted query <- $\mathbf{L}_1$ & $\cdots$ & $\mathbf{L}_i$ & $\cdots$ & $\mathbf{L}_n$ with sort constraint $\mathbf{C}$ and a clause $\mathbf{H}$ <- $\mathbf{L}'_1$ & $\cdots$ & $\mathbf{L}'_r$ with sort constraint $\mathbf{C}'$, if $\mathbf{L}_i$ is unified with $\mathbf{H}$ by θ, then the query becomes

$$\texttt{<-}\ (\mathbf{L}_1 \ \& \ \cdots \ \& \ \mathbf{L}'_1 \ \& \ \cdots \ \& \ \mathbf{L}'_r \ \& \ \cdots \ \& \ \mathbf{L}_n)\theta,$$

where the sort constraint of the new query is $(\mathbf{C} \ \& \ \mathbf{C}')\theta$.

Example 3.6 Following Example 3.3, the sort constraints for clauses

1. p(X) <- q(X)
2. q(red) <-
3. q(7) <-

are sort(X, colour), true, and true, respectively. The sort constraint of the query <- p(X) is sort(X, colour).

When p(X) is unified with the head of the first clause, the query becomes <- q(X) with sort constraint

(sort(X, colour) & sort(X, colour)),

which can be simplified to sort(X, colour). If X is instantiated to red, the sort constraint is satisfied, thus {X/red} is a computed answer. If X is instantiated to 7, the sort constraint cannot be satisfied, thus the instantiation leads to a failure. □

Further details of this approach will be given elsewhere [2].

4 Conclusions and Further Work

Soft sorting provides a sound theoretical basis for static and dynamic sorting (typing) in programming languages. This paper outlines a framework for softly sorted logic programming languages which overcomes limitations of strict sorting.

A declarative semantics for sorted logic programs with negation based on softly many-sorted languages has been introduced. The semantics is a modification of Clark's completion semantics for unsorted logic programs with negation. We also discussed sort checking and query evaluation procedures.

We are currently working on the extension of softly many-sorted languages to order-sorting. This is especially useful for extending the sorted logic programs introduced in this paper to parametric order-sorting.

Based on the above declarative semantics, further work on procedural semantics for our softly sorted logic programs and queries is needed, especially to develop practically efficient implementations.

References

[1] Cartwright, R. and Fagan, M., "*Soft Typing*", In *Proceedings of the ACM SIGPLAN'91 Conference on Programming Language Design and Implementation*, Toronto, Ontario, Canada, June 26-28, 1991, pages 278-292.

[2] Chen, J., "*Soft Sorting of First-Order Languages*", Ph.D. thesis, Department of Computer Science, The University of Queensland, to appear.

[3] Clark, K. L., "*Negation as Failure*", in Gallaire, H. and Minker, J., editors, *Logic and Data Bases*, Plenum Press, New York, pages 293-322, 1978.

[4] Dietrich, R. and Hagl, F., "*A Polymorphic Type System with Subtypes for Prolog*", In *Proceedings of 2nd European Symposium on Programming*, LNCS 300, Springer-Verlag, pages 79-93, 1988.

[5] Hanus, M., "*Horn Clause Programs with Polymorphic types: Semantics and Resolution*", In Diaz, J. and Orejas, F., editors, *Proceedings of the International Joint Conference on Theory and Practice of Software Development*, Barcelona, Spain, pages 225-240, Lecture Notes in Computer Science 352, Springer-Verlag, 1989.

[6] Hill, P.M. and Topor, R.W., "*A Semantics for Typed Logic Programs*", Department of Computer Science, University of Bristol, England. Technical Report TR-90-11, May 1990 (Revised December 1990).

[7] Lakshman, T.K. and Reddy, U.S., "*Typed Prolog: A Semantic Reconstruction of the Mycroft-O'Keefe Type System*", Department of Computer Science, University of Illinois at Urbana-Champaign, Urbana, Illinois 61801. Draft, February 1991. To appear in the proceedings of ILPS'91 at San Diego, California, USA.

[8] Lassez, J.-L. and Marriott, K., "*Explicit Representation of Terms Defined by Counter Examples*", *Journal of Automated Reasoning*, 3 (1987) 301-317.

[9] Lloyd, J.W., "*Foundations of Logic Programming*", (second edition), Springer-Verlag, 1987.

[10] Mycroft, A. and O'Keefe, R.A., "*A Polymorphic Type System for Prolog*", *Artificial Intelligence*, 23:295-307, 1984.

Modularity for Logic Programs

G. Antoniou
V. Sperschneider
University of Osnabrueck
Albrechtstrasse 28
D-4500 Osnabrueck
Germany

Abstract

We present a module concept for logic programming with formal interfaces, motivated by work in algebraic specification. We discuss aspects of semantics and correctness of such modules. Further we describe how to build larger logic programs from single modules by so called module operations, and derive results concerning compositionality of semantics and correctness preservation.

1 Introduction

In the present paper we introduce a framework for modular design, implementation, and verification of logic programs. It is our belief that, besides types and good declarative semantics ([9]), modularity is essential for achieving a breakthrough of logic programming in practical application.

We are motivated by work in the field of algebraic specification ([4], [7], [8]) and work on modules with imperative module body ([1], [2], [12], [13]). A logic program is thus seen as a collection of independent entities interacting with each other via import and export interfaces.

Let us now briefly describe our module concept. A module in our sense consists of four parts. The *export interface* describes the knowledge being offered to the public by the module, and is modelled as a logic program. The *import interface*, also a logic program, describes the information needed by the module in order to implement its functionality. This implementation is done in the module's *body*. Finally, import and export interfaces may be parametrized by a *parameter part* which is an arbitrary first order specification. The parameter part is freely instantiable and allows development of *generic modules*.

We have restricted attention to so called definite programs, i.e. Horn logic. The results can, however, be generalized in several directions (e.g. admitting stratified programs with their restricted use of negation).

Finally, we want to point out the difference between our modules and those already existing for Prolog systems (e.g. [5], [6], [10] and [15]). The fundamental difference is that all these attempts treat syntax-oriented approaches that are mainly concerned with name conflicts, whereas here we are rather focusing on formal semantical aspects of modularization, due to the existence of formal module interfaces. Let us briefly explain why we insist on this point.

It is our belief that the more logic programming finds application in practical problems, the more demands concerning quality will grow. As the history of data processing shows, testing of software is insufficient, since it can only find out erroneous behaviour but can never guarantee absense of errors. Therefore verification techniques for logic programs and rigorous approaches to program development will have to be used.

As we have already pointed out, structured knowledge based systems consist of modules interacting with each other. Following the lines of algebraic specification ([7]), we model such systems as results of so called *module operations* which describe ways of putting modules together. Here we shall discuss the composition operation; union and actualization have been treated in [3].

2 Basic notions of logic programming

We use here standard notions and notation for logic programming as can be found in [11] or [13]. We consider *definite logic programs* (in this paper often called logic program) defined as sets of definite program formulas. In some proofs we shall use infinite programs for technical reasons, but the logic programs in the modules are, of course, finite. We say that a logic program P *defines a predicate* p if p occurs in the head of a formula in P, while P *uses* a predicate p if p occurs in the body of some formula in P.

The least *Herbrand model* of logic program P is denoted by $\mathcal{M}_P$ and is defined as the set of all ground atoms in a given signature Σ that logically follow from P (this makes sense also for infinite P). There is a well known approximation of $\mathcal{M}_P$ making use of an increasing union of Herbrand models $\mathcal{I}_n(P)$ for $n = 0, 1, 2, \ldots$ (see [11]).

When trying to describe some domain with logic programs it is often necessary to use auxiliary predicates. In these cases it is usually desirable that the definition of the new predicates does not change the meaning of the old ones. This idea leads to the concept of conservative extensions.

Let Q be a definite logic program and M a set of predicates. We say that Q is *conservative with respect* to M if Q does not define predicates from M. Predicates of M may thus be only used, but not defined, in the body of rules in Q.

Let P and Q be definite logic programs over the same set of function symbols. We say that $P \cup Q$ is a *conservative extension* of P if Q is conservative w.r.t. the set of predicates occurring in P. The following lemma expresses the main property of conservative extensions.

Lemma Let P and Q be definite logic programs over the same set of function symbols such that $P \cup Q$ is a conservative extension of P. Then

$$\mathcal{M}_{P \cup Q} \cap H(P) = \mathcal{M}_P$$

where $H(P)$, the so-called Herbrand base, denotes the set of ground atoms $p(t_1, \ldots, t_k)$ with predicate p occurring in P.

Proof One direction is trivial, the other is shown by proving $\mathcal{I}_n(P \cup Q) \cap H(P) \subseteq \mathcal{M}_P$ by induction on n (see [14]). $\square$

The lemma states thus that conservatively extending P to $P \cup Q$ does not affect the semantics of predicates in P.

3 The module concept

3.1 Module syntax

A *logic module* Mod consists of a set Ω of function symbols, a parameter part PAR, an export interface EXP, an import interface IMP and an implementation part $BODY$. Its components are as follows:

- PAR consists of a set of predicates Σ_{par} and a first order axiom set Par over $\Sigma_{par} \cup \Omega$, the *constraints* of Mod.

- EXP consists of a set of predicates Σ_{exp} disjoint from Σ_{par}, and a definite logic program Exp over $\Sigma_{par} \cup \Sigma_{exp} \cup \Omega$. Exp must be conservative w.r.t. Σ_{par}. Certain predicates from Σ_{exp} are distinguished as *exported* predicates (these are made available to module users), while the remaining ones are called *auxiliary*.

- IMP consists of a set of predicates Σ_{imp} disjoint from $\Sigma_{par} \cup \Sigma_{exp}$, and a definite logic program Imp over $\Sigma_{par} \cup \Sigma_{imp} \cup \Omega$. Imp must be conservative w.r.t. Σ_{par}. Certain predicates from Σ_{imp} are distinguished as *imported* predicates (these are made visible to the outside), while the remaining ones are called *auxiliary*.

- $BODY$ consists of a set of auxiliary predicates Σ_{body} disjoint from $\Sigma_{par} \cup \Sigma_{exp} \cup \Sigma_{imp}$, and a definite logic program $Implem$ over $\Sigma_{par} \cup \Sigma_{body} \cup \Omega \cup \{p \in \Sigma_{exp} | p \text{ exported }\} \cup \{p \in \Sigma_{imp} | p \text{ imported}\}$. It is required that this program is conservative w.r.t. $\Sigma_{par} \cup \Sigma_{imp}$. □

Remarks

1. In the definition above, constants and function symbols are treated as *global*, meaning that they are common to all module parts. This view is compatible with module concepts in several Prolog systems like Quintus Prolog. How local functions can be used is discussed in [3], while in a paper under preparation we are discussing modules combining functional and logic programming.

2. The role of auxiliary predicates in the module interfaces and in the body is different. The former ones are only used to *describe* properties of imported or exported predicates. It is neither admitted to ask a query to the module using an auxiliary predicate of the export interface nor to use an auxiliary predicate of the import interface in the module body. The latter ones are parts of the defining programs in the module body and thus play a role in the module semantics. Of course, they are invisible from the outside as they are neither imported nor exported.

An example can be found in figure 1.

The module shows an implementation of cycle-free path searching in a directed graph. Naturally, the graph is used as a parameter of the module. The usual logic programming implementation is included in the module body, while the imported and exported predicates occur in the import and export interface respectively. The meaning (semantics) of these predicates is described in form of logic programs. Note that the export interface is also a logic program for path searching, a readable but not runnable one. Our idea is that effective and efficient implementations are used in the body, while they are described by more abstract logic programs in the interfaces (with no emphasis on efficiency).

3.2 Module semantics and correctness

Definition Given a logic module Mod, a *parameter model* $\mathcal{P}$ of *Mod* is a (perhaps infinite) set of program formulas in the signature $\Sigma_{par} \cup \Omega$ extended by an arbitrary set $Const(\mathcal{P})$ of new constants such that $\mathcal{M}_{\mathcal{P}}$ is a model (in the sense of predicate logic) of *Par*. The set of new constant symbols may depend on $\mathcal{P}$.

<table>
<tr>
<td>

EXPORT

Exported predicates: path (X,Y)
Auxiliar predicates: none
Definitions:
path(X,X).
path(X,Y):-edge(X,Y), diff(X,Z), path(Z,Y).

</td>
<td rowspan="3">

PARAMETER

Predicates:

edge(X,Y), diff (X,Y)

Constraints:

diff$(X,Y) \leftrightarrow \neg X = Y$

</td>
</tr>
<tr>
<td>

IMPLEMENTATION

Auxiliar predicates: restrictedPath $(X, Y,$ ForbiddenList$)$
Definitions:
path(X,Y) : − restrictedPath $X, Y, [X])$.
restrictedPath(X,X,L).
restrictedPath(X,Y,L) : −
edge(X,Z),
new(Z,L),
restrictedPath$(Z,Y,[Z|L])$.

</td>
</tr>
<tr>
<td>

IMPORT

Imported predicates: new (X,L)
Auxiliar predicates: none
Definitions:
new$(X,[\,])$.
new$(X,[Y|L])$:- diff(X,Y), new(X,L).

</td>
</tr>
</table>

Figure 1

Definition (Algebraic approach)
Let a logic module Mod and a parameter model $\mathcal{P}$ of Mod be given. The following logical notions must be read w.r.t. the set of functions $\Omega \cup Const(\mathcal{P})$. We define

$$\begin{aligned} &export_{Mod}(\mathcal{P}) = \mathcal{M}_{\mathcal{P} \cup Exp} \\ &import_{Mod}(\mathcal{P}) = \mathcal{M}_{\mathcal{P} \cup Imp} \\ &implement_{Mod}(\mathcal{P}) = \mathcal{M}_{import_{Mod}(\mathcal{P}) \cup Implem} \end{aligned}$$

Hence $export_{Mod}(\mathcal{P})$ describes the requirements to module semantics, while $implement_{Mod}(\mathcal{P})$ describes the actual semantics of the module as it is implemented. The module is thus called correct if these two views are equivalent. More formally: Mod is called *correct* iff for every parameter model $\mathcal{P}$ of Mod, every exported predicate q and all ground terms $t_1, \ldots, t_n$
$q(t_1, \ldots, t_n) \in export_{Mod}(\mathcal{P}) \Leftrightarrow q(t_1, \ldots, t_n) \in implement_{Mod}(\mathcal{P})$
□

This algebraic approach may be criticized as referring to infinite objects at two places: First we could imagine that a model $\mathcal{P}$ of Par is given by a finite logic program P such that $\mathcal{M}_P = \mathcal{P}$. Second, the semantics construction contains nested application of the least Herbrand operator:

$$implement_{Mod}(\mathcal{P}) = \mathcal{M}_{\mathcal{M}_{\mathcal{P} \cup Imp} \cup Implem} = \mathcal{M}_{\mathcal{M}_{\mathcal{M}_P \cup Imp} \cup Implem} \quad \square$$

This construction of nested $\mathcal{M}$-operators cannot be treated by usual logic programming. The question arises what happens if we flatten the structure above and consider the logic program $P \cup Imp \cup Implem$. It turns out that for logic modules this approach is equivalent to the algebraic one (But note that this has to do with the specific form of the module implementation part, i.e. the conservativity conditions; in general such an equivalence does not hold). Note though that the new correctness notion still refers to Herbrand algebras that are usually infinite. The reader may find in [14] a finitary proof strategy for module verification.

Theorem (Rule handling of module semantics and correctness)
Let Mod be a module and P a logic program such that $\mathcal{M}_P$ is a model of Par. Define $rule\_implement_{Mod}(P) = \mathcal{M}_{P \cup Imp \cup Implem}$. Then

$$rule\_implement_{Mod}(P) = implement_{Mod}(\mathcal{M}_P).$$

Proof Follows immediately from the following lemma, noting that Imp is a conservative extension of $\mathcal{M}_P$ and $Implem$ is a conservative extension of $\mathcal{M}_{\mathcal{M}_{\mathcal{P} \cup Imp}}$. □

The following lemma states that when considering conservative extensions of a definite logic program P, it doesn't make any difference whether we use program P directly or all ground atoms that follow from P.

Lemma Let $P$and Q be definite logic programs over the same set of function symbols such that $P \cup Q$ is a conservative extension of P. Then

$$\mathcal{M}_{\mathcal{M}_P \cup Q} = \mathcal{M}_{P \cup Q}$$

Proof Note that by the conservativity condition the same ground atoms $p(t_1, \ldots, t_n)$ with p occurring in P follow from P as from $P \cup Q$ as from $\mathcal{M}_P \cup Q$. So we need only prove the claim for ground atoms $q(t_1, \ldots, t_n)$ with q not occurring in P. One direction is trivial since the formulas in $\mathcal{M}_P$ follow from P. By induction on n we shall show that $q(t_1, \ldots, t_n) \in \mathcal{I}_n(P \cup Q)$ implies $\mathcal{M}_P \cup Q \models q(t_1, \ldots, t_n)$. Nothing is to be shown for $n = 0$.

Assume that $q(t_1, \ldots, t_n) \in \mathcal{I}_{n+1}(P \cup Q) - \mathcal{I}_n(P \cup Q)$. Then there is a ground instance $B\sigma \leftarrow B_1\sigma, \ldots, B_m\sigma$ of a program formula $B \leftarrow B_1, \ldots, B_m$ of $P \cup Q$ such that $q(t_1, \ldots, t_n) = B\sigma$ and $B_1\sigma, \ldots, B_m\sigma \in \mathcal{I}_n(P \cup Q)$. As q does not occur in P, $B \leftarrow B_1, \ldots, B_m$ belongs to Q. By induction hypothesis we know that $B_1\sigma, \ldots, B_m\sigma$ follow from $\mathcal{M}_P \cup Q$. Then also $q(t_1, \ldots, t_n) = B\sigma$ follows from $\mathcal{M}_P \cup Q$ and we are through. □

It should be noted that the above result does not hold without the conservativity condition. Let for example P be the program $\{p(a), p(X) \leftarrow q(X)\}$ and Q be $\{q(b)\}$. Then $\{p(a), q(b)\} = \mathcal{M}_{\mathcal{M}_P \cup Q} \neq \mathcal{M}_{P \cup Q} = \{p(a), q(b), p(b)\}$.

4 Building modular logic programs

4.1 The approach of module operations

How can big and complex logic programs be developed based on the module concept as discussed so far? All important parts of the system are developed as separate modules, and what has to be done is to put these modules together in such a way that the information needed in some module, i.e. its import interface, is obtained from the export side of other modules. A modular logical program is thus built by putting modules together that are combined by gluing together the module interfaces of several modules. In general, the approach consists in first solving the problem on a high level of abstraction and then realizing the needed information in the form of a **hierarchy of modules**.

The simplest situation is that the information needed by module $M1$ is obtained by the export interface of a module $M2$. In this case there must be some kind of mapping of the import interface of $M1$ to the export interface of $M2$. Just as in the theory of algebraic specification there is the concept of 'specification morphism', here we must define the notion of 'logic program morphism'. Our intention is that when having a morphism $h : P \rightarrow Q$, then Q restricted to the image of P has the same semantical behaviour as P. Let us now give a formal definition.

Definition Let P and Q be definite logic programs over the same set of functions, conservative w.r.t. a first order specification Par. Let h be a mapping from the set of predicates of P to the set of predicates of Q such that $h(p)$ has the same arity as p. We call h a *logic program morphism* from P to Q w.r.t. Par, if for all predicates

p in P, models P of Par, and ground terms $t_1, \ldots, t_n$

$$p(t_1, \ldots, t_n) \in \mathcal{M}_{P \cup P} \Leftrightarrow h(p)(t_1, \ldots, t_n) \in \mathcal{M}_{\mathcal{P} \cup Q}. \quad \Box$$

Now that we know how we can combine module interfaces in a reasonable way, we come to the problem of defining the semantics and correctness of modular logic programs. One possibility is, of course, to give new definitions of how these systems are built up, what their meaning is, and how modular programs can be put together to produce more complex ones. This approach would thus require several new semantical definitions.

Following the tradition of algebraic modules ([e.g. [7]) we have chosen here another way: We define some *module operations* describing ways of putting modules together. The major point is that the result of such operations is described as a single module. Modelling modular logic programs this way brings the following advantages:

- we have already clear semantics and correctness notions for modular systems and do not need new ones that would complicate the situation
- module operations may be combined in a compositional way, i.e. the results of some module operations can be used as arguments of another

Naturally we have to pay a price for these advantages: We must show that our definition of an operation's result is reasonable, i.e. matches our intuition of the operation considered. In particular, we show the following plausibility results:

- **compositionality of semantics:** The semantics of the result must be naturally expressible in terms of the semantics of the argument modules, and additionally match our intuition of the operation's meaning
- **correctness preservation:** Correctness of the result follows directly from the correctness of the modules used as arguments of the operation

4.2 Composition

One fundamental way of putting modules together is hierarchical combination: The predicates imported by module M1 are mapped to predicates exported by module $M2$.

Given are thus modules $M1 = (PAR, EXP1, IMP1, BODY1)$ and $M2 = (PAR, EXP2, IMP2, BODY2)$ with disjoint sets of predicates (e.g. names indexed by the module name), as well as a logic program morphism h from the import interface of $M1$ to the export interface of $M2$ w.r.t. Par. Note that, by definition of modules and morphisms, $M1$ and $M2$ are considered as using the same set of functions. Our aim is to describe this modular system as a single module $M3 = (PAR, EXP3, IMP3, BODY3)$. This is done in the following way:

- The parameter part of $M3$ is PAR.
- The import interface $IMP3$ of $M3$ is $IMP2$.

- The export interface $EXP3$ of $M3$ is $EXP1$.
- The body $BODY3$ of $M3$ consists of the auxiliary predicates of $BODY1$ and $BODY2$, and of the logic program $Implem2 \cup h(Implem1)$ ($h(Implem1)$ is obtained from $Implem1$ by replacing all occurrences of predicates p from Σ_{exp1} by $h(p)$).

$M3$ has thus the same appearance to the outside that we would expect from the composition of $M1$ and $M2$: The predicates of $EXP1$ are defined based on the knowledge available in $IMP2$.

According to our approach we must now show that our definition is meaningful. In particular, we have to show the following:

- $M3$ is indeed a module, i.e. the conditions concerning disjointness of predicates and conservativity are fulfilled.
- The semantics of $M3$ matches our intuition of the composition operation. Note that by 'semantics' we mean here $implement_{M3}(\mathcal{P})$, since $export_{M3}(\mathcal{P})$ is already given as $export_{M1}(\mathcal{P})$ and this is what we would expect.
- If $M1$ and $M2$ are correct, then $M3$ is also correct.

Lemma $M3$ as introduced above is a well-defined logic module.
Proof The disjointness and conservativity conditions are easily checked. □

Theorem

a) Let $M2$ be correct. Then, for all predicates p exported by $M1$ (so also by $M3$), all models $\mathcal{P}$ of Par, and ground terms $t_1, \ldots, t_n$

$$p(t_1, \ldots, t_n) \in implement_{M3}(\mathcal{P}) \Leftrightarrow p(t_1, \ldots, t_n) \in implement_{M1}(\mathcal{P})$$

b) $M1$ and $M2$ correct $\Rightarrow$ $M3$ correct.

Proof

a) First we show the direction from the right to the left. We need the following

Lemma

(1) $\forall p \in \Sigma_{par} p(t_1, \ldots, t_n) \in implement_{M1}(\mathcal{P})$

$$\Rightarrow p(t_1, \ldots, t_n) \in implement_{M3}(\mathcal{P})$$

(2) If $M2$ is correct, then for all p in Σ_{impl}

$$p(t_1, \ldots, t_n) \in implement_{M1}(\mathcal{P}) \Rightarrow h(p)(t_1, \ldots, t_n) \in implement_{M3}(\mathcal{P}).$$

Proof of the Lemma

(1) Follows from the facts that

$$p(t_1,\ldots,t_n) \in implement_{M1}(\mathcal{P}) \text{ implies } p(t_1,\ldots,t_n) \in \mathcal{P}$$

(by the conservativity conditions) and that $\mathcal{P}$ is part of $implement_{M3}(\mathcal{P})$.

(2) We know from $p(t_1,\ldots,t_n) \in implement_{M1}(\mathcal{P})$ that $p(t_1,\ldots,t_n) \in \mathcal{M}_{Impl}$ because of the conservativity conditions on $M1$. By definition of h follows $h(p)(t_1,\ldots,t_n) \in \mathcal{M}_{\mathcal{P}\cup Exp2}$, i.e. $h(p)(t_1,\ldots,t_n) \in export_{M2}(\mathcal{P})$. As $M2$ is correct, we conclude

$$h(p)(t_1,\ldots,t_n) \in implement_{M2}(\mathcal{P}) \subseteq implement_{M3}(\mathcal{P}).$$

□

Now we are able to prove our claim that for all $p \in \Sigma_{exp1}$, $p(t_1,\ldots,t_n) \in implement_{M1}(\mathcal{P})$ implies $p(t_1,\ldots,t_n) \in implement_{M3}(\mathcal{P})$. This is shown by proving

$$p(t_1,\ldots,t_n) \in \mathcal{I}_k(\mathcal{P} \cup Impl \cup Impleml) \Rightarrow implement_{M3}(\mathcal{P}) \models p(t_1,\ldots,t_n)$$

for all k using induction on k. Nothing must be shown for $k = 0$. Now let $p(t_1,\ldots,t_n) \in \mathcal{I}_{k+1}(\mathcal{P} \cup Impl \cup Impleml)$. If $p(t_1,\ldots,t_n) \in \mathcal{I}_k(\mathcal{P} \cup Impl \cup Impleml)$ then we are done by the induction hypothesis. Else there must be a ground instance $B\sigma \leftarrow B_1\sigma,\ldots,B_m\sigma$ of a program formula $B \leftarrow B_1,\ldots,B_m$ of $P \cup Impl \cup Impleml$ such that

$$p(t_1,\ldots,t_n) = B\sigma \text{ and } B_1\sigma,\ldots,B_m\sigma \in \mathcal{I}_k(\mathcal{P} \cup Impl \cup Impleml) \qquad (*)$$

We know that $B \leftarrow B_1,\ldots,B_m$ belongs to $Impleml$. Thus $B \leftarrow h(B_1),\ldots,h(B_m)$ belongs to $h(Impleml) \subseteq Implem3$ (with the reading $h(q) = q$ for $q \notin \Sigma_{impl}$). Using the induction hypothesis and the lemma above we may conclude from $(*)$ that $h(B_1\sigma),\ldots,h(B_m\sigma) \in implement_{M3}(\mathcal{P})$. It follows then that $p(t_1,\ldots,t_n) = h(B\sigma) = B\sigma \in implement_{M3}(\mathcal{P})$.

This completes the proof in one direction. The opposite direction is shown in an analogous way using the following

Lemma

(1) $\forall p \in \Sigma_{par} p(t_1,\ldots,t_n) \in implement_{M3}(\mathcal{P})$

$$\Rightarrow p(t_1,\ldots,t_n) \in implement_{M1}(\mathcal{P})$$

(2) If $M2$ is correct, then for all p in Σ_{impl}

$$h(p)(t_1,\ldots,t_n) \in implement_{M3}(\mathcal{P}) \Rightarrow p(t_1,\ldots t_n) \in implement_{M1}(\mathcal{P}).$$

b) For all exported predicates p and ground terms $t_1,\ldots,t_n$

$p(t_1,\ldots,t_n) \in export_{M3}(\mathcal{P}) \Leftrightarrow$ (by definition)
$p(t_1,\ldots,t_n) \in export_{M1}(\mathcal{P}) \Leftrightarrow$ ($M1$ is correct)
$p(t_1,\ldots,t_n) \in implement_{M1}(\mathcal{P}) \Leftrightarrow$ (by a))
$p(t_1,\ldots,t_n) \in implement_{M3}(\mathcal{P})$ □

5 Conclusion and future work

We have presented a theory of building modular logic systems. In our approach we restricted our attention to Horn logic because it is a fragment of predicate logic that is well understood, has efficient proof theory (*SLD*-resolution) and is broadly applied in praxis.

We gave a module concept with formal interfaces and discussed its semantics and correctness. Further we discussed how modular programs may be built out of single modules by gluing together their interfaces. The module operation of composition was introduced, and results concerning semantics and correctness were derived. The operations of union (for combining the export interfaces of modules) and actualization (for adapting the parameter parts of modules in order to allow their composition) have been studied in [3].

There remains though much to be done. A first point would be to extend the presented theory beyond *Horn logic*. This could be either done uniformly in all module parts (normal programs, arbitrary logic programs, many-sorted logic) or only in the module interfaces, i.e. the knowledge base would still consist of definite logic clauses but the interfaces would be first order theories. Indeed, this is the approach taken in the theory of algebraic modules (the implementation part uses initial semantics, whereas all models of interfaces are considered).

Another idea is to investigate more powerful implementation parts including negation and other impure features. We are working on a module concept with general logic programs (in the sense of [11]) based on *SLDNF*-resolution.

Finally, it appears interesting to investigate the significance of our approach to modularization of knowledge based systems, an issue that is currently gaining more and more attention.

References

[1] Antoniou G. Modules and Verification. In: Rattray R., Clark R.G. (eds) The Unified Computation Laboratory, Oxford University Press 1992

[2] Antoniou,G. & Sperschneider,V. On the Verification of Modules. CSL' 89, Springer LNCS, 1989

[3] Antoniou, G. & Sperschneider,V. A Horn-Logic Approach to Modular KBS. OSM Technical Report, Fachbereich 6, University of Osnabrueck 1991

[4] Blum, E.K., Ehrig, H. and Parisi-Presicce, F. Algebraic Specification of Modules and Their Basic Interconnections. JCSS 34, pp. 293-339, 1987

[5] Chan, Y. C. and Poterie, B. Modules in Prolog. British Standards Institution — IST/5/15 Prolog, Document PS/185, 1987

[6] Dietrich, R. A Preprocessor Based Module System for Prolog. In: Proc. TAPSOFT 89, 126-139, Springer LNCS, 1989

[7] Ehrig, H. and Mahr, B. Fundamentals of Algebraic Specification Vol. 2. Springer 1990

[8] Fey, W. Introduction to Algebraic Specification in ACT TWO. Bericht 86-13, FB 20, TU Berlin, 1986

[9] Hill, P.M. & Lloyd, J.W. The Goedel Report. TR-91-02, Computer Science Department, University of Bristol 1991

[10] Lindenberg, N. et al. KA-Prolog: Sprachdefinition. Interner Bericht 5/87 Universit Karlsruhe 1987

[11] Lloyd, J.W. Foundations of Logic Programming. 2. ed., Springer 1987

[12] Reif, W. A Logical Theory of Module Correctness. Dissertation, Fakultat fr Informatik, Universit Karlsruhe 1991

[13] Sperschneider, V. and Antoniou, G. Logic: A Foundation for Computer Science. Addison-Wesley 1991

[14] Sperschneider, V. Modularity and Verification in Logic Programming. Technical Report P 132, Dep. of Mathematics and Computer Science, University of Osnabrueck 1990

[15] Szeredi, P. Module Concepts for Prolog. In: Proc. Workshop on Prolog Programming Environments, Linkoping 1982, 69 - 80

SEL Compiler & Abstract Analyzers

Giancarlo Succi, Giuseppe A. Marino, Giancarlo Colla, Diego Cò, Sergio Novella, Amedeo Pata, Alexandro Regoli & Luca Viganò
DIST, Università di Genova
Genova, Italia

Abstract

This paper aims to evidence the potentialities of Prolog in the realization of a compiler and of some preprocessors for a subset equational language (SEL). Logic languages exhibit "implicit parallelism", which can be divided into "process parallelism" and "data parallelism". While most of the approaches are focussed on the former, in this paper we analyze the latter: we present the architecture and instruction set of a virtual machine (the SAM) which aims to exploit the data parallelism present in programs written in SEL and thus to speed up the execution of SEL on standard architectures and to be the starting point of a data parallel implementation. The general structure of the SAM resembles that of the WAM, apart from not needing unification capabilities. Specialized instructions have been adjoined in order to handle efficiently equational and subset assertions dealing with sets, and to point out their data parallelism. The implementation of SEL is very similar to that of Prolog, since it exploits an abstract machine (SAM) which is very similar to the WAM of Prolog. The paper also contains a description of the strategies adopted during the realizations of all the phases of the compilation and of the abstract analyzers.

1 Introduction

Logic languages define explicitly the logic of programs, leaving implicit the control, and therefore they seem quite suited for an implicit parallel implementation. It is possible to approach this problem in different ways, but researchers have been focusing mostly on "process parallelism". This form of parallelism identifies processes that may be executed in parallel and assign some of them to the available processors. *And-* , *Or-* and *Stream-* parallelism belong to this class. Our aim is to exploit another possible approach, i.e., the "data parallel" one. Its philosophy consists of identifying clusters of data on which to apply the same operation. Hence the main point is to develop a new logic language or to introduce a proper data structure tailored to obtain a high degree of data parallelism. SEL, a logic language based on set data structure, seems to be well suited for this purpose. The parallel implementation of this language needs both efficient standard compilation from the high level language into a machine instruction language and an abstract analysis that identifies the data parallelism in the source program. The best choice for these tasks seems to be Prolog.

2 SEL: Subset Equational Language

This section is a brief introduction to the SEL and to the data parallel approach to logic programming; this section can be skipped by those already inside these topics. SEL, the Subset Equational Language, was developed by Jayaraman et al. [JN88] at UNC/Chapel Hill and at SUNY/Buffalo. The main feature of this language is the set data structure, because lots of people have experience from very different fields in representing problems as relation between sets. A SEL program consists of two kinds of assertions:

- **equational assertion** of the kind $f(terms) = expr$.
  the function f is applied to the ground instances of *terms* and returns the ground instances of *expr*;
- **subset assertion** of the kind *f(terms) contains expr*.
  the set function f is applied to the ground instances of *terms* and returns a new subset that is generated by the join of the ground instances of *expr*.

Some examples of SEL programs can help to understand this approach.

```
square(X) = X.
squareSet({X|_}) contains {X*X}.
```

The first assertion computes the square of a given element, the second one computes the set of the squares of a given set. Some remarkable features are present in this simple situation, i.e., the *multiple matching* and the *collect_all assumption*.

- **multiple matching**: since no order is imposed over the elements of a set, a matching of the kind

  ```
  {X|_}
  ```

  produces the matching of X all over the elements of the argument set.
- **collect_all assumption**: which states that the result of set function calls is the union of all subsets obtained by all the subset assertions matching the ground terms with every possible matching.

A data parallel implementation of SEL on a SIMD architecture can perform this operation in just one shot. It is necessary that the argument set has already been distributed among the available processors of the parallel machine. This task is performed at compile-time by a Prolog abstract analyzer that identifies not only a shared base of the set elements, but also the life time of these objects during the program execution. Moreover, it is possible to identify the size of the object involved in the parallel execution in order to save a large amount of memory.
In the same way it behaves the cartesian product of two sets:

```
cartProd({X|_},{Y|_}) contains {[X,Y]}.
```

However, more complicate patterns may be executed, such as:

```
perms({}) = {[]}.
perms({x|t}) contains distr(x,perms(t)).
distr(x,{t|_}) contains {[x|t]}.
```

This assertion computes all possible permutations of the elements of the set. In order to obtain an efficient "data parallelism", it is necessary to generate all the sets matching the pattern in linear time and the application to all the sets of **distr**.

3 The SAM

In this chapter we will see the description of the abstract machine used in the implementation of SEL. As in Prolog, we can separate the execution of SEL programs into two different phases [JN88]:

- compilation, from SEL language to SAM assembler
- execution of the SAM code on the virtual SAM architecture

and these correspond to two different phases of the implementation:

- the development of a compiler targeted to the *abstract machine*
- the implementation of the abstract machine on the *real architecture*

The **SAM** belongs to the **WAM** [AK90] family, since its general structure resembles quite a lot that of the WAM; however it does not need full unification capabilities, therefore there is no need of the "trail" and faster **store** and **match** instructions replace the **unify** instructions. The SAM can be viewed as a sister of the SEL-WAM [Nai88] from which it inherits most of the implementation strategies, which are extended with environment trimming, table of constants and the capability of handling functors.

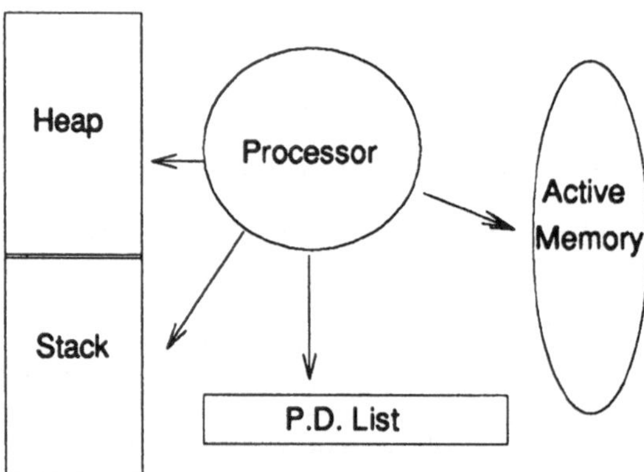

Figure 1: General Structure of the SAM

Figure 1 outlines the general structure of the SAM: in addition to the s-tandard 4 components -heap, stack, push-down list and processor- there is the

Active Memory,[1] *viz.* a memory whose cells both store data and perform computations. Its aim is to hold the sets so that data parallel operation can be executed on them.

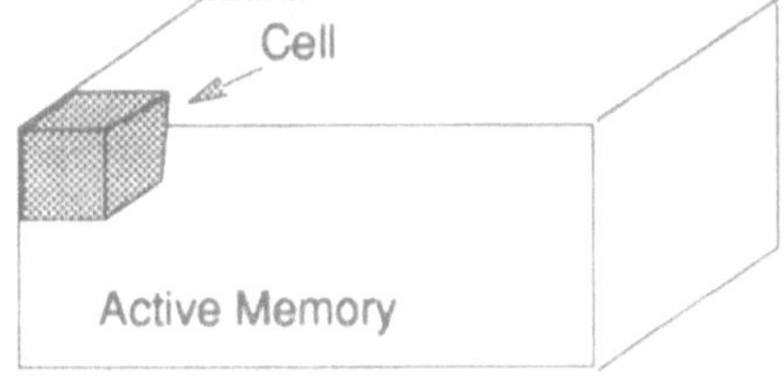

Figure 2: The Active Memory

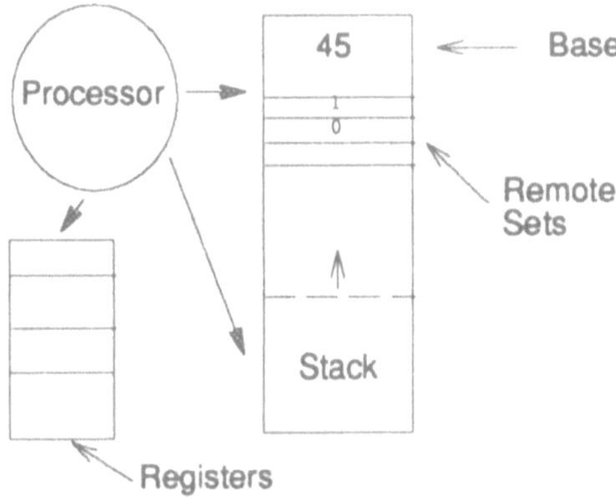

Figure 3: Structure of a Cell

Figures 2 and 3 detail the structure of the AM: it is a multidimensional array of cells where each cell is composed of three elements: a processor, a set of registers and memory. The memory is organized into two parts: a stack, for performing local computations, and a region for keeping set elements, which are stored using *basing* techniques: when there are some sets differing from one-another only by a few elements, it may be useful to store in the processing memory a superset of all of them, the *base*, and to represent each of the original sets (called *remote sets*) with a bit-vector (a 1 in its i-th position means that the i-th element of the base belongs to the remote set, and a 0 that it does not).

The SAM takes advantage of three main situations to exploit the data parallelism of problems, *viz.* when there are *mappings* of one set into another, when there are *filters* applied to a set, and when there are *foldings* of a set in a single element. When there is a map of one set into another, for instance in the set theoretic definition:

$$set2 = f(x) : x \in set1$$

[1] Form here it will be referred to as AM.

it is possible to compute **set2** in one shot applying **f** to all the elements of **set1** in parallel, as shown in figure 4.
Likewise if there is a filter like:

$$remote2 = x : x \in remote1, p(x)$$

remote2 can be computed in constant time (see Figure 5). Foldings are definitions of the kind:

$$f(\{\}) = k.$$
$$f(\{x|t\}) = z(x,f(t)).$$

Here it is possible to perform a tree-like computation in order to determine the result, as shown in figure 6, where **z** is applied to **a** and **b**, to **c** and **d**, to **e** and **f**, to **g** and **h** and to **i** and **l** at once, and then to each pair of results, and so on, until there is only one element left. Note that this class of operations is not deterministic, since no order is imposed on the elements of sets, e.g., the (pseudo) function **nonDet**:

$$nonDet(\{\}) = 0.$$
$$nonDet(\{x|t\}) = minus(x,nonDet(t)).$$

applied to the set {1,2,3} can give 0, 2 or 4 as result, depending on which matching we choose, as shown in figure 5. However [MS89] demonstrated that if the folding function is commutative and associative the result is the same no matter of the matching; hence since **plus** is both associative and commutative, the result of applying **det**:

$$det(\{\}) = 0.$$
$$det(\{x|t\}) = plus(x,det(t)).$$

to {1,2,3} is always 6.

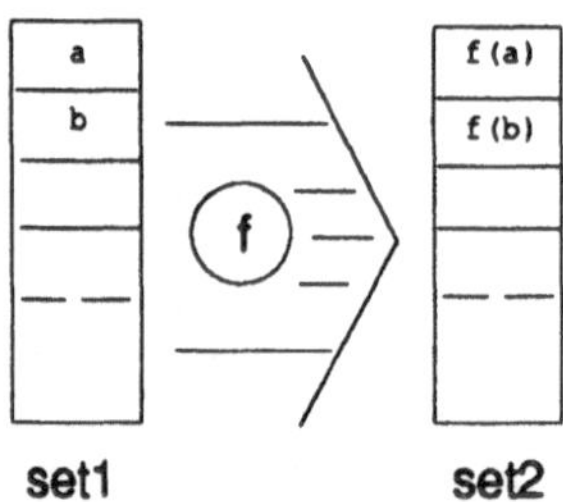

Figure 4: **set2** is obtained mapping **set1** through **f**

3.1 Data Objects

The types of data objects handled by the SAM are: atoms, integers, variables, boolean values, lists and sets. In the SEL language every term is represented by a word containing a value and a tag. The representation of lists or sets is obtained with a sequence of tagged pointer pairs, for the *head* and *tail* of them.

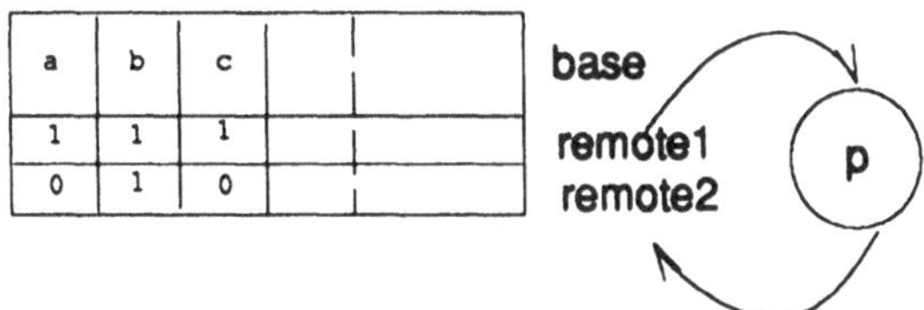

Figure 5: `remote2` is computed filtering `remote1` with `p`

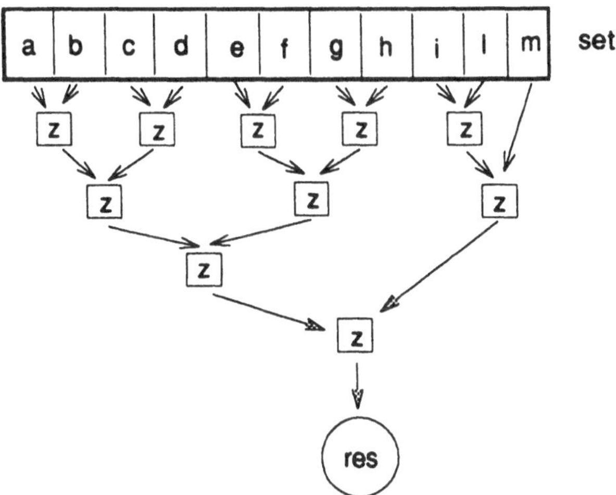

Figure 6: The `result` is determined `folding` `set` with `z`

3.2 Data Areas

The code area, the Stack and the Heap, are the main data areas and hold all the compiled code.

- **Stack** is used to store, in an appropriate environment, all permanent variables associated with a clause. It is possible also to have a continuation performed by a *continuation code pointer* and a *continuation environment pointer*. For instance, when there are multiple subset rules, a choice point is created. It contains all information necessary to restore an earlier state of computation. This information consists of: pointer to the other subset rule or the branch pointers *B1...Bm*, all argument registers *A1...An*, the continuation program pointer *CP*, the current environment pointer *CE*, the last choice point *LCP* and the mode register *M*.

- **Heap** is used to store all structured objects. Anyway, when the structures are created on the Heap, they are not retracted like in the case of the Prolog WAM.

3.3 Registers

The registers used during an execution of a SEL program to store the current state are:

- **P** program pointer (to the code area)
- **CP** continuation pointer (to the code area)
- **CE** current environment (on the local stack)
- **LCP** last choice point (on the local stack)
- **H** top of heap
- **S** structure pointer (to the heap)
- **CB** current branch point register
- **M** mode register
- **A1,A2,...An** argument registers
- **X1,X2,...Xn** temporary registers
- **B1,B2,...Bn** branch pointers (to the code area)

As in the WAM, the A registers and X registers are identical, but they are used for different purposes: the first to pass the arguments of a function call, the others to hold the value of temporary variables.

3.4 SAM Instruction Set

SEL programs are compiled into instructions for an abstract machine (the SAM) similar to the WAM for Prolog. In general, each SEL symbol corresponds to one instruction. The entire instruction set can be divided into a number of classes. We describe compilation of SEL programs by describing each class of instructions.

- The **get** instructions correspond to the terms in the head of a rule, and are responsible for matching the rule against the argument of the function call, which are in the **A registers**.
- The **store_indirect** instructions are used to return the result of the function call, and are generated for the last argument of a function.
- The **match** instructions are used to match arguments of lists or sets in the head of a rule.
- The **put** instructions are used to load the registers with the arguments before a function call is made.
- The **store** instructions are used to load arguments of lists and sets.
- The **procedural** instructions are used for control transfer, function invocation and environment allocation. They are:

- The **allocate** instruction appears at the beginning of any equality rule that has two function calls in its body (in its flattened form - see section 4), or any subset rule that has one function call.
- The **execute** instruction is used to call the last function in the body of any equality rule.
- The **proceed** instruction ends an equality rule with no function calls in its body. All functions in the body of a subset rule and all functions in an equality rule except the last one are invoked with a **call** instruction.
- The **save_choice_point?** instruction appears after the head and before the body of each subset rule.

- The **indexing** instructions are used to index among the definitions for one function.
  - The **try_equ_else** instruction appears before every equality rule which has another equality rule, with the same type of first argument, following it.
  - The **try_sub_and** instruction precedes the definition of every rule which has a subset rule, with the same type of first and the subset rules after. In both cases the argument is the code pointer for the next rule.
  - The **switch_on_ground_term Lc,Ll,Ls** is used to do clause indexing. This instruction appears at the beginning of any function that is defined with multiple rules having different first argument. **Lc** , **Ll** , **Ls** are the addresses of the definitions which have a constant, a list or a set as their first argument respectively.

- The **mapping** instructions are used to manage the operations which iterate over the elements of a set having the shape of generating a new set whose elements are functions of the elements of the original one; these mappings can be divided in three categories, depending on the space they need to perform the matching process (which is a multiple matching):
  - **Constant space**
  - **Quadratic space**
  - **Linear space**

- The **insert** instructions have a critical role for performing mappings and filters since they can act in parallel on all the AM cells of a set.

4 Implementing SEL Compiler

The first step of the compilation is flattening all expressions of the program. Flattening corresponds to transforming an expression into its *disembodied form*, a sequence of variable assignments only of the form **Xi = f(Xi1,...,Xin)**, to reflect leftmost innermost reduction order. For example, flattening:

```
append([],Y) = Y.
append([H|T],Y) = [H|append(T,Y)].

permutations({}) = {[]}.
permutations({X|T}) contains distr(X,permutations(T)).
distr(X,{Y|_}) contains {[X|Y]}.
```

produces:

```
append([],Y) = Y.
append([H|T],Y) = [H|T1] :- append(T,Y) = T1.

permutations({}) = {[]}.
permutations({X|T}) contains V1 :-
            permutations(T) contains V2, distr(X, V2) = V1.
```

and flattening

```
f(X) = g(h(i(X))).
```

becomes

```
f(X) = Z :- i(X) = W, h(W) = Y, g(Y) = Z.
```

In the description that follows, we assume that we are dealing with a flattened SEL program. From the description of SEL it suffices that, in order to generate a SAM assembler code, we need recognize only two SEL assertions:

- **equational assertion**: in the form *head :- body.*
- **subset assertion**: in the form *head contains body.*

And, for any assertion, we must recognize only a few SEL patterns:

- **atom**: a string beginning with a low-case character or anything within *'anything'*.
- **variable**: a string beginning with an upper-case character or with the character '_'.
- **functor**: in the form of: *identifier(X1,X2,...)* where X's may be variables or atoms.
- **list**: in the form of:

  ```
  [ H | T ]
  [ H | _ ]
  [ H | [ ]]
  ```

  where H and T may be variables, atoms or functors.
- **set**: in the form of:

```
{ H | T }
{ H | _ }
{ H | { }}
```

where H and T may be variables, atoms or functors.

Therefore the resulting Prolog program that can parse a SEL program is very simple. It involvs only three logical modules:

- **Flattener**: that generates, by reading the SEL program, a SEL flattened program.
- **Reader**: that reads the SEL flattened program with the predefined prolog predicate **read** and gives its output to next module.
- **Prolog Grammar**: that scans the result produced by the Reader and generates the parse-tree corresponding to the SEL flattened program.

As we have just said, in general each SEL symbol corresponds to a SAM assembler instruction. Then, after arriving at a leaf of the parsing tree generated by the grammar, we can immediately generate the SAM assembler instruction corresponding to the Token recognized.

4.1 A Little Example

Now, as a further explanation of concepts just expressed, is presented the SAM compilation of a little fragment of SEL program:

```
[ H | T ]
```

It is assumed to be the body of an equational assertion, for example:

```
function( H, T) = [ H | T ].
```

After the action of the Reader the fragment of Prolog Grammar that analyzes the pattern list is the following:

```
                                .
                                .
body_list(A,F)          --> b_open_sq(A,B),
                            b_head(B,C),
                            b_tail(C,D),
                            b_close_sq(E,F).
                                .
                                .
b_open_sq([A|B],B)      --> {A = '[',
                            gen_cod(store_ind_list(Ai))}.
                                .
                                .
b_head(A,C)             --> atomo(A,B),
                            is_mid(B,C),
                            {gen_cod(store_value(A))}.
```

```
                        .
                        .
b_tail(A,B)       --> atomo(A,B),
                      {gen_cod(store_value(A))}.
                        .
                        .
b_close_sq([A|B],B) --> {A = ']'}.
                        .
                        .
is_mid([A|B],B)   --> {A = '|'}.
                        .
                        .
atomo([A|B],B)    --> {atomic(A)}.
                        .
```

The predicate **gen_cod/1** simply writes on the output file the SAM assembler instruction corresponding to its argument.

In our example, SAM assembler code produced is:

```
STORE_IND_VALUE Ai
STORE_VALUE Vi
STORE_VALUE Vj
```

where **Ai** is the Argument register in which the result has to be returned, **Vi** and **Vj** are two temporary registers into which atoms **h** and **t** were previously loaded.

4.2 Using Prolog: Reasons and Gains

The reasons for the choice of Prolog to create a compiler for Subset-Equational programs are substantially these:

- Using **DCG Prolog Grammars** makes the generation of the parsing trees of a program very easy. In fact, to obtain an efficient and clear parser, we have only to specify, using Prolog formalism, the complete SEL language grammar. Furthermore, as subproducts (almost free of charge) of parsing tree generation, we can obtain:
  - *Consistency Checking*: a SEL program, which satisfies the grammar, is sure to be syntactically correct.
  - *Type Checking*: during parsing it is easy to verify Type Consistency of program's rules.
  - *Error Management*: during parsing it is also always possible to find out errors and to give some useful diagnostic informations to the users.
- **SAM code generation** can be bound to the leaves of the parsing tree as *Semantic Actions* during the expansion of the tree itself.
- **Compiler Maintenance** will be easier than using any imperative language. Future changes in the Semantics of SEL language will involve only few modifications to the parser written in Prolog (*e.g.* some Prolog clauses will be added and others will be deleted).

5 Abstract Analyzers

Abstract analyzers play an important role in the construction of an efficient implementation of a logic language. Their goal is to evidence relevant properties of the program, simply throughout its analysis and not its execution. With the help of these informations, the compiler will then be able to write a fast and concise code. The abstract analyzers discussed in this article are very relevant both for the sequential implementation and the parallel implementation on the SAM. The goals of our analyzers are:

- **Persistency Analysis**, that is composed of:
  - Shared Bases Analysis
  - Shared Structures Analysis
  - Destructive Update Analysis
- **Object Size Analysis**

6 Persistency Analyses

Persistency analysis should offer a measurement of the lifetime of objects at compile-time. This problem is undecidable, and therefore we will focus our discussions on approximations through estimations, knowing that it is important not to underestimate the lifetime of objects, i.e. the analyses must always find all allocated objects. These analyses allow us to save process memory space, which is very relevant. Therefore our approach is highly set-oriented. We can distinguish three different kinds of analyses:

- **Shared Bases Analysis**, which allows us to adopt a common base in order to represent remote sets;
- **Shared Structures Analysis**, which allows us to find which objects can be shared among different structures;
- **Destructive Update Analysis**, which allows us to identify the possibility of destructing and simultaneously updating a set, instead of constructing and allocating a new one.

6.1 Shared Bases Analysis

The goal is to find out which are the bases that are needed by a program, in order to be then able to determine which sets can share these bases. This analysis consists of three different phases:

a. Set-Flattening

b. Graph-Representation of connected components

c. Analysis of graph-connectivity

The first step consists of performing a flattening of the clauses, this means, as was seen before, that the clauses must be rewritten to a flattened form which contains only ground terms and variables. Every non-ground term is to be substituted by a variable, which will then be unified to the non-ground term, and added to the body of the clause. E.g.:

```
set_cancel([{a}|T]) = [a|set_cancel(T)]
```

becomes (in a flattened form):

```
set_cancel(Z) = Y :-  Z = [{a}|T], Y = [a|set_cancel(T)]
```

The second step consists of performing a set-flattening, i.e. the flattened clauses are rewritten in a set-flattened form which doesn't explicitly contain sets. The clause set_cancel will therefore become (in a set-flattened form):

```
set_cancel(Z) = Y :-  Z = [W|T], W = {a},
                      Y = [a|set_cancel(T)]
```

It is relevant to remark that even nested sets have to be set-flattened;e.g.: an expression like g({{a}|T},N) is transformed to g(W,N), and the equalities W = {Z|T}, Z = {a} are added to the body of the clause. The final result of both flattening and set-flattening is to have all the non-ground terms and all the explicit sets handled by the clause at term-depth 1. Having obtained the set-flattened form of the clause, it is very simple to detect all the sets contained in the clause itself, as we just need to scan the body. Each set explicitly encountered in the body is associated to a node of the graph, and an arc will connect each couple of nodes sharing an element or a subset. The analysis of all the clauses will hence permit the construction of a graph corresponding to the SEL program. The graph is not totally connected, but it is formed by several groups of connected nodes, each node standing for an explicit set. We will associate a different base to each single group of nodes. Therefore each single set of a particular group will be represented on the corresponding shared base at compile-time. Since Prolog doesn't explicitly permit the management of graphs, we have represented the graph with the help of a list, whose single elements correspond to different nodes. In our program, however, we have chosen not to consider the arcs between nodes, but just to detect and represent which nodes are connected to which. Therefore we have adopted as a structure a list of lists, where each sub-list represents a set of connected nodes which are likely to share the same base.
Example :

functors = [g/1].
f({x|_},{y|_},{z|_}) contains {x|{y|{g(z)}}}.

```
Graph Structure :   [[W1,W2,W4,W5,W6],[W3]]
ConnectedComps :   [[W1 = {x|_}, W2 = {y|_}, W4 = {x|W5},
      W5 = {y|W6}, W6 = {g(z)}],[W3 = {z|_}]]
Out = [SuperBase1:[W1 = {x|_}, W2 = {y|_}, W4 = {x|W5},
      W5 = {y|W6}, W6 = {g(z)}],SuperBase2:[W3 = {z|_}]].
```

6.2 Shared Structures Analysis

The active memory of the SAM is strictly limited. The structure of the SAM, whose standard part derives from the WAM, identifies therefore the sets of sets as a target of the shared structure. Aiming to save memory space, we should analyze if and when some sets can be shared on multiple sets, thus allowing them to adopt the same (and shared) structure. As outlined before, this problem is undecidable, but we can implement and utilize an algorithm that will always overestimate the sharingness of a SEL variable, thus possibly inducing us to consider a non-shared variable as "shared". Anyway we can say that the algorithm will never fail, i.e. a shared variable will always be marked as "shared", and never as "non-shared".

The algorithm is very general: it can be applied to any shared structure, and not simply to sets. The strategy is to verify if an object may depend on the result: we analyze the flow of every object of the clause. The algorithm will produce an output consisting of two lists: one list contains the shared objects, the other the non-shared ones. We are forced to handle the non-shared objects, in order to prevent infinite computations. This approach increases the speed of the algorithm, and, most of all, it does not negatively affect the successful result of computation: if an argument is non-shared, the correspondent branch of the computation will be cut, thus leading to the same result. Recursive calls must be handled very carefully, as they are likely to produce infinite loops. To prevent them, a table of the active computations is used, which allows us to test the arguments currently under analysis. This abstract analysis always comes to an end, since the number of clauses of a SEL program is always finite. The results collected in this analysis will serve as input of the DUA.

6.3 Destructive Update Analysis

In this analysis we examine the problem of the destructive update of the data structures. This requirement is again imposed by the bonds of the active memory of the SAM: we need to determine where and when it is possible to make the destructive update of a certain object. The strategy used is, like in the SSA, very general, but we specially concentrate our efforts on sets. The algorithm begins by analyzing each clause by itself, and it marks (on the base of some given rules) the objects that can be considered as potentially destructable. The recursive calls are treated as in the SSA. The management of the branch-points must be very careful: in multiple assertions, the same objects may be reused in successive backtrackings and a destructive update on these objects would be very harmful. The final output will provide a list of all the objects that may be destructively updated, in a safe and concise manner.// This is a very difficult problem: we are presently working on a rough implementation of this algorithm.

7 Object Size Analysis

Assuming an execution on a parallel machine, we need to know the dimensions of the objects of the program, in order to properly allocate the sets at compile-time. In this analysis these dimensions have been expressed as functions of the

input sizes. This problem is again undecidable, and therefore we look again for a size-approximation through an algorithm based on statistics. This algorithm has been developed by Debray, Lin and Hermenegildo [DLH90], and it works on relational Prolog-like languages. We first analyze the equational assertions and then the subset assertions. The algorithm begins by set-flattening all the assertions of the SEL program, as in the SBA. We use this set-flattened form to build the Data Dependency Graph (DDG) that highlights the program control flow. We can obtain the dimension relations between the program objects by analyzing the DDG. From these relations we must resume some closed formulae (i.e.: difference equations) for size computation. We can distinguish two cases for the construction of these difference equations: non-recursive clauses need only a standard analysis, whereas recursive clauses need a formula normalization.
The results obtained by the equational assertions analysis will be utilized in the subset assertions analysis. There are again two different situations: multiple subset assertions with the same left-hand side, and implicit iterations on the arguments of a set. With the help of two different algorithms, we will be able to produce two approximations of the results dimensions.

8 Conclusions, Related Work, Future Trends

In this paper we have described a new abstract machine for the execution of subset logic languages, the SAM. Its aims are to speed up the execution of SEL on standard architectures and to be the starting point of a data parallel implementation.
Presently we have almost completed the SAM implementation on a RISC Sun4 architecture, and we are in the process of developing a prototypic version of it on the Connection Machine. The first performance figures that we have obtained from the Sun implementation are encouraging both in absolute terms and in comparison with the SEL-WAM.
In the meanwhile we are building the basis for the forthcoming development of a debugger, and we are presently working on the realization of a graphical programming environment, capable of been transported to different systems.

References

[AK90] H. Aït-Kaci. *The WAM: A (Real) Tutorial.* Digital - Paris Research Laboratory, January 1990.

[DLH90] S. K. Debray, N. W. Lin, and M. Hermenegildo. Task Granularity Analysis in Logic Programs. In *ACM SIGPLAN 90*, pages 174–188, 1990.

[JN88] B. Jayaraman and A. Nair. Subset-Logic Programming: Application and Implementation. In *5th International Logic Programming Conference*, Seattle, August 1988.

[MS89] J. Marino and G. Succi. Data Structure for the Parallel Execution of Functional Languages. In G. Gries and J. Hartmanis, editors, *PARLE '89*, pages 346–356. Springer-Verlag, June 1989.

[Nai88] A. Nair. Compilation of Subset-Logic Programs, December 1988. University of North Carolina at Chapel Hill – Master Thesis.

Disciplined Exceptions in Logic Programming

Timothy K. Shih, Ruth E. Davis, and Fuyau Lin
Dept. of Computer Engineering, Santa Clara University
Santa Clara, CA 95053
U.S.A.
email: TSHIH@SCU.BITNET

Abstract

This paper [1] presents a disciplined exception mechanism to cope with program failure and a continuation mechanism for labels and jumps. We separate error detection from error handling. The discussion includes exception signals, handlers, and exception continuations for logic programs. Short examples illustrate the difficulty of recovering from error conditions in logic programs using traditional control constructs, and show how easily they can be handled using our approach.

1 Introduction

An exception occurs when some condition prevents a program from proceeding in the normal manner. When an exception is raised, an exception handler is invoked (which may involve some recovery mechanism or simply the display of an error message), and the computation proceeds from some continuation. Exceptions in a Lisp program can be dealt with by using the `catch` and the `throw` primitives so that whenever a throw form is evaluated (as an exception occurs), the value of its second argument (as the raised signal) immediately becomes the value of the surrounding `catch` with a matching identifier. The computation proceeds from the surrounding `catch` form (as the exception continuation). Similarly, an exception in a C program can be dealt with by using the `setjmp` and the `longjmp` UNIX system calls such that `setjump` provides the exception continuation and `longjump` raises the exception. Exceptions are called *conditions* in PL/I. An exception handler is declared by a `ON` statement and an exception is raised explicitly by a `SIGNAL` statement. Unless otherwise specified by the handler, after the handler is called, control will return to the point that issues the signal. In Ada, an exception is raised by a `raise` statement. A handler for each exception can be defined in a program unit within which an exception might be raised. When an exception is raised, the handler is executed followed by the termination of the program unit. If the currently executing unit does not provide a handler, the exception is propagated to the dynamically enclosing unit. In CLU, an exception can be raised by a procedure through a `signal` instruction. When an exception is raised, the procedure returns to its immediate caller, which is responsible for providing a handler for

[1] The work was supported by the University IBM Research Award Grant No. 5-28618 at Santa Clara University.

the exception. Other exception handling facilities have been provided by Bliss and ML. Some Prolog interpreters provide `catch/2` and `throw/0` predicates that support limited exception handling. In this paper, we discuss a systematic exception handling mechanism including predicates for exception signals, exception handlers, and exception continuations that specify where to continue the computation after the exception. Exception continuations discussed in this paper include retrying, resumption, termination, and alternation.

The execution of a terminating Prolog goal consists of a finite sequence of deduction steps. Each step selects a subgoal and either rewrites the subgoal or fails. The rest of the execution continues in a similar manner until the empty goal list is deduced or the original goal fails. A continuation in the language Scheme [6, 1, 16] is a function that represents the remainder of a program. A continuation can be created at a given time, assigned to a variable, returned as a result, and invoked at another program execution point. Algorithms and semantics for the implementation of continuation objects in Scheme are developed in [6, 16]. Continuations are used in developing formal semantics of programming languages as well as some applications such as program exception handling, backtracking, coroutine mechanisms, and unrestricted branching mechanisms.

We need a representation of the continuation object that will keep track of *what's happened so far* and *what remains to be done* in a deduction. This representation can be asserted to the global database of Prolog or passed between two predicates so that logic programs can manipulate continuations. We use this deduction status representation to provide labels and jumps in logic programs.

We discuss the representation of continuation objects in the next section. Predicates for creating labels and performing jumps are discussed in section three. Section four deals with the implementation of the exception handling mechanism. We discuss some examples using continuations in section five. Section six gives a summary and some possible extensions.

2 Representation of Deduction Status

A continuation can be described as the necessary information to save the state of a deduction. If we can keep all information in the previous deduction steps, after a suspension, we can go back to continue the suspended deduction. One way of implementing a continuation in Prolog is to give the continuation a name and to assert it in a global table. This operation associates a continuation with a name so that it can be saved and invoked at a later execution point. Before we define the representation of the *continuation object*, some terminology and data structures used in our implementation are presented.

For a predicate consisting of n clauses, the *clause selection pattern* (`CSPAT`) of the calling subgoal is an *n-tuple* where each item in the *n-tuple* is either "0" (available for selection) or "1" (clause has been selected or head does not unify with call). The *ancestor goal list* (`AGL`) at a deduction point is a list of 4-tuples that represents the path from the root to the current deduction point in the search tree. Each 4-tuple represents information about a deduction step on the search path, the top 4-tuple represents only partial information about the current deduction step (as the `MGU` and `CSPAT` are instantiated after a choice of clause to use has been made). A 4-tuple consists of:

```
<GL, IDX, CSPAT, MGU>
```

where **GL** is the goal list of the deduction step, **IDX** is the index of the selected subgoal in **GL**, **CSPAT** is the clause selection pattern of the clauses for the selected subgoal in **GL**, and **MGU** is the most general unifier of the selected subgoal in **GL** and head of the clause selected. Each 4-tuple describes a choice on the path from the current deduction step back to the root of the search tree. The ancestor goal list describes a deduction status. The *continue point* of a deduction step is the time point after a subgoal is selected and before the clause selection process begins. The representation of a *continuation object* in our meta-level interpreter is a pair:

```
<DVT, AGL>
```

where **DVT** is the *delay variable table*, and **AGL** is the *ancestor goal list*. The delay variable table **DVT** is used to keep information needed in the implementation of *delay* subgoals that are provided in the system (but are beyond the scope of this paper).

The ancestor goal list is a sequence of deduction steps that are treated as non-separable primitive operations. A program can continue from the continue point of any deduction step in the sequence, but not from any other time point within a deduction step (e.g. the middle of a unification process). Since the continue point is the time point after a subgoal is selected and before the clause is selected, the **MGU** of the first 4-tuple in the **AGL** of a continuation object is always undefined. Note that, by default, when a subgoal is first selected, its clause selection pattern consists entirely of zeros (none of the clauses has been tried). When a continuation is saved, the clause selection pattern in the top 4-tuple of the ancestor goal list may contain `0`'s and `1`'s.

3 Labels and Jumps

In this section, three continuation primitives are introduced. The predicate `assert_continuation(C)` has the following operational semantics: The subgoal succeeds immediately with the side effect of binding a unique label to C, and asserting a system fact

```
continuation_object(C, <DVT, AGL>)
```

which associates the current continuation with the given label. If two continuations are asserted with the same label, the second assertion will override the first. This assertion is different from the one of `assert/1` in that a continuation database is separated from the regular Prolog program database altered by `assert/1` or `retract/1`.

The predicate `call_continuation(C)` has the following operational semantics: If a continuation object associated with the label `C` is not defined, the calling subgoal fails. Otherwise, the current deduction process is aborted, and the deduction process associated with label `C` is invoked.

Using the above two primitives, a deduction point in the search space can be saved, and a control transfer that allows a jump from the current deduction point to a previously saved deduction point is possible. In order to undo the side effect made by predicate **assert_continuation(C)**, the third predicate **retract_continuation(C)** is also provided. The implementation will simply retract the continuation object asserted.

3.1 Why Continuation Jumps

Most programs containing unrestricted branching statements to create loops can be rewritten by using structured looping statements such as the *while do*, *repeat until*, and *for* constructs. This is true in procedural programming language which allows programmers take explicit control of their program continuations (i.e. as non-multitasking languages are deterministic and the execution sequences of programs are manipulated directly by the programmer). Without using unrestricted branching statements, the programmers are forced to use structured looping statements. Hence a structural program is easier to understand and maintain. However, the flexibility of control is reduced.

Prolog is one of the most popular logic languages for artificial intelligence programming. In the development of expert systems, information can be provided by the user through an interactive process. Some implementations of expert systems may assert facts provided by the user; these facts and part of the previous search space may need to be searched again to find possible solutions to a query. If the previous search space is large, and the expert system engineer knows that only a small portion of the search space may contain new solutions, it is desired to re-search only that small portion of space. If the implementation language is Prolog, there is no easy way for the engineer to resume a portion of previously searched space. However, using our continuation jump mechanism, this is possible, as illustrated in the next section.

3.2 An Example

We consider a sample program shown in the Logic Program Listing window of figure 1. Figure 1 also shows a sample section of a logic programming environment [25, 9, 10]. The search space for this program is shown in figure 2.

Since **goal(X)** is the only subgoal at point 0, it is selected. Clause 1 of predicate **goal** is selected, and **goal(X)** is rewritten to the new goal at point 1. The original goal **goal(X)** in the ancestor goal list of point 1 with the clause select pattern **[1,0,0]** indicating the first clause of predicate **goal** has been selected. Thus the first clause of predicate **goal** can not be selected again while backtracking. Note that at each step, the clause select pattern applies to the selected subgoal. The new goal at point 1 is to be solved. Suppose the subgoal **test1** is selected at this time, the only clause of predicate **test1** is used. Predicate **test1** succeeds and a new goal is shown at point 2. At point 2, the current continuation is asserted with a unique name **cont1**. The assertion succeeds immediately. When **cont1** is invoked later, the deduction continues from point 2.

At point 3, since clause **exist1** (which is a dynamic predicate) is undefined, the subgoal **exist1(X)** fails. The backtrack selector is called and **goal(X)** at point 0 is retried. The second clause of predicate **goal** is attempted since the clause select pattern for **goal(X)** in the ancestor goal list is **[1,0,0]**. The

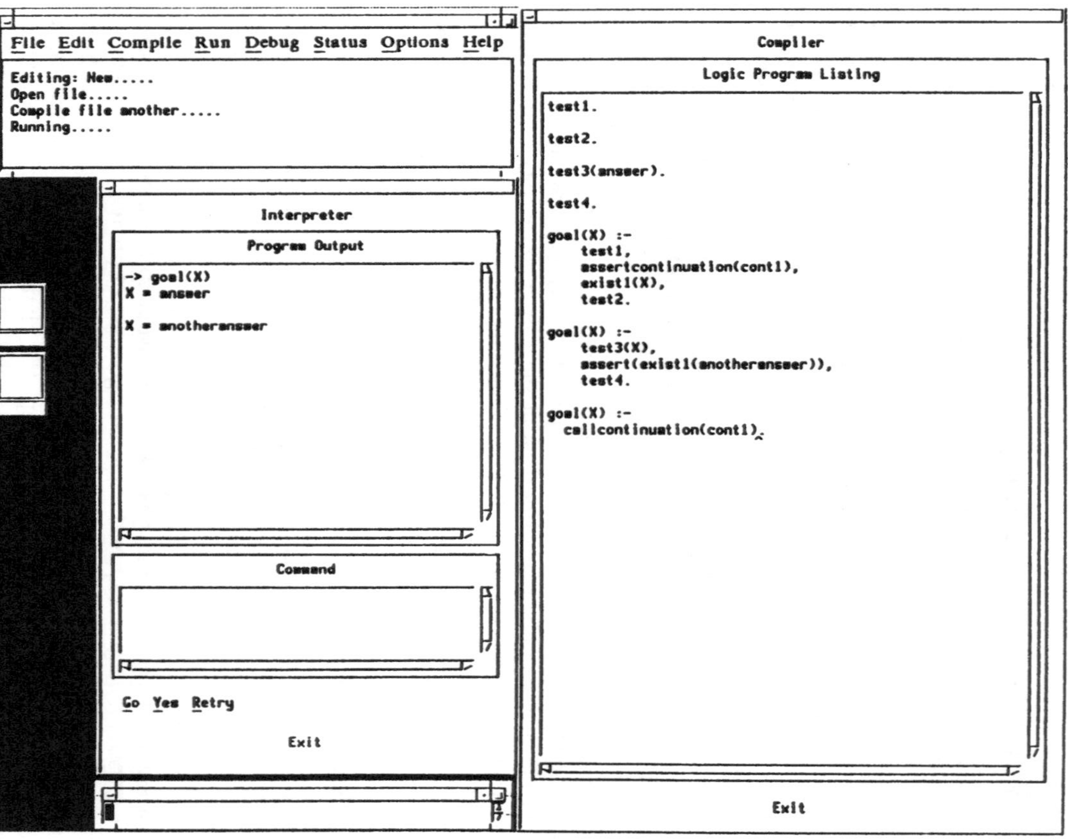

Figure 1 A sample program with a continuation jump

interpreter finds the first answer **answer** at point 6. A retry command (a ";" followed by a return) is provided by the user, so the interpreter seeks for possible alternative solutions.

A **call_continuation** is invoked at point 7 with the continuation **cont1**. This call aborts the current deduction. The deduction continues from **cont1**. A transfer is made from point 7 to point 2. Since **exist1/1** was asserted at point 5, the second answer of **goal(X)** is found at point 8.

Using label and jump, point 2 and point 3 are re-searched directly. Suppose, in another similar program, there are a large number of rewriting steps inbetween point 1 and point 2, but those steps do not affect finding the solution at point 8. It is difficult, or even impossible to use traditional Prolog constructs to skip the redundent search space in between point 1 and point 2. Perhaps, a call to **goal(X)** can be added some where in the program. But that will introduce even more redundent search.

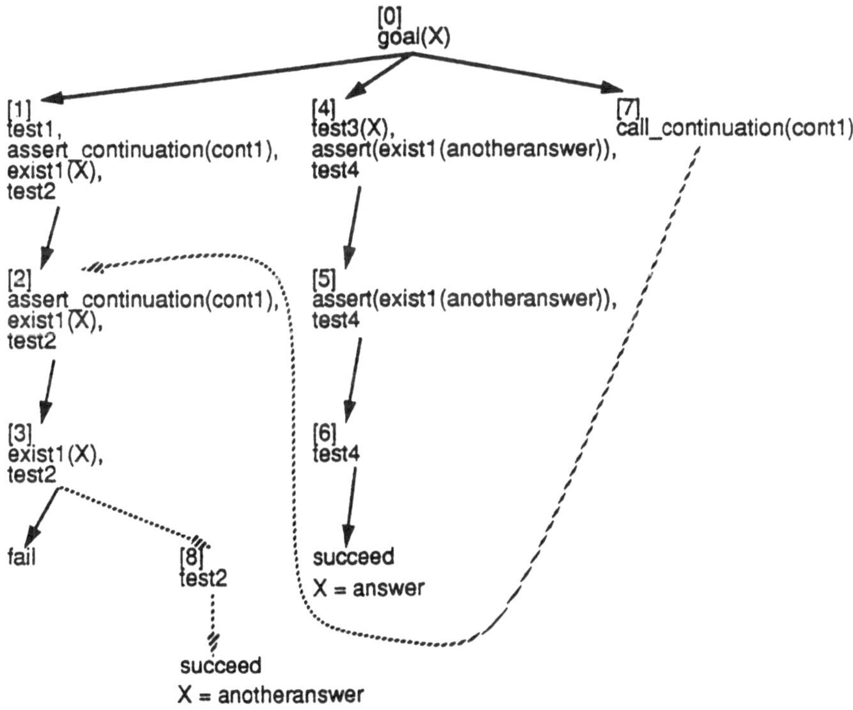

Figure 2 Search space of the sample program in figure 1

4 Implementation Model for Exception

Many implementations of exception mechanisms have been proposed [14, 23, 15, 29, 30]. In a typical Prolog system, on an error condition, a system predicate prints an error message and fails, aborts the computation, or leaves one in the debugger. We want to make it possible to trap undesired events and to specify suitable responses to such events. In this way, the behaviour of the system becomes more predictable even in anomalous situations.

We propose a facility to separate the exception handling from the algorithm. The exception handling mechanism is implemented in an interpreter using continuation subgoals and the appropriate calling sequence to the exception handler. For simplicity, we only consider software detectable exceptions. That is, the hardware failures or operating system environment failures are not considered in the discussion. For an exception handling mechanism, we need to consider:

- How is an exception raised?
- How is an exception handled?
- Where do we proceed after an exception is handled?

In our specification language, the user is asked to provide information for these actions through an exception signal, an exception handler, and an exception continuation. The syntax of the signal, handler, and continuation is as follows:

- Signal:

```
exception_raise(Etype, <Arg_list>),
exception_resume(Etype, <Arg_list>), or
exception_abort(Etype, <Arg_list>)
```

- Handler:

```
exception_handler(Etype, <Arg_list>) :-
  handler_body.
exception_handler(Etype, <Arg_list>) :-
  .....
```

- Continuation:

```
exception_continue(Etype), or
exception_skip(Etype)
```

where **Etype** can be bound to any atom denoting the unique name of the exception, **<Arg_list>** is an argument list of zero or more arguments to be passed to a handler. The handler consists of one or more handler clauses. An exception handler will only be invoked when the exception it handles is raised, it can not be invoked directly by an ordinary subgoal call.

Exception signals are explicitly specified by the user to raise the exception. When the exception signal is raised by **exception_raise**, the handler is called, and then computation continues from a previously defined exception continuation. Error messages and/or recovery actions are defined in the handler clause body. If the call to a handler succeeds and an exception continuation is defined, the computation continues from the exception continuation (e.g. defined by **exception_continue** or **exception_skip**). If the call fails, the system prints a message indicating the inadequate control of an exception, and the computation is aborted. The two exception continuation subgoals (i.e. **exception_continue** and **exception_skip**) are special subgoals explicitly provided by the user in his/her program. The subgoal succeeds immediately, and it defines where computation should continue after successful handling of the indicated exception. Retrying can be specified by asserting the exception continuation at a place before the exception occurs by using **exception_continue**. The **exception_skip** subgoal indicates that an alternative search path should be attempted.

When an exception signal is raised by **exception_resume**, the handler is called. And the computation after the **exception_resume** call is then resumed. This mechanism proceeds as if the **exception_resume** call is substituted by a call to the exception handler. However, an exception handler is a special predicate defined for a unique exception. It will only be called when an exception is raised. If the call to the exception handler fails, a control error message is printed. When the exception signal is raised by **exception_abort**, the handler is called, and the computation is then aborted.

In summary, we have three ways to raise an exception:

- retrying or alternation: An exception continuation is asserted in the first clause defining **goal1**, and the exception is raised in the first clause defining **goal2**. After executing the exception handler, computation continues from the point immediately following the **exception_continue** subgoal.

  ```
  goal  :- goal1, ..., goal2.
  goal1 :- ...,
           exception_continue(exception_type),
           ... .
  goal1 :- ... .
  goal2 :- ...,
           exception_raise(exception_type, arg1, arg2, ...).
  exception_handler(exception_type, arg1, arg2, ...) :-
           handler_body.
  exception_handler(exception_type, arg1, arg2, ...) :-
           ... .
  ```

  Similar to the case of retrying, alternation can be made by replacing **exception_continue** by **exception_skip** which abandons the clause in which the exception is declared and causes backtracking to an alternative clause for the parent goal. If there is no other alternative of **goal1** exists, backtracking is applied to an upper level (i.e. the next alternative of **goal**).

- resumption: After an exception handler is called, the computation resumes from **goal1** and **goal2** in **goal**.

```
goal :- ...,
        exception_resume(exception_type, arg1, arg2, ...),
        goal1,
        goal2.
```

- termination: If **exception_resume** is replaced by **exception_abort**, the computation ends after calling the exception handler.

4.1 Why Exception Handling

To increase the readability of the program and to indicate the programmer's assumptions about the expected and unexpected events, it is desirable to be able to divide the program into several units. Some units handle the usual events and can detect the occurrence of anomalous or exceptional conditions. The occurrence of an exception implicitly transfers control to an appropriate unit, the exception handler, that deals with the exception.

In some cases we cannot predict the behaviour of a failure. However, we want to take control and cope with failures whenever possible. Such run-time recovery from failures is the goal of exception mechanisms. The hallmark of high-quality logic programs is robustness. However, the limitations of the execution mechanism must be taken into account. A run-time error occurs when the machine cannot determine the result of a computation due to abnormal conditions. Thus an exception handling mechanism is necessary.

In an event driven style of programming, the response to a particular event is a specific transaction. Usually, the transaction is decomposed to several substeps. In case of the failure of a transaction, the transaction needs to *undo* all previous substeps. One elegant way to undo the intermediate steps is to go back to the spot where the transaction began to try again, or to another spot where an alternative solution is possible. Our exception handling mechanism implements this approach.

4.2 An Example

The example in figure 3 shows a typical bank withdraw transaction. Predicate **bankwithdraw** reads an account number and an amount that the customer want to withdraw after initiating account balances and asserting an exception continuation. The **withdraw** predicate checks if there is enough money in the account. Since the amount requested (i.e. 200) exceeds the balance of account **acc1** (i.e. 100), **enoughmoney** fails, a signal is raised, the message in the handler is displayed, and the computation continues from the exception continuation (the **write(account)** subgoal in predicate **bankwithdraw**). A withdraw of 120 from account **acc1** fails again. And finally, a withdraw of 60 from the same account succeeds.

If the handler fails, **system_error_handler(nomoney)** (internal to our system) is called and our interpreter prints an error message to indicate a possible exception control error.

As shown in the example, a withdraw transaction consists of several substeps (i.e. reads an account number, reads an amount to withdraw, checks for balance, calculates for new balance, updates balance, and indicates the transaction succeeds). In the case of failure (i.e. not enough money in the account

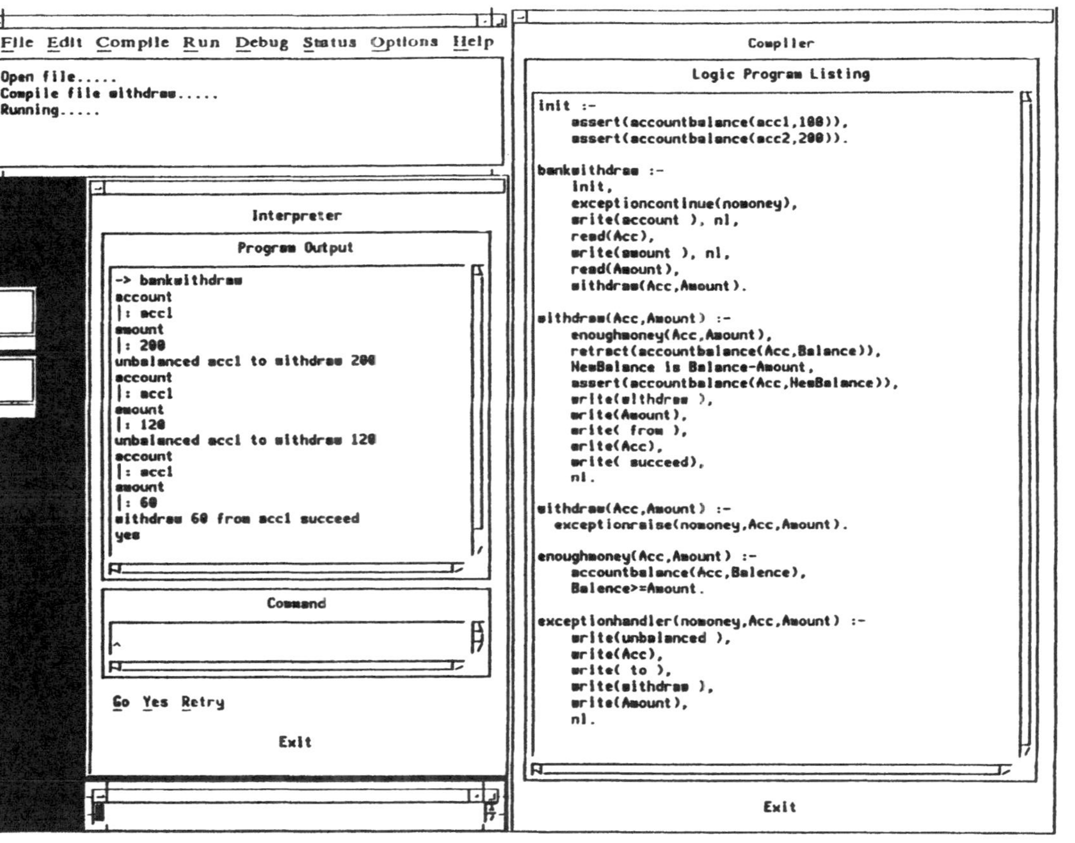

Figure 3 A sample program with exception handling

acc1), the first three substeps need to be done again. Our exception handling mechanism allows the logic program to undo these substeps. That is, the variable binding due to read/1 in predicate bankwithdraw is undone as if the computation proceeds from reading the account number at the first time. This is totally different from applications using a repeat-fail[2] combination to create an iteration loop, since subgoals in each iteration are re-visited again at the next level of search tree. The search tree becomes deeper and deeper as the iteration proceeds. But this never happens in out exception handling mechanism.

5 Two Examples

To illustrate the behaviour of the continuation discussed, we consider a sample program shown below. The search space is shown in figure 4 and the ancestor goal list is shown in Table 1 with the details of MGUs omitted.

```
% the first sample program

a(X, Y, Z) :- b(X, Y), c(Z).
a(X, Y, Z) :- f(Z).
b(X, Y).
b(X, Y) :- e(X, Y).
c(6).
e(1, 2).
f(3).

?- a(1, 2, 3).
```

Since a(1, 2, 3) is the only subgoal at point 0, it is selected. The undefined MGU is represented by the three question marks. Clause 1 of predicate a is selected, and a(1, 2, 3) is rewritten to the new goal b(1, 2), c(3). The original goal a(1, 2, 3) is in the ancestor goal list of point 1 with the clause select pattern [1, 0] indicating the first clause of predicate a has been selected. Thus the first clause of predicate a can not be selected again. This completes one deduction step.

The new goal b(1, 2), c(3) at point 1 is solved. Suppose the subgoal b(1, 2) is selected at this time, and the first clause of predicate b is used, the new goal becomes c(3). And the original goal b(1, 2), c(3) with clause select pattern [1, 0], indicating the first clause of predicate b was used, is in the ancestor goal list of point 2. Note that at each iteration, the clause select pattern only applies to the selected subgoal. In this case it is b(1, 2).

---

[2]The repeat/0 predicate can be defined as:

```
repeat.
repeat :- repeat.
```

Table 1: The ancestor goal list of the first sample program

Point	The ancestor goal list
0	`[<[a(1, 2, 3)], 1, [0, 0], ???>]`
1	`[<[b(1, 2), c(3)], 1, [0, 0], ???>,`
	`<[a(1, 2, 3)], 1, [1, 0], MGU>]`
2	`[<[c(3)], 1, [0], ???>,`
	`<[b(1, 2), c(3)], 1, [1, 0], MGU>,`
	`<[a(1, 2, 3)], 1, [1, 0], MGU>]`
3	`[<[e(1, 2), c(3)], 1, [0], ???>,`
	`<[b(1, 2), c(3)], 1, [1, 1], MGU>,`
	`<[a(1, 2, 3)], 1, [1, 0], MGU>]`
4	`[<[c(3)], 1, [0], ???>,`
	`<[e(1, 2), c(3)], 1, [1], MGU>,`
	`<[b(1, 2), c(3)], 1, [1, 1], MGU>,`
	`<[a(1, 2, 3)], 1, [1, 0], MGU>]`
5	`[<[f(3)], 1, [0], ???>,`
	`<[a(1, 2, 3)], 1, [1, 1], MGU>]`
final	`[<[f(3)], 1, [1], MGU>,`
	`<[a(1, 2, 3)], 1, [1, 1], MGU>]`

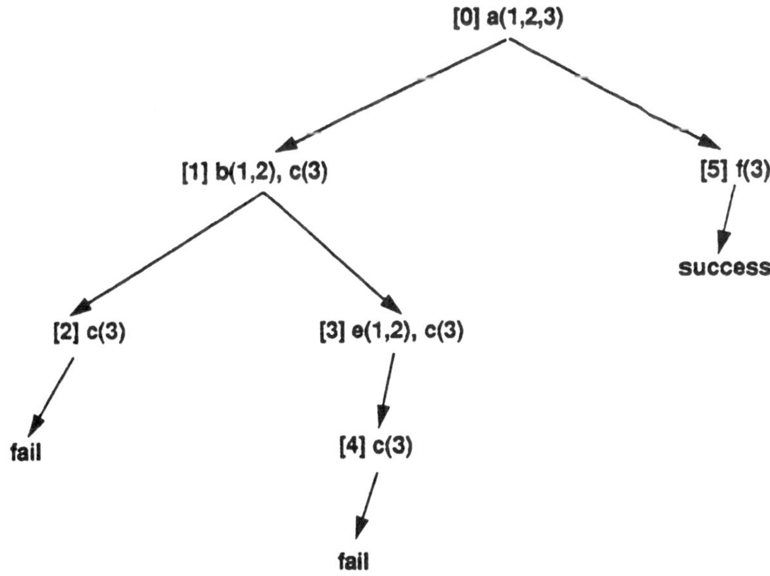

Figure 4 Search space of the first sample program

At point 2, the new goal `c(3)` matches no clause head so that the backtrack selector is called and `b(1, 2)` at point 1 is retried. Only the second clause of predicate `b` can be selected since the clause select pattern for `b(1, 2)` in the ancestor goal list is `[1, 0]`. The new goal is `e(1, 2), c(3)` and the goal `b(1, 2), c(3)` with clause select pattern `[1, 1]` is kept in the ancestor goal list of point 3.

To continue the process, the goal `e(1, 2), c(3)` at point 3 is tried, and failed at point 4. Since the second and the third 4-tuples in the ancestor goal list of point 4 have clause select pattern of the selected subgoal all filled with 1's (i.e. `[1]` for `e(1, 2)` and `[1, 1]` for `b(1, 2)`), backtracking is applied to retry `a(1, 2, 3)`. The second clause of predicate `a` is selected at point 0. The new goal becomes `f(3)`, and finally it succeeds.

If the exception handling is added to the above program example,

```
% the second sample program

a(X, Y, Z) :- exception_skip(errorb), b(X, Y), c(Z).
a(X, Y, Z) :- f(Z).
b(X, Y) :- exception_raise(errorb, X, Y).
b(X, Y) :- e(X, Y).
c(6).
e(1, 2).
f(3).

exception_handler(errorb, X, Y) :-
   write('error data '),
   write(X), write(Y).
?- a(1, 2, 3).
```

The search tree is shown in figure 5. And the ancestor goal list is shown in table 2. Since `exception_skip/1` and `exception_raise/n` are system predicates, the internal execution steps are not shown in the search tree.

Table 2: The ancestor goal list of the second sample program

Point	The ancestor goal list
0	[<[a(1,2,3)],1,[0,0],???>]
1	[<[exception_skip(errorb),b(1,2),c(3)],1,[0],???>, <[a(1,2,3)],1,[1,0],MGU>]
2	[<[b(1,2),c(3)],1,[0],???>, <[exception_skip(errorb),b(1,2),c(3)],1,[1],MGU>, <[a(1,2,3)],1,[1,0],MGU>]
3	[<[exception_raise(errorb,1,2),c(3)],1,[0],???>, [<[b(1,2),c(3)],1,[1],MGU>, <[exception_skip(errorb),b(1,2),c(3)],1,[1],MGU>, <[a(1,2,3)],1,[1,0],MGU>]
4	[<[f(3)],1,[0],???>, <[a(1,2,3)],1,[1,1],MGU>]
errorb	= <DVT,[<[a(1,2,3)],1,[1,0],???>]>

Note that at point 1, the current continuation is

```
<DVT, [<[exception_skip(errorb), b(1, 2), c(3)], 1, [0], ???>,
      <[a(1, 2, 3)], 1, [1, 0], MGU>]>
```

When `exception_skip(errorb)` is recognized, the top 4-tuple in the ancestor goal list is popped, `AGL` becomes

```
<DVT, [<[a(1, 2, 3)], 1, [1, 0], MGU>]>
```

and the `MGU` is reset. Thus, `assert_continuation` associates `errorb` with

```
<DVT, [<[a(1, 2, 3)], 1, [1, 0], ???>]>
```

When `errorb` is raised, `a(1, 2, 3)` will be attempted again but with the clause selection pattern `[1, 0]`, causing the second clause of predicate `a` to be selected for rewriting.

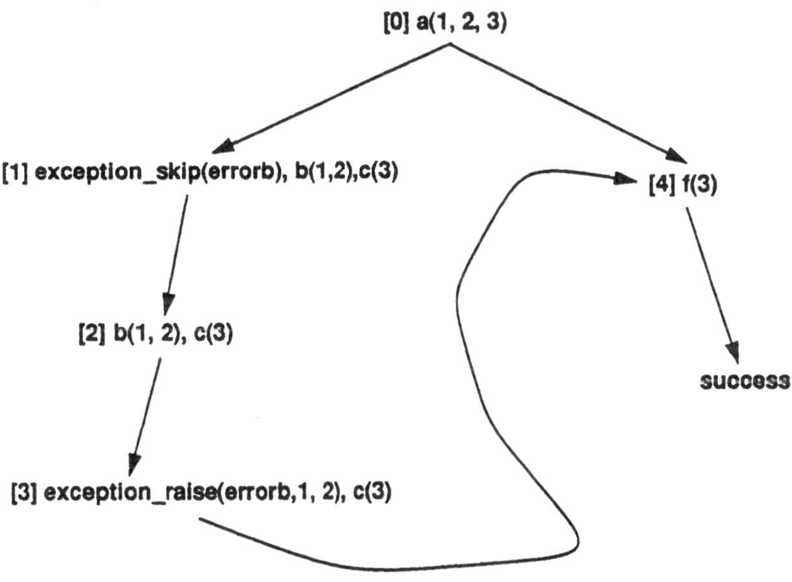

Figure 5 Search space of the second sample program

6 Summary

The representation of a continuation object discussed allows a program execution status to be saved and resumed at a later time. This mechanism is similar to the `call/cc` special form in the language Scheme. In our continuation passing style interpreter, three predicates dealing with the continuation objects were provided. And their operational semantics and implementation details were discussed. The continuation predicates are used in the implementation of exception handling facilities.

We can also apply the continuation mechanism to different areas other than exception handling:

- Intelligent backtracking: The continuation representing the usual evaluation sequence of a logic program is called the success continuation. The failure continuation is called when backtracking is needed. The failure continuation applied could be the most recent choice point continuation in terms of the chronological backtracking, but might be a more efficient choice point when implementing intelligent backtracking.
- Coroutine mechanism: A system of continuations that activate one another can be used to design a coroutine system. When a coroutine is invoked, the current active continuation is saved in a local control state of the coroutine, a jump (i.e. a continuation call) is made to transfer control to another coroutine. The coroutine special form in the language Scheme is constructed by using continuations. Intelligent backtracking and coroutine mechanism are discussed in [26].
- Iteration: Fail-driven loops are claimed to be a bad programming style. Even the `repeat/0` predicate, widely available in Prolog systems, does not allow one to directly specify the termination condition. Our continuation mechanism can be used in the implementation of structured iterative constructs. For instance, a *while construct* can be translated statically:

```
predicate :-
  goals,
  while test_predicates,
  loop_goals,
  end_while,
  other_goals.
```

  where `test_predicates` is a subgoal or a conjunction of subgoals. And `goals`, `loop_goals`, and `other_goals` can be any Prolog predicates, `while` and end_while are reserved words. The above example can be translated to

```
predicate :-
  goals,
  assert_continuation(while#),
  ( test_predicates,
    loop_goals
  ; retract_continuation(while#)
  ), !,
  ( call_continuation(while#)
  ; true
  ), !,
  other_goals.
```

A continuation associated with the while construct (e.g. **while#**, where **#** is a unique number for each of the while construct) is asserted before the loop starts. If the **test_predicates** succeed, the **loop_goals** are solved. And a continuation call is made to the beginning of the loop. If the call to **test_predicates** fail, the unique continuation associated with the while construct is retracted, and the computation proceeds from **other_goals**.

The main contributions of this paper are twofold: firstly, we provide a representation of continuation objects, and a control mechanism for assigning labels and performing jumps in a logic program. This introduces great flexibility of control for logic program execution. Various other control primitives such as coroutining can be built using continuations. Secondly, we presented logic program exception handling facilities based on the continuation mechanism. An exception continuation is invoked to jump away from the normal flow of the program. Thus the error recovery routine is executed directly and right after the exception is raised instead of using cuts and backtracking to an appropriate choice point to continue the computation. With these control facilities, our logic programming system provides a flexible and efficient environment for logic programmers.

An interpreter is running under Unix using X11/Motif Window system on a HP 9000 workstation. The behaviour of the interpreter is as expected and its performance is tolerable (in a small constant factor compared to the underlying Prolog system). We are working on optimizing the data structure to reduce the space required by the representation of continuations. We are investigating the benefits of logic programs that incorporate control primitives and continuation calls. The flexibility of the continuation style interpreter is expected to be of major benefit.

References

[1] Harold Abelson and Gerald Jay Sussman, Structure and Interpretation of Computer Programs, the MIT Press, 1985.

[2] M. Bruynooghe and D. De Schreye and B. Krekels, "Compiling Control," In Proceedings 1986 Symposium on Logic Programming, 1986, pp 70–77.

[3] A. Bundy, "A Broader Interpretation of Logic in Logic Programming," In R. Kowalski and K. Bowen, editors, Logic Programming: Proceedings of the Fifth International Conference and Symposium, The M.I.T. Press, 1988, pp 1624–1648.

[4] K. L. Clark and F. G. McCabe and S. Gregory, "IC-PROLOG Language Features," In K. Clark and S. A. Tarnlund, editors, Logic Programming, Academic Press, 1982, pp 253–266.

[5] K. L. Clark and S. Gregory, "Notes on Systems Programming in Parlog," In Fifth Generation Computer Systems, North Holland, 1984.

[6] Willian Clinger, "The Scheme 311 Compiler, an Exercise in Denotational Semantics," In Conference Record of the 1984 ACM Symposium on Lisp and Functional Programming, 1984.

[7] R. E. Davis, "Runnable Specification as a Design Tool," In K. Clark and S. A. Tarnlund, editors, Logic Programming, Academic Press, 1982, pp 141–149.

[8] R. E. Davis, "Keeping the Logic in Logic Programming," Santa Clara University, 1984.

[9] R. E. Davis, "Supporting the Specification of Logic Programs," In proceedings of the 24th Hawaii International Conference on System Sciences, 1991, pp 228–237.

[10] R. E. Davis and T. K. Shih, "A CASE for Logic Programming," In Proceedings of The Tenth International Conference of The Chilean Computer Science Society, 1990, pp 73–84.

[11] Yves Deville, Logic Programming: Systematic Program Development, Addison Wesley, 1990.

[12] Z. Farkas and P. Szeredi and E. Santane Toth, "LDM: A Program Specification Support System," In Proceedings of the First International Logic Programming Conference, 1982, pp 123–128.

[13] H. Gallaire and C. Lasserre, "Metalevel Control for Logic Programs," In K. Clark and S. A. Tarnlund, editors, Logic Programming, Academic Press, 1982, pp 173–185.

[14] Carlo Ghezzi and Mehdi Jazayery, "Programming Language Concepts," Wiley, 1982.

[15] J. B. Goodenough, "Exception Handling: Issues and Proposed Notation," comm. ACM 16 12 (Dec. 1975), pp 683–696.

[16] Christopher T. Haynes, Daniel P. Friedman and Mitchell Wand, "Continuations and Coroutines," ACM, Vol. 8, 1984, pp 293–298.

[17] Christopher T. Haynes, "Logic Continuations," The Journal of Logic Programming, 4(2), 1987, pp 157–176.

[18] R. Kowalski, "Algorithm = Logic + Control," Communications of the ACM, 22(7), 1979, pp 424–431.

[19] M. Meier and H. Grant, "SEPIA Programming Environment,"In Proceedings of the NACLP'89 Workshop on Logic Programming Environments: The Next Generation, 1989, pp 103–114.

[20] L. Naish, Negation and Control in Prolog, Lecture Notes in Computer Science, volume 238, Springer-Verlag, 1986.

[21] L. M. Pereira, "Logic Control With Logic," In Proceedings of the First International Logic Programming Conference, 1982, pp 9–18.

[22] A. Porto, "Epilog: A Language for Extended Programming in Logic," In Proceedings of the First International Logic Programming Conference, 1982, pp 31–37.

[23] A. C. Reeves, D. A. Harrison, A. F. Sinclair, P. Williamson, "Gerald: An Exceptional Lazy Functional Programming Language," in Functional Programming, Proceeding of the 1989 Glasgow Workshop, 21-23 August 1989, Fraserburgh, Scotland, 1989.

[24] E. Y. Shapiro, "A Subset of Concurrent Prolog and Its Interpreter," Weizmann Institute of Science, 1983.

[25] Timothy Shih, Ruth Davis, and Rob Langsner. "A Specification Processing Environment for Making Well Engineered Logic Programs," In *Proceeding of the second golden west international conference*, 1992.

[26] Timothy Shih and Ruth Davis. "Intelligent Backtracking and Control based on a Deduction Status Representation in Logic Programming," In *Proceeding of the second golden west international conference*, 1992.

[27] Sten Ake Tarnlund, "Logic Programming - From a Logic Point of View," In Proceedings 1986 Symposium on Logic Programming, 1986, pp 96–103.

[28] T. Vasak and J. Potter, "Metalogical Control for Logic Programs," The Journal of Logic Programming, 2(3), 1985, pp 203–220.

[29] S. Yemini and D. M. Berry, "A Modular Verifiable Exception Handling Mechanism," ACM TOPLAS, Vol 7, No 2, 1985, pp 214-243.

[30] S. Yemini and D. M. Berry, "An Axiomatic Treatment of Exception Handling in an Expression Oriented Language," ACM TOPLAS, Vol 9, No 3, 1987, pp 390-407.

Parallelism

On the Semantics of Concurrent Constraint Programming

Frank S. de Boer
Technische Universiteit Eindhoven,
P.O. Box 513, 5600 MB Eindhoven, The Netherlands
email: wsinfdb@tuewsd.win.tue.nl

Catuscia Palamidessi
Dipartimento di Informatica, Università di Pisa
Corso Italia, 40, I56125 Pisa, Italy
email: katuscia@dipisa.di.unipi.it

Abstract

One of the main aims of this paper is to show that the nature of the communication mechanism of concurrent constraint languages is essentially different from the classical paradigms of CCS, CSP and ACP. We define indeed a compositional semantics based on linear sequences, while more complicated structures, like trees and failure sets, are needed to model compositionally CCS, CSP and ACP. From this model we are able to derive a fully abstract semantics by imposing some saturation conditions, that model the monotonic nature of communication in concurrent constraint languages. Finally, we show that if we eliminate the consistency check, and drop the distinction between success and deadlock, then our model is isomorphic to the semantics based on Scott's closure operators proposed in [SRP91].

Note: The research of Frank S. de Boer was partially supported by the Dutch REX (Research and Education in Concurrent Systems) project and by the ESPRIT project SPEC (Formal Methods and Tools for the Development of Distributed and Real-Time Systems).

1 Introduction

There have been several proposals to extend logic programming with the constructs for concurrency, aiming at the development of a concurrent language which would maintain the typical advantages of logic programming: declarative reading, computations as proofs, amenability to meta-programming etc. Examples of concurrent logic languages include PARLOG [CG86], Concurrent Prolog [Sha83, Sha86], Guarded Horn Clauses [Ued87, Ued88] and their so-called *flat* versions. Concurrent constraint programming ([Sar89, SR90, SRP91]), which profited in part of the ideas developed by Maher in the ALPS paradigm ([Mah87]), represents one of the most successful proposals in this area.

Concurrent constraint (cc) programming presents two new perspectives on the underlying philosophy of logic programming. One is the replacement of the concept of unification over the Herbrand universe by the more general notion of *constraint* over an arbitrary domain. This is in a sense a 'natural' development: the idea was already introduced in logic programming by Jaffar and Lassez ([JL87]) and combined with concurrent features by Maher ([Mah87]). The other is the introduction of extra-logical *operators* typical of the imperative concurrent paradigms, like CCS ([Mil80]), TCSP ([BHR84]) and ACP ([BK86]); in particular, the *choice* (+), the *action prefixing* ($\rightarrow$), and the *hiding* operator ($\exists$). Additionally, concurrent constraint programming embodies an explicit characterization of the *control* mechanisms for communication and synchronization by means of the introduction of two kinds of actions (*ask* and *tell*). These control features were present in concurrent logic languages, but they were hidden in various ways: the choice was represented by alternative clauses, hiding by local (existentially quantified) variables, prefixing by guards and commitment, communication by sharing of variables, and synchronization by restrictions on the unification algorithm.

There are many advantages in an explicit representation of these concurrency control mechanisms by means of operators. First of all, they are 'isolated' and therefore the laws of their behaviour can be understood better. For instance, one of the problems in studying the semantics of concurrent logic programming is that the choice mechanism is 'mixed up' with recursion, since a clause is in general a recursive definition. Second, the standard tools developed in the theory of concurrency can be applied more easily. Third, a 'reconciliation' with the declarative principles of logic programming is more feasible, once the basic limitations are well understood. For instance, the conditions which rule the behaviour of *ask* and *tell* can be described in a logical way ([Mah87]), thus providing the synchronization mechanism with a 'declarative flavour' that was missing in the 'restricted-unification' approach.

This paper addresses the problem of a compositional and fully abstract semantics for concurrent constraint languages. Compositionality is considered one of the most desirable characteristics of a formal semantics, since it provides a basis for program verification and modular design. The difficulty in obtaining this property depends upon the *operators* of the language, the behaviour we want to describe (*observables*), and the degree of *abstraction* we want to reach. A compositional model is called *fully abstract* (with respect to some operators and observables) if it identifies programs that behave in the same way under all the possible contexts. A fully abstract model can be considered to be *the* semantics of a language since all the other compositional semantics can be reduced to it by abstracting redundant information. Full abstraction is important, for instance, to decide correctness of program transformation techniques. If a fully abstract model distinguishes the transformed program from the original one then the transformation is not correct (in the sense that it does not preserve the same behaviour under composition).

The compositional description of deadlock is one of the main semantic problems of concurrent languages. For languages like CCS, TCSP and ACP it is well-known that (linear) sequences are not sufficient. On the other hand, trees encode redundant branching information. In order to abstract from it two main approaches have been proposed. One is based on equivalence relations on trees (for instance, bisimulation [Par81]), and the other on grouping the *branching information* in sets (for instance, *failure sets* [BHR84]). In general, failure set semantics is more abstract than bisimulation and has proved to be fully abstract for the above languages.

With respect to compositionality, concurrent constraint and concurrent logic languages have previously been regarded just as a particular case of the classic paradigms. Therefore, the problem has been approached by the standard methods. De Bakker and Kok [dBK88, Kok88] and De Boer et al. [dBKPR89a, dBKPR89b] use tree-like structures labeled with functions on substitutions. More simple tree-like structures, labeled by constraints, are used by Gabbrielli and Levi [GL90]. Saraswat and Rinard ([SR90]) use similar structures modulo equivalence relations based on bisimulation; Gerth et al. ([GCLS88]) and Gaifman et al. ([GMS89]) use refusal pairs like in the failure semantics ([BHR84]), although in [GCLS88] the refusal set is reduced to be a singleton.

We think that concurrent logic and concurrent constraint languages require a different approach. In this paper we study the version of cc programming as defined in [SR90], which can be regarded as a generalization of most of the flat concurrent logic languages, including the 'more powerful' ones like Flat Concurrent Prolog. See [Sar89] for a detailed list of the logic languages which are subsumed by the cc paradigm, and the corresponding justification.

In cc programming there are essentially two kinds of actions: $ask(\theta)$ and $tell(\theta)$, where θ is a constraint. During the execution all processes share a common store, that represents the constraints established up to that moment. Communication is modeled by adding (telling) consistently some constraint to the store. Synchronization is achieved by checking (asking) if the store entails a given constraint; if not, the process suspends.

It is interesting to compare this cc paradigm with CCS. We can translate CCS by interpreting the action a as telling the constraint $x = a$, and the complementary action $\bar{a}$ as asking if $x = a$ is entailed by the store. The main difference is that complementary actions do not synchronize anymore. Indeed, telling a constraint will never suspend. In other words, the communication mechanism of concurrent logic languages is intrinsically *asynchronous*. The following example shows that this leads to an essentially different deadlock behaviour.

Example 1.1 Let $A_1 = \bar{a}\bar{b} + \bar{a}\bar{c} + \bar{a}\bar{d}$ and $A_2 = \bar{a}\bar{b} + \bar{a}(\bar{c} + \bar{d})$. In any compositional semantics for CCS these two processes must be distinguished. Indeed, they behave differently under the context $A = a(b + c)$. The process A_1 can deadlock, by choosing the third branch, while A_2 cannot. In the formalism of [SR90], this example can be translated as follows.

$$\begin{aligned} A_1 = \ & (\mathbf{ask}(x = a) \rightarrow \mathbf{ask}(y = b) \rightarrow \mathbf{Success}) \\ & + \\ & (\mathbf{ask}(x = a) \rightarrow \mathbf{ask}(y = c) \rightarrow \mathbf{Success}) \\ & + \\ & (\mathbf{ask}(x = a) \rightarrow \mathbf{ask}(y = d) \rightarrow \mathbf{Success}) \end{aligned}$$

$$\begin{aligned} A_2 = \ & (\mathbf{ask}(x = a) \rightarrow \mathbf{ask}(y = b) \rightarrow \mathbf{Success}) \\ & + \\ & (\mathbf{ask}(x = a) \rightarrow (\ (\mathbf{ask}(y = c) \rightarrow \mathbf{Success}) \\ & \qquad\qquad\qquad\quad + \\ & \qquad\qquad\qquad\quad (\mathbf{ask}(y = d) \rightarrow \mathbf{Success})\ ) \end{aligned}$$

and

$$A = \ (\mathbf{tell}(x = a) \rightarrow (\ (\mathbf{tell}(y = b) \rightarrow \mathbf{Success}) + (\mathbf{tell}(y = c) \rightarrow \mathbf{Success}) \ )$$

In this translation, both A_1 and A_2 have the same behaviour. The process A_2 can deadlock by choosing the second alternative, because A can independently decide to produce $y = b$ (after $x = a$). Figure 1 illustrates this example.

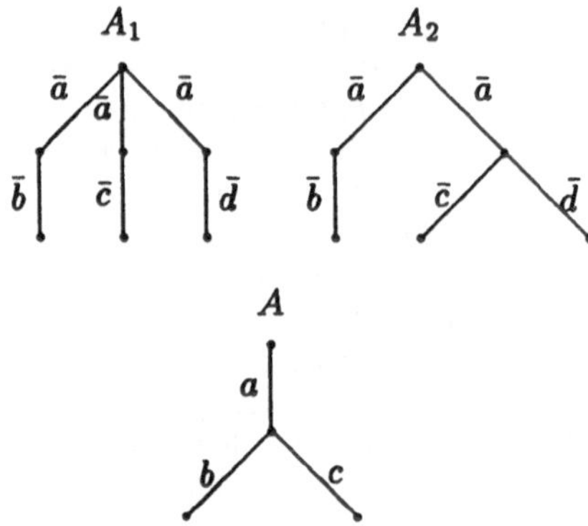

Figure 1: In concurrent constraint programming A cannot distinguish A_1 and A_2.

Actually, in concurrent logic languages we cannot express a context "strong" enough to distinguish between A_1 and A_2 above. The reason is that, due to the asynchronous nature of *tell*, the choice guarded by tell is a *local choice*. This is shown by the following example.

Example 1.2 In an asynchronous reading of CCS along the line of the translation given above, $A_1 = a(b + c)$ is equivalent to $A_2 = ab + ac$ under every context. After the production of a, A_1 can proceed to produce either b or c in the same way as A_2 does.

This example may induce one to believe that simple sequences of constraints are sufficient for obtaining compositionality. This is not the case, because the choice guarded by ask is a *global choice*.

Example 1.3 The process $A_1 = \bar{a}(\bar{b} + \bar{c})$ is not congruent to $A_2 = \bar{a}\bar{b} + \bar{a}\bar{c}$. They are distinguished by the context $A = ab$ (A_2 can deadlock while A_1 cannot).

However, the nature of the global choice in concurrent logic and concurrent constraint languages is essentially different from the one of CCS. Indeed, it only depends upon the result of the past behaviour of the system, i.e. upon the constraint contained in the store.

This remark indicates a possible way to solve the problem of compositionality. Given a sequence of constraints representing the computation of a process with respect to an arbitrary environment, we add the information about who is the producer of each constraint, either the process or the environment. If the store determined by such a sequence does not provide the process with the necessary information to proceed, then the process will deadlock, assuming that the environment does not produce anymore constraint. The composition of different processes then simply amounts to verifying that the assumptions made by one process about its environment are indeed validated by the other processes.

We define the compositional semantics of a process by means of a transition system. The configurations consist of a process and a store, represented as a sequence of constraints. A transition of the environment is modeled by adding an input constraint to the store. This kind of transition, that does not occur in the usual description of CCS, allows us to obtain a compositional operational semantics based on (sets of) sequences ended by a termination mode. These sequences are essentially different from the *scenarios* of [Sar85]. In that paper the input substitutions correspond solely to assumptions about the environment which are necessary for the process to proceed. As a consequence, compositionality is there obtained only for the success set. The input-output sequences we use have been introduced in [GCLS88] as one component of the domain of the denotational semantics, the other ingredient being the suspension set. Because of what is stated above, this suspension set could have been reduced to a simple termination mode.

The language described in [GCLS88] contains non-monotonic test predicates in the guards. Non-monotonic means that a predicate can be true on a certain store and false in a bigger store. For instance, the non-monotonic predicate $var(x)$ is true in the empty store and false in the store $x = a$. The language we consider is monotonic, in the sense that an *ask* being enabled depends monotonically upon the store. With respect to the problem of full abstraction, this feature causes the sequences to contain too much information. Indeed, they encode the order and the granularity in which constraints have been produced, details that cannot be sensed by monotonic contexts. This is mainly due to the fact that monotonic contexts cannot be specified to ask (only) a specific constraint, they can always proceed when stronger constraints are provided. Therefore a process producing first $x = a$ and then $y = b$ cannot be distinguished from a process that is also able to produce $x = a$ and $y = b$ at the same time: all contexts that are enabled by the store $x = a$ will also be enabled by the store $x = a \wedge y = b$. More generally, the reaction of any context is invariant with respect to the logical equivalence of the conjunction of the constraints produced by the process. Therefore, the final step to achieve full abstraction will consist of some closure conditions that represent this equivalence.

To our knowledge, the first proposal of a compositional semantics based on linear sequences for these kinds of languages has been given in [dBP90a, dBP90b]. Those papers, however, deal with concurrent logic languages, which are based on substitutions and have no explicit choice operator (it is 'hidden' in the clause union). The compositionality is treated there only with respect to the parallel operator. Later on, the same technique to obtain a fully abstract semantics has been extended and applied to cc languages ([dBP91]). The results in the present paper concerning full abstraction rely on [dBP91]. We have introduced here some improvements in the technique. In particular, our model consists now of *modular* sequences only, where every element is *closed* with respect to all variables but the global ones. From a technical point of view it is easier to deal with such sequences, because of the absence of nested local environments. Conceptually, they reflect faithfully the monotonic evolution of the store, as it is visible at the global level, and provide a purely logical meaning to the notion of a local state. At the level of the language we distinguish now between hiding in the constraints (existential quantification) and hiding in the program (locality). This makes the hiding operator more easy to model and to understand, and separates clearly the control component from the logical component in the suspension mechanism.

A completely different approach has been developed in [SRP91] for a version of concurrent constraint programming in which the consistency check is not supported, which can be seen as a sublanguage of the one we consider here; we will come back to this in Section 6. The basic idea consists of denoting processes as Scott's closure operators, which have the nice property of being representable by the set of their fixpoints. The operators of the language can then be described as operations on those sets. In particular, parallelism can be modeled simply by intersection. We show that if in our semantics we identify success and deadlock then we obtain a model which, restricted to the sublanguage mentioned above, is isomorphic with the one in [SRP91]. This by the way means that the notion of observables adopted in [SRP91] does not distinguish between deadlock and success. The underlying idea is that the only thing an external observer is able to detect is the maximal progress made by the process, in terms of constraints accumulated on the store when the process stops. The reasons why it stops cannot be observed. Dropping the distinction between success and deadlock was already present in concurrent logic programming ([Rin87]).

1.1 Plan of the paper

In the next section we give the definition of constraint system. In Section 3 we introduce the concurrent constraint paradigm; we describe its computational model by means of a transition system, and we formalize the notion of observables $\mathcal{O}$. In Section 4 we enrich the transition system so as to obtain a compositional semantics $\mathcal{D}$, correct with respect to $\mathcal{O}$, by simply collecting sequences of transitions. In Section 5 we present a semantics $\mathcal{A}$ which results from a 'saturation' of $\mathcal{D}$ and which is fully abstract with respect to $\mathcal{O}$. In Section 6 we discuss the relation between reactive sequences and Scott's closure operators. Due to space limitations, we have omitted the proofs, which can be found in the full paper ([dBP92]).

2 Constraint systems

The definition of constraint system we give here is a slightly modified version of the one described in [SR90], which follows Scott's treatment of information system ([Sco82]).

We first need to introduce the notion of *simple constraint system*. In the following, $\mathcal{P}(\mathcal{S})$ is the set of all subsets of $\mathcal{S}$.

Definition 2.1 A *simple constraint system* is defined as a structure $\langle \mathcal{S}, \vdash \rangle$, where $(\sigma, \theta \in) \mathcal{S}$ is a non-empty (denumerable) set of *primitive constraints* and $\vdash \subseteq \mathcal{P}(\mathcal{S}) \times \mathcal{S}$ is an entailment relation satisfying the following conditions:

(i) if $\sigma \in c$ then $c \vdash \sigma$, and

(ii) if $c \vdash \sigma$ and $\forall \theta \in c.\, d \vdash \theta$ then $d \vdash \sigma$.

Now extend $\vdash$ to a relation on $\mathcal{P}(\mathcal{S}) \times \mathcal{P}(\mathcal{S})$ as follows:

$$c \vdash d \text{ iff } \forall \theta \in d.\, c \vdash \theta.$$

It is easy to see that $\vdash$ is a preorder. Denote by $\sim$ the associated equivalence relation:

$$c \sim d \text{ iff } c \vdash d \;\wedge\; d \vdash c.$$

We use the notation $[c]$ to indicate the equivalence class of c, namely

$$[c] = \{d \mid c \sim d\}.$$

The ordering relation induced by $\vdash$ on $\mathcal{P}(\mathcal{S})_{/\sim} \times \mathcal{P}(\mathcal{S})_{/\sim}$ is still denoted by $\vdash$.

Definition 2.2 The *constraint system* generated by $\langle \mathcal{S}, \vdash \rangle$ is the structure $\langle \mathcal{P}(\mathcal{S})_{/\sim}, \vdash \rangle$.

The structure $\langle \mathcal{P}(\mathcal{S})_{/\sim}, \vdash \rangle$ is a complete lattice with ordering relation $[c] \leq [d]$ iff $[d] \vdash [c]$. The least element, denoted by *true*, is given by $[\emptyset] = \{c \mid \emptyset \vdash c\}$. The greatest element, denoted by *false* (or *inconsistency*), is given by $[\mathcal{S}] = \{c \mid c \vdash \mathcal{S}\}$. The *lub* operation, denoted by $\wedge$, is given by:

$$[c] \wedge [d] \;=\; [c \cup d]$$

It is easy to see that this definition is *correct*, i.e., it does not depend upon the choice of representative of the class, and that it actually corresponds to the *lub*. Furthermore, it can be naturally extended to arbitrary sets of elements, thus showing that $\langle \mathcal{P}(\mathcal{S})_{/\sim}, \vdash \rangle$ is in fact a complete lattice.

For the sake of simplicity, we will indicate the equivalence class $[c]$ by c.

Note. The standard definition of constraint system includes a restriction (compactness) on the entailment relation which has the effect of turning the structure $\langle \mathcal{P}(\mathcal{S})_{/\sim}, \vdash \rangle$ into a *complete algebraic* lattice. This guarantees that every element of the domain can be generated as the result of a (possibly infinite) computation.

In order to formalize the hiding operator it will be helpful to introduce the notion of *cylindric constraint system*, which is based on the theory of cylindric algebras ([HMT71]). In the following, $\mathcal{P}_{\mathrm{fi}}(\mathcal{S})$ denotes the set of the finite subsets of $\mathcal{S}$.

Definition 2.3 (Cylindric constraint system) Let *Var* be a (denumerable) set of variables $x, y, z, \ldots$ and let $\langle \mathcal{S}, \vdash \rangle$ be a simple constraint system. Assume that for each $x \in \mathit{Var}$ a function $\exists x : \mathcal{P}_{\mathrm{fi}}(\mathcal{S}) \rightarrow \mathcal{P}_{\mathrm{fi}}(\mathcal{S})$ is defined such that for any $c, d \in \mathcal{P}_{\mathrm{fi}}(\mathcal{S})$:

(i) $c \vdash \exists x(c)$,

(ii) if $c \vdash d$ then $\exists x(c) \vdash \exists x(d)$,

(iii) $\exists x(c \wedge \exists x(d)) \sim \exists x(c) \wedge \exists x(d)$,

(iv) $\exists x(\exists y(c)) \sim \exists y(\exists x(c))$.

Then $\langle \mathcal{P}(\mathcal{S})_{/\sim}, \vdash \rangle$ is a *cylindric constraint system.*

We will denote $\exists x(c)$ by $\exists x.c$ and, for a set $X = \{x_1, \ldots, x_n\}$, we will denote $\exists x_1 \ldots \exists x_n.c$ by $\exists X.c$.

In order to model the hiding operator of the language we have to introduce the notion of *renaming*. Following [SRP91], we formalize this notion by means of the 'diagonal formulas' ([HMT71]).

Definition 2.4 (Diagonal elements) Let *Var* be a (denumerable) set of variables $x, y, z, \ldots$ and let $\langle \mathcal{S}, \vdash \rangle$ be a simple constraint system. For $x, y \in Var$, the elements $d_{xy} \in \mathcal{S}$ are *diagonal elements* iff they satisfy the following:

(i) $\emptyset \vdash d_{xx}$,

(ii) if $x \not\equiv y$ then $\{d_{xy}\} \sim \exists z(\{d_{xz}, d_{zy}\})$,

(iii) $\{d_{xy}\} \wedge \exists x(c \wedge \{d_{xy}\}) \vdash c$.

If $\mathcal{S}$ models the equality theory, then the elements d_{xy} can be thought of as the formulas $x = y$.

We define the renaming $c[x/y]$ of x by y in a constraint c as the formula $\exists x(c \wedge \{d_{xy}\})$. The *simultaneous* renaming $c[X/Y]$ of the variables X by the variables Y in c can be defined analogously, we only need to extend the notion of diagonal elements to tuples of variables.

Example 2.5 Consider an alphabet consisting of a (denumerable) set of variables $x, y, z, \ldots$, a set of function symbols $f, g, \ldots$, and the equality predicate $=$. Let $(t, u \in)T$ be the set of terms over the alphabet. The *Herbrand constraint system* $\langle H, \vdash \rangle$ is the structure generated by the simple constraint system $\langle Eq, \vdash \rangle$, where Eq is the set of equations on T, and $\vdash$ is the entailment relation generated by Clark's equality axioms [Cla79]. This stucture can be extended to a cylindric constraint system by adding the the set of *existentially quantified conjunctions of equations* The diagonal elements are, as stated before, the formulas of the form $x = y$.

In the following, our examples will deal with constraint systems containing (existentially quantified) equalities on the Herbrand domain.

3 The language

Concurrent constraint programming was proposed by Saraswat [Sar89, SR90, SRP91]. We follow here the definition given in [SR90], which is more general than the later formulations, because it deals with a more general notion of guard (the so-called *atomic tell*). In this version, concurrent constraint programming can be regarded as a generalization of most of the concurrent logic languages, including the 'more powerful' ones like (Flat) Concurrent Prolog[1].

We assume given a cylindric constraint system $\langle \mathcal{C}, \vdash \rangle$ on a set of variables *Var*. The description of the language is parametric with respect to it, and so it is the semantical construction we develop in this paper.

For reasons which will be clarified later, we assume *Var* to be partitioned into *LVar*, the *logical variables*, and *PVar*, the *program variables*.

In the following, $A, B, \ldots$ range over the set of processes, $p, q, r, \ldots$ range over procedure names, and $X, Y, Z, \ldots$ range over subsets of *Var*. In addition, the notation $\vec{\chi}$ indicates a sequence of the form $\chi_1, \ldots, \chi_n$.

The processes are described by the following grammar

$$A ::= \mathbf{Success} \mid \mathbf{Fail} \mid \mathbf{ask}(c) \rightarrow A \mid \mathbf{tell}(c) \rightarrow A \mid A + A \mid A \parallel A \mid \exists X.A \mid p(\vec{t})$$

Success and **Fail** represent successful and failing termination. The basic actions are given by **ask**(c) and **tell**(c) constructs, where c is a *basic constraint*, i.e. a constraint which is equivalent to a finite set of simple constraints. We require the bound variables of the constraint c in **ask**(c) [**tell**(c)] to be logical variables, and the free variables of c to be program variables. The process **ask**$(c) \rightarrow A$ waits until the store entails c and then it behaves like A. The process **tell**$(c) \rightarrow A$ adds c to the store and then it behaves like A. They both fail when c is inconsistent with the store. The operators $\parallel$ and $+$ are the parallel composition and the nondeterministic choice, respectively. $\exists X.A$ is like the process A, with the variables in $X \subseteq PVar$ seen as *local*. Finally, $p(\vec{t})$ is a procedure call, p is the name of the procedure, and $\vec{t}$ is the list of the actual parameters. The meaning of a process is given with respect to a set W of procedure declarations of the form $p(\vec{x})$:- A. Given the list of actual parameters $\vec{t}$, an *instantiation* of $p(\vec{x})$:- A is an object of the form $p(\vec{t})$:- $\exists X.A'$, where A' is obtained from A by simultaneously replacing every (occurrence of a) formal parameter by its corresponding actual parameter, and by renaming all the other variables so to avoid clashes with $\vec{t}$. The set of variables X denote the local variables of A', i.e. the variables of A' which do not occur in $\vec{t}$. We denote by $Inst(W)$ the set of the instantiations of the clauses in W. In the sequel, unless stated otherwise, we assume W to be fixed, so we omit reference to it.

The distinction between logical variables and program variables is introduced to emphasize the difference between the operational meaning of the local variables of a process, on the one hand, and logical meaning of the bound variables of a tell [ask] action, on the other hand.

3.1 The operational model and the observables $\mathcal{O}$

The operational model is described by a transition system $T = (Conf, \longrightarrow)$. The configurations *Conf* are pairs consisting of a process or a *termination mode*, and a constraint representing the store. The termination modes *ss*, *ff* and *dd*, indicate success, failure and deadlock respectively. The rules of T are described in Table 1.

Notice that parallelism is described as interleaving. Furthermore, the plus operator models global non-determinism in the sense that the choices of a

[1] In its 'pure' version, i.e. without built-in predicates.

Rule	Transition	Condition
R1	$\langle \mathbf{Success}, c\rangle \longrightarrow \langle ss, c\rangle$	
R2	$\langle \mathbf{Fail}, c\rangle \longrightarrow \langle f\!f, c\rangle$	
R3	$\langle \mathbf{ask}(c'), c\rangle \longrightarrow \langle ss, c\rangle$	if $c \vdash c'$
R4	$\langle \mathbf{ask}(c'), c\rangle \longrightarrow \langle dd, c\rangle$	if $c \wedge c' \not\sim \mathit{false}$ and $c \not\vdash c'$
R5	$\langle \mathbf{tell}(c'), c\rangle \longrightarrow \langle ss, c \wedge c'\rangle$	if $c \wedge c' \not\sim \mathit{false}$
R6	$\langle \mathbf{tell}(c'), c\rangle \mid \langle \mathbf{ask}(c'), c\rangle \longrightarrow \langle f\!f, c\rangle$	if $c \wedge c' \sim \mathit{false}$
R7	$\langle p(\vec{t}), c\rangle \longrightarrow \langle A, c\rangle$	if $p(\vec{t}) :\!-\, A \in \mathit{Inst}(W)$
R8	$\dfrac{\langle g, c\rangle \longrightarrow \langle ss, c'\rangle \mid \langle \alpha, c\rangle}{\langle g \rightarrow A, c\rangle \longrightarrow \langle A, c'\rangle \mid \langle \alpha, c\rangle}$	if $\alpha \in \{f\!f, dd\}$
R9	$\dfrac{\langle A[Y/X], c\rangle \longrightarrow \langle A', c'\rangle}{\langle \exists X.A, c\rangle \longrightarrow \langle A', c'\rangle}$	if Y 'fresh'
R10	$\dfrac{\langle A, c\rangle \longrightarrow \langle A', c'\rangle \mid \langle ss, c'\rangle}{\begin{array}{c}\langle A \parallel B, c\rangle \longrightarrow \langle A' \parallel B, c'\rangle \mid \langle B, c'\rangle \\ \langle B \parallel A, c\rangle \longrightarrow \langle B \parallel A', c'\rangle \mid \langle B, c'\rangle\end{array}}$	
R11	$\dfrac{\langle A, c\rangle \longrightarrow \langle A', c'\rangle \mid \langle ss, c'\rangle}{\begin{array}{c}\langle A + B, c\rangle \longrightarrow \langle A', c'\rangle \mid \langle ss, c'\rangle \\ \langle B + A, c\rangle \longrightarrow \langle A', c'\rangle \mid \langle ss, c'\rangle\end{array}}$	
R12	$\dfrac{\langle A, c\rangle \longrightarrow \langle dd, c\rangle \quad \langle B, c\rangle \longrightarrow \langle \alpha, c\rangle}{\begin{array}{c}\langle A \parallel B, c\rangle \longrightarrow \langle \alpha, c\rangle \\ \langle B \parallel A, c\rangle \longrightarrow \langle \alpha, c\rangle \\ \langle A + B, c\rangle \longrightarrow \langle dd, c\rangle \\ \langle B + A, c\rangle \longrightarrow \langle dd, c\rangle\end{array}}$	if $\alpha \in \{f\!f, dd\}$
R13	$\dfrac{\langle A, c\rangle \longrightarrow \langle f\!f, c\rangle}{\begin{array}{c}\langle A \parallel B, c\rangle \longrightarrow \langle f\!f, c\rangle \\ \langle B \parallel A, c\rangle \longrightarrow \langle f\!f, c\rangle\end{array}}$	
R14	$\dfrac{\langle A, c\rangle \longrightarrow \langle f\!f, c\rangle \quad \langle B, c\rangle \longrightarrow \langle f\!f, c\rangle}{\begin{array}{c}\langle A + B, c\rangle \longrightarrow \langle f\!f, c\rangle \\ \langle B + A, c\rangle \longrightarrow \langle f\!f, c\rangle\end{array}}$	

Table 1: The Transition System T. The '|' is an abbreviation for alternative transitions.

process depend on the current store which is subject to modifications by the external environment.

The result of a terminating computation consists of the final store (up to logical equivalence), together with the termination mode. This is formally represented by the notion of *observables*.

Definition 3.1 The observables are given by the function

$$\mathcal{O}[\![A]\!] = \{\langle \exists X.c, \alpha\rangle \mid \langle A, \mathit{true}\rangle \longrightarrow^* \langle \alpha, c\rangle\}_\sim,$$

where X are all the variables in c which do not occur in A, the subscript $\sim$ denotes the closure under constraint equivalence, and $\longrightarrow^*$ denotes the transitive closure of $\longrightarrow$.

In the following examples, we assume the constraint system to contain the standard equality theory.

Example 3.2 It is worthwhile noticing the difference between the processes $\exists x.\mathbf{ask}(x = a)$ and $\mathbf{ask}(\exists x.x = a)$. The first process will deadlock in the empty store (*true*): *true* does not imply $y = a$ for any variable y. On the other hand the second process will terminate successfully: *true* obviously does imply $\exists x.x = a$.

Example 3.3 Consider the process A defined as follows:

$$A = \mathbf{tell}(x = a) \rightarrow \mathbf{ask}(y = f(a)) \rightarrow \mathbf{Success}.$$

Starting with the empty store (*true*), the process will first tell (add to the store) the constraint $x = a$, and then it will block on the execution of **ask**, since $x = a$ does not entail $y = f(a)$. Therefore what we observe out of the execution of A is

$$\mathcal{O}[\![A]\!] = \{\langle x = a, dd\rangle\}_\sim.$$

Consider now the processes

$$B_1 = \mathbf{tell}(y = f(x)) \rightarrow \mathbf{Success},$$

$$B_2 = \exists x.\mathbf{tell}(y = f(x)) \rightarrow \mathbf{Success}.$$

The observables are:

$$\mathcal{O}[\![B_1]\!] = \{\langle y = f(x), ss\rangle\}_\sim,$$

$$\mathcal{O}[\![B_2]\!] = \{\langle \exists z.y = f(z), ss\rangle\}_\sim.$$

Let's now consider the processes $A_1 = A \parallel B_1$ and $A_2 = A \parallel B_2$. After the first step of A and the execution of B_1, the store is $x = a \wedge y = f(x)$, which entails $y = f(a)$. Therefore A_1 can successfully terminate:

$$\mathcal{O}[\![A_1]\!] = \{\langle x = a \wedge y = f(x), ss\rangle\}_\sim.$$

This is not the case for A_2, since after the first step of A and the execution of B_2, the store is $x = a \wedge \exists z.y = f(z)$, which does not entail $y = f(a)$. Therefore A_2 will still deadlock:

$$\mathcal{O}[\![A_2]\!] = \{\langle x = a \wedge \exists z.y = f(z), dd\rangle\}_\sim.$$

Example 3.4 The following is a simple example showing that $\mathcal{O}$ is not compositional. Consider the processes

$$A_1 = \mathbf{ask}(x = a) \rightarrow \mathbf{Success},$$

and

$$A_2 = \mathbf{ask}(x = b) \rightarrow \mathbf{Success}.$$

We have that $\mathcal{O}[\![A_1]\!] = \mathcal{O}[\![A_2]\!] = \{\langle true, dd \rangle\}$. However, for $A = \mathbf{tell}(x = a) \rightarrow \mathbf{Success}$, we have

$$\mathcal{O}[\![A_1 \parallel A]\!] = \{\langle x = a, ss \rangle\},$$

whereas

$$\mathcal{O}[\![A_2 \parallel A]\!] = \{\langle x = a, ff \rangle\}.$$

4 A compositional semantics based on sequences

In this section we define a compositional model $\mathcal{D}$ based on linear sequences which describe the interaction between a process and its environment in terms of the evolution of the common store. Updates to the common store by the environment will be indicated by the label a (*assume*), while updates by the process itself will be labeled by t (*tell*). Thus these sequences encode the assumptions on the environment and the consequent reactions of the process, and we will call them *reactive sequences*[2]. Such a sequence will also encode the hiding of local variables, by means of existential quantifiers. We will only use *modular* sequences, namely sequences where every variable is either a global variable (never quantified) or it is local (existentially quantified) in every element in which it occurs.

We give now some technical definition. In the following, ℓ ranges over $\{\mathrm{a}, t\}$.

The function *Estore* represents the constraint associated with a sequence.

(i) $Estore(\lambda) = true$ (λ is the empty sequence),

(ii) $Estore((\exists X.c)^{\ell} \cdot s) = \exists X.c \wedge Estore(s)$.

Note that, for modular sequences, $Estore(s)$ coincides with the conjunction of the elements of s. Furthermore, for every sequence there is a modular sequence which is equivalent with respect to *Estore*.

The function *Store* represents the constraint associated with a sequence *local* to a process, as it is *seen* by the process.

(i) $Store(\lambda) = true$,

(ii) $Store((\exists X.c)^{\mathrm{t}} \cdot s) = c \wedge Store(s)$,

(iii) $Store((\exists X.c)^{\mathrm{a}} \cdot s) = (\exists X.c) \wedge Store(s)$.

[2] This term 'reactive' is also used in [GMS89] to denote sequences of ask-tell constraints. Note however that in [GMS89] an ask constraint is not an assumption about the environment, but the minimal store which is needed for the process to proceed, as in the case of the scenarios.

Given a sequence s we define

(i) $FV(s)$, the free variables of s (the global variables),

(ii) $BV(s)$, the bound program variables of s (the local variables),

(iii) $BV^{\ell}(s)$ $[FV^{\ell}(s)]$, $\ell \in \{a, t\}$, the bound [free] program variables of s occurring in constraints labeled by ℓ. The local variables introduced by the process itself are given by $BV^{t}(s)$ and those introduced by the environment by $BV^{a}(s)$,

(iv) $var(\chi)$, the program variables of the object χ (process, sequence ...).

To define the compositional semantics we use a transition system T' (see Table 2). The configurations are pairs $\langle A, s\rangle$, such that *Estore*(s) is consistent.
The difference with the transition system T consists mainly in rule **R15′**, which models the interaction with the environment. Note that a process A is not immediately affected by actions made by the environment (only its future behaviour will depend on them). An arbitrary constraint can be added (by the environment) consistently to the store without changing the state of A. In other words, A can make an ***arbitrary assumption*** about the store.
The correspondence between T and T' is expressed by the following lemma.

Lemma 4.1 *The rules* **R1′-R14′** *of* T' *mimic the rules* **R1-R14** *of* T, *in the sense that if*

$$\langle A, s\rangle \longrightarrow \langle A', s'\rangle$$

is a **Ri′** *transition step in* T', *then*

$$\langle A, Store(s)\rangle \longrightarrow \langle A', Store(s')\rangle$$

is a **Ri** *transition step in* T.

The semantics $\mathcal{D}$, based on the transition system T', delivers sets of reactive sequences, ended by a termination mode $\alpha \in \{ss, ff, dd, \perp\}$. A reactive sequence ending in $\perp$ represents an *unfinished* computation. On the other hand, a reactive sequence ending in one of the other termination modes represents a *completed* computation in the sense that *both* the process and the environment are terminated. In the case of a successfully terminated sequence this implies that both the process and the environment are successfully terminated, whereas, in the case of a deadlocking sequence, this implies that the process itself is suspended and the environment is either suspended too or has successfully terminated. However, since detection of a failure propagates through the whole system, a sequence will end in failure in case the process itself fails.
We need to introduce a notion of unfinished computations for a compositional treatment of failure in the presence of infinite processes.

Example 4.2 Consider the process $p(x)$, with $p(x)$:- **tell**$(x = f(z)) \rightarrow p(z)$. Since there are no terminating computations of $p(x)$, in the absence of a representation of unfinished computations, its semantics will be empty. However, when $p(x)$ is put in parallel with **Fail**, we get as observable results all the pairs $\langle \exists z.x = f^{n}(z), ff\rangle$, where $f^{0}(z) = z$ and $f^{n+1}(z) = f(f^{n}(z))$.

Rule	Transition	Condition
R1′	$\langle \mathbf{Success}, s\rangle \longrightarrow \langle ss, s\cdot \mathit{true}^t\rangle$	
R2′	$\langle \mathbf{Fail}, s\rangle \longrightarrow \langle \mathit{ff}, s\rangle$	
R3′	$\langle \mathbf{ask}(c), s\rangle \longrightarrow \langle ss, s\cdot \mathit{true}^t\rangle$	if $Store(s) \vdash c$
R4′	$\langle \mathbf{ask}(c), s\rangle \longrightarrow \langle dd, s\rangle$	if $Estore(s\cdot c) \not\sim \mathit{false}$ and $Store(s) \not\vdash c$
R5′	$\langle \mathbf{tell}(c), s\rangle \longrightarrow \langle ss, s\cdot {c'}^t\rangle$	if $Estore(s\cdot c) \not\sim \mathit{false}$ where $c' = Estore^t(s\cdot c)$
R6′	$\langle \mathbf{tell}(c), s\rangle \mid \langle \mathbf{ask}(c), s\rangle \longrightarrow \langle \mathit{ff}, s\rangle$	if $Estore(s\cdot c) \sim \mathit{false}$
R7′	$\langle p(\vec{t}), s\rangle \longrightarrow \langle A, s\cdot \mathit{true}^t\rangle$	if $p(\vec{t})$:- $A \in Inst(W)$
R8′	$\dfrac{\langle g, s\rangle \longrightarrow \langle ss, s'\rangle \mid \langle \alpha, s\rangle}{\langle g \rightarrow A, s\rangle \longrightarrow \langle A, s'\rangle \mid \langle \alpha, s\rangle}$	if $\alpha \in \{\mathit{ff}, dd\}$
R9′	$\dfrac{\langle A[Y/X], s\rangle \longrightarrow \langle A', s\cdot c^t\rangle}{\langle \exists X.A, s\rangle \longrightarrow \langle A', s\cdot(\exists Y.c)^t\rangle}$	if $Y \cap Var(A, s) = \emptyset$
R10′	$\dfrac{\langle A, s\rangle \longrightarrow \langle A', s\cdot c^t\rangle \mid \langle ss, s\cdot c^t\rangle}{\begin{array}{c}\langle A \parallel B, s\rangle \longrightarrow \langle A' \parallel B, s\cdot c^t\rangle \mid \langle B, s\cdot c^t\rangle \\ \langle B \parallel A, s\rangle \longrightarrow \langle B \parallel A', s\cdot c^t\rangle \mid \langle B, s\cdot c^t\rangle\end{array}}$	if $(BV(c) \setminus BV^t(s)) \cap var(B) = \emptyset$
R11′	$\dfrac{\langle A, s\rangle \longrightarrow \langle A', s\cdot c^t\rangle \mid \langle ss, s\cdot c^t\rangle}{\begin{array}{c}\langle A + B, s\rangle \longrightarrow \langle A', s\cdot c^t\rangle \mid \langle ss, s\cdot c^t\rangle \\ \langle B + A, s\rangle \longrightarrow \langle A', s\cdot c^t\rangle \mid \langle ss, s\cdot c^t\rangle\end{array}}$	
R12′	$\dfrac{\langle A, s\rangle \longrightarrow \langle dd, s\rangle \quad \langle B, s\rangle \longrightarrow \langle \alpha, s\rangle}{\begin{array}{c}\langle A \parallel B, s\rangle \longrightarrow \langle \alpha, s\rangle \\ \langle B \parallel A, s\rangle \longrightarrow \langle \alpha, s\rangle \\ \langle A + B, s\rangle \longrightarrow \langle dd, s\rangle \\ \langle B + A, s\rangle \longrightarrow \langle dd, s\rangle\end{array}}$	if $\alpha \in \{\mathit{ff}, dd\}$
R13′	$\dfrac{\langle A, s\rangle \longrightarrow \langle \mathit{ff}, s\rangle}{\begin{array}{c}\langle A \parallel B, s\rangle \longrightarrow \langle \mathit{ff}, s\rangle \\ \langle B \parallel A, s\rangle \longrightarrow \langle \mathit{ff}, s\rangle\end{array}}$	
R14′	$\dfrac{\langle A, s\rangle \longrightarrow \langle \mathit{ff}, s\rangle \quad \langle B, s\rangle \longrightarrow \langle \mathit{ff}, s\rangle}{\begin{array}{c}\langle A + B, s\rangle \longrightarrow \langle \mathit{ff}, s\rangle \\ \langle B + A, s\rangle \longrightarrow \langle \mathit{ff}, s\rangle\end{array}}$	
R15′	$\langle A, s\rangle \mid \langle ss, s\rangle \longrightarrow \langle A, s\cdot c^a\rangle \mid \langle ss, s\cdot c^a\rangle$	if $Estore(s\cdot c) \not\sim \mathit{false}$, $FV(c) \cap BV^t(s) = \emptyset$, $BV(c) \cap Var(A) = \emptyset$

Table 2: The Transition System T'

So, despite our interest in finite computations only, we need to represent the finite approximations of infinite computations for a proper treatment of failure. The semantics $\mathcal{D}$ is given below:

$$\begin{array}{rll} \mathcal{D}[\![A]\!] = & \{s \cdot ss & \mid \langle A, true \rangle \longrightarrow^* \langle ss, s \rangle\} \\ \cup & \{s \cdot ff & \mid \langle A, true \rangle \longrightarrow^* \langle ff, s \rangle\} \\ \cup & \{s \cdot dd & \mid \langle A, true \rangle \longrightarrow^* \langle dd, s \rangle\} \\ \cup & \{s \cdot \bot & \mid \langle A, true \rangle \longrightarrow^* \langle A', s \rangle\} \end{array}$$

The observables can be retrieved from $\mathcal{D}$ by first selecting those sequences entirely composed of tell constraints and ended by ss, ff, or dd. This amounts to requiring that the store has evolved only by updates of the process and that the computation has reached a final state. Then we abstract from the particular order in which the constraints have been produced, and close under logical equivalence. This procedure is described by the operator *Result*:

$$Result(S) = \{\langle Estore(s), \alpha \rangle \mid s \cdot \alpha \in S \ \wedge \ s = c_1^t \cdot \ldots \cdot c_n^t \ \wedge \ \alpha \in \{ss, ff, dd\}\}.$$

Theorem 4.3 (Correctness of $\mathcal{D}$) $\mathcal{O}[\![A]\!] = Result(\mathcal{D}[\![A]\!])_{/\sim}$.

It is interesting to see how the semantics $\mathcal{D}$ encodes the additional branching information necessary for a compositional description. Consider the following typical example:

Example 4.4 Let

$$A_1 = \mathbf{tell}(true) \rightarrow (\ \mathbf{ask}(x = a) \rightarrow \mathbf{Success} \ + \ \mathbf{ask}(x = b) \rightarrow \mathbf{Success} \ )$$

and

$$A_2 = (\mathbf{tell}(true) \rightarrow \mathbf{ask}(x = a) \rightarrow \mathbf{Success}) \ + \ (\mathbf{tell}(true) \rightarrow \mathbf{ask}(x = b) \rightarrow \mathbf{Success})$$

We have that $\langle (x = a)^{\mathrm{a}}, ff \rangle \in \mathcal{D}[\![A_2]\!] \setminus \mathcal{D}[\![A_1]\!]$.

4.1 Compositionality of $\mathcal{D}$

The operational semantics defined in the previous section is shown to be compositional by defining the semantic operators $\rightsquigarrow$, $\tilde{\|}$, $\tilde{+}$ corresponding to the operators of the language: $\rightarrow$, $\|$, $+$ and $\exists X$. Here we give only $\tilde{\|}$, the others definitions can be found in the full paper ([dBP92]).

To define $\tilde{\|}$ we first define the corresponding partial and nondeterministic operator, then we extend it to sets. This operator is similar to the one specified in [GCLS88] for sequences of substitutions. It allows the combination of sequences of assume/tell constraints that are equal at each point, apart from the modes, thus modeling the interaction of a process with its environment. It differs from the (more popular) interleaving operator in that it applies to sequences already containing all the information concerning the way in which processes interleave (the assumptions specify 'where' and 'what'). Hence the application of $\tilde{||}$ amounts to verifying that the assumptions made by one process are indeed validated by the other process (i.e. it tells or assumes the same constraints). In the positive case, the elements of the resulting sequence are labeled by tell whenever they are labeled by tell in at least one of the two sequences, by assume otherwise (a constraint is produced by a pair of parallel processes whenever it is produced by at least one of the two).

(i) $s_1 \cdot \alpha_1 \tilde{||} s_2 \cdot \alpha_2 = s_2 \cdot \alpha_1 \tilde{||} s_1 \cdot \alpha_2$

(ii) $c^{\mathrm{a}} \cdot s_1 \cdot \alpha_1 \tilde{||} c^{\ell} \cdot s_2 \cdot \alpha_2 = c^{\ell} \cdot (s_1 \cdot \alpha_1 \tilde{||} s_2 \cdot \alpha_2)$

(iii) $\alpha \tilde{||} ss = \alpha$

(iv) $\alpha \tilde{||} ff = ff$

(v) $dd \tilde{||} dd = dd$

(vi) $\perp \tilde{||} \perp = \perp$

Since arbitrary assumptions can always be made, it is sufficient to consider the cases listed above, and to leave $\tilde{||}$ undefined on the sequences of different kind. The extension to sets is defined in the obvious way:

$$S_1 \tilde{||} S_2 = \{ s_1 \cdot \alpha_1 \tilde{||} s_2 \cdot \alpha_2 \mid s_1 \cdot \alpha_1 \in S_1 \ \wedge \ s_2 \cdot \alpha_2 \in S_2 \}.$$

We have following theorem:

Theorem 4.5 *$\mathcal{D}$ is compositional with respect to all the operators of the language.*

As a consequence of this theorem, the equivalence relation associated with $\mathcal{D}$, defined as

$$A_1 \approx_{\mathcal{D}} A_2 \ \textit{iff} \ \mathcal{D}[\![A_1]\!] = \mathcal{D}[\![A_2]\!],$$

is a congruence.

This congruence is not able to identify processes having, in all contexts, the same final results (observables). A first reason is that it does not abstract from *silent steps*[3]. Consider the following:

Example 4.6 Let

$$A_1 = \mathbf{ask}(x = a) \rightarrow \mathbf{ask}(y = b) \rightarrow \mathbf{Success}$$

and

$$A_2 = \mathbf{ask}(x = a \wedge y = b) \rightarrow \mathbf{Success}.$$

Then $A_1 + A_2$ and A_1 give the same final results in all contexts, but $(x = a \wedge y = b)^{\mathrm{a}} \cdot true^{t} \cdot ss \in \mathcal{D}[\![A_1 + A_2]\!]$, whereas $(x = a \wedge y = b)^{\mathrm{a}} \cdot true^{t} \cdot ss \notin \mathcal{D}[\![A_1]\!]$. In fact A_1, under the assumption $x = a \wedge y = b$, must perform two silent steps before terminating. The corresponding sequence is $(x = a \wedge y = b)^{\mathrm{a}} \cdot true^{t} \cdot true^{t} \cdot ss$

[3] In this framework, a step is silent if does not modify the store; for instance, a step adding *true* is always silent.

This congruence, however, is large enough to capture equivalence of processes that react (stepwise) in the same way to any environment (taking silent steps into account). This notion of equivalence, is coarser than bisimulation and it is even coarser than failure semantics.

Example 4.7 Let A_1 and A_2 be the two processes in Example 1.1 in the introduction. Then the reaction of A_1 and A_2 with respect to an arbitrary environment will be exactly the same at each step, and indeed $A_1 \approx_{\mathcal{D}} A_2$.

As a consequence $\approx_{\mathcal{D}}$ is coarser than *reactive equality*, the congruence based on bisimulation defined in [SR90].

However, one may argue that this notion of equivalence is too fine and that it would be more interesting, for instance, to abstract from silent steps or, even, from intermediate steps (i.e. to identify processes that give, in all contexts, the same final results).

In the next section we introduce a semantics $\mathcal{A}$ that is fully abstract, i.e. it identifies processes that give the same observables in any context.

5 A fully abstract semantics

The operational semantics defined in the previous section is not fully abstract with respect to the observables. Like CCS, silent steps cause unnecessary distinctions, but this is only part of the the reason. More generally, the problem is that sequences contain redundant information about the order and the granularity in which constraints are added to the store.

Example 5.1 Let B_1 and B_2 be defined as follows:

$$\begin{aligned} B_1 = \ & (\mathbf{tell}(c_1) \rightarrow \mathbf{tell}(c_2) \rightarrow \mathbf{Success}) \\ & + \\ & (\mathbf{tell}(c_1 \wedge c_2) \rightarrow \mathbf{Success}) \end{aligned}$$

and

$$B_2 = \ \mathbf{tell}(c_1) \rightarrow \mathbf{tell}(c_2) \rightarrow \mathbf{Success}.$$

Of course, $B_1 \not\approx_{\mathcal{D}} B_2$, but still, in every context, they will produce the same final results. This is because of the monotonicity of communication: we cannot define an environment that accepts both c_1 and c_2 and not $c_1 \wedge c_2$.

In general, the reaction of a process to a certain sequence of actions will only depend upon the (logical) final content of the store. Therefore, we must eliminate distinctions between logically equivalent subsequences. One way to do this is to *saturate* a set of denotations by adding, for any sequence s, all those sequences that differ only for a logically equivalent subsequence (**C1**). This operation, however, is not enough: as it will introduce new possible interleaving points we need a rule (**C2**) which allows the addition of assumptions, provided that it does not add any new information.

Definition 5.2 Given a set of modular sequences S, the *saturation* of S, $Sat(S)$, is the minimal set of modular sequences which contain S and satisfies the conditions **C1** and **C2** of Table 3.

C1	if $s_1 \cdot c_1^\ell \ldots c_n^\ell \cdot s_2 \cdot \alpha \in S$ and $Estore(s_1 \cdot c_1^\ell \ldots c_n^\ell) \sim Estore(s_1 \cdot d_1^\ell \ldots d_m^\ell)$ then $s_1 \cdot d_1^\ell \ldots d_m^\ell \cdot s_2 \cdot \alpha \in S$
C2	if $s_1 \cdot s_2 \cdot \alpha \in S$ and $Estore(s_1 \cdot s_2) \sim Estore(s_1 \cdot c \cdot s_2)$ then $s_1 \cdot c^{\mathrm{a}} \cdot s_2 \cdot \alpha \in S$

Table 3: The saturation conditions

Sometimes it will be convenient to apply the saturation operator also on sets of sequences s (without termination mode), with the obvious meaning.

Remark 5.3 *The conditions* **C1** *and* **C2** *preserve the meaning of a sequence. Namely, if* $s.\alpha \in Sat(\{s'.\alpha'\})$ *(abbrev.* $Sat(s'.\alpha')$*), then* $Estore(s) \sim Estore(s')$ *holds.*

Remark 5.4 *The saturation operator is idempotent, namely*

$Sat(Sat(S)) = Sat(S)$.

We want to obtain a fully abstract semantics by applying the saturation operator to the semantics $\mathcal{D}$. However, as the closure under the conditions **C1** and **C2** abstracts from silent steps we loose the compositionality with respect to the choice operator. Examples of this phenomenon are the (weak) bisimulation semantics for CCS, and the *reactive equivalence* semantics defined in [SR90]. Essentially this problem arises because the distinction is lost between a computation that deadlocks [fails] immediately, and a computation that deadlocks [fails] after some silent steps. They should be distinguished, since the composition of these computations with a successful alternative choice gives different results (the second may still deadlock [fail] while the first cannot). In our framework it is possible to solve the problem in a quite simple way. We just need to introduce a distinction between two kinds of termination modes, representing the immediate and the not immediate deadlock and failure. For technical reasons we need to have this distinction also for the unfinished. Thus we add the new termination modes dd_ι, ff_ι and $\perp_\iota$: ff_ι and dd_ι are intended to describe computations in which the process *immediately* fails and suspends respectively. A sequence ending in $\perp_\iota$ will correspond to an unfinished computation in which the process has not performed any step. We introduce the new termination modes by the following modification of the semantics $\mathcal{D}$. The notation S_T stands for the subset of sequences of S in which there occurs a tell constraint, and S_A denotes the subset of sequences of S which consists only of assume constraints.

$$
\begin{array}{rlll}
\mathcal{D}_\iota[\![A]\!] = & \{s \cdot ss & \mid \langle A, \mathit{true}\rangle \longrightarrow^* \langle ss, s\rangle\} \\
\cup & \{s \cdot ff & \mid \langle A, \mathit{true}\rangle \longrightarrow^* \langle ff, s\rangle\}_T \\
\cup & \{s \cdot ff_\iota & \mid \langle A, \mathit{true}\rangle \longrightarrow^* \langle ff, s\rangle\}_A \\
\cup & \{s \cdot dd & \mid \langle A, \mathit{true}\rangle \longrightarrow^* \langle dd, s\rangle\}_T \\
\cup & \{s \cdot dd_\iota & \mid \langle A, \mathit{true}\rangle \longrightarrow^* \langle dd, s\rangle\}_A \\
\cup & \{s \cdot \perp & \mid \langle A, \mathit{true}\rangle \longrightarrow^* \langle A', s\rangle\}_T \\
\cup & \{s \cdot \perp_\iota & \mid \langle A, \mathit{true}\rangle \longrightarrow^* \langle A', s\rangle\}_A
\end{array}
$$

The semantics $\mathcal{A}$ is defined as follows:

$\mathcal{A}[\![A]\!] = Sat(\mathcal{D}_\iota[\![A]\!])$.

The equivalence defined by $\mathcal{A}$ is still more refined than the equivalence induced by $\mathcal{O}$. In fact, the observables can be retrieved from $\mathcal{A}$, by application of the operator *Result*.

Lemma 5.5 $Result(\mathcal{D}_\iota[\![A]\!]) = Result(\mathcal{D}[\![A]\!])$.

By Lemma 5.5 and Remark 5.3 we obtain

Theorem 5.6 (Correctness of $\mathcal{A}$) $Result(\mathcal{A}[\![A]\!]) = \mathcal{O}[\![A]\!]$.

Next we consider the compositionality of $\mathcal{A}$. To this purpose, we introduce the new semantics operators $\tilde{\leadsto}_\iota$, $\tilde{\|}_\iota$, and $\tilde{+}_\iota$. Here we give only the definition of $\tilde{\|}_\iota$, the others can be found in the full paper ([dBP92]).

The parallel operator $\tilde{\|}_\iota$ is defined as the operator $\tilde{\|}$ plus the following:

(i) $f\!f_\iota \tilde{\|}_\iota \alpha = f\!f_\iota$, $\alpha \in \{f\!f_\iota, dd_\iota, \perp_\iota\}$

(ii) $f\!f_\iota \tilde{\|}_\iota \alpha = f\!f$, $\alpha \in \{ss, f\!f, dd, \perp\}$

(iii) $dd_\iota \tilde{\|}_\iota dd_\iota = dd_\iota$

(iv) $dd_\iota \tilde{\|}_\iota \alpha = dd \tilde{\|} \alpha$, $\alpha \in \{ss, f\!f, dd\}$

(v) $\perp_\iota \tilde{\|}_\iota \perp_\iota = \perp_\iota$

(vi) $\perp_\iota \tilde{\|}_\iota \perp = \perp$

We have the following theorem:

Theorem 5.7 *$\mathcal{A}$ is compositional with respect to all the operators of the language.*

As a consequence we have that the equivalence relation associated to $\mathcal{A}$, defined as

$A_1 \approx_{\mathcal{A}} A_2$ *iff* $\mathcal{A}[\![A_1]\!] = \mathcal{A}[\![A_2]\!]$,

is a congruence.

Processes A_1 and A_2 of Example 4.7 and processes B_1 and B_2 of Example 5.1 are equivalent ($A_1 \approx_{\mathcal{A}} A_2$ and $B_1 \approx_{\mathcal{A}} B_2$). In the following we prove that $\approx_{\mathcal{A}}$ is the coarsest equivalence that preserves the five operators described above, and that is correct w.r.t. the observables. The basic lines of the proof are the following. Given two processes A_1, A_2 with a different semantics $\mathcal{A}$, we build a context that is able to 'detect' this difference at the observational level.

To construct the distinguishing context we will follow different strategies, depending upon the kind of termination mode (immediate or not immediate).

For the sequences ending with the not immediate termination modes (ss, $f\!f$, dd and $\perp$) the definition of the distinguishing context is *uniform*, in the following sense: given a modular sequence $s \cdot \alpha$ we define a *context* $C[\;] = C(s \cdot \alpha) \parallel [\;]$ such that the process $C(s \cdot \alpha)$ 'recognizes' $s \cdot \alpha$.

Definition 5.8 Let s be a modular sequence and $\alpha \in \{ss, ff, dd, \bot\}$. We define the process $C(s{\cdot}\alpha)$ by induction on the length of s.

(i) $C(ss) = C(ff) = C(dd) =$ **Success**, and $C(\bot) =$ **Fail**,

(ii) $C(c^{\mathbf{a}}{\cdot}s{\cdot}\alpha) = \mathbf{tell}(c) \rightarrow C(s{\cdot}\alpha)$,

(iii) $C(c^{t}{\cdot}s{\cdot}\alpha) = \mathbf{ask}(c) \rightarrow C(s{\cdot}\alpha)$.

The following proposition states that a process $C(s{\cdot}\alpha)$ recognizes the sequence $s{\cdot}\alpha$. Namely, $C(s{\cdot}\alpha)$ generates $\bar{s}{\cdot}\bar{\alpha}$, where $\bar{s}$ denotes the 'mirror' of s, i.e. $\overline{c^{\mathbf{a}}{\cdot}s} = c^{t}{\cdot}\bar{s}$ and $\overline{c^{t}{\cdot}s} = c^{\mathbf{a}}{\cdot}\bar{s}$, and

$$\bar{\alpha} = \begin{cases} ss & \textit{if } \alpha \in \{ss, ff, dd\} \\ ff & \textit{otherwise.} \end{cases}$$

Proposition 5.9 *For any modular sequence $s \cdot \alpha$ with $\alpha \in \{ss, ff, dd, \bot\}$ we have $\bar{s}{\cdot}\bar{\alpha} \in \mathcal{A}[\![C(s{\cdot}\alpha)]\!]$.*

Let the context $C[\,] = C(s{\cdot}\alpha) \parallel [\,]$. As a consequence of this proposition, we have that $\langle Estore(s), \alpha\rangle \in \mathcal{O}[\![C[A_1]]\!] \setminus \mathcal{O}[\![C[A_2]]\!]$ if $\alpha \neq \bot$ and $\langle Estore(s), ff\rangle \in \mathcal{O}[\![C[A_1]]\!] \setminus \mathcal{O}[\![C[A_2]]\!]$ if $\alpha = \bot$. It is possible to prove that every other sequence $s'{\cdot}\alpha$ recognized by $C(s{\cdot}\alpha)$ that gives the same result as $s{\cdot}\alpha$ must generate $s{\cdot}\alpha$ by application of the saturation operator. Then we reason by contradiction: given a sequence $s{\cdot}\alpha$ in the semantic difference (say, $s{\cdot}\alpha \in \mathcal{A}[\![A_1]\!] \setminus \mathcal{A}[\![A_2]\!]$), if the process $C(s{\cdot}\alpha)$ doesn't induce a difference in the observables, then there exists an other sequence $s'{\cdot}\alpha$ ($s'{\cdot}\alpha \in \mathcal{A}[\![A_2]\!]$) recognized by the process that produces the same result. But, since $\mathcal{A}$ is closed, the presence of $s'.\alpha$ implies the presence of $s{\cdot}\alpha$, and this contradicts the assumption.

For sequences ending in an immediate termination mode ($ff_\iota, dd_\iota, \bot_\iota$), the definition of the distinguishing context involves, of course, the operator $+$. For instance, the case $\alpha = ff_\iota$ is treated by defining a context of the form $C[\,] =$ $\mathbf{tell}(c) \rightarrow (((\mathbf{tell}(\mathit{true}) \rightarrow \mathbf{Fail}) \parallel [\,]) + \mathbf{ask}(c'))$, where c' is such that $c \not\vdash c'$. We have in fact a distinguishing sequence $\langle c, dd\rangle \in \mathcal{O}[\![C[A_1]]\!] \setminus \mathcal{O}[\![C[A_2]]\!]$.

Theorem 5.10 (Full abstraction of $\mathcal{A}$) *For arbitrary processes A_1, A_2 such that $\mathcal{A}[\![A_1]\!] \neq \mathcal{A}[\![A_2]\!]$ there exists a context $C[\,]$ such that $\mathcal{O}[\![C[A_1]]\!] \neq \mathcal{O}[\![C[A_2]]\!]$.*

6 Reactive sequences versus closure operators

In this section we show that if we eliminate the consistency check, and drop the distinction between success and deadlock, then the model $\mathcal{D}$ of the previous sections can be expressed in terms of Scott's *closure operators*. On this basis we prove the isomorphism of our restricted model with the model developed in [SRP91].

The consistency check requires one to perform, before executing an action of the form $tell(\alpha)$, a test on the consistency of α with respect to the current store. If α is inconsistent with the current store then we choose another possibility, and only if there are no other possibilities is a failure generated. When the consistency check is not supported then $tell(\alpha)$ just adds α to the store regardless of whether or not it will lead to an inconsistent situation (*false*). The two kinds of tell are called *atomic tell* and *eventual tell* respectively in [SR90]. The different definitions of this operation are already present in the literature concerning concurrent logic programming, where the consistency check is usually called *atomic unification* (this explains the terminology "atomic tell": unification on the Herbrand universe corresponds, roughly, to adding a constraint to the store). An example of a language with atomic unification is Concurrent Prolog ([Sha86]), an example of a language *without* atomic unification is the language of Guarded Horn Clauses ([Ued87]).

Note that the inconsistent store is a situation of no recovery, since it is the top of the lattice, and the store can only evolve monotonically. Inconsistency is regarded as the *most undesirable* situation, the *failure* of the computation. Obviously, the languages with atomic tell are more powerful, since processes can be specified which will try to avoid inconsistency, if possible.

Concurrent constraint without a consistency check can be defined within our framework in two equivalent ways:

(i) by eliminating some rules in the transition system (essentially the ones concerning failure), or

(ii) by restricting the syntax of the language; more precisely, by forbidding the occurrence of a tell-guard in a plus context (thus eliminating escape possibilities when a failure is detected).

We adopt here the first solution, which is to our taste more elegant.

Concerning the distinction between deadlock and success in the observables, by dropping it we renounce to the possibility of distinguishing processes which have terminated, and would not react to any 'stimulus', from processes which are just stuck on some input and which would still produce information once this input is provided.

Example 6.1 Consider the two processes

$$\begin{aligned} A_1 = \; & (\mathbf{tell}(\mathit{true}) \rightarrow \mathbf{tell}(x = a, y = b) \rightarrow \mathbf{Success}) \\ & + \\ & (\mathbf{tell}(\mathit{true}) \rightarrow \mathbf{ask}(x = a) \rightarrow \mathbf{tell}(x = a, y = b) \rightarrow \mathbf{Success}) \\ & + \\ & (\mathbf{tell}(\mathit{true}) \rightarrow \mathbf{Success}) \end{aligned}$$

$$\begin{aligned} A_2 = \; & (\mathbf{tell}(\mathit{true}) \rightarrow \mathbf{tell}(x = a, y = b) \rightarrow \mathbf{Success}) \\ & + \\ & (\mathbf{tell}(\mathit{true}) \rightarrow \mathbf{Success}) \end{aligned}$$

The semantics proposed in [SRP91] does not distinguish between A_1 and A_2, whereas the semantics presented in previous sections does. In fact, the second branch of A_1 can generate deadlock (depending upon the store) whereas this possibility is excluded in A_2. If we drop the distinction between success and deadlock then also our model would identify A_1 and A_2.

The identification of deadlock and success is maybe questionable from the practical point of view, but it allows to obtain an elegant representation of the

rR1	$\langle \mathbf{ask}(c'), c\rangle \longrightarrow \langle ss, c\rangle$	**if** $c \vdash c'$
rR2	$\langle \mathbf{tell}(c'), c\rangle \longrightarrow \langle ss, c \wedge c'\rangle$	
rR3	$\langle p(\vec{t}), c\rangle \longrightarrow \langle A, c\rangle$	**if** $p(\vec{t})$:- $A \in Inst(W)$
rR4	$\dfrac{\langle g, c\rangle \longrightarrow \langle ss, c'\rangle}{\langle g \rightarrow A, c\rangle \longrightarrow \langle A, c'\rangle}$	
rR5	$\dfrac{\langle A[Y/X], c\rangle \longrightarrow \langle A', c \wedge c'\rangle}{\langle \exists X.A, c\rangle \longrightarrow \langle A', c \wedge c'\rangle}$	**if** Y 'fresh'
rR6	$\dfrac{\langle A, c\rangle \longrightarrow \langle A', c'\rangle \mid \langle ss, c'\rangle}{\begin{array}{c}\langle A \parallel B, c\rangle \longrightarrow \langle A' \parallel B, c'\rangle \mid \langle B, c'\rangle \\ \langle B \parallel A, c\rangle \longrightarrow \langle B \parallel A', c'\rangle \mid \langle B, c'\rangle\end{array}}$	
rR7	$\dfrac{\langle A, c\rangle \longrightarrow \langle A', c'\rangle \mid \langle ss, c'\rangle}{\begin{array}{c}\langle A + B, c\rangle \longrightarrow \langle A', c'\rangle \mid \langle ss, c'\rangle \\ \langle B + A, c\rangle \longrightarrow \langle A', c'\rangle \mid \langle ss, c'\rangle\end{array}}$	

Table 4: The restricted Transition System rT

reactive sequences in terms of closure operators. The rest of this section is devoted to investigating this characterization.

The transition system for concurrent constraint without consistency check and without deadlock recognition is given in Table 4. From it we can derive the notion of observables (still denoted by $\mathcal{O}$) in the same way as before.

6.1 The restricted model

To define the compositional semantics we adopt the same 'pruning' (elimination of the rules for failure and deadlock) on the transition system T'. The new transition system, rT', is given in Table 5.

Based on rT' a semantics $\mathcal{D}$ is defined in the same way as before. All the results of previous section hold for $\mathcal{D}$ and $\mathcal{O}$. In particular, the compositionality of $\mathcal{D}$ and the correctness of $\mathcal{D}$ with respect to $\mathcal{O}$. Finally, we obtain the fully abstract model $\mathcal{A}$ for our sublanguage by applying the saturation operator Sat to $\mathcal{D}$. Observe that only one termination symbol remains there: ss[4]. Thus we can drop it from the reactive sequences of $\mathcal{A}$.

[4]Actually, for being compositional with respect to the plus, we would still need a distinction between immediate and not immediate termination. This is not needed in [SRP91] because they adopt a restriction in the use of the plus operator, namely they prefix by guards (ask operations) the processes to be put in an alternative choice. In other words, instead of the simple plus, they consider an operator of the form $\sum_1^n \mathbf{ask}(c_i) \rightarrow [\ ]_i$. In order to compare our approach to the approach in [SRP91] we impose here the same restriction.

Table 5: The Transition System rT'

rR1'	$\langle \mathbf{ask}(c), s\rangle \longrightarrow \langle ss, s\cdot true^t\rangle$	**if** $Store(s) \vdash c$
rR2'	$\langle \mathbf{tell}(c), s\rangle \longrightarrow \langle ss, s\cdot c'^t\rangle$	
rR3'	$\langle p(\vec{t}), s\rangle \longrightarrow \langle A, s\cdot true^t\rangle$	**if** $p(\vec{t})$:- $A \in Inst(W)$
rR4'	$\dfrac{\langle g, s\rangle \longrightarrow \langle ss, s'\rangle}{\langle g \rightarrow A, s\rangle \longrightarrow \langle A, s'\rangle}$	
rR5'	$\dfrac{\langle A[Y/X], s\rangle \longrightarrow \langle A', s\cdot c^t\rangle}{\langle \exists X.A, s\rangle \longrightarrow \langle A', s\cdot(\exists Y.c)^t\rangle}$	**if** $Y \cap Var(A,s) = \emptyset$
rR6'	$\dfrac{\langle A, s\rangle \longrightarrow \langle A', s\cdot c^t\rangle \mid \langle ss, s\cdot c^t\rangle}{\begin{array}{l}\langle A \parallel B, s\rangle \longrightarrow \langle A' \parallel B, s\cdot c^t\rangle \mid \langle B, s\cdot c^t\rangle \\ \langle B \parallel A, s\rangle \longrightarrow \langle B \parallel A', s\cdot c^t\rangle \mid \langle B, s\cdot c^t\rangle\end{array}}$	**if** $(BV(c) \setminus BV^t(s))$ $\cap var(B) = \emptyset$
rR'	$\dfrac{\langle A, s\rangle \longrightarrow \langle A', s\cdot c^t\rangle \mid \langle ss, s\cdot c^t\rangle}{\begin{array}{l}\langle A + B, s\rangle \longrightarrow \langle A', s\cdot c^t\rangle \mid \langle ss, s\cdot c^t\rangle \\ \langle B + A, s\rangle \longrightarrow \langle A', s\cdot c^t\rangle \mid \langle ss, s\cdot c^t\rangle\end{array}}$	
rR8'	$\langle A, s\rangle \mid \langle ss, s\rangle \longrightarrow \langle A, s\cdot c^a\rangle \mid \langle ss, s\cdot c^a\rangle$	**if** $Estore(s\cdot c) \not\rightarrow false$, $FV(c) \cap BV^t(s) = \emptyset$, $BV(c) \cap Var(A) = \emptyset$

6.2 Closure operators

A closure operator on a lattice $\langle L, \leq\rangle$ is a function $\Psi : L \rightarrow L$ which is *idempotent*, *monotonic* and *extensive*. More formally:

(i) $\forall x \in L.\ \Psi(\Psi(x)) = \Psi(x)$,

(ii) $\forall x, y \in L.\ x \leq y \Rightarrow \Psi(x) \leq \Psi(y)$,

(iii) $\forall x \in L.\ x \leq \Psi(x)$.

Closure operators have the following nice property: they are completely determined by their range, which coincide with the set of their fixpoint. In fact, if $R \subseteq L$ is the range of a closure operator Ψ, we can retrieve Ψ as follows

$$\Psi(x) = min\{y \in R \mid\ x \leq y\}.$$

We can also prove that, given a set R, if every subset of R which is bounded from below admits the least element, then R is the range of a closure operator. In the following, we will identify Ψ and its range.

Closure operators are used in [SRP91] to give semantics to determinate cc programming, namely cc programming without nondeterministic choice. A priori the absence of nondeterministic choice does not imply that the language is deterministic, because the parallel operator might re-introduce nondeterminism. In the case in which the consistency check is not supported, however, it is possible to prove a sort of confluence property, which causes a system to always reach the same final store from a given initial store. A determinate cc process can therefore be seen as a function from store to store. Furthermore, the way in which the process transforms the store satisfies the properties mentioned above, hence this function is actually a closure operator. The fact that closure operators can be represented as sets allows us to define the semantic correspondents of the operators of the language as operators on sets. In the case of the merge operator this is particularly convenient, in fact it just corresponds to set intersection.

Concerning the nondeterminate case, the behaviour of a process cannot be described anymore as a *single* function from the initial store to the final store, we need at least a set of functions. This turns out to be sufficient to obtain compositionality ([SRP91]). Actually it is sufficient to consider a special class of functions: the so-called bounded trace operators. A bounded trace operator (bto) is a closure operator Ψ which is defined on a sublattice of L of the form

$$\downarrow c = \{x \in L \mid x \leq c\}$$

wher c is an element of L. Moreover, the inverse of Ψ, defined as

$$\Psi^{-1} = (\downarrow c \setminus \Psi) \cup \{c\}$$

is a closure operator on $\downarrow c$ as well.

Also in [SRP91] full abstraction is obtained by applying a saturation condition: if denotation of a process contains a bto Ψ, then it contains also all the other bto's on the same domain which are superset of Ψ.

6.3 Correspondence between reactive sequences and bounded trace operators

The following definition builds a mapping $\mathcal{F}$ from reactive sequences (without termination modes) to bto's.

Definition 6.2 Let s be a modular sequence. We define the bto $\mathcal{F}(s)$ by induction on the length of s.

(i) $\mathcal{F}(\lambda)(c) = c$,

(ii) $\mathcal{F}(c^t \cdot s)(c') = c' \wedge \mathcal{F}(s)(c)$,

(iii) $\mathcal{F}(c^{\mathrm{a}} \cdot s)(c') = \text{if } c' \vdash c \text{ then } \mathcal{F}(s)(c) \text{ else } c'$.

It is easy to prove that this definition gives indeed a bto, with domain $\downarrow \mathit{Estore}(s)$.

We consider now the opposite function $\mathcal{G}$ which associates a reactive sequence with a bto.

Definition 6.3 Let Ψ be a bto. We define the reactive sequence $\mathcal{G}(\Psi)$ as follows

$$\Psi(true)^t \cdot \Psi^{-1}(\Psi(true))^a \cdot \Psi(\Psi^{-1}(\Psi(true)))^t \ldots$$

The sequence ends when the application of Ψ or Ψ^{-1} doesn't give any new contribution to the store, i.e. when the sequence reaches a fixpoint of Ψ or Ψ^{-1}.

It is possible to prove that $\mathcal{F}$ is surjective and $\mathcal{G}$ is injective. Furthermore $\mathcal{F}(\mathcal{G}(\Psi)) = \Psi$, whereas $\mathcal{G}(\mathcal{F}(s))$ is in general different from s. We call $\mathcal{G}(\mathcal{F}(s))$ the *canonical representant* of s. The sequences s and $\mathcal{G}(\mathcal{F}(s))$ are equivalent with respect to the saturation conditions: each of them can generate the other by saturation.

Proposition 6.4 *Let s be a reactive sequence. Then*

(i) $s \in Sat(\mathcal{G}(\mathcal{F}(s)))$ *and*

(ii) $\mathcal{G}(\mathcal{F}(s)) \in Sat(s)$.

Another important property is the following: Consider two bto's Ψ and Φ such that $\Psi \subseteq \Phi$. Then $\mathcal{G}(\Phi)$ is a sequence which *asks more* than $\mathcal{G}(\Psi)$ in some points. Note that this corresponds to obtaining $\mathcal{G}(\Phi)$ from $\mathcal{G}(\Psi)$ by application of the saturation condition **C2**. Therefore we have that our saturation includes the saturation by supersets (upward closure) required in [SRP91]

Proposition 6.5 *Let Ψ and Φ be two bto's. Then $\Psi \subseteq \Phi$ iff $\mathcal{G}(\Phi) \in Sat(\mathcal{G}(\Psi))$.*

From Propositions 6.4 and 6.5 we derive that the set of saturated sets of reactive sequences and the set of upward closed sets of bto's are isomorphic. This isomorphism is given by the extension of $\mathcal{F}$on sets. Of course, its inverse is given by the extension of $\mathcal{G}$ on sets. Furthermore, it is possible to show that this isomorphism is preserved by the semantics operators of the language, in the following sense:

Proposition 6.6 *For every operator op of the language, let $\widetilde{op}$ be the corresponding semantics operator of our approach, and $\widehat{op}$ the corresponding semantic operator as defined in [SRP91]. Then, for $S_1, \ldots, S_n$ saturated sets of sequences we have*

$$\mathcal{F}(\widetilde{op}(S_1, \ldots, S_n)) = \widehat{op}(\mathcal{F}(S_1), \ldots, \mathcal{F}(S_n))),$$

and for $T_1, \ldots, T_n$ upward closed sets of bto's we have

$$\mathcal{G}(\widehat{op}(T_1, \ldots, T_n)) = \widetilde{op}(\mathcal{G}(T_1), \ldots, \mathcal{G}(T_n))).$$

From Proposition 6.6 we finally derive:

Theorem 6.7 *The fully abstract semantics $\mathcal{A}$ presented in this paper and the semantics defined in [SRP91] are isomorphic.*

The representation of the semantics in terms of upward closed sets of bto's has the advantage that full abstraction is very easy to prove. Given a bto Ψ belonging to (the denotation of) a process A and not to B, we consider a context $C[\,]$ consisting of the process $\{\Psi^{-1}\}$ in parallel, i.e. $C[\,] = \{\Psi^{-1}\} \parallel [\,]$. Then $\Psi \widehat{\parallel} \Psi^{-1} = \Psi \cap \Psi^{-1}$ is a singletone c (the lub of their domain) and it constitutes an observable distinction, in fact $c \in C[A]$ and $c \notin C[B]$. To prove the last fact we use the upward closedness: if by contradiction $c \in C[B]$ then B would contain a bto $\Phi \subseteq \Psi$. But then, since B is upward closed, it would contain Ψ as well.

7 Conclusions and future work

We have presented a semantics for concurrent constraint programming which is fully abstract with respect to finite observables and the operators of choice, parallelism, prefixing and hiding. It would be interesting to extend our results to a notion of observables that includes infinite behaviours.

We are currently investigating the possibility of giving an axiomatization (in the style of Process Algebra) for the equivalence induced by our compositional models.

Another topic of future research is the development, in our semantics framework, of a tool for the static analysis of programs (in particular, deadlock analysis).

Acknowledgements We are much indebted to Jan Willem klop for stimulating discussions. We thank the members of the C.W.I. concurrency group, J.W. de Bakker, F. Breugel, A. de Bruin, E. Horita, P. Knijnenburg, J. Kok, J. Rutten, E. de Vink and J. Warmerdam for their helpful comments on preliminary versions of this paper.

References

[BHR84] S.D. Brookes, C.A.R. Hoare, and W. Roscoe. A theory of communicating sequential processes. *Journal of ACM*, 31:499–560, 1984.

[BK86] J.A. Bergstra and J.W. Klop. Process algebra: specification and verification in bisimulation semantics. In *Mathematics and Computer Science II*, CWI Monographs, pages 61 – 94. North-Holland, 1986.

[CG86] K.L. Clark and S. Gregory. PARLOG: parallel programming in logic. *ACM Trans. on Programming Languages and Systems*, (8):1–49, 1986.

[Cla79] K.L. Clark. Predicate logic as a computational formalism. Res. Report DOC 79/59, Imperial College, Dept. of Computing, London, 1979.

[dBK88] J.W. de Bakker and J.N. Kok. Uniform abstraction, atomicity and contractions in the comparative semantics of Concurrent Prolog. In *Proc. of the International Conference on Fifth Generation Computer Systems*, pages 347–355, Tokyo, Japan, 1988. OHMSHA, LTD. Extended Abstract, full version available as CWI report CS-8834.

[dBKPR89a] F.S. de Boer, J.N. Kok, C. Palamidessi, and J.J.M.M. Rutten. Control flow versus logic: a denotational and a declarative model for Guarded Horn Clauses. In A. Kreczmar and G. Mirkowska, editors, *Proc. of the Symposium on Mathematical Foundations of Computer Science*, volume 379 of *Lecture Notes in Computer Science*, pages 165–176. Springer-Verlag, 1989.

[dBKPR89b] F.S. de Boer, J.N. Kok, C. Palamidessi, and J.J.M.M. Rutten. Semantic models for a version of PARLOG. In Giorgio Levi and Maurizio Martelli, editors, *Proc. of the Sixth International Conference on Logic Programming*, Series in Logic Programming, pages 621–636, Lisboa, 1989. The MIT Press. Extended version in *Theoretical Computer Science*, 86(1):3 – 33, 1991.

[dBP90a] F.S. de Boer and C. Palamidessi. Concurrent logic languages: Asynchronism and language comparison. In *Proc. of the North American Conference on Logic Programming*, Series in Logic Programming, pages 175–194. The MIT Press, 1990. Full version available as technical report TR 6/90, Dipartimento di Informatica, Università di Pisa.

[dBP90b] F.S. de Boer and C. Palamidessi. On the asynchronous nature of communication in concurrent logic languages: A fully abstract model based on sequences. In J.C.M. Baeten and J.W. Klop, editors, *Proc. of Concur 90*, volume 458 of *Lecture Notes in Computer Science*, pages 99–114, Amsterdam, 1990. Springer-Verlag. Full version available as Technical Report CSN 90/17, Technische Universiteit Eindhoven.

[dBP91] F.S. de Boer and C. Palamidessi. A Fully Abstract Model for Concurrent Constraint Programming. In S. Abramsky and T.S.E. Maibaum, editors, *Proc. of TAPSOFT/CAAP*, volume 493 of *Lecture Notes in Computer Science*, pages 296–319. Springer-Verlag, 1991.

[dBP92] F.S. de Boer and C. Palamidessi. On the semantics of Concurrent Constraint Programming. Technical Report, Dipartimento di Informatica, Università di Pisa, 1992.

[GCLS88] R. Gerth, M. Codish, Y. Lichtenstein, and E. Shapiro. Fully abstract denotational semantics for Concurrent Prolog. In *Proc. of the Third IEEE Symposium on Logic In Computer Science*, pages 320–335. IEEE Computer Society Press, New York, 1988.

[GL90] M. Gabbrielli and G. Levi. Unfolding and fixpoint semantics for concurrent constraint logic programs. In H. Kirchner and

W. Wechler, editors, *Proc. of the Second Int. Conf. on Algebraic and Logic Programming*, Lecture Notes in Computer Science, pages 204–216, Nancy, France, 1990. Springer-Verlag.

[GMS89] H. Gaifman, M. J. Maher, and E. Shapiro. Reactive Behaviour semantics for Concurrent Constraint Logic Programs. In E. Lusk and R. Overbeck, editors, *North American Conference on Logic Programming*, 1989.

[HMT71] L. Henkin, J.D. Monk, and A. Tarski. *Cylindric Algebras (Part I)*. North-Holland, 1971.

[JL87] J. Jaffar and J.-L. Lassez. Constraint logic programming. In *Proc,. of ACM Symposium on Principles of Programming Languages*, pages 111–119. ACM, New York, 1987.

[Kok88] J.N. Kok. A compositional semantics for Concurrent Prolog. In R. Cori and M. Wirsing, editors, *Proc. Fifth Symposium on Theoretical Aspects of Computer Science*, volume 294 of *Lecture Notes in Computer Science*, pages 373–388. Springer-Verlag, 1988.

[Mah87] M. J. Maher. Logic semantics for a class of committed-choice programs. In Jean-Louis Lassez, editor, *Proc. of the Fourth International Conference on Logic Programming*, Series in Logic Programming, pages 858–876, Melbourne, 1987. The MIT Press.

[Mil80] R. Milner. *A Calculus of Communicating Systems*, volume 92 of *Lecture Notes in Computer Science*. Springer-Verlag, New York, 1980.

[Par81] D.M.R. Park. Concurrency and automata on infinite sequences. In P. Deussen, editor, *Proc. of the 5th GI conference*, Lecture Notes in Computer Science, pages 167–183. Springer-Verlag, 1981.

[Rin87] G.A. Ringwood. Pattern-Directed, Markovian, Linear Guarded Definite Clause Resolution. Technical report, Imperial College, London, 1987.

[Sar85] V.A. Saraswat. Partial Correctness Semantics for CP($\emptyset$, $|$, &). In *Proc. of the Conference on Foundations of Software Computing and Theoretical Computer Science*, volume 206 of *Lecture Notes in Computer Science*, pages 347–368. Springer-Verlag, 1985.

[Sar89] V.A. Saraswat. *Concurrent Constraint Programming Languages*. PhD thesis, Carnegie-Mellon University, January 1989. Published by The MIT Press, U.S.A., 1990.

[Sco82] D. Scott. Domains for denotational semantics. In *Proc. of ICALP*, 1982.

[Sha83] E.Y. Shapiro. A subset of Concurrent Prolog and its interpreter. Technical Report TR-003, Institute for New Generation Computer Technology (ICOT), Tokyo, 1983.

[Sha86] E. Y. Shapiro. Concurrent Prolog: A progress report. *Computer*, 19(8):44–58, 1986.

[SR90] V.A. Saraswat and M. Rinard. Concurrent constraint programming. In *Proc. of the seventeenth ACM Symposium on Principles of Programming Languages*, pages 232–245. ACM, New York, 1990.

[SRP91] V.A. Saraswat, M. Rinard, and P. Panangaden. Semantics foundations of Concurrent Constraint Programming. In *Proc. of the eighteenth ACM Symposium on Principles of Programming Languages*. ACM, New York, 1991.

[Ued87] K. Ueda. Guarded Horn Clauses. In E. Y. Shapiro, editor, *Concurrent Prolog: Collected Papers*. The MIT Press, 1987.

[Ued88] K. Ueda. Guarded Horn Clauses, a parallel logic programming language with the concept of a guard. In M. Nivat and K. Fuchi, editors, *Programming of Future Generation Computers*, pages 441–456. North Holland, Amsterdam, 1988.

L2||O2: Operational and Declarative Semantics*

E. Pimentel
J.M. Troya

Dpto. de Lenguajes y Ciencias de la Computación. Universidad de Málaga
Málaga - SPAIN

Abstract

In this paper we define the L2||O2 language incorporating the typical mechanisms of the object oriented programming into concurrent logic languages. This language is defined in the framework of the Parlog language, which contributes with its declarative style and its concurrence, considering objects as perpetual processes and message passing as the data stream among shared variables. The possibility of defining classes recursively, to extend the inheritance relation with the use relation, to link objects dynamically, to inherit private predicates plus some implementation issues, as well as the definition of the declarative semantics, distinguishes our proposal from others. Although we have implemented the whole language, in order to simplifiy the declarative semantics, we consider a subset of this, including the more relevant aspects of the object oriented method: class definition, creation of instances, inheritance, use relation, messages among objects. The operational semantics of this subset is given in terms of a transition relation which is defined by using the transition relation corresponding to the concurrent logic language considered. Only the success set is modelled. On other hand, the declarative semantics is defined as the least fixpoint of an immediate consequences operator. This is achieved by making use of an extended notion of Herbrand base and interpretations, enriched with variables and with annotations. The basic mathematical structure is the set of finite streams of substitutions. In order to relate both semantics, we show a result that permits us to establish the success set (given by the operational semantics) of a goal in terms of the least fixpoint of the operator defined.

1 Introduction

Concurrent logic languages [1] support the object-oriented paradigm considering objects as perpetual processes, and the messages between them as information transfer by means of shared variables [2]. Based on this idea a number of object-oriented extensions of concurrent logic languages have been proposed: Vulcan [3], Polka [4], Mandala [5]). These extensions provide some of the main characteristics in the object-oriented paradigm: inheritance (by delegation), encapsulation, hiding information, etc. All these proposals use the logic component in the integration to obtain very expressive object-oriented programming languages. However, the semantic aspects of these extensions have not been dealt with in depth. Only some references to the simple semantics of the kernel language used in the implementation have been made [3].

The need to formally define the computation models of the object-oriented languages is obvious. In this sense, a number of operational and denotational semantics for some mechanisms and languages have been proposed [6,7,8]. Likewise, the facility of defining

* This work was supported by the project CICYT-TIC 340/90

declarative semantics for the logic languages has also been extended to the object-oriented extensions [9]. Our aim is to exploit the possibility of defining formal semantics for the concurrent logic languages, in order to give a declarative semantics for a subset of the L2||O2 language proposed in [10]. This subset incorporates the main object-oriented mechanisms with the concurrent logic languages.

In Section 2 we introduce an object-oriented view of the concurrent logic languages and we consider an operational and a declarative semantics for a version of the Parlog language. In Section 3 we define the L2||O2 language and we illustrate it with some examples showing the difference between the client and inheritance relations. Later, a subset of L2||O2 is considered, and its operational semantics, based on a transition relation, is defined in order to obtain all computed answer substitutions corresponding to all successfully terminating computations of a given goal. We extend the approach used in [10] to define a declarative semantics for a version of Parlog, in order to achieve a declarative semantics for a subset of the integration proposed [11]. The two semantics are related by giving an equivalence between them in terms of the least fixpoint of an immediate consequences operator.

2 Concurrent logic languages. An object-oriented view

The commited choice logic languages, whose more outstanding representatives are Parlog [12], Concurrent Prolog [13] and GHC [14], are characterized by the appearance of guards in the clauses, such that the general aspect of one of them is:

$$H <- G_1, G_2, \ldots, G_n : B_1, B_2, \ldots, B_m.$$

where the goals G_i form the guard of the clause, and B_j its body.

Another characteristic of these languages is the distinction between input arguments and output arguments; either by means of a mode declaration (Parlog), adding '?' after the variable (CP), or including the input constraint in the execution model (GHC).

The reduction of an atomic goal is made by choosing a clause from the candidates nondeterministically, and substituting it by the clause body. When a choice is done, it cannot be undone (commit). The set of candidate clauses for a goal is composed of those clauses whose input variables in the head match the corresponding variables in the goal.

The concurrence is obtained due to AND-stream parallelism. Thus, the goal

?- producer(S),consumer(S).

where the arguments of *producer* and *consumer* are input and output variables, respectively, can be solved by suspending the evaluation of *consumer(S)* until *producer* produces a value for *S*. The concurrence is effective due to the partial binding, that is, a predicate will generate a list incrementally.

Finally, another significant characteristic of our proposals is back communication (incomplete messages). For example, the clause:

p(success(Ok),V) <- c(V) : Ok = ok.

will return ok on the Ok variable, if V satisfies c, although the first argument of p is declared as input.

2.1 Operational and declarative semantics

An operational and a fixpoint semantics based on the computations rules of GHC and Concurrent Prolog are found in [15]. Similar work is found in [10] with a version of Parlog. An operational semantics of a version of Parlog is given in the above-mentioned work considering the transition relation $\rightarrow_{\text{Parlog}} \subseteq (\mathcal{G}^{+}\times\Sigma)^2$ ($\mathcal{G}$ being the set of goals and Σ the set of substitutions). $\rightarrow_{\text{Parlog}}$ describes the situations in which a transition can be made. The parallel execution of a conjunction is modelled by interleaving. The input and output constraints are established by means of two most general unifiers: mgu_i and mgu_o.

After this, a declarative semantics, based on a fixpoint of an immediate consequence operator, is defined making use of an extended notion of Herbrand base and interpretations, enriched with variables and annotations in a similar way to [15].

2.2 Objects as perpetual processes

AND-stream parallelism and partial binding permit us to identify objects as perpetual processes. This is obtained by defining the objects behaviour by means of predicates consisting of recursive clauses. This will create a process with permanent activity. On the other hand, the communication among objects will be achieved by message sending, using the shared variables. These are the communication channels.

This approach is used in the implementation of Vulcan and Polka. Our proposal is based on the same method also, but there are some differences with respect to them. For example, our language explicitly distinguishes the client and inheritance relations; it permits the recursive class definition (it is possible to use the same class that is being defined), the private predicates are inherited, it is possible to establish a linking between two objects by means of a message. Moreover, in the language implementation, we construct the perpetual processes using metacalls: if the message processed belongs to the class of the object that received it, then a recursive call is made; but if the message belongs to an inherited class, the metacall maintains the self object. This technique simplifies the processing of messages sent to *self*. In [5] the metacalls are used to implement the inheritance, but they can produce undesired side effects.

3 The L2||O2 language

The syntax, semantics and implementation of the L2||O2 language which we define are based on those of Parlog++ and Polka, although they present significant differences as we have mentioned.

3.1 Syntax and operational characteristics

The syntactic outline of a class definition in the language proposed is:

<class> [<channels>] [; <channels>]
[**inherit** <classes>]
state <state_vars>
[**use** <calls>]
messages
EGHCs
end.

where

<classes> ::= <class> {',' <class>}
<class> ::= *Parlog identifier*
<channels> ::= <channel> {',' <channel>}
<channel> ::= *Parlog variable*
<state_vars> ::= <state_var> {',' <state_var>}

```
<state_var>   ::= Parlog term not ground
<calls>       ::= <call> {',' <call>}
<call>        ::= <class> '(' <channels> ')'
```

and EGHCs are a sequence of extended guarded Horn clauses whose syntax and semantics we will study below.

The interface of a class instance will be given by its input and output channels. They are declared after the class name (the output channels appear after ;). A class will always have an input channel I(c) (c being the class name) in addition to those appearing in the declaration. The state of an object will be determined by the structures in the *state* clause. The encapsulating and hiding information issues related with the instance variables will be similar to Smalltalk; in our context, it means that the state access will be made using incomplete messages. Message processing will be determined by the extended guarded clauses. These clauses have the following syntax:

[[I] ?] H <- G : B.

where I will be an input channel of the class or an output channel of an object in *use*. If I is not present, we consider I(c). The non-extended guarded Horn clauses correspond to private predicates. There can appear in B primitives of message passing as *O ! m*, *m* being a term (or *last*, indicating the closure of the channel *O*) and *O* either an output channel of the class, an input channel of some instance in *use*, an argument of the head (dynamic linking), a name of any inherited class, or one the key word *self*. The message *m* can be also a sequence of messages.

The behavior of a point can be described in L2||O2 as follows:

```
point
state X,Y
messages
   ? init(A,B)        <- nonvar(A),nonvar(B) : X is A, Y is B.
   ? x(A)             <- var(A) : A is X.
   ? x(A)             <- nonvar(A) : X becomes A.
   ? y(B)             <- var(B) : B is Y.
   ? y(B)             <- nonvar(B) : Y becomes B.
   ? move(A,B)        <- nonvar(A),nonvar(B): X becomes X+A, Y becomes Y+B.
   ? distance(P,D)    <- P ! x(X1), P ! y(Y1), distance(X1,Y1,X2,Y2,D).
   mode distance(?,?,?,?,^).
   distance(X1,Y1,X2,Y2,D) <-
        D1 is X1-Y1, D2 is X2-Y2, D3 is D1*D1+D2*D2, sqrt(D3,D).
end.
```

Because there are no variables after the class name, the only input channel will be I(point). The variables X and Y will determine the state of an instance, and their updating is made with the *becomes* primitive [16]. Note that private messages, as *distance/5* will be processed by Parlog clauses; we could use any other kernel concurrent logic language. On other hand, it is possible in L2||O2 to send messages along a channel provided by an argument of a method; e.g. in the clause corresponding to the distance method, we can use the first argument as a channel of any other object. This possibility is not considered in other proposals such as Polka, and it is very useful to connect objects dynamically.

The class instances are created from the *use* clause of a class or by means of a query. The queries will be made from that which we will call *top*, and this will be considered a special class, whose *use* section will contain the part of the query creating instances, and whose *messages* section will be composed of non-extended guarded Horn clauses. For example, the next query:

```
?- point(P1), point(P2), P2!init(2,0),
   P1!(init(1,2),move(1,0),distance(P2,D),x(X),y(Y),last).
```

will be made in the frame of a class *top* where the *use* section will contain: `point(P1)`, `point(P2)`. The rest of the calls will be considered the goal to solve.

To illustrate the client and inheritance relations, we give the class definition corresponding to a *segment* and a *particle*:

```
segment
use point(P1), point(P2)
messages
   ? origin(A,B)       <- P1 ! x(A), P1 ! y(B).
   ? extreme(A,B)      <- P2 ! x(A), P2 ! y(B).
   ? move(A,B)         <- P1 ! move(A,B), P2 ! move(A,B).
   ? length(L)         <- P1 ! distance(P2,L).
end.

particle
inherits point
state Weight
messages
   ? weight(M)         <- var(M)  : M is Weight.
   ? weight(M)         <- nonvar(M)  : Weight becomes M.
   ? attraction(P,A)   <- constant(G), self ! distance(P,D),
                          P ! weight(W), A is Weight*W*G/(D*D).
   mode constant(^).
   constant(6.67E-11).
end.
```

The first example shows how the segment class uses two instances of the class point, named P1 and P2, respectively. In the second one the particle class inherits from the point class. The instances of the segment and particle classes can be created with calls in the *top* as:

```
?- particle(P), segment(S), P!(init(1,1),weight(10),x(X1),y(Y1), ...),
   S!(origin(0,0),extreme(X1,Y1), ...).
```

This query creates a particle and a segment joining it to the point (0,0).

3.2 Operational semantics

In order to simplify the declarative semantics of the language, which will be defined later, we will consider some limitations on the constructions of L2||O2. Starting from now the only channels in a class definition will be the input channels, and in the expressions *O!m*, *m* will be a term (or *last*) and *O* will be an input channel of some instance in *use*. That is, the input channels of an object in use are considered output channels for the current object.

So, this section does not include the definition of the message sending to *self*. For the same reason we will not consider the message sending on channels provided as arguments of some message. The operational definition and implementation of these mechanisms do not present any problem (we have a prototype working), but the declarative semantics can become very confusing.

Suppose the general description of a class is:

c I1,I2,...,In
inherit c1,c2,...,ch
state t1,t2,...,ts
use $d_1(I^1_0,\ldots,I^1_{n_1})$,...,$d_k(I^k_0$,...,$I^k_{n_k})$
messages
...
end

Formally, a class will be given by:

$$c : \{ \mathcal{I}_c, \mathcal{S}_c, inh_c, use_c, \mathcal{M}_c \},$$

where c belongs to the set of class names $\mathcal{C}$, and

$\mathcal{I}_c = [I_0,I_1,\ldots,I_n]$, being $I_0 = I(c)$
$\mathcal{S}_c = \{t_1,t_2,\ldots,t_s\}$
$inh_c = \{c_1,c_2,\ldots,c_h\}$
$use_c = \{(d_1,I^1_0,\ldots,I^1_{n_1})$,...,$(d_k,I^k_0$,...,$I^k_{n_k})$
$\mathcal{M}_c$ is the set of clauses processing the messages of the class c.

And a program will be given by a set of classes

$$\mathcal{P} \subseteq \{ c:\{\mathcal{I}_c,\mathcal{S}_c,inh_c,use_c,\mathcal{M}_c\}, c\in \mathcal{C}\}$$

In the following, we will consider all the *becomes* operations in an EGHC grouped at the end of its body. That is, the EGHCs will have the following aspect:

$$[[I]\ ?]\ H \text{ <- } G : B,B_{bcc}.$$

We will base the operational semantics of the language on the transition systems. The transition systems permit us to determine the semantics of a program in terms of transitions between configurations. The execution of a program is modelled by a configuration sequence with transitions between them, starting with an initial configuration.

Our aim is to operationally model the set of answers for a given goal in the *top*. A query in the *top* will be divided into two parts: the creation of instances, and the goals to solve. So, if G is a conjunction of goals, we will distinguish G_{use} and G_{goal}, such that $G=G_{use},G_{goal}$. G_{use} will create the instances, and G_{goal} should be solved.

We define $\mathcal{O} : \mathcal{G}^+ \rightarrow \mathcal{P}(\Sigma)$ by

$\mathcal{O}[true] = \{\varepsilon\}$
$\mathcal{O}[G] = \{ \sigma_{|var(G)} \mid <(G;\ S_i;\ \varepsilon)_{top};\ \varepsilon> \rightarrow^* <(true;\ S_f;\ \varepsilon)_{top};\ \sigma>$,
where $S_i=\{(O,\_,o\_c) : O$ is an argument of an atom in $G_{use}\}$
and $S_f=\{(O,[last|\_],o\_c) : O$ is an argument of an atom in $G_{use}\}$ }

The success set for G is given by $\mathcal{O}[G]$: it contains all computed answer substitutions corresponding to all successfully terminating computations. These result of all possible transitions from the top object, whose state is composed by all arguments of any atom in G_{use} flagged as output channels (o_c). The final state must be composed by the same channels, but containing the *last* message .

We can see that the operational semantics is defined in terms of the reflexive-transitive closure of a transition relation $\rightarrow$. This one is based on $\rightarrow_{Parlog}$.

A typical configuration for $\rightarrow$ will be composed of a sequence of tuples and a substitution. The tuples will model the state of each object. So, a tuple will consist of a class name, a sequence of goals, a set of terms and a substitution: (c, G, S, γ), $c \in \mathcal{C}$, $G \in \mathcal{G}^+$, $\gamma \in \Sigma$. The terms of S have the form:

(*var_name*, *value*, *type*),

being *var_name* $\in \mathcal{V}$ (set of variables), *type* $\in \{i\_c, o\_c, st\}$ (input channel, output channel and state) and *value* $\in \mathcal{T}$ (set of terms), such that if *type* $\in \{i\_c, o\_c\}$, then *value* is a list. Moreover, S can contain the special elements *f_m* (first message) and *f* (finished), which will allow the control of the arrival of the first and last messages. That is,

$$S \in \mathcal{S} = \mathcal{P}(\mathcal{V} \times \mathcal{T} \times \{i\_c, o\_c, st\} \cup \{f\_m, f\})$$

and the set of tuples will be

$$\Gamma_0 = \mathcal{C} \times \mathcal{G}^+ \times \mathcal{S} \times \Sigma$$

So, the set of configurations will be

$$\Gamma = \Gamma_0^+ \times \Sigma$$

and when $(c,G,S,M) \in \Gamma_0$ we will write $(G,S,M)_c$.

Each tuple $(G,S,\gamma)_c$ represents a particular state of a class instance (see figure). So, the behavior of an object is modelled by a class name c, a list of goals to solve G, an inner state S, and the renaming γ of the program $\mathcal{M}_c$ providing the connections with other objects.

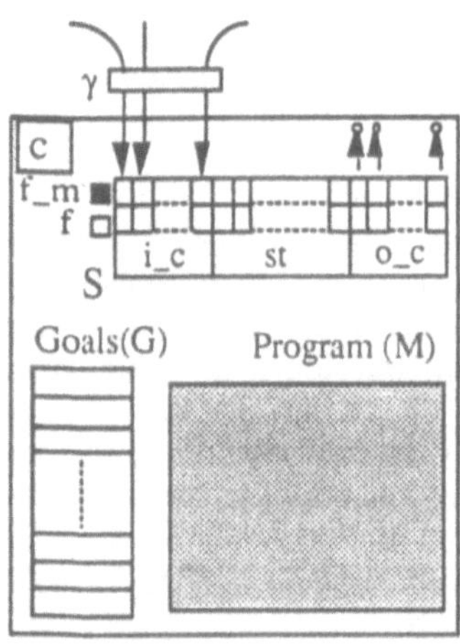

Before defining the relation $\rightarrow \subseteq \Gamma^2$ we will establish some aspects of the notation.

If $(\gamma,\lambda) \in \rightarrow$ we will write $\gamma \rightarrow \lambda$.

Given the sequence of input channels $\mathcal{I}_c$, we define $\overline{\mathcal{I}_c}$ as the closure of $\mathcal{I}_c$ with respect to the inheritance relation, that is, the list obtained by adding all the inherited input channels:

$$\overline{\mathcal{I}_c} = \begin{cases} \overline{\mathcal{I}_{c_1}} + \ldots + \overline{\mathcal{I}_{c_h}} + \mathcal{I}^*_c, & \text{if } inh_c = \{c_1, c_2, \ldots, c_h\} \\ \mathcal{I}^*_c, & \text{if } inh_c = \emptyset \end{cases},$$

$\mathcal{I}_c^*$ being the list $\mathcal{I}_c$ without I(c), and + the concatenate operator. Similarly, $\overline{\mathcal{S}_c}$ is defined as

$$\overline{\mathcal{S}_c} = \begin{cases} \mathcal{S}_c \cup \left(\bigcup_{d\in \text{inh}_c} \overline{\mathcal{S}_d}\right) & \text{if } \text{inh}_c \neq \emptyset \\ \mathcal{S}_c \quad \text{if } \text{inh}_c = \emptyset \end{cases}$$

We suposse the state variables in different classes are disjoint.

On the other hand, for any $c\in C$, we define

$pos_c : \text{inh}_c \rightarrow \{1..\#\text{inh}_c\}$

such that for any $d\in \text{inh}_C$, $pos_c(d)$ represents the position occupied by d in the *inherit* clause of c. This will permit us to assign an order to the multiple inheritance.We also define $anc : \mathcal{C} \rightarrow 2^{\mathcal{C}}$ and $pri_C : anc(c) \rightarrow \{0,...,\#anc(c) - 1\}$ as

$$anc(c) = \{c\} \cup \left(\bigcup_{d\in \text{inh}_c} anc(d)\right)$$

$$pri_c(a) = \begin{cases} pos_e(a) + \sum\limits_{\substack{a\notin \text{inh}_d \\ pri_c(d)<pri_c(e)}} \#\text{inh}_d, & \text{being } c\neq a\in \text{inh}_e \text{ and } e\in anc(c) \\ 0 \quad \text{if} \quad a=c \end{cases}$$

Given c, *anc*(c) provides a set containing all its inherited classes (directly or indirectly, i. e. the ancestors of c), and pri_C an inheritance priority. Both together formally represent the inheritance graph.

If γ is the substitution $\{V_1/V_1',...,V_n/V_n'\}$, $\mathcal{M}$ is a set of EGHCs for a class c and V_i belongs to $\overline{\mathcal{I}_c}$, we will denote $\mathcal{M}_\gamma$ as the set of clauses after formally substituting the variable V_i by V_i'.

On the other hand, if $S\in \mathcal{S}$, then we define $\eta_S=\{X/x : (X,x,st) \in S\}\in\Sigma$, and if B_{bec} is a conjunction of becomes operations then $bec(B_{bec}, S)$ is the new state resulting from S after changing (X,v,st) to (X,t,st) when X *becomes* t is in B_{bec}.

If C=(I?H<-G:B) is an EGHC, we call h_C to H, and i_c_C to I. If C = (H<-G:B) then i_c_C will be considered $\emptyset$.

Finally, *add*(S,I,m) with $(I,V,ch)\in S$, is the new state after substituting (I,V,ch) with (I,V+m,ch); and *ext*(S,I,m) with $(I,[m|M],ch)\in S$ is the new state after substituting (I,[m|M],ch) with (I,M,ch); where $ch\in \{i\_c, o\_c\}$.

3.3 Definition of the transition relation

We define $\rightarrow$ as the smallest relation verifying:

a) Creation of instances

$$\frac{\begin{array}{l} d{:}\{\mathcal{I}_d,\mathcal{S}_d,\text{inh}_d,\text{use}_d,\mathcal{M}_d\} \in \mathcal{P}, \text{ with } \#\overline{\mathcal{I}_d}=n \\ S' = \{(I_i,\_,o\_c)\}_{i=0..n} \\ S'' = \{(I_i,\_,i\_c)\}_{i=0..n} \cup \{(t,\_,st)\}_{t\in\overline{\mathcal{S}_d}} \cup \{f\_m\} \\ \text{If } \overline{\mathcal{I}_d}=[J_1,...,J_n] \text{ we consider } \gamma=\{I(d)/I_0, J_i/I_i\} \end{array}}{<(d(I_0,I_1,...,I_n),G;\ S;\ \gamma)_c;\ \sigma> \ \rightarrow\ <(G;\ S\cup S';\ \gamma)_c,\ (true;\ S'';\ \gamma)_d;\ \sigma>}$$

When a d-instance is created in the context of a class c, the state S of the c-instance is modified by S' and a new object appears with state S". The connection between both is made by considering all input channels of the d-instance as output channels of the c-instance. This information can be accessed by the d-instance by means of γ'.

Note that we are not considering the possibility of sharing channels among an object and its providers (those appearing in *use*). To achieve this sharing we would have to compose γ and γ' in the d-object. We have not found a convincing reason that justifies it.

b) Message sending

$$\frac{\begin{array}{l}(I,M,o\_c)\in S_1,\ M\neq[last|\_]\\ (I,N,i\_c)\in S_2\\ S_1' = add(S_1,I,m\sigma)\\ S_2' = add(S_2,I,m\sigma)\end{array}}{<(I!m,\ G_1;\ S_1;\ \gamma_1)_c,\ (G_2;\ S_2;\ \gamma_2)_d;\ \sigma> \rightarrow <(G_1;\ S_1';\ \gamma_1)_c,\ (G_2;\ S_2';\ \gamma_2)_d;\ \sigma>}$$

When a message is sent on an output channel, the transition is allowed if the same channel appears in another object state as input.

c) Message reception

i) First message

$$\frac{\begin{array}{l}f\_m\in S,\ \exists\ (I,M,i\_c)\in S,\ \text{with M non-variable}\\ \text{Let } use_c = \left\{ (d_i,I_0^i,\ldots,I_{n_i}^i) \right\}_{i=1..k} \text{ be}\\ S' = S\backslash\{f\_m\}\end{array}}{<(G;\ S;\ \gamma)_c;\ \sigma> \rightarrow <(G, \bigwedge_{i=1}^{i=k} d_i(I_0^i,\ldots,I_{n_i}^i);\ S';\ \gamma)_c;\ \sigma>}$$

The objects that will be used by the current instance are created only when this receives the first message. It permits a class to use an instance of itself. Therefore it is possible to construct recursive structures. For example, the class

```
snake
state Is_tail
use point(Head),snake(Body)
messages
   ? born(X,Y)        <- Head ! init(X,Y), Is_tail becomes yes.
   ? grow(X,Y)        <- Is_tail=no : Body ! grow(X,Y), Is_tail becomes no.
   ? grow(X,Y)        <- Is_tail=yes : Body ! born(X,Y), Is_tail becomes no.
   ? move(A,B)        <- Is_tail=no : Head ! move(A,B), Body ! move(A,B).
   ? move(A,B)        <- Is_tail=yes : Head ! move(A,B).
end.
```

defines the behaviour of a snake composed of a point (Head) and another snake (Body). So, when a process corresponding to an object snake is created, two more objects (a point, and another snake) must be created, but only when the snake receives a message. This is obtained storing the *f_m* flag in the state of a snake until the first message arrives.

ii) Message processing (applying inheritance)

$$\frac{\begin{array}{l}(I,[m|M],i\_c)\in S,\ m\neq last\\ \exists\ c\in anc(a) : \forall\ b\in anc(a) \text{ with } pri_a(b) < pri_a(c) \text{ it holds}\\ \quad \forall D\in (\mathcal{M}_b)_\gamma\ \neg\exists\ mgu_i(m\sigma,h_D) \text{ with } i\_c_D=I,\\ \exists\ (I?h \text{ <- } F{:}B)\in_* (\mathcal{M}_c)_\gamma\ (?h\text{<-}F{:}B \text{ if } I=I(a)) \text{ and } \exists\ \theta=mgu_i(m\sigma,h) \text{ such that}\\ \quad <F;\ \theta> \rightarrow_{Parlog} <true;\ \sigma'>\\ S'=ext(S,I,m)\end{array}}{<(G;\ S;\ \gamma)_a;\sigma> \rightarrow <(G,B;\ S';\ \gamma)_a;\ \sigma\sigma'>}$$

When a message is found on an input channel in the state S of an instance of the class a, and there is some ancestor c of a with an adequate clause to process the message, then the body of this clause is added to the pending goals of the object, the state is modified and the substitution is updated with the new bindings.

iii) Last message

$$\frac{\forall\ (I,M,i\_c) \in S\ ,\ M=[\mathit{last}|\_] \quad S'=S \cup \{f\}}{<(G;\ S;\ \gamma)_a;\ \sigma> \rightarrow <(G, \wedge_{(O,v,o\_c)\in S} O!\mathit{last};\ S';\ \gamma)_a;\ \sigma>}$$

If the *last* message is on all input channels of an object, then the same message will be put on all output channels of the object, and the *finished* flag (*f*) is joined to its state.

$$\frac{f \in S}{<(\mathit{true};\ S;\ P)_c, L;\ \sigma> \rightarrow <L;\ \sigma>}$$

d) Goal reduction

i) Private predicates

The private predicates reduction is accomplished by considering that they can be inherited. The necessary conditions to make the transition are similar to that of message processing. In this occasion an output unification can be produced because the arguments of a clause can be declared as output.

$$\frac{\begin{array}{l}\exists\ c \in \mathit{anc}(a) : \forall\ b \in \mathit{anc}(a) \text{ with } \mathit{pri}(b) < \mathit{pri}(c) \text{ it holds} \\ \quad \forall D \in (\mathcal{M}_b)_\gamma \text{ with } i\_c_D = \emptyset\ \neg\exists\ \mathrm{mgu}_i(g\sigma, h_D), \\ \exists\ (h \leftarrow F{:}B) \in (\mathcal{M}_c)_\gamma \text{ and } \exists\ \theta = \mathrm{mgu}_i(g\sigma, h) \text{ such that} \\ \quad <F;\ \theta> \rightarrow_{\mathrm{Parlog}} <\mathit{true};\ \sigma'>\end{array}}{<(g,G;\ S;\ \gamma)_a;\ \sigma> \rightarrow <(\mathit{outunif}(g\sigma, h\sigma'), B, G;\ S;\ \gamma)_a;\ \sigma\sigma'>}$$

ii) Output unification

$$\frac{\exists\ \mathrm{mgu}_O(g\sigma, h\sigma'),}{<(\mathit{outunif}(g\sigma, h\sigma'), B;\ S;\ \gamma)_a;\ \sigma\sigma'> \rightarrow <(B;\ S;\ \gamma)_a;\ \sigma\,\mathrm{mgu}_o(g\sigma, h\sigma')\eta_S>}$$

iii) Becomes

$$\frac{(X,v,st) \in S \quad S' = S \setminus \{(X,v,st)\} \cup \{(X,t,st)\}}{<(X\ \mathit{becomes}\ t, B;\ S;\ \gamma)_a;\ \sigma> \rightarrow <(B;\ S';\ \gamma)_a;\ \sigma>}$$

The transition of X *becomes* t is made by substituting the value of X in S by t.

e) Interleaving

The parallel execution of the goals conjunction in an object and the concurrence between objects are modelled by interleaving.

i) Objects interleaving

$$\frac{<K;\ \sigma> \rightarrow <K';\ \sigma'>}{\begin{array}{l}<K,L;\ \sigma> \rightarrow <K',L;\ \sigma'> \\ <L,K;\ \sigma> \rightarrow <L,K';\ \sigma'>\end{array}}$$

ii) Goals interleaving

$$\frac{<(A;\ S;\ \rho)_c, L;\ \sigma> \ \rightarrow\ <(A';\ S';\ \rho')_c, L';\ \sigma'> \mid <(true;\ S';\ \rho')_c, L';\ \sigma'>}{\begin{array}{l}<(A,B;\ S;\ \rho)_c, L;\ \sigma> \ \rightarrow\ <(A',B;\ S';\ \rho')_c, L';\ \sigma'> \mid <(B;\ S';\ \rho')_c, L';\ \sigma'> \\ <(B,A;\ S;\ \rho)_c, L;\ \sigma> \ \rightarrow\ <(B,A';\ S';\ \rho')_c, L';\ \sigma'> \mid <(B;\ S';\ \rho')_c, L';\ \sigma'>\end{array}}$$

The use of $\rightarrow_{Parlog}$, mgu_i and mgu_o does not limit the definition of $\rightarrow$. It is possible to adjust the semantics proposed to any concurrent logic language.

3.4 Declarative semantics

As we have mentioned before, to define the declarative semantics we will use some concepts which will be explained briefly here. For a full presentation we refer to [10].

3.4.1 Annotated variables

Annotation can occur on a variable in the goal, and it means that such a variable is located in an argument declared as input, and therefore cannot be bound, during the derivation step, before commitment.

We will denote the set of annotated variables by $\mathcal{V}^-$. If $X \in \mathcal{V}$ then $X^- \in \mathcal{V}^-$, and it means that the X variable is affected by an input constraint. The set of terms $\mathcal{T}$ is extended on the new set of variables $\mathcal{V} \cup \mathcal{V}^-$. If $t \in \mathcal{T}$ then t^- is the term obtained by replacing in t every variable $X \in \mathcal{V}$ by X^-.

A substitution σ is now a mapping $\sigma\colon \mathcal{V} \cup \mathcal{V}^- \rightarrow \mathcal{T}$, such that $\sigma(X) \neq X$ only for a finite number of Xs. In order to model the difference between producing and receiving a binding we introduce an asymmetry in the application of a substitution σ to a term (or atom, or formula) t.

$$t\sigma = \begin{cases} \sigma(X) & \text{if } t = X \in \mathcal{V} \\ \sigma(X^-) & \text{if } t = X^- \in \mathcal{V}^- \text{ and } \sigma(X^-) \neq X^- \\ \sigma(X) & \text{if } t = X^- \in \mathcal{V}^- \text{ and } \sigma(X^-) = X^- \\ f(t_1\sigma, \dots, t_n\sigma) & \text{if } t = f(t_1, \dots, t_n) \end{cases}$$

So, $\sigma(X^-)$ can result in $\sigma(X)^-$, instead of $\sigma(X)$. Therefore, when an annotated variable is bound to a term t, all the variables occurring in t come under the influence of the input-mode constraint.

The set of substitutions is factorized with respect to the equivalence relation $\sigma_1 \equiv \sigma_2$ iff $\forall\ X \in \mathcal{V} \cup \mathcal{V}^-$, $X\sigma_1 = X\sigma_2$. So, a substitution σ will indicate its equivalence class.

3.4.2 Parallel composition

Intuitively, parallel composition is the formalization of a basic operation performed by the parallel execution model of logic programs. If two atoms in the same goal are solved in parallel, the associated computed answer substitutions have to be combined to obtain the final result. The combination is obtained by using parallel composition.

Given a set of sets of terms T, σ is an unifier for T if:

$$\forall\ S \in T : \forall\ t_1, t_2 \in S,\ t_1\sigma = t_2\sigma \text{ and } t_1^-\sigma = t_2^-\sigma$$

The set of mgu's of T is denoted by mgu(T).

In the following, $S(\sigma)$ will be the set of sets $\{\{X,t\} \mid X/t \in \sigma\}$, σ being a substitution.

We define the parallel composition $\hat{o}$ of two substitutions σ_1 and σ_2 as follows:

$$\sigma_1 \hat{o} \sigma_2 = mgu(S(\sigma_1) \cup S(\sigma_2))$$

And, if Θ_1, Θ_2 are sets of substitutions,

$$\Theta_1 o \Theta_2 = \bigcup_{\sigma_i \in \Theta_i} \sigma_1 \hat{o} \sigma_2$$

We will denote the sets $\{\sigma\}\hat{o}\Theta$ and $\Theta\hat{o}\{\sigma\}$ by $\sigma\hat{o}\Theta$ and $\Theta\hat{o}\sigma$ respectively.

3.4.3 Sequences of substitutions

When the input constraints are present, it is not sufficient to only consider a substitution in order to declaratively model the computed bindings. In [Levi & Palamidessi 87] it is shown that a flat representation of the computed bindings is not powerful enough to model the effects of the possible interleavings in the execution of the atoms in a goal. We need to register in some sense the whole history of the execution of the atom, and therefore we have to deal with sequences of substitutions. But it is not sufficient to consider Σ^+, because in order to represent the *critical sections* given by the input unification and the guard evaluation of Parlog, we need to separate a subsequence from the rest.

So, a finite sequence of substitutions, s, is defined by the following syntax:

$$s ::= \sigma \mid [s] \mid s_1.s_2$$

The squared brackets are used to delimit the critical sections. Their meaning will be clarified by the definition of the *interleaving operator* ||.

$$\begin{aligned} s_1 \| s_2 = \; & \{\sigma.s \mid \exists\, s' : \sigma.s'=s_1,\ s \in s' \| s_2\} \\ \cup \; & \{\sigma.s \mid \exists\, s' : \sigma.s'=s_2,\ s \in s' \| s_1\} \\ \cup \; & \{[s'].s \mid \exists\, s'' : [s'].s''=s_1,\ s \in s'' \| s_2\} \\ \cup \; & \{[s'].s \mid \exists\, s'' : [s'].s''=s_2,\ s \in s'' \| s_1\} \end{aligned}$$

The operator || returns the set of sequences obtained by merging the substitutions of both sequences, but by maintaining the critical sections.

Finally, we introduce the notion of *result R* of a sequence s (or a set of sequences S) of substitutions:

$$E(\Theta) = \{\sigma \in \Theta \mid \sigma_{|\mathcal{V}^-} = \varepsilon\}$$

$$\begin{aligned} R(\sigma) &= E(\{\sigma\}) \\ R([s]) &= disann(R(s)) \\ R(s_1.s_2) &= R(R(s_1)\hat{o}s_2) \\ R(S) &= \bigcup_{s \in S} R(s), \end{aligned}$$

where *disann*(s) removes all the annotations in s.

The result of a sequence is obtained by performing the parallel composition of each element in the sequence with the next one, and by checking that the partial result does not map annoted variables. After a critical section, the input constraints are released. $E(\Theta)$ eliminates from Θ all the substitutions mapping annoted variables.

The parallel composition $\hat{o}$ of a set of substitutions Θ with a sequence s is defined by:

$$\Theta\hat{o}s = \bigcup_{\sigma \in \Theta} \sigma\hat{o}s$$

where

$\sigma\hat{o}s = (\sigma\hat{o}\sigma').s'$, with $s=\sigma'.s'$, and
$\sigma\hat{o}[s] = [\sigma\hat{o}s]$

3.4.4 Least fixpoint semantics

In this section we introduce the notion of interpretations, and we define a continuous mapping (associated with the program) on interpretations. The least fixpoint of this mapping will be used to define the declarative semantics. Such a mapping is an extension of the immediate consequence operator for Parlog.

The Herbrand base with variables $\mathcal{B}$ associated with the program $\mathcal{P}$ is the set of all possible atoms that can be obtained by applying the predicates of $\mathcal{P}$ to the elements of $\mathcal{C}$, including I!t with $I\in\mathcal{V}$ and $t\in\mathcal{C}$. It can be interpreted as the special predicate *send* applied to I, and t: I!t $\equiv$send(I,t).

An interpretation J of $\mathcal{P}$ is a set of elements of the form $<(A,S,\gamma)_c;s>$, where $A\in\mathcal{B}$, $S\in\mathcal{S}$, $\gamma\in\Sigma$, $c\in\mathcal{C}$ and s is a sequence of substitutions on $\mathcal{V}$ and $\mathcal{C}$. $<(A,S,\gamma)_c;s> \in J$ can be read declaratively as A is true in the context of c and γ, given the state S, under the sequence of substitutions s. $\mathcal{J}$ will denote the set of all the interpretations of $\mathcal{P}$.

$\mathcal{J}$ is a complete lattice with respect to set-inclusion, where the empty set $\emptyset$ is the minimum element, and set union and set intersection are the *lub* and the *glb* operations, respectively.

In the following, we use the notation $\bar{s}$ to denote a sequence of sequences of substitutions $s_1...s_n$. Moreover, if $\bar{s}=s_1...s_n$ and $A=A_1,...,A_n$, then $<(A,S,\gamma)_c;\bar{s}>$ stands for $<(A_1,S,\gamma);s_1>,...,<(A_n,S,\gamma);s_n>$, and $\|(\bar{s})$ stands for $s_1\|...\|s_n$.

We are now in a position to define the mapping $T : \mathcal{J}\rightarrow\mathcal{J}$, associated with a program $\mathcal{P}$, as follows:

$$T(J) = T_1(J) \cup T_2(J) \cup T_3(J)$$

where

$T_1(J)=$ { $<(A,S,\gamma)_c;s>$ | $\exists$ H< -G : B,$B_{bec} \in (\mathcal{M}_d)_\gamma$, $d\in anc(c)$,
$\exists$ $\bar{s}'$, $\bar{s}''$ locally independent on G,B,A, and $S'\in\mathcal{S}$, so that
$<(G,S',\gamma)_c; \bar{s}'>,<(B,S',\gamma)_c; \bar{s}''> \in J$, $S=bec(B_{bec},S')$ and
$s \in [mgu_i(A^-,H).(\|(\bar{s}'))].mgu_o(A,H).\eta_{S'}.(\|(\bar{s}''))$ },

$T_2(J)=$ { $<(O!A,S,\gamma)_c;s>$ | $\exists$ $(d,I_1,...,I_n)\in use_c$ with $I_i=O$,
$\exists$ I?H<-G : B,$B_{bcc} \in (\mathcal{M}_e)_{\gamma'}$, $e\in anc(d)$ and $\gamma'\in\Sigma$,
$\exists$ $\bar{s}'$,$\bar{s}''$ locally independent on G,B,A, and $S'\in\mathcal{S}$, so that
$<(G,S',\gamma')_d;\bar{s}'>,<(B,S',\gamma')_d;\bar{s}''> \in J$, $f\notin S'$, and
$s \in [mgu_i(A^-,H).(\|(\bar{s}'))].\eta_{S'}.(\|(\bar{s}''))$ }, and

$T_3(J)=$ { $<(O!last,S,\gamma)_c;s>$ | $\exists$ $(d,I_1,...,I_n)\in use_c$, with $I_i=O$,
$\exists$ $<(true, S',\gamma')_d;s>\in J$, with $(O,V,i\_c)\in S'$ and $f\notin S'$ }.

The local independence of a sequence $s_1...s_n$ of sequences of substitutions with respect to a conjunction of goals $A_1,...,A_m$ ($n\leq m$) means that the variables modified by every substitution in s_i and occurring in the conjunction, are variables from A_i.

Note that the definition of T is composed of three parts. The first one, T_1 corresponds to the private predicates, which includes the possibility of inheriting them. $A\in\mathcal{B}$ is derived from J in the c context, if there exits $\gamma\in\Sigma$ and a clause in $(\mathcal{M}_d)_\gamma$ (d being an ancestor of c), such that its guard and its body are true in a state S', which is updated to

S. This happens under the sequence composed of the critical section containing the mgu_i of $A^{\cdot}$ and the head of the clause, and the sequence resulting from the guard evaluation. This critical section is followed by the mgu_o, the substitution generated by the change of state, and a sequence resulting from the body. Similarly, the second part, T_2, models the message processing; and the last one, T_3, the last message on a channel.

Proposition. T is continuous.

Proof. The continuity of T is proved by showing the equality:

$$\mathrm{lub}(T(\mathcal{H})) = T(\mathrm{lub}(\mathcal{H})),$$

for any directed subset of $\mathcal{J}$, $\mathcal{H}$. One of the inclusions is obvious because T is monotonic. The other inclusion is derived by considering each one of the three branches of the definition of T. Given $\langle(A,S,\gamma)_c;s\rangle \in T(\mathrm{lub}(\mathcal{H}))$, if there exist $\langle(G,S',\gamma)_{c_i}.\bar{s}'\rangle,\langle(B,S',\gamma)_c; \bar{s}''\rangle \in \mathrm{lub}(\mathcal{H})$, with s, s', s'' suitably related, then we can consider H_1 and H_2 such that $\langle(G,S',\gamma)_{c_i}.\bar{s}'\rangle \in H_1$ and $\langle(B,S',\gamma)_c; \bar{s}''\rangle \in H_2$. Because $\mathcal{H}$ is directed, $H_0 \in H$ will exist so that $\langle(G,S',\gamma)_{c_i}.\bar{s}'\rangle,\langle(B,S',\gamma)_c; \bar{s}''\rangle \in H_0$, and therefore, $\langle(A,S,\gamma)_c;s\rangle \in T(H_0) \subseteq \mathrm{lub}(T(\mathcal{H}))$. If any of the other two possibilities is found, the result is proved in a similar way.

So, its least fixpoint $\mathrm{lfp}(T)$ exists, and $\mathrm{lfp}(T) = \bigcup_{n\geq 0}T^n(\emptyset)$. We define the least fixpoint semantics associated with $\mathcal{P}$ as the set $\mathcal{F}(\mathcal{P})=\mathrm{lfp}(T)$. The following theorem gives a relation between both semantics defined.

Theorem. If $G=G_{use},G_{goal}$ and $S_f=\{(O,[last|\_],o\_c) : O$ is an argument of an atom in $G_{use}\}$, then:

$$\mathcal{O}[G] = \{\sigma \mid \exists\, \bar{s} \text{ loc. indep. on } G_{goal} : \langle(G_{goal};S_f;\varepsilon)_{top};\bar{s}\rangle \in \mathcal{F}(\mathcal{P}) \text{ and } \sigma \in R(\|(\bar{s})_{|var(G)})\}$$

Proof. Let σ be an element of $\mathcal{O}[G]$. Then

$$\langle L_0;\varepsilon\rangle \rightarrow \langle L_1;\sigma_1\rangle \rightarrow \ldots \rightarrow \langle L_n;\sigma_n\rangle,$$

where $L_0=(G;S_i;\varepsilon)_{top}$, $L_1=(true;S_f;\varepsilon)_{top}$ and $\sigma_n=\sigma$. Let's suppose $G_{goal}=G_1,G_2,\ldots,G_n$, and let's consider one of them G_i. Let $s_i=\alpha_{i1}.\alpha_{i2}\ldots\alpha_{im}$ be the substitutions (chosen from $\sigma_1\ldots\sigma_n$) involved in the reduction of G_i, and with annotations in the variables corresponding to input-constrained arguments of the clauses used in the resolution. Although laborious, it is easy to show that $\langle(G_i;S_f;\varepsilon)_{top};s_i\rangle \in T^n(\emptyset)$, i.e. $\langle(G_i;S_f;\varepsilon)_{top};s_i\rangle \in \mathrm{lfp}(T)$, and, moreover, $\sigma \in R(s_1\|s_2\|\ldots\|s_n)$. The opposite inclusion is derived via similar reasoning.

4 Conclusions and future work

Formal definitions of object-oriented computing can provide a specification of the more relevant mechanisms of this paradigm and establish a solid basis for the design of object-oriented languages. This is particularly important for concurrent object oriented programming. Fixpoint semantics have been used to specify logic languages and different kinds of extensions. In this paper, we have shown how the semantics of concurrent logic languages can be extended to object-oriented extensions defining the operational and declarative semantics of the more relevant aspects of the integration of both paradigms. This allows a clearer distinction to be made between inheritance and client relations and modeling the message-passing mechanism.

We have implemented a first version of the L2||O2 language, including all mechanisms described in the third section. We are working now in the distribution of objects based on a distributed implementation of the Parlog language. On the other hand, the operational and declarative semantics are defined, and we are studying the definition of a simple compositional semantics.

5 References

[1] Shapiro E. The Family of Concurrent Logic Programming Languages. In: ACM. Computing Surveys, vol 21, 3. 1989. pp. 413- 510.

[2] Shapiro E, Takeuchi A. Object Oriented Programming in Concurrent Prolog. In: New Generation Computing, 1. 1983. pp. 25-48.

[3] Kahn K, Tribble E.D, Miller M.S, Bobrow D.G. Vulcan: Logical Concurrent Objects. In: Shriver & Wegner(eds). Research Directions in Object-Oriented Programming. MIT Press. 1987. pp. 75-112.

[4] Davison A. Polka: A Parlog Object-Oriented Language. PhD thesis. University of London. 1989.

[5] Ohki M, Takeuchi A, Furukawa K. An Object-Oriented Programming Language Based on the Parallel Logic Programming Language KL1. In: Proc. of the 4th Int. Conf. on Logic Programming. MIT Press. Cambridge (Mass) 1987. pp. 894-909.

[6] Cook W. A denotational Semantics of Inheritance. PhD thesis. Brown University, Providence. Rhode Island, 1989.

[7] Yelland P.M. First Steps Towards Fully Abstract Semantics for Object Oriented Languages. In: Proc. of the Third European Conf. on Object-Oriented Prog. ECOOP 89. Cambridge Univ. Press.

[8] AGHA, G. ACTORS: A model of Concurrent Computation in Distributed Systems. The MIT Press, 1986.

[9] Monteiro L, Porto A. A Transformational View of Inheritance in Logic Programming. In Proc. of the 7th Int. Conf. on Logic Programming. MIT Press, 1990.

[10] Pimentel E, Troya J.M. A Concurrent Object Oriented Logic Language. In: Atti del Sesto Convegno sulla Prog. Log. GULP'91.

[11] Gallardo M.M, Pimentel E, Troya J.M. Definición Formal de un Subconjunto de L2||O2. In Jornadas sobre Programación Declarativa. Málaga, 1991.

[12] Clark K, Gregory S. PARLOG: Parallel Programming in Logic. In: ACM Transactions on Programming Languages and Systems, vol 8, 1. 1986.

[13] Shapiro E. A subset of Concurrent Prolog and its interpreter. Tech. Report. The Weizmann Institute of Science, 1983.

[14] Ueda K. Guarded Horn Clauses. ICOT Tech. Report TR-103, Institute for New Generation Computer Technology. Tokyo, 1985.

[15] Levi G, Palamidessi C. An approach to the declarative semantics of synchronization in logic languages. In: Proc. of the 4th Int. Conf. on Logic Programming. MIT Press. 1987. pp. 877-893.

[16] Davison A. Parlog ++: A Parlog Object Oriented Language. Tech. Report. The Parlog Group. Dpt. of Computing. Imperial College. London 1990.

[17] Boer F.S, Kok J.N, Palamidessi C, Rutten J.M.M. Semantic models for a version of PARLOG. In: Proc. of the 4th International Conference on Logic Programming. MIT Press. Cambridge (Mass.) 1987. pp.894-909.

The DelPhi Multiprocessor Inference Machine

W.F. Clocksin
Computer Laboratory, University of Cambridge
New Museums Site, Pembroke Street, Cambridge CB2 3QG

Abstract

In 1986 I proposed a new principle of executing Horn Clause programs with low overhead on multiple processors. This method does not involve the sharing of memory or the copying of computation state between processors. Under certain conditions, the method has the remarkable property of executing a given program in the minimum time theoretically required. Such optimal operation is not always possible, but performance of the implemented system is such as to render it of practical use. This paper describes the experience of implementing the method on a network of processors and of executing programs according to the method. This paper is more a retrospective than a tutorial, and so readers are referred to previous papers for introductory material and technical details.

History of the DelPhi Principle

After a departmental seminar in 1986 in which the distinguished visiting speaker (Professor D. H.D. Warren) described the state-of-the-art in parallel (multiprocessor) Prolog machines (*Cf* [7]), some colleagues (Hiyan Alshawi, Roger Needham, David Wheeler) and I came to the conclusion that current work was neglecting or palliating the memory and communications contention problems that naturally arise when executing Prolog on such machines. We considered that even the extreme case of *random search* of the proof tree resulting from the Horn clause program and goal clause – if conducted quickly enough – might in certain circumstances be more efficient than the sophisticated and intricate methods being investigated at that time (*e.g.* sharing and cacheing of variable bindings, load balancing by arbitration among processors, shared memory computer architecture). The idea behind random search is to randomly *enumerate* paths through a proof tree and *test* them for success or failure. This is extremely easy to implement, so the question then became how this might be done efficiently and completely, and whether there might exist a natural way of accomplishing this by means of multiple processors. For example, the enumeration task can be distributed, and individual tests may proceed independently on distinct processors.

Following from this discussion, I devised the DelPhi principle [2,4,5], which states that the construction of computation state for each path (from the topmost goal node to a given terminal node) of a OR-only proof tree should be computed by a single processor associated with the path. Given multiple processors, the way to deploy them according to this principle is to enumerate all paths of the proof tree, and to associate each path with a processor. A path is represented by an *oracle*, a list of the nodes along a path. An oracle always begins with the root node of the tree, and terminates with either a success or failure node. The important thing about an oracle is that it is compact and context-free (contains no computation state such as variable bindings). For example, the complete OR-only binary tree of depth n has 2^n oracles, which are all binary strings of length n bits. Because a path of an OR-only tree contains no decisions and does not require state from 'across' the tree, a given processor in possession of the program is in principle capable of computing the path (choosing clauses as directed by the oracle and performing a series of unifications) without further inter-processor communications until the oracle is exhausted. A tree containing AND nodes may be converted to an OR-only forest by standard methods. Assuming the two subpaths of a binary AND-node are to be executed in sequence, the execution may be determined by an oracle string of the length of the sum of the lengths of the two subpaths. In practice, the forest is not constructed, but is tracked as execution proceeds (see Figs. 1,4 in [2]) using a stack.

In practice, the number of oracles will outnumber the number of available processors, and it is necessary to adopt an execution strategy that enumerates and allocates oracles in 'rounds', using information from each round to adjust the enumeration strategy. In principle, if on the first round an oracle terminated by a success node is executed, then the system will have found a solution in the minimum number of steps. Because the overhead required to enumerate and distribute oracles is very small (as they are context-free bit-strings), finding the solution in a minimum number of steps approximates to finding the solution in the minimum amount of time. Whether a successful oracle is allocated in an early 'round' depends on the ratio between the number of distinct paths and the number of available processors, and also on a random variable determined by the location of the goal in the proof tree.

Because in practice there are more paths than processors, strategies are an important part of any implementation, and are discussed in general in [5] and in detail in [6], but will not be further considered here. The strategies discussed in [5] require a limited amount of interprocessor communication, but improved strategies developed in [6] introduce load balancing together with limited backtracking without the need for interprocessor communication. The interesting point remains that even without such strategies, the simple DelPhi principle can give a practical and efficient implementation. The reason is that the outcome of an oracle test gives information about the shape and extent of the proof tree, and thus can influence the enumeration of oracles. For example, if an oracle is found to fail, there is no need to enumerate the oracles that extend it. This is not heuristic, but fact. The basic DelPhi implementation makes use of several such facts even before (heuristic) strategies are considered.

The DelPhi machine, so named because of the famous Oracle of Delphi, was predicted to have the following three characteristics.

(*i*) The best performance would be observed for highly nondeterministic programs of the type encountered by AI researchers. For more deterministic programs (such as matrix multiplication), no speedup would be observed as more processors were added. This is because deterministic problems are AND-heavy, making it necessary to search the major part (if not all) of the proof tree before the solution may be found. In the DelPhi context, this results in oracle strings of a length related to the number of nodes (leaves plus internal nodes) of the proof tree.

(*ii*) For nondeterministic problems, as the number of processors is increased, the machine would exhibit speedups until a certain point (that is, until no more or-parallelism is possible), but that the execution time should then *not increase significantly* as more processors are added without limit. I call this property 'monotonic execution' for lack of a better term (monotonic parallel time complexity is not what is being discussed here). This characteristic is unjustifiably neglected in the logic programming community. Most shared-memory systems do not exhibit monotonic execution because performance begins to decrease as processors are added beyond the bandwidth contention limit. Monotonic execution is a priority when considering a future in which the number of available processors is large (*i.e.* 10^n for $n > 3$) and unknown. Monotonic execution is essential for 'MIP-mopping': efficient utilisation of otherwise unused processor cycles on networks of thousands of distributed workstations. Monotonic execution is possible for the DelPhi machine because the processors are passive recipients of oracle strings. Processors do not need to communicate between themselves or solicit work, vices which increase network demand (or shared-memory contention) by (at least) the square of the number of processors.

(*iii*) Given that oracles are compact and context-free, and that the speed of computation does not depend significantly on interprocessor communication, it is feasible to use a relatively 'low tech' implementation based on distributed workstations connected by an Ethernet. This requires no special hardware, and allows harmonious integration with other network users. Furthermore, because the processing of an oracle string is an atomic operation, it can be abandoned and restarted on another processor if the processor it was first assigned to crashes during execution. This robustness property is also important when considering 'MIP mopping'.

The DelPhi machine was intended to offer an ordinary Prolog top-level, and to conceal all the details of parallelism implementation from the user. Therefore, the principal groundrule was to support ordinary Prolog, without the use of programmer-supplied annotations. It was also considered necessary to retain the full non-determinism of Prolog, as this is a characteristic that renders it useful to AI-style programming. It was also considered important to retain extralogical primitives such as the 'cut', even if their use limits the parallelism that can be exploited by the system. Input/output primitives were not to be supplied.

After a number of interpreted uniprocessor simulators (which I implemented in Prolog as it happens), Hiyan Alshawi [1] implemented a DelPhi model in Prolog on a network of five Sun workstations connected by an Ethernet. Oracles were represented as lists of integers, and were transmitted to processors by user-language-level I/O streams. Despite the efficiency limitations engendered by the need for the entire system to be implemented in Prolog, this system did demonstrate speedups related to the number of processors made available.

Or-Parallel Implementation

In 1987 it was decided to proceed with a compiler-based implementation on a network of 20 VAXstation-2000's running Ultrix and connected by an Ethernet. A number of refinements were made to the DelPhi model concerning the shortening of oracle strings when certain deterministic motifs appear in programs, and concerning the treatment of extralogical primitives such as the 'cut'. I devised new WAM instructions for choosing clauses based on the input oracle, and modified the SB-Prolog compiler and runtime-system accordingly. Oracles were represented as blocks of binary data. Carole Klein wrote routines that interfaced the SB-Prolog runtime-system to the Unix socket I/O level, organised the system on a client-server model, and made it usable by the summer of 1989. Details of the implementation and an investigation of various execution strategies are given in [6].

The system behaved as predicted, with the appropriate speedups, monotonicity, and robustness. Given that the predictions were considered idealistically optimistic, everyone was surprised by the extent to which the actual performance was more favourable than expected. Typical system behaviour is illustrated in the following graph, showing performance of the system on the nondeterministic 8-Queens problem:

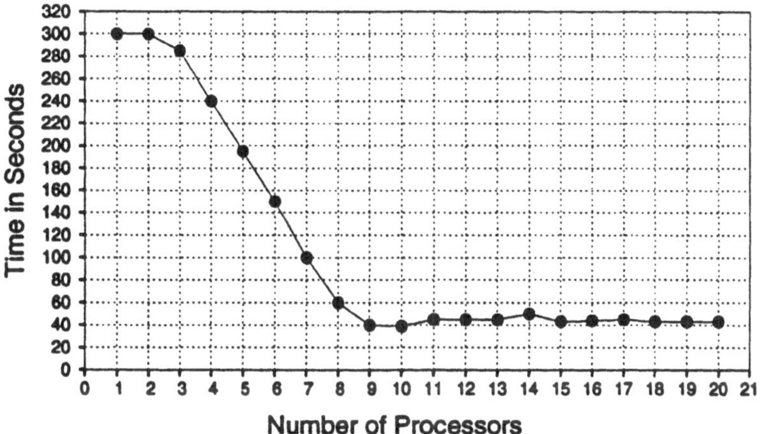

All timings in this paper are 'wall clock' times from start of goal to output of final solution, and include all setup costs and logging of results in ASCII files. Although not all researchers take such overheads into account, it is best to include them as they are unavoidable in any real system.

The concept of 'monotonicity' employed here is not the same as the mathematical textbook definition: I judge the above data to exhibit monotonicity (up to the known extent of the data) notwithstanding the presence of small fluctuations, notably the 'blip' at 14 processors. I interpret these as random fluctuations in system load and network congestion (the network is shared with about a hundred other users). They are not due to systematic increases in computation overhead, and thus are not comparable to the synchronisation and contention overheads obtained in shared memory systems.

Quite a different performance is shown for a deterministic problem: multiplication of matrices. The following graph shows performance on two problems: multiplication of two 20×20 matrices (the lower datapoints depicted as dots) and two 40×40 matrices (the upper datapoints depicted as triangles):

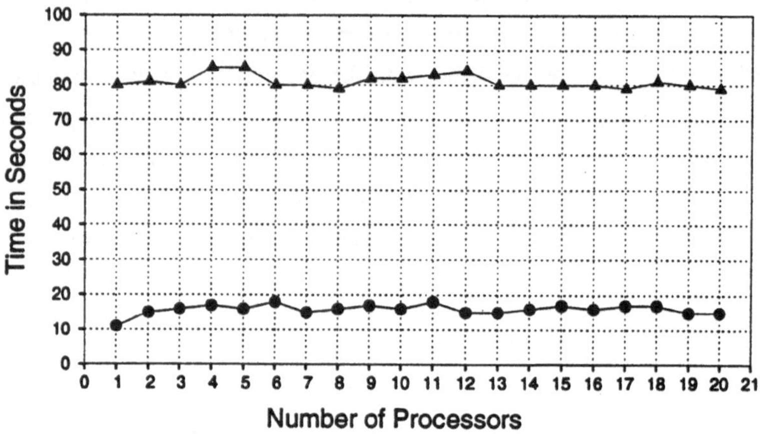

For a deterministic problem of this type there is no overt advantage arising from the use of Or-parallelism, and no speedup is seen when the number of processors is increased. However, there are two key observations to make. First, there is a relatively stable execution speed independent of the number of processors used, and therefore clear evidence of monotonic execution. Second, supposing an average execution time of 15s for the 20×20 matrix and given the complexity of matrix multiplication (n^3), execution times of about 120s would be predicted for the 40×40 matrix if there were no advantage in using multiple processors. However, the advantage in this case is demonstrated by the relatively small increase in computation time (*i.e.* less than a factor of 2^3) when the problem size is doubled. This is because processing relatively longer oracle strings (which is done without interprocessor communication and therefore without interruption) better pays back the cost of oracle management, and because the number of oracles to processed is related to the number of elements in the result matrix (*i.e.* a factor of n^2).

And/Or Parallel Implementation

Given that deterministic programs are not speeded up by adding more processors to the Or-parallel system, it was decided to attempt an And/Or-parallel implementation to determine whether any of the advantages of the DelPhi approach could be applied to deterministic problems in which communication across the proof tree can be used to establish consistent solution sets. Karen Wrench (now Bradshaw) devised and implemented a two-stroke computation cycle, also on a client-server model, in which partial solutions are generated by DelPhi-like oracle testing and sent to 'answer servers' where they are compared to form the solution. It was known at the outset that such a system had built-in performance limitations of the type found in shared-memory systems, but the purpose of the investigation was to determine the feasibility of a distributed and/or-parallel implementation and its characteristic behaviour. The performance on nondeterministic programs was comparable to the Or-parallel implementation for both speedup and monotonicity: the extra overhead introduced by the And/Or-parallel implementation was negligible. The performance graph for the 8-Queens problem illustrates this (in all the following graphs, the curve shown is the mean of ten observations, and thus exhibits the unrealistic smoothness of the mean):

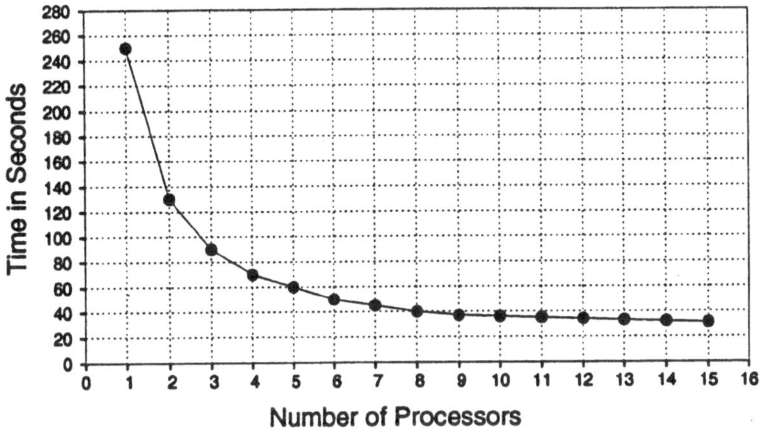

For deterministic problems, the most favourable performance was seen on the Discrete Fourier Transform (DFT), in which a random order-64 complex polynomial is evaluated at the powers of its 64th roots of unity according to the recursive Danielson-Lanczos decomposition (see [3] for how to do this in Prolog):

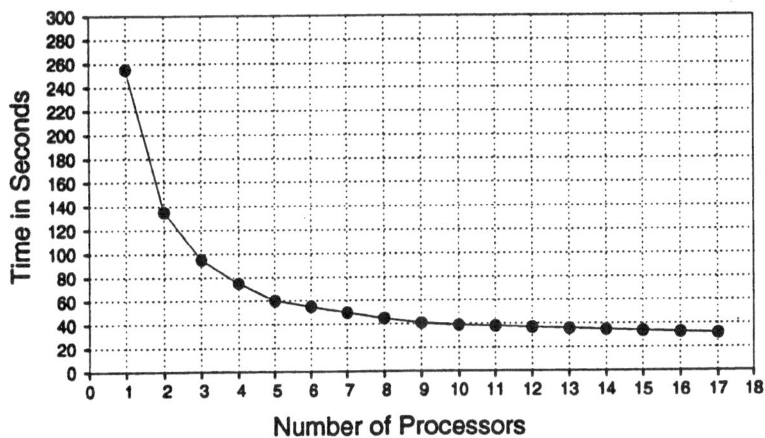

However, no convincing speedups were demonstrated for other deterministic programs such as sorting and graph colouring. For example, the following graph shows performance on Quicksorting random 1000-element lists:

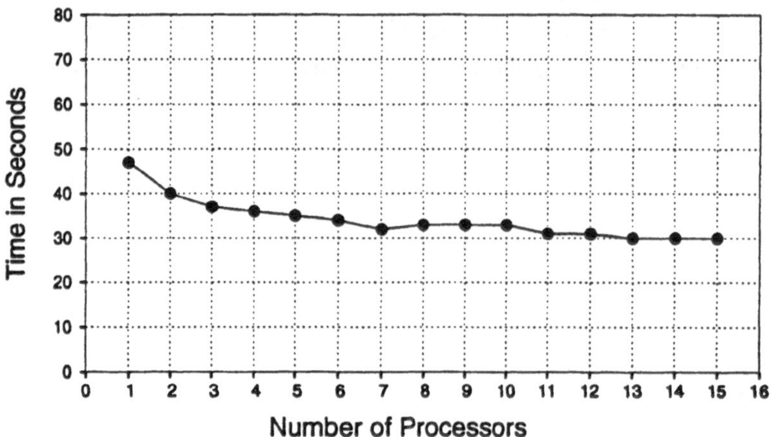

We suspect that the granularity of the problem is the deciding factor: the distributed element of computation in sorting and map colouring (simple comparisons) is too fine-grained to be expect to cover the cost of distribution, but the distributed element of computation in the DFT (basically following one path through a D-L decomposition) is sufficiently large. Also, graph problems in particular seem to be sensitive to the disposition of processors for reasons that are not entirely understood.

Discussion

It is tempting to criticise the DelPhi method on the questions of 'fairness' of load balancing and recomputation overhead. However, careful consideration shows these criticisms to be based on misleading intuitions about how time is spent in a distributed network of processors. The primary criterion of performance is the time taken for the whole system to execute the program. Questions of 'fairness' of processor load are secondary and irrelevant if they do not engage with the criterion for minimum execution time. Without analysing the program in advance, it is impossible to determine whether a given load balancing strategy is useful or fair, and under real conditions it is not obvious that a balanced or 'fair' load gives the fastest performance. The run-time load balancing strategies reported in [6,7] are heuristic and offer improvements in certain cases, although they must be put into perspective as additions to the simple DelPhi model.

Likewise, the criticism that recomputation leads to inefficiencies fails to appreciate that the *reason* for multiple processors in the DelPhi model is to quickly follow multiple paths that have subpaths in common. The critic might propose an 'efficient' alternative to DelPhi that arranges that unique subpaths are executed only once (or at least minimised) by means of task switching and sharing of variable bindings, but this is a false economy based on an intuition of what is more appropriate for sequential monoprocessors. Using the DelPhi model, common subpaths are followed by distinct processors because it is more efficient to use a unit amount of time to perform calculation than it is to perform communication. On a distributed multiprocessor the overheads of communication, synchronisation, and sharing program state (data structure) required to ensure minimal recomputation far exceed the amalgamated overhead of the DelPhi model.

Current Status

An improved distributed or-parallel system is currently being used on an experimental basis on the laboratory's local area network, where a 50-processor (DECstation 3000's) system is being implemented and tested by Paul Barham as part of a final year undergraduate project. This implementation has identified and remedied shortcomings in the Klein implementation concerning the interface to network communication routines. By using more and faster processors it is hoped to observe system behaviour in a larger environment, thus gaining a more realistic assessment of the potential of DelPhi for 'MIP-mopping'. Also, it is necessary to have a better theoretical grasp of what the DelPhi principle makes possible, and what its limitations are. It is clear that the expectations of system behaviour engendered by the new implementation have outgrown the broadband network, and an alternative is required. A more comprehensive performance evaluation with standard benchmarks is needed, and it is hoped to undertake this in the coming year.

Acknowledgements

I thank Donald Gaubatz and Brian Rees for arranging an equipment donation from a Digital Equipment Corporation External Research Grant, without which this work would not have been possible. I thank Hiyan Alshawi, Carole Klein and Karen Wrench for their collaboration during this project, and Roger Needham and David Wheeler for fruitful discussions. I especially thank Carole Klein and Karen Wrench for their care in acquiring the performance data. The or-parallel performance graphs were replotted from data in [6]; the and/or-parallel performance graphs were replotted from data in [9]. Any errors deriving from replotting are entirely my responsibility.

References

1. H. Alshawi and D.B. Moran. The Delphi model and some preliminary experiments. *Proc 5th Conf Symp Log Prog* (ed Kowalski and Bowen), MIT Press, 1578-1589.

2. W.F. Clocksin, 1987. Principles of the DelPhi parallel inference machine. *Computer Journal* **30**(5), 386-391.

3. W.F. Clocksin, 1988. A technique for translating clausal specifications of numerical methods into efficient programs. *Journal of Logic Programming* **5**, 231-242

4. W.F. Clocksin and H. Alshawi, 1986. A method for efficiently executing Horn Clause programs using multiple processors. Technical Report CCSC-3, SRI International (Cambridge Computer Science Centre).

5. W.F. Clocksin and H. Alshawi, 1988. A method for efficiently executing Horn Clause programs using multiple processors. *New Generation Computing* **5**, 361-376.

6. C.S. Klein, 1991. Exploiting or-parallelism in Prolog using multiple sequential machines. PhD dissertation. Reprinted as Technical Report 216, Computer Laboratory, University of Cambridge.

7. D.H.D. Warren, 1987. OR-parallel execution models of Prolog. Technical Report, Department of Computer Science, University of Manchester.

8. K.L. Wrench, 1990. A distributed and-or parallel prolog network. PhD dissertation. Available in summary form as Technical Report 212, Computer Laboratory, University of Cambridge.

Applications in Logic

Horn Clause Logic 1992

Wilfrid Hodges
School of Mathematical Sciences
Queen Mary and Westfield College, University of London

Abstract

We ask why Horn clause logic is useful for logic programming. The main reasons seem to lie in a connection between Horn clause logic and algebraic closure operators, and in the fact that recursively enumerable sets can be encoded in initial models of Horn clause theories. The existence of good algorithms for handling algebraic closure operators is also important. We review the other main characteristic properties of Horn clause logic, and ask what they are good for in logic programming and more generally in computer science. We make some polemical remarks about generic models, generalisations of Horn clause logic, and the Byrne-Johnson-Laird theory of syllogisms.

Let me open with some personal remarks. I work in mathematical logic, more precisely in model theory. I gave my first course in Horn clause logic in 1972. It included a proof calculus for Horn clause logic and quite a lot on the construction of colimit structures in classes of models of Horn clause theories. At that time I had barely heard of computer science. I first began to talk seriously to computer scientists in 1985, and very soon I became aware of the fact that they tend to be interested in Horn clause logic.

This fact was puzzling. Horn clause logic is very pretty and I always regarded it as a hobby of mine, but as logics go, it's distinctly limited. Why should people want to confine themselves to this form of logic when there is such a wealth of other logical languages, starting with full first-order logic?

Part of the answer, clearly, is that computer science exploits some special features of Horn clauses. In the literature there are various attempts to say what those features are. Some of these attempts are more convincing than others. One can also ask how the various features relate to each other. In this talk I aim to survey the ground and reach some conclusions. The questions asked are partly mathematical, but they are also partly about the reasons why people do certain things. Reasons shift with time, and so I put the date in my title.

Horn clauses have a number of distinctive properties. These mainly fall under five heads, which I list at once with typical examples. Some terms will be defined later.

Properties of proof systems. Horn clause theories allow positive unit refutations and input refutations. (Kuehner [1], Henschen & Wos [2])

Properties of the consequence relations. If a Horn clause theory entails "A or B" then either it entails A or it entails B. (McKinsey [3], Miller [4])

Generic models. A strict Horn clause theory T has a model in which positive existential sentences are true if and only if they are deducible from T. (Makowsky [5])

Colimit properties of the class of models. For every diagram of models of a strict Horn clause theory there is an explicit construction for the colimit of the diagram. (Mal'tsev [6], Reichel [7])

Limit properties of the class of models. The class of models of a Horn clause theory is closed under taking direct products and substructures. (McKinsey [3], Mal'tsev [6]).

Makowsky [5], in his paper on "Why Horn formulas matter in computer science", notes that first-order logic is used in several areas of computer science (he mentions in particular specification of data structures, relational data bases and logic programming), and he asks why it is that "Horn formulas are the right class of formulas to be used" in these contexts. His answer is that "Horn formulas play such an important role in the various branches of computer science" because they are "exactly the framework in which the notion of a generic example can be applied". We shall examine this claim in due course. But I think there is a prior question: why use logic at all?

In fact the number of places in which computer scientists explicitly use formal logic is rather limited (just as it is with mathematicians). It includes formal software verification, where as far as I know nobody uses Horn clause logic. It also includes the explicit study of formal deduction as in automated deduction or databases.

But if we turn to Prolog, for example, it's not clear that we have to mention logic at all in order to understand what Prolog is. I have in front of me a recent paper of Colmerauer [8] where he says that he is going to present the foundations of Prolog III "by means of simple mathematical concepts without explicit recourse to first-order logic". In fact most textbooks of Prolog get by with very few references to formal deduction after the obligatory first section on logical notation. Now it's a fruitless question whether Prolog "really is Horn clause logic". Obviously there are large parts of Prolog that you can explain that way, and many people find the logical explanation helpful. What I think we can sensibly try to do is to ask *what mathematical properties of Prolog can be explained in terms of logic, and why the logic in question has to be Horn clause logic.*

In order to answer this question, I want to add a sixth distinctive feature of Horn clause logic to the five just listed. In some sense I think it is more fundamental than any of them.

1 Closure operators

There is a time-hallowed description of what computing is about, which we owe to Emil Post [9]. According to Post's account, computing is about collecting up (he says "generating") sets of strings of symbols. Let me start to formalise this idea.

A *closure operator* C on a set Ω is a function which takes each subset X of Ω to a subset $C(X)$ of Ω, subject to the following laws:

- $X \subseteq C(X) = C(C(X))$.
- If $X \subseteq Y$ then $C(X) \subseteq C(Y)$.

The set $C(X)$ is called the *closure* of X. We say that a subset X of Ω is *closed* with respect to the closure operator C if X has the form $C(Y)$ for some $Y \subseteq \Omega$ (or equivalently, if $X = C(X)$). The collection of closed subsets of Ω forms a complete lattice of subsets of Ω, and the greatest lower bound of a set of closed sets is their intersection.

Closure operators appear in every branch of mathematics, and in most areas of life where mathematics can be applied. For example:

1. Ω is the set of all sentences of some logical language. Let $C(X)$ be the set of all logical consequences of the set X.
2. Ω is the set of all grammatical expressions of some language. Let $C_1(X)$ be the set of all grammatical expressions that can be built up by combining the expressions in X, and let $C_2(X)$ be the set of all grammatical constituents of expressions in X (counting an expression as a constituent of itself).
3. Ω is the set of elements of a group. Let $C_1(X)$ be the subgroup generated by X, and let $C_2(X)$ be the normal subgroup generated by X.

All these examples have a feature in common. We say that a closure operator C is *algebraic* if it has the further property:

If $x \in C(Y)$ then there is a finite subset F of Y such that $x \in C(F)$.

This property can be recognised from the lattice of closed sets:

FACT 1 *Let C be a closure operator on a set Ω. The following are equivalent:*

1. *C is algebraic.*
2. *The union of an increasing chain of closed sets is closed.*

This fact is proved in Cohn [10] pp. 41-47, together with various other facts about closure operators.

Now we can introduce Horn clauses. A *propositional Horn clause* is a formula of one of the forms

$$q,$$
$$p_1 \& \cdots \& p_n \rightarrow q,$$
$$\bot,$$
$$p_1 \& \cdots \& p_n \rightarrow \bot$$

where $p_1, \cdots, p_n, q$ are propositional letters and $\bot$ stands for absurdity. We call the clause *strict* (or *definite*) if $\bot$ doesn't occur in it.

THEOREM 2 *Let Ω be a set, and consider a propositional language which has a distinct propositional letter p_x for each element x of Ω. If C is an algebraic closure operator on Ω, then there is a strict propositional Horn theory T such that for every subset X of Ω,*

$$C(X) = \{y \in \Omega : \{p_x : x \in X\} \cup T \vdash p_y\}.$$

Conversely if T is any strict propositional Horn theory, the function C defined by the equation above is an algebraic closure operator.

The proof is easy from the definitions. This theorem doesn't quite say that strict propositional Horn clauses correspond one-to-one to algebraic closure operators. There is some slippage at both ends. In the first place, given a strict propositional Horn theory T, we get a closure operator out of it by attaching to each propositional symbol p a distinct element x of a set Ω, so that p is p_x. Obviously this can be done in arbitrarily many different ways. So *a strict propositional Horn theory uniformly describes a family of isomorphic algebraic closure operators.*

In the second place, even when the propositional letters are attached to elements of some set Ω, there can be two different strict propositional Horn theories which describe the same algebraic closure operator. For example if Ω is the set $\{1, 2, 3\}$ and C is the closure operator which takes $\emptyset$ to $\emptyset$ and every other set to Ω, then C can be represented by the Horn theory

$$p_1 \rightarrow p_2,$$
$$p_1 \rightarrow p_3,$$
$$p_2 \rightarrow p_1,$$
$$p_2 \rightarrow p_3,$$
$$p_3 \rightarrow p_1,$$
$$p_3 \rightarrow p_2,$$

but it can equally well be represented by the theory

$$p_1 \rightarrow p_2,$$
$$p_2 \rightarrow p_3,$$
$$p_3 \rightarrow p_1.$$

The difference between these two theories is that for the first of them, each element of $C(X)$ can be inferred in a single deductive step, whereas for the second it may take two steps (e.g. to put 3 into $C(\{1\})$). So *strict propositional Horn theories describe not just the set $C(X)$, but also the steps by which one can reach $C(X)$ from X.*

Let us go back for a moment to Post's picture of computing as generating a stream of strings. Post's imagery is a little peculiar; it suggests that computing is a matter of spewing out strings of symbols ad infinitum. A fairer description of computing would be this: a program describes an algebraic closure operator C on a set Ω and a subset X (maybe empty) of Ω. When we run the program, we determine whether or not a given element y of Ω lies in $C(X)$. Now if C is described by a strict propositional Horn theory T, then T gives us a (nondeterministic) procedure for testing whether y is in $C(X)$. Namely we look for clauses

$$p_a \& \cdots \& p_k \rightarrow p_y$$

and then we look for clauses finishing with $p_a, \cdots, p_k$, and so on; we stop looking for clauses involving p_x when $x \in X$. This is exactly the Kowalski procedural interpretation of Horn clause logic, as in Kowalski [11]. To sum up so far:

> Strict propositional Horn logic = uniform family of algebraic closure operators + procedure for testing membership of closures of sets.

The restriction to strict is not really significant here. We can earmark an element y of Ω by adding to Ω a new element $\perp$ and putting $\perp$ into $C(\{y\})$. Then testing whether $y \in C(X)$ is equivalent to testing whether $\perp \in C(X)$, which gives us a uniform style.

2 Added structure

The step from propositional Horn logic to Horn clause logic is more subtle. Let me take it in slow motion. Imagine that Ω is the set of positive integers, and we have propositional Horn clauses

$$p_1 \rightarrow p_2,$$
$$p_2 \rightarrow p_3,$$
$$p_3 \rightarrow p_4,$$
etc.

Here the closed sets are the final segments of the positive integers. Note that the clauses are all in a uniform style. We can represent this by adding the successor function S as a piece of structure to the set Ω, and then writing just one rule:

$$\text{For each } n, \; p_n \rightarrow p_{Sn}.$$

Turning this into logical symbols,

$$\forall n \; (p(n) \rightarrow p(S(n))).$$

Here we have a Horn clause; I remind you that a Horn clause is the same thing as a propositional Horn clause except that the propositional letters are replaced by arbitrary atomic formulas and we bind all the variables by universal quantifiers at the beginning. The recipe for finding the Horn clause in our example was:

> *Simplify the theory of the closure operator by defining structure on Ω and describing the rules uniformly in terms of the structure.*

This immediately raises the question: What other kinds of structure can we impose on Ω so as to simplify the Horn clause description?

Here are two examples. First, suppose Ω has the form of a cartesian product $A \times B$. Then we can represent the elements a of A by 1-ary relation symbols R_a and the elements b of B by constant symbols c_b, so that the pair $\langle a, b \rangle$ can be represented by the string $R_a(c_b)$. Possibly we can describe the closure operator by a set of rules which are uniform in the elements b; then we can quantify them out and write for example

$$\forall x\ (R_a(x) \rightarrow R_{a'}(x)).$$

This way we get a Horn clause. But maybe the rules are uniform in the elements a; then we get a higher-order Horn clause

$$\forall R\ (R(c_b) \rightarrow R(c_{b'})).$$

Formally these two moves—to first-order or to higher-order Horn clauses—are exactly parallel.

Or second, we can suppose that some of the elements of Ω can be identified with finite sequences of other elements of Ω. If we combine this added structure with the one just described, we find ourselves writing Horn clauses such as

$$\forall x_1 \forall x_2\ ((R_a(x_1, x_2) \rightarrow R_{a'}(x_1, x_2)).$$

But equally well the uniformities might go the other way, so that we find ourselves writing

$$\forall R_1 \forall R_2\ ((R_1, R_2)(c_b) \rightarrow (R_1, R_2)(c_{b'})).$$

In terms of higher order logic this is gibberish. From our present point of view it makes exactly as much sense as the previous formula, but with left to right reversed.

In short,

> *By exploiting extra structure on the set Ω, we can sometimes find uniformities which allow us to reduce the theory of a closure operator to a Horn clause theory. But the same kinds of uniformity can equally well lead to higher-order Horn clauses, or to "clauses" which have no immediate logical interpretation.*

Dale Miller and his group [14] have started to explore the higher order devices. I don't know whether it's lack of imagination or something more fundamental that has stopped us investigating the more bizarre possibilities. (In his talk at the conference, Lincoln Wallen emphasised that in logic programming a system of proof rules is not going to serve its purpose unless people can recognise the rules as meaning something. Of course the same applies here.)

There are some representation theorems which say that in a computing context "first-order Horn clauses are always enough". But they don't necessarily say that a first-order Horn clause representation is always the most natural way of handling a particular closure operator, or that the reduction to first-order Horn clauses is straightforward; so I don't think they should put us off searching for other ways of doing it.

The classic representation theorem of this kind is due to Raymond Smullyan [12], and it runs as follows in our terminology.

THEOREM 3 *Let A be a finite alphabet $\{a_1, \cdots, a_n\}$ and Ω the set of all finite strings of symbols from A; let C_0 be a recursively enumerable subset of Ω. Then there is a finite strict Horn clause theory T with a 1-ary relation symbol R such that*

1. *For each string s in* Ω, $s \in C_0$ *if and only if* $T \vdash R(s)$.

2. *T uses no structure on* Ω *except the concatenation relation and the sets* $\{a_1\}, \cdots, \{a_n\}$.

This can be converted into a result saying that if the relation "$y \in C(\{x\})$" is recursively enumerable, then it can be defined by a finite strict Horn clause theory using only concatenation and the names of the letters of the alphabet. In fact Smullyan's result reduces the notion of recursively enumerable set to something purely algebraic, and one can use it as a good starting-point for elegant treatments of recursion theory.

3 Proof-theoretic properties

For the rest of this talk I shall review the other five distinctive properties of Horn clauses that were mentioned at the beginning.

The first in the list was a theorem of Kuehner [1]:

THEOREM 4 *Let T be a minimally inconsistent clausal theory. Then T admits a unit resolution refutation if and only if T can be brought to Horn form by renaming. The unit refutation then becomes a positive unit refutation.*

(Renaming means replacing some relation symbols by their negations, consistently throughout the theory. A unit refutation is one in which at least one of the parents in each step consists of a literal; it's positive if this literal is an atomic formula.)

The theorem stands on its own. I know no way of putting it into a more general context. From the point of view of logic, it's limited because we are already given the theory in clausal form. The theorem can't be translated into a theorem about closure operators, because it is specifically about the steps used to build up the closure, and we have seen that these steps are not uniquely determined by the closure itself.

Kuehner's theorem gets practical importance from a theorem of Chang [13] which doesn't mention Horn clauses: If a set T of clauses contains all its unit factors, then T has a unit refutation if and only if T has a resolution refutation in which each step has an input clause as one of the parents. Put together, these theorems lead directly to SLD-resolution for Horn clauses, and it's well known that one can describe a core part of Prolog in terms of resolution proofs of this kind.

Nadathur and Miller [14] cite four properties of Horn clause theories T (where ϕ, ψ are goal formulas, and I have paraphrased a little):

i. If $T \vdash \exists x \phi(x)$ then there is a ground term t such that $T \vdash \phi(t)$.

ii. If $T \vdash \phi \wedge \psi$ then $T \vdash \phi$ and $T \vdash \psi$.

iii. If $T \vdash \phi \vee \psi$ then $T \vdash \phi$ or $T \vdash \psi$.

iv. If ϕ is atomic and $T \vdash \phi$, then either ϕ comes from some sentence in T by substitution, or T contains a sentence with a substitution instance of the form $\alpha \rightarrow \phi$ such that $T \vdash \alpha$.

Of these, (ii) is a property of logical consequence and hardly distinctive for Horn clauses. Property (iv) is perhaps a little too close to the definition of "Horn" to help us forward. The interesting property is (iii), which was noted by McKinsey [3] in the paper in which Horn clauses were first introduced. In fact it holds for disjunctions of any size, even infinite.

THEOREM 5 *Let T be a clausal theory (or more generally a first-order theory in which every axiom is the universal quantification of a quantifier-free formula). The following are equivalent.*

1. *T is logically equivalent to a Horn clause theory.*

2. *For every set U of ground atomic formulas, if $T \cup U$ entails a disjunction of atomic formulas, then it already entails one formula of the disjunction.*

To get (1) from (2) in the theorem, express each clause in T as a disjunction $(\neg\phi_1 \vee \cdots \vee \neg\phi_m \vee \psi_1 \vee \cdots \vee \psi_n)$ where $\phi_1, \cdots, \psi_n$ are atomic. Then T entails this disjunction, so $T, \phi_1, \cdots, \phi_m$ entails the disjunction $\psi_1 \vee \cdots \vee \psi_n$, and by (2) in the theorem it entails one disjunct, say ψ_i. Then the original clause in T can be replaced by

$$\phi_1 \& \cdots \& \phi_m \rightarrow \psi_i$$

which is Horn.

The other direction in the theorem goes back almost directly to the explanation in terms of closure operators. Property (2) says that if C is the closure operator defined by T, and $C(U)$ contains either ϕ_1 or ...or ϕ_n, then it must contain at least one of these. Strictly the matter is a little more complicated because of the implied universal quantification of $\phi_1 \vee \cdots \vee \phi_n$, but the argument is a refinement of the one just given.

In fact property (iii) of Nadathur and Miller holds for arbitrary Horn theories (with any quantifiers) and arbitrary disjunctions of positive formulas. I say no more about this, except that it is proved by using direct products.

Property (i) of Nadathur and Miller is really a combination of property (iii) and another result which holds for all clausal theories T: if T entails $\exists x \phi(x)$ where ϕ has no quantifiers, then T entails some disjunction of formulas $\phi(t)$ where t are terms. This is sometimes known as Herbrand's theorem.

The proof of Herbrand's theorem, and one or two other arguments given just above, can be put into an elegant form by using some model theory. But note that nothing we have said so far involves the existence of any "models" of a Horn clause theory except for the set Ω. Let me just say, without labouring it, that *if T is a Horn clause theory, then there is a natural way of interpreting all the closed sets of the closure operator defined by T as models of T; every model of T is given in this way.* To study the models is really to study the closed sets.

In particular there is a unique model (up to isomorphism) of T determined by the closure of the empty set. This model is the initial model; we shall discuss it in the next two sections. The idea of the initial model goes back in some crude form to Grassmann [15] in the middle of last century, but modern treatments begin with Smullyan [12], who calls it the *minimal model.*

4 Genericity

Following Makowsky [5], let us say that a structure M is an *atomic-generic* model of a theory T if

- M is a model of T;
- If A is any atomic sentence of the language of T, then M is a model of A if and only if T entails A.

Let us say that M is a *term model* of T if M is a model of T and every element of M is named by a ground term. The following fact is a restatement of a result in Mal'tsev [6].

THEOREM 6 *Let T be a first-order theory. Then the following are equivalent:*

1. *For every set S of atomic sentences, the theory $T \cup S$ has an atomic-generic term model.*
2. *T is logically equivalent to a strict Horn clause theory.*

We can drop the word "strict" if we add the condition that $T \cup S$ is consistent.

The atomic-generic term model of $T \cup S$ is in fact its initial model. If we regard a logic program as a strict Horn clause theory, then its atomic-generic term model is its least Herbrand model.

As mentioned earlier, Makowsky claims that this theorem explains "why Horn formulas play such an important role in the various branches of computer science". He goes on to mention logic programming explicitly.

It is not at all obvious that the existence of atomic-generic term models has anything to do with logic programming. In the course of his paper Makowsky mentions three ways in which they might be connected:

First argument. "Logic programs allow a procedural interpretation, because there is a *unique* "generic" mathematical structure in which to interpret logic programs."

I don't understand this argument. The procedural interpretation is not a semantic interpretation; it doesn't depend on our being able to interpret logic programs in any structure. Van Emden and Kowalski [16] argue that "in the procedural interpretation, operational semantics is proof theory and fixpoint semantics is model theory". What they show is that the procedural interpretation *can be described* by means of Herbrand models, not that the procedural interpretation *exists* because of the Herbrand models. I return to this below.

Second argument. At the beginning of his paper, Makowsky points out that sometimes we check that something must always be true by finding a typical or "generic" case where it is true. This suggests the following explanation of logic programming. Suppose T is a Horn clause theory and A is an atomic sentence; we want to tell whether A is deducible from T. So we look at an atomic-generic model G of T to see whether or not A is true in G. If it is then it is deducible from T; if not, not.

Unfortunately this is not a correct description of what happens in logic programming. The only way we know that an atomic sentence A is true in the generic model G is by deducing A from T; so the procedure suggested is completely circular. There has been no forward movement.

Third argument. Makowsky holds that the existence of atomic-generic models for Horn clause theories "guarantees that ... "negation as failure" for logic programming [is a] reasonable concept". He says this without explanation, but I suppose we can fill it out as follows.

At a first approximation, we can say that the goal **not**(A) succeeds if and only if the statement A is not deducible from the program. This gives a logical interpretation of **not** in Prolog. If A is an atomic sentence (a ground fact), then since the least Herbrand model is an atomic-generic model of the program, it follows that **not**(A) succeeds if and only if the formula $\neg A$ is true in the least Herbrand model. So we can think of **not** as being a genuine logical negation. This makes it reasonable.

This explanation is in my words, not Makowsky's, but I hope it is fair to his intentions. It seems to me he has a point, but he overstates it. The notion "A is not deducible from the program" is just as reasonable as the notion "A is not true in the least Herbrand model of the program". We don't get any further *justification* by switching from provability to truth.

What we do get is a benefit of a different kind. ***When a logic computation derives an atomic sentence A from a Horn clause theory T, we can think of it as checking that A is true in a certain fixed model of T.*** This gives us two distinct birthday presents. First, it offers us a convenient mental picture, which is one reason why John Lloyd's book [17] is so elegant. Second, if we do want to use Prolog to compute the properties of a particular structure, the atomic-generic term model of our program is quite likely to be a good approximation to the structure that we had in mind. (One should see the connection between the closed-world assumption and the atomic-generic term model in this light.)

That said, the atomic-generic term model tells us essentially nothing about why Prolog works as a programming language. The most that we can extract from Mal'tsev's theorem along these lines is that if Prolog is extended to allow program clauses which are not Horn, then a description of how Prolog works will have to be more complicated—for example using several jointly generic models, as Minker [18] does. (Shepherdson [19] has a very cogent critique of some remarks I made in a preprint in 1985 in the same general direction as Makowsky.)

I know much less about databases and expert systems, but as far as I can see, generic models are relevant to them in much the same way as for logic programming. Here the computation is explicitly about theories. If the theories can be written as Horn clause theories, then their generic term models are a way of making them concrete; the generic term models are also quite likely to resemble the intended model if there is one.

Let us go back for a moment to Makowsky's second argument. Recall that he suggests we can derive A from T by checking that A is true in "typical" models of T. At first sight this looks a little like semantic resolution, where we help a proof along by consulting a model. In fact it is completely different: in semantic resolution we use the model to guide the search for a proof, but the proof once found is a self-contained formal demonstration.

In a recent book, Johnson-Laird and Byrne [20] suggest that in everyday life we do in fact make deductions by reading off what is true in models. They also argue that we find deductions hard in proportion to the number of models that we need to examine. To check this, they consider all 27 forms of premise which lead to valid syllogisms, and they quote some experiments which measured how hard the resulting syllogisms are by seeing how many people in a sample could deduce the correct conclusion. The ten easiest deductions turn out to be exactly those where (according to their account) only one model is needed. Since Johnson-Laird and Byrne suggest that their approach should be useful for artificial intelligence, one wonders if they really have put their finger on an automatable way of making deductions by testing in models.

Unfortunately their account of what they mean by a "model" is barely coherent—to the point that we have no way of telling whether they have correctly counted the number of models needed for each syllogism. (Also there are several things in the text which suggest that a Byrne-Johnson-Laird "model" isn't so much a model as a theory.) It seems to me the artificial intelligence community can safely wait a while until the psychologists have got their act together.

Be that as it may, I thought it might be interesting to take the data of Byrne and Johnson-Laird, and put it through the Horn clause mangle. Each of the syllogisms that they consider can be turned into a straightforward deduction of an atomic sentence from a Horn clause theory by applying one or more of the following transformations:

I. Instantiating, i.e. assuming "a is a P" and proving "a is a Q" where a is a new constant (rather than proving the non-atomic sentence "All Ps are Qs").

R. Renaming, i.e. transposing the two predicates "x is a P" and "x is not a P" throughout.

C. Conversion, i.e. replacing "No P is a Q" or "Some P is a Q" by the logically equivalent "No Q is a P" or "Some Q is a P" respectively.

S. Skolemising, i.e. replacing "Some P is a Q" by "a is a P and a Q".

E. Existentialising, i.e. adding "a is a P" to express that a named class is not empty.

The results are quite striking. The 27 forms of syllogism fall into three groups according to what transformations are needed. The groups are as follows (where each number n represents a syllogism which n per cent of the subjects got right).

1. *Syllogisms which need at most one of R and S, and don't involve E.* There are ten: 89, 88, 86, 79, 75, 74, 70, 69, 68, 63.

2. *Syllogisms which need both R and S, but don't involve E.* There are twelve: 51, 41, 38, 38, 34, 31, 28, 26, 23, 20, 19, 15.

3. *Syllogisms which need E.* There are five: 19, 16, 15, 11, 8.

The three groups all occupy non-overlapping intervals of the range from 0 to 100, except for two of the syllogisms in the second group; these happen to need C as well as R and S. Moreover 19 is the only syllogism in the third group which doesn't also need R. So a closer look at the transformations which are needed will give an almost perfect division into intervals.

For comparison, here are the Byrne-Johnson-Laird groupings by "numbers of models". The one-model syllogisms are exactly our first group. The two-model syllogisms are 51, 41, 34 and 31. All the rest are three-model. I haven't done the statistical analysis, but it seems clear that our division matches the data a little better than the Byrne-Johnson-Laird one, and it has the advantage that it means something precise and simple. I wouldn't dream of suggesting a psychological theory to explain it.

5 Properties of the class of models

An *initial model* of a theory T is a model of T which has a unique homomorphism to each other model of T. Historically this idea comes from presentations of groups, as studied by von Dyck in 1882. These presentations are equational theories. It was Mal'tsev [6] who showed that the same machinery works equally well for strict Horn clause theories. In fact he showed the following result.

THEOREM 7 *Let T be a first-order theory. Then the following are equivalent:*

1. *For every set S of atomic sentences, $T \cup S$ has an initial model.*

2. *T is logically equivalent to a strict Horn clause theory.*

This is really another statement of Theorem 6 above. The initial model of a strict Horn clause theory is determined only up to isomorphism; but the proof of Theorem 7 gives us a concrete choice of this structure as a term algebra.

For mathematicians, Theorem 7 shows that the class of models of a strict Horn theory, regarded as a category with homomorphisms for morphisms, admits colimits of all diagrams. I am not sure how much interest there is in this for computer scientists, except for two consequences. The first is the fact that strict Horn clause theories have initial models (i.e. colimits of the empty diagram).

It is often said that this fact is important because it implies that Horn clause theories have a model in a canonical way; we can specify the initial model by giving the theory. If a logical theory is consistent but not Horn, then in general it has lots of models but there is no straightforward and natural way of picking out just one of them. This line of argument has led people to look for analogues of initial models for other kinds of theory.

I have to dissent. I don't know any place in computer science where it makes sense to look for just one model of a theory, but it doesn't matter which model. And if it matters which model we get, then it matters whether or not the initial model is the right one. For example, Horn clause theories are often used to specify datatypes; the datatype is the initial model of the theory. If we wanted to specify a stack of finite height, then there's no point in taking a model which is not a stack of finite height but happens to be a model of the same Horn clause theory.

In short, the significant thing about initial models for computer science is not that they exist, but that *they were the structures we wanted to specify anyway*. This is a quite remarkable fact, and I don't have any "explanation" of it, except to point to Smullyan's theorem mentioned earlier, that any recursively enumerable set can be represented by the initial model of a finite Horn clause theory. Note that once again the Horn clause theory is being used to define not a class of structures, but the minimal closed set of a closure operator.

There is a second consequence of Mal'tsev's result which has some computational significance. This is the existence of left adjoints to forgetful functors between classes of models of strict Horn clause theories. These left adjoints are known as "free functors", and they play a role in the semantics of parametrised algebraic specifications (see for example Ehrig and Mahr [21]).

Malt'sev's theorem (Theorem 7 above) tells us that a *first-order theory* can be put in strict Horn clause form if it has certain properties. In fact Mal'tsev did better than this; he gave purely structural conditions on a class of structures which are equivalent to its being the class of models of a Horn clause theory. I quote another result from his paper [6].

THEOREM 8 *Let K be a class of structures. Then K is the class of models of a strict Horn clause theory if and only if it has the properties:*

- *K is closed under direct products (including the trivial product 1).*
- *If every finitely generated substructure of a structure M is embeddable in some structure in K, then M is in K.*

However, Mal'tsev did assume that the structures were structures in the conventional mathematical sense: sets with relations and total functions defined on them. For computational purposes it's not at all clear that this notion of "structure" is adequate; there is every reason to try to generalise Mal'tsev's result to broader notions of structure. (Mal'tsev would certainly have approved. He was one of the pioneers of many-sorted structures.)

For example, the fact that algorithms don't always terminate is a strong reason for allowing partial functions.

In another direction, we saw earlier that the base set Ω of a closure operator can carry some structural features which are not at all in line with conventional model theory.

One fairly natural generalisation of the notion of "structure" is to allow the elements to be grouped in sorts, and to introduce partial functions F whose domains are identified by relation symbols R_F. Theorems 7 and 8 generalises painlessly to this kind of structure. (For direct products one has to define the product on each sort separately.) Also no damage is done if we impose a Horn clause condition on the sorts. For example we can partially order the sorts by inclusion; note that inclusion is expressed by

$$\forall x \; (x \text{ is of sort } \sigma \rightarrow x \text{ is of sort } \tau).$$

which is a Horn clause.

Tarlecki [22] follows another line by generalising Mal'tsev's ideas directly to institutions. His setting is very abstract, and it is not clear how many concrete examples it has which are not reducible to the models of a Horn clause theory of a more conventional kind.

The connection between direct products and the other properties of Horn clauses is, roughly speaking, that the set of atomic sentences true in a direct product is the intersection of the atomic sentences true in the factors. This relates to the fact that the family of closed sets of a closure operator is closed under intersection.

I passed on quickly from Theorem 8, as if it couldn't have any computational interest. But in fact it does have some computational implications, of at least two kinds. The first is rather theoretical: Theorem 8 gives us a technique for showing that certain sentences can't be rewritten as Horn clauses. For example if M is a model of $(p \& \neg q)$ and N is a model of $(\neg p \& q)$, then both M and N are models of $(p \vee q)$, but the direct product $M \times N$ is not. It follows that $(p \vee q)$ is not logically equivalent to a set of Horn clauses, and hence can't be written in Prolog without using non-logical features such as negation or cut. The practical interest of this technique is probably rather limited. In Prolog it's no big deal to tell when a program can be written without using negation or cut.

The second is more down-to-earth. Before stating it I quote a result of Weinstein (which appears in Galvin [23]). I shall not explain the notions involved, except to say that an $\forall_2$ sentence consists of universal quantifiers, then existential quantifiers, then a quantifier-free formula; so every Horn clause is an $\forall_2$ sentence.

THEOREM 9 *If A is an $\forall_2$ first-order sentence, then the following are equivalent.*

1. *A is preserved in direct products.*
2. *A is equivalent to an $\forall_2$ Horn sentence.*

Fagin [24] shows that several important types of database dependency are preserved in direct products (this has a concrete meaning, as he shows). Since database dependencies can be written in $\forall_2$ form, it follows that they can be written as Horn sentences. He uses this as a basis for classifying database dependencies. Of course we could have found the Horn forms without knowing Weinstein's theorem; but Weinstein's theorem was an encouragement to look for them.

6 Generalising Horn clause theories

Theorems 7 and 8 are only two of a bunch of related theorems which characterise strict Horn clause theories in terms of their models. There is another way of generalising these results. Instead of broadening the notion of a structure, we can put weaker conditions on the models and broaden the notion of a Horn clause theory. For example Volger [25] characterises those first-order theories whose class of models is closed under direct products and (images of) equalisers—an equaliser is a particular sort of substructure. Classes closed under direct products and equalisers are very close to Horn clause theories, as the following theorem shows.

THEOREM 10 *Let K be a class of structures (possibly many-sorted) which is closed under direct products (including 1), equalisers and filtered colimits (all in the sense of the category of sets). Then there is a definable expansion of the structures in K, adding partial function symbols, which makes K into the class of models of a strict Horn clause theory.*

Here one should also mention FL sketches, as for example in Barr [26]. We can think of these as a categorical device for catching what is essential to Horn clause theories. If T is a strict Horn clause theory in a language whose only relation symbol is equality, then one can translate T into an FL sketch, which is a category with the property that the functors from the sketch to the category of sets correspond naturally to the models of T. Barr says that there are FL sketches which can't be translated into Horn clause theories; but this is because he restricts himself to languages whose only relation symbol is equality, and which have no partial function symbols. If we allow partial functions with relation symbols defining their domains, there is no problem about representing each FL sketch by a strict Horn clause theory. Theorem 10 suggests that it is going to be difficult to reach a genuinely broader notion of Horn clause class by way of sketches or any similar device. (Of course one can experiment with models which are functors to other categories besides sets.)

In 1976 I put an infinitary version of Theorem 10 into a preprint, and the referee convinced me rather easily that it was of no interest to anyone, so it was left out of the paper that was eventually published. Has the situation changed since 1976? Maybe. In the theoretical computer science literature one certainly comes across classes of structure which obey weaker closure conditions than those in Theorem 8. The class of small categories is one example. Another example is higher-type algebras as studied by Meinke [27]. For reasons stated earlier, I look with a jaundiced eye at attempts to find initial structures in these classes; there is no special virtue in being initial, unless the initial models happen to be the ones that interested us in the first place. Still, there is mathematics to be done here.

7 Conclusions

To summarise, Horn clause theories play three main roles in computer science today:

- They describe computation with algebraic closure operators.
- Through their initial models they specify structures which encode recursively enumerable sets.
- In a number of significant cases their initial models are datatypes which are important for reasons not connected with their Horn clause description.

The first and second of these roles are closely connected, and they both rest on theorems about the representation of r.e. sets. (The first role also depends on the existence of good algorithms for handling algebraic closure operators. Often these algorithms can be written in terms of automated deduction.) The third role seems to be a freak fact of nature, not an instance of any general theorem.

On the the negative side, the uses of Horn clause theories in computer science seem to owe much less to:

- Generic models.

- Properties of the class of all models of a strict Horn clause theory.

Generic models are a useful aid to thinking and teaching, both for Prolog and databases, but they play no essential role. At some points in specification theory it's useful to consider the class of all models of a Horn clause theory; parametrised datatypes are a case in point. Closure under direct products has also thrown some light on database dependencies.

I hardly need add that none of these comments are meant to discourage anybody from trying any approach that he or she thinks could be helpful.

Acknowledgements

I thank the organisers of the ALPUK meeting for a very successful occasion, and the referees of this paper for their corrections and helpful suggestions.

References

[1] Kuehner D. Some special purpose resolution systems. In: Meltzer B, Michie D (eds) Machine Intelligence. Halsted Press New York, 1972, pp 117–128.

[2] Henschen LJ, Wos L. Unit refutations and Horn sets. JACM 1974; 21:590–605.

[3] McKinsey JCC. The decision problem for some classes of sentences without quantifiers. J Symbolic Logic 1943; 8:61–76.

[4] Miller D. Abstractions in logic programs. In: Odifreddi P (ed) Logic and Computer Science. Academic Press London, 1990, pp 329–359.

[5] Makowsky JA. Why Horn formulas matter in computer science: initial structures and generic examples. J Comp Sys Sci 1987; 34:266–292.

[6] Mal'tsev AI. Quasiprimitive classes of abstract algebras (Russian). Doklady Akad Nauk SSSR 1956; 108:187–189. Translated in Mal'cev AI. The Metamathematics of Algebraic Systems. North-Holland Amsterdam, 1971, pp 27–31.

[7] Reichel H. Initially restricting algebraic theories. In: Dembiński P (ed) Proc. 9th MFCS, Ryszyna, Lecture Notes in Comp Sci 88. Springer Berlin, 1980, pp 504–514.

[8] Colmerauer A. An introduction to Prolog III. In: Lloyd JW (ed) Computational Logic. Springer Berlin, 1990, pp 37–79.

[9] Post E. Recursively enumerable sets of positive integers and their decision problems. Bull Amer Math Soc 1944; 50:284–316.

[10] Cohn PM. Universal Algebra. Reidel, Dordrecht, 1981.

[11] Kowalski RA. Logic for Problem Solving. North-Holland, New York, 1979.

[12] Smullyan RM. On definability by recursion. Bull Amer Math Soc 1956; 62:601.

[13] Chang CL. The unit proof and the input proof in theorem proving. JACM 1970; 17;698–708.

[14] Nadathur G, Miller D. Higher-order Horn clauses. JACM 1990; 37:777–814.

[15] Grassmann HG. Die lineale Ausdehnungslehre, ein neuer Zweig der Mathematik dargestellt und durch Anwendungen auf die übrigen Zweige der Mathematik, wie auch auf Statik, Mechanik, die Lehre von Magnetismus und die Krystallonomie erläutert. Stettin 1844.

[16] Van Emden MH, Kowalski RA. The semantics of predicate logic as a programming language. JACM 1976; 23:733–742.

[17] Lloyd JW. Foundations of logic programming. Springer, Berlin, 1984.

[18] Minker J. On indefinite databases and the closed world assumption. In: Loveland DW (ed) 6th Conference on Automated Deduction. Springer Berlin, 1982, pp 292–308 (Lecture Notes in Comp Sci 138).

[19] Shepherdson JC. Negation in logic programming. In: Minker J (ed) Foundations of Deductive Databases and Logic Programming. Morgan Kaufmann, Los Altos, 1988, pp 19–88.

[20] Johnson-Laird PN, Byrne RMJ. Deduction. Lawrence Erlbaum Associates, Hove and London, 1991.

[21] Ehrig H, Mahr B. Fundamentals of algebraic specification I. Springer Berlin, 1985.

[22] Tarlecki A. On the existence of free models in abstract algebraic institutions. Theor Comp Sci 1985; 37:269–304.

[23] Galvin F. Horn sentences. Ann Math Logic 1970; 1:389–422.

[24] Fagin R. Horn clauses and database dependencies. JACM 1982; 29:952–985.

[25] Volger H. Preservation theorems for limits of structures and global sections of sheaves of structures. Math Zeitschrift 1979; 166:27–53.

[26] Barr M. Models of Horn theories. In: Gray JW, Scedrov A (eds) Categories in Computer Science and Logic. Contemporary Mathematics 92. Amer Math Soc 1989, pp 1–7.

[27] Meinke K. Universal algebra in higher types. Theor Comp Sci (to appear).

Wilfrid Hodges
School of Mathematical Sciences
Queen Mary and Westfield College
Mile End Road
London E1 4NS
W.Hodges@qmw.ac.uk

From a Hilbert Calculus to its Model Theoretic Semantics

Dov Gabbay
Imperial College, Dept. of Computing
180 Queens Gate
London SWZ 2AZ, England

Hans Jürgen Ohlbach
Max–Planck–Institut für Informatik
Im Stadtwald
Saarbrücken 11, Germany *

Abstract

There are different ways of constructing a logic. One possibility is to define a Hilbert calculus, i.e. a kind of grammar that produces all formulae to be considered true. A logic can also be defined by a model theoretic semantics for the logical connectives in the language. In this paper a general theory is presented for the transition from a Hilbert calculus to its model theoretic semantics such that soundness and completeness are automatically guaranteed.

For a given Hilbert calculus we start with a general neighbourhood semantics for n-place connectives. This semantics does not impose any built-in properties. A quantifier elimination algorithm is used to translate Hilbert axioms and rules into corresponding semantic properties. By proving certain key lemmas from these semantic properties, neighbourhood semantics can be systematically strengthened up to a version of the semantics which has as many Hilbert axioms built in as possible. The work is still incomplete and will be continued.

Key Words: Logic, Hilbert calculus, model theoretic semantics, correspondence theory.

1 Introduction

Traditionally the way, new logics have been developed so far, is to concentrate on one or a few specific features and build a logic or a class of logics around it. For example modal logic is built around the two modal operators $\Box$ and $\Diamond$ and a corresponding possible worlds semantics. Relevance logic is built around the implication and the intuition that all assumptions should be used in the proofs. The construction and investigation of these logics was a scientific enterprise which sometimes took decades. From a practical point of view,

*This work was supported by the ESPRIT project 3125 MEDLAR, by the "Sonderforschungsbereich" 314, "Künstliche Intelligenz und wissensbasierte Systeme" of the German Research Council (DFG) and by the MFT funded project 'LOGO'. The first author is a SERC/UK Senior Research Fellow.

however, the outcome is still not satisfactory. Having these different types of logics which quite often have nothing to do with each other is like for example having one programming language with recursion and another one with arrays, but no language with both. Therefore there is a need, not only for combining existing logics with different features, but also for developing new logics that suit particular applications. If the development of a new logic is application driven, it should be an engineering issue that does not divert from the work on the application itself.

In this paper we make a first step in supporting the development of logics by a powerful meta theory. The meta theory provides procedures and general proofs such that the construction of a specific logic really becomes an exercise which can be automated to a large extent. The process of developing a theory for going from a purely syntactic Hilbert calculus to a model theoretic semantics consists of the following parts:

Part 1: We have to find a language in which both the Hilbert calculus as well as its semantics can be formulated. Fortunately it turned out that predicate logic is the adequate language. Sometimes, however, second-order predicate logic is needed.

Part 2: Suppose there is a Hilbert calculus that defines a logic $\mathcal{L}$ containing some connectives C_i and this Hilbert calculus HK is formalized in a certain way in predicate logic. In this formulation all $\mathcal{L}$-formulae are represented as terms. For each connective C_i we need to find a definition of its semantics. This semantics should also be formalized in predicate logic. The semantics definition SD expresses a logical equivalence which can act as a rewrite rule for eliminating all occurrences of C_i, thus translating $\mathcal{L}$-fomulae into predicate logic.

The first property we have to ensure is that adding the semantics definitions does not change the logic. Schematically that means for every $\mathcal{L}$-formula F:

$$HK \models F \text{ iff } HK \cup SD \models F.$$

Ensuring this property goes along with finding an appropriate semantics SD at all, and finding it as automatically as possible. To this end we start with a very weak (neighbourhood-) semantics which guarantees this property without any conditions on the Hilbert calculus at all. In a sequence of steps, which can be automated to a great extend, this weak semantics is strengthened such that as many Hilbert axioms as possible become tautologies in the semantics in the same sense as for example the Necessitation Rule and the K-Axiom for modal logic are tautologies in the standard Kripke semantics (see sections 4, 6). In this way an optimal semantics is eventually obtained.

Part 3: Given a semantics SD, the Hilbert calculus HK has to be translated into an equivalent set of axioms in terms of the semantic notions only. For example, if SD specifies standard relational Kripke semantics for the modal $\Box$-operator, the Hilbert axiom $\Box P \Rightarrow P$ is translated into the reflexivity of the accessibility relation. The translation of Hilbert axioms into semantic properties turns out to be a quantifier elimination problem in second-order predicate logic. In another paper [GO92] we have defined the so called SCAN algorithm which can be used for this purpose (see section 5). What we get is, again schematically, for every $\mathcal{L}$-formula F:

$$HK \cup SD \models F \text{ iff } HK_{sem}(SD) \cup SD \models F$$

where $HK_{sem}(SD)$ denotes the translated Hilbert axioms and rules. The translation of the Hilbert axioms of course depends on the semantics SD. Since SD can actually act as rewrite rules for translating $\mathcal{L}$-formulae into predicate logic, we finally end up with

$$HK_{sem}(SD) \cup SD \models F \text{ iff } HK_{sem}(SD) \models SD(F)$$

That means, theorem proving for the new logic $\mathcal{L}$ can be realized by theorem proving in predicate logic.

All these parts are described in detail in the subsequent chapters.

2 Hilbert Calculi

There are basically two different ways for specifying a logic, either by an Hilbert calculus, or by a model theoretic semantics. A Hilbert calculus consists of some axioms, i.e. formulae or formula schemata respectively which are a priori considered true, together with some production rules for generating from the axioms other formulae which are also to be considered true. Lukasiewicz' axiomatization of the implicational fragment of propositional logic is an example of a Hilbert calculus:

Example 2.1 (Implicational Fragment of Propositional Logic)

Axiom: $((P \to Q) \to R) \to ((R \to P) \to (S \to P))$

Rule: $P, \quad P \to Q \quad \vdash \quad Q$ (Modus Ponens)

◁

Implicitly there is always a substitution rule allowing to consider the propositional variables $(P, Q, R, \ldots)$ as place holders for more complex formulae. It is, however, important to notice that the propositional variables of the Hilbert rules cannot be instantiated by any syntactically correct formula, but only in such a way that the preconditions of the rule become Hilbert axioms or formulae generated in previous steps, i.e. the preconditions are formulae which are already shown to be tautologies in the new logic.

Specification of a logic via a Hilbert calculus is the method of choice when there is no precise idea about the semantics of the logical connectives in the new logic. As an example, suppose, *Want*, *Believe* and *because*–operators are to be defined. Nobody has an idea what these notions mean in precise mathematical terms. But everybody would agree to some basic correlations between them, for example if you want R because you believe that R implies Q then in reality you want Q, or formally

$$((Want\ R)\ because\ Believe(R \Rightarrow Q)) \Rightarrow Want\ Q$$

This is an Hilbert axiom that correlates the *Want*–Operator with *Believe*, *because* and $\Rightarrow$. Thus, a Hilbert calculus is a device for approximating intuitive notions in a logical framework. Unfortunately a Hilbert calculus is the worst basis for automating reasoning in the so specified logic. Reasoning by means of an Hilbert calculus amounts to enumerating all theorems and checking if a given formula is among them. The basis for efficient reasoning methods in a logic is a model theoretic semantics which maps syntactic items to simple and well known mathematical objects, sets, functions, relations etc. A model theoretic semantics provides a notion of semantic truth which, of course, has to coincide with the syntactic truth defined by the Hilbert calculus. The resolution calculus for first-order predicate logic is a striking example that shows how to obtain from a notion of semantic truth an efficient syntactic reasoning system.

The development of a logic up to a level where an automatic reasoning system can be implemented consists therefore of the steps

Hilbert calculus $\rightarrow$ model theoretic semantics $\rightarrow$ automatable calculus

Richard Routley and Bob Meyer have proved that every sentential logic, i.e. a logic specified by a Hilbert calculus has a two-valued semantics [RM76]. This proof, however, is merely an existential proof. In this paper we show how to compute a semantics and how to improve the computed semantics with a general method. Thus, this paper solves the problems Routley and Meyer have stated in their conclusion.

2.1 Our Meta Logic

In order to construct from a Hilbert calculus its model theoretic semantics in a systematic and automatable way, a meta language is necessary in which both sides can be formalized. It turned out that in the very first step, modal logic is an appropriate choice. (In the sequel we assume the reader to be familiar with modal logic, cf. [Che80].) In a second step we shall get rid of modal logic and work in predicate logic. With modal logic it is possible to encode the informal requirement that a Hilbert axiom is to be understood as a tautology, i.e. true under all circumstances — true in all possible worlds. Hilbert axioms F are therefore written as $Box\ Pr(F)$ where the formula F of the new logic is encoded as a term and the predicate Pr is to be read as 'provable'. Thus, all connectives in the new logic are encoded as ordinary function symbols. We write Box instead of the usual $\Box$ when we use modal logic as meta logic. Since modal logic will be used as object logic in many examples, the familiar $\Box$-operator is reserved for the object logic.

An even stronger reason for taking modal logic as meta logic comes from the definition of the Hilbert rules. Encoding rules like Modus Ponens $P, P \rightarrow Q \vdash Q$ in predicate logic, for example as

$$Pr(P) \wedge Pr(P \rightarrow Q) \Rightarrow Pr(Q)$$

cannot capture the requirement that the premises ought to be tautologies and not just formulae which happen to be true just be chance. Therefore the correct encoding in modal logic is:

$$Box\ Pr(P) \wedge Box\ Pr(P \rightarrow Q) \Rightarrow Box\ Pr(Q)$$

Thus, a Hilbert calculus becomes nothing else than a special set of modal Horn clauses. For example the Hilbert calculus of example 2.1 is encoded:

Example 2.2 (Hilbert System for Modal Logic K)
Axiom: $\forall P, Q, R, S\ Box\ Pr(((P \rightarrow Q) \rightarrow R) \rightarrow ((R \rightarrow P) \rightarrow (S \rightarrow P)))$
Rule: $\forall P, Q\ Box\ Pr(P) \wedge Box\ Pr(P \rightarrow Q) \Rightarrow Box\ Pr(Q)$

As a further example, in order to extend the Hilbert system[1] from propositional logic to the propositional modal logic K (this time as *object logic*), the K-Axiom

$$\forall P, Q\ Box\ Pr(\Box(P \rightarrow Q) \rightarrow (\Box P \rightarrow \Box Q))$$

and the 'Necessitation Rule'

$$\forall P\ Box\ Pr(P) \Rightarrow Box\ Pr(\Box P)$$

have to be added. ◁

The Necessitation Rule shows clearly that modal logic as meta logic is necessary. Interpreting the $\Box$–operator for example as the temporal *henceforth*–operator and writing the Necessitation Rule in predicate logic $\forall P\ Pr(P) \Rightarrow Pr(henceforth\ P)$, the instantiation $Pr(raining) \Rightarrow Pr(henceforth\ raining)$ is derivable, which would be a disaster.

From a syntactic point of view, the *Box*–operator could be ignored so far. What we have is essentially a set of Horn clauses which generates by forward reasoning all theorems of the object logic. In principle, all theorems of the logic can now be derived with a predicate logic theorem prover. Already for simple theorems, however, the search space may become so large that it becomes almost impossible to prove them. Although a Hilbert system is a Horn theory, this is an example where Prolog execution immediately loops. [MW92] gives an overview about what can be done with current theorem proving technology.

The first step in transforming a syntactic Hilbert system into something which can be handled more efficiently is to get rid of the *Box*–operator by translating the modal formulae into predicate logic. Exploiting the possible worlds semantics of the *Box*–operator one can translate a modal formula $Box\ Pr(F)$ into a predicate logic formula $\forall w\ R(w_0, w) \Rightarrow H(F, w)$. R is the accessibility relation, w_0 is the initial or actual world respectively and $H(F, w)$ expresses that F holds in world w. Actually the target logic for this translation has to be a *two–sorted* version of predicate logic. The two sorts are needed for separating terms denoting worlds from terms representing formulae of the new logic. Since this distinction is so obvious it will not be mentioned in the rest of the paper.

The special structure of the Hilbert axioms in modal logic formulation allows to take a fixed initial world w_0 and to hide this world by abbreviating $R(w_0, w)$ with $A(w)$. The precise reason for this shortcut is the following: We are interested in proving theorems from the Hilbert axioms, i.e. we want to prove *Hilbert-System* $\models$ $Box\ Pr(F)$ for a given formula F. If this is a theorem in modal logic (as meta logic) it must be true for all frames and all actual worlds. Therefore one can choose one 'arbitrary but fixed' world w_0 as initial world in the modal interpretation. (Proving the theorem by refuting the negation, one gets w_0 explicitly as Skolem constant.)

---

[1] With 'Hilbert system' we mean an Hilbert calculus encoded in modal logic.

The worlds for which $A(w)$ holds are sometimes called 'actual worlds' [HC68]. It is the distinction between worlds and actual worlds which prevents the constructed logic of being automatically closed under logical equivalences.

All these informal considerations are made precise by the next definition.

Definition 2.3 (Syntactic and Semantic Hilbert System)
In the sequel let $\mathcal{L}$ denote the new logic to be constructed.

- A (propositional) $\mathcal{L}$–formula is a formula constructed from infinitely many propositional variables and the $\mathcal{L}$–connectives in the usual inductive way.
- A *syntactic Hilbert system* $HS_P = HA \cup HR$ for a logic $\mathcal{L}$ consists of Hilbert axioms HA and Hilbert rules HR.
  A Hilbert axiom is just a $\mathcal{L}$-formula where all propositional variables are taken to be place holders for arbitrary $\mathcal{L}$-formulae. All instances of the Hilbert axioms are $\mathcal{L}$-tautologies.
  A Hilbert rule has the form $G_1, \ldots, G_n \vdash G$
  where G and the G_i are $\mathcal{L}$–formulae with propositional variables. If instances $G'_1, \ldots, G'_n$ of $G_1, \ldots, G_n$ are all $\mathcal{L}$-tautologies then the corresponding instance G' of G is an $\mathcal{L}$-tautology.
- A *semantic Hilbert system* HS_H is a syntactic Hilbert system with every literal F replaced with
  $\forall w\ A(w) \Rightarrow H(F, w)$. All free variables are universally quantified. F is now encoded as a term in predicate logic.

◁

For example for the modal logic K (Example 2.2), we get

Example 2.4 (Semantic Hilbert System for Modal Logic K)

<u>Axioms</u>: $\forall P, Q, R, S \quad \forall w\ A(w) \Rightarrow H(((P \rightarrow Q) \rightarrow R) \rightarrow ((R \rightarrow P) \rightarrow (S \rightarrow P)), w)$

$\forall P, Q \quad \forall w\ A(w) \Rightarrow H(\Box(P \rightarrow Q) \rightarrow (\Box P \rightarrow \Box Q), w)$

<u>Rules</u>: $\forall P, Q \quad (\forall w\ A(w) \Rightarrow H(P, w)) \wedge (\forall w\ A(w) \Rightarrow H(P \rightarrow Q, w)) \Rightarrow (\forall w\ A(w) \Rightarrow H(Q, w))$

$\forall P \quad (\forall w\ A(w) \Rightarrow H(P, w)) \Rightarrow (\forall w\ A(w) \Rightarrow H(\Box P, w))$

◁

The definition 2.3 of syntactic Hilbert systems excludes certain constructs which are sometimes used. Excluded are syntactic constraints on the structure of the $\mathcal{L}$–formulae in the Hilbert axioms and rules. For example constraints like "If the connective X does not occur in the scope of connective Y then ..." cannot be represented. Quantifier rules like $F(t) \vdash \exists x\ F(x)$ also cannot be represented because $F(t)$ means that t is contained syntactically in F and all its occurrences have to be replaced with x. This excludes the treatment of Hilbert axiomatizations of quantifiers. For our purpose, this is actually not necessary, because the quantifiers can be introduced directly on the semantic level (c.f. example 6.1,9).

In the sequel we do no longer distinguish between Hilbert axioms and Hilbert rules. They all can be treated the same way and therefore the notion Hilbert axiom means both of them.

The detour via modal logic as meta logic gives us immediately the equivalence of the syntactic and semantic Hilbert systems with respect to provability of $\mathcal{L}$-formulae.

Proposition 2.5 ()
If HS_P is a syntactic Hilbert calculus for a logic $\mathcal{L}$ HS_H is its semantic counterpart (def. 2.3), and F is a $\mathcal{L}$-formula then ($\models$ is semantic consequence)

$$HS_P \vdash F \text{ iff } HS_S \models \forall w\ A(w) \Rightarrow H(F, w).$$

Proof: The proof is a straightforward consequence of the detour via modal logic as meta logic and the soundness and completeness of the so called relational translation from modal logic into predicate logic [Ohl91]. ◁

3 Semantics Definitions

So far, the step from syntactic to semantic Hilbert systems is only a syntactic transformation in the meta formalism which does not yet give any new insight. But this gives the formal basis within which to express the desired semantics of the logical connectives in the same system and then to reason about the combined system consisting of a syntactic characterization of true formulae and a corresponding semantic characterization.

In the sequel a special notation for truth sets of formulae will be used:

Definition 3.1 (Truth Sets)
The expression $\xi(v_1, \ldots, v_n)\varphi(v_1, \ldots, v_n)$ where $\varphi(v_1, \ldots, v_n)$ is a formula with free variables $v_1, \ldots, v_n$ denotes the truth set of φ. That means

$$\mathit{interpretation}(\xi(v_1, \ldots, v_n)\varphi(v_1, \ldots, v_n)) = \{(v_1, \ldots, v_n) \mid \varphi(v_1, \ldots, v_n) \text{ is true}\}$$

If φ is just a predicate symbol, we sometimes write
$\|\varphi\|$ for $\xi(v_1, \ldots, v_n)\varphi(v_1, \ldots, v_n)$. ◁

A brief look at the semantics of logical connectives in existing logics shows that there are different possibilities. The simplest version is to use just predicate logic semantics. The formula

$$\forall P, Q\ \forall w\ H(P \& Q, w) \Leftrightarrow (H(P, w) \wedge H(Q, w))$$

for example expresses that $P \& Q$ is true in a world w if and only if both P and Q are true in that world. That means the connective & is given the semantics of the predicate logic $\wedge$. Notice that the 'Holds' predicate H permits the usage of ordinary predicate logic for expressing semantics of connectives.

As another example, the standard Kripke semantics of the $\Box$-operator can be expressed in our system with

$$\forall P\ \forall w\ H(\Box P, w) \Leftrightarrow (\forall v\ \mathcal{R}(w, v) \Rightarrow H(P, v).$$

A similar formula expresses a possible worlds semantics of the arrow connective '$\rightarrow$':

$$\forall P, Q\ \forall w\ H(P \rightarrow Q, w) \Leftrightarrow (\forall v_1, v_2\ \mathcal{R}(w, v_1, v_2) \Rightarrow (H(P, v_1) \Rightarrow H(Q, v_2))).$$

As it is known from modal logic, the relational semantics is not the only possibility for the semantics of the $\Box$-operator. There is also neighbourhood (or minimal model) semantics [Che80]:

$$\forall P\ \forall w\ H(\Box P, w) \Leftrightarrow \mathcal{N}(w, \xi(v) H(P, v))$$

where $\mathcal{N}$ is the neighbourhood relation which relates each world with its neighbourhood structure as a set of sets of worlds. $\Box P$ is true in a world w if P itself is true *exactly* in one of w's neighbourhoods.

Neighbourhood semantics can be extended to n-place connectives. For a two-place connective '$\rightarrow$' it may be:

$$\forall P, Q\ \forall w\ (H(P \rightarrow Q, w) \Leftrightarrow \mathcal{N}_{\rightarrow}(w, \xi(v_1, v_2)(H(P, v_1) \Rightarrow H(Q, v_2)))$$

There is a large number of different schemes for semantics definitions. So far we have considered only generalisations to n-place connectives of predicate logic, relational, and neighbourhood semantics. The methodology we are proposing, however, is independent of the particular type of semantics. The generalisations are listed in the next definition.

Definition 3.2 (Semantics Definitions)
A semantics definition for an n-place connective C is a formula of the form

$$\forall F_1, \ldots, F_n\ \forall w\ H(C(F_1, \ldots, F_n), w) \Leftrightarrow \Phi$$

where the formula Φ does not contain the connective C.
Some sample types of semantics definitions are:
Type P (for predicate logic):
$\forall F_1, \ldots, F_n\ \forall w\ H(C(F_1, \ldots, F_n), w) \Leftrightarrow \Psi_C(H(F_1, w), \ldots, H(F_n, w)))$

Type R (for relational):
$\forall F_1, \ldots, F_n\ \forall w\ H(C(F_1, \ldots, F_n), w) \Leftrightarrow$
$\forall v_1, \ldots, v_n\ \mathcal{R}_C(w, v_1, \ldots, v_n) \Rightarrow \Psi_C(H(F_1, v_1), \ldots, H(F_n, v_n)))$
where $\mathcal{R}_C$ is the $n+1$-place accessibility relation.

Type N (for neighbourhood):
$\forall F_1, \ldots, F_n\ \forall w\ H(C(F_1, \ldots, F_n), w) \Leftrightarrow$
$\mathcal{N}_C(w, \xi(v_1, \ldots, v_n)\Psi_C(H(F_1, v_1), \ldots, H(F_n, v_n)))$
where $\mathcal{N}_C$ is the neighbourhood relation,
i.e. a relation between a world and sets of n-tuples of worlds (neighbourhoods)[2].

In all three cases Ψ_C is a propositional function like $\Rightarrow$, $\wedge$ etc. This function has to be provided by the developer of the logic. It is this point where he/she can put some intuition about the semantics of the connectives into the procedure.
To simplify matters we assume that Ψ_C does not contain redundant arguments, i.e. for every argument a there is a set of other arguments such that when the truth value of a is switched, then Ψ_C switches.

In principle we can also define the semantics of quantifiers in this framework:

$$\forall F\ \forall x\ \forall w\ (H(forall(x, F), w) \Leftrightarrow \forall y\ (y = x \wedge exists(y, w)) \Rightarrow H(F, w)$$

This expresses that *forall* x F is true in the world w if F holds in w for all objects existing in that world. The condition $y = x$ is necessary to identify the object and meta variables. ◁

---

[2] This version of general neighbourhood semantics differs from the general semantics, Routley and Meyer used [RM75]. Their version is $w \models C(F_1, \ldots, F_n)$ iff $\mathcal{N}_C(w, \|F_1\|, \ldots, \|F_n\|)$. This version is not very suitable for strengthening it to relational semantics.

Definition 3.3 (Translation into Predicate Logic)
If SD is a set of semantics definitions for the connectives occurring in an $\mathcal{L}$–formula F then let $SD(H(F,w))$ be the result of applying the semantics definitions as rewrite rules as long as possible. After exhaustive application of SD, $SD(H(F,w))$ contains no further $\mathcal{L}$–connectives, but only literals $H(P,\ldots)$ with atomic Ps, which in turn can be written as $P(\ldots)$. Therefore this process can be called "translation of F into predicate logic." ◁

Obviously for each connective, one of the above (or other) types of semantics definitions have to be chosen. But how? The constraint which has to be ensured is that adding a semantics definition to a Hilbert system does not change the logic $\mathcal{L}$. In this case we say that the semantics definition is sound and complete.

Theorem 3.4 (Neighbourhood Semantics are Sound and Complete)

Adding a neighbourhood semantics definition SD (def. 3.2) for a connective C to a Hilbert system does not change the logic $\mathcal{L}$, i.e. for all $\mathcal{L}$-formulae F

$$HS \models \forall w\ A(w) \Rightarrow H(F,w) \text{ iff } HS \cup \{SD\} \models \forall w\ A(w) \Rightarrow H(F,w)$$

Proof: Let $SD = \forall F_1,\ldots,F_n\ \forall w\ H(C(F_1,\ldots,F_n),w) \Leftrightarrow$
$\mathcal{N}(w,\xi(v_1,\ldots,v_n)\Psi(H(F_1,v_1),\ldots,H(F_n,v_n)))$
be a semantics definition of neighbourhood type.
Adding a formula to a set of predicate logic formulae does not turn theorems into non-theorems (predicate logic is monotonic.) Therefore the 'if'–direction is obvious.

For showing the 'only-if'–direction, suppose $HS \cup \{SD\} \models \forall w\ A(w) \Rightarrow H(F,w)$. Let $\Im$ be a model for HS. The structure of the proof is to show that $\Im$ can be extended to satisfy SD without changing the interpretation of the symbols in $A(w) \Rightarrow H(F,w)$. Therefore the extended interpretation satisfies $HS \cup \{SD\}$, and because this is assumed to entail the right hand side, both the extended and the original interpretation satisfy $\forall w\ A(w) \Rightarrow H(F,w)$. Thus, $HS \models \forall w\ A(w) \Rightarrow H(F,w)$.
To implement this idea, an appropriate neighbourhood relation $\mathcal{N}_{\Im'}$ as denotation for $\mathcal{N}$ in $\Im'$ is to be constructed.
Let $\mathcal{N}_{\Im'}(w,N)$ iff $N = \{(v_1,\ldots,v_n) \mid \Im \models \Psi(H(F_1,v_1),\ldots,H(F_n,v_n))\}$ for some $F_1,\ldots,F_n$ with $\Im \models H(C(F_1,\ldots,F_n),w)$. That means, the neighbourhoods of the worlds w consist of the truth sets of those formulae $C(F_1,\ldots,F_n)$ which are true in w. Obviously this satisfies the "$\Rightarrow$"–part of SD.
In order to show the "$\Leftarrow$"–part of SD, we need to ensure that different formulae really have different truth sets. Now let $G_1,\ldots,G_n$ such that N is the truth set of $\Psi(H(G_1,v_1),\ldots,H(G_n,v_n))$ and $\Im' \models \mathcal{N}(w,N)$, but $\Im$ does not satisfy $H(C(G_1,\ldots,G_n),w)$. We want this to be come impossible. The idea is to add sufficiently many non-actual worlds such that this can no longer happen.
According to the construction of the interpretation of $\mathcal{N}$, there must be
$F_1,\ldots,F_n$ with
$\Im \models H(C(F_1,\ldots,F_n),w)$ and $\forall v_1,\ldots,v_n\ (v_1,\ldots,v_n) \in N$ iff
$\Im \models \Psi_C(H(F_1,v_1),\ldots,H(F_n,v_n))$
If one of the G_i is different to F_i we construct a third interpretation $\Im''$ by adding a non-actual world u_i (i.e. $A(u_i)$ is false) where $H(F_i,u_i)$ is false and

$H(G_i,u_i)$ is true. Since all the Hilbert axioms have the condition $A(w) \Rightarrow \ldots$, this does not change the truth value of the Hilbert axioms. However, we find some u_i where the truth value of
$\Psi(H(F_1,v_1),\ldots,H(F_{i-1},v_{i-1}),H(F_i,u_i),H(F_{i+1},v_{i+1}),\ldots,H(F_n,v_n))$
is different to the truth value of
$\Psi(H(G_1,v_1),\ldots,H(G_{i-1},v_{i-1}),H(G_i,u_i),H(G_{i+1},v_{i+1}),\ldots,H(G_n,v_n))$
(Ψ_C is assumed to contain no redundant arguments).
This operation can be done sufficiently often such that finally there is an interpretation $\Im'''$ where no syntactically different formulae have the same truth set. In this interpretation the $\Leftarrow$-part of SD is also satisfied. That means $\Im''' \models HS \cup \{SD\}$ and thus $\Im''' \models \forall w\ A(w) \Rightarrow H(F,w)$. Since $\Im'''$ agrees with $\Im$ on the actual worlds $A(w)$, we find $\Im \models \forall w\ A(w) \Rightarrow H(F,w)$.
This finishes the 'only-if'-part of the proof. ◁

This proof has an interesting and useful corollary. The construction of the semantics for the neighbourhood predicate $\mathcal{N}$ ensures that the sets of n-tuples of worlds which form a neighbourhood of a given world are not arbitrary sets, but truth sets of some formulae $\Psi(P_1(v_1),\ldots,P_n(v_n))$.

Corollary 3.5 (Neighbourhood Predicates)
The following axiom is satisfied by the constructed interpretation for the neighbourhood relation in the proof of theorem 3.4:

$$\begin{aligned}&\forall M\ \forall w\ \mathcal{N}(w,\|M\|) \Rightarrow\\ &\exists P_1,\ldots,P_n\ \forall v_1,\ldots,v_n\ M(v_1,\ldots,v_n) \Leftrightarrow \Psi(P_1(v_1),\ldots,P_n(v_n)).\end{aligned}$$

n-place predicates satisfying this axiom are called *neighbourhood predicates*. Being a neighbourhood predicate depends on the function Ψ which in turn depends on the connective C. Since in most cases it is obvious which Ψ and which C is meant, we do not mention this explicitly.

In the sequel $\mathcal{NP}(M)$ means that M is a neighbourhood predicate, i.e. it satisfies the above axiom.

The extensions of neighbourhood predicates are called *neighbourhood sets*. (Sometimes we do not distinguish between N as a neighbourhood predicate and $\|N\|$ as a neighbourhood set.) ◁

The above axiom is a tautology for one-place connectives like the modal logic $\Box$-operator. For more complex connectives, however, this property is nontrivial and may turn out to be helpful (see theorem 4.4 and example 6.4).

If nothing is known about the logic $\mathcal{L}$, neighbourhood semantics can always be used. In this case the developer of the logic has to choose only the propositional function Ψ_C for each connective C. If the choice is inappropriate, nothing serious does happen at this stage. What usually will happen, however, is that the semantics cannot be strengthened with the mechanisms shown below. For example if the Hilbert calculus contains the axiom $\Box P \Rightarrow \neg P$ and the identity function is chosen for $\Psi_\Box$ this axiom corresponds to the property $\forall w, N\ \mathcal{N}(w,\|N\|) \Rightarrow \neg N(w)$ of the neighbourhood structure. This Hilbert axiom is however inconsistent with standard relational Kripke semantics for the $\Box$-operator. Therefore neighbourhood semantics cannot be strengthened to relational semantics. If instead $\neg$ is chosen for $\Psi_\Box$, strengthening to relational semantics is possible and yields the reflexivity of the accessibility relation as corresponding property.

Neighbourhood semantics is very complex and therefore not very satisfactory. If it can be shown that the Hilbert calculus actually supports a stronger semantics, things become much easier. First of all, stronger semantics means that some Hilbert axioms become automatically tautologies in that semantics. For example, Necessitation Rule and the K-Axiom are tautologies in the standard relational semantics of the modal $\Box$–operator, whereas they need not be true in neighbourhood semantics. Therefore in the stronger semantics one needs no longer worry about these axioms and can ignore them. Secondly, stronger semantics are in general much better to understand, show more about the structure of the logic, are much simpler to handle, and therefore a better basis for developing automated reasoning methods.

A systematic method for strengthening the semantics will be presented in the next section.

4 Strengthening the Semantics

The way we propose for strengthening the semantics of a connective is as follows: Suppose you are given a Hilbert system together with some semantics definitions of the connectives. If you manage to prove from these two parts certain key lemmas, then — by our meta theorems — you are entitled to exchange a semantics definition with a stronger one. The key lemmas which have to be proved depend on the pair weaker semantics, stronger semantics. In this section we shall provide schemata for the key lemmas for the following transitions:

- transition from semantics *with* the actual world predicate A to semantics *without* the actual world predicate A,
- transition from neighbourhood semantics to relational semantics,
- transition from relational semantics to predicate logic semantics.

The first transition, dropping the actual world predicate, involves all connectives at once which still have neighbourhood or relational semantics. The other transitions, however, are individual to each connective. That means you may be able to strengthen the semantics for one connective, but not for the other connectives.

The definitions and meta theorems about the strengthening method are given in this section. All conditions for strengthening the semantics are sufficient and not necessarily necessary. In the subsequent sections, we shall present methods for mechanizing these transitions.

The first theorem states the general condition for eliminating the A–predicate.

Theorem 4.1 (Elimination of the A–Predicate)
If for a Hilbert system HS together with semantics definitions for the connec-

tives the following 'Deletion Lemmas' can be proved:

For all connectives C with neighbourhood semantics:
$$\forall N, M \quad \forall v_1, \ldots, v_n\ A(v_1) \wedge \ldots \wedge A(v_n) \Rightarrow (N(v_1, \ldots, v_n) \Leftrightarrow M(v_1, \ldots, v_n)) \Rightarrow \forall w\ A(w) \Rightarrow (\mathcal{N}_C(w, \|N\|) \Leftrightarrow \mathcal{N}_C(w, \|M\|))$$

For all connectives C with relational semantics:
$$\forall w\ A(w) \Rightarrow \forall v_1, \ldots, v_n\ \mathcal{R}_C(w, v_1, \ldots, v_n) \Rightarrow (A(v_1) \wedge, \ldots \wedge A(v_n))$$

then $\forall w\ A(w)$ can be assumed true.

Proof: For the connectives with neighbourhood semantics the condition means that two neighbourhood sets whose intersection with the set of actual worlds is identical are either both in or both not in the neighbourhood of the actual worlds. The condition for the connectives with relational semantics means that worlds which are accessible from actual worlds are again actual worlds. These two conditions imply that the denotation of the 'world'–sort can be reduced to the set of actual worlds without changing the truth of the Hilbert axioms and the semantics definitions. With other words, if $HS \cup SD$ is satisfied by all 'reduced' interpretations, it is also satisfied by the original interpretations. In the reduced interpretations, however, $\forall w\ A(w)$ is true in general. ◁

The parts of the Hilbert system allowing to get rid of the A–predicate are in general rules expressing in some sense closedness under equivalence. We shall see that in the case of modal logic it is the presence of the ME-Rule, $P \Leftrightarrow Q \vdash \Box P \Leftrightarrow \Box Q$ which allows for proving these two conditions. And in fact, it is well known that the ME-Rule permits to drop the distinction between actual worlds and all worlds.

4.1 From Neighbourhood Semantics to Relational Semantics

It is also well known from modal logic that the semantics can be strengthened from neighbourhood to relational semantics if the neighbourhood structure is closed under intersection and supersets, i.e. if the intersection of two neighbourhoods of a world is again a neighbourhood of this world, and if all supersets of a neighbourhood of a world are also neighbourhoods of this world. Closedness under intersection permits the definition of an accessibility relation by saying that those worlds which are contained in the intersection of all neighbourhoods of a given world are in fact the accessible worlds.

The generalisation of the first condition, closedness under intersection, to arbitrary n-place connectives, however, is not straightforward. As we already have pointed out (corollary. 3.5), neighbourhood sets are truth sets of formulae and therefore they have a certain structure. The intersection of two such neighbourhood sets, however, has in general not this structure. Instead of requiring that the intersection of two neighbourhoods contains again a neighbourhood, we have to weaken this to the requirement that there is a neighbourhood set contained in the intersection of two neighbourhood sets.

Unfortunately, it can be shown that the intersection of two neighbourhood sets contains not always a neighbourhood set. Whether or not there is a neighbourhood set contained in the intersection of two neighbourhood sets depends on the structure of the Ψ–function used for defining the semantics of the connective. If all the arguments of this function have only one polarity, either positive or negative[3], then the intersection of two neighbourhood sets is again a neighbourhood set. This property holds for the propositional functions, $\neg, \wedge, \vee, \Rightarrow$, but it does not hold for example for $\Leftrightarrow$. Therefore the transition from neighbourhood semantics to relational semantics works only for this restricted case.

Let us illustrate the idea for formalizing 'neighbourhood intersection with the '$\rightarrow$'-connective whose neighbourhood semantics is:

$$H(F \rightarrow G, w) \Leftrightarrow \mathcal{N}(w, \xi(x,y)(H(F,x) \Rightarrow H(G,y)))$$

Let $||N||$ and $||M||$ be two neighbourhoods for a world w. As neighbourhood sets, $||N||$ and $||M||$ are truth sets of some formulae (cf. 3.5). That means there exist P_N and Q_N as well as P_M and Q_M such that

$$\begin{array}{l} \forall x, y\ N(x,y) \Leftrightarrow (P_N(x) \Rightarrow Q_N(y)) \text{ and} \\ \forall x, y\ M(x,y) \Leftrightarrow (P_M(x) \Rightarrow Q_M(y)). \end{array}$$

The largest neighbourhood set $||K||$ which is contained in $||N|| \cap ||M||$ is now defined by

$$\forall x, y\ K(x,y) \Leftrightarrow ((P_N(x) \vee P_M(x)) \Rightarrow (Q_N(y) \wedge Q_M(y)))$$

The right hand side formula is in fact equivalent to

$$(P_N(x) \Rightarrow Q_N(y)) \wedge (P_N(x) \Rightarrow Q_M(y)) \wedge (P_M(x) \Rightarrow Q_N(y)) \wedge (P_M(x) \Rightarrow Q_M(y))$$

And this is the structure we are using for defining 'neighbourhood intersection.'

Definition 4.2 (Neighbourhood Intersection)
'Neighbourhood intersection' $N \sqcap M$ between two neighbourhood predicates N and M (def. 3.5) is defined as follows:

$$\begin{array}{l} \forall P_{1N}, \ldots, P_{nN}, P_{1M}, \ldots, P_{nM} \\ ((\forall v_1, \ldots, v_n\ N(v_1, \ldots, v_n) \Leftrightarrow \Psi(P_{1N}(v_1), \ldots, P_{nN}(v_n))) \wedge \\ (\forall v_1, \ldots, v_n\ M(v_1, \ldots, v_n) \Leftrightarrow \Psi(P_{1M}(v_1), \ldots, P_{nM}(v_n)))) \\ \Rightarrow (\forall v_1, \ldots, v_n\ (N \sqcap M)(v_1, \ldots, v_n) \Leftrightarrow \bigwedge_{i_1=N,M,\ \ldots\ ,i_n=N,M} \Psi(P_{1i_1}(v_1), \ldots, P_{ni_n}(v_n))) \end{array}$$

◁

Lemma 4.3 (Neighbourhood Intersection is a Neighbourhood Set)
If in the propositional function Ψ which is used for the semantics definition of a connective C no propositional variable occurs with undefined polarity then
(1) neighbourhood intersection $N \sqcap M$ (def. 4.2) between two neighbourhood predicates N and M is again a neighbourhood predicate, i.e. it satisfies the axiom in corollary 3.5 and
(2) $||N \sqcap M|| \subseteq (||N|| \cap ||M||)$

[3] The polarity is of an argument P_i of a propositional function $\Psi(P_1, \ldots, P_n)$ is defined as follows: Write Ψ in clause form and check whether P_i occurs only positively or negatively. For example in $\Psi(P,Q) = P \Rightarrow Q$, P has negative and Q has positive polarity. In $\Psi(P,Q) = P \Leftrightarrow Q$ neither P nor Q have a unique polarity.

Proof: of (1): First of all we show by induction on n for an arbitrary propositional function Ψ whose propositional variables occur only with positive or negative polarity:
forall $P_{1N},\ldots,P_{nN},P_{1M},\ldots,P_{nM}$ exists $Q_1,\ldots,Q_n$ such that

$$\bigwedge_{i_1=N,M,\ \ldots\ ,i_n=N,M} \Psi(P_{1i_1}(v_1),\ldots,P_{ni_n}(v_n)) \Leftrightarrow \Psi(Q_1,\ldots,Q_n)$$

Let $n=1$. For $n=1$, Ψ is either the identity or it is the negation.
If Ψ is the identity we choose $Q(v) \Leftrightarrow (P_{1N}(v) \wedge P_{1M}(v))$.
If Ψ is the negation we choose $Q(v) \Leftrightarrow (P_{1N}(v) \vee P_{1M}(v))$.
Thus we get $\Psi(P_{1N}(v)) \wedge \Psi(P_{1M}(v)) \Leftrightarrow \Psi(Q(v))$.
Let $n>1$. Assume the last argument of Ψ occurs only with positive polarity in Ψ. The proof has to exploit that every prepositional function $\Psi(P_1,\ldots,P_n)$ where P_n occurs only with positive polarity can be rewritten as
$(\Psi'(P_1,\ldots,P_{n-1}) \vee P_n) \wedge \Psi''(P_1,\ldots,P_{n-1}))$.
We have

$$\bigwedge_{i_1=N,M,\ \ldots\ ,i_n=N,M} \Psi(P_{1i_1}(v_1),\ldots,P_{ni_n}(v_n))$$

$$\Leftrightarrow \bigwedge_{i_1=N,M,\ \ldots\ ,i_{n-1}=1,M} \Psi(P_{1i_1}(v_1),\ldots,P_{n-1i_{n-1}}(v_{n-1}),P_{nN}(v_n)) \wedge$$
$$\bigwedge_{i_1=N,M,\ \ldots\ ,i_{n-1}=1,M} \Psi(P_{1i_1}(v_1),\ldots,P_{n-1i_{n-1}}(v_{n-1}),P_{nM}(v_n))$$

$$\Leftrightarrow \bigwedge_{i_1=N,M,\ \ldots\ ,i_{n-1}=1,M} [(\Psi'(P_{1i_1}(v_1),\ldots,P_{n-1i_{n-1}}(v_{n-1})) \vee P_{nN}(v_n)) \wedge$$
$$\Psi''(P_{1i_1}(v_1),\ldots,P_{n-1i_{n-1}}(v_{n-1}))] \wedge$$
$$\bigwedge_{i_1=N,M,\ \ldots\ ,i_{n-1}=1,M} [(\Psi'(P_{1i_1}(v_1),\ldots,P_{n-1i_{n-1}}(v_{n-1})) \vee P_{nM}(v_n)) \wedge$$
$$\Psi''(P_{1i_1}(v_1),\ldots,P_{n-1i_{n-1}}(v_{n-1}))]$$

$$\Leftrightarrow [\bigwedge_{i_1=N,M,\ \ldots\ ,i_{n-1}=1,M} (\Psi'(P_{1i_1}(v_1),\ldots,P_{n-1i_{n-1}}(v_{n-1}))] \vee P_{nN}(v_n)) \wedge$$
$$\bigwedge_{i_1=N,M,\ \ldots\ ,i_{n-1}=1,M} \Psi''(P_{1i_1}(v_1),\ldots,P_{n-1i_{n-1}}(v_{n-1})) \wedge$$
$$[\bigwedge_{i_1=N,M,\ \ldots\ ,i_{n-1}=1,M} (\Psi'(P_{1i_1}(v_1),\ldots,P_{n-1i_{n-1}}(v_{n-1}))] \vee P_{nM}(v_n)) \wedge$$
$$\bigwedge_{i_1=N,M,\ \ldots\ ,i_{n-1}=1,M} \Psi''(P_{1i_1}(v_1),\ldots,P_{n-1i_{n-1}}(v_{n-1}))$$

$$\Leftrightarrow [\bigwedge_{i_1=N,M,\ \ldots\ ,i_{n-1}=1,M} (\Psi'(P_{1i_1}(v_1),\ldots,P_{n-1i_{n-1}}(v_{n-1}))]$$
$$\vee (P_{nN}(v_n) \wedge P_{nM}(v_n)) \wedge$$
$$\bigwedge_{i_1=N,M,\ \ldots\ ,i_{n-1}=1,M} \Psi''(P_{1i_1}(v_1),\ldots,P_{n-1i_{n-1}}(v_{n-1}))$$

with induction hypothesis:

$$\Leftrightarrow \quad \Psi'(Q_1(v_1),\ldots,Q_{n-1}(v_{n-1})) \vee$$
$$(P_{nN}(v_n) \wedge P_{nM}(v_n)) \wedge \Psi''(Q_1(v_1),\ldots,Q_{n-1}(v_{n-1}))$$
$$\Leftrightarrow \quad \Psi(Q_1(v_1),\ldots,Q_n(v_n)) \qquad (Q_n(v_n) =_{def} (P_{nN}(v_n) \wedge P_{nM}(v_n)))$$

If the last argument of Ψ occurs only with negative polarity we choose $Q_n(v_n) = (P_{nN}(v_n) \vee P_{nM}(v_n))$.

Let

$$\forall v_1, \ldots, v_n \; N(v_1, \ldots, v_n) \Leftrightarrow \Psi(P_{1N}(v_1), \ldots, P_{nN}(v_n)) \text{ and}$$
$$\forall v_1, \ldots, v_n \; M(v_1, \ldots, v_n) \Leftrightarrow \Psi(P_{1M}(v_1), \ldots, P_{nM}(v_n))$$

The previous result gives immediately the solution to the main problem:

$$\begin{aligned} \forall v_1, \ldots, v_n \; (N \sqcap M)(v_1, \ldots, v_n) \quad \Leftrightarrow & \bigwedge_{i_1=N,M, \ \ldots \ ,i_n=N,M} \Psi(P_{1i_1}(v_1), \ldots, P_{ni_n}(v_n)) \\ & \Leftrightarrow \Psi(Q_1(v_1), \ldots, Q_n(v_n)) \end{aligned}$$

Since both $\Psi(P_{1N}(v_1), \ldots, P_{nN}(v_n))$ and $\Psi(P_{1M}(v_1), \ldots, P_{nM}(v_n))$ are among the conjuction

$$\bigwedge_{i_1=N,M, \ \ldots \ ,i_n=N,M} \Psi(P_{1i_1}(v_1), \ldots, P_{ni_n}(v_n)),$$

$(N \sqcap M)(v_1, \ldots, v_n)$ implies $N(v_1, \ldots, v_n)$ and $M(v_1, \ldots, v_n)$, and therefore we conclude

(2): $(\|N \sqcap M\|) \subseteq (\|N\| \cap \|M\|)$. ◁

The next theorem formalizes sufficient conditions under which the semantics can be strengthened from relational to neighbourhood semantics.

Theorem 4.4 (Strengthening Lemma to Relational Semantics)
If for a Hilbert system together with semantics definitions for its connectives the following two facts can be proved for a particular connective C with neighbourhood semantics definition SD_N:

- the neighbourhood structure $\mathcal{N}$ for a connective C is closed under 'neighbourhood intersection', i.e. the 'Intersection Lemma'

  $$\forall N, M (\forall w \; (\mathcal{N}(w, \|N\|) \wedge \mathcal{N}(w, \|M\|)) \Rightarrow \mathcal{N}(w, \|N \sqcap M\|))$$

  holds and

- the neighbourhood structure contains supersets, i.e. the 'Superset Lemma'

  $$\forall N, M \; \|N\| \subseteq \|M\| \wedge \mathcal{NP}(M) \Rightarrow \forall w \; \mathcal{N}(w, \|N\|) \Rightarrow \mathcal{N}(w, \|M\|)$$

  holds,

then relational semantics can be adopted for the connective C.

Proof: We construct for every model $\Im$ for $HS \cup \{SD_N\}$ a denotation for the accessibility relation $\mathcal{R}$ and show that the extended interpretation satisfies the relational semantics definition

$$\begin{aligned} SD_R = \forall F_1, \ldots, F_n \; \forall w \quad & H(C(F_1, \ldots, F_n), w) \Leftrightarrow \forall v_1, \ldots, v_n \\ & \mathcal{R}(w, v_1, \ldots, v_n) \Rightarrow \Psi(H(F_1, v_1), \ldots, H(F_n, v_n)). \end{aligned}$$

The accessibility relation is constructed from the neighbourhood structure by making the neighbourhood intersection of all neighbourhoods of the world w accessible from w:

$$\mathcal{R}(w, w_1, \ldots, w_n) \text{ iff } (w_1, \ldots, w_n) \in \bigsqcap_N \mathcal{N}(w, N)$$

The rest of the proof is the same as in the modal logic case.
That means, instead of proving for a given formula F the theorem $HS \cup \{SD_N\} \models \forall w\ H(F,w)$ one can prove $HS \cup \{SD_R\} \models \forall w\ H(F,w)$. $\triangleleft$

The transition from relational to predicate logic semantics is straightforward.

Theorem 4.5 (Strengthening Lemma to Predicate Logic Semantics)

If the accessibility relation $\mathcal{R}_C$ collapses to a point relation, i.e. the 'Collapsing Lemma'

$$\begin{array}{l}\forall w\, \mathcal{R}_C(w,\ldots,w) \wedge \\ \forall w, v_1,\ldots,v_n\, \mathcal{R}_C(w,v_1,\ldots,v_n) \Rightarrow (w = v_1 \wedge \ldots \wedge w = v_n)\end{array}$$

can be proved then the relational semantics of the connective C can be strengthened to predicate logic semantics.

Proof: If the accessibility relation collapses to a point relation, obviously the relational semantics definition

$$\begin{array}{ll}\forall F_1,\ldots,F_n\, \forall w & (H(C(F_1,\ldots,F_n),w) \Leftrightarrow \forall v_1,\ldots,v_n \\ & \mathcal{R}_C(w,v_1,\ldots,v_n) \Rightarrow \Psi_C(H(F_1,v_1),\ldots,H(F_n,v_n)))\end{array}$$

is equivalent to predicate logic semantics definition

$$\forall F_1,\ldots,F_n\, \forall w\ (H(C(F_1,\ldots,F_n),w) \Leftrightarrow \Psi_C(H(F_1,w),\ldots,H(F_n,w)))$$

$\triangleleft$

5 Quantifier Elimination

Most of the formulae that appeared so far contained quantifiers over predicate variables. They are second–order in nature. Since our main goal is to automate the process of semantics generation, and second–order logic is much more difficult to mechanize than first–order logic, a method for manipulating second–order problems into first–order problems is very helpful. In [GO92] we have developed a (still incomplete) algorithm which can compute for second–order formulae of the kind $\exists P_1,\ldots,P_k\ \Phi$ where Φ is a first–order formula, an equivalent first–order formula — if there is one. Since $\forall P_1,\ldots,P_k\ \Phi \Leftrightarrow \neg\exists P_1,\ldots,P_k\ \neg\Phi$ this algorithm can also be applied to our case. Related methods can also be found in [Ack35, Ack54, Sza92, BGW92, Sim92].

The definition of the algorithm is:

Definition 5.1 (The SCAN Algorithm)
Input to SCAN is a formula $\alpha = \exists P_1,\ldots,P_n\ \psi$ with predicate variables $P_1,\ldots,P_n$ and an arbitrary first–order formula ψ.
Output of the SCAN — if it terminates — is a formula φ_α which is *logically equivalent* to α, but not containing the predicate variables $P_1,\ldots,P_n$.
SCAN performs the following three steps:

1. ψ is transformed into clause form using second order skolemization. That means the resulting formula has the form: $\exists P_1, \ldots, P_n \exists f_1, \ldots, f_n \psi'$ where the f_i are the Skolem functions and ψ' is a set of clauses. From the algorithm's point of view, the quantifier prefix can be ignored. Therefore ψ' is treated as an ordinary clause set with the usual Skolem constants and functions.

2. All C–resolvents and C–factors with the predicate variables $P_1, \ldots, P_n$ have to be generated. C–resolution ('C' for constraint) is defined as follows:

$$\frac{\begin{array}{ll} P(s_1, \ldots, s_n) \vee C & P(\ldots) \text{ and } \neg P(\ldots) \\ \neg P(t_1, \ldots, t_n) \vee D & \text{are the } \textit{resolution literals} \end{array}}{C \vee D \vee s_1 \neq t_1 \vee \ldots \vee s_n \neq t_n}$$

   and the C-factorization rule is defined analogously:

$$\frac{P(s_1, \ldots, s_n) \vee P(t_1, \ldots, t_n) \vee C}{P(s_1, \ldots, s_n) \vee C \vee s_1 \neq t_1 \vee \ldots \vee s_n \neq t_n}.$$

   Notice that only C-resolutions between different clauses are allowed (no self resolution). A C-resolution or C-factorization can be optimized by destructively resolving literals $x \neq t$ where the variable x does not occur in t with the reflexivity equation. C–resolution and C–factorization takes into account that second order quantifiers may well impose conditions on the interpretations which must be formulated in terms of equations and inequations.

   As soon as *all* resolvents and factors between a particular literal and the rest of the clause set have been generated (the literal is 'resolved away'), the clause containing this literal must be deleted (purity deletion). If all clauses are deleted this way, this means that α is a tautology.

   All equivalence preserving simplifications may be applied freely. These are for example:

   - Tautologous resolvents can be deleted.
   - Subsumed clauses can be deleted.
   - Subsumption factoring can be performed. Subsumption factoring means that a factor subsumes its parent clause. This may be realized by just deleting some literals. For example $Q(x), Q(a)$, where x is a variable, can be simplified to $Q(a)$.
   - Subsumption resolution can also be performed. Subsumption resolution means that a resolvent subsumes its parent clause, and this again may be realized by deleting some literals [OS91] (see also example 6.2,9). For example the resolvent between P, Q and $\neg P, Q, R$ is just Q, R such that $\neg P$ can be deleted from the clause.

   If an empty clause is generated, this means that α is contradictory.

3. If the previous step terminates and there are still clauses left then reverse the skolemization. If this is not possible, the only chance is to take parallel Henkin quantifiers [Hen61] (see example 6.2,7) or leave the second–order quantification.

◁

The next example illustrates the different steps of the SCAN algorithm in more detail. The input is:
$\exists P\, \forall x, y\, \exists z\, (\neg P(a) \vee Q(x)) \wedge (P(y) \vee Q(a)) \wedge P(z)$. In the first step the clause form is to be computed:

$$\begin{array}{ll} C_1 & \neg P(a), Q(x)) \\ C_2 & P(y), Q(a) \\ C_3 & P(f(x,y)) \end{array}$$

f is a Skolem function.

In the second step of SCAN we begin by choosing $\neg P(a)$ to be resolved away. The resolvent between C_1 and C_2 is $C_4 = Q(x), Q(a)$ which is equivalent to $Q(a)$ (this is one of the equivalence preserving simplifications). The C-resolvent between C_1 and C_3 is $C_5 = (a \neq f(x,y), Q(x))$. There are no more resolvents with $\neg P(a)$. Therefore C_1 is deleted. We are left with the clauses

$$\begin{array}{ll} C_2 & P(y), Q(a) \\ C_3 & P(f(x,y)) \\ C_4 & Q(a) \\ C_5 & a \neq f(x,y), Q(x) \end{array}$$

Selecting the next two P-literals to be resolved away yields no new resolvents. Thus, C_2 and C_3 are simply to be deleted as well. All P-literals have now been eliminated. Restoring the quantifiers we then get

$$\forall x\, \exists z\, Q(a) \wedge (a \neq z \vee Q(x))$$

as the final result (y is no longer needed.)

6 Towards Mechanization of Semantics Generation

The purpose of this section is to demonstrate the application of SCAN for reducing the second-order character of our theory in most of the cases to first-order such that standard first-order theorem provers can be used.

6.1 Neighbourhood Predicates

The axiomatization of a neighbourhood predicate N for a connective C, according to the definition in 3.5, is

$$\exists P_1, \ldots, P_n\, \forall v_1, \ldots, v_n\; N(v_1, \ldots, v_n) \quad \Leftrightarrow \quad \Psi_C(P_1(v_1), \ldots, P_n(v_n))$$

If N is given as a concrete predicate, this formula can be converted into an equivalent first-order formula by eliminating the predicate variables P_i. For the elementary choices for Ψ_C, SCAN yields:

- $\Psi_C = \mathit{identity}$: $(\exists P\, \forall v\; N(v) \Leftrightarrow P(v)) = \mathit{true}$
- $\Psi_C = \mathit{negation}$: $(\exists P\, \forall v\; N(v) \Leftrightarrow \neg P(v)) = \mathit{true}$

- $\Psi_C = conjuction$: $(\exists P_1, P_2 \forall v_1, v_n\ N(v_1, v_2) \Leftrightarrow (P_1(v_1) \wedge P_2(v_2))$
Application of SCAN:

  Clause Form: $\neg N(v_1, v_2), P_1(v_1)$
  $\neg N(v_1, v_2), P_2(v_2)$
  $N(v_1, v_2), \neg P_1(v_1), \neg P_2(v_2)$

  P_1, P_2 resolved away: $\forall v_1, v_2, v_1', v_2'\ N(v_1, v_2) \vee \neg N(v_1, v_2') \vee \neg N(v_1', v_2)$

- $\Psi_C = disjunction$: $(\exists P_1, P_2 \forall v_1, v_n\ (v_1, v_2) \in N \Leftrightarrow (P_1(v_1) \vee P_2(v_2))$
$\Leftrightarrow \forall v_1, v_2, v_1', v_2'\ \neg N(v_1, v_2) \vee N(v_1, v_2') \vee N(v_1', v_2)$
(analogous to the previous case.)

- $\Psi_C = implication$: The result is the same as the previous one.

In case the neighbourhood predicate N occurs universally quantified, the resulting formulae are still second-order. Therefore the above equivalences represent only partial solutions.

6.2 Simplification of Hilbert Axioms

All semantics definitions (def. 3.2) have the form

$$\forall F_1, \ldots, F_n \forall w\ H(C(F_1, \ldots, F_n), w) \Leftrightarrow \Phi$$

The left to right part of these formula can serve as a rewrite rule for eliminating the logical connectives from literals $H(t, w)$ in the first formulation of the Hilbert axioms. If finally the first argument of the 'Holds'-predicate H is atomic, then we write instead of, say, $H(P, w)$, simply $P(w)$.

In formalizing neighbourhood semantics we used the ξ-operator for denoting truth sets. This notation is not very suitable for automated reasoning. With the following trick it can be (almost) eliminated. Suppose a ξ-operator occurs inside a formula ϕ, i.e. $\phi = \forall P_1, \ldots, P_m\ \phi'(\xi(v_1, \ldots, v_n)\theta(v_1, \ldots, v_n))$ where $P_1, \ldots, P_m$ are the predicates occurring in θ. This formula can be transformed into the equivalent formulation:
$\forall P_1, \ldots, P_m \forall N\ (\forall v_1, \ldots, v_n\ N(v_1, \ldots, v_n) \Leftrightarrow \theta(v_1, \ldots, v_n)) \Rightarrow \phi'(||N||)$

These transformations are illustrated with a number of examples. The examples are chosen to demonstrate certain techniques and phenomena. In all the examples the implication sign $\Rightarrow$ has the semantics of material implication: $\forall P, Q \forall w\ H(P \Rightarrow Q, w) \Leftrightarrow (H(P, w) \Rightarrow H(Q, w))$

Example 6.1 (Rewriting Hilbert Axioms and Rules)

1. *ME-Rule* for the modal $\Box$-operator:
$P \Leftrightarrow Q \vdash \Box P \Leftrightarrow \Box Q$.
H-Formulation with actual world predicate A:
$\forall P, Q\ (\forall w\ A(w) \Rightarrow (H(P, w) \Leftrightarrow H(Q, w))) \Rightarrow$
$(\forall w\ A(w) \Rightarrow (H(\Box P, w) \Leftrightarrow H(\Box Q, w)))$.
Neighbourhood semantics for $\Box$:
$\forall P \forall w\ H(\Box P, w) \Leftrightarrow \mathcal{N}_\Box(w, ||P||)$.
Rewritten ME-Rule:
$\forall P, Q\ (\forall w\ A(w) \Rightarrow (P(w) \Leftrightarrow Q(w))) \Rightarrow$
$(\forall w\ A(w) \Rightarrow (\mathcal{N}_\Box(w, ||P||) \Leftrightarrow \mathcal{N}_\Box(w, ||Q||)))$.

2. *Necessitation Rule*:
   $P \vdash \Box P$.
   H-Formulation without actual world predicate A:
   $\forall P\ (\forall w\ H(P,w)) \Rightarrow (\forall w\ H(\Box P,w))$.
   Rewritten Necessitation Rule with neighbourhood semantics:
   $\forall P\ (\forall w\ P(w)) \Rightarrow (\forall w\ \mathcal{N}_\Box(w, \|P\|))$

3. *K-Axiom*:
   $\Box P \Rightarrow (\Box(P \Rightarrow Q) \Rightarrow \Box Q)$.
   H-Formulation without actual world predicate A:
   $\forall P, Q\ \forall w\ H(\Box P, w) \Rightarrow H(\Box(P \Rightarrow Q), w) \Rightarrow H(\Box Q, w)$.
   Rewritten K-Axiom with neighbourhood semantics:
   $\forall P, Q\ \forall w\ \mathcal{N}_\Box(w, \|P\|) \Rightarrow \mathcal{N}_\Box(w, \xi v P(v) \Rightarrow Q(v)) \Rightarrow \mathcal{N}_\Box(w, \|Q\|)$.
   Elimination of the ξ-notation:
   $\forall P, Q\ \forall N (\forall v\ N(v) \Leftrightarrow (P(v) \Rightarrow Q(v)))$
   $\Rightarrow (\forall w\ \mathcal{N}_\Box(w, \|P\|) \Rightarrow (\mathcal{N}_\Box(w, \|N\|) \Rightarrow \mathcal{N}_\Box(w, \|Q\|)))$.

4. *T-Axiom* in modal logic:
   $\Box P \Rightarrow P$.
   H-formulation without actual world predicate A:
   $\forall P\ \forall w\ H(\Box P, w) \Rightarrow H(P, w)$.
   Relational semantics for the $\Box$-operator:
   $\forall P\ \forall w\ H(\Box P, w) \Leftrightarrow (\forall v\ \mathcal{R}_\Box(w, v) \Rightarrow H(P, v))$.
   Rewritten T-Axiom:
   $\forall P\ \forall w\ (\forall v\ \mathcal{R}_\Box(w, v) \Rightarrow P(v)) \Rightarrow P(w)$.

5. *Collapsing Axiom*:
   $P \Rightarrow \Box P$
   H-formulation without actual world predicate A:
   $\forall P\ \forall w\ H(P, w) \Rightarrow H(\Box P, w)$.
   Rewritten using relational semantics:
   $\forall P\ \forall w\ P(w) \Rightarrow (\forall v\ \mathcal{R}_\Box(w, v) \Rightarrow P(v))$.

6. *K4-Axiom* of modal logic:
   $\Box P \Rightarrow \Box\Box P$.
   H-Formulation without actual world predicate A:
   $\forall P\ \forall w\ H(\Box P, w) \Rightarrow H(\Box(\Box P), w)$.
   Rewritten K4-Axiom using relational semantics for $\Box$.
   $\forall P\ \forall w\ (\forall v\ \mathcal{R}_\Box(w, v) \Rightarrow P(v))$
   $\Rightarrow (\forall v\ \mathcal{R}_\Box(w, v) \Rightarrow (\forall v'\ \mathcal{R}_\Box(v, v') \Rightarrow P(v')))$.

7. *McKinsey Axiom* in modal logic:
   $\Box\Diamond P \Rightarrow \Diamond\Box P$. ($\Diamond P$ abbreviates $\neg\Box\neg P$)
   H-Formulation:
   $\forall P\ \forall w\ H(\Box(\Diamond P), w) \Rightarrow H(\Diamond(\Box P), w)$.
   Relational semantics for $\Diamond$:
   $\forall P\ \forall w\ H(\Diamond P, w) \Leftrightarrow (\exists v\ \mathcal{R}_\Box(w, v) \wedge H(P, v))$.
   Rewritten McKinsey Axiom using relational semantics for $\Box$ and $\Diamond$:
   $\forall P\ \forall w\ (\forall v\ \mathcal{R}_\Box(w, v) \Rightarrow H(\Diamond P, v)) \Rightarrow (\exists v\ \mathcal{R}_\Box(w, v) \wedge H(\Box P, v))$,
   and further to
   $\forall P\ \forall w\ (\forall v\ \mathcal{R}_\Box(w, v) \Rightarrow (\exists v'\ \mathcal{R}_\Box(v, v') \wedge P(v')))$
   $\Rightarrow (\exists v\ \mathcal{R}_\Box(w, v) \wedge (\forall v'\ \mathcal{R}_\Box(v, v') \Rightarrow P(v')))$.

8. *Löb Axiom:*
   $\Box(\Box P \Rightarrow P) \Rightarrow \Box P$.
   H-Formulation:
   $\forall P\ \forall w\ H(\Box(\Box P \Rightarrow P), w) \Rightarrow H(\Box P, w)$.
   Rewritten using relational semantics:
   $\forall P\ \forall w\ (\forall v\ \mathcal{R}_\Box(w,v) \Rightarrow H(\Box P \Rightarrow P, v)) \Rightarrow (\forall v'\ \mathcal{R}_\Box(w,v) \Rightarrow H(P,v))$,
   and further to:
   $\forall P\ \forall w\ (\forall v\ \mathcal{R}_\Box(w,v) \Rightarrow$
   $((\forall v'\ \mathcal{R}_\Box(v,v') \Rightarrow P(v')) \Rightarrow P(v)) \Rightarrow (\forall v\ \mathcal{R}_\Box(w,v) \Rightarrow P(v))$.

9. *Barcan Formula* in modal logic:
   $\Box\forall x\ P(x) \Rightarrow \forall x\ \Box P(x)$.
   H-Formulation:
   $\forall P\ \forall w\ H(\Box(\mathit{forall}(x, P(x))), w) \Rightarrow H(\mathit{forall}(x, \Box(P(x))), w)$.
   Semantics of $\forall$:
   $\forall F\ \forall x\ \forall w\ (H(\mathit{forall}(x,F), w) \Leftrightarrow (\forall y\ (y = x \wedge \mathit{exists}(y,w)) \Rightarrow H(F,w))$.
   Rewritten Barcan Formula with relational semantics for $\Box$:
   $\forall P\ \forall w\ (\forall v\ \mathcal{R}_\Box(w,v) \Rightarrow H(\mathit{forall}(x, P(x)), v)) \Rightarrow$
   $(\forall y\ (y = x \wedge \mathit{exists}(y,w)) \Rightarrow H(\Box(P(x)), w))$,
   and further to
   $\forall P\ \forall w\ (\forall v\ \mathcal{R}_\Box(w,v) \Rightarrow (\forall y\ (y = x \wedge \mathit{exists}(y,v)) \Rightarrow H(P(x), v)))$
   $\Rightarrow (\forall y\ (y = x \wedge \mathit{exists}(y,w)) \Rightarrow (\forall v\ \mathcal{R}_\Box(w,v) \Rightarrow H(P(x), v)))$.
   Simplified notation:
   $\forall P\ \forall w\ (\forall v\ \mathcal{R}_\Box(w,v) \Rightarrow (\forall y\ \mathit{exists}(y,v) \Rightarrow P(y,v))) \Rightarrow$
   $(\forall y\ \mathit{exists}(y,w) \Rightarrow (\forall v\ \mathcal{R}_\Box(w,v) \Rightarrow P(y,v)))$.

10. *Modus Ponens* with neighbourhood semantics:
    P and $P \rightarrow Q \vdash Q$.
    H-Formulation with actual world predicate A:
    $\forall P, Q\ ((\forall w\ A(w) \Rightarrow H(P,w)) \wedge$
    $(\forall w\ A(w) \Rightarrow H(P \rightarrow Q, w))) \Rightarrow (\forall w\ A(w) \Rightarrow H(Q,w))$.
    Neighbourhood semantics for '$\rightarrow$':
    $\forall P, Q\ \forall w\ H(P \rightarrow Q, w) \Leftrightarrow \mathcal{N}_\rightarrow(w, \xi(u,v)(H(P,u) \Rightarrow H(Q,v)))$.
    Rewritten Modus Ponens:
    $\forall P, Q\ ((\forall w\ A(w) \Rightarrow H(P,w)) \wedge$
    $(\forall w\ A(w) \Rightarrow \mathcal{N}_\rightarrow(w, \xi(u,v)(H(P,u) \Rightarrow H(Q,v)))))$
    $\Rightarrow (\forall w\ A(w) \Rightarrow H(Q,w))$.
    Elimination of the ξ-notation:
    $\forall P, Q\ \forall N\ (\forall u, v\ N(u,v) \Leftrightarrow (P(u) \Rightarrow Q(v))) \Rightarrow$
    $((\forall w\ A(w) \Rightarrow P(w)) \wedge (\forall w\ A(w) \Rightarrow \mathcal{N}_\rightarrow(w, \|N\|))) \Rightarrow (\forall w\ A(w) \Rightarrow Q(w))$.

11. *Modus Ponens* with relational semantics. H-Formulation without actual world predicate A:
    $\forall P, Q\ (\forall w\ H(P,w)) \wedge (\forall w\ H(P \rightarrow Q, w))) \Rightarrow (\forall w\ H(Q,w))$.
    Relational semantics for '$\rightarrow$':
    $\forall P, Q \forall w\ H(P \rightarrow Q, w) \Leftrightarrow (\forall u, v\ \mathcal{R}_\rightarrow(w,u,v) \Rightarrow (H(P,u) \Rightarrow H(Q,v)))$.
    Rewritten Modus Ponens:
    $\forall P, Q\ (\forall w\ P(w)) \wedge (\forall w\ (\forall u, v\ \mathcal{R}_\rightarrow(w,u,v) \Rightarrow (P(u) \Rightarrow Q(v)))))$
    $\Rightarrow (\forall w\ Q(w))$.

12. *Łukasiewicz Axiom* (ex. 2.1) with neighbourhood semantics:
    $((P \rightarrow Q) \rightarrow R) \rightarrow ((R \rightarrow P) \rightarrow (S \rightarrow P))$.

H-Formulation with actual world predicate A:
$\forall P,Q,R,S\ \forall w\ A(w) \Rightarrow H(((P \rightarrow Q) \rightarrow R) \rightarrow ((R \rightarrow P) \rightarrow (S \rightarrow P)), w)$.
Rewritten using neighbourhood semantics for '$\rightarrow$' (see ex. 10):
$\forall P,Q,R,S\ \forall w\ A(w) \Rightarrow \mathcal{N}_{\rightarrow}(w, \xi(u,v)(H(((P \rightarrow Q) \rightarrow R), u) \Rightarrow H(((R \rightarrow P) \rightarrow (S \rightarrow P)), v)))$.
Elimination of the ξ-notation:
$\forall P,Q,R,S\ \forall K\ (\forall u,v\ K(u,v) \Leftrightarrow (H(((P \rightarrow Q) \rightarrow R), u) \Rightarrow H(((R \rightarrow P) \rightarrow (S \rightarrow P)), v))) \Rightarrow \forall w\ A(w) \Rightarrow \mathcal{N}_{\rightarrow}(w, \|K\|)$.
Further rewriting with neighbourhood semantics:

$$\begin{aligned}
&\forall P,Q,R,S\ \forall K\ (\forall u,v\ K(u,v) \Leftrightarrow \\
&(\mathcal{N}_{\rightarrow}(u, \xi(u_1,v_1)(H(P \rightarrow Q, u_1) \Rightarrow H(R, v_1))) \Rightarrow \\
&\qquad \mathcal{N}_{\rightarrow}(v, \xi(u_2,v_2)(H(R \rightarrow P, u_2) \Rightarrow H(S \rightarrow P, v_2)))))) \\
&\Rightarrow \forall w\ A(w) \Rightarrow \mathcal{N}_{\rightarrow}(w, \|K\|).
\end{aligned}$$

After a further sequence of eliminations of the ξ-notation and rewritings:

$$\begin{aligned}
&\forall P,Q,R,S\ \forall K,L,M,N,I,J \\
&\qquad ((\forall u,v\ N(u,v) \Leftrightarrow (P(u) \Rightarrow Q(v))) \wedge \\
&\qquad (\forall u,v\ I(u,v) \Leftrightarrow (R(u) \Rightarrow P(v))) \wedge \\
&\qquad (\forall u,v\ J(u,v) \Leftrightarrow (S(u) \Rightarrow P(v))) \wedge \\
&\qquad (\forall u,v\ L(u,v) \Leftrightarrow (\mathcal{N}_{\rightarrow}(u, \|N\|) \Rightarrow R(v))) \wedge \\
&\qquad (\forall u,v\ M(u,v) \Leftrightarrow (\mathcal{N}_{\rightarrow}(u, \|I\|) \Rightarrow \mathcal{N}_{\rightarrow}(v, \|J\|))) \wedge \\
&\qquad (\forall u,v\ K(u,v) \Leftrightarrow (\mathcal{N}_{\rightarrow}(u, \|L\|) \Rightarrow \mathcal{N}_{\rightarrow}(v, \|M\|)))) \\
&\Rightarrow \forall w\ A(w) \Rightarrow \mathcal{N}_{\rightarrow}(w, \|K\|).
\end{aligned}$$

13. *Lukasiewicz Axiom* (ex. 12) with relational semantics:
H-Formulation without actual world predicate A:
$\forall P,Q,R,S\ \forall w\ H(((P \rightarrow Q) \rightarrow R) \rightarrow ((R \rightarrow P) \rightarrow (S \rightarrow P)), w)$.
Rewritten using relational semantics for '$\rightarrow$' (see ex. 11):
$\forall P,Q,R,S\ \forall w\ \forall u,v\ \mathcal{R}_{\rightarrow}(w,u,v) \Rightarrow (H((P \rightarrow Q) \rightarrow R), u) \Rightarrow H((R \rightarrow P) \rightarrow (S \rightarrow P), v))$.
and after a further sequence of rewritings:

$$\begin{aligned}
&\forall P,Q,R,S\ \forall w\ \forall u,v\ \mathcal{R}_{\rightarrow}(w,u,v) \Rightarrow \\
&((\forall u_1,v_1\ \mathcal{R}_{\rightarrow}(u,u_1,v_1) \Rightarrow \\
&((\forall u_3,v_3\ \mathcal{R}_{\rightarrow}(u_1,u_3,v_3) \Rightarrow (P(u_3) \Rightarrow Q(v_3))) \Rightarrow R(v_1))) \\
&\ \Rightarrow (\forall u_2,v_2\ \mathcal{R}_{\rightarrow}(w,u_2,v_2) \Rightarrow ((\forall u_4,v_4\ \mathcal{R}_{\rightarrow}(u_2,u_4,v_4) \Rightarrow (R(u_4) \Rightarrow P(v_4))) \\
&\ \Rightarrow (\forall u_5,v_5\ \mathcal{R}_{\rightarrow}(v_2,u_5,v_5) \Rightarrow (S(u_5) \Rightarrow P(v_5)))))).
\end{aligned}$$

◁

All transformations in the examples above are simple rewritings which can be easily mechanized. They do, however, not yet solve the main problem, getting a first-order version of the axioms. When equivalent first-order versions of the Hilbert axioms are available then automated reasoning is feasible.

The structure of the Hilbert axioms rewritten with relational semantics is $\forall P_1,\ldots,P_n\ \phi$ where ϕ is a normal first-order formula. This structure is perfectly suitable for the SCAN algorithm (def. 5.1). The next step in manipulating these axioms is therefore to negate them, apply SCAN, and negate the result.

The structure of the Hilbert axioms rewritten with neighbourhood semantics, however, is more complicated. They contain still literals $\mathcal{N}(\ldots, \|N\|)$

which are 'more second-order' in nature than the others because formulae occur as arguments of literals. The idea for getting rid of these structures is to replace neighbourhood predicates with predicates directly denoting their extension. That means instead of $\mathcal{N}(\ldots, \|N\|)$ we simply write $\mathcal{N}(\ldots, N)$ and instead of $N(x, y)$ we write $(x, y) \in N$. This is equivalent notation if the N is a constant symbol or existentially quantified. If N, however, is universally quantified — and this is in most examples the case — then this notation is only an approximation. In $\forall N\ N(x, y)\ \ldots$ the N can be instantiated with an arbitrary formula with two free variables whereas in $\forall N\ (x, y) \in N\ \ldots$, N can only be instantiated with terms. To fill this gap, a number of axioms are needed which ensure a term representation for the relevant formulae. In general, of course, there is no sufficient finite number of axioms. Things are somewhat simpler in our application because the neighbourhood predicates are not arbitrary predicates, but they have a certain minimal structure (corollary 3.5):

$$\forall M\ \mathcal{NP}(M) \Rightarrow \exists P_1, \ldots, P_n\ \forall v_1, \ldots, v_n\ M(v_1, \ldots, v_n) \Leftrightarrow \Psi(P_1(v_1), \ldots, P_n(v_n))$$

From this requirement a set of axioms is derivable which reconstructs a number of relevant formulae as terms in the '$(x, y) \in N$'-formulation. The idea is as follows: The formula

$$\forall P_1, \ldots, P_n\ \exists N\ \forall v_1, \ldots, v_n\ N(v_1, \ldots, v_n) \Leftrightarrow \Psi(P_1(v_1), \ldots, P_n(v_n))$$

which is a tautology in second-order predicate logic is reformulated as

$$\forall P_1, \ldots, P_n \exists N\ \forall v_1, \ldots, v_n\ (v_1, \ldots, v_n) \in N \Leftrightarrow \Psi(P_1(v_1), \ldots, P_n(v_n))$$

which is no longer a tautology because N is now a term which is used as name for a formula with the appropriate structure. Unfortunately this is also no first-order formula. First-order versions are obtained by instantiating the P_i with concrete formulae, like *true*, *false*, A (actual world predicate), $\mathcal{N}(M)$ (neighbourhood relation without the 'world argument') etc. For example for the neighbourhood semantics of the '$\rightarrow$' connective (example 6.1,10) relevant instances are:

$$\begin{array}{ll} \forall K, L & \exists N\ \forall u, v\ (u, v) \in N \Leftrightarrow (\mathcal{N}_{\rightarrow}(u, K) \Rightarrow \mathcal{N}_{\rightarrow}(v, L)) \\ \forall L & \exists N\ \forall u, v\ (u, v) \in N \Leftrightarrow \mathcal{N}_{\rightarrow}(v, L) \\ \forall L & \exists N\ \forall u, v\ (u, v) \in N \Leftrightarrow (A(u) \Rightarrow \mathcal{N}_{\rightarrow}(v, L)) \\ \forall K & \exists N\ \forall u, v\ (u, v) \in N \Leftrightarrow (\mathcal{N}_{\rightarrow}(u, K) \Rightarrow A(v)) \\ & \exists N\ \forall u, v\ (u, v) \in N \Leftrightarrow A(v) \end{array}$$

It is an open problem whether this method yields a sufficient approximation of the second-order nature of neighbourhood semantics.

Using these ideas we finish the transformation of the Hilbert axioms into their semantic counterparts for the examples in 6.1.

Example 6.2 (Translating Hilbert Axioms)

1. *ME-Rule* for the modal $\Box$-operator: $P \Leftrightarrow Q \vdash \Box P \Leftrightarrow \Box Q$.
   Rewritten (6.1,1):
   $\forall P, Q\ (\forall w\ A(w) \Rightarrow (P(w) \Leftrightarrow Q(w))) \Rightarrow$

$(\forall w\ A(w) \Rightarrow (\mathcal{N}_\Box(w, \|P\|) \Leftrightarrow \mathcal{N}_\Box(w, \|Q\|)))$.
Approximative first–order formulation:
$\forall P, Q\ (\forall w\ A(w) \Rightarrow (w \in P \Leftrightarrow w \in Q))) \Rightarrow$
$(\forall w\ A(w) \Rightarrow (\mathcal{N}_\Box(w, P) \Leftrightarrow \mathcal{N}_\Box(w, Q)))$.

2. *Necessitation Rule*: $P \vdash \Box P$.
Rewritten (6.1,2): $\forall P\ (\forall w\ P(w)) \Rightarrow (\forall w\ \mathcal{N}_\Box(w, \|P\|))$.
Approximative first–order formulation: $\forall P\ (\forall w\ w \in P) \Rightarrow (\forall w\ \mathcal{N}_\Box(w, P))$.

3. *K-Axiom*: $\Box P \Rightarrow (\Box(P \Rightarrow Q) \Rightarrow \Box Q)$.
Rewritten (6.1,3):
$\forall P, Q\ \forall N (\forall v\ N(v) \Leftrightarrow (P(v) \Rightarrow Q(v))) \Rightarrow$
$(\forall w\ \mathcal{N}_\Box(w, \|P\|) \Rightarrow (\mathcal{N}_\Box(w, \|N\|) \Rightarrow \mathcal{N}_\Box(w, \|Q\|)))$.
Approximative first–order formulation:
$\forall P, Q\ \forall N (\forall v\ v \in N \Leftrightarrow (v \in P \Rightarrow v \in Q)) \Rightarrow$
$(\forall w\ \mathcal{N}_\Box(w, P) \Rightarrow (\mathcal{N}_\Box(w, N) \Rightarrow \mathcal{N}_\Box(w, Q)))$.

4. *T-Axiom* in modal logic: $\Box P \Rightarrow P$.
Rewritten (6.1,4): $\forall P\ \forall w\ (\forall v\ \mathcal{R}_\Box(w, v) \Rightarrow P(v)) \Rightarrow P(w)$.
Negated (in order to apply SCAN): $\exists P\ \exists w\ (\forall v\ \mathcal{R}_\Box(w, v) \Rightarrow P(v)) \wedge \neg P(w)$.

Clause form:	$\neg\mathcal{R}_\Box(w, v), P(v)$ $\neg P(w)$	(w is a Skolem constant)
P resolved away:	$\neg\mathcal{R}_\Box(w, w)$	
Negated:	$\forall w\ \mathcal{R}_\Box(w, w)$	(reflexivity)

5. *Collapsing Axiom*: $P \Rightarrow \Box P$
H-formulation without actual world predicate A:
$\forall P\ \forall w\ H(P, w) \Rightarrow H(\Box P, w)$.
Rewritten (6.1,5): $\forall P\ \forall w\ P(w) \Rightarrow (\forall v\ \mathcal{R}_\Box(w, v) \Rightarrow P(v))$.
Negated (in order to apply SCAN): $\exists P\ \exists w\ P(w) \wedge (\exists v\ \mathcal{R}_\Box(w, v) \wedge \neg P(v))$.

Clause form:	$P(w)$ $\mathcal{R}_\Box(w, v)$ $\neg P(v)$	(v, w are Skolem constants)
P resolved away:	$\mathcal{R}_\Box(w, v)$ $w \neq v$	
Negated:	$\forall w, v\ \mathcal{R}_\Box(w, v) \Rightarrow w = v$	(atomicity)

6. *K4-Axiom* of modal logic: $\Box P \Rightarrow \Box\Box P$.
Rewritten (6.1,6):
$\forall P\ \forall w\ (\forall v\ \mathcal{R}_\Box(w, v) \Rightarrow P(v)) \Rightarrow (\forall v\ \mathcal{R}_\Box(w, v) \Rightarrow (\forall v'\ \mathcal{R}_\Box(v, v') \Rightarrow P(v')))$.
Negated (in order to apply SCAN):
$\exists P\ \exists w\ (\forall v\ \mathcal{R}_\Box(w, v) \Rightarrow P(v)) \wedge (\exists v\ \mathcal{R}_\Box(w, v) \wedge (\exists v'\ \mathcal{R}_\Box(v, v') \wedge \neg P(v')))$.

Clause form:	$\neg\mathcal{R}_\Box(w, x), P(x)$ $\mathcal{R}_\Box(w, v)$ $\mathcal{R}_\Box(v, v')$ $\neg P(v')$	(only x is a variable)

P resolved away: $\neg\mathcal{R}_\Box(w,v')$
$\mathcal{R}_\Box(w,v)$
$\mathcal{R}_\Box(v,v')$

Negated: $\forall w,v,v'\ \mathcal{R}_\Box(w,v)\wedge\mathcal{R}_\Box(v,v')\Rightarrow\mathcal{R}_\Box(w,v')$
(transitivity)

7. *McKinsey Axiom*: $\Box\Diamond P\Rightarrow\Diamond\Box P$
Rewritten (6.1,7):
$\forall P\ \forall w\ (\forall v\ \mathcal{R}_\Box(w,v)\Rightarrow(\exists v'\ \mathcal{R}_\Box(v,v')\wedge P(v')))\Rightarrow$
$(\exists v\ \mathcal{R}_\Box(w,v)\wedge(\forall v'\ \mathcal{R}_\Box(v,v')\Rightarrow P(v')))$
Negated (in order to apply SCAN):
$\exists P\ \exists w\ (\forall v\ \mathcal{R}_\Box(w,v)\Rightarrow\exists v'\ (\mathcal{R}_\Box(v,v')\wedge P(v')))\wedge$
$(\forall v\ \mathcal{R}_\Box(w,v')\Rightarrow\exists v'\ (\mathcal{R}_\Box(v,v')\wedge\neg P(v')))$

Clause form:
$\neg\mathcal{R}_\Box(w,x),\mathcal{R}_\Box(x,f(x))$
$\neg\mathcal{R}_\Box(w,x),P(f(x))$
$\neg\mathcal{R}_\Box(w,y),\mathcal{R}_\Box(y,g(y))$
$\neg\mathcal{R}_\Box(w,y),\neg P(g(y))$
(x replaces the first v, y replaces the second v, f is the Skolem function for the first v', g is the Skolem function for the second v')

P resolved away:
$\neg\mathcal{R}_\Box(w,x),\mathcal{R}_\Box(x,f(x))$ (Quantifier prefix: $\exists f,g\ \forall x,y$)
$\neg\mathcal{R}_\Box(w,y),\mathcal{R}_\Box(y,g(y))$
$\neg\mathcal{R}_\Box(w,x),\neg\mathcal{R}_\Box(w,y),f(x)\neq g(y)$

unskolemized with second-order Henkin quantifiers [Hen61]:

$$\exists w\begin{pmatrix}\exists f\ \forall x\\ \exists g\ \forall y\end{pmatrix}\begin{array}{l}(\mathcal{R}_\Box(w,x)\Rightarrow\mathcal{R}_\Box(x,f(x)))\wedge\\(\mathcal{R}_\Box(w,y)\Rightarrow\mathcal{R}_\Box(y,g(y)))\wedge\\(\neg\mathcal{R}_\Box(w,x)\vee\neg\mathcal{R}_\Box(w,y)\vee f(x)\neq g(y))\end{array}$$

negated:

$$\forall w\begin{pmatrix}\forall f\ \exists x\\ \forall g\ \exists y\end{pmatrix}\begin{array}{l}((\mathcal{R}_\Box(w,x)\Rightarrow\mathcal{R}_\Box(x,f(x)))\wedge\\(\mathcal{R}_\Box(w,y)\Rightarrow\mathcal{R}_\Box(y,g(y))))\Rightarrow\\(\mathcal{R}_\Box(w,x)\wedge\mathcal{R}_\Box(w,y)\wedge f(x)=g(y))\end{array}$$

The McKinsey Axiom is an example where the corresponding property of the accessibility relation is *not* first-order axiomatizable.

8. *Löb Axiom*: $\Box(\Box P\Rightarrow P)\Rightarrow\Box P$.
Rewritten (6.1,8):
$\forall P\ \forall w\ (\forall v\ \mathcal{R}_\Box(w,v)\Rightarrow((\forall v'\ \mathcal{R}_\Box(v,v')\Rightarrow P(v'))\Rightarrow P(v))\Rightarrow(\forall v\ \mathcal{R}_\Box(w,v)$
$\Rightarrow P(v))$.
Negated (in order to apply SCAN):
$\exists P\ \exists w\ (\forall v\ \mathcal{R}_\Box(w,v)\Rightarrow((\forall v'\ \mathcal{R}_\Box(v,v')\Rightarrow P(v'))$
$\Rightarrow P(v))\wedge(\exists v\ \mathcal{R}_\Box(w,v)\wedge\neg P(v))$.

Clause form:
$\neg\mathcal{R}_\Box(w,x),\mathcal{R}_\Box(x,f(x)),P(x)$
$\neg\mathcal{R}_\Box(w,x),\neg P(f(x)),P(x)$
(only x is a variable, f is the Skolem function for v')
$\mathcal{R}_\Box(w,v)$
$\neg P(v)$

P resolved away:
$\mathcal{R}_\Box(w,v)$
$(\bigvee_{k=0}^{n}\neg\mathcal{R}_\Box(w,f^k(v))),\mathcal{R}_\Box(f^n(v),f^{n+1}(v))$
for $n=0,\ldots,\infty$

Negated: $\forall f\ \forall w,v\ \mathcal{R}_{\Box}(w,v) \Rightarrow$
$\exists n \geq 0 \bigwedge_{k=1}^{n} \mathcal{R}_{\Box}(w, f^k(v)) \wedge \neg\mathcal{R}_{\Box}(f^n(v), f^{n+1}(v))$

This is the 'finite chain condition'. It is also not first-order axiomatizable. The symptom for the presence of a second-order property of the accessibility relation is the loop in the attempt to resolve P away. By observing its behaviour, it is however very easy to find the characteristic pattern.

9. *Barcan Formula*: $\Box\forall x\ P(x) \Rightarrow \forall x\ \Box P(x)$
   Rewritten (6.1,9):
   $\forall P\ \forall w\ (\forall v\ \mathcal{R}_{\Box}(w,v) \Rightarrow (\forall y\ exists(y,v) \Rightarrow P(y,v))) \Rightarrow$
   $(\forall y\ exists(y,w) \Rightarrow (\forall v\ \mathcal{R}_{\Box}(w,v) \Rightarrow P(y,v)))$
   Negated (in order to apply SCAN):
   $\exists P\ \exists w\ (\forall v\ \mathcal{R}_{\Box}(w,v) \Rightarrow (\forall y\ exists(y,v) \Rightarrow P(y,v))) \wedge$
   $(\exists y\ exists(y,w) \wedge (\exists v\ \mathcal{R}_{\Box}(w,v) \wedge \neg P(y,v)))$

   Clause form: $\neg\mathcal{R}_{\Box}(w,v'), \neg exists(y',v'), P(y',v')$
   $exists(y,w)$ (only y', v' are variables)
   $\mathcal{R}_{\Box}(w,v)$
   $\neg P(y,v)$

   P resolved away: $exists(y,w)$
   $\mathcal{R}_{\Box}(w,v)$ (resolving with $\mathcal{R}_{\Box}(w,v)$
   $\neg exists(y,v)$ preserves equivalence)

   negated: $\forall w,v\ \mathcal{R}_{\Box}(w,v) \Rightarrow (\forall y\ exists(y,w) \Rightarrow exists(y,v))$
   (Increasing Domain)

10. *Modus Ponens* with neighbourhood semantics: P and $P \rightarrow Q \vdash Q$
    Rewritten (6.1,10):
    $\forall P,Q\ \forall N\ (\forall u,v\ N(u,v) \Leftrightarrow (P(u) \Rightarrow Q(v))) \Rightarrow$
    $((\forall w\ A(w) \Rightarrow P(w)) \wedge (\forall w\ A(w) \Rightarrow \mathcal{N}_{\rightarrow}(w, \|N\|))) \Rightarrow (\forall w\ A(w) \Rightarrow Q(w))$
    Negated (in order to apply SCAN for eliminating P and Q):
    $\exists P,Q\ \exists N\ (\forall u,v\ N(u,v) \Leftrightarrow (P(u) \Rightarrow Q(v))) \wedge$
    $(\forall w\ A(w) \Rightarrow P(w)) \wedge (\forall w\ A(w) \Rightarrow \mathcal{N}_{\rightarrow}(w, \|N\|))) \wedge (\exists w\ A(w) \wedge \neg Q(w))$

    Clause form: $\neg N(u,v), \neg P(u), Q(v)$
    $N(u,v), P(u)$
    $N(u,v), \neg Q(v)$
    $\neg A(w), P(w)$
    $\neg A(w), \mathcal{N}_{\rightarrow}(w, \|N\|)$
    $A(a)$ (a is a Skolem constant,all
    $\neg Q(a)$ other variables are universal.)

    P, Q resolved away: $\neg N(u,v), N(u,v'), N(u',v)$
    $\neg N(u,v), \neg A(u), N(u',v)$
    $\neg N(u,a), \neg A(u)$
    $\neg N(u,a), N(u,v')$
    $\neg A(w), \mathcal{N}_{\rightarrow}(w, \|N\|)$

    Negated:
    $\forall N\ ((\forall u,v\ (\exists v'\ (N(u,v') \Rightarrow A(u))) \Rightarrow (N(u,v) \Rightarrow \forall u'\ N(u',v))) \wedge$
    $(\forall w\ A(w) \Rightarrow \mathcal{N}_{\rightarrow}(w, \|N\|))) \Rightarrow (\forall a\ \exists u\ N(u,a) \wedge \exists v'\ N(u,v') \Rightarrow A(u))$.

A straightforward proof shows that this generalizes to
$\forall N\ ((\forall u,v\ (\exists v'\ (N(u,v') \Rightarrow A(u))) \Rightarrow (N(u,v) \Rightarrow \forall u'\ N(u',v))) \wedge$
$(\forall w\ A(w) \Rightarrow \mathcal{N}_{\rightarrow}(w, \|N\|))) \Rightarrow (\forall u,v\ N(u,v) \wedge A(u))$

Things become slightly simpler in this case if the actual world predicate A is always true:
$\forall N\ ((\forall u,v,u',v'\ (N(u,v) \vee N(u,v') \vee N(u',v)) \wedge (\forall w\ \mathcal{N}_{\rightarrow}(w, \|N\|))) \Rightarrow$
$\forall u,v\ N(u,v)$
In both cases the second-order character of the resulting axiom can again be approximated by replacing the neighbourhood predicate with the neighbourhood set.

11. Rewritten *Modus Ponens* with relational semantics (6.1,11):
$\forall P,Q\ (\forall w\ P(w)) \wedge (\forall w\ (\forall u,v\ \mathcal{R}_{\rightarrow}(w,u,v) \Rightarrow (P(u) \Rightarrow Q(v))))) \Rightarrow (\forall w\ Q(w))$.
Negated (in order to apply SCAN for eliminating P and Q):
$\exists P,Q\ (\forall w\ P(w)) \wedge (\forall w\ (\forall u,v\ \mathcal{R}_{\rightarrow}(w,u,v) \Rightarrow (P(u) \Rightarrow Q(v))))) \wedge \exists w \neg Q(w)$.

clause form:	$P(w)$	
	$\neg\mathcal{R}_{\rightarrow}(w,u,v), \neg P(u), Q(v)$	(a is a Skolem constant
	$\neg Q(a)$	all other variables are universal)
P,Q resolved away.	$\neg\mathcal{R}_{\rightarrow}(w,u,a)$	
Negated:	$\forall a\ \exists w,u\ \mathcal{R}_{\rightarrow}(w,u,a)$	

12. *Łukasiewicz Axiom* with neighbourhood semantics:
$((P \rightarrow Q) \rightarrow R) \rightarrow ((R \rightarrow P) \rightarrow (S \rightarrow P))$
Rewritten (6.1,12):
$\forall P,Q,R,S\ \forall K,L,M,N,I,J$
$((\forall u,v\ N(u,v) \Leftrightarrow (P(u) \Rightarrow Q(v))) \wedge$
$(\forall u,v\ I(u,v) \Leftrightarrow (R(u) \Rightarrow P(v))) \wedge$
$(\forall u,v\ J(u,v) \Leftrightarrow (S(u) \Rightarrow P(v))) \wedge$
$(\forall u,v\ L(u,v) \Leftrightarrow (\mathcal{N}_{\rightarrow}(u, \|N\|) \Rightarrow R(v))) \wedge$
$(\forall u,v\ M(u,v) \Leftrightarrow (\mathcal{N}_{\rightarrow}(u, \|I\|) \Rightarrow \mathcal{N}_{\rightarrow}(v, \|J\|))) \wedge$
$(\forall u,v\ K(u,v) \Leftrightarrow (\mathcal{N}_{\rightarrow}(u, \|L\|) \Rightarrow \mathcal{N}_{\rightarrow}(v, \|M\|))))$
$\Rightarrow \forall w\ A(w) \Rightarrow \mathcal{N}_{\rightarrow}(w, \|K\|)$
This example is too complicated to be done by hand. Eliminating P, Q, R, S with an implemented SCAN procedure yields:

$$
\begin{array}{ll}
\forall K, L, M, N, I, J & \\
\forall x, y, z, u & \neg N(x,y) \vee N(x,z) \vee N(u,y) \wedge \\
\forall x, y & L(x,y) \vee \mathcal{N}_{\rightarrow}(x, \|N\|) \wedge \\
\forall x, y, z & I(x,y) \vee N(y,z) \wedge \\
\forall x, y, z & J(x,y) \vee N(y,z) \wedge \\
\forall x, y, z & L(x,y) \vee I(y,z) \wedge \\
\forall x, y & \neg L(x,y) \vee \neg \mathcal{N}_{\rightarrow}(x, \|N\|) \vee L(z,y) \wedge \\
\forall x, y, z, u & \neg I(x,y) \vee I(x,z) \vee \neg N(y,u) \vee N(v,u) \wedge \\
\forall x, y, z, u & \neg I(x,y) \vee I(x,z) \vee J(u,y) \wedge \\
\forall x, y, z, u & \neg I(x,y) \vee J(z,y) \vee \neg L(u,x) \vee \neg \mathcal{N}_{\rightarrow}(u, \|N\|) \wedge \\
\forall x, y, z, u & \neg I(x,y) \vee I(z,y) \vee \neg L(u,x) \vee \neg \mathcal{N}_{\rightarrow}(u, \|N\|) \wedge \\
\forall x, y, z, u & \neg J(x,y) \vee J(x,z) \vee \neg N(y,u) \vee N(v,u) \wedge \\
\forall x, y, z, u & \neg J(x,y) \vee J(x,z) \vee I(u,y) \wedge \\
\forall x, y, z, u, v & \neg L(x,y) \vee \neg \mathcal{N}_{\rightarrow}(x, \|N\|) \vee \neg I(y,z) \vee \neg N(z,u) \vee N(v,u) \wedge \\
\forall u, v & M(u,v) \Leftrightarrow (\mathcal{N}_{\rightarrow}(u, \|I\|) \Rightarrow \mathcal{N}_{\rightarrow}(v, \|J\|)) \wedge \\
\forall u, v & K(u,v) \Leftrightarrow (\mathcal{N}_{\rightarrow}(u, \|L\|) \Rightarrow \mathcal{N}_{\rightarrow}(v, \|M\|)) \\
\multicolumn{2}{l}{\Rightarrow \forall w\ A(w) \Rightarrow \mathcal{N}_{\rightarrow}(w, \|K\|)}
\end{array}
$$

13. Rewritten *Lukasiewicz Axiom* with relational semantics (6.1,13):

$$
\begin{array}{l}
\forall P, Q, R, S\ \forall w \\
\forall u, v\ \mathcal{R}_{\rightarrow}(w,u,v) \Rightarrow ((\forall u_1, v_1\ \mathcal{R}_{\rightarrow}(u,u_1,v_1) \Rightarrow \\
((\forall u_3, v_3\ \mathcal{R}_{\rightarrow}(u_1,u_3,v_3) \Rightarrow (P(u_3) \Rightarrow Q(v_3))) \Rightarrow R(v_1))) \\
\ \Rightarrow (\forall u_2, v_2\ \mathcal{R}_{\rightarrow}(w,u_2,v_2) \Rightarrow ((\forall u_4, v_4\ \mathcal{R}_{\rightarrow}(u_2,u_4,v_4) \Rightarrow (R(u_4) \Rightarrow P(v_4))) \\
\ \Rightarrow (\forall u_5, v_5\ \mathcal{R}_{\rightarrow}(v_2,u_5,v_5) \Rightarrow (S(u_5) \Rightarrow P(v_5)))))).
\end{array}
$$

Eliminating P, Q, R, S with SCAN yields:

$$
\begin{array}{l}
\forall a, b, c, d, e, h, k\ (\mathcal{R}_{\rightarrow}(a,b,c) \wedge \mathcal{R}_{\rightarrow}(c,d,e) \wedge \mathcal{R}_{\rightarrow}(e,h,k)) \\
\ \Rightarrow \exists u, v\ \mathcal{R}_{\rightarrow}(b,u,v) \wedge \mathcal{R}_{\rightarrow}(d,v,k) \wedge \forall x, y\ \mathcal{R}_{\rightarrow}(u,x,y) \Rightarrow k = x.
\end{array}
$$

◁

Notice that the SCAN algorithm performs an equivalence preserving transformation. Therefore only those manipulations of Hilbert axioms and rules which replace neighbourhood predicates by their truth sets are approximations and thus, potentially incomplete.

We turn now to the mechanization of the transitions from weaker to stronger semantics.

6.3 Deletion of the Actual World Predicate

According to theorem 4.1 a proof of the following lemma

$$
\begin{array}{l}
\forall N, M\ \forall v_1, \ldots, v_n\ A(v_1) \wedge \ldots \wedge A(v_n) \Rightarrow (N(v_1, \ldots, v_n) \Leftrightarrow M(v_1, \ldots, v_n)) \\
\qquad \Rightarrow \forall w\ A(w) \Rightarrow (\mathcal{N}_C(w, \|N\|) \Leftrightarrow \mathcal{N}_C(w, \|M\|))
\end{array}
$$

for all connectives with neighbourhood semantics permits the elimination of the actual world predicate A (if there are no connectives with relational semantics). If this formula is proven by refuting its negation, N and M get existentially quantified. Therefore these neighbourhood predicates can safely be replaced with their truth sets:

$$\forall N, M\ \forall v_1, \ldots, v_n\ A(v_1) \wedge \ldots \wedge A(v_n) \Rightarrow ((v_1, \ldots, v_n) \in N \Leftrightarrow (v_1, \ldots, v_n) \in M) \Rightarrow \forall w\ A(w) \Rightarrow (\mathcal{N}_C(w, N) \Leftrightarrow \mathcal{N}_C(w, M))$$

This is a normal first-order formula. For $n = 1$ the formula

$$\forall N, M\ (\forall w\ A(w) \Rightarrow (w \in N \Leftrightarrow w \in M)) \Rightarrow (\forall w\ A(w) \Rightarrow (\mathcal{N}(w, N) \Leftrightarrow \mathcal{N}(w, M)))$$

is already the formula that has been obtained by translating the ME-Rule for the $\square$-operator (example 6.2,1). Thus, eliminating the A-predicate for modal logic is straightforward. We have, however, not yet succeeded in proving that the A-predicate can also be eliminated for the Lukasiewicz example. In this case it has should be proved that the formulae 6.2,12 and 10 imply the Deletion Lemma.

6.4 From Neighbourhood to Relational Semantics

In order to prove that relational semantics for a given connective is complete, according to theorem 4.4 the following lemmas have to be proved

$$\forall N, M\ (\forall w\ (\mathcal{N}(w, \|N\|) \wedge \mathcal{N}(w, \|M\|)) \Rightarrow \mathcal{N}(w, \|N \sqcap M\|)) \text{ and}$$
$$\forall N, M\ \|N\| \subseteq \|M\| \wedge \mathcal{NP}(M) \Rightarrow \forall w\ \mathcal{N}(w, \|N\|) \Rightarrow \mathcal{N}(w, \|M\|).$$

The first one, the 'Intersection Lemma', is not yet in a form suitable for automated treatment. Using the definition of 'neighbourhood intersection' (def. 4.2), and exploiting corollary 3.5 it can be written in the following form:

$$\begin{aligned}
&\forall N, M, K\ \forall P_{1N}, \ldots, P_{nN}, P_{1M}, \ldots, P_{nM} \\
&\quad ((\forall v_1, \ldots, v_n\ N(v_1, \ldots, v_n) \Leftrightarrow \Psi(P_{1N}(v_1), \ldots, P_{nN}(v_n))) \wedge \\
&\quad (\forall v_1, \ldots, v_n\ M(v_1, \ldots, v_n) \Leftrightarrow \Psi(P_{1M}(v_1), \ldots, P_{nM}(v_n))) \wedge \\
&\quad (\forall v_1, \ldots, v_n\ K(v_1, \ldots, v_n) \Leftrightarrow \bigwedge_{i_1=N,M,\ \ldots\ ,i_n=N,M} \Psi(P_{1i_1}(v_1), \ldots, P_{ni_n}(v_n)))) \\
&\Rightarrow (\forall w\ (\mathcal{N}(w, \|N\|) \wedge \mathcal{N}(w, \|M\|)) \Rightarrow \mathcal{N}(w, \|K\|))
\end{aligned}$$

This simplifies considerably for concrete connectives.

Example 6.3 (for Intersection Lemmas)
For or the $\square$-operator and $\Psi = \mathit{identity}$ the intersection lemma is:

$$\begin{aligned}
&\forall N, M, K\ \forall P_1, P_2((\forall v\ N(v) \Leftrightarrow P_1(v)) \wedge (\forall v\ M(v) \Leftrightarrow P_2(v)) \wedge \\
&\quad (\forall v\ K(v) \Leftrightarrow (P_1(v) \wedge P_2(v)) \\
&\quad \Rightarrow (\forall w\ (\mathcal{N}_\square(w, \|N\|) \wedge \mathcal{N}_\square(w, \|M\|)) \Rightarrow \mathcal{N}_\square(w, \|K\|))
\end{aligned}$$

The two variables P_1 and P_2 are superfluous. The final first-order version is therefore as expected:

$$\begin{aligned}
&\forall N, M, K\ (\forall v\ v \in K \Leftrightarrow (v \in N \wedge v \in M) \\
&\quad \Rightarrow (\forall w\ (\mathcal{N}_\square(w, \|N\|) \wedge \mathcal{N}_\square(w, \|M\|)) \Rightarrow \mathcal{N}_\square(w, \|K\|))
\end{aligned}$$

The intersection lemma for our second major example, the '$\rightarrow$'-connective, is not quite so simple:

$$\begin{aligned}&\forall N, M, K\ \forall P_{11}, P_{21}, P_{12}, P_{22},\\ &\quad ((\forall v_1, v_2\ N(v_1, v_2) \Leftrightarrow (P_{11}(v_1) \Rightarrow P_{21}(v_2))) \wedge\\ &\quad ((\forall v_1, v_2\ M(v_1, v_2) \Leftrightarrow (P_{12}(v_1) \Rightarrow P_{22}(v_2))) \wedge\\ &\quad (\forall v_1, v_2\ K(v_1, v_2) \Leftrightarrow ((P_{11}(v_1) \vee P_{12}(v_1)) \Rightarrow ((P_{21}(v_2) \wedge P_{22}(v_2))))\\ &\Rightarrow (\forall w\ (\mathcal{N}_{\rightarrow}(w, N) \wedge \mathcal{N}_{\rightarrow}(w, M)) \Rightarrow \mathcal{N}_{\rightarrow}(w, K)) \quad \text{(see theorem 4.3)}\end{aligned}$$

In this particular case it is not possible to eliminate the P-predicates completely with the SCAN algorithm because it simply does not terminate. Fortunately this is not necessary. Since the formula has to be proven, it can be negated and then refuted. Negation makes all second-order predicates existentially quantified. Therefore the resolution process of the SCAN algorithm is automatically integrated in the overall resolution proof. ◁

The formulation of the 'superset lemma' which is suitable for automated proofs is obtained by expanding the 'neighbourhood predicate' condition $\mathcal{NP}(M)$ using the formulation of subsection 6.1.

Example 6.4 (for Superset Lemmas)
The superset lemma for the □-operator becomes simply the normal superset condition:

$$\forall N, M\ N \subseteq M \Rightarrow \forall w\ \mathcal{N}_{\Box}(w, N) \Rightarrow \mathcal{N}_{\Box}(w, M)$$

The corresponding lemma for the '$\rightarrow$'-connective is

$$\begin{aligned}&\forall N, M\ N \subseteq M \wedge (\forall u, v, u', v'\ (u, v) \notin M \vee (u, v') \in M \vee (u', v) \in M)\\ &\Rightarrow \forall w\ \mathcal{N}(w, N) \Rightarrow \mathcal{N}(w, M)\end{aligned}$$

◁

It is well known that the Necessitation Rule and the K-Axiom in modal logic entail closedness under intersection and supersets and therefore allow for the transition to relational semantics. We should be able to prove this with the machinery developed so far.
The translation of the Necessitation Rule is (6.2,2):

(1) $\forall P\ (\forall w\ w \in P \Rightarrow (\forall w\ \mathcal{N}_{\Box}(w, P))$.

The translation of the K-Axiom Rule is (6.2,3):

(2) $\forall P, Q\ \forall N(\forall v\ v \in N \Leftrightarrow (v \in P \Rightarrow v \in Q))$
$\Rightarrow (\forall w\ \mathcal{N}_{\Box}(w, P) \Rightarrow (\mathcal{N}_{\Box}(w, N) \Rightarrow \mathcal{N}_{\Box}(w, Q)))$.

An informal proof for closedness under supersets is:
Suppose $\mathcal{N}_{\Box}(w, N)$ and $N \subseteq M$. Then $\overline{N} \cup M = W$ where W means the set of all worlds and $\overline{N}$ is the complement of N. From (1), $\mathcal{N}_{\Box}(w, \overline{N} \cup M)$ follows, and from (2) $\mathcal{N}_{\Box}(w, M)$.

The proof for the closedness under intersection exploits the closedness under supersets:
Suppose $\mathcal{N}_{\Box}(w, N)$ and $\mathcal{N}_{\Box}(w, M)$. It is $M \subseteq (\overline{N} \cup (N \cap M))$ and therefore $\mathcal{N}_{\Box}(w, \overline{N} \cup (N \cap M))$ and thus, by (2) $\mathcal{N}_{\Box}(w, N \cap M)$.
Both proofs can of course by done with an automated theorem prover. We have, however, not yet succeeded in proving these lemmas for the Lukasiewicz example.

6.5 From Relational to Predicate Logic Semantics

The key condition for permitting the transition from relational to predicate logic semantics is the 'Collapsing Lemma' (4.5)

$$\begin{aligned}&\forall w\ \mathcal{R}(w,\ldots,w)\wedge\\&\forall w,v_1,\ldots,v_n\ \mathcal{R}(w,v_1,\ldots,v_n)\Rightarrow(w=v_1\wedge\ldots\wedge w=v_n)\end{aligned}$$

This formula schema is already in pure first-order form and therefore ready to be used. For modal logic it is the Hilbert axiom $\Box P\Leftrightarrow P$ which forces the accessibility relation to collapse into a point relation. And in fact, both parts of the equivalence have been translated. The left to right part is example 6.2,4: $\forall w\ \mathcal{R}_\Box(w,w)$. The right to left part is example 6.2,5: $\forall w,v\ \mathcal{R}_\Box(w,v)\Rightarrow w=v$ and both together make up the Collapsing Lemma.

The Collapsing Lemma for the '$\rightarrow$'-connective is:

$$(\forall w\ \mathcal{R}(w,w,w))\wedge\forall w,u,v\ \mathcal{R}(w,u,v)\Rightarrow(w=u\wedge w=v)$$

This should be provable from the translated Modus Ponens rule 6.2,11 and the translated Lukasiewicz axiom 6.2,13. And in fact, a proof has been found, both manually (Dov Gabbay and Mark Reynolds), as well as automatically (Bill McCune and Larry Wos with the OTTER theorem prover). A key step in the proof, however, is to prove the lemma $\forall x,y,z,u,v\ (R(x,y,z)\wedge R(u,v,x))\Rightarrow v=z)$ first.

7 Further Results

7.1 Comparison with the Sahlquist Theorem

Hilbert axioms like the McKinsey axiom or Löb's axiom specify properties of the accessibility relation which cannot be axiomatized in first-order logic. There are, however, large classes of axioms which correspond to first-order properties of the accessibility relation. For example there is a theorem by Sahlquist that states that all modal formulae of the form $\phi\Rightarrow\psi$ characterize first-order axiomatizable frames where

- ϕ is a conjunction from the forms P, $\Box P$, $\Box\Box P\ldots,\top,\bot$, using only $\wedge,\vee$ and $\Diamond$, (i.e. no negations and no $\Diamond$s in the scope of $\Box$es) while
- ψ is any negation free modal formula.

By the following arguments it can be seen that these formulae are in the domain of the SCAN algorithm.

Since neither ϕ nor ψ have negations, translation of the negated axiom schema yields clauses of the following structure: $P_i(a)$, $P_1(x_1)$, ... $P_1(x_n)$, $P_2(y_1)$, ... from ϕ and $\neg P_i(a)$, $\neg P_j(x_j)$, $\neg P_j(f(x_j))\ldots$ from $\neg\psi$. (a comes from the initial existential quantifier)

There are two important points. First of all, the clauses originating from ϕ have only positive occurrences of the non-$\mathcal{R}$ predicates while the clauses originating from ψ have only negative occurrences. Since in ϕ no $\Diamond$s are in the scope of $\Box$es, and all $\Box$es are immediately in front of the predicates, the P_i have at most the constant a or variables as arguments. Moreover, the variables of all positive predicates are different. Because of these facts, there is no possibility to build up nested terms by resolution or factorization. Even in the resolvents, all positive predicates have variables different from the negative ones. Thus, no nontrivial recursion is possible and no inequations between different Skolem functions are produced.

That means the resolution eventually produces only tautologies or subsumed clauses. After it stops, no new terms appeared, there are no inequations between Skolem functions, and therefore first–order reversing the Skolemization is always possible. Therefore SCAN always succeeds with a first–order result.

7.2 From Semantic Properties to Hilbert Axioms

We have seen how to generate semantics for Hilbert systems using a quantifier elimination procedure. Sometimes, the other way round, translation of semantic conditions into Hilbert axioms, is also needed. As the next example shows, it turns out that in the formulation with the H–predicate, this direction can be reduced to a theorem proving task. The idea is to prove constructively the existence of a formula which holds in all worlds.

Example 7.1 (for constructing Hilbert Axioms from Semantics)
We want to construct in standard modal logic $\Box P \rightarrow \Box\Box P$ from the transitivity of the accessibility relation.
From the axioms
(all f all w (H(b(f),w) ⇔ (all v (R(w,v) ⇒ H(f,v))))). (Semantics of □)
(all f all g all w (H(i(f,g),w) ⇔ (H(f,w) ⇒ H(g,w)))). (Semantics of material implication)
(all x all y all z ((R(x,y) & R(y,z)) ⇒ R(x,z))). (Transitivity)
and the negated theorem
-(exists f all w (H(f,w) & -$ans(f))). ($ans collects the bindings of f)
where 'b' denotes the □–operator and 'i' denotes the arrow connective, the 23rd proof, the theorem prover OTTER [McC90] found, actually constructed the desired formula.

```
11 [ur,10,8]      $ans(i(x,y)) | -H(y,g(i(x,y))).
13 [ur,10,7]      $ans(i(x,y)) | H(x,g(i(x,y))).
17 [ur,11,5]      $ans(i(x,b(y))) | -H(y,f(y,g(i(x,b(y))))).
18 [ur,11,4]      $ans(i(x,b(y))) | R(g(i(x,b(y))),f(y,g(i(x,b(y))))).
24 [ur,17,5]      $ans(i(x,b(b(y)))) | -H(y,f(y,f(b(y),g(i(x,b(b(y))))))).
25 [ur,17,4]      $ans(i(x,b(b(y)))) |
                  R(f(b(y),g(i(x,b(b(y))))),f(y,f(b(y),g(i(x,b(b(y))))))).
63 [ur,24,3,13]   $ans(i(x,b(b(y)))) | $ans(i(b(y),z)) |
                  -R(g(i(b(y),z)),f(y,f(b(y),g(i(x,b(b(y)))))))
115 [ur,63,9,18]  $ans(i(x,b(b(y)))) | $ans(i(b(y),b(z))) |
                  -R(f(z,g(i(b(y),b(z)))),f(y,f(b(y),g(i(x,b(b(y))))))).
116 [115,25]      -$ans(i(b(x),b(b(x)))).
                  This term represents the desired formula □P ⇒ □□P
```

Unfortunately there is not only one formula which holds in all worlds. This is the reason why the theorem prover generates a lot of proofs. Therefore each result has to be checked by translating it back into its semantic counterpart (using quantifier elimination) and proving the equivalence with the original formula. This cycle can also be fully automated. $\triangleleft$

8 Limitations of our Methodology

Our methodology is based on a quantifier elimination algorithm. For this purpose we developed the SCAN algorithm. It does surprisingly well even in those pathological cases as Löb's axiom (ex. 6.2,8) or McKinsey's axiom (ex. 6.2,7) where the correspondence axiom is second-order. There are, however, a number of built in limitations which require further investigation.

Combination of Axioms

A Hilbert calculus consists in general of several axioms and rules. They all have to be processed by the SCAN algorithm. If all correspondence axioms are first-order definable, they can be processed one by one and the overall result is just the conjunction of the individual result. This is no longer so simple when some of the axioms are actually second-order.

As it was noticed, the characteristic property for the McKinsey axiom is only second-order definable. Combined with the transitivity axiom $\Box P \Rightarrow \Box\Box P$ (ex. 6.2,6), however, these two define atomicity $\forall x\ \exists y\ (\mathcal{R}(x,y) \land \forall z\ \mathcal{R}(y,z) \Rightarrow z = y))$ [vB84, page203] which is obviously a first-order definable property.

Applied to the McKinsey axiom, SCAN actually computes this property if the critical clause which prevents the first-order unskolemization is replaced with its factor. Although we have some ideas, why transitivity might in this particular case enable this operation, we are far from having a general theory for processing combinations of axioms with these strange properties. Actually the proof that the McKinsey axiom together with the transitivity axiom correspond to atomicity requires the axiom of choice. Therefore no simple solution of this problem is to be expected.

Conditions on the Assignment

The model theoretic semantics of several logics is not only defined via properties of the possible worlds structure alone. Relevance logic, for example, which has a semantics for the '$\rightarrow$'-connectives in terms of a ternary accessibility relation (cf. def. 3.2) has a condition on the assignment of the propositional variables. The condition is:

$$\forall P\ \forall u,v\ \mathcal{R}(0,u,v) \land H(P,u) \Rightarrow H(P,v)$$

where 0 is a distinguished world. That means there is a built in restriction for the truth value of P.

A similar condition holds for intuitionistic logic. The semantics of the '$\rightarrow$'-connective in intuitionistic logic is defined by means of a binary accessibility relation $\leq$ which is actually a partial ordering.

$$\forall P,Q\ \forall w\ H(P \rightarrow Q, w) \Leftrightarrow \forall v\ w \leq v \Rightarrow (H(P,v) \Rightarrow H(Q,v))$$

The restriction on the assignment is:

$$\forall P\ \forall w\ H(P,w) \Rightarrow \forall v\ w \leq v \Rightarrow H(P,w)$$

i.e. if a proposition P is true at a world, it remains true at all "higher" worlds.

Applied to the axiom $P \rightarrow P$, for example with relevance logic semantics for $\rightarrow$, the SCAN algorithm computes $\forall v, w\ \mathcal{R}(0,v,w) \Rightarrow v = w$. That means the second and third argument of the accessibility relation collapse if the very natural axiom $P \rightarrow P$ is required and the standard process is applied. This makes the ternary relation $\mathcal{R}$ almost useless. The alternative, which has been chosen both for relevance logic and for intuitionistic logic, is to encode the $P \rightarrow P$ axiom into the restriction on the assignment. This keeps the third argument of the accessibility relation free to encode other phenomena. This condition can be obtained by the SCAN algorithm, if we do not insist on resolving away all P–literals.

That means, in order to deal with restrictions on the assignment, the control on the resolution process in SCAN has to be modified. Since this is a choice of the developer of the logic, it is, however, highly questionable whether this should be automated in some way. Once a restriction on the assignment has been accepted, this is a second–order formula which constraints the processing of the other Hilbert clauses within the SCAN algorithm. We have not yet investigated what the implications are.

Second–Order Semantics

An alternative to neighbourhood semantics, we gave for the '$\rightarrow$'–connective and which has also no built in properties is used in conditional logic:

$$\forall P, Q\ \forall w\ H(P \rightarrow Q, w) \Leftrightarrow f(w,P) \subseteq ||Q||.$$

f is the *accessibility function*, which has a formula as second argument. This is clearly a second–order formula already in the definition of the semantics for '$\rightarrow$'. Since SCAN is based on first–order predicate logic, it cannot work for this kind of semantics.

9 Conclusion

We have presented a general theory for the transition from a logic presented as a Hilbert calculus to its model theoretic semantics with emphasis to automate this process to a large extent by using standard first–order predicate logic reasoning. Although the technical details in the current state of the theory are limited to basic versions of neighbourhood and relational semantics, we think the underlying ideas are general enough to be extended for other kinds of semantics.

It turned out that most of the problems of the transition to model theoretic semantics can be reduced to quantifier elimination problems for second–order quantifiers over predicate variables. Therefore the kernel of our method is a quantifier elimination procedure. Although this procedure is still limited, surprisingly many problems which needed at good deal of experience and intuition of logicians can now be solved completely automatically.

References

[Ack35] Wilhelm Ackermann. Untersuchung über das Eliminationsproblem der mathematischen Logik. *Mathematische Annalen*, 110:390–413, 1935.

[Ack54] W. Ackermann. *Solvable Cases of the Decision Problem*. North–Holland Pu. Co., 1954.

[BGW92] Leo Bachmair, Harald Ganzinger, and Uwe Waldmann. Theorem proving for hierarchic first-order theories, 1992. To appear in Proc. ALP'92, Lecture Notes in Comp. Science.

[Che80] B. F. Chellas. *Modal Logic: An Introduction*. Cambridge University Press, Cambridge, 1980.

[GO92] Dov M. Gabbay and Hans Jürgen Ohlbach. Quantifier elimination for second order predicate logic. In *Proc. of KR92*. Morgan Kaufmann, 1992.

[HC68] G.E. Hughes and M.J. Cresswell. *An Introduction to Modal Logic*. Routledge, London, New York, 1968.

[Hen61] L. Henkin. Some remarks on infinitely long formulas. In *Infinistic Methods*, pages 167–183. Pergamon Press, Oxford, 1961.

[McC90] William McCune. OTTER 2.0. In Mark Stickel, editor, *Proc. of* 10th *Internation Conference on Automated Deduction, LNAI 449*, pages 663–664. Springer Verlag, 1990.

[MW92] William McCune and Larry Wos. Experiments in automated deduction with condensed detachment. In Deepak Kapur, editor, *Proc. of CADE 92*, 1992.

[Ohl91] Hans Jürgen Ohlbach. Semantics based translation methods for modal logics. *Journal of Logic and Computation*, 1(5):691–746, 1991.

[OS91] Hans Jürgen Ohlbach and Jörg H. Siekmann. The Markgraf Karl refutation procedure. In Jean Luis Lassez and Gordon Plotkin, editors, *Computational Logic, Essays in Honor of Alan Robinson*, pages 41–112. MIT Press, 1991.

[RM76] Richard Routley and Robert Meyer. Every Sentential Logic has a two valued semantics. Logique et Analyse n.s. vol. 19, pages345-365.

[Sim92] Harold Simmons. An algorithm for eliminating predicate variables from π_1^1 sentences, 1992.

[Sza92] Andrzej Szałas. On correspondence between modal and classical logic: Automated approach. Technical Report MPI–I–92–209, Max Planck Institut für Informatik, Saarbrücken, march 1992.

[vB84] Johan van Benthem. *D. Gabbay, F. Guenthner: Handbook of Philosophical Logic*, volume II, Extensions of Classical Logic of *Synthese Library Vo. 165*, chapter Correspondence Theory, page203. D. Reidel Publishing Company, Dordrecht, 1984.

Logic Programming via Proof-valued Computations*

David J. Pym
University of Edinburgh,Scotland, U.K.

Lincoln A. Wallen
University of Oxford,England, U.K.

Abstract

We argue that the computation of a logic program can be usefully divided into two distinct phases: the first being a proof-valued computation or proof-search; the second a residual computation, or answer extraction. Extension of extraction techniques to various theories then permits more extensive languages and proof procedures to be employed for the computational solution of problems.

We illustrate these ideas with a simple propositional logic and show that SLD-resolution computes presentations of proofs in which the residual computation may be interleaved with the proof-search, whereas a more general proof procedure yields shorter presentations of (the same) proofs, but which require more extensive residual computations.

1 Introduction

One often takes the result of a computation of a logic program $(\Gamma; \exists x\psi)$ to be a substitution of a term t for the (existentially quantified) variable of the query such that

$$\Gamma \quad \text{entails} \quad \psi[t/x];$$

indeed logic programs are usually modelled as sets of such substitutions [8]. This is a natural view to take since the substitutions typically carry information required by the user of the program.

However, since logical consequence is an abstract notion, our access to it is via concrete notions of deduction; *i.e.*, we construct a (finitary) proof that $\exists x\psi$ follows from Γ, and extract a term t from this proof. There are thus two distinct phases of computation:

- *proof-search:* the computation of a proof; and
- *residual computation:* the extraction of witnesses from that proof.

It is obvious that the residual computation is dependent on the result of the proof-search.

*This work was supported in part by ESPRIT BRA, "Logical Frameworks"; and U.K. SERC grant GR/G 58588, "Logical and Semantical Frameworks".

The output from the first computation (*i.e.*, the proof) is, we believe, more naturally seen as the result of the computation; so from this point of view *any* sound proof procedure for a logical language gives rise to a notion of computation, the values computed being proofs.[1] The belief that this view is inadequate as a basis for (the theory of) logic programming stems, it seems, from the belief that it is easier to program with predicates and objects satisfying them, than with formulae and proofs proving them. If one considers logical systems as represented in the LF [4], the calculation of objects satisfying predicates and of proofs proving formulae is achieved by the same mechanism.[2]

If we require that the residual computation be an operation of low complexity, severe restrictions on both the language for expressing our programs and on the proof procedures used as interpreters for them must be accepted. Horn clauses and SLD-resolution are perhaps the best known matching pair (though see the work of Miller *et al.* [11, 12]). However, extraction techniques have been developed for various theories (see for example [1, 18]) and it is the extent of this knowledge that sets a limit on the languages and proof procedures that can be used in the first phase of computation.

In this paper we begin an investigation of logic programming (or, more abstractly, proof-search) as proof-valued computation. We show that even in a simple propositional language well-known methods of proof-search compute interesting values. More specifically, that a cut-free sequent calculus is naturally interpreted as computing *constructions* of natural deduction proofs. These constructions are non-normal in the sense that they present normal natural deductions in a non-normal, and often more compact, manner. Such constructions require further *residual* computation to bring them to normal form. Although we do not treat quantifiers here, it becomes clear that witnesses for existential quantifiers would, in general, fail to be explicit in such constructions. The residual computation is effectively the second phase of answer extraction referred to above.

We show that an analytic (or cut-free) sequential formulation of SLD-resolution computes constructions requiring limited residual computation; so limited, in fact, that the residual computation may be safely interleaved with the proof-search. In a quantified setting this would yield, as expected, explicit witnesses on termination.

In further work, we hope to apply the techniques of this paper to logics determined by general, schematic classes of natural deduction rules [10, 15, 16].

Apart from its theoretical interest this approach to "computation via deduction" has a number of practical applications. One is to speed up computations that rely on Boolean (*i.e.*, ground) subcomputations. There is no need to construct normal proofs of such goals since answer extraction is not required. A second application is to support the integration of answer extraction and program extraction techniques. Extending a language with functional forms (say recursion or combinators for conditionals) permits the expression of answers to more complex queries and databases (*cf.* Gödel's Dialectica interpretation for Peano Arithmetic [3]). Such representations of answers may be manipulated,

[1] An important, yet informal, constraint on such proof procedures is that their behaviour be predictable enough for programmers to appreciate the relationship between the form of their axiomatisations and the behaviour of the proof procedure in its attempt find a solution.

[2] An elementary notion of logic programming for the type theory of the LF is discussed in [16, 17]; a more elaborate notion is developed in [13].

stored or even passed as input to other computations. In effect we are gaining a form of *modularity* in the expression (and computation) of answers. These ideas will be explored elsewhere.

2 Logical Background

It is well-known that, for certain subsystems of predicate logic, proofs of a sequent $\Gamma;\varphi$ within a (single-conclusioned) sequent calculus ($\boldsymbol{L}$) can be interpreted as constructing natural deductions ($\boldsymbol{N}$) of the succedent formula φ from the antecedent formulae Γ [19]. Let us denote this interpretation of sequent derivations by $[\![.]\!]^E$. Let $\boldsymbol{L}(l)$ denote the set of sequent derivations ($\vdash$) of l, and $\boldsymbol{N}(\Gamma;\varphi)$ the set of natural deductions ($\models$) of φ from Γ; *i.e.*,

$$\begin{aligned} \boldsymbol{L}(\Gamma;\varphi) &:= \{d \mid \vdash^d \Gamma;\varphi\} \\ \boldsymbol{N}(\Gamma;\varphi) &:= \{M \mid \Gamma \models^M \varphi\}. \end{aligned}$$

Then, for all sequents l,

$$d \in \boldsymbol{L}(l) \;\Rightarrow\; [\![d]\!]^E \in \boldsymbol{N}(l). \tag{1}$$

The interpretation induces an equivalence relation $\sim$ on $\boldsymbol{L}(l)$ by

$$d \sim d' \quad \text{iff} \quad [\![d]\!]^E = [\![d']\!]^E. \tag{2}$$

If we view sequent derivations as natural deduction-valued functions it is natural to call this an *extensional* equivalence relation.

The fact that distinct sequent derivations are extensionally equivalent in this sense has been used as a criticism of the sequent calculus and of predicate logic itself [2].

After defining this interpretation for a pure implicational language below, in § 5 we introduce an alternative interpretation, $[\![.]\!]^S$, which emphasises some intensional properties of derivations as *construction operations*. As an application of this (constructive) interpretation we show that a standard cut-free sequent calculus for the logic constructs *normal* natural deductions in a *non-normal* (and hence shorter) way. The presentation below follows [4].

A natural deduction system $\boldsymbol{N}$, for a *pure implicational propositional logic* is defined as follows. Let $n > 0$ be a fixed natural number. The set $\mathcal{F}$ of *formulae* is the smallest set containing the *propositional variables* $p_0, \ldots, p_n$ and such that $\varphi \supset \psi \in \mathcal{F}$ whenever $\varphi, \psi \in \mathcal{F}$. We shall use φ, ψ and χ (possibly subscripted) to denote formulae.

Given a countably infinite set of *assumption markers*, $\{\xi_i\}_{i<\omega}$, the set of *proof expressions* $\mathcal{N}$ is the smallest set containing $\text{HYP}_\varphi(\xi)$, $\text{IMP-I}_{\varphi,\psi}(\xi : M)$ and $\text{IMP-E}_{\varphi,\psi}(M, N)$ whenever $\varphi, \psi \in \mathcal{F}$, ξ is a marker and $M, N \in \mathcal{N}$. All occurrences of $\text{HYP}_\varphi(\xi)$ in the expression M in $\text{IMP-I}_{\varphi,\psi}(\xi : M)$ are considered bound; such bound occurrences of marked hypotheses correspond to discharged assumptions. Capture-avoiding substitution of expressions for free occurrences of subexpressions of the form $\text{HYP}_\varphi(\xi)$ is defined as usual. The *end formula* of a proof expression of the first kind is φ; of the second kind is $\varphi \supset \psi$; and of the third kind is ψ. If we want to emphasise the end formula φ of a proof expression M we shall write it as a superscript thus M^φ.

A *(proof) context* is a finite sequence of *declarations* of the form $\xi:\varphi$. Equality on contexts is taken up to permutation. We shall use Δ, possibly primed, to denote contexts. The *domain* of a context $\Delta = (\xi_i:\varphi_i)_{i<n}$, written dom$\Delta$, is the set of markers $\{\xi_i \mid i < n\}$. A context is said to be *well-formed* if its markers are pairwise distinct.

The set of well-formed context-expression pairs (Δ, M) is the smallest set satisfying:

N1. $(\Delta, \text{HYP}_\varphi(\xi))$ is well-formed whenever Δ is well-formed and $\xi:\varphi \in \Delta$;

N2. $(\Delta, \text{IMP-I}_{\varphi,\psi}(\xi:M)^{\varphi\supset\psi})$ is well-formed whenever $(\Delta, \xi:\varphi\,,\ M^\psi)$ is well-formed;

N3. $(\Delta, \text{IMP-E}_{\varphi,\psi}(M,N)^\psi)$ is well-formed whenever $(\Delta, M^{\varphi\supset\psi})$ and (Δ, N^φ) are well-formed.

We write $\Delta \models^M \varphi$ if (Δ, M^φ) is well-formed. It is clear that in such a case M is a derivation of its end formula from the formulae of Δ in the usual sense; derivations being natural deductions.

Note that our presentation of propositions and their natural deduction proofs differs from that of the Curry-Howard correspondence. We remark only that the generality of our analysis requires the distinction made by our definitions between markers in contexts and the variables of lambda terms.

3 Sequents, calculi and logic programming

A *sequent* is a (well-formed) context-formula pair, written $\Gamma;\varphi$. In terms of our sequential understanding of logic programming, the context or antecedent of the sequent, Γ, corresponds to the *program* and the succedent, φ, to the *goal*. Typically, Γ is a set of *clauses* and φ is of the form $\exists x\psi$. Such a sequent is traditionally interpreted as a request to calculate a term or *answer substitution*, t, such that the sequent $\Gamma;\psi[t/x]$ is provable. In order to determine that such a situation obtains, it is necessary to calculate both a term t and a proof of the sequent $\Gamma;\psi[t/x]$.

With the aforesaid understanding in mind, and using l, k, possibly subscripted, to denote sequents, we define

$$\boldsymbol{N}(\Gamma;\varphi) \ := \ \{M \in \mathcal{N} \mid \Gamma \models^M \varphi\}$$

and

$$\boldsymbol{N}_0(l) \ := \ \{M \in \boldsymbol{N}(l) \mid M \text{ normal}\},$$

where "normal" here is taken in the sense of Prawitz [14].

A (cut-free) sequent calculus ($\boldsymbol{L}$) for a pure implicational logic is defined as follows: for each sequent l consider a family of pairwise distinct variables $(\alpha^l_m)_{m<\omega}$. These variables are used to represent the unproved or *open* leaves of a derivation. The set of derivations of sequent l, denoted $\boldsymbol{D}(l)$, is the smallest set that contains the variables and is closed under the following rules:

L1. $\text{AXIOM}_{\Gamma,\varphi}(\xi) \in \boldsymbol{D}(\Gamma;\varphi) \quad \text{if} \quad \xi:\varphi \in \Gamma$;

$$\frac{}{\Gamma ; \varphi} \quad (\xi : \varphi \in \Gamma) \quad \text{L1}$$

$$\frac{\Gamma, \xi : \varphi ; \psi}{\Gamma ; \varphi \supset \psi} \quad (\xi \notin \mathrm{dom}\Gamma) \quad \text{L2}$$

$$\frac{\Gamma, \eta : \psi ; \chi \quad \Gamma ; \varphi}{\Gamma ; \chi} \quad (\xi : \varphi \supset \psi \in \Gamma) \quad \text{L3}$$

Figure 1: L1 – L3 displayed.

L2. $\text{IMP-R}_{\Gamma,\varphi,\psi}(\xi, d) \in \boldsymbol{D}(\Gamma; \varphi \supset \psi)$ if $d \in \boldsymbol{D}(\Gamma, \xi : \varphi; \psi)$ and $\xi \notin \mathrm{dom}\Gamma$;

L3. $\text{IMP-L}_{\Gamma,\varphi,\psi,\chi}(\eta, \xi, d, d') \in \boldsymbol{D}(\Gamma; \chi)$ if $d \in \boldsymbol{D}(\Gamma; \varphi)$, $d' \in \boldsymbol{D}(\Gamma, \eta : \psi; \chi)$, $\eta \notin \mathrm{dom}\Gamma$ and $\xi : \varphi \supset \psi \in \Gamma$.

If $d \in \boldsymbol{D}(l)$ we often write d^l.

In terms of our sequential understanding of logic programming, clauses L1 – L3, displayed as rules in Figure 1, should be considered to determine *reduction operators* — rules that are read from conclusion to premisses.[3] With this reading, SLD-resolution can be considered to amount to taking a specialised form of L3, namely $\text{L}_\iota 3$, *q.v.* § 6.

4 Completions and extensional equivalence

The traditional interpretation of the sequent calculus is that it builds normal natural deductions. In an (intuitionistic) first-order setting, such deductions contain explicit witnesses for existential quantifiers.

Let $V(d)$ denote the set of variables of a derivation d. A mapping that assigns a natural deduction $M \in \boldsymbol{N}(l)$ to each variable α^l, is called a *completion*[4].

Let ρ be a completion. The *extensional* interpretation relative to ρ, denoted $[\![\cdot]\!]^E_\rho$, is defined by recursion on the structure of sequent derivations as follows:

E0. $[\![\alpha]\!]^E_\rho = \rho(\alpha)$;

E1. $[\![\text{AXIOM}_{\Gamma,\varphi}(\xi)]\!]^E_\rho = \text{HYP}_\varphi(\xi)$;

E2. $[\![\text{IMP-R}_{\Gamma,\varphi,\psi}(\xi, d)]\!]^E_\rho = \text{IMP-I}_{\varphi,\psi}(\xi : [\![d]\!]^E_\rho)$;

E3. $[\![\text{IMP-L}_{\Gamma,\varphi,\psi,\chi}(\eta, \xi, d, d')]\!]^E_\rho =$
$$([\![d']\!]^E_\rho)[\text{IMP-E}_{\varphi,\psi}(\text{HYP}_{\varphi\supset\psi}(\xi), [\![d]\!]^E_\rho)/\text{HYP}_\psi(\eta)].$$

4.1 PROPOSITION *For any completion ρ, if $d \in \boldsymbol{D}(l)$ then $[\![d]\!]^E_\rho \in \boldsymbol{N}(l)$.*

[3] Kleene [6] explains this in the setting of the classical predicate calculus.

[4] This notion of completion is distinct from that of Clark [8].

$$\dfrac{\dfrac{}{\Gamma,\xi:\psi\supset\chi,\eta:\chi;\chi} \quad \dfrac{\dfrac{}{\Gamma,\xi:\psi\supset\chi,\zeta:\psi;\psi} \quad \Gamma,\xi:\psi\supset\chi;\varphi}{\Gamma,\xi:\psi\supset\chi;\psi}}{\dfrac{\Gamma,\xi:\psi\supset\chi;\chi \qquad\qquad \dfrac{\dfrac{}{\Gamma,\zeta:\psi;\psi} \quad \Gamma;\varphi}{\Gamma;\psi}}{\Gamma;\chi}}$$

$$\dfrac{\dfrac{\dfrac{\dfrac{}{\Gamma,\xi:\psi\supset\chi,\zeta:\psi,\eta:\chi;\chi} \quad \dfrac{}{\Gamma,\xi:\psi\supset\chi,\zeta:\psi;\psi}}{\Gamma,\xi:\psi\supset\chi,\zeta:\psi;\chi} \quad \dfrac{}{\Gamma,\zeta:\psi;\psi}}{\Gamma,\zeta:\psi;\chi} \quad \Gamma;\varphi}{\Gamma;\chi}$$

$$\Gamma = \{\xi_1:\varphi\supset\psi, \xi_2:\psi\supset(\psi\supset\chi)\}$$

Figure 2: Two extensionally equivalent derivations.

Define the relation of *extensional equivalence*, $\sim$, by

$$d \sim d' \quad \text{iff} \quad (\forall\rho)\, [\![d]\!]^E_\rho = [\![d']\!]^E_\rho .$$

Two extensionally equivalent derivations are shown in Figure 2; they are permutation variants of each other [5].

5 Constructions

The interpretation $[\![.]\!]^E_\rho$ above is suitable for interpreting the *results* of computations (searches) via the sequent calculus, *i.e.*, for interpreting sequent *proofs*. However, since the two derivations of Figure 2 require differing amounts of work to complete — assuming such completions exist — they represent clearly distinct *partial* computations. In this section we introduce an interpretation of derivations that captures this difference and is therefore suitable for interpreting states of computations (*i.e.*, partial derivations). The idea is very simple: we internalise the operation of substitution $[M^\varphi/\text{HYP}_\varphi(\xi)]$ rather than treating it as a metatheoretic operation.

The set of *constructions* $\mathcal{C}$ is defined to be the smallest set containing $\text{HYP}_\varphi(\xi)$, $\text{IMP-I}_{\varphi,\psi}(\xi:t)$, $\text{IMP-E}_{\varphi,\psi}(t,s)$ and $\text{SUB}(t, s/\text{HYP}_\varphi(\xi))$ whenever $\varphi,\psi \in \mathcal{F}$, ξ is a marker and $t, s \in \mathcal{C}$. End formulae of constructions are defined as for proof expressions with the addition that the end formula of a construction of the form $\text{SUB}(t, s/\text{HYP}_\varphi(\xi))$ is the end formula of t. The intended meaning of this construct is that construction s is substituted for (all) free occurrences of $\text{HYP}_\varphi(\xi)$ in t. It is clear that $\mathcal{N} \subset \mathcal{C}$.

The set of well-formed context-construction pairs (Δ, t) is the smallest set satisfying:

C1. $(\Delta, \text{HYP}_\varphi(\xi))$ is well-formed whenever Δ is well-formed and $\xi:\varphi \in \Delta$;

C2. $(\Delta, \text{IMP-I}_{\varphi,\psi}(\xi : t)^{\varphi \supset \psi})$ is well-formed whenever $(\Delta, \xi : \varphi, t^{\psi})$ is well-formed;

C3. $(\Delta, \text{IMP-E}_{\varphi,\psi}(t, s)^{\psi})$ is well-formed whenever $(\Delta, t^{\varphi \supset \psi})$ and (Δ, s^{φ}) are well-formed;

C4. $(\Delta, \text{SUB}(t, s^{\varphi}/\text{HYP}_{\varphi}(\xi)))$ is well-formed whenever (Δ, t) and (Δ, s) are well-formed.

We write $\Delta \models^{t} \varphi$ if (Δ, t^{φ}) is well-formed.

Define

$$\boldsymbol{C}(\Gamma; \varphi) \quad := \quad \{t \in \mathcal{C} \mid \Gamma \models^{t} \varphi\}.$$

Let $\rightarrow$ denote the reduction relation for substitution over constructions in the usual manner. Call a construction *explicit* if it contains no substitution redices. $\rightarrow$ is Church-Rosser and strongly normalising for well-formed constructions. Consequently the explicit form of a construction is unique. Substitution preserves well-formedness, and explicit constructions are normal deductions.

5.1 PROPOSITION *If $t \in \boldsymbol{C}(l)$, then:*

(i) If $t \rightarrow s$ then $s \in \boldsymbol{C}(l)$;

(ii) If s is the explicit form of t, then $s \in \boldsymbol{N}_0(l)$.

The *constructional* interpretation relative to a completion ρ, denoted $[\![.]\!]^{S}_{\rho}$, is defined inductively on the structure of sequent derivations as follows:

S0. $[\![\alpha]\!]^{S}_{\rho} = \rho(\alpha)$;

S1. $[\![\text{AXIOM}_{\Gamma,\varphi}(\xi)]\!]^{S}_{\rho} = \text{HYP}_{\varphi}(\xi)$;

S2. $[\![\text{IMP-R}_{\Gamma,\varphi,\psi}(\xi, d)]\!]^{S}_{\rho} = \text{IMP-I}_{\varphi,\psi}(\xi : [\![d]\!]^{S}_{\rho})$;

S3. $[\![\text{IMP-L}_{\Gamma,\varphi,\psi,\chi}(\eta, \xi, d, d')]\!]^{S}_{\rho} =$
$$\text{SUB}([\![d']\!]^{S}_{\rho}, \text{IMP-E}_{\varphi,\psi}(\text{HYP}_{\varphi \supset \psi}(\xi), [\![d]\!]^{S}_{\rho})/\text{HYP}_{\psi}(\eta)).$$

The counterpart to Proposition 4.1 is:

5.2 PROPOSITION *For any completion ρ, if $d \in \boldsymbol{D}(l)$ then $[\![d]\!]^{S}_{\rho} \in \boldsymbol{C}(l)$.*

6 Some results

Proposition 5.1(ii) tells us that the substitution reduction $\rightarrow$ embeds the set of constructions $\boldsymbol{C}(l)$ into the set of normal natural deductions $\boldsymbol{N}_0(l)$. (In fact the embedding is surjective.) As expected, $[\![.]\!]^{E}$ factors through $[\![.]\!]^{S}$ via reduction to explicit form using $\rightarrow^{*}$, the transitive closure of $\rightarrow$, *i.e.*,

$$[\![\cdot]\!]^{E} \quad = \quad (\rightarrow^{*} \circ \quad [\![\cdot]\!]^{S}).$$

In fact we can pick out a copy of $\boldsymbol{C}(l)$ in $\boldsymbol{N}(l)$.

Define a mapping $\tau : \mathcal{C} \rightarrow \mathcal{N}$ by recursion on the structure of constructions as follows:

$$\mathrm{SUB}\Big(\begin{array}{c}\xi:\psi\\ \vdots\\ \chi\end{array}\ t\ ,\ \begin{array}{c}\vdots\\ \psi\end{array}\ s\ /\,(\xi:\psi)\Big)\ \stackrel{\tau}{\longmapsto}\ \dfrac{\dfrac{\begin{array}{c}[\xi:\psi]\\ \vdots\ \ \tau(t)\\ \chi\end{array}}{\psi\supset\chi}\qquad \begin{array}{c}\vdots\ \ \tau(s)\\ \psi\end{array}}{\chi}$$

Figure 3: Identification of construction with non-normal deduction.

T1. $\tau(\mathrm{HYP}_\varphi(\xi)) = \mathrm{HYP}_\varphi(\xi)$;

T2. $\tau(\text{IMP-I}_{\varphi,\psi}(\xi:t)) = \text{IMP-I}_{\varphi,\psi}(\xi:\tau(t))$;

T3. $\tau(\text{IMP-E}_{\varphi,\psi}(t,s)) = \text{IMP-E}_{\varphi,\psi}(\tau(t),\tau(s))$;

T4. $\tau(\mathrm{SUB}(t^\chi, s/\mathrm{HYP}_\varphi(\xi))) = \text{IMP-E}_{\psi,\chi}(\text{IMP-I}_{\psi,\chi}(\xi:\tau(t))\ ,\ \tau(s))$.

It is perhaps easier to see the effect of this mapping pictorially in Figure 3, which illustrates an instance of T4: given a construction t of χ from assumption ψ, we can replace occurrences of the marker ξ, standing for occurrences of a (hypothetical) construction of ψ, by a construction s of ψ: the resulting construction, represented on the left of the $\mapsto$ in Figure 3, corresponds to the non-normal natural deduction tree on the right of the $\mapsto$ in Figure 3. Indeed, this situation is characteristic of T4, which distinguishes constructions from (normal) natural deductions as follows:

6.1 Proposition $\tau[\,\boldsymbol{C}(l)\setminus \boldsymbol{N}(l)\,]\cap \boldsymbol{N}_0(l) = \emptyset$.

Although τ maps true constructions to non-normal deductions, there is a class of non-normal deductions that are essentially normal. *Identity* reduction, $\rightarrow_\iota$, is a notion of reduction defined on proof expressions as follows:

$$\text{IMP-E}_{\psi,\psi}(\text{IMP-I}_{\psi,\psi}(\xi:\mathrm{HYP}_\psi(\xi))\ ,\ M)\quad\rightarrow_\iota\quad M.$$

This is a special case of normalisation [14]. Notice that the redex on the left is a particular case of the image under τ of a substitution (see T4 above). Let $=_\iota$ denote the congruence generated by $\rightarrow_\iota$ in the usual manner. Call $M\in\boldsymbol{N}(l)$ *ι-normal* if it is normal or ι-congruent to a normal deduction. Let $\boldsymbol{N}_\iota(l)$ denote the set of ι-normal deductions of l.

Let $\boldsymbol{L}_\iota$ denote the sequent calculus formed by replacing the IMP-L rule of $\boldsymbol{L}$ by the rule below; *cf.* §3. ($\boldsymbol{D}_\iota(l)$ denotes the derivations of l in $\boldsymbol{L}_\iota$.)

$\mathrm{L}_\iota 3$. $\text{IMP-L}_{\Gamma,\varphi,\chi,\chi}(\eta,\xi,d,\mathrm{AXIOM}_{(\Gamma,\eta:\chi),\chi}(\eta))\in\boldsymbol{D}_\iota(\Gamma;\chi)$ if $d\in\boldsymbol{D}_\iota(\Gamma;\varphi)$, $\eta\notin$ domΓ and $\xi:\varphi\supset\chi\in\Gamma$.

$\mathrm{L}_\iota 3$ is a derived rule of $\boldsymbol{L}$; *i.e.*, $\boldsymbol{D}_\iota(l)\subset\boldsymbol{D}(l)$. L3 is only admissible in $\boldsymbol{L}_\iota$. These rules are displayed in Figure 4. Notice that both rules make use of implicit contraction.

A completion is said to be *ι-normal* (resp. *normal*) if, for all α^l, $\rho(\alpha)\in\boldsymbol{N}_\iota(l)$ (resp. $\boldsymbol{N}_0(l)$).

IMP-L of $\boldsymbol{L}$	$\dfrac{\Gamma, \eta : \psi ; \chi \quad \Gamma ; \varphi}{\Gamma ; \chi}$	$\xi : \varphi \supset \psi \in \Gamma$
IMP-L of $\boldsymbol{L}_\iota$	$\dfrac{\overline{\Gamma, \eta : \chi ; \chi} \quad \Gamma ; \varphi}{\Gamma ; \chi}$	$\xi : \varphi \supset \chi \in \Gamma$

Figure 4: The rules L3 and $\mathrm{L}_\iota 3$ displayed.

6.2 PROPOSITION *(i)* $(\tau \circ [\![.]\!]_\rho^S)[\boldsymbol{D}_\iota(l)] = \boldsymbol{N}_\iota(l)$, *for all ι-normal ρ.*

(ii) $(\tau \circ [\![.]\!]_\rho^S)[\boldsymbol{D}(l)] \supset \boldsymbol{N}_\iota(l)$, *for all ι-normal ρ.*

Computations (searches) using the system $\boldsymbol{L}_\iota$ involve only ι-normal proofs whereas computations using the system $\boldsymbol{L}$ encounter a wider class of deduction. To this extent ι-normal proofs characterise the constructions that result from (an analytic account of) computations via SLD-resolution. Despite the fact that ι-normal proofs need not be normal, reduction to normal form can be performed on *partial* proofs and hence the residual computation can be interleaved with the primary computation.

$\boldsymbol{L}$, on the other hand, embodies a form of limited (analytic) cut on *left* or *negative* subformulae. Thus the construction of a proof ($[\![.]\!]^S$) may involve less work than the explicit presentation ($[\![.]\!]^E$) of that proof; the difference being measured by the effect of the elimination of the substitution operator. However, the substitution constructs *cannot* be eliminated until certain subproofs have been fully completed (those with $\eta : \psi$ in their antecedents).

It is obvious, though we shall not develop it here, that the extension of the constructional interpretation $[\![.]\!]_\rho^S$ to first-order programs would yield non-trivial residual computations.

References

[1] R.L. Constable *et al.*. Implementing mathematics with the NuPRL proof development system. Prentice Hall, 1986.

[2] J.-Y. Girard. Linear logic. *Theoret. Comput. Sci.*, 50(1), 1987.

[3] K. Gödel. Uber eine bisher noch nicht benützte Erweiterung des finiten Standpunktes, *Dialectica,* 12, 1958, pp.280–287; English translation, *J. Phil. Logic,* 9, 1980, pp.133–142.

[4] R. Harper, F. Honsell, G. Plotkin. A framework for defining logics. *J. ACM*, (to appear). (Preprint available as University of Edinburgh LFCS report ECS-LFCS-91-162, June 1991.)

[5] S.C. Kleene. Permutability of inferences in Gentzen's calculi **LK** and **LJ**. *Mem. Amer. Math. Soc.*, pages 1–26, 1952.

[6] S.C. Kleene. *Mathematical Logic.* Wiley and Sons, 1968.

[7] R. Kowalski and D. Kuehner. Linear resolution with selection function. *J. Artif. Int.*, 2:227–260, 1971.

[8] J. Lloyd. *Foundations of Logic Programming.* Springer-Verlag, 1984.

[9] D.W. Loveland. *Automated theorem proving: a logical basis.* Elsevier, 1979.

[10] P. Martin-Löf. On the meanings of the logical constants and the justifications of the logical laws. Technical Report 2, Scuola di Specializziazione in Logica Matematica, Dipartimento di Matematica, Università di Siena, 1985.

[11] D. Miller and G. Nadathur. Higher-order Logic Programming. Report MS-CIS-86-17, University of Pennsylvania, 1986.

[12] D. Miller, G. Nadathur, A. Ščedrov and F. Pfenning. Uniform Proofs as a Foundation for Logic Programming. *Ann. Pure and Appl. Logic,* 51, pp. 125–157, 1991.

[13] F. Pfenning. Logic programming in the LF logical framework. In: *Logical Frameworks*, G. Huet and G. Plotkin (editors), Cambridge University Press, 1991. pp. 149–181.

[14] D. Prawitz. *Natural deduction: a proof-theoretical study.* Almqvist & Wiksell, 1965.

[15] D. Prawitz. Proofs and the meaning and completeness of the logical constants. In: J. Hintikka, I. Niiniluoto and E. Saarinen (eds.) *Essays on Mathematical and Philosophical Logic*, pp. 25-40. D. Reidel, 1978.

[16] D.J. Pym. *Proofs, Search and Computation in General Logic.* Ph.D. thesis, University of Edinburgh, 1990. Available as report CST-69-90, Department of Computer Science, University of Edinburgh, 1990. (Also published as LFCS report ECS-LFCS-90-125.)

[17] D.J. Pym and L.A. Wallen. Proof-search in the $\lambda\Pi$-calculus. In: *Logical Frameworks*, G. Huet and G. Plotkin (editors), Cambridge University Press, 1991. pp. 309–340.

[18] W. Sieg. Herbrand analyses. *Arch. Math. Logic*, 30, pp. 409–441, 1991.

[19] J. Zucker. The correspondence between cut-elimination and normalisation. *Ann. Math. Logic*, 7:1–112, 1974.

An Amalgamated Temporal Logic

Yuejun Jiang & Barry Richards
Department of Computing
Imperial College
London SW7 2BZ

Abstract

There are two typical ways to formalize reasoning over time. The first is in a modal logic where time is characterized implicitly through tense operators. The second addresses time explicitly in a first-order theory, where the reasoning is itself essentially first order. In this paper we shall introduce an amalgamated temporal logic which combines the tense operators of the modal approach with the referential aspects of the first-order approach.

The modal operators of the new logic, called IQ-C, include the familiar tense operators plus a few new ones; together they allow complex temporal propositions to be represented in a compact form. Unlike standard modal temporal logics, IQ-C contains terms which refer to times; this allows the logic to characterize certain temporal properties and operators which cannot be axiomatized or defined by conventional modal operators. IQ-C is expressively complete over any connected flow of time, and has several other interesting theoretical properties, some of which will be developed in this paper.

Most interval logics take one of two approaches to temporal assertions; either they analyze assertions for intervals in terms of assertions at points, or they treat intervals as primitive, allowing assertions for intervals but not at points. IQ-C allows assertions both for intervals and at points, and treats them as independent; this yields a special degree of semantic discrimination and at the same time simplifies the representation of several temporal properties. In this paper we shall outline the IQ-C framework, specifying its special features and defining its semantics. We shall also extend a method of skolemization, which is designed to support a resolution based approach to the proof theory. This will be sketched in some detail, with a view to providing a preliminary account of the basic proof theory. A complete specification of the deductive theory, together with relevant proofs, will be developed elsewhere.

Keywords: Intervals, Points, Temporal Representation and Expressiveness, Homogeneity, Skolemization, and Modal Theorem Proving.[1]

---

1 The work reported in this paper was supported in part by a grant from the Information

1 Introduction

Intervals can be formalized implicitly through Priorean tense operators [Humberstone 79], but this approach is seen to be inadequate for certain applications which may reason about intervals. In the case of planning, for example, it is felt that intervals must be represented explicitly to allow a sufficiently rich and efficient form of reasoning. This is manifest in the approaches of Allen [84], McDermott [82] and Shoham [87]. These first-order formalizations, however, suffer either from an unclear semantics or an inability to represent complex temporal notions. The purpose of this paper is to develop an amalgamated temporal logic of intervals which combines the virtues of the modal approach with those of the first-order approach. The amalgamation can be seen to involve a partial integration of meta-level and object-level features in the sense of Bowen & Kowalski [82]. The modal operators of the object language will, as expected, quantify over intervals, but intervals can also be referred to by terms in the language.

Intervals are taken to be essential for reasoning about actions and properties since they typically have duration and hence may overlap in complex ways. But intervals raise several new questions for the formalization of time. One concerns the characterization of truth-for-an-interval and the degree to which it is homogeneous. Some properties would seem to be true for an interval without necessarily being true for all its subintervals. Consider the property of averaging 60 mph over a particular interval; this surely can be true even though for some subinterval the average speed is more (or less) than 60 mph. A rather different case concerns the homogeneity of the denotation of terms. For example, if the proposition "John Major is Prime Minister" is true for an interval, it is natural to assume that the proposition is true for the subintervals of the interval and that "John Major" names the same person throughout. But consider the proposition "The Prime Minister leads the government." If this proposition is true for an interval, it must surely be true for all the subintervals of the interval. This does not, however, imply the "The Prime Minister" names the same individual in each subinterval.

Another question relates to the characterization of the structure of time. The properties of density and discreteness, for example, require special treatment if the 'basic' units of time are taken to be intervals; density and discreteness are essentially pointlike properties. But admitting (or extracting) points to capture these properties gives rise to a problem with the characterization of continuous change. The continuity of time cannot be axiomatized in first-order logic, although it can in a modal logic. Although continuity may not be a problem for a purely interval-based logic [Allen 83], reasoning with points

---

Engineering Directorate/ Science and Engineering Research Council: "Temporal Databases and Planning" Grant No. 1320.

is an essential aspect of reasoning about time. But then how can a 'mixed' ontology of time, one which involves both points and intervals, be integrated into a single theory? This is one of the fundamental questions we shall explore in this paper.

Let us start with the reified approach to temporal logic. Here propositions take the form of properties which are indexed to time by means of a special predicate, e.g. "Hold". For example, the representation of the proposition "John is married to Sue in the interval 78 to 89" is something like "Hold([78,89], Married(John, Sue))". The expression "Married(John, Sue)" refers to a property, viz. the property of John's being married to Sue; the term "[78,89]" refers to an interval whose end points are 78 and 89; and the predicate "Hold" is a two-place relation, relating the property to the interval. The non-reified analysis of the proposition is rather different [Quine 60]. Time is treated as an additional argument of the predicate "married", yielding a regimentation something like "Married([78,89], John, Sue)". There is clearly no need to reify properties in this formulation.

The reified approach is exemplified in Allen's temporal logic [Allen 84]. This formulation, however, does not provide a clear semantic account of complex properties, particularly of properties involving quantification. A modified version of the reified approach is given in [McDermott 82], where properties are treated semantically as sets of times, analogous to the way temporal propositions are treated in modal logic. 'Boolean' combinations of properties are derived by set theoretical operations, e.g. intersection and union, from the component properties. This approach still cannot deal with 'universal' properties, e.g. the property of everyone's loving Sue, although Shoham [87] further refines the strategy to remove this limitation. Shoham's formulation (STL) reinstates 'atomic' properties as propositions, and does not invoke complex properties. There are just complex propositions, which are formed using the connectives and quantifiers with their standard meanings. This approach remains essentially first order, even though there is an underlying modal semantics. In fact, Baccus et al [92] have shown that everything which can be expressed in STL can also be expressed in their non-reified logic (BTK). Since BTK is a first-order theory, STL is essentially also first order.

In contrast, the amalgamated logic IQ-C, which we shall develop, is fundamentally modal in that the denotation of formulas is interpreted uniformly as intensional. Although it is possible to refer explicitly to time in IQ-C, there are no first-order temporal quantifiers, as there are in STL and BTK. The only form of temporal quantification in IQ-C is through temporal operators, e.g. the Priorean operators F (Future) and P (Past). There are also some non-Priorean temporal operators which are used to capture aspects of the temporal structure that cannot be reflected in terms of F and P alone. For example, the irreflexivity of time cannot be expressed using just F and P, although it can be in any first-order approach such as STL and BTK. The new operators of IQ-C allow irreflexivity to be captured, even though there is no explicit quantification over time. But in contrast to STL and BTK, IQ-C can also capture certain second-order properties, like the continuity of time.

It was noted in Baccus et al [92] that STL has a special limitation which BTK does not, viz. terms cannot be temporally indexed. In IQ-C, however, terms can be indexed to times. The key to this and other features of the language lies in the method of treating homogeneity, which is defined through a modal operator and hence is not primitive to the system. The modal aspects of the language are fully characterized in a special purpose modal resolution proof procedure. The capacity to refer to time explicitly in the language serves to control the process of modal reasoning, as well as to simplify temporal representation.

The combination of modality and explicit temporal reference in IQ-C is developed in the spirit of the original temporal logic IQ [Richards et al 89]. The major difference lies in the status of homogeneity, which is taken as a primitive notion in IQ and interpreted so as to generate the need for a third truth value. A proposition, when evaluated at an interval, may be either true, false, or neither nor false, depending upon the denotations of its terms and predicates in the subintervals of the evaluation interval. IQ-C, however, is a bivalent logic in which the denotation of an expression for an interval does not depend upon its denotation in any of the subintervals. This is tantamount to saying that IQ-C assigns denotations heterogeneously. The logic can, nevertheless, represent the homogeneity restrictions invoked in IQ and can reason about them. In effect, IQ-C is more expressive than IQ. Moreover, the deducibility relation satisfies certain standard conditions, e.g. the bivalent form of the deduction theorem.

This paper is organized as follows. In Section 2 we examine certain issues relating to intervals, points and homogeneity, and provide the motivation for the logic to be presented. In Section 3 we describe the syntax and semantics of IQ-C, and in Section 4 we explore the expressive power of the logic by considering a range of temporal properties and structures. Finally, we develop a preliminary account of a modal resolution proof procedure in Section 5. Here we extend an approach to skolemization, which is well suited to an amalgamated logic like IQ-C.

2 Intervals, Points and Homogeneity

In point-based temporal logics the denotation of a formula in a model is taken to be the set of points at which it is true. The concept of 'true at a point' is assumed to be unproblematic. In interval-based temporal logics, however, the concept of 'true for an interval' is not so simple. Where φ is an atomic proposition, some would say that φ is true for an interval i if and only if it is true at the beginning of i. While this might be a useful definition, it is certainly not intuitive from the perspective of applications in artificial intelligence. A more appropriate definition might be the following: φ is true for i if and only if it is true for all its subintervals. Hamblin [71] suggests that if the truth of φ for i is to be homogeneous, then the logic should be three-valued. The proposition φ might fail to be true in two ways: it might be homogeneously false for i, or it may be false only for some subinterval of i. Humberstone [79] accommodates this by introducing two forms of negation, one which is bivalent and the other 'intuitionistic'. Richards & Bethke [89] indicate, however, that this may not be sufficient to avoid invoking a third truth value. How is the denotation of a term to be defined with respect to an interval? In some cases it would seem that a term can denote an object for an interval only if it denotes that object for all the subintervals of the interval. Where this condition fails to hold, the term fails to denote, and any formula containing this term must then be neither true nor false for the given interval. Richards & Bethke take this as a third truth value.

Richards & Bethke develop a logic, viz. IQ, on the assumption that all atomic propositions must be homogeneously true; that is, an atomic proposition is true for an interval only if it is true for all its subintervals. But not all atomic propositions seem to satisfy this restriction. Recall the property of averaging 60 mph for some interval of time; the proposition "Max drove at an average speed of 60 mph", when evaluated at a particular interval, may be true for that interval even though it is false for some of its subintervals. This is not to say, of course, that there are not some propositions which are homogeneous; indeed atomic propositions may typically be homogeneous.

In IQ-C we adopt what may be called the heterogeneous approach to the truth of atomic formulas; an atomic formula may be true for an interval even though it is false for some subintervals. To assert that a particular proposition (atomic or otherwise) is true at an interval i, we follow the IQ strategy and use an operator, here *At*. Where φ is any proposition, $At(i, \varphi)$ says that φ is true at the interval i. If φ is an atomic proposition, say of the form $P(a)$, this means that the denotation of a at i belongs to the denotation of P at i. Here there are no homogeneity assumptions. If we want to assert that $P(a)$ is homogeneously true, we need to invoke another operator *Ah*: where ψ is any proposition, $Ah(\psi)$ is true for an interval if only if ψ is true for all the subintervals of that interval. The formula $At(i, Ah(P(a)))$ asserts that $P(a)$ is homogeneously true for the interval i. On the assumption that a is an individual constant, the denotation of a is defined to be rigid, that is, it is the same object for all intervals.

We accommodate non-rigid designators by allowing terms to be indexed explicitly to interval terms. Thus, if a is an individual constant and t an interval term, we admit $a(t)$ as a term. The denotation of $a(t)$ depends upon the denotation of t. In the next section we shall give a precise definition of the denotation of terms such as $a(t)$, which will characterize the conditions under which they are non-rigid.

So far we have spoken only of intervals. Points might be taken as the limiting case of intervals, but this need not be the case. Humberstone and Allen regard intervals as primitive and hence give no status to points. Allen notes that in an interval structure which admits points, it can sometimes be difficult to decide what truth value to assign to a proposition at a point. Suppose that two intervals meet at some point, and that φ is true for one interval and $\neg\varphi$ is true for the other. What is true at the point? If both are true at the point, we violate consistency; if neither is true, we lose the principle of excluded middle. To make just one true we seem to have to choose arbitrarily. This apparently awkward problem can be sidestepped by avoiding points altogether. Unfortunately, the need for points in temporal representation and reasoning seems inevitable.

It is partly for this reason that Allen & Hayes [87] and Halpern & Shoham [88] consider strategies for constructing points from intervals. They do not, however, give a fully adequate treatment of truth at a point. Allen & Hayes say that a proposition (property) is true at a point if and only if it is contained in an interval where the proposition is true. This suggestion is not always correct. Consider the case of a ball which is thrown upwards and falls back. Although the ball's velocity is non-zero in both the upward and downward intervals, its velocity is zero at the meeting point of the two intervals. This point is not contained in any interval where the velocity of the ball is zero.

To resolve this and other problems, Galton [90] proposes a classification of properties into two types: state-of-position and state-of-motion. Properties of state-of-position can hold at isolated instants. If having zero velocity is classified as a state-of-position property, it can hold at the meeting point of two non-zero intervals. In general, if a state-of-position property holds throughout an interval, then it must also hold at the limits of that interval. Properties of state-of-motion, however, do not hold at isolated instants. A state-of-motion property holds at an instant if and only if it holds throughout some interval within which that instant falls. On Galton's reckoning it is possible for the ball to have zero velocity and to be moving at the same point, without falling into contradiction. The former property is a state-of-position property while the latter is a state-of-motion property. By definition these are not in conflict. Although Galton's classification may be sensible, it is semantically insecure since it presupposes Allen's approach to properties, which is not entirely satisfactory.

In IQ-C we take the view that it is better to admit points from the beginning and construct intervals from points. As for the apparently awkward problem of relating properties for intervals to properties at points, we assume that these are generally independent; truth for an interval and truth at a point are separate notions, which may or may not be related. That is, a property may be true at a point, although not true for an interval containing that point; conversely, a property may be true for an interval, although not true at all the points in that interval. This allows IQ-C to reflect Galton's distinctions, although in a somewhat different way.

Two different kinds of homogeneity can be defined in IQ-C, viz. interval-homogeneity and homogeneity simpliciter. A property is said to be interval-homogeneous for an interval if it holds for all the non-point subintervals of that interval. Since intervals are constructed from points in IQ-C, points can be seen as the limiting case, hence the need to distinguish non-point subintervals. An example of an interval-homogeneous property is non-zero velocity. A object might have non-zero velocity in all non-point subintervals of an interval but not at every point. This is the case for the trajectory of the ball whose velocity at the turning point is zero; its velocity for every non-point subinterval is non-zero but its velocity at the apex is zero.

It is natural to wonder whether interval-homogeneity can, as it were, be inherited from truth at all the points of the interval. If a property is true at all the points of an interval, does it hold interval-homogeneously for the interval as a whole? Consider a ball rolling along a flat surface. At each time point it is true that the ball is located at exactly one spatial point. And for any non-point interval of such time points it is clear that the ball is located at more than one spatial point. This suggests that interval-homogeneity is not inheritable from truth at all points of an interval. We might, nevertheless, want to say that a property holds at all points of an interval, without saying anything about the subintervals of that interval. There is an operator in IQ-C which allows such assertions to be made.

To enrich the expressive flexibility of IQ-C we type the modal operator Ah to reflect the domain of the implicit quantifier. Recall that above we said that $Ah\varphi$ is true for an interval i if and only if φ is true for all the subintervals of i. We now refine this into three different cases, viz. Ah_i, Ah_p and Ah_{ip}. Ah_i quantifies over all non-point subintervals, Ah_p only over point subintervals and Ah_{ip} over all subintervals. These are precisely defined in the next section. It will also be convenient to type the other modal operators, e.g. F and P, in a similar way. For example, there will be three different future tense operators, viz. F_i, F_p and F_{ip}. If typing were to increase the complexity of reasoning, the strategy might not be such a good idea, but fortunately, this is not the case in IQ-C.

3 The Logic IQ-C

3.1 Syntax of IQ-C

The language of IQ-C is a many-sorted first order modal language. There are two distinct sorts of terms, viz. temporal and non-temporal, and for each there are three types, constants, variables and function terms. The basic vocabulary of IQ-C includes the following.

1) A set of **non-temporal** expressions where,
   - x is a variable,
   - c is a constant,
   - P^n is an n-ary predicate,
   - f^n is an n-ary function.

2) A set of **temporal** expressions where,
   - tx is a variable,
   - tc is a constant,
   - tf^n is an n-ary function.

The set of temporal terms is defined straightforwardly.

3) The set of **temporal terms** is the smallest set containing,
   - all temporal variables
   - all temporal constants,
   - all expressions of the form $tf^n(t_1, \ldots, t_n)$, where $t_1, \ldots, t_n$ are temporal terms.

The envisaged interpretation of temporal terms is that they designate points of time.

Intervals will be designated in terms of their end points. For this purpose we introduce a special set of interval terms.

4) Where t_1 and t_2 are temporal terms, an **interval term** is any expression which conforms to exactly one of the following.
   - $[t_1, t_2]$ (closed),

- $(t_1, t_2]$ (left open),
- $[t_1, t_2)$ (right open),
- (t_1, t_2) (open).

For convenience we refer to an arbitrary interval term as $\{t_1, t_2\}$.

The set of non-temporal terms requires a somewhat more complicated definition, since these terms can be temporally indexed by interval terms.

5) The set of **non-temporal terms** is the smallest set containing,
   - all non-temporal variables,
   - all non-temporal constants,
   - all expressions of the form $c\{t1, t2\}$, where $\{t_1, t_2\}$is an interval term,
   - all expressions of the form $f^n(nt_1, ..., nt_n)\{t1, t2\}$, where $nt_1, ... , nt_n$ are non-temporal terms and $\{t_1, t_2\}$ is an interval term.

The atomic formulas of IQ-C include a special formula $\top$ and otherwise are defined as one would expect.

6) An **atomic formula** is either $\top$ or any expression of the form $P^n(nt_1, ..., nt_n)$, where $nt_1, ... , nt_n$ are non-temporal terms.

As we mentioned in the previous section, there are several modal operators in IQ-C, all indexed with a type.

7) The **modal operators** are Ah_{type}, As_{type}, F_{type}, P_{type}, G_{type} and H_{type}, where *type* may be either *i*, *p* or *ip*.

For example, G_i, G_p and G_{ip} are all modal operators; sometimes we shall abbreviate G_{ip} simply as G. The same holds, mutatis mutandis, for each of the other operators. IQ-C has the standard boolean connectives, but quantifiers only for the non-temporal variables. In effect, the quantifiers are restricted to non-temporal domains; there are no explicit temporal quantifiers, only temporal operators which quantify implicitly. There are, however, two substitution operators which will be used like lambda abstraction to bind temporal variables.

8) $L^{\ulcorner}tx$ and $L^{\urcorner}tx$ are **substitution operators.**

These will be explained below when we define their semantics. We are now in a position to define the formulas of IQ-C.

9) The set of **formulas** of IQ-C is the smallest set of expressions containing,

- the atomic formulas,
- $\neg\varphi$ and any formula of the form $(\varphi \vee \psi)$, provided φ and ψ are formulas,
- $\exists x\varphi$, provided φ is a formula and x is a non-temporal variable,
- $L^{\ulcorner}tx\varphi$ and $L^{\urcorner}tx\varphi$, provided φ is a formula and tx is temporal variable,
- $At(it, \varphi)$, $Ah_{type}\varphi$, $As_{type}\varphi$, $F_{type}\varphi$, $P_{type}\varphi$, $G_{type}\varphi$ and $H_{type}\varphi$, provided it is an interval term and φ is a formula.

All free occurrences of the non-temporal variable x in φ are bound in the formula $\exists x\varphi$; and
all free occurrences of the temporal variable tx in φ are bound in the formulas $L^{\ulcorner}tx\varphi$ and $L^{\urcorner}tx\varphi$.

Although we have indicated roughly how some of the formulas of IQ-C are to be read, it is perhaps best to define their semantics precisely before we attempt to identify the intuitive content.

3.2 Semantics of IQ-C

The semantics of IQ-C is characterized with respect to a point structure.

10) A point structure **T** is a pair (T, <) where,

- T is a nonempty set (of points),
- < is an ordering on T.

11) A model **M** on **T** is a quadruple (D, I, $\ll$, Φ) satisfying the following conditions.

- D and I are disjoint nonempty sets (of individuals and intervals);
- I is a subset of the power set P of T such that,
  - all singletons in P are in I,
  - i is in I only if for all for t_1 and t_2 in i and all t such that $t_1 \leq t \leq t_2$, t is in i,
  - the empty set is not in I;
- $\ll$ is a partial ordering of I such that for all i and j in I, i $\ll$ j if and only if for all t_1 in i and t_2 in j $t_1 < t_2$;
- Φ is a (meaning) function such that,
  - for each temporal constant tc, $\Phi(tc)$ is an element in T,
  - for each temporal function tf^n, $\Phi(tf^n)$ is a function from T^n to T,
  - for each non-temporal constant c, $\Phi(c)$ is a function from I to D,
  - for each non-temporal predicate P^n, $\Phi(P^n)$ is a total function from I to

a function from D^n to {true, false},

- for each non-temporal function f^n, $\Phi(f^n)$ is a total function from I to a function from D^n to D.

We next define the denotation of a term in a model with respect to an assignment to the variables.

12) An **assignment** g is a function such that,

- for each temporal variable, $g(tx)$ is an element of T,
- for each non-temporal variable, $g(x)$ is an element of D.

We shall refer to the denotation of a term t in a model **M** under the assignment g as $//t//^g$. Explicit reference to the model is unnecessary here.

13) The denotation of a **temporal term** in **M** is defined as follows.

- For each variable tx, $//tx//^g$ is $g(tx)$,
- For each constant tc, $//tc//^g$ is $\Phi(tc)$,
- For each function term of the form $tf^n(t_1, \ldots, t_n)$, $//tf^n(t_1, \ldots, t_n)//^g$ is $\Phi(tf^n)(//t_1//^g, \ldots, //t_n//^g)$.

Note that the denotations of temporal terms are not intensional entities, i.e. functions from temporal indices to extensions.

14) The denotation of a **non-temporal term** in **M** is an intensional entity defined with respect to the set of intervals. Intervals will be designated as {s, e}, where s is the 'left' limiting point and e the 'right' limiting point of the interval.

- For each variable x, $//x//^g\{s, e\}$ is $g(x)$,
- For each constant c, $//c//^g\{s, e\}$ is $\Phi(c)\{s, e\}$,
- For each term of the form $c\{t_1, t_2\}$, $//c\{t_1, t_2\}//^g\{s, e\}$ is $\Phi(c)\{//t_1//^g, //t_2//^g\}$,
- For each term of the form $f^n(nt_1, \ldots, nt_n)\{t_1, t_2\}$, $//f^n(nt_1, \ldots, nt_n)\{t_1, t_2\}//^g\{s, e\}$ is $\Phi(f^n)\{//t_1//^g, //t_2//^g\}(//nt_1//^g\{//t_1//^g, // t_2//^g\}, \ldots, //nt_n//^g\{//t_1//^g, //t_2//^g\})$.

Note that the denotations of indexed terms, i.e. those indexed with interval terms, are constant functions; such terms are sometimes called rigid designators.

Finally, we are in a position to specify the truth definition of IQ-C. Like non-temporal terms, formulas in IQ-C denote intensions from the set of intervals to truth values.

15) Where σ is any formula, we say that σ is true in **M** under the assignment g for the interval {s, e}, abbreviated as **M**, g, {s, e} $\models \sigma$, provided the following holds.

- Where σ is $\top$, **M**, g, {s, e} $\models \top$,

- Where σ is of the form $P^n(nt_1, ..., nt_n)$,
  $\mathbf{M}, g, \{s, e\} \models P^n(nt_1, ..., nt_n)$, iff
  $\Phi(P^n)\{s, e\}(//nt_1//^g\{s, e\}, ..., //nt_n//^g\{s, e\})$.
- Where σ is of the form $\neg\varphi$,
  $\mathbf{M}, g, \{s, e\} \models \neg\varphi$ iff not $\mathbf{M}, g, \{s, e\} \models \varphi$.
- Where σ is of the form $(\varphi \vee \psi)$,
  $\mathbf{M}, g, \{s, e\} \models (\varphi \vee \psi)$ iff $\mathbf{M}, g, \{s, e\} \models \varphi$ or $\mathbf{M}, g, \{s, e\} \models \psi$.
- Where σ is of the form $\exists x\varphi$,
  $\mathbf{M}, g, \{s, e\} \models \exists x\varphi$ iff $\mathbf{M}, g^*, \{s, e\} \models \varphi$ for some assignment g^* which differs fromg at most in way it assigns to x.
- Where σ is of the form $L^l tx\varphi$,
  $\mathbf{M}, g, \{s, e\} \models L^l tx\varphi$ iff $\mathbf{M}, g^*, \{s, e\} \models \varphi$ for the assignment g^* which is exactly like g except that $g^*(tx)$ is s.
- Where σ is of the form $L^r tx\varphi$,
  $\mathbf{M}, g, \{s, e\} \models L^r tx\varphi$ iff $\mathbf{M}, g^*, \{s, e\} \models \varphi$ for the assignment g^* which is exactly like g except that $g^*(tx)$ is e.
- Where σ is of the form $At(\{t_1, t_2\}, \varphi)$,
  $\mathbf{M}, g, \{s, e\} \models At(\{t_1, t_2\}, \varphi)$ iff $//t_1//^g$ is s, $//t_2//^g$ is e and $\mathbf{M}, g, \{s, e\} \models \varphi$.

Here we need to distinguish the *type* of an interval. An interval is a *p-interval* if it is an interval consisting of a single point; it is an *i-interval* if it consists of more than one point; and it is an *ip-interval* if it is either of *type p* or *type i*..

We continue the definition.

- Where σ is of the form $As_{type}\varphi$,
  $\mathbf{M}, g, \{s, e\} \models As_{type}\varphi$ iff there is a *type-subinterval* $\{s^*, e^*\}$ of $\{s, e\}$, such that $\mathbf{M}, g, \{s^*, e^*\} \models \varphi$.
- Where σ is of the form $Ah_{type}\varphi$,
  $\mathbf{M}, g, \{s, e\} \models Ah_{type}\varphi$ iff for all *type-subintervals* $\{s^*, e^*\}$ of $\{s, e\}$ $\mathbf{M}, g, \{s^*, e^*\} \models \varphi$.
- Where σ is of the form $F_{type}\varphi$,
  $\mathbf{M}, g, \{s, e\} \models F_{type}\varphi$ iff there is a *type-interval* $\{s^*, e^*\}$ such that $\{s, e\} \ll \{s^*, e^*\}$ and $\mathbf{M}, g, \{s^*, e^*\} \models \varphi$.
- Where σ is of the form $P_{type}\varphi$,
  $\mathbf{M}, g, \{s, e\} \models P_{type}\varphi$ iff there is a *type-interval* $\{s^*, e^*\}$ such that $\{s^*, e^*\} \ll \{s, e\}$ and $\mathbf{M}, g, \{s^*, e^*\} \models \varphi$.
- Where σ is of the form $G_{type}\varphi$,
  $\mathbf{M}, g, \{s, e\} \models G_{type}\varphi$ iff for all *type-intervals* $\{s^*, e^*\}$ such that $\{s, e\} \ll \{s^*, e^*\}$ $\mathbf{M}, g, \{s^*, e^*\} \models \varphi$.
- Where σ is of the form $H_{type}\varphi$,

M, g, {s, e} ⊨ $H_{type}\varphi$ iff for all type-intervals {s*, e*} such that {s*, e*} ≪ {s, e}M, g, {s, e} ⊨ φ.

It should be emphasized that in IQ-C the notion of truth in a model under an assignment is bivalent; in this respect it differs significantly from IQ, which is a many-valued system. As a result, the definitions of validity and consequence in IQ-C are purely classical.

16) An IQ-C formula is **true in a model M** (simpliciter) iff it is true in **M** under all assignments for all intervals.
An IQ-C formula is **valid in a class of point structures** iff it is true (simpliciter) in all models on those point structures.
An IQ-C formula is **satisfiable** iff it is true in some model **M** under an assignment for some interval.

Since IQ-C has a classical semantics, the boolean connectives for conjunction, implication and bi-implication, and the universal quantifier can be introduced with their standard definitions. It will also be noted that the following pairs of formulas are all equivalent: *($Ah_{type}\varphi$, $\neg As_{type}\neg\varphi$) ($G_{type}\varphi$, $\neg F_{type}\neg\varphi$), and ($H_{type}\varphi$, $\neg P_{type}\neg\varphi$).* Having introduced three different types of homogeneity into the logic, which are reflected in three homogeneity operators, we are committed to typing the other modal operators in a similar way. This may look aesthetically cluttered, but it will subsequently be seen to allow a certain expressive efficiency. Moreover, it will not overly complicate the deductive theory.

4 Expressiveness of IQ-C

In this section we shall illustrate the expressiveness of IQ-C by considering a number of cases. We begin with the basic interval relations of Allen [83], which can all be captured using modal operators of the sort found in Halpern & Shoham [88]. Since Allen's logic assumes time to be linear, we shall take the intended class of point structures to be linear when giving the various IQ-C translations. This assumption is not essential restriction on the expressiveness of IQ-C, but it makes the discussion here more convenient.

We shall now show how to translate the modal operators, which are similar to those in Halpern & Shoham, into IQ-C. We shall represent these operators in a way which reveals their intended meaning. Consider the formula *EQUAL* σ (with the operator *EQUAL*), which is interpreted as saying that σ is true in an interval which equals the interval of evaluation. To capture this in IQ-C we use the substitution operators L^{t}_{x} and

$L^{\lceil}tx$ and the modal At.

17) $L^{\{}tx\, L^{\lceil}tyAt(\{tx, ty\}, \sigma)$

Recall that,

18) M, g, {s, e} $\models L^{\{}tx\, L^{\lceil}tyAt(\{tx, ty\}, \sigma)$ iff M, g^*, {s, e} $\models At(\{tx, ty\}, \sigma)$ for the assignment g^* which is exactly like g except that $g^*(tx)$ is s and $g^*(ty)$ is e.

This is tantamount to saying that the formula $L^{\{}tx\, L^{\lceil}tyAt(\{tx, ty\}, \sigma)$ is true at the interval {s, e} provided σ is true at the interval {s, e}, which is just what the formula *EQUAL* σ asserts.

Take another example, viz. *BEFORE* σ, this is interpreted as saying that σ is true in an interval which is before the interval of evaluation. It is translated into IQ-C as follows.

19) $L^{\{}tx\, L^{\lceil}tyAt(\{tx, ty\}, P\sigma)$

Here there is no restriction on the type of the past tense operator P; it quantifies freely over intervals and points. Note that (19) is true (in a model) at a particular evaluation interval provided σ is true in an interval which is before the interval of evaluation.

The translation of the formula *MEET* σ is slightly more complicated. This formula is said to be true at an interval of evaluation iff σ is true at an interval which meets the evaluation interval. Here the intended meaning of *MEET* is "is adjacent to". To translate this into IQ-C we need to indicate how to assert that two intervals meet. Since IQ-C refers to intervals in terms of their boundary points, there are essentially two ways of specifying the meet relation: the right-open interval $\{t_1, t_2)$ meets the left-closed interval $[t_2, t_3\}$; and the right-closed interval $\{t_1, t_2]$ meets the left-open interval $(t_2, t_3\}$. To take account of this in the translation we need to resort to a disjunction.

20) $L^{\{}tx\, L^{\lceil}tyAt(\{tx, ty\}, FPL^{\{}tzAt(\{tz, tx], \sigma)) \vee$
$L^{\{}tx\, L^{\lceil}tyAt(\{tx, ty\}, FPL^{\{}tzAt(\{tz, tx), \sigma))$.

Here again there is no need to specify the type of modal operators involved since this will take care of itself.

Referring to intervals by means of their boundary points may sometimes be inconvenient, but it can also be useful. Consider the formula *BEGIN* σ, which says that

σ is true in an interval which begins (is an initial segment of) the evaluation interval. This is translated as follows.

21) $L^{\int}tx\ L^{\ulcorner}tyAt(\{tx, ty\}, FPL^{\ulcorner}tzAt(\{tx, tz\}, \sigma)\ \&\ FPAt(\{tz, ty\}, T)))$

The modal operators corresponding to the remaining basic interval relations, of which there are ten, can be handled similarly within the resources of IQ-C. It can also be shown that everything expressible in the logic of Halpern & Shoham [88] can be captured in IQ-C, although we shall not undertake the exercise here.

It is significant, though not surprising, that IQ-C can express the *CHOP* operators defined in Venema [90]. The formula $CHOP(\varphi, \psi)$ is said to be true at an interval iff φ is true in a proper initial segment of the interval and ψ is true in the remaining final segment of the interval. This is rendered in IQ-C as follows.

22) $L^{\int}tx\ L^{\ulcorner}tyAt(\{tx, ty\}, FPL^{\ulcorner}tzAt(\{tx, tz\}, (\varphi\ \&\ FPAt(\{tz, ty\}, \psi))))$

There exist similar translations for the operators *F-CHOP* and *I-CHOP*. $F\text{-}CHOP(\varphi, \psi)$ is said to be true at an interval iff φ is true for that interval and ψ is true for a proper final segment of it. And $I\text{-}CHOP(\varphi, \psi)$ is said to be true at an interval iff φ is true for that interval and ψ is true for an initial segment of it. None of these operators can be defined using a finite number of "standard" modal operators, e.g. of the sort used in Halpern & Shoham [88]. In effect, Halpern & Shoham cannot define the *CHOP* operators.

For the sake of completeness it may be mentioned that IQ-C can define the *SINCE* and *UNTIL* operators of Kamp [76]. $UNTIL(\varphi, \psi)$ is said to be true at a point (of evaluation) iff there is a future point at which φ is true and for all intervening points (including the evaluation point) ψ is true at that point. This is expressed by the following formula.

23) $L^{\int}txF(\varphi\ \&\ H(PAt(\{tx, tx\}, T) \rightarrow \psi)))$

A similar formula expresses $SINCE(\varphi, \psi)$. For further details of the expressive relation between languages like IQ-C and the logic of *SINCE* and *UNTIL*, see Hirsch [90].

It is well known that the standard Priorean operators (*F, P, G and H*) are not sufficient to formulate an axiom which is true only if time is irreflexive, that is, if the ordering relation on the set of times is irreflexive. This can of course be easily expressed in first order logic by this formula, where the quantifier ranges over times: $\forall x \neg x < x$. An appropriate formula, however, does exist in IQ-C, viz.

24) $L^{\lceil}tx\, L^{\ulcorner}ty(At(\{tx, ty\}, T) \rightarrow \neg FAt(\{tx, ty\}, T))$.

It should be noted that this axiom holds not only for point intervals but or intervals in general. A similar formula can express the proposition that time is asymmetric, which again is first-order expressible but not definable by the standard Priorean operators. Two formulas are needed to express this in IQ-C, viz.

25) $L^{\lceil}tx\, L^{\ulcorner}ty(At(\{tx, ty\}, k) \rightarrow \neg FFAt(\{tx, ty\}, T))$
$L^{\lceil}tx\, L^{\ulcorner}ty(At(\{tx, ty\}, k) \rightarrow \neg PPAt(\{tx, ty\}, T))$

Linearity is another such property of time, but unlike the above cases it is essentially a point property; that is, the axiom does not apply to intervals in general, but only to point-intervals. The appropriate first order formulation is $\forall x \forall y(x < y \vee y < x \vee x = y)$, where the quantifiers are assumed to range just over point intervals. This is captured by the following IQ-C axiom; note that the antecedent is true only for point intervals.

26) $L^{\lceil}txAt(\{tx, tx\}, T) \rightarrow (At(\{t, t\}, T) \vee PAt(\{t, t\}, T) \vee FAt(\{t, t\}, T))$

It is of course obvious that IQ-C can express everything expressible with the Priorean operators, including such second order properties as the continuity of time and well-foundedness.[2]

Since IQ-C is basically an interval logic, it is important to note that it can express interval properties such as left and right monotonicity, which are specified respectively in the following first-order formulas.

27) $\forall x1 \forall x2 \forall y1 \forall y2 \forall z1 \forall z2(\{x1, x2\} \ll \{y1, y2\} \;\&\; \{z1, z2\} \subseteq \{x1, x2\} \rightarrow z2 < y1)$
$\forall x1 \forall x2 \forall y1 \forall y2 \forall z1 \forall z2(\{x1, x2\} \ll \{y1, y2\} \;\&\; \{z1, z2\} \subseteq \{y1, y2\} \rightarrow x2 < z1)$

Left monotonicity is captured by these two IQ-C schemas, where φ is any formula.

28 $F\varphi \rightarrow AhF\varphi$

---

2 It is perhaps worth mentioning that IQ-C does not have full first-order expressiveness, since disconnected flows of time are admitted within the point structure. As a result, we cannot always assert truly In IQ-C that φ is true somewhere, when it is. This occurs if φ is true at some time contained in a disconnected flow of time, i. e. in a flow of time disconnected from the time of evaluation (assertion).

$P\varphi \rightarrow AhP\varphi$

The key here is the special IQ-C operator *Ah*. Right monotonicity is expressed by two slightly different schemas.[3]

29) $FAs\varphi \rightarrow F\varphi$
$FAs\varphi \rightarrow P\varphi$

Left and right monotonicity are conditions which are normally imposed on any admissible interval structure; that is, they are properties which are assumed to hold in the minimal interval logic. Another property, called convexity, is also usually taken to be among those which hold in the minimal interval logic. For the record this property is defined in this way.

30) $\forall x1 \forall x2 \forall y1 \forall y2 \forall z1 \forall z2((\{y1, y2\} \ll \{z1, z2\} \,\&\, \{y1, y2\} \subseteq \{x1, x2\}) \rightarrow$
$x2 < z1 \vee \exists u1 \exists u2(\{u1, u2\} \subseteq \{z1, z2\} \,\&\, \{u1, u2\} \subseteq \{x1, x2\}))$

Unlike some interval logics, convexity does not generally hold in IQ-C and hence, not in the minimal system. It is straightforward to construct an IQ-C formula which expresses convexity, but such a formula is not true in all the "minimal" models.

5 A Resolution Proof Method for IQ-C

Baccus et al [92] suggest that temporal reasoning is best treated within a first order theory because first order proof mechanization is well developed. While this is certainly the dominant approach to temporal reasoning, and is effectively followed even in modal treatments [Ohlbach 88], we shall take another approach. As we noted above, IQ-C (like other modal temporal languages) can express properties of time which cannot be formulated in first order logic. We should like to bring the corresponding logics within the proof mechanization framework. We should also like to show how IQ-C logics can be naturally assimilated within the strategy of resolution theorem proving. It is well known that modal logics present certain awkward problems for modal theorem proving, some of which are particular to the resolution approach. IQ-C can circumvent these in a clear and straightforward way.

The step towards obtaining a resolution system is to show that every IQ-C formula is equivalent to a formula in negation normal form.

---

3 This is not to suggest there is a "left/right" duality between *Ah* and *As*. These two operators are indeed duals of each other, but this is independent of left and right monotonicity.

31) **Definition:** An IQ-C formula is in negation normal form (NNF) iff all the negation signs in the formula are in front of either an atomic formula or a formula of the form $At(\{t_1, t_2\}, \top)$.

Theorem: Every IQ-C formula is equivalent to an IQ-C in NNF.

Since IQ-C is classical, the usual equivalences hold, including De Morgan's laws, the double negation rule and the interdefinability of $\forall$ and $\exists$ using negation. It is also immediately obvious that the following equivalences hold.

32)
$$\neg F_{type}\sigma \equiv G_{type}\neg\sigma \qquad \neg G_{type}\sigma \equiv F_{type}\neg\sigma$$
$$\neg P_{type}\sigma \equiv H_{type}\neg\sigma \qquad \neg H_{type}\sigma \equiv P_{type}\neg\sigma$$
$$\neg As_{type}\sigma \equiv Ah_{type}\neg\sigma \qquad \neg Ah_{type}\sigma \equiv As_{type}\neg\sigma$$
$$\neg L^{l}tx\sigma \equiv L^{l}tx\neg\sigma \qquad \neg L^{r}tx\sigma \equiv L^{r}tx\neg\sigma$$

Recall that "type" has three instantiations, viz. i, p and ip representing respectively quantification over non-point intervals, point intervals and arbitrary intervals. There is only one special case we have to consider, viz. $\neg At(\{t_1, t_2\}, \sigma)$. This is treated as follows.

33) $$\neg At(\{t_1, t_2\}, \sigma) \equiv \neg At(\{t_1, t_2\}, \top) \vee At(\{t_1, t_2\}, \neg\sigma)$$

Using (33) together with the other equivalences, we can find for any IQ-C formula an equivalent formula in NNF. In the following sections we shall consider just the NNF fragment of IQ-C. In particular, skolemization will be defined only with respect to this fragment.

5.1 Skolemization

It is well known that skolemization presents a problem for modal systems. In general, existential quantifiers cannot be moved outside the scope of universal modal operators, which in IQ-C are the operators G, H and Ah. To solve this problem we extend a scheme for indexing skolem terms, which was first adumbrated in Jiang [86] and subsequently developed in Jiang [90].[4] The basic idea is to attach to each skolem term substituted an integer name which records the number of modal operators (other than At)within whose scope the term falls. Using this device, we can skolemize the

---

4 Jiang [90] sketches the history of the idea and some related work. Among those cited are McCarthy [79], Barden [86], Konolige [86], Jiang [86, 88], Wallen [87], Jackson & Reichgelt [87], Wilks & Ballim [87], de la Quintana [88]. Full references can be found in Jiang [90].

existential quantifiers in the formula as if the formula were in prenex normal form. For example, consider the formula $\forall xG\exists yP^{2}(x,y)$, where x and y are non-temporal variables. The skolem term used to skolemize the existential quantifier $\exists y$ is determined in the normal way; in this case it is the term $f(x)$ since y falls within the scope of the universal quantifier $\forall x$. When this is substituted, the term is indexed with the integer name "1", viz. as $f(x)^{1}$, indicating that it falls within the scope of just one modal operator, viz. G. The resulting formula is $\forall xGP^{2}(x, f(x)^{1})$. In contrast, the formula $\forall x\exists yGP^{2}(x, y)$ is skolemized as $\forall xGP^{2}(x, f(x)^{0})$; the index "0" signifies that the skolem term does not fall within the scope of any modal operator.

For the sake of semantic simplicity we assume a constant domain semantics for the first-order quantifiers; that is, the domain of the quantifiers remains the same irrespective of the interval of evaluation. Thus the formula $G\forall xP^{2}(x, f(x)^{1})$ is equivalent to the formula $\forall xGP^{2}(x, f(x)^{1})$, and similarly for the formulas $F\forall xP^{2}(x, f(x)^{1})$ and $\forall xFP^{2}(x, f(x)^{1})$. We could, however, allow the domain of the quantifiers to vary from interval to interval. This would have the benefit of simplifying the treatment of skolemization (given below), but at the expense of complicating the logic.

We apply the same basic indexing strategy to skolemize the occurrences of the substitution operators L^{ℓ} and L^{r}, except that in this case the skolem terms will always be indexed temporal variables. There is no need to introduce any new skolem constants, as there is for first order quantification, since 'quantification' over time is performed only by modal operators. There is, however, an added dimension of complexity. Since the substitution operators are themselves indexed by 'ℓ' and 'r', the skolem variables will have to be similarly indexed to reflect which operator binds the variable. Let us consider a case of skolemization involving three occurrences of the substitution operators, viz. the formula $\forall xFL^{\ell}txL^{r}tyHL^{\ell}tzP^{3}(x, c\{tx, ty\}, b\{tz, tz\})$, where P^{3} is a three-place predicate and the expressions $c\{tx, ty\}$ and $b\{tz, tz\}$ are complex terms. Note that the subformula $L^{\ell}txL^{r}tyHL^{\ell}tzP^{3}(x, c\{tx, ty\}, b\{tz, tz\})$ falls within the scope of just one modal operator, viz. F. To skolemize the operator $L^{\ell}tx$ the indexing convention requires that the skolem term have a double index, viz. the number 1 (to record that the term falls within the scope of one modal operator), and 'ℓ' to indicate that the operator removed is itself indexed by "ℓ". Here the requisite skolem term is $tx^{1,\ell}$; note that the indexed variable is the same as the variable in the operator skolemized. Since the next substitution operator $L^{r}ty$ also falls only within the scope of F, it is skolemized using the variable $ty^{1,r}$; note that 'r' appears in the second coordinate of the index. The final operator $L^{\ell}tz$ occurs within the scope of both F and H, and is accordingly skolemized in terms of the variable $tz^{2,\ell}$. As a result, the given formula $\forall xFL^{\ell}txL^{r}tyHL^{\ell}tzP^{3}(x, c\{tx, ty\}, b\{tz, tz\})$ is fully skolemized as $\forall xFHP^{3}(x, c\{tx^{1,\ell}, ty^{1,r}\}, b\{tz^{2,\ell}, tz^{2,\ell}\})$. It should perhaps be mentioned that there is no need to take account of the universal quantifier $\forall x$ in the skolemization process since temporal variables are independent of non-temporal quantifiers.

We now define the skolemization of a NNF formula σ, which is denoted as $SK_n(\sigma)$. Here the subscript n records the number of modal operators which have scope over σ.

34) **Definition:** To skolemize σ, we first initialize to $SK_0(\sigma)$, and apply the following inductive definition. For convenience we specify more cases than appear in the inductive definition of a formula, which is given above in (9). The following definition applies to **constant domain logics** only. For variable domain logics it is necessary to make a small adjustment, which is indicated in a footnote below.

- If φ is an atomic formula or its negation, $SK_n(\varphi)$ is φ;
- If φ is of the form $\neg At(\{t_1, t_2\}, T)$, $SK_n(\varphi)$ is φ;
- If φ is of the form $(\alpha \vee \beta)$, $SK_n(\varphi)$ is $(SK_n(\alpha) \vee SK_n(\beta))$;
- If φ is of the form $(\alpha \;\&\; \beta)$, $SK_n(\varphi)$ is $(SK_n(\alpha) \;\&\; SK_n(\beta))$;
- If φ is of the form $\Delta\psi$, $SK_n(\varphi)$ is $\Delta SK_{n+1}(\psi)$, where Δ is F, P, G, H, As or Ah;
- If φ is of the form $At(\{t_1, t_2\}, \psi)$, $SK_n(\varphi)$ is $At(\{t_1, t_2\}, SK_n(\psi))$;
- If φ is of the form $\forall x\psi$, $SK_n(\varphi)$ is $\forall x SK_n(\psi)$; [5]
- If φ is of the form $\exists x\psi$, $SK_n(\varphi)$ is $SK_n(\psi[f(y_1, \ldots, y_k)^n/x])$, where f is a new non-temporal skolem function and $y_1, \ldots, y_k$ are the free non-temporal variables in ψ other than x;
  if ψ has no free variables other than x, $SK_n(\varphi)$ is $SK_n(\psi[c^n/x])$, where c is a new non-temporal skolem constant;[6]
- If φ is of the form $L^l tx\psi$, $SK_n(\varphi)$ is $SK_n(\psi[tx^{n,l}/tx]$, where tx is a temporal variable;
  if φ is of the form $L^r tx\psi$, $SK_n(\varphi)$ is $SK_n(\psi[tx^{n,r}/tx]$, where tx is a temporal variable.

Theorem: An IQ-C formula is satisfiable iff its skolemization is satisfiable.

To prove this theorem we must first specify the role of the numerical indices on the skolem terms. They serve only one function, viz. to record the scope of skolem terms

---

5 For variable domain logics the clause involving the universal quantifier should read as follows:
- If φ is of the form $\forall x\psi$, $SK_n(\varphi)$ is $SK_n(\psi[x^n/x])$.

Note that this clause generates skolem variables indexed with integer names. Skolemization for constant domain logics never yields skolem variables indexed with integer names.

6 Note that $\psi[f(y1, \ldots, yk)^n/x]$ is the formula which is just like ψ except that the term $f(y1, \ldots, yk)^n$ is substituted for every free occurrence of x in ψ.

with respect to the modal operators in the formula. As a result, the interpretation of skolem terms must be treated in a special way.

To specify the general procedure for treating skolem terms in a formula σ, we must first indicate how 0-indexed terms are interpreted. There are two cases to consider, viz. temporal and non-temporal terms, and there are two points to emphasize. First, skolemization yields no non-temporal variables which are indexed with integer names. Second, in the case of temporal terms skolemization gives indices involving integer names only to temporal variables. To capture both cases we require two definitions.

Let $\sigma(t0_1, \ldots, t0_n)$ be the formula σ whose 0-indexed non-temporal skolem terms are $t0_1, \ldots, t0_n$. Given the method of constructing $t0_1, \ldots, t0_n$, we assume that each t_i ($1 \leq i \leq n$) in σ, i.e. each $t0_i$ with the 0-index removed, has been added to the language of σ. On the assumption that each such t_i has also been assigned an interpretation in the model **M**, we can define the conditions under which $\sigma(t0_1, \ldots, t0_n)$ is true in **M** under an assignment g for an interval {s, e}.

35) **M**, g, {s, e} $\models \sigma(t0_1, \ldots, t0_n)$ iff **M***, g, {s, e} $\models \sigma(t1\{s', e'\}, \ldots, tn\{s', e'\})$, where s' and e' are new temporal constants added to the language and **M*** is exactly like **M** except $//s'//^{\beta}$ is s and $//e'//^{\beta}$ is e.

Let us illustrate (35) since it is both unusal and essential. Note that the interval term {s', e'} has been added as an index on each term t_i, and by construction t_i itself will not already have an interval index. The import of (35) emerges clearly in this formula $GP^1(c0)$.

36) **M**, g, {s, e} $\models GP^1(c0)$ iff there is an **M*** which is exactly like **M** except that $//s'//^{\beta}$ is s and $//e'//^{\beta}$ is e, and **M*** g, {s, e} $\models GP^1(c\{s', e'\})$; and **M***, g, {s, e} $\models GP^1(c\{s', e'\})$ iff for all {s*, e*} such that {s, e} $\ll$ {s*, e*} $\Phi(P^1)$\{s*, e*\}$(//c//^{\beta}\{//s'//^{\beta}, //e'//^{\beta}\})$.

Note that the term c is interpreted with respect to the interval of evaluation {s, e}, and not the interval {s*, e*}. This allows just the sort of flexibility required to handle skolem terms in a temporal logic.

A similar, but slightly different, clause specifies the interpretation of 0-indexed temporal terms. Recall that the skolemization process, specified in (34), introduces only temporal variables which are numerically indexed; no constant terms are required. But the indices are, as we illustrated earlier, slightly more complex; for example, the skolem terms are either of the form $tx^{i,l}$ or $tx^{i,r}$, where i is the numerical coordinate. Intuitively the coordinate 'l' is used to indicate that the assignment to the variable tx is to be the left coordinate of the evaluation interval, and 'r' that it is the right coordinate. We shall refer to 'l' and 'r' arbitrarily as d. Consider the formula $\sigma(tx^{0,d_1}, \ldots, tx^{0,d_n})$, whose 0-indexed skolem variables are $tx^{0,d_1}, \ldots, tx^{0,d_n}$, with each occurrence of d_i being either 'l' or 'r'.

37) $\mathbf{M}, g, \{s, e\} \models \sigma(tx^{0,d_1}, \ldots, tx^{0,d_n}),)$ iff $\mathbf{M}, g^*, \{s, e\} \models \sigma(tx_1, \ldots, tx_n)$, where g^* is exactly like g except that for each tx_i $(1 \leq i \leq n)$ $g^*(tx_i)$ is s if d in tx^{0,d_i} is 'l' and e if d is 'r'.[7]

Again an example might be helpful. Take the formula $At(\{tx^{0,r}, ty^{0,l}\}, T)$; we have deliberately reversed 'l' and 'r' to illustrate how they work.

38) $\mathbf{M}, g, \{s, e\} \models At(\{tx^{0,r}, ty^{0,l}\}, T)$ iff $\mathbf{M}, g^*, \{s, e\} \models At(\{tx, ty\}, T)$, where g^* is exactly like g except $g^*(tx)$ is e and $g^*(ty)$ is s.

We are now in a position to extend the truth definition to skolemized formulas. Where φ is any formula of the language (including skolemized formulas), we say that the formula φ^{dec} is exactly like φ except that all the integer names on the skolem terms in φ are 'decremented' by one.

39) Where σ is any non-skolemized formula, definition (15) specifies $\mathbf{M}, g, \{s, e\} \models \sigma$. We now extend the definition to cover formulas containing skolem terms; (35) and (37) are repeated as the first two clauses.

- If σ contains n 0-indexed non-temporal skolem terms $t^0{}_1, \ldots, t^0{}_n$, $\mathbf{M}, g, \{s, e\} \models \sigma$ iff $\mathbf{M}^*, g, \{s, e\} \models \sigma(t1\{s', e'\}, \ldots, tn\{s', e'\})$, where s' and e' are new temporal constants added to the language and $\mathbf{M}^*$ is exactly like $\mathbf{M}$ except that $/\!/s'/\!/^{\mathcal{B}}$ is s and $/\!/e'/\!/^{\mathcal{B}}$ is e.
- If σ contains n zero indexed temporal skolem terms $tx^{0,d_1}, \ldots, tx^{0,d_n}$, $\mathbf{M}, g, \{s, e\} \models \sigma$ iff $\mathbf{M}, g^*, \{s, e\} \models \sigma(tx_1, \ldots, tx_n)$, where g^* is exactly like g except that for each tx_i $(1 \leq i \leq n)$ $g^*(tx_i)$ is s if d in tx^{0,d_i} is 'l' and e if d is "r".

---

7 To accommodate variable domain logics where indexed non-temporal variables will occur, it is necessary to add a further clause. Let $\sigma(x^0{}_1, \ldots, x^0{}_n)$ be the formula 0-indexed non-temporal variables are $x^0{}_1, \ldots, x^0{}_n$.

- $\mathbf{M}, g, \{s, e\} \models \sigma(x^0{}_1, \ldots, x^0{}_n)$ iff $\mathbf{M}, g^*, \{s, e\} \models \sigma(x_1, \ldots, x_n)$, where g^* is exactly like g except that for each x_i $(1 \leq i \leq n)$ $g^*(x_i)$ is an element in the domain associated with the interval $\{s,e\}$.

- If σ is of the form $As_{type}\varphi$ and contains no zero indexed skolem terms, $M, g, \{s, e\} \models As_{type}\varphi$ iff there is a *type-subinterval* $\{s^*, e^*\}$ of $\{s, e\}$, such that $M, g, \{s^*, e^*\} \models \varphi^{dec}$;
- Similar clauses hold for each of the other modal operators. That is, if σ is of the form $Ah_{type}\varphi$, $F_{type}\varphi$, $P_{type}\varphi$, $G_{type}\varphi$, or $H_{type}\varphi$, and contains no 0-indexed skolem terms, then the corresponding clause of (15) applies with φ^{dec} occurring in the definiens.
- All other clauses of (15) remain the same.

The proof of Theorem (34), viz. that every IQ-C formula is satisfiable iff its skolemization is, proceeds in the normal way.

5.2 Clausal Form

The next step is to specify when an IQ-C formula is in clausal form.

40) **Definition:** Let σ be a skolemized IQ-C formula. We say that σ is in clausal form iff it is a disjunction where each disjunct is either a literal (a positive or negative atomic formula), $\neg At(t, T)$ or a formula of the form $At(t, \varphi)$ or $\Delta\varphi$, where φ is in clausal form and Δ is a modal operator.

Theorem: Every skolemized IQ-C formula σ can be transformed into a formula $C(\sigma)$ which is a conjunction of formulas in clausal form such that σ is satisfiable iff $C(\sigma)$ is satisfiable.

The proof of theorem (40) is quite straightforward. As we mentioned above, the usual classical equivalences hold in IQ-C. In addition, the following hold for any IQ-C formulas φ and ψ.

41)
- $At(\{t_1, t_2\}, (\varphi \ \& \ \psi)) \equiv (At(\{t_1, t_2\}, \varphi) \ \& \ At(\{t_1, t_2\}, \psi))$;
- Where Δ is either *G, H, or Ah,*
  $\Delta_{type}(\varphi \ \& \ \psi) \equiv (\Delta_{type}\varphi \ \& \ \Delta_{type}\psi)$;
- Where Γ is either *F, P or As,*
  $\Gamma_{type}(\varphi \vee \psi) \equiv (\Gamma_{type}\varphi \vee \Gamma_{type}\psi)$,
- $\Gamma_{type}(At(\{t_1, t_2\}, \varphi) \ \& \ At(\{t_1, t_2\}, \psi)) \equiv$
  $(\Gamma_{type}At(\{t_1, t_2\}, \varphi) \ \& \ \Gamma_{type}At(\{t_1, t_2\}, \psi))$,
  where t_1 *and* t_2 are any temporal terms.

There is only one type of case which requires special treatment. Consider the following formula, where Γ is either *F, P or As,* and φ and ψ are **atomic** formulas.

42) $\Gamma_{type}(\varphi \ \& \ \psi)$

It is obvious that (42) is not equivalent to this formula.

43) $\Gamma_{type}\varphi \ \& \ \Gamma_{type}\psi$

However, it can be immediately verified that (42) is equivalent to the following.

44) $\Gamma_{type}L^{\ell}tx L^{r}ty At(\{tx, ty\}, (\varphi \ \& \ \psi))$

Skolemizing the substitution operators yields this formula,

45) $\Gamma_{type}At(\{tx^{1,\ell}, ty^{1,r}\}, (\varphi \ \& \ \psi))$

which is by (41) equivalent to the following.

46) $\Gamma_{type}At(\{tx^{1,\ell}, ty^{1,r}\}, \varphi) \ \& \ \Gamma_{type}At(\{tx^{1,\ell}, ty^{1,r}\}, \psi)$

To generalize the exemplified strategy, suppose that we wish to translate a skolemized formula of the form $\Gamma_{type}(\varphi \ \& \ \psi)$ into clausal form, where φ and ψ are now any formulas.

47) If φ is of the form $At(\{tx^{i,\ell}, ty^{i,r}\}, \alpha)$ and ψ of the form $At(\{tx^{i,\ell}, ty^{i,r}\}, \beta)$,
- $\Gamma_{type}(\varphi \ \& \ \psi)$ translates to
  $(\Gamma_{type}At(\{tx^{i,\ell}, ty^{i,r}\}, \alpha) \ \& \ \Gamma_{type}At(\{tx^{i,\ell}, ty^{i,r}\}, \beta))$;

Otherwise,
- $\Gamma_{type}(\varphi \ \& \ \psi)$ translates to $\Gamma_{type}L^{\ell}tx L^{r}ty At(\{tx, ty\}, (\varphi \ \& \ \psi))$, which is then skolemized to $\Gamma_{type}At(\{tx^{i,\ell}, ty^{i,r}\}, (\varphi \ \& \ \psi))$, where i records the number of modal operators with scope over $At(\{tx^{i,\ell}, ty^{i,r}\}, (\varphi \ \& \ \psi))$.

Although we shall not prove the result, it should be intuitively clear that any skolemized formula can be translated into a formula in clausal form such that the skolemized formula is satisfiable iff its clausal form translation is satisfiable.

5.3 Resolution Rules

We are now ready to outline a modal resolution proof system for the clausal form fragment of IQ-C. The immediate aim is to lay the foundations of an approach to modal resolution which can cover a comprehensive range of temporal logics, including those which cannot be translated into first order logic. Unfortunately, we cannot here develop and explore the various logics which fall within the framework; this will have to be left to another occasion [Jiang & Richards 92]. Moreover, we shall not attempt to provide a fully precise specification of the proof system. We shall instead present the basic rules of the system, which are intended to specify the minimal temporal logic of intervals; and we shall define the unification procedures which are appropriate to constant domain logics.

It is perhaps worth emphasizing that since IQ-C is an interval-based system, the resolution rules must take account of this. Here the typing of modal operators is relevant. Although we shall indicate appropriate typing restrictions in the rules, we shall not attempt to explicate their significance. The broad task is to draft the basic system in some detail, with a view to identifying the dimensions of temporal reasoning which we intend to be integrate into IQ-C. Further elaboration will be required to establish that the integration has actually been achieved.

We turn first to unification. The essential step is to extend unification to cover indexed terms. There are two types of indices to be considered in IQ-C, viz. interval indices as in the expression$c[s, e]$ and indices involving integer-names which occur in skolem terms. To facilitate the general account of unification we shall adopt a strategy for representing all term in the language. Here the language is the skolemized clausal form fragment of IQ-C. We define the representation of terms in two stages, first for temporal terms and then for non-temporal terms.

48) Representation of **temporal terms**

- For a skolem variable of the form $tx^{n,d}$, where n is an integer name and$d$ is either 'l' or 'r', $REP[tx^{n,d}] = (tx, (n, d))$.
- For a constant of the form tc, $REP[tc] = (tc, \_)$.
  NB Here "_" is to be read like a dummy variable in Prolog.
- For a term of the form $tf^m(t_1, \dots, t_m)$, where $t_1, \dots, t_m$ are temporal terms, $REP[tf^m(t_1, \dots, t_m)] = (tf^n(REP[t_1], \dots, REP[t_m]), \_)$.

These are the only types of temporal terms which appear in the given fragment of IQ-C.

49) Representation of **non-temporal terms**

- For a variable of the form x,
  $REP[x] = (x, \_)$.

- For a skolem variable of the form x^n, where n is an integer name,
  $REP[x^n] = (x, n)$.[9]
- For a constant of the form c,
  $REP[c] = (c, \_)$.
- For a constant of the form $c\{t1, t2\}$, where $t1$ and $t2$ are temporal terms,
  $REP[c\{t1, t2\}] = (c\{t1, t2\}, \_)$.
- For a skolem constant of the form c^n, where n is an integer name,
  $REP[c^n] = (c, n)$.
- For a term of the form $f^m(nt_1, \dots, nt_m)$, where $nt_1, \dots, nt_m$ are non-temporal terms,
  $REP[f^m(nt_1, \dots, nt_m)] = (f^m(REP[nt_1], \dots, REP[nt_m]), \_)$.
- For a term of the form $f^m(nt_1, \dots, nt_m)^n$, where n is an integer name and $nt_1, \dots, nt_m$ are non-temporal terms,
  $REP[f^m(nt_1, \dots, nt_m)] = (f^m(REP[nt_1], \dots, REP[nt_m]), n)$.

These are the only types of non-temporal terms which appear in the given fragment of IQ-C.

We can now define unification for constant domain logics. Although we shall not treat variable domain logics, it should perhaps be noted that the skolemization procedure for such logics differs slightly from that for constant domain logics.[10]

50) **Unification for constant domain logics**
Note that skolemization for constant domain logics yields no non-temporal variables indexed with integer names. Here two terms are said to unify provided that each of the coördinates in their representation unify in the standard sense.
NB The dummny variable, like any variable, is assumed to unify with anything.

Consider these two terms, $c\{s, e\}$ and $c\{tx^{0,\ell}, e\}$. They are represented respectively as $(c\{(s,\_), (e,\_)\}, \_)$ and $(c\{(tx, (0,\ell)), (e,\_)\}, \_)$. By definition (50) these representations can be seen to unify. Note, in addition, that the representation of the non-temporal variable x, viz. $(x, \_)$, also unifies with $(c\{(s,\_), (e,\_)\}, \_)$.

For variable domain logics all non-temporal variables will be indexed with integer-name indices.[11] This complicates the unification procedure somewhat. We shall develop this in detail in Jiang & Richards [92].

---

9 This clause actually not required for the fragment of IQ-C used in constant domain logics. Recall that the skolemization procedure never yields skolem variables indexed with integer names.

10 See definition (34).

11 See the clause involving the universal quantifier in definition (34).

For the sake of brevity, we shall sometimes abuse notation, although hopefully not at the cost of clarity. We shall sketch the rules by inductively defining $Res(\varphi, \psi)\theta$, which is understood as referring to the resolvent of φ and ψ under the unification θ. In general, where σ is any clause, we read $(\sigma)\theta$ as the instantiation of σ by θ.

In the following rules we shall use φ^{inc} to denote the formula which is just like φ except that all the integer names on the skolem terms (both temporal and non-temporal) are 'incremented' by one. Conversely, φ^{dec} is used to refer to the formula which is like φ except that all the integer names on the skolem terms are 'decremented' by one.

51) **Resolution Rules**

1 Base clause
If φ is the literal $P^n(t_1, \ldots, t_n)$ and ψ is the literal $\neg P^n(s_1, \ldots, s_n)$,
$Res[\varphi, \psi]\theta = \neg T$, if $t_1, \ldots, t_n$ unifies with $s_1, \ldots, s_n$ under θ.
($\neg T$ is henceforth abbreviated as $\bot$.)

2 $Res[(\varphi \vee \alpha), (\psi \vee \beta)]\theta = Res[\alpha, \beta]\theta \vee (\varphi \vee \psi)\theta$, if α and β are disjuncts.
NB A disjunct is either a literal, a formula preceded by a modal operator, a formula of the form $At(\{t_1, t_2\}, \varphi)$ or a formula of the form $\neg At(\{t_1, t_2\}, T)$.

3 Factorization
If $Res[\alpha, \neg\beta]\theta' = \bot$,
$Res[(\varphi \vee \alpha \vee \beta), \psi]\theta = Res[(\varphi \vee \alpha)\theta', \psi]\theta''$,
where $\theta = \theta' + \theta''$.

4 $Res[At(\{t_1, t_2\}, \varphi), At(\{t_1, t_2\}, \psi)]\theta = At(t_1, t_2\}, Res[\varphi, \psi]\theta.$

5 $Res[At(\{t_1, t_2\}, \varphi), \psi]\theta = Res[As(\{t_1, t_2\}, \varphi), \psi]\theta.$

6 $Res[At(\{t_1, t_2\}, \varphi), \psi]\theta = At(\{t_1, t_2\}, Res[\varphi, \psi]\theta.$

7 $Res[(At(\{t_1, t_2\}, \varphi) \vee \psi), \alpha]\theta = (At(\{t_1, t_2\}, (\psi \vee Res[\varphi, \alpha]\theta)))\theta.$

8 $Res[At(\{t_1, t_2\}, \varphi), \neg At(\{t_1, t_2\}, T)]\theta = \bot.$

9 $Res[At(\{t_1, t_2\}, T), Ahip\varphi]\theta = At(\{t_1, t_2\}, \varphi^{dec}).$

10 $Res[At(\{t_1, t_2\}, \varphi), \psi]\theta = At(\{t_1, t_2\}, Res[As\varphi_i^{inc}, \psi]\theta).$

11 $Res[At(\{t_1, t_2\}, At(\{t_1, t_2\}, \varphi)), \psi]\theta = Res[At(\{t_1, t_2\}, \varphi), \psi]\theta.$

12 $Res[At(\{t_1, t_2\}, At(\{t_3, t_4\}, \varphi)), \psi]\theta =$
$Res[(At(\{t_1, t_2\}, At(\{t_3, t_4\}, \varphi))\theta', \psi]\theta'',$
where θ' is the unification between $\{t_1, t_2\}$ and $\{t_3, t_4\}$ and
$\theta = \theta' + \theta''$.

13 $Res[At(\{t_1, t_2\}, At(\{t_3, t_4\}, \varphi)), \psi]\theta =$
$Res[At\{t_3, t_4\}, At(\{t_1, t_2\}, \varphi)), \psi]\theta.$

14 If Ω^1 and Ω^2 are either *Ah* or *As*,
$Res[At(\{t, t\}, (\varphi \vee \Omega^1{}_{type}\psi)), \alpha]\theta =$
$Res[At(\{t, t\}, (\varphi \vee \Omega^2{}_{type}\psi)), \alpha]\theta.$

15 If Ω is either *Ah* or *As*,
$Res[At(\{t, t\}, (\varphi \vee At(\{t, t\}, \psi)]\theta =$
$Res[At(\{t, t\}, (\varphi \vee \Omega_{type}\psi^{inc})), \psi]\theta.$

16 If Γ and M are pairwise instantiated as $<G, F>$, $<G, G>$, $<H, P>$, $<H, H>$,
$<Ah, As>$ *or* $<Ah, Ah>$,
$Res[\Gamma_{type1}\varphi, M_{type2}\psi]\theta = M_{type2}Res[\varphi, \psi]\theta,$
where $type2 \leq type1$.
NB The order of types is as follows: $p < ip$ and $i < ip$.

17 If E is either *F*, *P or As*,
$Res[E_{type}(At(\{t_1, t_2\}, \varphi) \vee \psi), E_{type}(At(\{t_1, t_2\}, \alpha) \vee \beta)]\theta =$
$E_{type}At(\{t_1, t_2\}, Res[\varphi, \alpha]\theta) \vee (E_{type}\psi \vee E_{type}\beta)\theta.$

18 If Ω is either *Ah* or *As*,
$Res[Ah_{type1}\varphi, \Omega_{type2}\psi]\theta = \Omega_{type2}Res[As_{type1}\varphi^{inc}, \psi]\theta,$
where $type2 \leq type1$.

19 If Π is either *G* or *F*,
$Res[\varphi, \Pi_{type}\psi]\theta = \Pi_{type}Res[P_{ip}(\varphi^{inc})^{inc}, \psi^{dec}]\theta,$

20 If Ξ is either *H* or *P*,
$Res[\varphi, \Xi_{type}\psi]\theta = \Xi_{type}Res[F_{ip}\varphi^{inc})^{inc}, \psi]\theta,$

21 If Π is either G or F, Ω either Ah or As,
$Res[G_{type1}\varphi, \Pi_{type2}\Omega_{type3}\psi]\theta = \Pi_{type2}Res[Ah_{type1}\varphi^{inc}, \Omega_{type3}\psi]\theta$,
where $type2 \leq type1$ and $type\ 3 \leq type2$.

22 If Ξ is either H or P, Ω either Ah or As,
$Res[H_{type1}\varphi, \Xi_{type2}\Omega_{type3}\psi]\theta = \Xi_{type2}Res[Ah_{type1}\varphi^{inc}, \Omega_{type3}\psi]\theta$,
where $type2 \leq type1$ and$type\ 3 \leq type2$.

23 There are also two control rules.
$Res[\varphi, \psi]\theta = Res[\psi, \varphi]\theta$
$Res[\varphi, Res[\psi, \varphi]\theta]\theta = Res[\varphi, \psi]\theta$

This completes the set of basic resolution rules, which determines the minimal temporal logic. To distinguish other temporal logics we shall simply add appropriate rules. For example, to capture the transitivity of time, we add the following rule.

52) **Transitivity**

24 If Γ and M are instantiated pairwise as either $<G, F>$, $<G, G>$, $<H, P>$, $<H, H>$, $<Ah, As>$ or $<Ah, Ah>$,
$Res[\Gamma_{type1}\varphi, M_{type2}\psi]\theta = M_{type2}Res[\Gamma_{type1}\varphi^{inc}, \psi]\theta$,
where $type2 \leq types\ 1$.

In addition to the resolution rules, there are the following reduction rules.

53) **Reduction rules**

25 $\top \vee \varphi = \top$

26 $\bot \vee \varphi = \varphi$

27 $M_{type}\top = \top$
where M is either G, F, H, P, Ah or As.

28 $E_{type}\bot = \bot$
where E is either F, P or As.

29 $At(\{t_1, t_2\}, \top) = \top$

30 $At(\{t_1, t_2\}, \bot) = \bot$

31 $Ah_{type}\bot = \bot$
where $type$ is either ip or p.

There is also one special reduction rule which is applicable only in **serial** structures.

32 $\Gamma_{type}\bot = \bot$

where Γ is G or H.

Let us now illustrate the rules with a couple of examples. We shall consider only propositional cases, since examples involving unification would add a dimension of 'tedious' detail. To show whether a formula σ is a theorem, we first take its negation $\neg\sigma$, then skolemize this and translate the result into a conjunction of formulas in clausal form. From the set of conjuncts (of clauses), we then attempt to derive $\bot$ using the resolution and reduction rules. Consider the IQ-C formula $FFH\varphi \rightarrow F\varphi$, where φ is an atomic formula. Note that $\neg FFH\varphi \rightarrow F\varphi$ is equivalent to $(FFH\varphi \;\&\; G\neg\varphi)$, which is a conjunction of formulas in clausal form.

54) To show that $\bot$ can be derived from $\{(FFH\varphi,\; G\neg\varphi\}$.

•	$Res[FFH\varphi, G\neg\varphi]$	
•	$FRes[G\neg\varphi, FFH\varphi]$	by rule 23
•	$FRes[\neg\varphi, FH\varphi]$	by rule 16
•	$FFRes[P\neg\varphi, H\varphi]$	by rule 19
•	$FFRes[H\varphi, P\neg\varphi]$	by rule 23
•	$FFPRes[\varphi, \neg\varphi]$	by rule 16
•	$FFP\bot$	by rule 1
•	$\bot$	by three uses of rule 28

Let us take another example, viz. $((F\varphi \vee P\varphi \vee \varphi) \rightarrow FP\varphi)$. This formula is valid in the class of point structures where time is serial and transitive; time is said to be serial (in the future) if for all points of time there is a point in the future of it. This formula cannot be deduced in the minimal system, although it can if we add the transivity rule (24) and the serial rule (32). Using the same strategy exemplfied above, the task is,

55) To show that $\bot$ can be derived from $\{(F\varphi \vee P\varphi \vee \varphi),\; GH\neg\varphi\}$.

i)	$(F\varphi \vee P\varphi \vee \varphi)$	
ii)	$GH\neg\varphi$	
iii)	$Res[(F\varphi \vee P\varphi \vee \varphi), GH\neg\varphi]$	
iv)	$(F\varphi \vee P\varphi \vee Res[\varphi, GH\neg\varphi])$	by rule 2
v)	$(F\varphi \vee P\varphi \vee GRes[P\varphi, H\neg\varphi])$	by rule 19
vi)	$(F\varphi \vee P\varphi \vee G\bot)$	by rule 16
vii)	$(F\varphi \vee P\varphi)$	by rule 32 (serial rule)

viii)	$Res[GH\neg\varphi, (F\varphi \vee P\varphi)]$	by resolution on (ii) and (vii)
ix)	$(F\varphi \vee Res[GH\neg\varphi, P\varphi])$	by rule 2
x)	$(F\varphi \vee GRes[H\neg\varphi, PP\varphi])$	by rule 19
xi)	$(F\varphi \vee GPRes[H\neg\varphi, P\varphi])$	by rule 24
xii)	$(F\varphi \vee GPP\bot)$	by rule 16
xiii)	$F\varphi$	by rule 28 twice and 32
xiv)	$Res[GH\neg\varphi, F\varphi]$	by resolution on (ii) and (xiii)
xv)	$FRes[GH\neg\varphi, \varphi]$	by rule 24 (transitivity rule)
xvi)	$FGRes[H\neg\varphi, P\varphi]$	by rule 19
xvii)	$FGP\bot$	by rule 16
xviii	$\bot$	by rule 28 and 32, & rule 28 again

We must leave the discussion of soundness and completeness to another time.[12]

6 References

M Abadi (1989) "The power of temporal proofs" *Theoretical Computer Science 52.*

J Allen (1983) "Maintaining knowledge about temporal intervals" *CACM 26 Vol 11.*

J Allen (1984) "Towards a general theory of action and time" *Journal of Artificial Intelligence 23.*

J Allen & P Hayes (1987) "Moments and points in an interval-based temporal logic" *IJCAI 87.*

Y Auffray et al (1990) "Strategies for modal resolution: results and problems" *Journal of Automated Reasoning.*

F Baccus, J Tenenberg & J Koomen (1991) "A non-reified temporal logic" *Journal of Artificial Intelligence 52.*

J van Benthm (1983) *The Logic of Time* Reidel Publishing Co.

J van Benthem (1984) "Correspondence Theory" in D Gabbay & F Guenthner (eds), *Handbook of Philosophical Vol 2* Reidel Publishing Co.

P Blackburn (1990) *Reasoning in and about Time* PhD thesis, University of Edinburgh.

K Bowen & R Kowalski (1982) "Amalgamating language and metalanguage in logic programming" in K Clark, S Tarnlund (eds.) *Logic Programming* Academic Press.

J Burgess (1984) "Basic tense logic" in D Gabbay & F Guenthner (eds), *Handbook of*

[12] The IQ approach to temporal logic was first adumbrated in Richards [86], and has been subsequently developed and explored in a number of papers (see references). The broad aim has been to define an interval temporal logic (with modal operators) which can meet the expressive requirements of artificial intelligence and cognitive science. The present paper represents a further step in this direction. In subsequent papers we shall provide proofs of the theorems cited, together with adjustments imposed on unification by different logics. In the meantime it should perhaps be said that this paper is the product of an invited contribution to ALPUK 92, and hence is not intended as a definitive account of the logic presented.

Philosophical Logic Vol 2 Reidel Publishing Co.

F Del Cerro & A Herzberg (1992) "Modal Theorem Proving and its applications to epistemic and temporal logics" *Studia Logica*, to appear.

T Dean & D McDermott (1987) "Temporal database management" *Journal of Artificial Intelligence 32.*

A Galton (1990) "A critical examination of Allen's theory of action and time" *Journal of Artificial Intelligence 42.*

J Halpern & Y Shoham (1986) "A propositional modal logic of time intervals" *IEEE Symposium on Logic in Computer Science.*

C Hamblin (1971) "Instants and Intervals" *Studium Generale 27.*

R Hirsch (1991) "The expressive power of IQ" *Technical Report*, Department of Computing, Imperial College.

L Humberstone (1979) "Interval semantics for tense logic: some remarks" *Journal of Philosophical Logic 8.*

Y Jiang (1986) *A Formalism for Representing Qualified Knowledge* PhD thesis, University of Manchester.

Y Jiang (1990) "An epistemic model of logic programming" *New Generation Computing 8.*

Y Jiang & B Richards (1992) "A general proof procedure for the temporal logic IQ-C" forthcoming.

Y Jiang, B Richards & H Choi (1991) "Actions and noninterference conditions" *Proceedings of 1st World Conference on Fundamentals of Artificial Intelligence* Paris.

J Kamp (1968) *Tense Logic and the Theory of Linear Order*, PhD thesis, UCLA.

R Kowalski & M Sergot (1986) "A logic-based calculus of events" *New Generation Computing 4.*

P Ladkin (1987) "Models of axioms for time intervals" *AAAI 87.*

J McCarthy & P Hayes (1969) "Some philosophical problems from the standpoint of artificial intelligence" *Machine Intelligence 4.*

D McDermott (1982) "A temporal logic for reasoning about process and plans" *Cognitive Science 6.*

H Ohlbach (1986) "A resolution calculus for modal logics" *CADE 86.*

W Quine (1960) *Word and Object* MIT Press.

B Richards (1986) "Tenses, temporal quantifiers and semantic innocence", in E LePore *Truth and Interpretation* Oxford Press.

B Richards et al (1989) *Temporal Representation and Inference* Academic Press.

B Richards, Y. Jiang & H. Choi (1991) "On interval-based planning: An IQ strategy" *ISMIS 6.*

Y Shoham (1987) "Temporal logics in AI: Semantical and ontological considerations" *Journal of Artificial Intelligence 33.*

Y Venema "Expressiveness and completeness of an interval tense logic" *Notre Dame Journal of Formal Logic 31.*

Y Venema "A modal logic for chopping intervals" *Journal of Logic and Computation 1.*

Tutorials

An Introduction to Gödel

A. Bowers
Department of Computer Science, University of Bristol
Bristol BS8 1TR

P.M. Hill
School of Computer Studies, University of Leeds
Leeds, LS2 9JT

Abstract

The logic programming language Gödel is a new language with functionality and expressiveness similar to Prolog, but greatly improved declarative semantics compared with Prolog. Facilities provided by Gödel include types, meta-programming, control annotations, modules, and input/output. This paper is an introduction and tutorial for Gödel.

Contents

1 Introduction

The logic programming language Gödel[1] is a new language with functionality and expressiveness similar to Prolog, but greatly improved declarative semantics compared with Prolog. This paper is an introduction to the language and is not meant to be a complete guide. A comprehensive description of all the facilities of Gödel is given in the Gödel Report [7].

The main facilities provided by Gödel are as follows:

- types
- modules
- control
  - control declarations
  - constraint solving
  - pruning operator
- meta-programming
- input/output

In later sections of this tutorial, we will introduce these facilities and other features of Gödel, illustrating them with examples. In this section we will motivate these facilities.

1.1 Motivation

Consider, first, the types. The reasons for having types in logic programming languages are well known. The major reason is for knowledge representation. Intended interpretations in most logic programming applications are typed and hence using a typed language is the most direct way of capturing the relevant knowledge in the application. Furthermore, type declarations can help catch programming errors. For example, in an untyped language, simple typographical errors often lead to bizarre program behaviour which can only be identified by laborious tracing of the program. In contrast, in a typed language, many such errors can be caught by the compiler. It is nearly always easier to correct an error caught by the compiler than it is to discover and correct an error that leads to wrong program behaviour. Our experience with the Gödel type system supports the contention that it greatly decreases the effort required for program development and greatly increases the likelihood of correctness of programs compared with untyped languages.

Consider, next, the advantages of a module system. The usual software engineering reasons for having a module system are well known: it provides a way of writing large programs so that components of the program don't interfere with one another because of name clashes and allows implementation

[1] The name Gödel is appropriate since the key concept of the language's approach to meta-programming is representation (i.e. naming), which was introduced by Gödel in his incompleteness result. Alternatively, Gödel can be regarded as an acronym formed from God's Own DEclarative Language.

details to be hidden. The Gödel module system divides a module into two parts, called *export* and *local*. The export part of a module has declarations for symbols that may be used in either part of the module and in other modules which import it. The local part of a Gödel module contains statements defining the predicates declared in the export part, and declares any additional symbols used by these definitions. The module system is used in the design of Gödel to separate the optional features from the underlying language. Thus Gödel consists of a small core language together with a set of useful *system modules* defining *system predicates*.

We now consider Gödel's control facilities. Gödel has a computation rule which may select a literal other than the leftmost literal in a goal. The Gödel computation rule ensures safeness by delaying negative literals until they are ground. The computation rule is controlled by means of **DELAY** control declarations, which are syntactic variants of the **when** declarations of NU-Prolog [14] and cause certain calls to be delayed until they are sufficiently instantiated. These declarations can be used to assist termination, improve efficiency, and control pruning. Furthermore, a programmer can specify co-routining behaviour by means of these declarations. Many of Gödel's system predicates have **DELAY** declarations.

Gödel has constraint solving capabilities in the domains of integers and rationals. Gödel can solve systems of (not necessarily linear) constraints which involve integers, variables which range over bounded intervals of integers, and the usual functions and predicates with integer arguments. It can also solve systems of linear constraints involving rationals, variables ranging over the rationals, and the usual functions and predicates with rational arguments.

It was argued in [8] that a sound pruning operator does have an important place in logic programming languages even though it will affect the completeness. Hence, the Gödel pruning operator has been designed so that the underlying logic component of a program can be obtained by stripping away all the commits. The Gödel pruning operator, called commit, is based on the commit of the concurrent languages [13]. There are two special forms of this commit, the bar commit | and one-solution commit {...}. The Gödel bar commit is almost the same as the commit of the concurrent languages. The informal procedural meaning of the bar commit is that it finds only one solution for a guard and prunes all other statements in the definition which contain a commit. The one solution commit finds just one solution for the formula in the scope of its brackets. Details of both of these operators this are given in Section 6. We envisage Gödel programmers writing almost all their programs with just these two pruning operators. However, Gödel source-level tools, such as partial evaluators and program transformers, will require the flexibility of the general form of the Gödel commit. This is because more complex definitions requiring the general form can easily be obtained from definitions using the | and {...} notation after a single unfolding step. Note that the Gödel commit only has a procedural semantics.

Next we turn to Gödel's meta-programming facilities. A meta-program is a program which uses another program (the object program) as data. Meta-programming techniques underlie many of the applications of logic programming. For example, knowledge base systems consist of a number of knowledge bases (the object programs), which are manipulated by interpreters and assimilators (the meta-programs). Other important kinds of software, such as debuggers, compilers, and program transformers, are meta-programs.

Within the framework of the appropriate representation, a meta-program is a (typed) first order theory and the meta-logical predicates of Prolog, such as *var*, *nonvar*, *assert*, and *retract*, have declarative counterparts. The representation supported in Gödel is called the *ground* representation. In this representation, object level expressions are represented by ground terms at the meta-level. In particular, in the ground representation, an object level variable is represented by a ground meta-level term. The ground representation is a standard tool in mathematical logic. Using this representation, it is possible to give appropriate definitions for declarative counterparts of the static meta-logical predicates of Prolog, such as *var* and *nonvar*. Furthermore, in Gödel, object programs are represented not as meta-programs, but instead as meta-level terms [2]. It is straightforward with this representation to give appropriate definitions for declarative counterparts of the dynamic meta-logical predicates of Prolog, such as *assert* and *retract* [5]. Gödel provides considerable support for the ground representation for the reasons given above.

Finally we turn to the facilities for input and output. Gödel provides a number of system modules dedicated to input and output. Apart from the usual file handling, these modules support the reading to and writing from files of individual characters, numbers, and complete Gödel programs and theories. The module system of Gödel can be used to separate those parts of the program that depend on these system modules from other parts of the program. Thus, by placing modules that use predicates defined in these system modules, as high as possible, preferably at the top in the module hierarchy, other modules in the program that do not depend on these system modules will have a declarative semantics.

1.2 An Example

Before describing the Gödel system in more detail, we present a small example program `M1` to give the flavour of programming in Gödel.

The simplest form of a Gödel program like `M1` consists of a single module. Such a module begins with a declaration whose keyword `MODULE` is followed by the name of the module. The declarations beginning with the key words `BASE`, `CONSTANT`, `FUNCTION`, `PREDICATE` define the language of the program. These are explained in the next section.

The example program `M1` defines the predicates `Append` and `Append3` for appending lists of days of the week. Note that variables are denoted by identifiers beginning with a lower case letter and constants by identifiers beginning with an upper case letter.

Before we can run queries for this program, it must be compiled and loaded into the Gödel system. This is done by entering commands at the Gödel system prompt. Commands to the system begin with a semi-colon to distinguish them from goals; for example the command `;c` compiles a module and `;l` loads a program. The Gödel prompt consists of the name of the currently loaded program in square brackets followed by a left arrow. Initially no program is loaded. Once a program has been loaded, it can be queried by entering goals for the program at the system prompt. A goal for `M1` can be any first order formula in the language of `M1`. Answer bindings will be displayed for the free

```
MODULE    M1.

BASE      Day, ListDay.
CONSTANT  Monday, Tuesday, Wednesday, Thursday, Friday,
          Saturday, Sunday : Day.
CONSTANT  Nil : ListDay.
FUNCTION  Cons : Day * ListDay -> ListDay.

PREDICATE Append : ListDay * ListDay * ListDay.
Append(Nil,x,x).
Append(Cons(u,x),y,Cons(u,z)) <-
          Append(x,y,z).

PREDICATE Append3 : ListDay * ListDay * ListDay * ListDay.
Append3(x,y,z,u) <-
          Append(x,y,w) &
          Append(w,z,u).
```

variables of the goal. Typing a semi-colon at this point causes Gödel to search for another solution, whereas any other input terminates the query.

The transcript below shows an example session using **M1**.

```
% goedel
Goedel 0.22
Type ;h for help.
[] <- ;c M1.

Reading file "M1.loc" ...

Parsing module "M1" ...

Compiling module "M1" ...

Module "M1" compiled
[] <- ;l M1.
Loading program "M1" ...
[M1] <- Append(Cons(Monday,Nil),Nil,Cons(Monday,Nil)).
Yes
[M1] <- Append(Nil,Cons(Monday,Nil),Nil).
No
[M1] <- Append(Cons(Monday,Nil),Cons(Tuesday,Nil),x).

x = Cons(Monday,Cons(Tuesday,Nil)) ?
Yes
[M1] <- Append3(Cons(Monday,Nil),x,y,
                Cons(Monday,Cons(Tuesday,Nil))).
```

```
x = Nil,
y = Cons(Tuesday,Nil) ? ;

x = Cons(Tuesday,Nil),
y = Nil ? ;
No
[M1] <- ;q.
%
```

2 Types

In this section we describe the Gödel type system giving details of the various kinds of language declarations which are used to define typed first order languages.

2.1 Many-Sorted Types

The Gödel type system is based on many-sorted logic with generic polymorphism. We first discuss the many-sorted aspect ([3], [10]) of the type system.

The language declarations begin with the keywords **BASE**, **CONSTRUCTOR**, **CONSTANT**, **FUNCTION**, **PROPOSITION**, or **PREDICATE**. These declarations declare the *symbols* of the language, which belong in one of the *categories*: bases, constructors, constants, functions, propositions, and predicates. In module **M1**, the language declaration beginning with the keyword **BASE** declares **Day** and **ListDay** to be *bases*, which are the only types for the language of the module **M1** (more complex types will be introduced shortly). The next three declarations declare the constants, functions, and predicates of the language. The first part of the **CONSTANT** declaration declares **Nil** to be a constant of type **ListDay**. The second part declares **Monday**, **Tuesday**, etc., to be constants of type **Day**. The **FUNCTION** declaration declares **Cons** to be a binary function which maps a tuple of arguments, where the first argument is of type **Day** and the second argument is of type **ListDay**, to a term of type **ListDay**. The **PREDICATE** declaration declares **Append** and **Append3** to be predicates with arguments of type **ListDay**. A proposition is declared with a **PROPOSITION** declaration. So, for example, a module may contain the declaration

```
PROPOSITION  P,Q.
```

which declares **P** and **Q** to be propositions. In general, apart from the keyword, an identifier before the : in a language declaration is the *name* of the symbol being declared. However, within the context of a single module, we identify a symbol with its name.

The language declarations in **M1** define a many-sorted language (in the sense of [3]) and the statements in **M1** are written in this language. Module **M1** forms a complete Gödel program. In this case, a goal for the program must be written in the same many-sorted language as the statements. Typical goals for **M1** are:

```
<- Append3(Cons(Monday,Nil), Cons(Tuesday,Nil), Nil, x).
<- Append3(x, y, z, Cons(Monday,Cons(Tuesday,Nil))).
```

Note that every base type used in a constant, function, or predicate declaration must be declared. Moreover, every constant, function, proposition, and predicate used in a statement or goal must be declared. The types of variables are not declared, but are assigned using the positions of the variables in each statement and the language declarations given. Each occurrence of a variable in a statement must have the same assigned type. If there is such an assignment of types, then it is unique. For example, for module `M1`, the variable `x` in the first statement is assigned the type `ListDay`. In the second statement, the variable `u` is assigned the type `Day`, and the variables `x`, `y`, and `z` are assigned the type `ListDay`. There is no requirement that a variable have the same type in different statements. For example, in the second statement of module `M1`, the variable `u` is assigned the type `Day` and, in the third statement, `u` is assigned the type `ListDay`. Each statement in `M1` is a formula in the typed language defined in `M1`. However, given the declarations

```
BASE          Day, People.
PREDICATE     P : Day * People.
```

the expression

```
P(x,x).
```

is not a formula in the declared language, since there is no type which can be assigned to `x` to satisfy the declaration for `P`.

2.2 Parametric Types

Next we introduce the second aspect of the type system, which is generic polymorphism. For this form of polymorphism, it is convenient to have a more structured language for the types. The type language we use here is constructed using bases, constructors, and parameters. The bases are the simple "constant" types described above and declared as `Day` and `ListDay` in `M1`.

Module `M2`, which is a variation of module `M1`, demonstrates the use of *constructors*. The main difference between the two modules is that, in module `M2`, a unary constructor `List` has been declared. In this module, the ground types are `Day`, `List(Day)`, `List(List(Day))`, ... Every base and constructor[2] used in a module must be declared. The ground types are obtained by forming all "ground terms" using the bases as "constants" and the constructors as "functions" of the appropriate arity.

However with just bases and constructors, it is still not possible to define generic constants, functions or predicates. For example, the `Append` predicate is normally written so that it can append lists with arguments of any type, whereas, in `M2`, it can only append lists whose arguments are of type `Day`. For this we require *parameters* which are "type variables". The use of parameters is illustrated by module `M3`.

The logic on which module `M3` is based is called *polymorphic many-sorted logic*. In module `M3`, `a` is a *parameter*. A parameter can be instantiated to any type of the language of the logic. Like variables, parameters are not declared. For a typed language for this logic, we need to extend the concept of a type.

[2]Note that a constructor itself is not a type.

```
MODULE    M2.

BASE      Day.
CONSTANT  Monday, Tuesday, Wednesday, Thursday, Friday,
          Saturday, Sunday : Day.

CONSTRUCTOR  List/1.
CONSTANT  Nil : List(Day);
FUNCTION  Cons : Day * List(Day) -> List(Day).

PREDICATE Append : List(Day) * List(Day) * List(Day).
Append(Nil,x,x).
Append(Cons(u,x),y,Cons(u,z)) <-
          Append(x,y,z).

PREDICATE Append3 : List(Day) * List(Day) * List(Day) *
                                                   List(Day).
Append3(x,y,z,u) <-
          Append(x,y,w) &
          Append(w,z,u).
```

```
MODULE    M3.

BASE      Day.
CONSTANT  Monday, Tuesday, Wednesday, Thursday, Friday,
          Saturday, Sunday : Day.

BASE      People.
CONSTANT  Fred, Bill, Mary : People.

CONSTRUCTOR List/1.
CONSTANT  Nil : List(a);
FUNCTION  Cons : a * List(a) -> List(a).

PREDICATE Append : List(a) * List(a) * List(a).
Append(Nil,x,x).
Append(Cons(u,x),y,Cons(u,z)) <-
          Append(x,y,z).

PREDICATE Append3 : List(a) * List(a) * List(a) * List(a).
Append3(x,y,z,u) <-
          Append(x,y,w) &
          Append(w,z,u).
```

In such a language, a type is a "term" constructed using the bases as "constants", the parameters as "variables", and the constructors as "functions". Thus, for module **M3**, the following are types: **List(List(Day))**, **List(a)**, and **a**. A *ground* type (also called a *monotype*) is a type not containing parameters. Thus the set of ground types for module **M3** is **Day**, **People**, **List(Day)**, **List(People)**, **List(List(Day))**, ...

A symbol is *polymorphic* if its declaration contains a parameter; otherwise, we say it is *monomorphic*. We can understand a polymorphic symbol as representing a collection of monomorphic symbols. For example, the **CONSTANT** declaration for the polymorphic constant **Nil** in module **M3** could be regarded as a countably infinite set of declarations for constants with types **List(***t***)**, where *t* ranges over all ground types.

The definition of a formula in a polymorphic many-sorted language is given in Chapter 11 of the Gödel Report and also in [9]. It is decidable whether an expression is a formula or not. For example, consider module **M3**. During checks that the expressions in **M3** are formulas in the language defined by the language declarations, the variable **u** in the second statement for **Append** has the type **a** assigned, and the variables **x**, **y**, and **z** have the type **List(a)** assigned. The type checker assumes the most general possible assignment of types to the variables so that the statement is a formula. It can be shown that such an assignment is unique apart from the choice of parameters in the types. Consider, also, the module **ParametricTypes** below. The variable **x** has most general type **a** in the atom **Q(x)** and **M** in the atom **P(F(x))**. Thus the variable **x** has most general type **M** in **P(F(x)) <- Q(x)** because the types of the two occurrences of **x** in the statement can be unified to give the type **M**. Thus the argument **F(x)** of **P** has type **L(M)** in this statement.

```
MODULE          ParametricTypes.

BASE            M.
CONSTRUCTOR     L/1.
FUNCTION        F : a -> L(a).

PREDICATE       P : L(M); Q : a.
P(F(x)) <- Q(x).
```

We need to extend the usual definitions of interpretation, model, logical consequence, and so on, to polymorphic many-sorted logic. For a typed language for this logic, an interpretation has a domain corresponding to every ground type[3]. Then a constant such as **Nil** in module **M3** with polymorphic type **List(a)** is assigned one or more domain elements, one in the domain of each ground type which can be obtained by instantiating **a** in **List(a)** with all possible ground types. In a similar way, one can define the assignments to functions and predicates. The definitions of model, logical consequence, and so on, also generalise from a (monomorphic) many-sorted language to a polymorphic many-sorted language.

[3]These domains can be regarded as disjoint, but this is not essential.

For a module such as **M3** which does not depend upon other modules, the *language of the module* is the polymorphic many-sorted language defined by the language declarations in the module.

A *Gödel statement*[4] in a module is a formula in the language of the module having the form either **A** or **A <- W**, where **A** is an atom, called the *head* of the statement, and **W** is a formula, called the *body* of the statement. Any variables in **A** and any free variables in **W** are assumed to be universally quantified at the front of the statement. In addition, each statement must satisfy a condition on the types of the arguments in the head. This condition will be given shortly.

A *Gödel goal* for a Gödel program consisting of a single module[5] has the form **<- W**, where **W** is a formula in the language of the module. **W** is called the *body* of the goal. Any free variables in **W** are assumed to be universally quantified at the front of the goal.

Module **M3** forms a complete Gödel program on its own. Typical Gödel goals for this program could be:

```
<- Append3(Cons(Monday,Nil), Cons(Tuesday,Nil), Nil, x).
<- Append3(x, y, z, Cons(Fred,Cons(Bill,Cons(Mary,Nil)))).
```

When a Gödel goal is given for a Gödel program consisting of a single module[5], the goal is first checked to make sure it is a formula in the language of the module. A desirable requirement of a type system is that goals can then be run with no run-time type checking. However, we need to impose two conditions to ensure this property holds. The first, called the *head condition*, is applied to a program statement:

- There is an assignment of types to the variables in the statement such that the tuple of types of the arguments of the head in the statement is the same as the type declared for the predicate in the head.

Note that the head condition is satisfied by the statement in **ParametricTypes** and also each statement in module **M3**. The second condition, called *transparency*, is applied to a function declaration:

- Every parameter in the declaration occurs in its range type[6].

Then, under the assumptions that each statement satisfies the head condition and each function declaration the transparency condition, it can be shown that no run-time type checking is needed. In other words, a Gödel program and goal can be run under the usual (untyped) SLDNF-resolution and it is guaranteed that no type error will occur. For the proof of this, the reader is referred to [9, theorem 5.7]. The head and transparency conditions are very general and natural, so their imposition rarely causes any inconvenience.

Lists are a common data structure. Thus there is a system module **Lists** in Gödel which provides a constructor **List** of arity 1 for list processing. **Lists** also provides a constant **Nil** and a function **Cons**, whose declarations are:

```
CONSTANT   Nil : List(a).
FUNCTION   Cons : a * List(a) -> List(a).
```

[4]Later we shall extend this definition to include commits.

[5]The module must also be open. See Section 5 for the definition of an open module.

[6]The range type of a function declaration is the type on the right of the arrow.

The usual [...] and | syntax for lists is allowed in Gödel and is syntactic sugar for **Nil** and **Cons**. Thus the list

```
Cons(Fred,Cons(Bill,Cons(Mary,Nil)))
```

can be written more conveniently as

```
[Fred,Bill,Mary]
```

A collection of useful list processing predicates, including **Append**, is defined in **Lists**. These predicates together with **List**, **Nil**, and **Cons** are available for use in any module containing an **IMPORT** module declaration for **Lists**. We shall see the way **Lists** exports these in Section 5. In general, if a module imports from another module, it imports *all* the symbols exported by the other module.

Module **M4** is a version of module **M1** that illustrates the use of **Lists**. The constructor **List**, the constant **Nil**, the function **Cons**, and the predicate **Append**, provided by **Lists** are used in **M4**. Modules **M4**, **Lists**, and **Integers** (which is imported by **Lists**, see Section 4), together form a Gödel program. Typical Gödel goals for this program could then be:

```
<- Append3([Monday], [Tuesday], [], x).
<- Append3(x, y, z, [Fred,Bill,Mary]).
```

```
MODULE    M4.

IMPORT    Lists.

BASE      Day, People.
CONSTANT  Monday, Tuesday, Wednesday, Thursday, Friday,
          Saturday, Sunday : Day;
          Fred, Bill, Mary : People.

PREDICATE Append3 : List(a) * List(a) * List(a) * List(a).
Append3(x,y,z,u) <-
          Append(x,y,w) &
          Append(w,z,u).
```

2.3 Operators

It is often convenient to employ prefix, infix, or postfix notation instead of the standard logical notation for terms and atoms. For example, we usually prefer to write `1 + 2` instead of `+(1,2)`, `x < y` instead of `<(x,y)`, and `x * y + z` instead of `(x * y) + z`. For this reason, Gödel provides a mechanism for declaring *operators*, which are functions or predicates using this notation.

FUNCTION declarations allow fixity, precedence, and associativity of unary or binary functions to be declared by means of optional *function indicators*.

The form of an indicator for an infix binary function must be either `xFx(`N`)`, `xFy(`N`)`, or `yFx(`N`)`. Each of **xFx**, **xFy**, and **yFx** is a *specifier*. The N, which is a positive integer, is the *precedence*. The **x** and **y** indicate associativity. For example, the module **Integers** provided by the system contains the following function declarations.

```
FUNCTION    * : yFx(520) : Integer * Integer -> Integer;
            + : yFx(510) : Integer * Integer -> Integer;
            - : yFx(510) : Integer * Integer -> Integer.
```

These declarations allow the use of infix notation. For example, the specifier **yFx** in the declaration for **+** in **Integers** indicates that **+** is infix so that `x + y` can be written instead of `+(x,y)`, and `x + (y + z)` instead of `+(x,+(y,z))`.

However, with the fixity information alone, we must always bracket subterms with structure. For a term containing functions with distinct precedences, the precedence information is used to disambiguate the meaning of the term in the absence of brackets. The precedence rule is that *the higher its precedence, the more tightly a function binds its arguments*[7]. For example, the precedence `510` for **+** and the precedence **520** for ***** in **Integers** indicate that the term `x * y + z` means `(x * y) + z` and not `x * (y + z)`. If the latter meaning is intended, then the term must be written with explicit bracketing to indicate this. In general, precedence (and associativity) information in indicators can always be over-ridden by explicit bracketing.

The associativity information is needed when a term contains functions with the same precedence. The specifier **xFy** means the function is right associative, **yFx** means the function is left associative, and **xFx** means the function is non-associative. For example, the indicator **yFx(510)** for **+** declares it to be infix and left associative. So the term `x + y + z` means `(x + y) + z` and not `x + (y + z)`. Also the indicator **yFx(520)** for ***** declares it to be infix, and left associative with a higher precedence than **+**. So the term `x * (y + z) * w` means `(x * (y + z)) * w`. More formally, in an indicator with precedence N, an **x** indicates that the argument in that position must have precedence strictly greater than N and a **y** indicates that the argument in that position must have precedence greater than or equal to N. For this purpose, the precedence of a term is the precedence of its top-level function, where the precedence of a function without an indicator is taken to be (plus) infinity. The precedence of variables, constants, and terms enclosed in brackets is also assumed to be (plus) infinity.

The general form of a unary function indicator is either `xF(`N`)`, `Fx(`N`)`, `yF(`N`)`, or `Fy(`N`)`, where the specifier is either **xF**, **Fx**, **yF**, or **Fy**, and N, which is a positive integer, is the precedence. **Fx** and **Fy** indicate prefix, and **xF** and **yF** indicate postfix. The **x** and **y** have the same meanings as for binary functions.

For example, the module **Integers** also contains the following function declaration.

```
FUNCTION    - : Fy(530) : Integer -> Integer.
```

So the unary **-** is a prefix operator which is right associative with precedence `530`. Thus the term `-x + y` means `(-x) + y` and the term `- -x` means `-(-x)`.

[7]This is the convention most other languages use, but the opposite to Prolog.

PREDICATE declarations have an optional fixity declaration using a *predicate indicator*. Predicate indicators consist solely of a *specifier* which indicates the fixity of the predicate. The specifier for a binary infix predicate is **zPz**. A specifier for a unary predicate is either **Pz**, indicating that the predicate is prefix, or **zP**, indicating that the predicate is postfix.

For example, **Integers** contains the declaration

```
PREDICATE =< : zPz : Integer * Integer.
```

which declares =< to be an infix predicate. Thus we write 3 =< 2 instead of =<(3, 2). Unfortunately, it is possible to write ambiguous expressions using operators. If the parser is unable to disambiguate an operator expression, then the expression will be rejected. As far as the user is concerned, the simplest remedy is to help the parser by bracketing the subterms. Note that prefix and postfix binary functions and predicates are not allowed.

3 Quantifiers and Connectives

In the examples in Section 2, all the statements are in the form of Horn clauses. However, Gödel allows the use of arbitrary formulas in the bodies of statements and goals. In this section, we examine the use of this facility in more detail.

3.1 Quantifiers and Basic Connectives

In Gödel, conjunction is denoted by &, disjunction by \/, negation by ~, left implication by <-, right implication by ->, and equivalence by <->. The universal and existential quantifiers are denoted by **ALL** and **SOME**. Each quantifier has two arguments, the first being a list of the quantified variables and the second the scope of the quantifier. Note that the types of the quantified variables are not declared. The types of these variables are assigned by the type checker along with the types of the other variables in the statement or goal.

As an example, module **Sets** below defines the subset predicate, where sets are represented by lists. The predicate **Subset** can be used to check that one set is a subset of another. Thus, for example, the goal[8]

```
<- Subset([1,3,2],[4,3,2,1]).
```

succeeds and the goal

```
<- Subset([1,5,2],[4,3,2,1]).
```

fails. However, it cannot be used to *generate* subsets of a given set. The reason is that the implementation involves transforming the program to normal form [10, page 113] and then running the normal form under SLDNF-resolution. If either argument of **Subset** is non-ground, then the resulting computation will flounder, that is, reach a goal consisting of only non-ground negative literals. Fortunately, in practice, floundering is rarely a problem once the limitations of the proof procedure are understood.

Allowing an arbitrary formula to appear in the body of a goal is very useful for querying databases, such as the module **DB**.

---

[8] Note that the integers are available in the module **Sets** since they are imported via **Lists**. See Section 5.

```
MODULE    Sets.

IMPORT    Lists.

PREDICATE Subset : List(a) * List(a).
Subset(x,y) <-
              ALL [z] (Member(z,y) <- Member(z,x)).
```

```
MODULE    DB.

BASE      People.
CONSTANT  Fred, Mary, George, James, Jane, Sue : People.

PREDICATE Ancestor, Parent, Mother, Father : People * People.

Ancestor(x,y) <-
          Parent(x,z) &
          Ancestor(z,y).
Ancestor(x,y) <-
          Parent(x,y).

Parent(x,y) <-
          Mother(x,y).
Parent(x,y) <-
          Father(x,y).

Father(Fred, Mary).
Father(George, James).

Mother(Sue, Mary).
Mother(Jane, Sue).
```

A typical goal to the program consisting of this module could query if every person with a mother also has a father.

```
<- ALL [x] (SOME [z] Father(z,x) <- SOME [y] Mother(y,x)).
```

Taking advantage of the notational convention that '_' in a body stands for a unique variable existentially quantified at the front of the atom in which it appears, the previous goal can be written more compactly as follows.

```
<- ALL [x] (Father(_,x) <- Mother(_,x)).
```

Another goal could try to find a mother who has no father.

```
<- SOME [z] Mother(x,z) & ~ SOME [y] Father(y,x).
```

Using the underscore notation, this can be written as follows.

```
<- Mother(x,_) & ~ Father(_,x).
```

Sometimes a programmer may only be interested in the values of a subset of the free variables in the body of a goal. In this case, the unwanted variables can be masked out using the following colon notation. For example, suppose the goal was to find all grandparents of Jane.

```
<- x : Parent(x,y) & Parent(y,Jane).
```

The "`x :`" reads "find the `x` such that". In general, there can be zero or more variables before the colon, separated by commas. It is an error if a variable appears before the colon but is not a free variable in the body of the goal. Note that the colon notation can only be used in goals.

3.2 Conditionals

The connectives and quantifiers introduced so far provide an expressive language in which to write goals and statements. However, there are situations where it is advantageous to provide constructs with specialised procedural semantics. The most common such situation is when a programmer wants to use a formula of the form

(*Condition* & *Formula1*) \/ (~*Condition* & *Formula2*).

in a body. Although this formula is written with the connectives introduced so far, the approach has the disadvantage that *Condition* will be computed twice. Obviously, if *Condition* is computationally expensive, this is undesirable. For this reason, Gödel has constructs with specialised procedural semantics to avoid this inefficiency. These constructs, which we call *conditionals*, are due to Naish [11] and are available in the NU-Prolog system [14]. The conditionals have the four forms:

I-T: IF *Condition* THEN *Formula1*.
IS-T: IF SOME [*x1*,...,*xn*] *Condition* THEN *Formula1*.
I-T-E: IF *Condition* THEN *Formula1* ELSE *Formula2*.
IS-T-E: IF SOME [*x1*,...,*xn*] *Condition* THEN *Formula1* ELSE *Formula2*.

In each case *Condition*, *Formula1*, and *Formula2* must be formulas. Note that, if the *Condition* is of the form **SOME** [*x1*,...,*xn*] *W*, then it must be bracketed. The formulas *Condition*, *Formula1*, and *Formula2* are called the *condition part*, *then part*, and *else part*, respectively, of the conditional.

As an example of the use of a conditional, we give a definition of the predicate **Max**, which computes the maximum of its first two arguments.

```
Max(x,y,z) <- IF x =< y THEN z = y ELSE z = x.
```

The meaning of this is that **Max(x,y)** is true if either **x =< y** and **z = y** or **x > y** and **z = x**. Procedurally, as soon as **x =< y** is ground, this inequality is tested. If the call to **x =< y** succeeds, then **z** is bound to the value of **y**. If the call fails, then **z** is bound to the value of **x**.

More formally, the meanings of the conditionals are:

I-T: *Formula1* \/ ~*Condition*.
IS-T: (SOME [*x1*,...,*xn*] (*Condition* & *Formula1*)) \/
~ SOME [*x1*,...,*xn*] *Condition*.
I-T-E: (*Condition* & *Formula1*) \/ (~*Condition* & *Formula2*).
IS-T-E: (SOME [*x1*,...,*xn*] (*Condition* & *Formula1*)) \/
(~ SOME [*x1*,...,*xn*] *Condition* & *Formula2*).

We now give the procedural semantics of the conditionals. The essential requirement is soundness.

If a conditional occurs in a goal, it will be *delayed* until it is certain that calling *Condition* will not bind any free variables in **SOME** [*x1*,...,*xn*] *Condition* (resp., *Condition*) in conditionals IS-T and IS-T-E (resp., I-T and I-T-E)[9]. In the current Gödel implementation, conditionals are delayed until there are no such free variables, but more sophisticated implementations are possible, for example where *Condition* consists of a single equality literal. A conditional is only selected if it is not nested in the then or else part of another conditional and is not delayed. Once a conditional has been selected, the procedural semantics is as follows:

1. *Condition* is called.

2. If the call to *Condition* succeeds, *Formula1* is called. In the case of the conditionals IS-T and IS-T-E, the system may subsequently backtrack to *Condition*, eventually finding all solutions to **SOME** [*x1*,...,*xn*] (*Condition* & *Formula*).

3. If the call to *Condition* finitely fails, then, for I-T and IS-T, the conditional succeeds and, for I-T-E and IS-T-E, *Formula2* is called.

Nesting of these conditionals in the then part and else part is allowed although the condition part cannot contain a conditional. This allows a straightforward simulation of a case statement. In Chapter 3 of the Gödel Report, it is shown that the procedural semantics for each form of the conditional is sound.

The forms IS-T and IS-T-E are non-standard uses of the **SOME** in the conditionals in that the quantification extends over *Condition* and *Formula1*. However, from a programming viewpoint, this non-standard use is very convenient.

[9] *Condition* is an arbitrary formula so it will generally have both bound and free variables.

This is illustrated in the module **AssocList** below, which defines the predicate **Lookup** for looking up or inserting into an association list. The list consists of pairs having an integer key in the first argument and a string in the second. (See the module **Strings** in Section 5.) The definition of **Lookup** is due to Naish [11]. If **Lookup** is called with its first and third arguments instantiated, and there is a pair in the association list having key value equal to the first argument, it returns all such pairs. If it is called with the first and third argument, and possibly the second argument, instantiated and there is no pair in the association list having key value equal to the first argument, it inserts the pair containing the first and second arguments into the association list. Note the quantification of the variable **v** over the condition and the then-part, and how this gives the required behaviour of **Lookup**.

```
MODULE    AssocList.

IMPORT    Strings.

BASE      Pairs.
FUNCTION  Pair : Integer * String -> Pairs.

PREDICATE  Lookup : Integer * String * List(Pairs) * List(Pairs).
Lookup(key, value, assoc_list, new_assoc_list) <-
          IF SOME [v] Member(Pair(key,v), assoc_list) THEN
              value = v &
              new_assoc_list = assoc_list
          ELSE
              new_assoc_list = [Pair(key,value) | assoc_list].
```

---

4 Equality and Numbers

In this section, we discuss the equality predicate and also the *arithmetic* modules which provide the integers, rationals, and floating-point numbers.

4.1 Equality

Equality is a distinguished predicate in logic because it is so fundamental. The same is true of the equality and disequality predicates in Gödel which have the following declarations.

```
PREDICATE =, ~=  : zPz : a * a.
```

Equality and disequality are built into the system and are available in every module without being imported.

Each Gödel program has an associated equality theory. First we consider Gödel programs that do not include any of the arithmetic modules. The definition of = is given by a theory consisting of the usual equality axioms in first order theories with equality together with a typed form of the Clark equality axioms. We illustrate this by giving the equality theory for the program which consists just of the module **M3**. First we give the equality axioms that hold in first order theories with equality.

```
x = x.
(x1 = y1) & (x2 = y2) -> (Cons(x1,x2) = Cons(y1,y2)).
(x1 = y1) & (x2 = y2) -> ((x1 = x2) -> (y1 = y2)).
(x1 = y1) & (x2 = y2) & (x3 = y3) -> =
                        (Append(x1,x2,x3) -> (Append(y1,y2,y3)).
(x1 = y1) & (x2 = y2) & (x3 = y3) & (x4 = y4) ->
                 (Append3(x1,x2,x3,x4) -> (Append3(y1,y2,y3,y4)).
```

The first axiom is reflexivity. The first and third axioms are generic in the sense that the variables in these axioms can be assigned a parameter type. These will be present in the equality theory of every Gödel program. These generic axioms imply that in a model of the theory the interpretations of the = predicates corresponding to the various domains must be equivalence relations on those domains. The second to fifth axioms together ensure that = has the usual substitutivity properties. Note that there is one of these axioms for each constant, function, and predicate of the language.

Next come the Clark equality axioms [10] for **M3**.

```
~(Monday = Tuesday).
~(Monday = Wednesday).
        ⋮
~(Sunday = Saturday).
~(Fred = Bill).
~(Fred = Mary).
~(Bill = Mary).
~(Nil = Cons(x,y)).
```

~(Cons(*s*,*t*) = x), where *s* or *t* is a term containing **x**.

```
~(x1 = y1) \/ ~(x2 = y2) -> ~(Cons(x1,x2) = Cons(y1,y2)).
```

The above equality theory for **M3** implies that two terms in **M3** of the same type are equal if and only if they are syntactically identical. A model of such a theory is usually an Herbrand model with equality interpreted as identity[10].

For Programs that include one or more of the arithmetic modules, the equality theory consists of the two generic equality axioms, a first order equality axiom for each symbol of the language, a set of Clark equality axioms for each non-parametric type other than other than those defined in the arithmetic modules, and a set of equality axioms imported with the arithmetic modules. These equality axioms will be given later.

---

[10] In any case, the domains of the model must contain isomorphic copies of the corresponding Herbrand universes and equality must be interpreted as identity on these domains [10, p.103, problem 10].

The declarative semantics of Gödel programs is the completion semantics [10]. Thus the definitions of propositions and predicates (apart from those in the arithmetic modules which are treated differently) are completed and the equality theory added to form the completion of the program.

Although the definition of ~= is

```
x ~= y <-> ~(x = y).
```

it has a sophisticated implementation that does not require the disequality atom to be ground before it can be selected. A call to ~= may run even if it contains free variables. However, such a call will never bind any free variables in the call. Thus it will never create bindings for variables appearing elsewhere in the goal.

One subtle point when using underscores with ~= is worth noting. Recall that an underscore in an atom in a body means a unique variable existentially quantified at the front of the atom. If an underscore appears in S ~= T, where S and T are terms, we treat this as ~(S = T), in which case the underscore becomes a unique variable *universally* quantified at the front of S ~= T. So, for example, `x ~= [_|_]` means `ALL [u,v] x ~= [u|v]`, where `u` and `v` are unique variables. Thus the call `x ~= [_|_]` delays, `[] ~= [_|_]` succeeds, and `[`*s*`|`*t*`] ~= [_|_]` fails for any terms *s* and *t*. Note that `[`*s*`|`*t*`] ~= [_|_]` and `[`*s*`|`*t*`] ~= [y|z]` have different semantics. For instance, a goal of the form

```
<- [s|t] ~= [y|z].
```

is equivalent to

```
<- Some [y,z] [s|t] ~= [y|z].
```

so that the call `[`*s*`|`*t*`] ~= [y|z]` delays for any terms *s* and *t*.

In addition to the built-in predicates = and ~=, the system has the two built-in propositions, **True** and **False** with the obvious definitions. These are also available in every module without being imported.

4.2 Numbers

There are three arithmetic modules in Gödel: **Integers**, **Rationals**, and **Floats**. We first describe the **Integers** module.

The export part (except for the control declarations) of **Integers** is given below. The export part of a module contains language declarations for symbols that it makes available to other modules that import it. The keyword **CLOSED** indicates an export part of a module, plus a further property which we will discuss in Section 5.

The export part of the **Integers** declares a type **Integer** and constants 0, 1, 2, and so on. Since there are infinitely many non-negative integers and since the syntax does not support the declaration[11] of infinitely many symbols, the constant declaration is simply indicated by a comment in the export part of **Integers**. The system knows that **Integers** is to be treated specially in this regard. The usual functions and predicates required for integer arithmetic are provided by **Integers**.

[11]Such a syntax could be provided, but we do not consider it important enough just for this one case.

```
CLOSED     Integers.

BASE       Integer.

% CONSTANT  0, 1, 2, ... : Integer.

FUNCTION  ^   : yFx(540) : Integer * Integer -> Integer;
          -   : Fy(530) : Integer -> Integer;
          *   : yFx(520) : Integer * Integer -> Integer;
          Div : yFx(520) : Integer * Integer -> Integer;
          Mod : yFx(520) : Integer * Integer -> Integer;
          +   : yFx(510) : Integer * Integer -> Integer;
          -   : yFx(510) : Integer * Integer -> Integer;
          Abs : Integer -> Integer;
          Max : Integer * Integer -> Integer;
          Min : Integer * Integer -> Integer.

PREDICATE >  : zPz : Integer * Integer;
          <  : zPz : Integer * Integer;
          >= : zPz : Integer * Integer;
          =< : zPz : Integer * Integer;
          Interval : Integer * Integer * Integer.
```

The module **Integers** provides an equality theory for the terms of type **Integer**. To illustrate how the equality theory for the integers is used, suppose a module which imports **Integers** defines a predicate **P** as follows.

```
PREDICATE P : Integer * Integer.
P(x,x).
```

Then the goal

```
<- P(3 + 4, (17 Div 6) + 5).
```

succeeds.

A range expression of integers can be expressed using the notation *s* `=<` `x` `=<` *t*, where *s* and *t* are terms of type **Integer** and **x** is a variable. This is compiled into the atom **Interval(*s*,x,*t*)**.

As an example of the use of **Integers** consider the module **GCD** below. The predicate **Gcd** is intended to be true when its third argument is the greatest common divisor of the first two arguments. Note that **GCD** contains essentially a *specification* of **Gcd** rather than an efficient algorithm, such as the Euclidean algorithm.

Gödel can solve systems of (not necessarily linear) constraints which involve integers, variables which range over bounded intervals of integers, and the functions and predicates exported by **Integers** (including, of course, `=` and `~=`). For example, with **Integers** loaded, the goals

```
MODULE    GCD.

IMPORT    Integers.

PREDICATE Gcd : Integer * Integer * Integer.
Gcd(i,j,d) <-
          IF i = 0 & j = 0
          THEN d = 0
          ELSE CommonDivisor(i,j,d) &
               ~ SOME [e] (CommonDivisor(i,j,e) & e > d).

PREDICATE CommonDivisor : Integer * Integer * Integer.
CommonDivisor(i,j,d) <-
          IF i = 0 & j = 0
          THEN d = 0
          ELSE 1 =< d  =< Max(Abs(i),Abs(j)) &
               i Mod d = 0 &
               j Mod d = 0.
```

```
<- 32*4 >= (130 Mod 4).
<- x + 43 = 73 + (34 Mod 4).
<- 0 =< x =< 10  &  0 < y =< 10  &  35*x + 33*y =< 34.
<- 0 < x =< 10  &  x ~= 2  &  x^2 < 12.
```

succeed with the answer `x = 32` for the second goal, answer `x = 0` and `y = 1` for the third goal, and answers `x = 1` and `x = 3` for the fourth goal.

The module `Integers` conforms to the standard for the data type Integer in the Language Compatible Arithmetic Standard (LCAS) [1]. This is a draft ISO standard which specifies the essential properties of integer and floating-point numbers that can be relied on in writing portable software. The implementation of Gödel conforms to this standard.

Next we discuss the module `Rationals` which provides a similar collection of functions and predicates with rational arguments, as does `Integers` for integer arguments. The intended domain is the rationals Q. The various functions, such as +, -, etc., have their usual interpretation as mappings from $Q \times Q$ (or Q, as appropriate) into Q. Similarly, the various predicates, such as >, <, etc., have their usual interpretation on $Q \times Q$.

The function `//` of type `Integer * Integer -> Rational` is the function which is used in the usual construction of the rationals from the integers (see [12, pages 201–204]). However, a rational of the form `N//1` can be written as `N`. The system will assume by default that, if the `Rationals` module is loaded, then a number `N`, which could be an integer or a rational, is a rational provided there is no type information forcing it to have type `Integer`. Rational division in Gödel is denoted by `/`. Thus, `2/3` denotes the rational number 2/3. The module `Rationals` adds to the equality theory imported with the `Integers` using the terms constructed using the functions declared in this module. To illustrate the equality and the convention described above suppose the module

```
CLOSED     Rationals.

IMPORT     Integers.

BASE       Rational.

FUNCTION  //  : yFx(520) : Integer * Integer -> Rational;
          ^   : yFx(540) : Rational * Integer -> Rational;
          -   : Fy(530) : Rational -> Rational;
          *   : yFx(520) : Rational * Rational -> Rational;
          /   : yFx(520) : Rational * Rational -> Rational;
          +   : yFx(510) : Rational * Rational -> Rational;
          -   : yFx(510) : Rational * Rational -> Rational;
          Abs : Rational -> Rational;
          Max : Rational * Rational -> Rational;
          Min : Rational * Rational -> Rational.

PREDICATE >  : zPz : Rational * Rational;
          <  : zPz : Rational * Rational;
          >= : zPz : Rational * Rational;
          =< : zPz : Rational * Rational.
```

`Rationals` is loaded. Then the goal

```
<- x = 5 + 9/7.
```

succeeds with answer `x = 44/7` and the goal

```
<- x = 4/3 + 2/3.
```

succeeds with answer `x = 2`.

When giving answers, the system returns (non-zero) rationals in the form `N/M`, where `M>0` and `Gcd(N,M) = 1`. For example, the goal

```
<- x = -120/-25.
```

succeeds with answer `x = 24/5`.

Gödel solves systems of linear constraints involving rationals, variables of type `Rational`, and the functions and predicates exported by `Rationals`. For example, the goals

```
<- 3*x + 2*y = 3  &  (7/2)*x + y = 0.

<- 4*x + 5 >= 16  &  -x =< 2.
```

succeed with answer `x = -3/4` and `y = 21/8` for the first goal, and answer `x >= 11/4` for the second goal. Note that infinite precision rational arithmetic is provided.

There is also a system module `Floats` that provides floating point numbers and functions and predicates for manipulating these numbers and a system module **Numbers** that provides predicates for converting between the floating point numbers and the rationals. Details of these can be found in Chapter 4 of the Gödel Report.

5 Modules

We now turn to an explanation of the Gödel module system.

5.1 Module Declarations

Most modules consist of two parts, a local part and an export part. The *local part* of a module is indicated by a `LOCAL` or `MODULE` module declaration. The *export part* of a module is indicated by an `EXPORT` or `CLOSED` module declaration. In these declarations, the keywords `LOCAL`, `MODULE`, `EXPORT` and `CLOSED` are followed by the name of the module. In fact, a module may have a local and an export part, or just a local part, or just an export part.

The other kind of module declaration is the `IMPORT` declaration, which names the imported modules.

The export part of a module contains zero or more `IMPORT` declarations, language declarations, and control declarations. The local part of a module contains zero or more `IMPORT` declarations, language declarations, control declarations, and statements. If a module consists *only* of a local part, then this is indicated by using a `MODULE` declaration instead of a `LOCAL` declaration. The use of a `CLOSED` declaration instead of an `EXPORT` declaration will be explained later. To define the meaning of the module declarations, we introduce the following concepts.

We say that (the export part of) a module `M` *imports* a symbol `S` *from* a module `N` if

1. `S` is declared in the export part of `N`,
2. the (export part of) `M` contains a declaration of the form

   `IMPORT` m

   and
3. either $m \equiv$ `N`, or the export part of the module m imports `S` from `N`.

A symbol is *accessible to* the (export part of) a module if it is either declared in or imported into (the export part of) the module.

A module *exports* a symbol if the symbol is accessible to the export part of the module.

Only those symbols accessible to (the export part of) a module are available for use in (the export part of) the module. For instance, any bases or constructors that appear in a `CONSTANT`, `FUNCTION`, or `PREDICATE` declaration in the export part of a module must be accessible to the export part of that module. Moreover, only those constants, functions, propositions, and predicates accessible to a module can appear in statements in the local part of that module. We call the typed first-order language given by the symbols accessible to (the export part of) a module, the *(export) language* of that module.

Certain modules are provided by the system and are called *system modules*. For example, **Integers** and **Lists** are system modules. The complete set of system modules is given in Chapter 13 of the Gödel Report. Other modules are called *user-defined modules*.

We illustrate the module system with modules **M5** and **M6** below. Module **M5** has an export part and a local part. All the symbols accessible to the export part of **M5** are available for use by **M6**. In particular, the declarations for the bases **Day** and **People**, the constants **Monday**, **Fred**, and so on, and for the predicate **Append3** are available for use by other modules which import **M5**. The **IMPORT** declaration in the export part of **M5** makes the symbols exported by **Lists** available for use in **M5**. It also makes the symbols exported by **Integers** available for use in **M5**, since the export part of **Lists** imports **Integers**. Any module which imports **M5** automatically imports all the symbols exported by **Lists** and **Integers** and hence does not need to refer to **Lists** or **Integers** to make these available for use. The local part of **M5** contains the definition of the predicate **Append3**, which uses the definition of **Append** from **Lists**.

```
EXPORT    M5.

IMPORT    Lists.

BASE      Day, People.
CONSTANT  Monday, Tuesday, Wednesday, Thursday, Friday,
          Saturday, Sunday : Day;
          Fred, Bill, Mary : People.

PREDICATE Append3 : List(a) * List(a) * List(a) * List(a).
```

```
LOCAL     M5.

Append3(x,y,z,u) <-
          Append(x,y,w) &
          Append(w,z,u).
```

By contrast with module **M5**, module **M6** has only a local part. Hence its first module declaration uses the keyword **MODULE** instead of **LOCAL**. It imports all the symbols exported by **M5**, which include **Append3** together with all the symbols exported by **Lists** and **Integers**. Module **M6** contains the definition of the predicate **Member2**. **Member2(x,y,z)** is intended to be true if and only if **z** is a list which contains **x** and **y** as members so that **x** precedes **y** in the list.

The symbols exported by **Lists** are shown in its export part (which is complete except for the control declarations) below.

Note that the first module declaration in the export part of **Lists** contains the keyword **CLOSED** instead of **EXPORT**. A module is *closed* if its export part contains a **CLOSED** declaration and *open* if it is not closed. Closed modules allow some propositions or predicates declared in the module, which although

```
MODULE    M6.

IMPORT    M5.

PREDICATE Member2 : a * a * List(a).
Member2(x,y,z) <-
          Append3(u,[x|v],[y|w],z).
```

```
CLOSED     Lists.

IMPORT    Integers.

CONSTRUCTOR
          List/1.

CONSTANT  Nil : List(a).
FUNCTION  Cons : a * List(a) -> List(a).

PREDICATE Member : a * List(a);
          Append : List(a) * List(a) * List(a);
          Permutation : List(a) * List(a);
          Delete : a * List(a) * List(a);
          DeleteFirst : a * List(a) * List(a);
          Reverse : List(a) * List(a);
          Prefix : List(a) * Integer * List(a);
          Suffix : List(a) * Integer * List(a);
          Length : List(a) * Integer;
          Sorted : List(Integer);
          Sort : List(Integer) * List(Integer);
          Merge : List(Integer) * List(Integer) * List(Integer).
```

in principle have a definition via Gödel code, to be actually implemented by another method. All system modules are closed modules. At present, all user-defined modules must be open modules. The latter restriction will be removed once facilities are added to the language to allow programmers to call foreign languages in the local parts of modules.

A type `String` is defined in the system module `Strings` which provides a collection of useful predicates for processing strings. The export part of `Strings` (except for the control declarations) is given below. Note that there is no type for characters.

Strings are treated as an abstract data type. Thus it is not possible to directly access or display the constants and functions used in the (internal) representation of strings. However, as a convenience, Gödel provides the usual double quotes notation for strings as a kind of external notation for them. Thus `"ABC"` is the external notation for the string whose sequence of characters is `A`,`B`,`C`. Similarly, `""` is the external notation for the empty string. A double quote can appear in a string by use of the \ as an escape character, as in `"This is a string with a \" in it."`. The predicate `ListIntAsString` allows conversion between the list of ASCII codes of characters in a string and the string itself. Thus the call `ListIntAsString([77,111,110,100,97,121], x)` would bind `x` to the string whose external notation is `"Monday"`.

This external notation can be used to input string arguments in the following way. Suppose a predicate `P` having declaration

```
PREDICATE  P : String * ... .
```

appears in a program. Then an atom of the form `P("abc",...)`, for example, may appear in a statement or goal. Such an atom is expanded by the system into

```
P(x,...) & ListIntAsString([97,98,99],x).
```

This convention gives users all the convenience of the usual notation for inputting strings and, at the same time, respects the Gödel module conditions. A similar convention applies when the system displays a computed answer of type `String`. The predicate `ConcatStrings` concatenates strings, so that the call `ConcatStrings("MOD", "ULE", x)` would bind `x` to the string `"MODULE"`. The predicate `LengthString` gives the length of a string, so that the call `LengthString("MOD", x)` would bind x to `3`. The predicate `<` is lexicographic less than for strings, `>` is lexicographic greater than, and so on.

5.2 Module Conditions

A *Gödel program* with *main module* `M` is the smallest set of modules including `M` that is closed wrt to the modules named in the import declarations occurring in modules in the set. A module `M` is said to *depend* on a module `N` if the Gödel program with main module `M` includes `N`. A Gödel program must also satisfy a number of *module conditions*. These conditions allow independent compilation and protect procedures defined in one module from being modified by another module. The module conditions are as follows.

- No module may depend upon itself.

```
CLOSED      Strings.

IMPORT      Lists.

BASE        String.

PREDICATE   ListIntAsString : List(Integer) * String;
            ConcatStrings : String * String * String;
            FirstSubString : String * Integer * String;
            LastSubString : String * Integer * String;
            LengthString : String * Integer;
            > : zPz : String * String;
            < : zPz : String * String;
            >= : zPz : String * String;
            =< : zPz : String * String.
```

- For every name appearing in (the export part of) a module, there must be a symbol having that name accessible to (the export part of) the module.
- A module must declare every proposition or predicate defined in that module.
- In a module, a type in a constant declaration or the range type in a function declaration must be either a base type declared in the module or a type with a top-level constructor declared in the module.
- Distinct symbols cannot be declared in the same module with the same category, name, and arity[12].

The enforcement of the final module condition avoids unnecessary ambiguity, but at the same time allows considerable flexibility in overloading. The system uses all the type and indicator information to try to disambiguate the use of a name which could refer to different symbols and, in most cases, will be able to resolve the ambiguity. In those circumstances where it cannot resolve the ambiguity, an overloading error message is issued. Note that, a precondition for an overloading error is the *use* of a name for which there is more than one accessible symbol having this name. By the *use* of a name in a module we mean any appearance of the name except as an identifier declared in a language declaration. So, for example, it is always legal for a module to import two distinct symbols with the same name or to import a symbol with the same name as a symbol declared in the module if the name of these symbols is not used anywhere in the module. This requirement reduces the reporting of overloading errors to those that cause genuine difficulty.

Every symbol appearing in a goal for a Gödel program must be accessible to the main module. If the module is closed, then only those symbols accessible to the export part of the main module may be used.

[12]The arity of a base, constant, or proposition is 0.

As an example, {`M6, M5, Lists, Integers`} is a Gödel program with main module `M6`. Goals for this program could be

```
<- Member2(x,y,[Fred,Bill,Mary]).
<- w : Append3([1,3],[2,5,6],[4,5],z) & Sort(z,w).
```

6 Control

There are two aspects to control in Gödel. The first of these is the computation rule which determines the literal or conditional that will be selected in a goal. The second is Gödel's pruning operator which determines those subtrees that will be pruned from the search tree. We examine each of these in turn.

6.1 Computation Rule

Leaving aside pruning for the moment, the procedural semantics for Gödel is given by SLDNF-resolution[13] [10]. A Gödel program and goal are first transformed to normal form and then the normal goal is run for the normal program under SLDNF-resolution. The computation rule determines which literal or conditional in the current goal will be selected. The Gödel computation rule is partly built into the system and partly under the control of the programmer through explicit `DELAY` control declarations.

The major theoretical requirement of a computation rule is that it be *safe* [10], that is, select only negative literals (other than those of the form `s ~= t`, for which a weaker safeness condition is enforced) which are ground. When a computation rule is safe, a soundness theorem [10] guarantees that every (SLDNF) computed answer is correct (with respect to the completion semantics)[14]. Safeness is built-in to the Gödel system. Thus, whatever control might be specified by user-defined `DELAY` declarations, no non-ground negative literal (other than those of the form `s ~= t`) will ever be selected.

For an example of a `DELAY` declaration consider the predicates `Permutation` and `Sorted` from `Lists`. `Permutation` and `Sorted` have the following control declarations.

```
DELAY      Permutation(x,y) UNTIL NONVAR(x) \/ NONVAR(y).
DELAY      Sorted([]) UNTIL TRUE;
           Sorted([_]) UNTIL TRUE;
           Sorted([x,y|_]) UNTIL NONVAR(x) & NONVAR(y).
```

The `DELAY` declarations are syntactic variants of `when` declarations, which are due to Naish and available in the NU-Prolog system [14]. The meaning of the `DELAY` declaration for `Permutation` is that calls to `Permutation` will delay until either the first argument is not a variable or the second argument is not a variable. The meaning of the `DELAY` declaration for `Sorted` is as follows. If the argument of a call to `Sorted` is not an instance of either `[]`, `[_]`, or `[x,y|_]`, then the call delays. Thus the call `Sorted(x)` delays. If the argument of a call to `Sorted` has the form `[`s`,`t`|`r`]`, where either s or t is a variable, then

[13] Suitably modified to deal with constraints and conditionals.

[14] See also the remark on page 94 of [10] which shows that the weaker safeness condition enforced for the disequality predicate guarantees the soundness of its implementation.

the call delays. Thus the call **Sorted([1,x|y])** delays. If the argument of a call to **Sorted** is either [] or has the form [*r*] or [*s*,*t*|*r*], where *s* and *t* are not variables, then the call can proceed. Thus calls to **Sorted([])** and **Sorted([3,2|x])** can proceed. A **DELAY** declaration has the form:

DELAY *Atom* **UNTIL** *Condition*

where *Atom* is an atom and *Condition* is constructed using **NONVAR**(*var*), **GROUND**(*var*), **TRUE**, and the connectives **&** and \/. The variable *var* must occur in *Atom*. For example, the predicate < in the module **Strings** has the following **DELAY** declaration.

```
DELAY    x < y UNTIL GROUND(x) & GROUND(y).
```

This declaration delays calls to < until both its arguments are ground.

The following conditions are placed on **DELAY** declarations.

- A **DELAY** declaration for a predicate can only appear in the part of the module where the predicate is declared.
- No pair of *Atom*s in the set of **DELAY** declarations for a predicate can have a common instance.

The second condition simplifies the semantics and the implementation of **DELAY** declarations. Without it, a situation could arise where one declaration allowed a call to proceed, while another delayed it.

In a **DELAY** declaration **&** stands for conjunction, \/ for disjunction, **TRUE** for the truth value true. **NONVAR** is true if and only if its argument is a non-variable term, and **GROUND** is true if and only if its argument is a ground term. Now suppose an atom $A = Atom\,\theta$, for some substitution θ. Then we say that **A** *satisfies Condition* if $Condition\,\theta$ has truth value true using the above meanings given to the various connectives and reserved words. Otherwise, we say **A** does *not satisfy Condition*. For example, the atom **Permutation(x,[1|y])** is an instance of the atom in the **DELAY** declaration for **Permutation** and satisfies the corresponding condition, **Sorted([1,y|z])** and **Sorted([1,3|y])** are both instances of the third **DELAY** declaration for **Sorted** but only **Sorted([1,3|z])** satisfies the corresponding condition. A Gödel program and goal is transformed to normal form before execution. Thus the computation rule is only defined for a Gödel program and goal in normal form. We now explain what is meant by normal form.

A *constraint atom* is one of the following:

an atom whose arguments have type **Integer** and whose predicate is =, ~=, >, <, >=, =<, or **Interval**;

an atom whose arguments have type **Rational** and whose predicate is =, ~=, >, <, >=, or =<;

an atom whose arguments have type **Float** and whose predicate is = or ~=.

A *constraint literal* is either a constraint atom or a negative literal whose atom is a constraint atom with predicate =, ~=, >, <, >=, or =< (that is, not **Interval**). Other literals are called *non-constraint literals*. A literal is in *normal form* if either it is a constraint atom or a non-constraint literal.

A conditional is in *normal form* if the condition part is a conjunction of literals in normal form and the then and else parts are conjunctions of literals and/or conditionals in normal form[15]. Conditionals that are in normal form can be run under SLDNF-resolution using the procedural semantics described in Subsection 3.2.

A body is in *normal form* if it is a conjunction of literals and/or conditionals in normal form. A statement is in *normal form* if the body is in normal form and each term of type integer or rational in the head is a unique variable (wrt the statement). A goal is in *normal form* if has a normal body.

Now let `G` be a goal such that when all commits (see the next section) are removed from the body what remains is a goal in normal form. We have already defined the concept of a delayed conditional in a goal `G`, in Subsection 3.2. We now define the concept of a delayed non-constraint literal in `G`.

- A non-ground negative literal in `G` is *delayed*.
- A non-constraint atom in `G` of the form `s ~= t`, for which `s` and `t` unify but only by binding at least one (non-underscore) variable, is *delayed*.
- An atom in `G`, which has a common instance with some *Atom* in a `DELAY` declaration but is not an instance of this *Atom*, is *delayed*.
- An atom in `G`, which is an instance of an *Atom* in a `DELAY` declaration[16] but does not satisfy the corresponding condition *Condition*, is *delayed*.

Then the Gödel computation rule requires that the selected literal or conditional in `G` will be a constraint atom or a conditional or non-constraint literal that is not delayed. In the current sequential implementation it is normally the leftmost such literal or conditional that is selected. If `G` consists entirely of delayed literals and/or conditionals, then the computation halts with the error message that the computation has *floundered*[17].

6.2 Pruning

The most general form of the Gödel pruning operator, called *commit*, has the form `{...}_n`, of which two special cases have the form `|` and `{...}`. The general form of the commit is defined in Chapter 6 of the Gödel Report. We describe here with examples the special cases `|` and `{...}` only.

Consider the module `P1`, which is a variation of the module `Qsort` in Section 5 and for which the predicate `Quicksort` must be called with its first argument instantiated. Module `P1` uses the `|` version of the commit, which we call the *bar* commit. Declaratively, `|` is just conjunction. However, for convenience, either argument of `|` can be omitted, as in the first statement for `Quicksort3`. Each statement can contain at most one `|`. The *scope* of `|` is the formula to its left in the body of the statement. The order in which the statements are tried is not specified, so that commit does not have the sequentiality property of cut. The procedural meaning of `|` is that only one solution is found for the formula in its scope and all other branches arising from the statements containing a `|` are pruned while those without a `|` are not. Thus the meaning of `|` is close

[15] A more formal definition proceeds by induction on the number of conditionals in *Formula2*.

[16] There can be at most one such declaration.

[17] If a sub-computation of a computation flounders, then the computation also flounders.

to the commit of the concurrent logic languages. Note that, while a | commit would normally appear in *every* statement of a definition for which at least one | appears, this is not obligatory.

```
MODULE     P1.

IMPORT    Lists.


PREDICATE Quicksort : List(Integer) * List(Integer).
DELAY     Quicksort(x,_) UNTIL NONVAR(x).
Quicksort(x,y) <-
          Quicksort3(x,y,[]).


PREDICATE Quicksort3 : List(Integer) * List(Integer) *
                                                List(Integer).
DELAY     Quicksort3(x,_,_) UNTIL NONVAR(x).
Quicksort3([],xs,xs) <-
            |.
Quicksort3([x|xs],ys,zs) <-
            |
          Partition(xs,x,l,b) &
          Quicksort3(l,ys,[x|ys1]) &
          Quicksort3(b,ys1,zs).


PREDICATE Partition : List(Integer) * Integer * List(Integer) *
                                                List(Integer).
DELAY     Partition([],_,_,_) UNTIL TRUE;
          Partition([u|_],y,_,_) UNTIL NONVAR(u) & NONVAR(y).
Partition([],y,[],[]) <-
          |.
Partition([x|xs],y,[x|ls],bs) <-
          x =< y |
            Partition(xs,y,ls,bs).
Partition([x|xs],y,ls,[x|bs]) <-
          x > y |
          Partition(xs,y,ls,bs).
```

The **DELAY** declarations for **Quicksort** and **Quicksort3** delay calls to these predicates until their first argument is not a variable. The **DELAY** declaration for **Partition** ensures that either the first argument of a call to **Partition** will have its first argument the empty list, or the first element of the list in the first argument and the second argument will be known so that an arithmetic comparison between these can be carried out.

With these delay declarations, the statements for **Quicksort3** are mutually exclusive, in the sense that the system can commit to at most one of them. The same is true for **Partition**. Thus no answer will be pruned – only useless computation will be pruned. So, in this case, the commits enhance efficiency without affecting completeness. More generally, the commits can prune answers.

Next we illustrate the Gödel one-solution commit, written {...}. Consider the module P2. The intended meaning of **Perm** in **P2** is that it should be true when its first argument is a list of integers and its second argument is a permutation of the list in the first argument.

```
MODULE       P2.

IMPORT       Lists.


PREDICATE    Perm : List(Integer) * List(Integer).
DELAY        Perm(x,y) UNTIL NONVAR(x) \/ NONVAR(y).
Perm([],[]).
Perm([x|y],[u|v]) <-
             Del(u,[x|y],z) &
             Perm(z,v).


PREDICATE    Del : Integer * List(Integer) * List(Integer).
DELAY        Del(_,y,z) UNTIL NONVAR(y) \/ NONVAR(z).
Del(x,[x|y],y).
Del(x,[y|z],[y|w]) <-
             Del(x,z,w).
```

A goal such as

```
<- Perm([1,2,3],x).
```

will produce (in some order) the sequence of computed answers

```
x = [1,2,3]
x = [1,3,2]
...
x = [3,2,1]
```

If instead the goal was

```
<- {Perm([1,2,3],x)}.
```

then only one answer, `x = [1,3,2]`, say, would be produced. The scope of the one-solution commit {...} is the formula between the { and the }. When the scope is solved, all possible alternative solutions to the scope are pruned away. Of course, the one-solution commit can also be used in the bodies of statements in a program.

The bar commit and the one-solution commit provide programmers with powerful pruning facilities, which should suffice for the vast majority of programming tasks. However, source-level tools, such as program transformers and partial evaluators, have need of a more powerful pruning operator. The reason is that the class of programs containing | is not closed under even simple program transformations, such as unfolding. For this reason, Gödel has a more powerful pruning operator, {...}_n, which includes the | and {...} as special cases, and which gives a class of programs closed under the usual program transformations. This pruning operator was introduced in [8]. A more formal description of the procedural semantics of commit can be found in Chapter 6 of the Gödel Report [7].

7 Input/Output

The Gödel input and output facilities are provided by the system modules `IO`, `NumbersIO`, `ProgramIO`, and `TheoryIO`. The first two modules are discussed in this section. The last two are relevant for meta-programming applications and so the discussion of these is postponed to Section 8.

The basic module is `IO`, the export part (except for the `DELAY` declarations) of which is given below. Types `InputStream` and `OutputStream` are provided for input and output streams. To open a file for reading, the predicate `FindInput` is used. Its first argument is the name of a file (given as a string), the second argument is the new input stream, and the third argument contains either the constant `Found` or `NotFound` depending on whether the attempt to open the file was successful or not. Similarly, `FindOutput` is used to open a file for writing. The read predicates are `ReadChar`, which returns the ASCII code of the next character read from the open input stream, and `ReadString`, which returns a string of length 1 containing the next character read from the open input stream, assuming the end of the stream has not yet been reached. The write predicates are `WriteChar`, which writes the character whose ASCII code is the second argument to the open output stream, and `WriteString`, which writes the string of characters in the second argument to the open output stream. The predicate `EndInput` closes an open input stream and `EndOutput` closes an output stream.

As an example of the use of the module `IO`, the module `DisplayFile` below reads a file as input and displays it on standard output. Gödel's input and output system modules do not have a declarative semantics. So the use of these modules should be confined to as small a part of a Gödel program as possible. Let us say a module is an *input/output module* if it depends upon the module `IO`. Then the key idea is to have the input/output modules as high as possible, preferably at the top, of the module hierarchy of a program. In fact, a natural module structure is to have just the main module of a program importing the system input/output modules. In this case, all the other modules in the program have a declarative semantics. There is a strong incentive for programmers to adopt this kind of module structure, since it is only modules that are not input/output that the common tools of program transformation, declarative debugging, and so on, apply.

The system module `NumbersIO` provides input/output facilities for integers, rationals, and floating-point numbers. It also provides conversion between a

```
CLOSED     IO.

IMPORT     Strings.

BASE       InputStream, OutputStream, ResultOfFind.

CONSTANT   StandardInput : InputStream;
           StandardOutput, StandardError : OutputStream;
           Found, NotFound : ResultOfFind.

PREDICATE  FindInput : String * InputStream * ResultOfFind;
           FindOutput : String * OutputStream * ResultOfFind;
           FindUpdate : String * OutputStream * ResultOfFind;
           EndInput : InputStream;
           EndOutput : OutputStream;
           ReadChar : InputStream * Integer;
           ReadString : InputStream * String;
           WriteChar : OutputStream * Integer;
           WriteString : OutputStream * String;
           NewLine : OutputStream;
           Flush : OutputStream.
```

```
MODULE    DisplayFile.
IMPORT    Strings, IO.

PREDICATE Display : String.
DELAY     Display(x) UNTIL GROUND(x).
Display(file) <-
          FindInput(file, stream, result) &
          IF result = Found
          THEN ReadChar(stream, c) &
               DisplayStream(stream, c) &
               EndInput(stream)
          ELSE
               WriteString(StandardOutput, "File not found") &
               NewLine(StandardOutput).

PREDICATE DisplayStream : InputStream * Integer.
DELAY     DisplayStream(x,c) UNTIL GROUND(x) & GROUND(c).
DisplayStream(stream, c) <-
          IF c ~= -1
          THEN WriteChar(StandardOutput, c) &
               ReadChar(stream, c1) &
               DisplayStream(stream, c1).
```

number and its representation as a string which is often useful for input and output. Details of **NumbersIO** are given in Chapter 7 of the Gödel Report.

8 Meta-Programming

The ground representation is a scheme for representing typed languages, programs, goals, and theories as terms in a meta-language. In Gödel the details of the representation are not made explicit (for details of various ways of setting up a ground representation, see [2], [5], or [6]). Instead, following an abstract data type approach, Gödel provides, via the system modules **Syntax**, **Program**, and **Theory**, a set of predicates which allow a program that imports them to access and manipulate terms representing object expressions. The constants and functions actually used in the representation are hidden in the local part of these modules.

Gödel supports the ground representation of both Gödel programs and first-order theories, the former with the module **Program** and the latter with the module **Theory**. A third module, **Syntax**, provides facilities for the manipulation of the representations of object expressions common to both of the ground representations and is imported by both **Program** and **Theory**. The complete export parts of the system modules **Syntax**, **Program**, and **Theory** are given in Chapter 13 of the Gödel report.

In order to explain the ground representation we need to introduce the flat name of a symbol and the flat form of a Gödel program. For clarity in this discussion, what we called before the *name* of a symbol, we now call the *declared name* of the symbol. In the context of Gödel program, which normally consists of a number of modules, a symbol can always be uniquely identified by the quadruple consisting of the name of the module **M** in which the symbol is declared, the declared name **S** of the symbol, its category **C**, and its arity[18] **A**. Such a quadruple (**M**, **S**, **C**, **A**) is called the *flat name* of the symbol.

The *flat form* of a program **P** is the program obtained from **P** by replacing each occurrence of the declared name of a symbol in **P** by the flat name of the symbol. The *flat language of a program* **P** is the typed language given by the collection of language declarations in the flat form of **P**. It is the flat form of an object program that is represented in Gödel, because each symbol in the flat language has a unique name and therefore each name has a natural unique representation.

8.1 Syntax and Program

Here we briefly describe the modules **Syntax** and **Program**. The module **Syntax** imports all the symbols exported by **Integers**, **Lists**, and **Strings**. It also declares (amongst others) the following bases, which are required by the ground representation of languages.

```
BASE      OName, OType, OTerm, OFormula, OTypeSubst, OTermSubst,
          OVarTyping.
```

[18] For bases, constants, and propositions, the arity is extraneous, of course. We include it in these cases for uniformity.

OName is intended for terms representing the names of symbols; **OType**, **OTerm**, and **OFormula** are intended for terms representing types, terms, and formulas, respectively; **OTypeSubst** and **OTermSubst** are intended for terms representing type and term substitution; and **OVarTyping** is intended for terms representing a variable typing (a set of assignments of variables to types).

The module **Syntax** exports a large number of predicates for constructing object terms and formulas, for testing whether or not a given expression is of a certain form, and for performing a number of standard tasks such as the unification of two object terms. A brief discussion of a selection of these predicates follows, concentrating on those used in the examples in this section. To simplify the discussion, we adopt the convention that uppercase calligraphic symbols $\mathcal{U}$, $\mathcal{V}$, $\mathcal{W}$ ... denote the object-level expressions represented by Gödel variables u, v, w ... of type **OName**, **OType**, **OTerm**, **OFormula** etc.

```
PREDICATE And : OFormula * OFormula * OFormula;
          IsImpliedBy : OFormula * OFormula * OFormula;
          AndWithEmpty : OFormula * OFormula * OFormula;
          EmptyFormula : OFormula.
```

`And(u,v,w)` is true when $\mathcal{W}$ is the expression $\mathcal{U}$ & $\mathcal{V}$.
`IsImpliedBy(u,v,w)` is true when $\mathcal{W}$ is $\mathcal{U}$ <- $\mathcal{V}$.
`AndWithEmpty(u,v,w)` is true when $\mathcal{W}$ is formed as follows: if $\mathcal{U}$ is the empty formula, $\mathcal{W}$ is $\mathcal{V}$; otherwise if $\mathcal{V}$ is the empty formula, $\mathcal{W}$ is $\mathcal{U}$; otherwise $\mathcal{W}$ is $\mathcal{U}$ & $\mathcal{V}$.
`EmptyFormula(u)` is true when $\mathcal{U}$ is the empty formula.

```
PREDICATE Atom : OFormula;
          PredicateAtom : OFormula * OName * List(OTerm).
```

`Atom(u)` is true when $\mathcal{U}$ is an atom.
`PredicateAtom(u,p,[t1,...,tn])` is true when $\mathcal{U}$ is an atom, $\mathcal{P}$ is the name of the predicate in $\mathcal{U}$, and $\mathcal{T}_1, \ldots, \mathcal{T}_n$ are the arguments of $\mathcal{P}$ in $\mathcal{U}$.

```
PREDICATE EmptyTermSubst : OTermSubst;
          ComposeTermSubsts : OTermSubst * OTermSubst *
                                                      OTermSubst;
          RestrictSubstToFormula : OFormula * OTermSubst *
                                                      OTermSubst.
```

`EmptyTermSubst(s)` is true when $\mathcal{S}$ is the empty term substitution.
`ComposeTermSubsts(q,r,s)` is true when $\mathcal{S}$ is the substitution formed from the composition[19] of $\mathcal{Q}$ and $\mathcal{R}$.
`RestrictSubstToFormula(u,r,s)` is true when $\mathcal{S}$ is the substitution obtained by restricting $\mathcal{R}$ to the variables of the formula $\mathcal{U}$.

```
PREDICATE EmptyVarTyping : OVarTyping.
```

`EmptyVarTyping(v)` is true when $\mathcal{V}$ is an empty variable typing.

[19] defined in [10], page 21.

```
PREDICATE UnifyAtoms : OFormula * OFormula * OTermSubst;
          RenameFormula : List(OFormula) * List(OFormula) *
                                                  List(OFormula);
          Derive : OFormula * OFormula * OFormula * OFormula *
                                  OFormula * OTermSubst * OFormula.
```

`UnifyAtoms(u,v,s)` is true when $\mathcal{U}$ and $\mathcal{V}$ are atoms and $\mathcal{S}$ is their mgu. `RenameFormula([u1,...,un],[v1,...,vm],[w1,...,wm])` is true when $\mathcal{W}_1, \ldots, \mathcal{W}_m$ are the formulas obtained by making a specific renaming of the the free variables in $\mathcal{V}_1, \ldots, \mathcal{V}_m$ so that they are distinct from the free variables in the formulas $\mathcal{U}_1, \ldots, \mathcal{U}_n$.
`Derive(u,v,w,x,y,s,z)` is true when $\mathcal{U}$ <- $\mathcal{V}$ & $\mathcal{W}$ & $\mathcal{X}$ is a resultant with selected atom $\mathcal{W}$, $\mathcal{Y}$ is a statement, $\mathcal{S}$ is an mgu of $\mathcal{W}$ and the head of the $\mathcal{Y}$, and $\mathcal{Z}$ is the new resultant formed by resolving the given resultant and statement on atom $\mathcal{W}$.

The module `Program` imports `Syntax` and, in addition, declares the following bases required in the representation of a Gödel program.

```
BASE       OProgram, OModulePart, OCondition.
```

`OProgram` is intended for terms representing the flat form of Gödel programs. `OModulePart` is for constants representing the keywords `EXPORT`, `LOCAL`, `CLOSED` and `MODULE`, which distinguish the various kinds of module parts. Thus there are four constants of type `OModulePart` with declarations as follows.

```
CONSTANT  Export, Local, Closed, Module : OModulePart.
```

`OCondition` is intended for terms representing conditions in `DELAY` declarations.

In addition to these types, `Program` exports a large number of predicates, including predicates for translating between object-level expressions in the form of a string and the internal representations of these expressions, for inserting and deleting statements and declarations in a module, and for running goals for an object program. We now describe some of these predicates that are needed for the examples that follow.

The first predicate is used to determine whether a given object-level expression is a valid formula in the flat language of a particular program and in the context of a specific assignment of types to its free variables.

```
PREDICATE FormulaInProgram : OProgram * OVarTyping * OFormula *
                                                      OVarTyping.
```

`FormulaInProgram(p,u,v,w)` is true when $\mathcal{V}$ is a formula in the flat language of $\mathcal{P}$, and $\mathcal{W}$ is the variable typing obtained by combining variable typing $\mathcal{U}$ with the types of the free variables occurring in $\mathcal{V}$.

The next three predicates manipulate the statements of the object program.

```
PREDICATE StatementMatchAtom : OProgram * String * OFormula *
                                                        OFormula;
          DefinitionInProgram : OProgram * String * OName *
                                                  List(OFormula);
          InsDelStatement : OProgram * String * OFormula *
                                                        OProgram.
```

`StatementMatchAtom(p,m,u,v)` is true when `m` is the name of an open module in $\mathcal{P}$, $\mathcal{U}$ is an atom, and $\mathcal{V}$ is a statement in the module with a proposition or predicate in the head that is the same as that in $\mathcal{U}$.
`DefinitionInProgram(p,m,r,[u1,...,un])` is true when `m` is the name of an open module in $\mathcal{P}$, $\mathcal{R}$ is the flat name of a proposition or predicate declared in module `m`, and $\mathcal{U}_1,\ldots,\mathcal{U}_n$ are all the statements in the definition of $\mathcal{R}$.
`InsDelStatement(p,m,u,q)` is true when `m` is the name of an open module in $\mathcal{P}$, $\mathcal{U}$ is a statement in the flat language of $\mathcal{P}$, and $\mathcal{Q}$ is a program that differs from $\mathcal{P}$ only in that it also contains statement $\mathcal{U}$ in module `m`. The mode declarations for this predicate allow it to be used for both inserting and deleting statements from an object program.

The last two predicates allow conversion between the hidden ground representation and visible Gödel syntax.

```
PREDICATE StringToProgramFormula : OProgram * String * String *
                                                   List(OFormula);
          ProgramTermToString : OProgram * String * String *
                                                           OTerm.
```

`StringToProgramFormula(p,m,s,[u1,...,un])` is true when `m` is the name of a module in $\mathcal{P}$, and $\mathcal{U}_1,\ldots,\mathcal{U}_n$ are all formulas in the language of module `m` that can be obtained by parsing `s` using the grammar of Gödel. Note that multiple parses are possible because Gödel allows symbols to be overloaded.
`ProgramTermToString(p,m,s,t)` is true when `m` is the name of a module in $\mathcal{P}$, and `s` is a string representation of the term $\mathcal{T}$. Any subterms of the $\mathcal{T}$ not in the language of module `m` do not appear in the string.

As an example of the use of the module `Program`, we give below the module `Dynamic` that defines a predicate `RemoveAll`, a declarative counterpart of Prolog's *retractall*.

So that a meta-program can access the term representing an object program or object theory, Gödel provides system modules called `ProgramIO` and `TheoryIO`. `ProgramIO` exports predicates

```
PREDICATE GetProgram : InputStream * OProgram;
          PutProgram : OutputStream * OProgram.
```

which allow the ground representation of an object program to be read from or written to a file. `TheoryIO` exports similar predicates.

8.2 An Example Meta-Program

We now give another example to illustrate further the use of the Gödel meta-programming facilities. This example consists of the module `BreadthFirst` which implements a basic breadth-first interpreter for definite object programs. `BreadthFirst` maintains a queue of unexplored SLD-nodes, and performs its search by taking the first node from the queue, computing all the children of this node in the SLD-tree, and adding them to the end of the queue of unexplored nodes. Nodes are represented by the function `Node`, whose arguments are the resultant and substitution at the node. A check is made before starting the computation to ensure that `BreadthFirst` has been given a definite goal in the language of the object program.

```
MODULE    Dynamic.

IMPORT    Program.

PREDICATE RemoveAll : OProgram * String * OFormula * OProgram.
DELAY     RemoveAll(x,y,z,_)
                    UNTIL GROUND(x) & GROUND(y) & GROUND(z).
RemoveAll(prog, mod, atom, new_prog) <-
          Atom(atom) &
          RemoveAll1(prog, mod, atom, new_prog).

PREDICATE RemoveAll1 : OProgram * String * OLanguage *
                                          OFormula * OProgram.
RemoveAll1(prog, mod, atom, new_prog) <-
          IF SOME [prog1] Remove(prog, mod, atom, prog1)
          THEN RemoveAll1(prog1, mod, atom, new_prog)
          ELSE new_prog = prog.

PREDICATE Remove : OProgram * String * OFormula * OProgram.
Remove(prog, mod, atom, new_prog) <-
          StatementMatchAtom(prog, mod, atom, stmt) &
          IsImpliedBy(head, _, stmt) &
          RenameFormula([head], [atom], [atom1]) &
          UnifyAtoms(head, atom1, _) &
          InsDelStatement(new_prog, mod, stmt, prog).
```

The module TestBF imports BreadthFirst for the purposes of the demonstration. It also imports ProgramIO, which is needed to read in the object program, and a module called Answers which provides a predicate AnswerString, used to convert the ground representation of the answer substitution into the form of a string so that it can be displayed. AnswerString is implemented using predicates exported by Program.

```
EXPORT    BreadthFirst.

IMPORT    Program.

PREDICATE BreadthFirst : OProgram * OFormula * OTermSubst.
```

```
LOCAL     BreadthFirst.

BASE      SLDNode.
FUNCTION  Node : OFormula * OTermSubst -> SLDNode.
```

```
BreadthFirst(program, goal, computed_answer) <-
   ConjunctionOfAtoms(goal) &
   EmptyVarTyping(empty_var_types) &
   FormulaInProgram(program, empty_var_types, goal, _) &
   IsImpliedBy(goal, goal, resultant) &
   EmptyTermSubst(empty_subst) &
   Breadth(program, [Node(resultant, empty_subst)], answer) &
   RestrictSubstToFormula(goal, answer, computed_answer).

PREDICATE Breadth : OProgram * List(SLDNode) * OTermSubst.
Breadth(program, [Node(resultant, subst)|nodes], answer) <-
   IsImpliedBy(head, body, resultant) &
   IF EmptyFormula(body)
   THEN
      answer = subst \/
      Breadth(program, nodes, answer)
   ELSE
      Select(body, left, sel, right) &
      PredicateAtom(sel, predicate, _) &
      DefinitionInProgram(program, _, predicate, defn) &
      DeriveAll(defn, head, left, sel, right, subst, children) &
      Append(nodes, children, new_nodes) &
      Breadth(program, new_nodes, answer).

PREDICATE DeriveAll : List(OFormula) * OFormula * OFormula *
                OFormula * OFormula * OTermSubst * List(SLDNode).
DeriveAll([], _, _, _, _, _, []).
DeriveAll([stat|rest], head, left, sel, right, subst, nodes) <-
   RenameFormula([head, left, sel, right], [stat], [stat1]) &
   ( IF SOME [mgu, resultant]
        Derive(head, left, sel, right, stat1, mgu, resultant)
     THEN
        ComposeTermSubsts(subst, mgu, new_subst) &
        nodes = [Node(resultant, new_subst)|nodes1]
     ELSE
        nodes = nodes1
   ) &
   DeriveAll(rest, head, left, sel, right, subst, nodes1).

PREDICATE Select : OFormula * OFormula * OFormula * OFormula.
Select(atom, empty, atom, empty) <-
   Atom(atom) |
   EmptyFormula(empty).
Select(body, left, sel, right) <-
   And(left_body, right_body, body) |
   Select(left_body, left, sel, right1) &
   AndWithEmpty(right1, right_body, right).
```

```
EXPORT Answers.

IMPORT Program.

PREDICATE AnswerString : OProgram * String * OTermSubst * String.
DELAY     AnswerString(x,y,z,_)
                        UNTIL GROUND(x) & GROUND (y) & GROUND(z).
```

```
EXPORT TestBF.

IMPORT BreadthFirst, ProgramIO, Answers.
```

We shall use module **M1** given in Section 1 as the object program for the demonstration. Before the object program can be loaded by the **GetProgram** predicate, it must be compiled into its ground representation. The Gödel system provides a utility called the *program compiler* that creates the ground representation in a file with extension **.prm**. The program compiler is invoked by the command **;pc**. Gödel also provides a program decompiler, which will recover the text of the modules of a program from its ground representation.

In the transcript that follows, the **TestBF** program is loaded, and then the program compiler is used to generate the ground representation of **M1**. Finally, an example goal is given that reads in the object program, constructs the representation of a query given in the form of a string, calls **BreadthFirst** to evaluate the query, and translates the representation of the computed answer back into a string.

```
% goedel
Goedel 0.23
Type ;h for help.
[] <- ;l TestBF.
Loading program "TestBF" ...
Loading program "ProgramIO" ...
Loading program "Program" ...
Loading program "AVLTrees" ...
Loading program "Strings" ...
Loading program "Lists" ...
Loading program "Integers" ...
Loading program "Syntax" ...
Loading program "IO" ...
Loading program "BreadthFirst" ...
Loading program "Answers" ...
[TestBF] <- ;pc M1.

Reading file "M1.loc" ...
Parsing module "M1" ...
```

```
Ground representation of program "M1" is in file "M1.prm".
[TestBF] <- answer :
   FindInput("M1.prm", s, Found) &
   GetProgram(s, p) &
   StringToProgramFormula(p, "M1",
   "Append3(x, y, z, Cons(Monday, Cons(Tuesday, Nil)))", [w]) &
   BreadthFirst(p, w, a) &
   AnswerString(p, "M1", a, answer).

answer = "{x/Nil,y/Nil,z/Cons(Monday,Cons(Tuesday,Nil))}" ? ;

answer = "{x/Nil,y/Cons(Monday,Nil),z/Cons(Tuesday,Nil)}" ? ;

answer = "{x/Cons(Monday,Nil),y/Nil,z/Cons(Tuesday,Nil)}" ? ;

answer = "{x/Nil,y/Cons(Monday,Cons(Tuesday,Nil)),z/Nil}" ? ;

answer = "{x/Cons(Monday,Nil),y/Cons(Tuesday,Nil),z/Nil}" ?
Yes
[TestBF] <- ;q.
%
```

9 Semantics

We now outline the declarative and procedural semantics of Gödel programs.

First we remove the module structure of a program. Let P be a Gödel program. The *flat form* of a program P is obtained from P by replacing each occurrence of the declared name of a symbol in P by the flat name of the symbol[20]. The *flat language of a program* P is the typed language defined by the language declarations in the flat form of P. The *compacted form* of P is obtained by using the flat language of P as the language of the compacted form, the DELAY declarations of the flat form as the control declarations, and all the statements of the flat form of P as its statements. (Thus the compacted form of a program is obtained from the flat form by removing the module structure.)

9.1 Declarative Semantics

We now give the declarative semantics of a Gödel program and goal.

The *(typed) logic program* P' *underlying* P is obtained by using all the language declarations of the compacted form of P to define the language of P' and all the statements of the compacted form of P as its statements with all commits removed and all conditionals replaced by the formulas giving their meanings, as discussed in Subsection 3.2. A *goal* for the logic program P' is of the form <- W, where W is a formula in the typed language of P' not containing commits or conditionals. Any Gödel goal to P can be transformed to a goal for P' by deleting all commits, replacing any conditionals by the formulas giving their meanings, and replacing the declared names of all symbols in the goal by their flat names.

[20] The concepts *declared* name and *flat* name of a symbol are introduced in Section 8.

Then the declarative semantics of `P` is defined to be the completion[21] [10] `P'`, except for the predicates in the modules **`Integers`**, **`Rationals`**, and **`Floats`**, which use the theories given in their export parts. The completion of a many-sorted program is given in [10, page 145], except that we do *not* include axiom schema 9 (the domain closure axioms) of the equality theory. In fact, a straightforward generalisation of the definition of completion, as given in [10], is required to handle polymorphism. Such a generalisation is described in [4].

9.2 Procedural Semantics

Next we turn to the procedural semantics, for which the starting point is the compacted form of a Gödel program `P`. The first step is to transform the compacted form of the program and a corresponding goal into normal form. For this purpose, the transformations given in [8], which depend upon those given in [10, page 113], are employed. However, we need an extension of the definition of normal form and the transformations given in [8] to handle the constraints and conditionals. The definition of this extended version of normal form is that (excluding commits) each body is a conjunction of non-constraint literals, constraint atoms, and/or normal conditionals and, in the head of a statement, the only terms of type **`Integer`**, **`Rational`**, or **`Float`** are unique variables. The transformation from the compacted form of a program and a corresponding goal to this normal form is described in Chapter 9 of the Gödel Report.

The procedural semantics (excluding the commit, for the moment) is defined to be SLDNF-resolution [10], augmented with the mechanism described earlier for executing the conditionals and constraints. Since the head and transparency conditions are enforced, the untyped unification algorithm can be used (after the program and goal have been type checked). Note that the unification algorithm does the occur check wherever necessary, otherwise, incorrect answers may be computed, although there is substantial opportunity for analysing most occur checks away. The computation rule, although not completely specified, does satisfy the condition defined in Subsection 6.1. Thus the computation rule is guaranteed to be safe.

To complete the definition of the procedural semantics, we add the pruning operator commit, whose procedural semantics is given in Chapter 7 of the Gödel Report. Note that, to ensure the soundness of the procedural semantics, pruning is disabled when evaluating a negative call or running the condition in the conditionals.

Acknowledgements

Our first and principal acknowledgement is to John Lloyd who has led and encouraged the Gödel team (both designers and implementers). Without John there would be no Gödel language. Real thanks go to Jiwei Wang who has worked extremely hard on the project over the last few months to produce the current implementation. We would like to thank Alastair Burt who contributed much to the project in its initial stages. Thanks also to Andrea Domenici who

[21] It is possible to take a view of the declarative semantics of Gödel different from that of the completion. However, provided SLDNF-resolution is sound with respect to the chosen declarative semantics, very little depends upon the choice.

helped with the implementation of the parser. The second author is indebted to the Division of Artificial Intelligence (and in particular Dr A. Cohn) in Leeds for supporting and encouraging her work on Gödel. Finally, we would like to thank the many people who have contributed by means of comments, criticisms, and discussions to the shape of the language Gödel.

References

[1] *Language Compatible Arithmetic Standard, ISO/IEC 10967:1991*, March 1991. First Committee Draft (Version 3.1), JTC1/SC22/WG11 N229; X3T2 91-073.

[2] K.A. Bowen and R.A. Kowalski. Amalgamating language and metalanguage in logic programming. In K.L. Clark and S.-A. Tarnlund, editors, *Logic Programming*, pages 153–172. Academic Press, 1982.

[3] H. B. Enderton. *A Mathematical Introduction to Logic.* Academic Press, 1972.

[4] P. M. Hill. Typed logic programs and their completion. Technical Report 92.05, School of Computer Studies, 1992.

[5] P.M. Hill and J.W. Lloyd. Meta-programming for dynamic knowledge bases. Technical Report CS-88-18, Department of Computer Science, University of Bristol, 1988.

[6] P.M. Hill and J.W. Lloyd. Analysis of meta-programs. In H.D. Abramson and M.H. Rogers, editors, *Meta-Programming in Logic Programming*, pages 23–52. MIT Press, 1989. Proceedings of the Meta88 Workshop, June 1988.

[7] P.M. Hill and J.W. Lloyd. The Gödel report. Technical Report TR-91-02, Department of Computer Science, University of Bristol, 1991. Revised June 1992.

[8] P.M. Hill, J.W. Lloyd, and J.C. Shepherdson. Properties of a pruning operator. *Journal of Logic and Computation*, 1(1):99–143, 1990.

[9] P.M. Hill and R.W. Topor. A semantics for typed logic programs. In F. Pfenning, editor, *Types in Logic Programming.* MIT Press, 1992.

[10] J.W. Lloyd. *Foundations of Logic Programming.* Springer-Verlag, second edition, 1987.

[11] L. Naish. Negation and quantifiers in NU-Prolog. In E. Shapiro, editor, *Proceedings of the Third International Conference on Logic Programming*, London, pages 624–634. Lecture Notes in Computer Science 225, Springer-Verlag, 1986.

[12] H. Paley and P.M. Weichsel. *Elements of Abstract and Linear Algebra.* Holt, Rinehart and Winston, 1972.

[13] E. Shapiro. The family of concurrent logic programming languages. *ACM Computing Surveys*, 21(3):412–510, 1989.

[14] J. A. Thom and J. Zobel. Nu-prolog reference manual, version 1.3. Technical report, Machine Intelligence Project, Department of Computer Science, University of Melbourne, 1988.

Parallel Logic Programming in Strand: A Tutorial

John Florentin
and
Martin Gittins
Strand Software Technologies Ltd., Ver House,
Markyate, AL3 8JP, England.

Abstract

Strand is a logic programming language designed for efficient programming of parallel computers. This tutorial describes the syntax and semantics of Strand and illustrates some of the programming techniques that can be used to construct real Strand programs. The syntax is based on Prolog, but the semantics are quite different and Strand does not support those features of Prolog that might impair performance on real parallel machines. The absence of backtracking and unification reveals dataflow as the dominant feature of the computational model.

1 Logic Languages and Parallel Programming

Parallel execution goes naturally with logic programs since independent parts of a logical formula may be proved in any time order, or simultaneously. Prolog is the most widely recognised logic language and proposals for parallel execution of Prolog programs were made as soon as the language was developed. However, it was found that making minor modifications to the Prolog language to make parallelism possible produced an unsatisfactory result, and so a fundamental re-appraisal of parallel execution was needed.

This re-appraisal led to the emergence of logic languages designed from the outset for parallel execution. Some basic features of Prolog, like the sequential evaluation of goals and unification, were modified, or dropped. Shapiro [1] gives an extensive survey of the many parallel logic languages put forward up to 1989.

In the mid 1980's, while the re-consideration of parallelism in logic languages was under way, several computer manufacturers began to sell multi-processor machines intended to obtain high performance through parallel execution. In use, these multi-processor machines were found to be very difficult to program using conventional languages like Fortran.

The ideal solution to these programming difficulties seemed to be the introduction of a parallel logic language which could be implemented efficiently, could be ported readily across to several different machines, and which was easy to learn.

Strand [2] is the extreme point in a spectrum of languages, such as Parlog and Flat Concurrent Prolog, that explore the trade-offs of parallel logic programming. It has been implemented on both shared memory and distributed memory multi-processor machines, and is available as a commercially supported product, STRAND[88] [3].

It has been found that Strand is equally useful for implementing programs which run across a distributed network of machines. Strand is therefore also a language for distributed programming and it is being used more and more for this purpose.

Strand is the result of careful simplification and refinement of every feature of parallel logic programming. At the syntactic level Strand closely resembles Prolog, but its operation is different. Backtracking and unification have been replaced by pattern matching and a computational model based on dataflow concepts.

1.1 The Memory Model

At the programming level, Strand is best viewed as a language for multi-processor machines that supports a single shared name space.

In this model the shared name space, which holds all the variables and data values, can be accessed by many processors. The design of Strand takes care of all the complications of mapping this shared name space onto real shared memory or distributed memory machines. Programmers do not have to worry about clashes as different processors access the same variables or data structures.

2 The Strand Language

Strand programs manipulate *terms*. A term is a real number, an integer, a character string, a variable, a tuple, a list or a user defined datatype.

Variables follow the Prolog convention and start with a capital letter.

Tuples are fixed length vectors of terms written between curly brackets. An example of a tuple is `{myTuple, 2.1, 'ABC'}`. This tuple can also be written - `myTuple(2.1, 'ABC')`.

Lists are varying length sequences of terms written between square brackets. An example of a list is `[myList, 2.1, 'ABC']`.

In Strand, computations are carried out by *processes*. The process p with argument terms, T1, T2, .. Tn, is written: `p(T1,T2, .. Tn)`.

Processes resemble goals in Prolog in several respects, including defining structures as arguments in process definitions. However a different name is used because the computation associated with a Strand process can be either active or suspended. Suspended processes wait for data to be calculated by other parts of the computation, and resume activity when the data is available. Strand programs can therefore be event-driven, or, in Shapiro's terminology, reactive, rather than direct computations from input to results.

2.1 How Does a Strand Program Execute ?

A Strand program executes as a collection of parallel computations. New processes are created dynamically as a program executes. As each process completes its work, it disappears and the computational resources allocated to it are reclaimed automatically by the Strand garbage collector. Processes can spawn new processes as they execute. Thus, a Strand program executes as a constantly changing pool of processes.

A Strand process picks-up input data from the shared name space and places its computed results back in new locations in the name space. Because there is only one name space, the data output of one process can be read as input data to other processes. The shared data and variables in the name space connect the processes to each other forming a complete network.

2.2 An Example of a Strand Process

An example of a Strand process definition is:

```
twice(Number, Result) :- Number > 0 |
                         Result is 2*Number.
twice(Number, Result) :- Number =< 0 |
                         Result := 0.
```

In this definition of the twice process, Number is the input data store location and Result is the store location where the output is placed. The definition of twice has two cases, or clauses, which are selected for execution by the *guards* -

Number > 0 and

Number =< 0

A clause can only be selected if all of its arguments can be matched, and all of the guards succeed. Notice that the computed answer has to be assigned to a named location.

A computation, such as - Result is 2*Number, is called the *body* of the process. The computation of the body is spawned off as a new process separate from the original twice process.

Strand uses run-time typing and variables can be assigned data of any type; all data is tagged with its type. All variables behave like logic variables, values can be assigned to them only once, making Strand a *single assignment* language.

2.3 Non-Determinism in Strand

If the above definition of twice were changed to:

```
nonDtwice(Number, Result) :- Number >= 0 |
                             Result is 2*Number.
nonDtwice(Number, Result) :- Number =< 0 |
                             Result := 0.
```

an input data value of 0 in Number would make both guards true. In this situation one body - either, Result is 2*Number, or, Result := 0 - is selected. The system arbitrarily chooses which body will be selected. On different runs of the same program, in theory, different selections can occur. However, in practice, the system will make the same choices every time, but programmers should not assume this will always be the case. In particular there is no guarantee that different versions, or different machines will make the same selections .

This feature means that Strand is non-deterministic.

2.4 Starting Program Execution

A program could be started by the calls - `twice(3,W),twice(W,Y)`. Two twice processes are invoked simultaneously, the variable W being shared for communication. This creates a simple network of two processes communicating via the location W.
Note that the second process - `twice(W,Y)` - cannot actually start until the first process - `twice(3,W)` has completed. A Strand process with undefined input data does not crash, as would a conventional program. The Strand process waits for its input data to be defined elsewhere. When the input data becomes available, computation is resumed.

2.5 Suspending Process Execution

Suspension in process invocation is decided by matching the parameters in the process call against the parameters given in the process definition. The matching rules are best expressed as a table. Suppose that a call is made to a single-parameter process, `p(T1)`. At the time of the call T1 could be a be an undefined variable, or a defined data value such as an integer, or a data structure (see later). Suppose the process definition is of the form

```
p(T2) :- <guard> | <body>.
```

then the matching rules are given by table 1.

Table 1: Matching Rules for clause selection

	T1		
T2	Variable	Constant	Structure
Variable	T2 := T1	T2 := T1	T2 := T1
Constant	Suspend	Fail unless T2 = T1	Fail
Structure	Suspend	Fail	Match Args

Matching causes a process call to succeed, fail or be suspended. Failure, unlike in Prolog, has no real meaning and is a run-time error in Strand. A process can only suspend if there are one or more variables in the call that must be matched against data values or tested with guards. If a process suspends, the matching is restarted whenever one of the required variables is assigned a value. This may succeed or fail, or suspend again on the variables remaining in the call.

Failure in Strand represents an error in the program. For example an assignment error results from two (or more) attempts to assign the same variable. Programmers need to take care to design their programs to avoid this class of error. To allow tolerant code, for example in library routines, to detect this error but retain control an error trapping assign kernel is provided.

The effect of these rules can be understood from the simple examples shown in table 2, which include the effect of guard evaluation. When a process is suspended it waits for an event, which is the assignment of a value to a variable. Immediately the assignment takes place the process invocation is resumed. If the assigned value is appropriate then the matching will succeed, if not then the match fails.

The synchronising effect in the call twice(2,W),twice(W,Y), is that the first process reduces while the second twice process is suspended until W is assigned. The delay is caused by the underlying implementation of the '>=' and '=<' operations.

Table 2: Examples of matching

Call	Definition	Comment
p(3,Y)	p(X,Y) :- X > 0 | Y := 77.	Succeeds in head, guard and selects body.
p(W,Z)	p(X,Y) :- X > 0 | Y := 77.	Succeeds in head, guard suspends.
p(W,Z)	p(3,Y) :- Y := 77.	Suspends in head.
p(W,Z)	p(X,Y) :- Y is 2*X.	Succeeds in head, but the '*' operation suspends.

2.6 Data Structures in Strand

Strand has two built-in data structures - tuples and lists. Tuples are fixed length, single dimension, mixed data type, arrays, for example a tuple may be written {1, 2.0, Three, four}. Lists are variable length, mixed type, sequences written [1, 2.0, Three, four].

Lists may also be manipulated by writing a list pair in brackets: [head|tail]. For example if L is the list [1, 2, 3], then the term [0 | L] is the list [0, 1, 2, 3].

Data selection is carried out by exploiting the matching operation during process invocation. For example, a process definition which would select the second item from a three-element tuple could be written

```
select2({X,Y,Z}, Result) :- Result := Y.
```

When a call select2({1,2,3}, Second) is made Y will match 2, which will be assigned to Second.

The first item of a list can be selected by a process

```
selectFirst([Head | Tail], Result) :- Result := Head.
```

A call, selectFirst([1, 2, 3], First) will match Head to 1, which will be assigned to First.

There are a number of type coercion kernels built-in to Strand that convert between lists and tuples, and lists and strings, integers and reals. For example the call:

```
string_to_list("abc", L, [39]),
```

results in L being assigned the value: `[97,98,99,39]`, the third parameters being used as the 'tail' of the list, in a 'difference list' style.

2.7 Stream Communication

In the 'twice' example only one data value can be passed through the shared variable W during the course of a computation because W is a single assignment variable. We often wish to design programs with component processes which communicate many times during a computation

The effect of repeated communications between processes can be obtained by making use of lists which are used in a special way. Lists used in this way are called streams. Streams are lists of data items in which the tail of the list is instantiated progressively as computation proceeds. Streams allow sequences of data values to be passed through a shared name such as W.

Using the notation above, `[1,2 | Tail]` represents the stream with first item 1, second item 2, and Tail is a list of undefined variables.

The twice example could be re-written to accept a stream of numbers as input and give a stream of doubled numbers as output.

```
streamTwice([Head | Tail], ResultStream) :-
   Head > 0 |
          Temp is 2*Head,
          ResultStream:= [Temp | R],
          streamTwice(Tail, R).
streamTwice([Head | Tail], ResultStream) :-
   Head =< 0 |
          ResultStream:= [0 | R],
          streamTwice(Tail, R).
streamTwice([], ResultStream) :-
          ResultStream:= [].
```

Notice that the empty list case is needed to terminate the recursive calls of streamTwice.

3 Parallel Programming Paradigms in Strand

Strand is truly parallel because, in a process definition such as:

```
p(X,Y,Z) :- r(X,Y,Z), s(X,Y,Z), t(X,Y,Z).
```

the three processes on the right hand side, r(X,Y,Z), s(X,Y,Z), t(X,Y,Z), are all spawned in simultaneously. If the matching conditions are satisfactory the three processes all start together. Thus, there is no notion of sequencing in Strand program syntax. This process spawning policy can lead to a very rapid growth in the number of processes which are active simultaneously. In extreme cases this can overwhelm the hardware resouces of the computer. Rather than add extra control mechanisms in the run-time system to control this, it is the Strand philosophy that the programmer be able to throttle back such process explosions by use of the sequencing mechanisms described in the next section.

3.1 Forcing Sequential Execution in Strand

There are some program actions which it is essential to run in sequence, for example, in printing it might be necessary to output 'newline', 'print X', 'newline' in that order. A Strand program written naively will run the instructions in parallel so that the order of appearance of the newlines and print-out is not determined.

When needed, a programmer can control sequencing by using a flag parameter in the head. This determines when a process actually starts. The flag is set by one of the small number of Strand instructions which can instantiate variables after they have completed. For example, the instruction - `display("hello world")` - also has the form - `display("hello world",Flag)`. In this second form the variable `Flag` is assigned `true` only after `"hello world"` has been sent to the display device.

```
showHello :- display("hello world, ", Flag)!,
    showAgain(Flag).
showAgain(true) :- display("hello again")!.
```

`showAgain` will wait until `Flag` is set to *true*.

3.2 The Producer/Consumer Paradigm

A typical program exploiting the stream notion will include a producer process feeding data items to one or more consumer processes. A difficulty with producer/consumer pairs is that either the producer generates data faster than the consumer can process it, or alternatively the consumer waits for the producer. Programmers need some form of control. In Strand, control can be exercised by choosing a suitable form of stream handling.

Three outline programs below illustrate how control can be exercised by the programmer, each one consisting of a producer process and a consumer process. The three different simplified definitions are:

```
leading_prod(X) :-       X := [message|T], leading_prod(T).
trailing_con([H|T]) :- consume(H),trailing_con(T).

trailing_prod([H|T]) :- H := message, trailing_prod(T).
leading_con(X) :-        X := [H|T], consume(H), leading_con(T).

buff_prod([H|T]) :-    H := message, buff_prod(T).
buff_con([H|T]) :-     consume(H), buff_con(T).
control(N,X) :-    N > 0 | N1 is N - 1, X := [H|T], control(N1,T).
```

Note, in these examples the case of an empty input stream has been ignored, so that examples 1 and 2 loop forever.

The first variant is called with

```
leading_prod(A),trailing_con(A).
```

A is an undefined communication variable. When started, leading_prod can proceed immediately, while trailing_con suspends until a data structure is placed into the shared variable, A. Leading_prod pours out "messages". If trailing_con cannot consume messages fast enough there is a risk of over-flowing memory.

The second variant is called with

```
trailing_prod(A),leading_con(A).
```

In this definition leading_con creates a stream of variables by assigning to the common location A. If trailing_prod cannot produce 'message' items quickly enough, again there is a risk of running out of memory.

In the third variant the starting call for 10 messages is

```
control(10,X,Tail),buff_prod(X,Tail),buff_con(X).
```

Initially both producer and consumer await the creation of the stream X by the process named 'control'. Each time a variable is injected into X the producer comes out of suspension and sends a 'message'. Upon seeing the 'message' the consumer comes out of suspension and executes. After each activation, producer and consumer suspend awaiting the next pattern to arrive in X. In this example only 10 messages are transferred.

3.3 Pipeline Parallelism

Streams in Strand support the important pipeline parallel processing construct. A sequential computation, p followed by c, on a list of values, [v1, v2, v3, v4] can be parallelised as - p(v1), followed by p(v2) and c(p(v1)) in parallel, followed by p(v3) and c(p(v2)) in parallel, etc. The total time of computation is thus reduced by overlapping the p and c computations.

3.4 Object-Style Programming in Strand

Objects combine a data structure with a collection of procedures which act on the data structure. The data structure holds the state of the object. The procedures are invoked by sending messages to the object. Objects can be used to implement abstract data types or to support a style of program design in which objects represent real-world entities.

Strand processes with stream arguments are used to implement objects. The streams carry successive messages to the object. When a message arrives the process selects the appropriate clause and modifies its data state. During this computation the process spawns a new version of itself connected to the tail of the input stream. This new process handles the next message, perhaps starting to deal with the next message whilst the previous generation is still executing.

Objects execute in parallel. As an example consider a car object which holds the data speed. The car can respond to four messages -

new - which creates a new car object and initialises the speed
faster - which increases the speed by 10
slower - which decreases the speed by 10

remove - which removes the car

The definition of the car object is

```
car(Commands) :- car(Command1, 0).
car([faster | NextCommand], Speed) :- NewSpeed is Speed + 20,
                              car(NextCommand, NewSpeed).
car([slower | NextCommand], Speed) :- NewSpeed is Speed - 10,
                              car(NextCommand, NewSpeed).
car([remove], Speed) :- true.
```

The first call must be of the form car(Command1). Once a car has been created it is represented by the process resulting from the call to car, with an initial speed of zero. A message can be sent to this car by assigning a value to Command1, for example:

```
Command1 := [faster | Command2]
```

After this assignment is executed a new car process will be ready to handle a message assigned to Command2. This new process will encapsulate a second generation car object with Speed value of 20. The initial process disappears.

A subsequent assignment - Command2 := [slower | Command3] - will create a third generation of car process with Speed value 10. Again, the second generation process disappears. An assignment - CommandN := [remove] - will not spawn a new process, so that the car disappears entirely.

Two separate cars can be created by calls such as - car(First) and car(Second). Subsequent assignments like - First := [faster | First1], and Second := [slower | Second1] - retain the identities of the two distinct cars through the use of different streams.

Each car maintains its own state, Speed, and alters its state in response to messages received, but the representation of Speed is fully encapsulated inside the object.

4 Writing Strand Programs

A typical Strand program makes an initial call which sets-up a collection of concurrently executing processes. It is usual to write the initial call in some form like:

```
myProgram(data1, data2, EndResult) :-
            process1(data1, data2, Local1),
            process2(data1, data2, Local1, Local2),
            process3(Local2, EndResult).
```

Some further common program forms are filters and client/server combinations.

4.1 Filters

It is often useful to think of processes as having special roles. One important role is a filter. Filter processes take a stream as input and produce a modified stream as output. An example of a filter is the sift process in this Prime Number Sieve program shown in figure 1.

The processes in this example operate as follows:

`primes(N,Ps)` N is a positive integer input, Ps is an output list of integers - generates a stream, Ps, of prime numbers between 2.and N inclusive.

`integers(From,To,Ns)` From, To, are positive integers input, Ns is an output list of integers - generates a stream of all integers, Ns, between From and To inclusive.

`sift(Ns,Ps)` Ns is an input, Ps is an output, list of integers - Ps is Ns with the non-primes removed.

`filter(In,P,Out)` In is an input, Out is an output, list of integers, P is a input positive integer. Out is In with all multiples of P removed.

```
primes(N,Ps) :- integers(2,N,Ns), sift(Ns,Ps).
integers(From,To,Ns) :- From > To | Ns := [ ].
integers(From,To,Ns) :- From =< To |
                From1 is From + 1,
                Ns := [From1|Ns1],
                integers(From1,To,Ns1).
sift([P|Ns],Ps) :- Ps := [P|Ps1],
                filter(Ns,P,Ns1),
                sift(Ns1,Ps1).
sift([ ],Ps) :- Ps := [ ].
filter([X|In],P,Out) :- W is X//P,
                filter2([X|In],W,P,Out).
filter([ ],P,Out) :- Out := [ ].
filter2([X|In],0,P,Out) :- filter(In,P,Out).
filter2([X|In],W,P,Out) :- W =\= 0 |
                Out := [X|Out1],
                filter(In,P,Out1).
```

Figure 1. A prime number Sieve

4.2 Client/Servers

Roles frequently found for processes are clients and servers. One server may serve several clients.

An example of a server is the Pseudo-Random Number Generator shown in figure 2.

`random(Numbers,Seed)` Numbers is a stream into which successive random numbers are output, Seed is a start number input. A stream of new variable names is supplied to random which instantiates them to successive pseudo-random numbers.

rand(Numbers,Seed,Mult,Inc,Mod) Numbers and Seed are as above, Mult,Inc,Mod are inputs of hashing numbers.

To start to generate random numbers a call like, random([num(X1)|T1],56) must be made, when the first pseudo-random number will appear in X1. The next random number is generated in X2 when the assignment T1 := [num(X2)|T2] is made. Further pseudo-random numbers are generated by assignments, T2 := [num(X3)|T3], etc. The generation is stopped at stage n by the assignment Tn := [halt].

```
random(Numbers,Seed) :- rand(Numbers,Seed,25173,13849,65536).
rand([halt|T],N,Mult,Inc,Mod) :-
            display_nl('No more random numbers')!.
rand([num(X)|T],N,Mult,Inc,Mod) :-
            X is (Mult*N + Inc)//Mod,
            display_nl(X)!,
            rand(T,X,Mult,Inc,Mod).
```

Figure 2. A Pseudo-random number generator

5 Conclusion

This tutorial has introduced the basic ideas of Strand Programming, and how those can be realised on real parallel hardware. It has been a feature of the Strand project that as many implementations as possible should exist for real parallel machines, the latest developments addressing the issues of programming co-operating networks of work-stations. A multi-user multi-workstation environment has recently been constructed which is allowing Strand to be used for a new area of CSCW applications. An active area of investigation at the moment is the provision of additional data types in the language to support data parallelism, allowing the range of machines amenable to Strand implementations to include SIMD architectures.

6 References

1. Shapiro, E. The Family of Concurrent Logic Programming Languages, ACM Computing Surveys 1989; 21(3): 413-510.
2. Foster, I and Taylor, S, Strand: New Concepts in Parallel Programming, Prentice-Hall Inc New Jersey, 1989.
3. Strand Software Technologies, STRAND88 USER MANUAL, Buckingham Release, 1989.

Author Index

Published in 1990–91

AI and Cognitive Science '89, Dublin City University, Eire, 14–15 September 1989
A. F. Smeaton and G. McDermott (Eds.)

Specification and Verification of Concurrent Systems, University of Stirling, Scotland, 6–8 July 1988
C. Rattray (Ed.)

Semantics for Concurrency, Proceedings of the International BCS-FACS Workshop, Sponsored by Logic for IT (S.E.R.C.), University of Leicester, UK, 23–25 July 1990
M. Z. Kwiatkowska, M. W. Shields and R. M. Thomas (Eds.)

Functional Programming, Glasgow 1989
Proceedings of the 1989 Glasgow Workshop, Fraserburgh, Scotland, 21–23 August 1989
K. Davis and J. Hughes (Eds.)

Persistent Object Systems, Proceedings of the Third International Workshop, Newcastle, Australia, 10–13 January 1989
J. Rosenberg and D. Koch (Eds.)

Z User Workshop, Oxford 1989, Proceedings of the Fourth Annual Z User Meeting, Oxford, 15 December 1989
J. E. Nicholls (Ed.)

Formal Methods for Trustworthy Computer Systems (FM89), Halifax, Canada, 23–27 July 1989
Dan Craigen (Editor) and Karen Summerskill (Assistant Editor)

Security and Persistence, Proceedings of the International Workshop on Computer Architecture to Support Security and Persistence of Information, Bremen, West Germany, 8–11 May 1990
John Rosenberg and J. Leslie Keedy (Eds.)

Women into Computing: Selected Papers 1988–1990
Gillian Lovegrove and Barbara Segal (Eds.)

3rd Refinement Workshop (organised by BCS-FACS, and sponsored by IBM UK Laboratories, Hursley Park and the Programming Research Group, University of Oxford), Hursley Park, 9–11 January 1990
Carroll Morgan and J. C. P. Woodcock (Eds.)

Designing Correct Circuits, Workshop jointly organised by the Universities of Oxford and Glasgow, Oxford, 26–28 September 1990
Geraint Jones and Mary Sheeran (Eds.)

Functional Programming, Glasgow 1990
Proceedings of the 1990 Glasgow Workshop on Functional Programming, Ullapool, Scotland, 13–15 August 1990
Simon L. Peyton Jones, Graham Hutton and Carsten Kehler Holst (Eds.)

4th Refinement Workshop, Proceedings of the 4th Refinement Workshop, organised by BCS-FACS, Cambridge, 9–11 January 1991
Joseph M. Morris and Roger C. Shaw (Eds.)

AI and Cognitive Science '90, University of Ulster at Jordanstown, 20–21 September 1990
Michael F. McTear and Norman Creaney (Eds.)

Software Re-use, Utrecht 1989, Proceedings of the Software Re-use Workshop, Utrecht, The Netherlands, 23–24 November 1989
Liesbeth Dusink and Patrick Hall (Eds.)

Z User Workshop, 1990, Proceedings of the Fifth Annual Z User Meeting, Oxford, 17–18 December 1990
J.E. Nicholls (Ed.)

IV Higher Order Workshop, Banff 1990
Proceedings of the IV Higher Order Workshop, Banff, Alberta, Canada, 10–14 September 1990
Graham Birtwistle (Ed.)